INTERNATIONAL INDIANS & THE LAW

The daring publisher, Universal Law Publishing Company, among the foremost in the law publishing field and progressive in venturing to bring out rare legal literature of avant garde *character has rightly enriched the* corpus juris *of India*

Justice V R Krishna Iyer
Random Reflections, page 14

INTERNATIONAL INDIANS & THE LAW

ANIL MALHOTRA
RANJIT MALHOTRA

Foreword by

Soli J. Sorabjee

Former Attorney General for India

Preface by

Dr. Balram K. Gupta

Director, National Judicial Academy, Bhopal

Universal
Law Publishing Co. Pvt. Ltd.
NEW DELHI - INDIA

First Edition : 2010
Second Edition : 2012
Third Edition : 2015

ISBN: 978-93-5035-511-4

Published by

Universal
Law Publishing Co. Pvt. Ltd.
NEW DELHI - INDIA

A-58, G.T. Karnal Road Industrial Area,
(Near Azadpur Metro Station), Delhi-110033
Tel. : 011-47082254, 27458529, 27215334 Fax : 011-27458529
e-mail: unilaw@vsnl.com

- Showroom : C-27, Connaught Place, New Delhi-110001
- Sales : sales@unilawbooks.com
- Editorial : edit@unilawbooks.com
- Website : **www.unilawbooks.com**

Join us on Facebook www.facebook.com/unilawbooks

Recommended citation: Anil Malhotra & Ranjit Malhotra, *International Indians & the Law*, 3rd Edn. (New Delhi: Universal Law Publishing Co. Pvt. Ltd., 2015).

Computer Typeset at Aesthetic and *Printed* at Nice Printing Press, Delhi.

Dedicated
To our beloved parents

Justice, justice you shall pursue (Deut. 16:20)

Soli J. Sorabjee

Senior Advocate, Supreme Court of India
Former Attorney General for India

FOREWORD

Knotty legal issues and problems confront Non-Resident Indians and all those persons who may be closely or remotely associated with them. *International Indians and the Law* is an excellent compilation of articles written by celebrated authors in this field. The book sheds light on these multifarious problems and provides invaluable information.

The true merit of the book is that it is a focused study on every conceivable issue relating to NRIs such as marriage, divorce, spousal maintenance, child abduction, domestic and inter-country adoptions, succession, inheritance, probate and wills, nationality, immigration, citizenship as also the new generation questions on the issue of surrogate motherhood. The subject of marital agreements, human smuggling, immigration, managed migration, citizenship and nationality are grey areas which have been very well described and dealt with in the book. An emerging Indian jurisprudence on child laws has received special treatment in the book. Due to lack of authentic material and proper guidance on these new subjects, numerous fellow citizens are sometimes misguided to utilize channels of illegal immigration which at times impacts severely on their lives, highlighting the dire need expressed by the authors for a new central legislation on the much needed subject of human smuggling.

In this backdrop, the book is a good eye opener in highlighting these problem areas with practical answers. Likewise, the quest of the NRI to become an Indian citizen is well handled. In the myriad problematic zone of Family Law relating to abandoned spouses, divorce decrees by foreign courts, inter-parental child removal and inter-country adoptions, the book contains very good references which would provide realistic legal options. Surrogacy, an unchartered field, is dealt with admirable clarity. Beneficial laws promoting the cause of missing and abused children are well dealt with. The authors ken extends to NRI property conflicts relating to tenancy, succession and inheritance and provide simplified responses. Some original thoughts on reformatory ideas or examples for India to emulate, which have been derived from the authors' experience gained from foreign travels, are ingenious and thought provoking. Reports of some of the deliberations arising from participation in international conferences and seminars held in India on NRI legal issues and related matters are a worthwhile feature of the work and give it added dimension.

Exposition of the various aspects of the law is crafted in simple readable language. For those who need to delve into details, copious case law references can lead them to wider horizons. The book is an invaluable source of ready information. A remarkable feature of the work is the generous references to inter-country adoptions and Strasbourg jurisprudence, especially in context of the right to family life of the NRI community vis-a-vis family migration.

I, have no doubt that the book will be extremely useful to judges in India and abroad, to lawyers in India and overseas practitioners and also to foreign readers. The book will also provide excellent guidance to policy makers, foreign offices, Consular Directorates besides consular sections of Embassies and High Commissions worldwide by providing answers to the unresolved problems in new emerging areas of the vast Indian Diaspora scattered around the world. The authors deserve full marks for their original and sterling endeavour.

SOLI J. SORABJEE

29th September, 2014

Former Attorney General for India

National Judicial Academy
Bhadbhada Road, Bhopal- 462044
Tel: 0755-269-6766
E-mail: balramkgupta@nja.gov.in

Dr. Balram K Gupta
Director

PREFACE

This encyclopedic work on 'International Indians and The Law' includes 35 short write-ups and 14 long Chapters. It caters to a wide spectrum of an Audience. Literate Litigants. Lawyers. Judges. Family Courts and Forums dealing with family matters in India and beyond. Even those who are not involved in litigation, but are interested in taking well thought out decisions in the domain of marriage, divorce, adoption, surrogacy, inter-country parental child removal, maintenance, human smuggling (the list is unending), would find the book highly educative and informative.

This Book has been written in the language which is highly digestive and easily understood. The authors are a blend of academic and professional Lawyers. The Book is reflective of a sound academic base and a sounder and richer practical experience as professionals. The authors are active practitioners of private international law. The writing of the different chapters would show that different aspects, complex in nature and weaved in equally complex legal knots have been dealt with based upon cases argued by the author/s themselves as also the decisions of Constitutional Courts. Since the Book is based upon the experience of long many years at the Bar as also academic writings, the authors have been able to do justice wholesome in nature to such variety of problems, issues and disputes.

There are certain issues which warrant immediate consideration of the Indian Parliament. There are issues which need a review and a fresh look. There are issues which need change/changes in Law. In the ultimate, the authors have been able to bring out how the different courts have approached and dealt with different issues. The Book has been able to bring out the ever growing and emerging family jurisprudence. Normally, one would think that in private law, the Constitution would have no role to play. The Book breaks this myth. It shows that even in the field of private law like family law, it is not divorced say for instance from the umbrella of Article 21 of the Indian Constitution. In fact, by bringing the Constitutional focus, the authors have been able to penetrate the private law arena with public law. The dealing of various issues in the field of family law has a deep impact on the society. Consequently, the private field is merging into the public field. This mixing of the two helps in handling such issues keeping in view their impact on the public issues. Human Trafficking. Human Rights. Human Behaviour. These aspects are in Family Law

Jurisprudence. The authors of the Book have made a serious and sincere effort to make Family Law Jurisprudence wholesome in knitting most of the aspects of Private Law with a tinkering of Public Law. It is hoped that the weaving of the two would go a long way in developing healthy family jurisprudence.

September 26, 2014 **Balram K. Gupta**

PROFESSIONAL PROFILE
ANIL MALHOTRA

Anil Malhotra is a practising Advocate in India since October 15, 1983 at the Punjab and Haryana High Court at Chandigarh. He also appears as Counsel in the Supreme Court of India at New Delhi and before other High Courts, Commissions, Boards and Tribunals all over India.

Email:anilmalhotra1960@gmail.com

Educational Attainments

Qualified Bachelor of Science (1980) and Bachelor of Laws (Professional) (1983) Degrees from the Punjab University, Chandigarh. Attained his Master of Laws (LL.M) Degree from the University of London, London in November 1985. Studied comparative family law at the London School of Economics (LSE) as well as law and society in South Asia at The School of Oriental and African Studies (SOAS), University of London, London.

Court Representation

From January 1986 to August 1987, trained in the chambers of Mr. Kuldip Singh, Barrister at Law (retired Hon'ble Judge, Supreme Court of India). Since September 1987, he has been practicing independently and has his own independent office in Chandigarh. He has represented Punjab State Agricultural Marketing Board, Punjab State Electricity Board, Punjab Small Industries Sports Corporation, Markfed, Punjab State Warehousing Corporation, Punjab State Cooperative Banks, Punjab Urban Planning and Development Authority (PUDA), Food Corporation of India, Unit Trust of India, Hindustan Petroleum Corporation Ltd., Bharat Petroleum Corporation Ltd., Indian Oil Corporation Ltd., IBP Company Ltd., Steel Authority of India Ltd., Rashtriya Ispat Nigam Ltd., Council of Scientific Industrial Research (CSIR), Central Scientific Instruments Organization (CSIO), Post Graduate Institution of Medical Education and Research (PGIMER), Panjab University and Punjab and Haryana High Court in litigations at the Supreme Court, High Court, Central Administration Tribunal, Railway Claims Tribunal, Consumer Disputes Redressal Commissions, Company Law Board, MRTPC, Debt Recovery Tribunal and District Courts Chandigarh as an empanelled Counsel.

Has assisted the Punjab & Haryana High Court, Chandigarh as an Amicus Curiae in a large number of matters and has represented Punjab State Legal Services Authority as Counsel in legal aid matters referred for appearance in Courts.

From November 1997 till November 2000 had worked as Additional Central Government Standing Counsel in the Punjab and Haryana High Court at Chandigarh for representing Central Government Departments. Represented Armed Forces and all Paramilitary Organisations besides Ministries of the Government of India in all types of litigation at the High Court level. Actively assisted in Organising first ever Pension Adalat at the High Court for Ministry of Defence litigations. Worked as Standing Counsel for PGIMER, Chandigarh for three years for conducting cases at the High Court, Supreme Court and Consumer Commissions. Worked as Additional Government Pleader on Civil side by Chandigarh Administration in 2003. Appointed as Counsel of Chandigarh Housing Board for the year 2003.

Well conversant with independently conducting Civil, Service, Company, Matrimonial and allied litigation at the High Court and Supreme Court level. Have represented substantial number of private clients for the past almost three decades by filing and defending independent petitions at the High Court and other forums in matters relating to constitutional, civil, company, criminal, consumer and family disputes oriented litigation.

Professional Description

For over 28 years have had extensive exposure in handling civil, matrimonial, criminal and overseas litigation on behalf of non-resident Indians residing abroad. Have represented a large number of overseas clients in Indian courts and regularly opined on matters of Indian law in cases arising in related matters in foreign jurisdictions. Have conducted a vast variety of matters in Indian Courts pertaining to interpretation and application of foreign Court Orders regarding divorce decrees, child abduction, custody, maintenance, adoption and property related issues of non resident Indians. Have interacted extensively with a worldwide Indian population settled overseas in advising them regularly on all issues of civil, matrimonial and criminal law in India.

Have contributed significantly to issues of Inter-Country Adoptions, Inter-Parental Child Removal and Surrogacy by convening seminars, discussions and debates at the India International Centre, New Delhi and other law faculties in association with Law Commission of India and Mr Soli Sorabjee, Senior Advocate and Former Attorney General of India.

Have to his credit a number of Amicus and Joint Expert appointments by Courts in India and by Courts abroad to opine on issues of Indian law. Have assisted the Punjab and Haryana High Court, Chandigarh as Amicus Curaie in matters of Child Custody, repatriation of victims of illegal immigration and cases relating to compensation of victims of crimes and accidents.

Has been assessed to Income Tax since March 31,1997 and have a Permanent Account Number with the Income Tax Department.

International Memberships and Local Appointments

Member of Lawasia, International Law Association, International Bar Association, Commonwealth Lawyers Association and Indian Society of International Law besides being Country Representative (Family Law) Lawasia. His law firm, Malhotra & Malhotra Associates are empanelled Lawyers for several key embassies and High Commissions at New Delhi for advisory, opinion and other legal work.

Have given opinion and evidence as an Expert Witness on Indian Law in Foreign Courts to give joint expert reports. Have rendered reports on child abduction and surrogacy issues to foreign missions at New Delhi. Have conducted workshops and seminars at Embassies in New Delhi on issues relating to illegal immigration, human smuggling and the practice of surrogacy.

On January 29, 2007 was elected as Fellow of The International Academy of Matrimonial Lawyers, London.

In May 2010, the Executive Council of the International Law Association, London nominated him as the India Member of the International Family Law Committee of the International Law Association.

Was made the Indian family law Correspondent for the International Family Law journal published by Jordan Publishing Limited, Bristol, UK to which regular contributions are made in the area of Family Law.

Appointed Indian representative for Reunite Child Abduction Agency, UK.

Was appointed as Member of the Punjab Governance Reforms Commission and Chairperson of Task Force on Policy Procedures, Resolution and Grievances of NRIs by the Government of Punjab on June 13, 2012 and had compiled and prepared five reports in the year 2012 described as hereunder:

- First Report - Reform of NRIs Marriage Laws, Creation of Family Courts in Punjab alongwith a draft of a Compulsory Punjab Registration of Marriages Bill.
- Second Report - Curbing of Working of Unregistered Recruiting Agents in Punjab.
- Third Report-Return of Irregular Migrants to Punjab from Foreign Jurisdictions.
- Fourth Report - NRI's Property related problems – The Punjab Model.
- Fifth Report - Amendments proposed in The Punjab State Commission for Non-Resident Indians Act, 2011 (Punjab Act No.33 of 2011).

Assisted the Government of Punjab in drafting of Punjab Compulsory Registration of Marriages Act, 2012 and Punjab Prevention of Human Smuggling Act, 2012. Rendered further assistance in preparation of Punjab Travel Professionals Regulation Amendment Act, 2014.

Appointed as Advisor, Non-resident Indian (NRI) Affairs to Government of Punjab in January 2014.

Publications

As an author have to his credit substantial published work in international legal journals on issues relating to Inter-Parental Child Abduction, Surrogacy, Human Smuggling and other issues of Indian Matrimonial Law.

Have co-authored book titled "Acting for Non-resident Indian Clients" (London 2005) published by Jordan Publishing Limited, Bristol, UK.

Have authored booklet on "An Overview of Legal Issues" published by the Government of Punjab for the Punjabi NRI Sammelan held on January 5, 2008.

Have authored book titled "India, NRIs and the Law" published by Universal Law Publishing Company Private Limited, New Delhi (2009).

Have co-authored book titled "Indians, NRIs and the Law" published by Universal Law Publishing Company Private Limited, New Delhi (2011).

Co-authored booklet titled, "An Overview of Legal Issues-2013" published by the Government of Punjab, which was released at the Non-Resident Punjabi Sammelan, Chandigarh held on January 3-5, 2013.

Have co-authored book titled "Surrogacy in India – A Law in the making" published by Universal Law Publishing Company Private Limited, New Delhi (2013).

Co-authored booklet titled, "Promise to Performance – New Punjab NRI Laws, Commissions and Policies" published by the Government of Punjab, which was released at the Non-Resident Punjabi Sammelan held on January 10-11, 2014.

Have written regular newspaper articles on family law and allied issues with about 200 published articles to his credit in national Indian newspapers. Have participated in over 50 TV discussions on propositions related to Human Smuggling, Surrogacy, NRI problems and Family Law related subjects.

Co-authored book titled, "International Indians and the Law" published by Universal Law Publishing Company Private Limited, New Delhi (2014).

Have co-authored following chapters on Indian law from 2001-2014 in the International Survey of Family Law published on behalf of the International Society of Family Law by Jordan Publishing Limited, Bristol, UK :

Surrogacy for single and unmarried foreign persons : A challenge under Indian Law (2014)

Law and Surrogacy arrangements in India (2013)

Missing children in India: Suggestions, Remedies and Solutions (2012)

Custom as an important source of Hindu Law: its usage in International Family Migration (2011)

Alternative Dispute Resolution in Indian Family Law – Realities, Practicalities and Necessities (2010)

Conflict of laws in Inter-country Adoptions: The Indian perspective with special reference to the position after India ratified The Hague Convention on Adoptions (2009)

Inter-country Parental Child removal and the Law (2008)

Hindu Law and Uniform Civil Code–The Indian experience (2007)

Divorce nullity and related matters under The Hindu Marriage Act 1955 (2005)

Analysis of the law of marriage from an International perspective, under Hindu Law (2004)

Some perspectives on Indian Family Law (2001)

Teaching Experience

Was retained as Part-time Lecturer, Faculty of Laws, Panjab University, Chandigarh from 1986 to 1992 for teaching Professional Subjects to Final Year LLB Students at the Department of Laws, Panjab University, Chandigarh.

Lectured as a Resource Person in the National Conference of Judges of the District Judiciary and Family Courts on adjudication of Issues relating to Women and Children, held at the National Judicial Academy, Bhopal from September 6 to 8, 2013. Made presentations in Sessions on "Issues relating to Women and Children : International Law and its Impact on India", "NRI Marriages : Implications in Litigation relating to Women and Children", "Adoption and Surrogacy – Concerns and Judicial Responses"

Lectured as a Resource Person in the National Conference of Judges of the District Judiciary on adjudication of Issues relating to Women and Children, held at the National Judicial Academy, Bhopal from November 22 to 24, 2013. Made presentations in Sessions on "Issues relating to Women and Children : Child Abuse : Issue and Challenges, Custody of Child in NRI Cases, Adjudicating cases relating to Women and Children : Issues and Challenges, Protecting Rights of Women: International Initiate and National Perspective, Protection Rights of Women in Matrimonial Cases.

Lectured as a Resource Person in the Refresher-cum-Orientation Course for Judges of Subordinate Courts of Punjab, Haryana & Chandigarh, held at Chandigarh Judicial Academy, Chandigarh on March 15, 2014. Made presentations on "NRI Divorce Decrees and their recognition in Indian Courts" and on "India Inter-parental Child Removal and the Law".

Lectured as a Resource Person in the National Conference of Presiding Officers of Family Courts, held at the National Judicial Academy, Bhopal from April 11-13, 2014. Made presentations in Sessions on "NRI Marriages & Divorce", "Re-thinking Role of Lawyers in Family Courts" and "Matters relating to Custody and Guardianship: Issues and Challenges".

Lectured as a Resource Person in the National Conference of Presiding Officers of Family Courts, held at the National Judicial Academy, Bhopal from July 25-27, 2014 to make presentations in Sessions on "Judging Family Disputes: Issues & Concerns", "Effective Use of ADR methods in resolving Family Disputes: Role of Family Courts", "NRI Marriages and Divorce-Family Courts" and "Rethinking Role of Lawyers in Family Courts".

Lectured as a Resource Person in the National Conference of Presiding Officers of District Judiciary, held at the National Judicial Academy, Bhopal from September 12-14, 2014 on "Adjudication to issues relating to Women and Children" to make presentations in Sessions on "Adoptions and Guardianship of Children Role of Judiciary", "Crime against Children: Human Rights Perspective", "Surrogacy as an Emerging Concern : Judicial response" and "Juvenile Justice System in India : Achievements and shortfalls".

International Conference Participations

Presented a paper on "Enforcement of Foreign Judgments and Foreign Arbitral Awards in The Indian Civil Jurisdiction at the Civil And Syariah Family Law Potential Conflicts Session of the XIX Biennial Lawasia Conference, 20–24 March 2005, at the Gold Coast Queensland, Australia.

Presented a paper on "International Parental Child Abduction Law in The Indian Jurisdiction: Case Law Analysis and Procedural Safeguards," at 50th Anniversary conference of the Commonwealth Lawyers Association held at London from September 11-15, 2005.

Presented a paper on the "Enforcement of Foreign Judgments and Foreign Arbitral Awards in the Indian Civil Jurisdiction," at 72nd Biennial Conference of the International Law Association at Toronto, Canada from June 4-8, 2006.

Presented Paper on "Family Law and Religion -The Indian Experience" in the session on Cultural and Indigenous Issues in Family Law at the Australian National Family Law Conference held on October 24, 2006 at Perth in Australia.

Presented a paper titled "Migration: The Indian Experience and Managed Migration Experiments," at the Wilton Park Conference WP 890, on "Migration towards a Comprehensive Approach", held at San Lorenzo Ee El Escorial, Spain, from October 8-10, 2007, in Session 5 Titled Can Migration be Managed: What can be learnt from the Experiences of Sending and Receiving Countries.

Participated on invitation of the International Law Association as a Speaker at the 73rd ILA Biennial Conference held at Rio De Janerio, Brazil to speak at the session on Rights of Children on August 18, 2008, and made a presentation titled "India, Inter Country Parental Child Removal and the Law."

From December 4 to 6, 2008, on invitation from the British High Commission, New Delhi was invited to speak, participate and attend The 941st Wilton Park Conference on "The Future of Migration" held at Wilton Park, Wiston House, Steyning, West Sussex, UK and made a presentation on "Illegal Immigration from India." This meet was held in cooperation with the Institute for Public Policy Research, the Foreign and Commonwealth Office and the UK Border Agency,

Presented Paper titled "Challenges in Inter-Country Child Removal and The Indian Law" at the 11th Annual Family Law Conference held on March 12 and 13, 2009 in Cape Town organised by The Miller Du Toit Cloete Inc and The Law Faculty of The University of the Western Cape.

Was invited to speak on 'Inter-Parental Child Removal Issues" at the 11th Annual Family Law Conference at Cape Town, South Africa on March 12-13, 2009. Made a presentation on "Indian, Inter-parental Child Conflicts & the law."

Was invited to speak on "Inter-Parental Child Removal Issues" at the 16th Commonwealth Law Conference 2009 at Hong Kong on April 5-9, 2009. Made a presentation on Inter-Parental Child Abduction law in India.

Presented Paper titled, "All Aboard for The Fertility Express' in the Conference wrap up Session titled, "The Family Law Forum," at the Third Lawasia Children and The Law Conference 2009 held at Singapore from May 21-23, 2009.

Chaired Session titled, "Relocating the Child: Parental Movement and International Adoptions," at the Third Lawasia Children and The Law Conference 2009 held at Singapore from May 21-23, 2009.

Presented Paper titled "To Return or Not To Return: Hague Convention vs. Non-Convention Countries," in the Session titled, "Implementation of The Hague Convention: Practical Issues and Lessons Learnt," at the Third Lawasia Children and The Law Conference 2009 held at Singapore from May 21-23, 2009.

Was the only legal practitioner amongst Judges who had been invited to speak at the International Family Justice Judicial Conference for the Common Law & Commonwealth Jurisdictions held at Windsor, UK from August 4-7, 2009. Participated with a presentation on Cross border Child Removal Conflicts in India.

Was invited to speak on "Indian Civil Aspects of International Child Abduction Bill 2007 and the Indian Perspective on International Child Abduction" at the Conference on International Child Abduction, Relocation and Forced Marriage held from June 30 to July 2, 2010 at the London Metropolitan University, London. Made presentation on International Perspective of child abduction law in India.

Was invited as a Panelist in the 74th Biennial Conference of the International Law Association held in the Hague, Netherlands from August 15 to 19, 2010 to speak in the session on "Out of Concern for the Child : Transnational Co-operation in Cases of Child Protection, Maintenance and Abduction."

Invited and presented a paper on Surrogacy Titled "All Aboard for The Fertility Express" at the 14th Annual Family Law Conference 2011, Capetown, South Africa, organised By Miller Du Toit Cloete Inc And The University Of The Western Cape on March 17 and 18, 2011.

Participated in The 2nd International Family Law and Practice Conference 2013 on "Parentage, Equality and Gender" held by The Centre for Family Law and Practice, London Metropolitan University, London from July 3 to 5, 2013. Made presentations titled "Surrogacy: Imported from India, Need for a Regulatory Law" and "Abduction – To Return or not to Return".

Domestic Conference Participations

Presented a paper on "International Parental Child Abduction Law in the Indian Jurisdiction: Caselaw Analysis and Procedural Safeguards," at the private international law session of the Second International Conference organised by the Indian Society of International Law at New Delhi from November 14-17, 2004

As a Panelist made presentations and organised Seminar on "India's Role in Combating Inter-Country Parental Child Removal" at India International Centre, New Delhi on December 9, 2005.

Conducted a seminar at India International Centre, Lodhi Road, New Delhi on Conflict of Jurisdictions in Interparental Child Custody Disputes on May 5, 2006. Made a presentation on India's Role in Combating Inter-country Parental Child Removal in the international perspective.

Presented paper titled 'Conflicts of Jurisdiction in Interparental Child Custody Disputes – The Indian Experience' at the Indian Society of International Law's International Conference on Private International Law held on December 2-3, 2006 at New Delhi.

Organised in association with Department of Laws, Panjab University, Chandigarh, a Seminar on "NRIs Abandoned Brides – A Challenge to Meet" held at the Panjab University, Chandigarh, on February 13, 2007. Prepared and compiled a Report of the Seminar on the deliberations and conclusions drawn up in the Seminar on problems and legal issues arising out of abandoned brides in the Indian jurisdiction which was forwarded to National Commission for Women, New Delhi.

As knowledge partner with British High Commission, New Delhi, organized seminar on "Migration – Myths and Realities," on March 23, 2007 at Chandigarh and coordinated a Panel discussion on Illegal Immigration from India.

Presented paper titled "Rewriting Medical Jurisprudence – DNA Profiling Comes of Age" at a Seminar on Expert Witnesses and their Training held at Law Bhawan, Chandigarh on March 31, 2007.

As knowledge partner with Embassy of Italy, New Delhi and VFS Global Services Pvt. Ltd., organized seminar on "Destination Italy – The Right Way," on August 11, 2007 at Chandigarh and coordinated a Panel discussion on Managed Migration and legal channels of Immigration from India.

Presented papers titled "Breakdown Abroad, Divorce In India, Why Not ?," and "Adoption, Parentage And Surrogacy – A Maze or a Dilemma?," at the one day national seminar on "Family Law: Problems And Perspectives," organised by the Rajiv Gandhi National University Of Law, at Patiala, Punjab on September 8, 2007.

Presented a paper titled "Foreign Investments and International Law – Some Legal Perspectives," at a seminar titled "International Law on Foreign Investment," organised by the International Law Association, Regional Branch, India and its Chandigarh chapter in association with Confederation of Indian Industry, held on September 26, 2007.

Moderated a panel discussion on Legal Perspectives for Non-resident Indians held at the Punjabi NRI Sammelan, Chandigarh on January 5, 2008. Deliberated on Family Law, Property Law, Immigration related Issues and NRI problems of repatriation of funds besides fast track resolution of criminal cases of NRIs.

Presented a Paper in the State Level Seminar sponsored by Dean, College Development Council, Panjab University titled "Women Shackled in NRI

Weddings," on February 23, 2008 at Guru Gobind Singh College for Women, Sector 26, Chandigarh.

"Human Rights: Limitations and Judicial Review– The Indian Perspective", paper presented at the National Seminar on Globalization, Development and Human Rights : Issues and Challenges on March 11, 2008 at Department of Sociology, Panjab University, Chandigarh.

As knowledge partner with British High Commission, New Delhi, organized second seminar on "Managed Migration – Myths and Realities...One year on," on March 28, 2008 at Chandigarh and coordinated a Panel discussion on issues relating to effects of curbing Illegal Immigration from India.

Organised a seminar with Law Commission of India at the Army Institute of Law at Mohali on October 18, 2008 and delivered a lecture on India, Inter-Country Parental Child Removal and the Law, in a session chaired by The Chairman, Law Commission of India.

Organised a seminar at the India International Centre, New Delhi on February 13, 2009 on "Surrogacy – Bane or Boon". Made a presentation on the legal perspectives on Surrogacy existing in 2009 and as under the proposed law on surrogacy besides anomalies/lacunas under the proposed Bill on surrogacy.

In association with the Faculty of Laws, Panjab University, Chandigarh, organised a panel discussion titled, "Surrogacy: Bane or Boon" on March 4, 2009. Moderated a panel discussion on the Assisted Reproductive Technology (Regulation) Bill and Rules 2008 in a session presided over by the Chairman, Law Commission of India.

Invited to speak on NRI issues and problems in the field of Private International Law at the Army Institute of Law, Mohali (Punjab). The Ambassador of Italy, New Delhi delivered a talk on Public International Law on September 9, 2009. Made presentation on "Law for Non-Resident Indian Families, a Dilemma"

Was invited by the Government of India to make a special presentation on Property Problems of Non-Resident Indians at a special seminar held at New Delhi on January 7, 2010. Participated in deliberations and gave concluding notes on issues arising out of property disputes and legal propositions in India

Participated in the 17th Commonwealth Law Conference held from February 5-9, 2011 at Hyderabad by making interventions in sessions on Honour Crimes, Forced Marriages and Inter-Country Parental Child Removal issues prevailing in India.

Organised a book discussion on "Indians, NRIs and the Law" at the Institute for Development and Communication, Chandigarh, on November 19, 2011 chaired by Prof Sir Peter Gregson, Vice-Chancellor and President, Queens University, Belfast and co-chaired by Lord Diljit Rana, MBE, Member Parliament, UK.

Participated in a National Conference on 'Human Rights & Social Inclusion; Contemporary Concerns' Organised by The Department of Political Science, held at Jamia Millia Islamia University, New Delhi on November 23-24, 2011. Presented a paper on "Human Rights: Limitations and Judicial Review- The

Indian Perspective" and deliberated in Sessions on Human Rights and the Law.

Invited and made a Case Presentation on successful return of irregular migrants from Iraq at the National Consultation European Union Workshop, New Delhi on facilitating safe and Legal Migration and Preventing Irregular Migration on September 6-7, 2012 at Hotel Claridges, New Delhi.

Organised Symposium "International Family Law Inc. - International Parental Child Removal" as knowledge partners with the British High Commission, New Delhi at The India International Centre, New Delhi on May 13, 2013. Moderated a panel discussion by international experts and made a presentation on The position of India on Inter-Parental Child Removal Law.

Invited to Fourth Biennial Conferences of the Asian Society of International Law, "Asia & International Law in the Twenty-First Century: New Horizons" held at India Habitat Centre, New Delhi on November 14 to 16, 2013. Presented paper titled "Surrogacy Law arrangements in India" in the session on Conflict of Law relating to marriage, Adoption, Surrogacy & custody of children held on November 15, 2013 at the conference.

Chaired a Session on the theme of Domestic Violence and Female Foeticide at a National Seminar on "A World in Transition – New Challenges for Women Empowerment" held at Rajiv Gandhi National University of Law, Patiala in collaboration with Indian Council for Social Science Research, North West Regional Centre, Panjab University, Chandigarh on February 22, 2014. Made observations as Chair on pressing issues of female foetcide and violence at home.

Chaired a session on "The New Dimensions of Human Rights Violations in Contemporary Times : Challenges & Solutions" at the Army Institute of Law, National Seminar 2014, held on September 19-20, 2014 at Army Institute of Law, Mohali. Made concluding observations on emerging dimensions of Human Rights

PROFESSIONAL PROFILE
RANJIT MALHOTRA

Ranjit Malhotra, qualified as a lawyer in India in the year 1990 and was the first Indian lawyer to be awarded the prestigious Felix Scholarship to read for the LLM Degree at the School of Oriental and African Studies, University of London. He attained his Degree with merit in 1993, specialising in areas of private international law and South Asian family laws. He is an India-based lawyer handling substantial international work. He is a member of the International Bar Association and is presently the Newsletter Editor for the second term of the Family Law Section of the IBA and the past Co-Chair of the Family Law and Family Law Rights Section of Lawasia. He has also been the Regional Representative for India of the Migration and Nationality Law Committee of the IBA.

He is also a nominated life member of the Indian Society of International Law, Immigration Law Practitioners Association, London, American Immigration Lawyers Association, Washington, Reunite Child Abduction Agency in London, Indian Council of Arbitration at New Delhi, Lawasia at Australia, Fellow of the International Academy of Matrimonial Lawyers, Commonwealth Lawyers Association at London and International Law Association at London. He is also enrolled with The International Association of Youth And Family Judges And Magistrates.

He frequently travels abroad to present papers at international legal conferences. Mr. Ranjit Malhotra has travelled extensively in the UK, USA, Canada, Europe, South Africa, Australia and the far east including Japan, Philippines, Malaysia, Hong Kong, Singapore in connection with professional assignments as also to make presentation at international legal conferences.

He participated in the Lawasia biennial conference, held in Manila, Philippines in August 1997.

He had a presentation on, "Privatisation of Power Projects in India," at the International Business Law Conference of Lawasia, held in Tokyo on 9–10 November 1998.

He attended the conference organised by the Section on "Legal Practice of the International Bar Association," held in Boston, USA in the first week of June 1999.

He actively participated as a family law speaker with regard to wealth transfer issues for high net worth Individuals in the International Bar Association Annual Conference held at Amsterdam, Netherlands from 17–22 September 2000.

He was the only Indian speaker at the first AILA Global Immigration Summit held in New York in September 2002 and the second Summit in New York in October 2004. He also presented papers at the Global Immigration Conferences jointly organised by AILA, IBA and ILPA held in London in November 2007 and November 2009. Previously, he has made presentations at AILA Annual conferences held in New Orleans in 2003, Salt Lake City in 2005 and in Vancouver in 2008.

He presented a paper on "Foreign Entrepreneurs and Corporates Setting up Offices in India," at the Immigration and Big Business Session of the XIX Biennial Lawasia Conference, 20–24 March 2005, at the Gold Coast Queensland, Australia.

He spoke on "Ancillary Relief Issues under Hindu Law with special reference to Non-Resident Indians," at 50th Anniversary conference of the Commonwealth Lawyers Association held at London from 11 – 15 September 2005.

He had a presentation on "International Parental Child Abduction Law in the Indian Jurisdiction : Caselaw Analysis and Procedural Safeguards," at the XVII World Congress of the International Association of Youth and Family Judges and Magistrates held in Belfast, Northern Ireland from 27 August – 1 September 2006.

He analysed "Legal Practice and Procedure Governing Movement and Presence of Refugees in India: Need for Reform," at the 15th Commonwealth Law Conference held from 9–13 September 2007 at Nairobi, Kenya in the Session on Refugee and Immigration Law in the 'Constitutionalism, Human Rights, Governance and the Rule of Law' Stream.

In October 2007, he was nominated by the British High Commission, New Delhi, India to attend the Wilton Park Conference titled "WP 890 Migration Towards a Comprehensive Approach," held in Spain from 8-10 October 2007. He had attended another Wilton Park conference as a special invitee on migration issues in the UK in December 2008.

He made two presentations "All Aboard for The Fertility Express," on surrogacy issues in the Indian jurisdiction at The Family Law and Matrimonial Law Session held on 27 October 2009 and the second one on "Enforcement of Foreign Judgments and Foreign Arbitral Awards In The Indian Civil Jurisdiction," in the arbitration session as part of the New York State Bar Association, International Section Seasonal Meeting held in Singapore from 26–29 October 2009.

He closely analysed "Conflict of Law in Inter Country Adoptions: The Indian Perspective with Special Reference to the Position after India Ratifying The Hague Convention on Adoptions," at the European Chapter meeting of the International Academy of Matrimonial Lawyers held in Munich, Germany from 5 May to 9 May 2010.

He was invited to deliberate at the International Family Justice Judicial Conference for the Common Law & Commonwealth Jurisdictions held at Windsor, UK from 4-7 August 2009.

He was also invited by the Government of India to make a special presentation on Property Problems of Non-Resident Indians at a special seminar held at New Delhi on 7 January 2010, organised by the Government of India.

He made a detailed presentation in the session on "International Private Client Work, Mediation and Practice Management at the Third Annual India

Legal Practice Conference," organised by the Law Society of England and Wales from 21-24 June 2010, held in London, The United Kingdom.

Mr. Malhotra was invited as a Panellist in the 74th Biennial Conference of the International Law Association to be held in the Hague, Netherlands from 15 to 19 August 2010 to speak in the session on "Out of Concern for the Child: Transnational Co-operation in Cases of Child Protection, Maintenance and Abduction."

He was awarded the E. Michael Berger Scholarship Award [towards conference registration fees] to make a presentation at the 2011 AILA Annual Conference on Immigration Law held from 15-18 June, 2011 at San Diego, California.

He significantly analysed "Socio-legal perspective of forced marriages in the Indian context: perceptions and possible solutions," at the International Bar Association Annual Conference 2010 held in Vancouver, Canada from 3- 8 October 2010 at the family law session on Honour based violence, Child Brides and Forced Marriages – Protection of Human Rights.

That on a special invitation from the National Commission for Women, New Delhi, India he presented a paper on "NRI Marriages-Problems and Possible Solutions: The Punjab Perspective," at the seminar jointly organised by The National Commission for Women and The Ministry of Overseas Indian Affairs, held In New Delhi On 15 February 2011.

He was invited to present a paper on Surrogacy Titled "All Aboard for The Fertility Express," at the 14th Annual Family Law Conference 2011, Cape Town, South Africa, organised by Miller Du Toit Cloete Inc and The University Of The Western Cape on 17 and 18 March 2011.

In 2013, he made presentations at the international family law conferences organised by the Law Society of Australia at Sydney in March 2013, by the London Metropolitan University in July 2013 and at the International Bar Association conference held in Boston in October 2013.

He substantially assisted as knowledge partner in organising a Symposium "International Family Law Inc. - International Parental Child Removal," as knowledge partners with the British High Commission, New Delhi at The India International Centre, New Delhi on 13 May 2013.

He was invited as a speaker to the Fourth Biennial Conference of the Asian Society of International Law, "Asia and International Law in the Twenty-First Century: New Horizons," held at New Delhi, India on 14 to 16 November 2013. He presented a paper titled "Surrogacy Law arrangements in India," in the session on Conflict of Law relating to marriage, Adoption, Surrogacy and custody of children held on 15 November 2013 at the conference.

As part of the speaker series of the Programme on the Legal Profession Division, he was invited to lecture at the Harvard Law School on child abduction law issues with special reference to India as a non Hague Convention country, on 15 April 2014.

He had a substantial presentation on "Suggestive Cross Border Perspectives and Safeguards: For proposed Surrogacy Law in India," held at National Law University Conference at Delhi on 13-14 September 2014 and at the National Conference on "A policy dialogue on issues around Surrogacy in India," organised by the Centre for Social Research, in association with Heinrich Boll Stiftung at

New Delhi on 22-23 September 2014. The pre-legislative suggestions advanced by the author were reported as, "Legal tangles hurdle to commissioning couples- Experts call for regulations to check baby breeding cartels and child trafficking," in India's national newspaper The Hindu dated 28 September 2014.

He has also been actively and regularly involved in organising seminars on child issues in the international perspective, at the India International Centre, New Delhi.

He has substantial published work in different major jurisdictions to his credit. He is one of the principal authors in the published book [2005] titled "Acting for Non-resident Indian Clients," by Jordan Publishing Limited at Bristol in U.K. The book carries a foreword by the late Lord Slynn of Hadley, Senior Judge of the erstwhile House of Lords in London, U.K. This book was released in the House of Lords on 15 April 2005.

Mr. Ranjit Malhotra has co-authored book titled "Indians, NRIs and the Law," published by Universal Law Publishing Company Private Limited, New Delhi released in November 2011.

He has also co-authored book titled "Surrogacy in India – A Law in the making," published by Universal Law Publishing Company Private Limited, New Delhi, which was released in May 2013.

He is also co-authored for the Government of Punjab a booklet titled "Promise to Performance," on newly enacted state Government legislations, for the Non Resident Punjabi Sammelan held on 10-11 January 2014.

He is also the Indian family law Correspondent for the International Family Law journal and has been regularly co-authoring for more than last five years the India chapter in the worldwide annual family law survey titled "The International Survey of Family Law," an International Society of Family Law initiative. Both publications are published by Jordan Publishing Limited, Bristol, England.

Mr. Ranjit Malhotra, specialising in areas of private international law is a managing partner in his firm Malhotra & Malhotra Associates. The Firm has a broad-based practice with a reputation for offering a full range of quality personalised legal services. The firm has also been handling legal work for several Fortune 500 companies.

He also extensively advises foreign lawyers in the area of private international law, while acting on behalf of the non-resident Indian community, besides rendering expert testimony in foreign litigation, involving Indian laws.

Mr. Ranjit Malhotra has also been extensively handling inbound and outbound corporate immigration work for software companies, banks, consulting companies, multinationals etc. including lodging business and settlement applications at Embassies and Consulates throughout India. He has rich experience of consular representation.

His firm, Malhotra & Malhotra Associates, is on the panel of lawyers for eight major Embassies in New Delhi, including the American Embassy, Australian High Commission, British High Commission, Canadian High Commission, and New Zealand High Commission, Embassy of the Federal Republic of Germany, Embassy of Spain, Austrian Embassy, Embassy of Sweden at New Delhi, and the office of the Consul General of the American Embassy at Mumbai.

He can be contacted at malhotraranjitindia@rediffmail.com

CONTENTS

LONG CHAPTERS

SHORT CHAPTERS

TABLE OF CASES

A

B

C

N

S

T

U

V

W

X

Y

Z

Custom as an Important Source of Hindu Law—Its Usage in International Family Migration

INTRODUCTION

As practitioners in the area of private international law, when dealing with major embassies and high commissions in New Delhi on behalf of intending settlement applicants in the context of family migration, it is essential for foreign immigration and family law lawyers to understand the legal position in India as to family law issues. These issues include the statutory recognition of customary marriages and divorces and the registration of marriages under the provisions of the Hindu Marriage Act, 1955 (HMA, 1955) as applicable to non-resident Indians staying abroad. This is the main thrust of this chapter. Due to local variations and the recognition of customs under Indian law, immigration law at the Indian end has a very different complexion. These differences are critical to foreign immigration lawyers preparing immigration applications, at the initial stages of lodging the family reunion applications and of course in the event of any litigation before immigration adjudicators and tribunals.

Apart from statutory recognition by HMA, 1955, this chapter also traces the case-law on the subject of customary marriages and divorces. The case-law analysis is in chronological order from 1969 with reference to some very old decisions of the Privy Council to 2014 taking into account the important relevant judgments. The judgments quoted are of the Supreme Court of India and various High Courts in the country, especially the Punjab and Haryana High Court, within whose jurisdiction the bulk of the population of Punjabi origin resides, as well as the neighbouring states. Customary Karewa marriages are popular among certain agricultural sects in rural parts of Punjab. Also, it is manifest from the case-law analysis that customary marriages including the custom of Karewa marriages, which are defined below, have not been overruled, modified or diluted in any form at all.

Emphasizing that Karewa form of marriage is *"a social response to bring respectability to a widow through remarriage for which elaborate ceremonies are unnecessary"*, the Punjab and Haryana High Court in a erudite verdict rendered by Justice K. Kannan in *Darbara Singh* v. *Jaswant Kaur,* 2014 (1) RCR (Civil)

1004, with the aid of diligent research, very ably expounded the background and concept of Karewa marriage, which can be best relied upon by quoting the relevant extract from the judgment itself reading as follows:

> *"6. Any customary rite as spoken to by witnesses shall be taken as sufficient proof of marriage. We should indeed push for an agenda that approves of minimum formalities so long as the society recognizes them as sufficient. If after the ceremonies, however informal and modest they were, the man and woman lived together as husband and wife, that itself ought to be taken as sufficient. Every State has responded in its own way to approve of expression of intentions as sufficient to supplant elaborate ceremonies. In Tamil Nadhu, the suya mariyada (self-respect) was statutorily recognized by an amendment to the Hindu Marriage Act in 1967. In Punjab, it is karewa form which is the approved form of remarriage of a widow. Even a legislation legitimizing remarriage of widows will obtain its full value only if it approves of minimal ceremonies accompanying such functions as sufficient to validate the marriage. It will be abominable to look for ceremonies like saptapati, a la brahminical form, to legitimise a customary form of marriage prevalent among jat sikhs. Section 7(2) shall be construed to include any minimal ceremony, sans religiosity, so long as it is acceptable to the community. Available literature on the subject suggests that Widow re-marriage in the karewa form prevalent in Punjab is known 'as a marriage by a widow with the brother or some other male relative of her deceased husband and requires no religious ceremonies and confers all the rights of a valid marriage' (underlining mine; see 38 P.R. 1879; 316 of 1879; 26 P.R. 1880; 36 P.R. 1881; 48 P.R. 1890; 98 P.R. 1890; 54 P.R. 1900 - reproduced from punjabrevenue.nic.in). In the book Haryana: Past and Present by Suresh K. Sharma (Mittal Publications, 2006), it is stated (at page 45) "Karewa or a widow marrying one of the brothers of her deceased husband is known among the Jats, Ahirs, Gujars and Harijans is un-accompanied by ceremonies of any kind. The woman merely resumes her jewels and coloured clothes which she had ceased to wear on her husband's death. Sometimes, there is a public ceremony to give it a sanctimonious touch; generally living together is held to constitute karewa." In Women and Social Reform in Modern India: A Reader by Sumit Sarkar, and Tanika Sarkar, (Indiana University Press, 2008), the authors state: "The agrarian needs which allowed bride price also sanctified widow-remarriage. Like the former, this was also a feature which the agriculturist castes shared in common with the lower castes. However, the custom of widow-remarriage as followed here had special features of its own. Known as karewa, karao, or chaddal andazi, the custom was a throw back to the old Rig-vedic niyog (levirate marriage) which was prevalent in the geographical region of Haryana-Punjab and associated with the early vedic Aryan settlements. Karewa, a white sheet coloured at the corners, was thrown by the man over the widow's head signifying his acceptance of her as his wife. This custom represented social consent for cohabitation. There could be certain variations. For example, it could take the form of placing churis (glass bangles) on the widow's wrist in full assembly and sometimes even a gold nath (nose ring) in her nose and a red sheet over her head with a rupee tied in one of its corners. This could be followed by the distribution of gur (jaggery)*

or sweets. Significantly, this form of marriage was not accompanied by any kind of religious ceremony, as no woman could be customarily married twice, that is, go through the ceremony of biah (religious wedding). After Karewa the widow merely resumed her jewels and coloured clothes which she had ceased to wear on her husband's death. So much so sometimes mere cohabitation was considered sufficient to legitmize the relationship and it conferred all the rights of a valid marriage. [(underlining mine). Reference sourced to C.I. Tupper, The Punjab Customary Law (Calcutta: Government Printing 1881) Vol. 2, pp. 93, 123) See *also* E. Joseph, Customary Law of the Rohtak District, 1910 (Lahore: Govt. Printing, 1911), p. 45*]. If witnesses have spoken about the ceremonies, we shall not be looking towards elaborate forms to render invalid a lawful relationship. In this case, there was enough evidence of such customary practices as government texts and Punjabi (and Haryanvi as well) literature admit of."*

It is further pertinent to mention that Karewa marriage is just one of the many forms of customary marriages, but as a matter of fact customary marriages in India vary within different communities and regionally as well. Karewa marriage was defined way back by Sir W.H. Rattigan [in W.H. Rattigan *A Digest of Customary Law* (Allahabad: University Book Agency, 15th Edn., revised by Prakash Aggarawala, with a foreword by Dr. Bakshi Tek Chand, 1989) para 75 of Chapter 5], before the partition of India took place, as follows:

> *"A 'Karewa' marriage with the brother or some other male relative of the deceased husband requires no religious ceremonies, and confers all the rights of a valid marriage."*

The relevant case-law analysis on customary marriages and customary divorces in this chapter is to drive home the point that custom traditionally is an important source of Hindu law, and that continues to be the position.

FAMILY IMMIGRATION ISSUES

Indian marriages: registration of marriages – law and custom

Both formally registered and customary marriages are recognised under the laws of India. Visa officers have full information about the state of origin of the applicants. They are quite up to date on issues like land value, monies earned from cultivation per acre, Indian customs, etc. In Hindu marriage cases they view the *Saptapadi* photographs with a jeweller's focus. *Saptapadi* is the taking of seven steps by the bridegroom and the bride jointly before the sacred fire. The marriage becomes complete and binding when the seventh step is taken.

At the major embassies and high commissions in New Delhi including the office of the Canadian consulate at Chandigarh, the capital of the state of Punjab, most visa officers will be aware that in certain areas in the state of Punjab especially in Jalandhar and Hoshiarpur Districts, which are famous for outbound family migration, fake marriages are performed with all the pomp and show without the religious ceremonies actually taking place at all. This is to facilitate migration through the family route.

A typical case is where the British Asian boy or girl is from the Midlands in the UK or a spouse from Maryland in the USA or from areas having dense Indian population in Canada, who is being married to a spouse from the state of Punjab. And the parents, being wary of the outcome of the spouse application, insist on a contingent arrangement. In such a situation, a fake marriage certificate is submitted to the immigration authorities. In an attempt to safeguard the interests of their children, the parents fall prey to bad advice. It is sad to mention that dubious travel agents and unqualified local consultants thrive on this non-resident clientele.

Under section 8 of the HMA, 1955, the principal law governing Hindu marriages, registration of marriages is not compulsory. This is primarily because Hindu marriages and most marriages in India have always been performed in public with wide publicity. Section 8(2) provides that any state government may make rules for the compulsory registration of Hindu marriages. Furthermore, section 8(5) specifically expresses that failure to register a Hindu marriage does not affect its validity. Even where compulsory registration of marriage is laid down under the rules, non-registration does not affect the validity of the marriage, but merely entails a nominal fine. Moreover, mere registration of a marriage under section 8 will not *ipso facto* make the marriage valid.

In light of the prevailing law in India, registration of marriages in this region by non-resident Indians is only undertaken to satisfy the immigration authorities. It is not very difficult to obtain fake marriage certificates in the abovementioned areas of Punjab. Such false practices have a direct bearing on genuine applicants. Even their documentation and circumstances leading to the marriage are viewed cautiously.

Customary marriages are also performed in limited situations where one of the spouses is resident abroad. Generally, it is the husband who is resident abroad.

CUSTOM AS AN IMPORTANT SOURCE OF HINDU LAW

The HMA, 1955 is an Act of the Parliament of India to amend and codify the law relating to marriage among Hindus. At the outset, it is important to mention that section 5 of the HMA, 1955, which deals with the conditions for a valid Hindu marriage, also by virtue of section 5(iv), allows marriage within the prohibited degrees of relationship as and when permitted by the custom or usage governing the parties to the marriage, as is generally the situation in customary marriages. It is also important to mention that section 29 recognises customary marriages before the enactment of the HMA, 1955 while simultaneously recognising customary divorces even after the enactment of the HMA, 1955. To make matters explicitly clear customary divorces, subject to conditions of compliance, are clearly recognised under the provisions of section 29 of the HMA, 1955. Customary marriages within the prohibited degrees of relationship are specifically recognised by virtue of section 5(iv) of the HMA, 1955 after the legislation came into force, on 18 May 1955, and this continues to be the position to date.

It is important to consider the other relevant provisions of the HMA, 1955. The relevant sections relating to the territorial jurisdiction and the extraterritorial application are defined in section 1 of the HMA, 1955. The application of the said central legislation is defined in section 2, while the definition clause is contained in section 3. The conditions for a valid marriage are stipulated in section 5 and registration of marriages under the legislation is provided in section 8. The savings clause has explicit recognition in section 29.

The relevant sections of the HMA, 1955 with regard to the scope of the present chapter are reproduced below.

'**1. *Short title and extent.***—(1) *This Act may be called the Hindu Marriage Act, 1955.*

(2) It extends to the whole of India except the State of Jammu and Kashmir, and applies also to Hindus domiciled in the territories to which this Act extends who are outside the said territories.

2. *Application of Act.*—*(1) This Act applies—*

(a) to any person who is a Hindu by religion in any of its forms or developments, including a Virashaiva, a Lingayat or a follower of the Brahmo, Prarthana or Arya Samaj,

(b) to any person who is a Buddhist, Jaina or Sikh by religion, and to any other person domiciled in the territories to which this Act extends who is not a Muslim, Christian, Parsi or Jew by religion, unless it is proved that any such person would not have been governed by the Hindu law or by any custom or usage as part of that law in respect of any of the matters dealt with herein if this Act had not been passed.

Explanation.—The following persons are Hindus, Buddhists, Jainas or Sikhs by religion, as the case may be:—

(a) any child, legitimate or illegitimate, both of whose parents are Hindus, Buddhists, Jains or Sikhs by religion;

(b) any child, legitimate or illegitimate, one of whose parents is a Hindu, Buddhist, Jaina or Sikh by religion and who is brought up as a member of the tribe, community, group or family to which such parent belongs or belonged; and

(c) any person who is a convert or re-convert to the Hindu, Buddhist, Jaina or Sikh religion.

(2) Notwithstanding anything contained in sub-section (1), nothing contained in this Act shall apply to the members of any Scheduled tribe within the meaning of clause (25) of article 366 of the Constitution unless the Central Government, by notification in the Official Gazette, otherwise directs.

(3) The expression "Hindu" in any portion of this Act shall be construed as if it included a person who, though not a Hindu by religion, is, nevertheless, a person to whom this Act applies by virtue of the provisions contained in this section.

3. *Definitions.*—*In this Act, unless the context otherwise requires,—*

(a) the expressions "custom" and "usage" signify any rule which, having been continuously and uniformly observed for a long time, has obtained the force of law among Hindus in any local area, tribe, community, group or family: Provided that the rule is certain and not unreasonable or opposed to public policy; and

Provided further that in the case of a rule applicable only to a family it has not been discontinued by the family;

(b) "district court" means, in any area for which there is a city civil court, that court, and in any other area the principal civil court of original jurisdiction, and includes any other civil court which may be specified by the State Government, by notification in the Official Gazette, as having jurisdiction in respect of the matters dealt with in this Act;

(c) "full blood" and "half blood"– two persons are said to be related to each other by full blood when they are descended from a common ancestor by the same wife and by half blood when they are descended from a common ancestor but by different wives;

(d) "uterine blood"– two persons are said to be related to each other by uterine blood when they are descended from a common ancestress but by different husbands;

Explanation.—In clauses (c) and (d), "ancestor" includes the father and "ancestress" the mother;

(e) "prescribed" means prescribed by rules made under this Act;

(f)

(i) "sapinda relationship" with reference to any person extends as far as the third generation (inclusive) in the line of ascent through the mother, and the fifth (inclusive) in the line of ascent through the father, the line being traced upwards in each case from the person concerned, who is to be counted as the first generation;

(ii) two persons are said to be "sapindas" of each other if one is a lineal ascendant of the other within the limits of sapinda relationship, or if they have a common lineal ascendant who is within the limits of sapinda relationship with reference to each of them;

(g) "degrees of prohibited relationship"– two persons are said to be within the "degrees of prohibited relationship"—

(i) if one is a lineal ascendant of the other; or

(ii) if one was the wife or husband of a lineal ascendant or descendant of the other; or

(iii) if one was the wife of the brother or of the father's or mother's brother or of the grandfather's or grandmother's brother of the other; or

(iv) if the two are brother and sister, uncle and niece, aunt and nephew, or children of brother and sister or of two brothers or of two sisters;

Explanation.—For the purposes of clauses (f) and (g), relationship includes—

(i) relationship by half or uterine blood as well as by full blood;

(ii) illegitimate blood relationship as well as legitimate;

(iii) relationship by adoption as well as by blood; and all terms of relationship in those clauses shall be construed accordingly.'

It is important to mention that a definition similar to section 3(a) of the HMA, 1955 is also found in section 3(a) of the Hindu Adoptions and Maintenance Act 1956 (HAMA, 1956).

Section 5 of the HMA, 1955 prescribes the valid conditions for a Hindu marriage, which are stated below. It will be noticed that section 5(iv) explicitly recognises customary marriages.

'5. Conditions for a Hindu marriage

A marriage may be solemnised between any two Hindus, if the following conditions are fulfilled, namely:—

(i) neither party has a spouse living at the time of the marriage;

(ii) at the time of the marriage, neither party—

(a) is incapable of giving a valid consent to it in consequence of unsoundness of mind; or

(b) though capable of giving a valid consent, has been suffering from mental disorder of such a kind or to such an extent as to be unfit for marriage and the procreation of children; or

(c) has been subject to recurrent attacks of insanity;

(iii) the bridegroom has completed the age of twenty one years and the bride the age of eighteen years at the time of the marriage;

(iv) the parties are not within the degrees of prohibited relationship unless the custom or usage governing each of them permits of a marriage between the two;

(v) the parties are not sapindas of each other, unless the custom or usage governing each of them permits of a marriage between the two.'

Clearly, it will be noticed that section 5(iv) statutorily permits marriage between the degrees of prohibited relationship on the basis of custom or usage.

Section 8 of the HMA, 1955 provides for registration of marriages, and even validly performed customary marriages can be registered under section 8 of the HMA, 1955 which reads as follows:

'8. Registration of Hindu marriages

(1) For the purpose of facilitating the proof of Hindu marriages, the State Government may make rules providing that the parties to any such marriage may have the particulars relating to their marriage entered in such manner and subject to such conditions as may be prescribed in a Hindu Marriage Register kept for the purpose.

(2) Notwithstanding anything contained in sub-section (1), the State Government may, if it is of opinion that it is necessary or expedient so to do, provide that the entering of the particulars referred to in sub-section (1) shall be compulsory in the State or in any part thereof, whether in all cases or in such cases as may be specified, and where any such direction has been issued, any person contravening any rule made in this behalf shall be punishable with fine which may extend to twenty-five rupees.

(3) All rules made under this section shall be laid before the State Legislature, as soon as may be, after they are made.

(4) The Hindu Marriage Register shall at all reasonable times be open for inspection, and shall be admissible as evidence of the statements therein contained and certified extracts therefrom shall, on application, be given by the Registrar on payment to him of the prescribed fee.

(5) Notwithstanding anything contained in this section, the validity of any Hindu marriage shall in no way be affected by the omission to make the entry.'

Section 29 of the HMA, 1955 gives statutory recognition to customary divorce and the same is stated below for ease of reference.

'29. *Savings*

(1) A marriage solemnised between Hindus before the commencement of this Act, which is otherwise valid, shall not be deemed to be invalid or ever to have been invalid by reason only of the fact that the parties thereto belonged to the same gotra or pravara or belonged to different religions, castes or sub-divisions of the same caste.

(2) Nothing contained in this Act shall be deemed to affect any right recognised by custom or conferred by any special enactment to obtain the dissolution of a Hindu marriage, whether solemnised before or after the commencement of this Act.

(3) Nothing contained in this Act shall affect any proceeding under any law for the time being in force for declaring any marriage to be null and void or for annulling or dissolving any marriage or for judicial separation pending at the commencement of this Act, and any such proceeding may be continued and determined as if this Act had not been passed.

Nothing contained in this Act shall be deemed to affect the provisions contained in the Special Marriage Act, 1954 (43 of 1954) with respect to marriages between Hindus solemnised under that Act, whether before or after the commencement of this Act.'

ESSENTIALS OF A VALID CUSTOM

It is important to refer to the essential ingredients of a valid custom, which essentially require that the custom should be ancient, certain, reasonable and not opposed to public policy. In 1969, in *Rabindra Nath Dutta* v. *State,* AIR 1969 Cal 55 the Calcutta High Court laid down that the provisions of the HMA, 1955 do not provide for any particular kind or form of ceremonies to be observed in a Hindu marriage. The judgment at para 20, page 58 reads as follows:

'20. The Hindu Marriage Act, 1955 does not lay down any special or particular kind or form of ceremonies to be compulsorily observed in all Hindu marriages. In fact, the form of marriage, prescribed by the Sastras, is subject to modifications by custom or usage. But the expression "Customary Ceremonies" cannot be taken to mean that "Sastric Ceremonies" have been totally ignored. The expression "Customary Rites and Ceremonies" naturally means such sastric ceremonies, which the caste or community to which the party belongs is customarily following. For Customary rites and ceremonies to be accepted it must be shown that such custom as an essence of marriage ceremony had been followed definitely from ancient times and that the members of the Caste, Community or Sub-Caste had recognised such ceremonies as obligatory. Once it is proved by evidence what ceremonies had been followed as customary rites, it is no longer left to the will of the Caste, Community or Sub-Caste to alter them as the essence of custom is that on account of its definiteness it had been recognised and adopted by the caste or community with certainty and without any variation.'

The Supreme Court of India in the case of *Harihar Prasad Singh* v. *Balmiki Prasad Singh,* AIR 1975 SC 733, held that the specific family custom pleaded in a particular case should be proved. The initial onus lies on the plaintiffs to prove the special custom. It must be proved that the custom has been acted upon in practice for such a long period and with such invariability as to show that it has by common consent been submitted to as the established governing rule of the particular family.

TRADITIONAL REASONS AND OBJECTIVES BEHIND CUSTOMARY MARRIAGES

The *Chadar* ceremony (the second marriage which is one of the forms of Karewa marriage), is a brief marriage ceremony which is basically handing over the bride to the bridegroom. This custom of low-key marriages is uniformly followed within the Jatts and certain sections of the Sikh community and is an established ongoing practice of Karewa marriages within the Sikh community. There is no dispute as to the validity of such a custom.

This customary wedding ceremony is generally a small low-key ceremony. Given the circumstances of such a wedding, no celebrations are held at all. No guests are invited nor are any pictures taken at all. These Karewa marriages, generally as per custom, are usually performed in such a low-key manner. Following the tenets of the Sikh religion, no actual wedding ceremony is performed in a Sikh temple, unlike a wedding ceremony in normal circumstances. The main reason for following such a practice is that it is a remarriage of a widow, quite often within the immediate family itself.

Traditionally, one of the prime objectives of such a customary marriage is the rehabilitation of the widow within the family fold, and to retain the land holding within the family fold. Since, Karewa marriages emanate from the state of Punjab, which is known for its flourishing agriculture, the size of the land holdings have added significance for the family name. Land holdings in the state of Punjab are considered to be the pride of the family and more valuable than the family silver.

ADDITIONAL MODES OF PROVING VALID CUSTOMARY MARRIAGES: CREDIBLE EVIDENCE BY WAY OF AFFIDAVITS AND EXPERT LEGAL REPORTS

Evidence as to the usage and continuance of customary marriages and practices can be put forward in the shape of affidavits, to demonstrate the genuineness of the same to the satisfaction of the immigration authorities when they doubt the existence and usage of such customary practices. The claim may additionally be supported by expert reports from lawyers of repute, in the event of any post-refusal appeal proceedings or in any litigation in any foreign court or tribunal.

Such affidavits should be tendered by the aggrieved beneficiary applicant wife, and made by the *Sarpanch* (the elected village headman including several respectable elderly people from the village from different walks of life). There should be at least eight to ten such affidavits couched in very specific terms as to the applicability, specific practice, usage and continuity of the custom within the community.

The Supreme Court in *Harihar Prasad* (supra), AIR 1975 SC 733 has traced the history of the usage of the family customs, also placing reliance on some of the very early decisions of the Privy Council:

> '6. *Now on whom does the burden rest and what is the scope of the evidence that is admissible? The earliest decision on the question regarding proof of custom in variance of the general law is found in* Ramalakshmi Ammal *v.* Shivanatha Perumal, *(1872) 14 Moo Ind App 570 (585) (PC) to the effect:*
>
> > "It is of the essence of special usages modifying the ordinary law of succession that they should be ancient and invariable; and it is further essential that they should be established to be so by clear and unambiguous evidence. It is only by means of such evidence that the Courts can be assured of their existence, and that they possess the conditions of antiquity and certainty on which alone their legal title to recognition depends."'

This passage was quoted by this court with the approval in its decision in *Pushpavathi Vijayaram* v. *P. Visweswar*, AIR 1964 SC 118 and this court went on further to observe:

> '*In dealing with the family custom, the same principle will have to be applied, though, of course, in the case of a family custom, instances in support of the custom may not be as many or as frequent as in the case of customs pertaining to a territory or to the community or to the character of any estate. In dealing with family customs, the consensus of opinion amongst the members of the family, the traditional belief entertained by them and acted upon by them, their statements, and their conduct would all be relevant and it is only where the relevant evidence of such a character appears to the Court to be sufficient that a specific family custom pleaded in a particular case would be held to be proved,* Abdul Hussein Khan v. Bibi Sona, *AIR 1917 PC 181.*'

The observations of the Supreme Court of India back in 1964 in *Pushpavathi Vijayaram* v. *P. Visweswar*, were subsequently reiterated in *Harihar Prasad* in 1975.

Obviously, affidavits of local village people should state that the customary marriage of the applicant was on the basis of family custom, consensus of the applicant wife and also the family and the community and they acted accordingly upon the traditional belief entertained by them.

It should not be the case at all that the usage of the custom of Karewa marriage, other forms of customary marriages or divorces by either of the spouses with their consent and the support of the family has sprung up overnight, possibly to circumvent immigration rules. The pleaded custom should be supported by affidavits of respectable community members and there should exist no such infirmity in the pleadings made by them.

CUSTOMARY DISSOLUTION OF MARRIAGES, UNDER HMA, 1955, SECTION 29(2)

Customary dissolution of marriages is permitted under section 29(2) of the HMA, 1955. There is a direct judgment of the Jammu and Kashmir High Court in *Smt. Rano Devi* v. *Rishi Kumar*, AIR 1981 J&K 2.

The interpretation of section 29(2) of the HMA, 1955 in crystal clear terms reads as follows, at para 6, page 4 of the above mentioned case:

> *'It clearly states that marriage may be dissolved in accordance with a custom governing the parties, or under any other law providing for the same. This sub-section is couched in a stronger language and says that notwithstanding anything contained in the Act, including sections 4 and 13, a Hindu marriage may be dissolved even under the customary law of the parties, by adopting a mode different from the one provided under the Act. This is what has happened here also. Instead of approaching the District Court in a petition under section 13, the parties, by mutual agreement, dissolved their marriage by executing a deed of divorce, a mode permissible under the customs followed by them. The trial Court was, therefore, right in dismissing the appellant's petition on the ground that since the marriage between the parties already stood dissolved through a customary divorce, no decree for the restitution of conjugal rights could be passed in her favour.'*

There is a custom among the Sikh Jats of Amritsar, by which a husband can dissolve a marriage out of court, preferably by written instrument, which of course is saved by section 29(2) of the HMA, 1955. Thus, a second marriage after such a customary divorce was held not to be void. This was held in the case of *Balwinder Singh* v. *Gurpal Kaur*, AIR 1985 Del 14, which has elucidated the position of customary divorces in very eloquent terms in para 20 as follows:

> *'20. The upshot of the whole discussion, therefore is that there is ample oral as well as other evidence on record to warrant the conclusion that there does exist a custom amongst Sikh Jats of District Amritsar under which a marriage can be dissolved out of court preferably through a written instrument. The very fact that dissolution of marriage amongst Sikh Jats of that district has been taking place even after the enactment of the Act is in itself a strong proof of its recognition by the community concerned. It would show that despite the relief of dissolution of marriage by divorce being available under the Act people still prefer to resort to customary law rather than seek redress in a court of law under the Act. So,*

the mere fact that the appellant has not furnished any old instance would not undermine the evidentiary value of the instances cited by various witnesses in Court; rather they tend to establish beyond doubt that such a custom is firmly rooted and is still prevalent despite the remedy of divorce being available under statutory law. Hence, I hold accordingly.'

Quite often, there are refusal letters by the embassy authorities in instances of Karewa marriages or other forms of valid customary marriages. That such an assertion in the case of a valid customary marriage that the beneficiary has married her former brother-in-law, which of course is not legally sustainable also in light of the law laid down in *Parkash Chander* v. *Smt Parmeshwari*, AIR 1987 P&H 37. The most relevant paragraph relating to the interpretation of Karewa marriages reads as follows:

'12. The next question of definite importance which arises in this case is whether during the lifetime of Ishwar Singh who was very much present in the village, any Karewa marriage could be legally entered into between the respondent and the appellant, or had it in fact been so taken place. There is no doubt whatsoever in my mind that in the presence of Ishwar Singh, who was very much alive in the village, no valid marriage could take place between the parties. Such a marriage would be void in the face of the provisions of section 5(1) of the Act wherein it is laid down that a marriage may be solemnised between any two Hindus if neither party has a spouse living at the time of the marriage. It has been held by the Supreme Court in Mohd. Ikram Hussain *v.* State of Uttar Pradesh, *AIR 1964 SC 1625, that in view of provisions of sections 5 and 11 of the Act, such a marriage would be null and void. In para 74 of the* Digest of Customary Law *by Sir W.H. Rattigan (13th Edn.), it has been laid down that until the former marriage is validly set aside, a woman cannot marry a second husband in the lifetime of her first husband.'*

THE WIFE SHOULD NOT HAVE A LIVING SPOUSE FOR A VALID KAREWA MARRIAGE

It is very important that for a Karewa marriage to be valid the wife should have no living spouse at the time she solemnised her subsequent Karewa marriage.

In the abovementioned case of *Parkash Chander* (supra), AIR 1987 P&H 37, the Karewa marriage was held to be invalid because the original husband of the wife was subsequently found not to be dead. He was found to be alive after a certain period of time. Meanwhile, the wife had entered into a Karewa marriage with her brother-in-law. In this particular case, the wife pleaded the custom raising the presumption that, since her first husband had not been heard of for 7-8 years he was presumed to be dead. This contention was rejected outright on the ground that the alleged custom was contrary to section 108 of the Indian Evidence Act, 1872. The Punjab and Haryana High Court tersely held as follows:

'20. . . . In the instant case what the respondent had pleaded was that since Ishwar Singh, her husband, had not been heard of and his whereabouts were not known for a period of 7–8 years, she entered into a Karewa marriage with

the appellant. Therefore, it is not necessary to probe into the facts of the issue whether there is a custom prevalent in the community of the parties which permits dissolution of marriage on the ground that either party had been mentally insane, had become impotent or was incapable of performing the duties of husband/wife. The only aspect that needs examination and determination is whether a divorce is permissible in the community of the parties under custom where one of the spouses is unheard of or his whereabouts are not known. Before examination of this aspect of the issue, it has to be kept in mind that a custom to be valid must not contravene any express provision of the law. It should not be against public policy nor it should be contrary to justice, equity and good conscience and it should be ancient, certain and invariable. These ingredients of a valid custom are laid down in para 1 of Rattigan's Digest of Customary Law ibid . . .'

In the event of refusal of a settlement visa for a wife to join her husband overseas in the case of a valid customary marriage, support can very much be drawn by the beneficiary wife from these observations of the Punjab and Haryana High Court. This is to the effect that the custom of *Karewa* marriage pleaded by the beneficiary wife is very much valid, does not contravene any express provision of law and nor it is against public policy.

Under the provisions of the HMA, 1955 both parties to the marriage are at full liberty to solemnise their marriage by way of customary rites and ceremonies generally prevalent in their community. However, such ceremonies and rites should essentially fulfil the essential ingredients of a custom, as already stated above. But, if *Saptapadi* (taking of seven steps around the holy fire) and invocation before the sacred fire are made, the marriage is validly solemnised under the Shastric law.

CUSTOMARY MARRIAGES WILL NOT BE RECOGNISED IN THE ABSENCE OF COGENT RELIABLE PROOF

In a customary marriage case where there is no proof of custom nor is a customary marriage is pleaded, such a customary marriage will not be recognised. In this particular regard, it is important to note the observations of the Kerala High Court in *Chakki* v. *Ayyappan,* AIR 1989 Ker 89:

'10. *The appellant cannot succeed only by showing that in other marriages of the community there were exchange of rings and pooja and thali etc. Those can be accepted as requirements of customary marriage only if they are proved to be sufficiently ancient and definite and that members of the community recognise them as obligatory. It should also be shown that those formalities were unalterable. As we indicated earlier, there are no pleadings, much less any proof of an ancient, definite and unalterable custom in this regard.*'

By way of clarification, in this case, the marriage was held to be valid on the basis of the performance of the statutory essential requirement of a Hindu marriage, *i.e.,* invocation before the sacred fire, and *Saptapadi* (taking seven steps by the groom and bride jointly before the sacred fire).

KAREWA MARRIAGES GENERALLY PREDOMINANT IN AGRICULTURAL TRIBES OF PUNJABI ORIGIN

In *Garja Singh* v. *Surjit Kaur,* AIR 1991 P&H 177, it was held that a marriage will be valid only if the ceremony through which it is solemnised is sanctioned by the religion of either party as a customary ceremony. Therefore, merely going through some ceremonies like distribution of *Gur* and *Shakkar* (sugar) with the intention that the parties be taken to have been married will not make them the customary ceremonies prescribed by law or sanctioned by custom. Even in the general customary law in Punjab as applicable to the predominantly agricultural tribes, the *Karewa* marriage with the brother or some male relative of the deceased husband requires no religious ceremonies and confers all the rights of a valid marriage. However, the bride in this case had no connection whatsoever with the deceased, alleged to be her husband prior to the execution of the '*Karewa Nama*'. The marriage with a stranger has to be performed in accordance with the customary rites or ceremonies as prescribed by law. There was no allegation, much less proof, as to what were the customary ceremonies performed for solemnising the marriage between the deceased and the defendant claiming a share in the estate of the deceased, as his widow. This is also one of the judgments which categorically notices that such *Karewa* marriages are generally predominant in agricultural tribes of Punjabi origin.

CUSTOM SHOULD BE PROVED IN THE FOLLOWING TERMS

Furthermore, the Punjab and Haryana High Court in *Asha Rani* v. *Gulshan Kumar,* AIR 1995 P&H 287 has elaborated on the way in which custom should be proved:

> *'10. A custom must be proved to be ancient, certain and reasonable if it is to be recognised and acted upon by Courts of Law. The specific family custom pleaded in a particular case should be proved by the party pleading it. It must be proved that the custom has been acted upon in practice for such a long period and with such invariability, as to show that it has, by common consent, been submitted to as the established governing rule of the particular family. Custom no doubt can be proved by oral evidence of witnesses acquainted with custom, instances and general pronouncements. Section 29(2) of the Act does not disturb the position which a customary divorce occupied before the enactment of the Act.'*

As stated above, customary marriage and divorce, *qua* the aggrieved beneficiary applicant, can additionally be proved by key credible witnesses from the community and possibly community leaders as well, in the shape of affidavits.

NOT NECESSARY FOR PARTIES TO OBTAIN DIVORCE FROM COURT, ON GROUND ALREADY RECOGNISED BY CUSTOM

In *Rita Rani* v. *Ramesh Kumar,* 1995 (2) HLR 338 (P&H), it was held that, if there is a local custom by which marriage can be dissolved either by brotherhood or by executing an agreement, such a customary dissolution of marriage is saved by section 29(2) of the HMA, 1955. And more importantly the parties are not required to obtain a decree of divorce through a court, after such a customary divorce has been effected. The Punjab and Haryana High Court held as follows:

> '7. *Relying on* Balwinder Singh v. Smt. Gurpal Kaur, *AIR 1985 Del 14: 1985 (1) AIHLR 442 (Del);* Smt. Sudarshan Kaur v. Major Manmohan Singh Bhatt, *AIR 1978 P&H 115;* A Digest of Customary Law by Sir W.H. Rattigan *(14th Edn.), p. 470; and* Hindu Law by Mulla, *16th Edn., p. 745, he contended that from the pleadings and sole testimony of Ramesh Kumar, it is evident that in the cast of the parties, there is customary mode of marriage and customary mode of dissolution of marriage also. Therefore, Ramesh Kumar himself dissolved his earlier marriage with Rita Rani under this customary mode* i.e., *dissolution of marriage by "biradari". He stressed that under section 29(2) of the Act, it is not necessary for parties in any such case to go to Court to obtain divorce on ground recognised by custom. It is not the case of Ramesh Kumar that this customary mode of dissolution of marriage is either against the public policy or is not upheld by Courts.*'

The ruling in this case is of immense significance. It has been categorically held by the Punjab and Haryana High Court at Chandigarh in this case that it is not necessary for the parties to go to court on the ground that such a divorce is recognised by custom. Likewise, it is argued by analogy that it is not mandatory for the parties to the marriage as in the present case to go to court for validation of their customary marriage. Generally, there is an assertion in the refusal letters in settlement cases by the embassy authorities to the effect 'also please provide a court order stating that this relationship is allowed'. Clearly, in light of the settled position of law as stated above, the assertion of a court declaration by the embassy authorities to the effect that the relationship is permitted by law is not a sustainable action.

COURTS CAN TAKE JUDICIAL NOTICE OF GENERAL CUSTOMS

The Punjab and Haryana High Court in *Ranbir Kaur* alias *Harjit Kaur* v. *Gurnam Singh*, 1996 (2) HLR 71, held that the courts can take judicial notice of general customs. The court elaborated that the term 'general custom' is used in the sense that it has, by repeated recognition by courts over a period of time, become entitled to judicial notice. This judgment crystallises the law on judicial notice of general customs by consolidating the earlier case-law as follows:

> '8. *Whoever sets up a custom must prove the same. Sometimes the custom is recognised by Courts and it passes into the law of land. This question was considered by the Supreme Court in the case of* Ujagar Singh v. Mst. Jeo, *AIR 1959 SC 1041. In paragraph 14 it was held:*
>
> > *14. It therefore appears to us that the ordinary rule is that all customs, general or otherwise, have to be proved. Under section 57 of the Evidence Act however nothing need to be proved of which courts can take judicial notice. Therefore, it is said that if there is a custom of which the courts can take judicial notice, it need not be proved. The circumstances in which the courts can take judicial notice of a custom* **were stated** *by Lord Dunedin in* Raja Ram Rao *v.* Raja of Pittapur, *45 Ind* **App 148** *(154, 155): AIR 1918 PC 81 (83), in the following words, "When a* **custom or** *usage, whether in*

> *regard to a tenure or a contract or a family right, is repeatedly brought to the notice of the Courts of a country, the Courts may hold that custom or usage to be introduced into the law without necessity of proof in each individual case." When a custom has been so recognised by the courts, it passes into the law of the land and the proof of it then becomes unnecessary under section 57(1) of the Evidence Act. It appears to us that in the courts in the Punjab the expression "general custom" has really been used in this sense, namely, that a custom has by repeated recognition by courts, become entitled to judicial notice as was said in* Bawa Singh *v.* Mt. Taro, *AIR 1951 Punj 239; and* Sukhwant Kaur v. Balwant Singh, *AIR 1951 Punj 242."*

The judgment specifically highlights the importance of general custom. This term is used in the sense that the same by repeated recognition by the courts has become entitled to judicial notice.

Thus, it can be stated that the onus of proving and establishing a custom would lie on the party who claims its benefit. As already stated before, from the catalogue of evidence in the shape of affidavits furnished by the beneficiary applicant, other members of the family, as also by respectable people from the community, the practice of customary marriages and divorces can be proved successfully. Whether the same is acceptable for judicial notice or it is to be proven separately would depend on the facts and circumstances of each case. It is clear that, in the northern Indian state of Punjab, customary divorce and customary widow remarriage is an acceptable customary practice in some local communities. (For further details see Sir W.H. Rattigan *A Digest of Customary Law (in Punjab)*, 1880, and reprinted subsequently by other authors, which discusses in great detail customary law practices prevalent in Punjab in all walks of life.

The scheme and object of the HMA, 1955 are not to override any such custom which recognises divorce, and explicit recognition is given to the same by the saving clause contained in section 29(2). It is not necessary for parties in any such case to go to court to obtain divorce on the grounds that it is already recognised by custom. The custom, as elaborated above must be a valid custom. Section 29(2) saves customary divorce but the party relying on a custom needs to prove the existence of such custom and also that it is ancient, certain, reasonable and not opposed to public policy. In *Mariammal* v. *Padmanabhan*, AIR 2001 Mad 350, the Madras High Court overruled the finding of the trial court that there cannot be customary divorce after the coming into force of the HMA, 1955. It held that divorce was recognised by custom even before the Act, and after the Act courts also uphold the custom if not opposed to public policy.

From the discussion and the case-law analysis on section 29 of the HMA, 1955 it is manifest that the section specifically saves customs regarding marriage and divorce from the operation of the provisions of the HMA, 1955 and they are legally recognised. In *Jasbir Singh* v. *Inderjit Kaur*, AIR 2003 P&H 317, the husband sought annulment of his marriage on the ground that, at the time of marriage, his wife was already married. The wife's contention was that she had obtained a customary divorce from her previous husband and the petitioner was aware of this as he had seen the written deed of customary divorce; he was, therefore, estopped from taking the plea that the wife was already married and not divorced. The wife was a Jat Sikh from District Sangrur in Punjab. After going through the evidence, the court held that it was established that there is a custom among the Jat Sikhs of District Sangrur which permits divorce and the wife had obtained the divorce according to that custom. The validity of the custom being saved, it was not necessary for the parties to go to court to obtain divorce; it is open for the parties to dissolve the marriage out of court, in accordance with the custom. The court relied on, *inter alia, Gurdit Singh* v. *Mst Angrez Kaur,* AIR 1968 SC 142, where the apex court held that there can be valid divorce where custom allows dissolution, and on dissolution of a marriage by custom, the party can enter into second marriage in the lifetime of the first divorced spouse. The husband's petition for annulment was consequently dismissed in *Jasbir Kaur* (supra), AIR 2003 P&H 317 as, the wife having obtained customary divorce from her previous husband, the marriage with the petitioner was legal and valid. The Punjab and Haryana High Court on this case held as follows:

> *'9. In AIR 1978 P&H 98 (*supra*) relied upon by the learned counsel for the appellant-husband, it has been held that a party relying upon a particular custom is called upon to allege and to prove that custom. It was further held that entries in a Riwaj-e-am, which pertain to a special custom applicable to a locality or a class of persons, should also be presumed to be correct unless rebutted . . .'*

The Court further held:

> *'20. . . . In* Gurdit Singh *v.* Mst. Angrez Kaur, *AIR 1968 SC 142, it was held by the Hon'ble Supreme Court that a custom exists among the Hindu Jats of the Jalandhar District which permits a valid divorce by a husband of his wife which dissolves the marriage. It was further held that on the dissolution of such a marriage the divorced wife can enter into a valid marriage with a second husband in the lifetime of the first husband. The law laid down by this Court in (1962) Punj LR 1179, was affirmed by the Hon'ble Supreme Court, in the said authority. In* Balwinder Singh v. Smt. Gurpal Kaur, *1985 Marri LJ 414: AIR 1985 Del 14 it was held by the Delhi High Court that on a plain reading of section 29(2) of the Hindu Marriage Act, 1955, it is manifest that a marriage may still be dissolved in accordance with a custom governing the parties or under any other law providing for the same. It was further held that the validity of any custom recognising the right to dissolve a marriage is expressly saved by this sub-section. It was further held that as a necessary corollary, it follows that it would not be necessary for the parties in any such case to go to Court to obtain divorce on grounds recognised by custom and it would be open to dissolve the marriage out of Court in accordance with such custom. It was further held that the net result will be that a Hindu marriage may now be dissolved under section 13 of the Hindu Marriage Act, 1955 or under any other special enactment or in accordance with any custom applicable to the parties. Reliance was also placed on the law laid down by Hon'ble Court, in* Gurdit Singh's *case (supra), in respect of the existence of such a custom in District Jalandhar. It was also held that the existence of such a custom permitting dissolution of marriage by divorce amongst Hindu Jats was also prevalent in Districts surrounding Jalandhar, including Amritsar, Hoshiarpur and Ludhiana.*

21. In view of the above, in my opinion, it can safely be held that there is a custom among Jat Sikhs of District Sangrur, permitting dissolution of marriage by divorce through writing executed by the parties in this regard and such a divorce would be recognised, in view of section 29(2) of the Hindu Marriage Act, 1955 and the law laid down by the Hon'ble Supreme Court and Delhi High Court, in the cases referred to above. I am further of the opinion, that the learned Additional District Judge had rightly found that the marriage between the petitioner and respondent could not be annulled under section 11 of the Hindu Marriage Act, 1955, in as much as respondent had validly obtained a divorce from her previous husband Lachhman Singh, at the time when her marriage had taken place with the petitioner. Accordingly, I affirm the findings of the learned Additional District Judge in this regard.'

This ruling in *Jasbir Singh* (supra), laying in similar tenor to *Rita Rani* v. *Ramesh Kumar*, 1995 (2) HLR 338 (P&H) (*supra*) is again of immense significance. This is because it has been yet again categorically reiterated by the Punjab and Haryana High Court at Chandigarh that it is not necessary for the parties to go to court on the ground that such a divorce is recognised by custom. Hence, if the denial letter by the embassy authorities in the case of a valid Karewa marriage states to the effect 'also please provide a court order stating that this relationship is allowed', clearly this would not be legally sustainable according to the settled law, as elaborated above.

CUSTOMARY DISSOLUTION OF MARRIAGE DOES NOT REQUIRE VALIDATION FROM COURT – RECENT SUPREME COURT OF INDIA JUDGMENT

The Supreme Court of India in *Mahendra Nath Yadav* v. *Sheela Devi*, (2010) 9 SCC 484 upheld the judgment of the Allahabad High Court stating that the High Court rightly held that dissolution of marriage through the panchayat (local elected village council at the grassroot level) according to custom cannot be a ground for granting divorce under section 13 of the HMA, 1955. The facts of this case are as follows:

'4. According to appellant, it was customary in the locality and in the community to which both parties belong to have a divorce through the Panchayat. Thus, the Panchayat was convened on 7–6-1997. The said Panchayat decided that the appellant should pay a sum of Rs. 30,000 to the respondent's family. It was paid and a document was prepared which was duly signed by the parties. Thus, the marriage came to an end. In order to give legal effect to the said customary divorce, the appellant tried to persuade the respondent to get divorce from the Family Court under section 13B of the 1955 Act, by consent. However, she did not agree. Thus the appellant approached the Family Court by filing Petition No. 370 of 1998 under section 13 of the 1955 Act, seeking divorce on the ground of desertion and cruelty.

5. The respondent filed the counter-case i.e. *Petition No. 57 of 1999 under section 9 of the 1955 Act, for restitution of conjugal rights. The Family Court decreed the suit mainly on the ground that the marriage stood dissolved through Panchayat and dismissed the petition filed by the wife for restitution of conjugal rights vide order dated 15–09–2000. Being aggrieved, the respondent preferred appeals against both the orders before the High Court and the High Court has reversed the said order in both the cases. Hence this appeal.'*

The reasoning clearly elucidated by the apex court in not interfering with the judgment of the High Court is as follows:

'7. The High Court has rightly held that dissolution of marriage through Panchayat as per custom prevailing in that area and in that community permitted cannot be a ground for granting divorce under section 13 of the 1955 Act. We fully agree with the said decision for the reason that in case the appellant wanted a decree on the basis of customary dissolution of marriage through Panchayat held on 7–6-1997, he would not have filed a petition under section 13 of the 1955 Act. Filing this petition itself means that none of the parties was of the view that the divorce granted by the Panchayat was legal. In view of the above, we do not see any reason to interfere with the well-reasoned judgment of the High Court.'

DIFFERENT TYPES OF CUSTOMS

The Supreme Court of India in an elaborate judgment handed down in 2007 has very clearly elucidated the three types of different customs in the case of *Smt. Ass Kaur (Deceased) by LRs* v. *Kartar Singh (Dead) by LRs*, JT 2007 (9) SC 118.

One of the key issues in this case was succession rights on the basis of *Karewa* marriage:

'10. Hindu law recognises three types of customs: local custom, class custom and family custom. The courts below have held that the parties were governed by Zimindara custom. Whether the said custom is a general custom, or a special custom or for that matter a family custom has not been stated. The customary law prevailing in the State of Punjab has received a statutory sanction by reason of the Punjab Laws Act, 1872, sections 5 and 7 whereof read as under:

5. Decisions in certain cases to be according to Native law.—In questions regarding succession, special property of females, betrothal, marriage divorce, dower, adoption, guardianship, minority, bastardy, family relations, wills, legacies, gifts, partitions, or any religious usage or institution the rule of decision shall be—

(a) any custom applicable to the parties concerned, which is not contrary to justice, equity or good conscience, and has not been by this or any other enactment altered or abolished, and has not been declared to be void by any competent authority.

(b) the Muhammadan law, in cases where the parties are Muhammadans and the Hindu law, in cases where the parties are Hindus, except in so far as such law has been altered or abolished by legislative enactment, or is opposed to the provisions of this Act, or has been modified by any such customs as is above referred to.

7. Local customs and mercantile usages when valid.—All local customs and mercantile usages shall be regarded as valid, unless they are contrary to justice, equity or good conscience, or have, before the passing of this Act, been declared to be void by any competent authority.

11. Amongst the Sikh Jats of Punjab province, there exists a custom, where the widow marries her first husband's brother in the Karewa form, remarriage would not cause forfeiture of her own share.

12. In respect of Jats belonging to Ferozepur district, it has been held that a widow who remarried her first husband's brother succeeds to a co-widow in preference to collaterals. But the widow's right only accrues on husband's death, and if it does not accrue then, it cannot accrue later by the death of subsequent heir. The fact, if the widow is a Karewa widow it would not affect her right in a suit the parties to which were the two widows of a Manhas Rajput resident in the Shakargarh Tehsil of Gurudaspur District, had that [sic] the plaintiff (upon whom under the circumstances the onus lay) had failed to prove a custom in her favour, excluding the defendant, who was a co-widow by a Karewa marriage, from succeeding to a share in the deceased husband's estate. Even a woman who had contracted such marriage may not forfeit her life estate, if any, in her deceased husband's property despite the provisions of the Hindu Widows Remarriage Act, 1856. However, the said principle would not apply where a remarriage is not with the brother of her deceased but with some other relative.'

Furthermore, the apex court in paras 17 to 19 of its judgment has reiterated the settled position of law that courts can take judicial notice of custom and as and when the custom has been recognised by the courts, the same need not be proved. Paragraphs 17 to 19 at pages 123 and 124 read as follows:

'17. We may, however, notice that customary law has been recorded in Rattigan's Digest of Customary Laws. *The courts below have categorically held the law to be applicable in the instant case is the customary law having regard to the fact that the parties belonged to the community of Sidhu Jats.*

18. In R.B.S.S. Munnalal v. S.S. Rajkumar, *AIR 1962 SC 1493, this Court was considering the question as to whether a Jain widow could adopt a son to her husband without his express authority, being governed by the custom which had by long acceptance become part of the law applicable to them. Therein, it was observed:*

> *. . . It is well-settled that where a custom is repeatedly brought to the notice of the Courts of a country, the courts may hold that custom introduced into the law without the necessity of proof in each individual case . . .*

19. The court can also take judicial notice of such customs in terms of section 57 of the Evidence Act, 1872. As and when custom has repeatedly been recognised by the courts, the same need not be proved. Reference in regard to the Punjab 'general custom' may be made to Ujagar Singh *(supra), and* Bawa v. Taro, *AIR 1951 Punj 239.'*

The law reiterated and the law laid down by the Supreme Court of India in *Smt. Ass Kaur (Deceased)*, would clearly support the case of a beneficiary wife who is affected by the refusal of her settlement visa application. The apex court has yet again given clear-cut recognition to Karewa marriages, even in rights of succession. Furthermore, the observations in para 25 at pages 124 and 125 of the above judgment are also very important in a situation where a wife has performed a valid customary marriage:

'25. As statutory law did not exclude the applicability of the customary law, the principle that customary law would prevail over the statutory law would apply. It was so found by the courts below.'

The point to be conveyed is that, in the case of a valid customary marriage, the customary law would prevail over statutory law.

Lastly, in relation to the present judgment, support is drawn from the observations in para 29 at page 125 of the *Smt. Ass Kaur (deceased)*, JT 2007 (9) SC 118, judgment which reads as follows:

'29. In Daya Singh (dead) through L.Rs. *(supra), paragraph 23 of* Rattigan's Digest of Customary Law of Punjab *has been noticed. It was held:*

It is on the basis of this Customary Law that the reversioners succeeded in the suit filed by them questioning the gift made by the respondents['] mother to her. There is no doubt that Rattigan's work is an authoritative one on the subject of Customary Law in Punjab. This Court in Mahant Salig Ram *v.* Musammat Maya Devi *said:*

The customary rights of succession of daughters as against the collaterals of the father with reference to ancestral and non-ancestral lands are stated in para 23 of Rattigan's Digest of Customary Law. *It is categorically stated in sub-para (2) of that paragraph that the daughter succeeds to the self-acquired property of the father in preference to the collaterals even though they are within the fourth degree. Rattigan's work has been accepted by the Privy Council as a book of unquestioned authority in the Punjab. Indeed, the correctness of this para was not disputed before this Court in* Gopal Singh *v.* Ujagar Singh.'

The Andhra Pradesh High Court in 2008 has in relation to the constant usage of customary law has reiterated the relevant operative parts of earlier judgments of the Supreme Court of India and the Privy Council. This is in the case of Atluri Brahmanandam v. Anne Sai Bapuji, *2008 (2) AIHLR 432:*

'17. In Gokal Chand v. Parvin Kumari, *AIR 1952 SC 231, Supreme Court laid down general principles, to be kept in view, in dealing with the question of customary law. Inter alia it is laid down that, "a custom in order to be binding must derive its force from the fact that by long usage it has obtained a force of law, but English rule that, 'a custom in order that it may be legal and binding, must have been used so long that the memory of man runneth not to the contrary' should not be strictly applied to Indian conditions. All that is necessary to prove is that the usage has been acted upon in practice for such a long period and with such invariability as to show that it has, by common consent, been submitted to as the established governing rule of a particular locality".*

18. In Raja of Pittapur, *AIR 1918 PC 81, the Privy Council held as under:*

This proposition, it must be noted, does not negative the doctrine that there are members of the family entitled to maintenance in the case of an impartible zamindari. Just as the impartibility is the creature of custom, so custom may and does affirm a right to maintenance in certain members of the family. No attempt has been, as already stated, made by the plaintiff to prove any special custom in this zamindari. That by itself in the case of some claims would not be fatal. When a custom or usage, whether in regard to a tenure or a contract or a family right, is repeatedly brought to the notice of the Courts of a country, the Courts may hold that custom or usage to be introduced into the law without the necessity of proof in each individual case. It becomes in the end truly a matter of process and pleading.

19. In Bai Sakar *v.* Ismail Gafoor, *AIR 1937 Bom 65, Supreme Court laid down as under:*

The fact that a particular custom has been judicially recognized establishes that the custom is reasonable and not opposed to public policy so that it will be upheld whenever it is proved. This is the legal aspect of custom: Moult v. Halliday, *(1898) 1 QB 125. But, subject to what I shall presently state, judicial recognition of a custom in another suit leaves untouched the proof of the fact that the custom is applicable to the particular parties who are before the court.*

20. In Ujagar Singh, *AIR 1959 SC 1041, while observing that every general custom relied on [by] a person must be clearly proved to exist, the Supreme Court ruled that if the Court takes judicial notice of such custom under section 57 of Indian Evidence Act, 1872, no further proof is required. Keeping this in mind, the submission of learned Counsel for the appellant that the plaintiff did not plead and prove the existence of such custom is without any merit . . .'*

The Punjab and Haryana High Court in *Rajinder Kaur* v. *Kuldeep Singh,* 2011 (1) Haryana LR 205, refused to recognise a customary divorce in the absence of any evidence on record to prove that divorce through a *Panchyatnama* (written agreement executed before the local elected village council at the grassroot level), was actually permissible under any custom or usage prevalent in the society. In this particular case, the second marriage of the wife, without legally nullifying the earlier marriage, was held to be a nullity. The decree earlier passed by the trial court declaring the second marriage null and void on the petition of the husband was upheld by the High Court in no uncertain categorical terms.

Paragraph 11 at pages 207 and 208 of that judgment in this regard is most relevant and is reproduced hereunder:

'11. As already observed above learned matrimonial court also found as a fact, that no evidence was led to establish that there was any custom or usage prevalent in the community of the appellant under which divorce through writing of panchayatnama was permissible. Hon'ble Supreme Court in the case of M.M. Malhotra v. Union of India, *AIR 2006 SC 80, has laid down as under:—*

"11. For appreciating the status of a Hindu woman marrying a Hindu male with a living spouse some of the provisions of the Hindu Marriage Act, 1955 (herein referred to as the 'Marriage Act') have to be examined. Section 11 of

the Marriage Act declares such a marriage as null and void in the following terms:

> *11. 'Void marriage—Any marriage solemnised after the commencement of this Act shall be null and void and may, on a petition presented by either party thereto against the other party, be so declared by a decree of nullity if it contravenes any one of the conditions specified in clauses (i), (iv) and (v) of section 5.'"*

Clause (i) of section 5 lays down, for a lawful marriage, the necessary condition that neither party should have a spouse living at the time of the marriage. A marriage in contravention of this condition, therefore, is null and void. By reason of the overriding effect of the Marriage Act as mentioned in section 4, no aid can be taken of the earlier Hindu law or any custom or usage as a part of that law inconsistent with any provision of the Act. So far as section 12 is concerned, it is confined to other categories of marriages and is not applicable to one solemnised in violation of sections (i) of the Act. Sub-section (2) of section 12 puts further restrictions on such a right. The cases covered by this section are not void ab initio, *and unless all the conditions mentioned therein are fulfilled and the aggrieved party exercises the right to avoid it, the same continues to be effective The marriages covered by section 11 are void ipso jure, that is, void from the very inception, and have to be ignored as not existing in law at all if and when such a question arises. Although the section permits a formal declaration to be made on the presentation of a petition, it is not essential to obtain in advance such a formal declaration from a court in a proceeding specifically commenced for the purpose. The provisions of section 16, which is quoted below, also throw light on this aspect.*

"16. Legitimacy of children of void and voidable marriages:—

(1) Notwithstanding that a marriage is null and void under section 11, any child of such marriage who would have been legitimate if the marriage had been valid, shall be legitimate, whether such child is born before or after the commencement of Marriage Laws (Amendment) Act, 1976 (68 of 1976), and whether or not a decree of nullity is granted in respect of that marriage under this Act and whether or not the marriage is held to be void otherwise than on a petition under this Act.

(2) Where a decree of nullity is granted in respect of a voidable marriage under section 12, any child begotten or conceived before the decree is made, who would have been the legitimate child of the parties to the marriage if at the date of the decree it had been dissolved instead of being annulled, shall be deemed to be their legitimate child notwithstanding the decree of nullity.

Nothing contained in sub-section (1) or sub-section (2) shall be construed as conferring upon any child of a marriage which is null and void or which is annulled by a decree of nullity under section 12, any rights in or to the property of any person, other than the parents, in any case where, but for the passing of this Act, such child would have been incapable of possessing or acquiring any such rights by reason of his not being the legitimate child of his parents."

Sub-section (1), by using the words underlined above clearly implies that a: void marriage can be held to be so without a prior formal declaration by a court in a

> *proceeding. While dealing with cases covered by section 12, sub-section (2) refers to a decree of nullity as an essential condition and sub section (3) prominently brings out the basic difference in the character of void and voidable marriages as covered respectively by sections 11 and 12. It is also to be seen that while the legislature has considered it advisable to uphold the legitimacy of the paternity of a child born out of a void marriage, it has not extended a similar protection in respect of the mother of the child. The marriage of the appellant must, therefore, be treated as* null *and* void *from its very inception.*
>
> *In view of the authoritative pronouncement of Hon'ble Supreme Court marriage between thc parties was nullity, therefore, learned matrimonial court rightly allowed the petition and dissolved the marriage by way of a decree of nullity.'*

The judgment above is significant for two reasons. *First,* the court tersely refused to recognise an invalid customary marriage. *Secondly,* the judgment explicitly lays down that no formal declaration from the court of competent jurisdiction is necessary in the case of void *ipso jure* marriages.

It may also be added that in the illuminating judgment by Justice K. Kannan of the Punjab and Haryana High Court in *Darbara Singh* v. *Jaswant Kaur,* 2014 (1) RCR (Civil) 1004, it has been held that *Karewa* marriage among Jat Sikhs of Punjab is a valid form of marriage. In the instant case, the father of the widow tied a turban on the head of the younger brother of the late husband and he in turn put a chadar on the widow, after which *gur* was distributed. Expounding the social aspect of *karewa* marriages to bring respectability to young widows who were rehabilitated by marriage to the deceased husband's brother or any such relative, it was held that it is not expected that such forms of marriage would be attendant with any elaborate ceremonies. The Court ruled that mere execution of the *Karewanama,* even without proof of customary ceremony to celebrate a *karewa* marriage, would be sufficient proof of valid marriage and for conferring the status to the woman as that of a wife. Obviating the need for proof of elaborate ceremonies, the Court very rightly observed that, *"Even a legislation legitimizing remarriage of widows will obtain its full value only if it approves of minimal ceremonies accompanying such functions as sufficient to validate the marriage."* Consequently, the High Court upheld the decision of the Appellate Court finding the marriage to be true by accepting the *Karewanama* as evidence of such performance of *Karewa* marriage. Very aptly, the High Court thus recognized the consequential status of the wife as sufficient to claim possession as a heir by giving her preference over a son through a previous marriage without the necessity of going into the aspect of whether the *Karewanama* constituted a Will. This, in terms, was substantial justice and the true import of recognizing the evidentiary value of the *Karewa* marriage.

CONCLUSION

Clearly, it emerges that custom is an important source of Hindu law, having due statutory recognition by virtue of the saving clauses under the provisions of the Hindu Marriage Act, 1955. A huge amount of case-law is available on the subject.

There is a clear consistency of approach by the Supreme Court of India and various High Courts in different parts of the country in reiterating the earlier settled position of customary law with regard to marriage and divorce. The underlying aim of this chapter is to attempt to ensure that the principled approach in customary marriages and divorces, as applicable under the relevant provisions of the Hindu Marriage Act, 1955, is duly availed of by the parties to such genuine customary marriages and divorces in limited situations, especially in the area of international family migration.

Sometimes, from practical experience it is noticed that parties who genuinely perform customary marriages and enter into customary divorces depending on the facts and circumstances of each case, intending to join their spouses resident abroad on the basis of family reunion, in the context of the present chapter, are not properly and professionally guided. This of course results in outright refusals, at the hands of the embassy authorities. The problem is compounded by the fact of lack of specialist knowledge on the part of visa and consular officers, obviously for which they cannot be blamed. Clearly, this is an avoidable situation. The fact of the matter is that such a gap needs to be plugged appropriately by proper paperwork substantially highlighting the statutory provisions and the settled position of law.

Lastly, as it will be noticed that knowledge of Indian family law also becomes essential for foreign immigration lawyers acting on the behalf of sponsors in appeal proceedings in the event of unsuccessful applications. Specialist domestic family law expertise is pivotal in customary marriages and divorces. The relevant provisions of Indian law in this regard will hopefully prevent foreign practitioners from unwarily walking into traps created by conflicts between local Indian laws and laws of their own jurisdiction.

Conflict of Laws in Inter-Country Adoptions—The Indian Perspective with Special Reference to the Position After India Ratifying the Hague Convention on Adoptions

I. Introduction

At the outset it is important to emphasize that at present there exists no exclusive general law of adoption of children governing non-Hindus and foreigners. Adoption is permitted by statute among Hindus and by customs among some other communities. At present non-Hindus and foreigners can only be guardians under the Guardian and Wards Act, 1890. In India, in the last few years a new dimension has also emerged on account of tedious and complicated inter-country adoption laws and procedures. This gives rise to surrogacy arrangements, preferred especially by the Non-Resident Indians community resident overseas. This new emerging issue is also discussed in this chapter.

In actual practice, earlier foreign nationals and persons of Indian Origin domiciled overseas wishing to adopt children from India had to also obtain guardianship orders from the District Court or High Court, as the case may be, within whose territorial jurisdiction the child is residing. This was done with a view to later adopt the child formally under the legal system of the country of their habitual residence. However, with the enactment of the new CARA Guidelines of 2011, now the Courts have the power to directly grant a child to be placed in adoption and grant adoption orders if the adoptive parents want to adopt the child. There is no need to first take a Guardianship Order from an Indian Court and then adopt the child in the foreign country through their foreign laws. This is indeed a big step to simplify the procedures and provide for adoption through Indian law. A brief reference is also made to the enactment of the Juvenile Justice (Care and Protection) Act, 2000, subsequently amended by Act 33 of 2006, (hereinafter called JJ Act). This legislation introduces the concept of secular adoptions. This concept is discussed in the main body of the chapter, in a separate topic.

The topic of adoption gains importance in the light of the demand made recently in a case where adoption was demanded to be made a right under Part III of the Constitution as a Fundamental Right. In the recent case of *Shabnam Hashmi* v. *Union of India,* (2014) 4 SCC 1, a public spirited individual, filed a writ under article 32 of the Constitution for recognition of the right to adopt and to be adopted as a fundamental right under Part III of the Constitution and an alternative prayer requesting the Court to lay down optional guidelines enabling adoption of children by persons irrespective of religion, caste, creed etc. To this, the Apex Court in answer to the alternative prayer stated that the rules already prevailing in this context existed by quoting the steps taken by Government and other regulatory bodies in the following words in para numbers 2 and 3 of the judgment:

> "2. *The aforesaid alternative prayer made in the writ petition appears to have been substantially fructified by the march that has taken place in this sphere of law, gently nudged by the judicial verdict in* Lakshmi Kant Pandey *v.* Union of India *and the supplemental, if not consequential, legislative innovations in the shape of the Juvenile Justice (Care and Protection of Children) Act, 2000 as amended in 2006 (hereinafter for short the JJ Act, 2000) as also The Juvenile Justice (Care and Protection of Children) Rules promulgated in the year 2007 (hereinafter for short the JJ Rules, 2007).*
>
> 3. *The alternative prayer made in the writ petition may be conveniently dealt with at the outset.*
>
> *The decision of this Court in* Lakshmi Kant Pandey *(supra) is a high watermark in the development of the law relating to adoption. Dealing with inter-country adoptions, elaborate guidelines had been laid by this Court to protect and further the interest of the child. A regulatory body, i.e., Central Adoption Resource Agency (for short CARA) was recommended for creation and accordingly set up by the Government of India in the year 1989. Since then, the said body has been playing a pivotal role, laying down norms both substantive and procedural, in the matter of inter as well as in country adoptions. The said norms have received statutory recognition on being notified by the Central Government under rule 33(2) of the Juvenile Justice (Care and Protection of Children) Rules, 2007 and are today in force throughout the country, having also been adopted and notified by several states under the Rules framed by the states in exercise of the Rule making power under section 68 of the JJ Act, 2000."*

The Indian Ministry of Welfare, pursuant to the guidelines issued by the Supreme Court of India in a Public Interest Litigation petition, *Laxmi Kant Pandey* v. *Union of India,* AIR 1984 SC 469: (1984) 2 SCC 244: 1984 Cri LR (SC) 127, framed guidelines governing inter-country adoptions. This case was monitored by the Supreme Court from time-to-time until 1991, when the Court scrupulously reviewed the existing procedure and practices followed in inter-country adoptions. The main objective was to prevent trafficking of children and to protect the welfare of adopted children.

In the further supplemental judgment of *Laxmi Kant Pandey* v. *Union of India,* AIR 1986 SC 272: (1986) 1 SCWR 52: 1986 Cri LR (SC) 52, the Apex Court pointed out that ordinarily the Court, entertaining an application on behalf of a foreigner seeking to be appointed as a guardian of a child with a view to eventual adoption, should not insist on the foreigner making a deposit by way of securities for due performance of the obligations undertaken by him. More importantly, Justice Bhagwati in *Laxmi Kant Pandey* v. *Union of India*, (1987) 1 SCC 66: (1987) 1 SCWR 167: AIR 1987 SC 232, para 12 (at page 240) incorporated a vital note of clarification, as follows:

> *"... We would, therefore, direct that in case of a foreigner who had been living in India for one year or more, the home-study report and other connected documents may be allowed to be prepared by the recognized placement agency which is processing the application of such foreigner for guardianship of a child with a view to its eventual adoption and that in such a case the Court should not insist on sponsoring of such foreigner by a social or child welfare agency based in the country to which such foreigner belongs nor should a home-study report in case of such foreigner be required to be obtained from any such foreign social or child welfare agency, the home study report and connected documents prepared by the recognized placement agency should be regarded as sufficient."*

After the implementation of the initial guidelines in 1989, it was felt necessary to revise them. Accordingly, a taskforce comprising a cross-section of representatives of adoption agencies under the chairmanship of former Chief *Justice* of India, Mr. Justice P.N. Bhagwati, was constituted on 12 August, 1992. The taskforce submitted its report on 28 August, 1993, and the Indian Government accepted its recommendations. Accordingly, the Government of India circulated revised guidelines in 1994 (herein after 'the Guidelines') to regulate matters relating to the adoption of Indian children. These guidelines were published by the Government of India in the Gazette of India on 20 June, 1995. Subsequently, new further guidelines were placed from 14 February, 2006. CARA earlier had two sets of guidelines: Guidelines of 2004 that governed in-country adoption and Guidelines of 2006 that governed inter-country adoption. Yet, the latest enactment *i.e.*, Guidelines Governing the Adoption of Children, 2011 replaces all earlier guidelines and consolidates as well as updates the earlier two guidelines that were enacted. Talking on the retrospective applicability of these guidelines in different cases the Apex Court in the recent case of *Stephanie Joan Becker* v. *State*, AIR 2013 SC 3495: 2013 AIR SCW 4668: (2013) 2 SCALE 312 observed in para 9 as below:

> *"9. It will also be necessary at this stage to take note of the fact that the Guidelines of 2006 stand repealed by a fresh set of Guidelines published by Notification dated 24-6-2011 of the Ministry of Women and Child Development, Government of India under section 41(3) of the JJ Act. The time gap between the coming into effect of the provisions of section 41(3) of the JJ Act i.e. 22-08-2006 and the publication of the 2011 Guidelines by the Notification dated 24-6-2011 is on account of what appears to be various procedural steps that were undertaken including consultation with various bodies and the different State Governments. A reading of the Guidelines of 2011 squarely indicate that the procedural norms spelt out by the 2006 Guidelines have been more elaborately*

reiterated and the requirements of the pre-adoption process under rules 33(3) and (4) have been incorporated in the said Guidelines of 2011. As a matter of fact, by virtue of the provisions of rule 33(2) it is the Guidelines of 2011 notified under section 41(3) of the JJ Act which will now govern all matters pertaining to inter-country adoptions virtually conferring on the said Guidelines a statutory flavour and sanction."

Thus, making it clear as to when and in which cases these guidelines are to be made applicable, this chapter thus mentions the procedure set up under the new guidelines and also does a critical analysis of these latest guidelines in the main body of this chapter.

It may however be pertinent to point out that the Apex Court in *Anokha* v. *State of Rajasthan,* 2004 (1) HLR 351: AIR 2004 SC 2820: 2004 AIR SCW 1363, has held that the above guidelines would not be applicable where the child is living with his or her biological parent(s) who have agreed that he or she is to be given in adoption to a known couple who may be of foreign origin. The Court in such cases had to deal with the application under section 7 of the Guardianship and Wards Act, 1890 and dispose of the same after being satisfied that the child is being given in adoption voluntarily with the parents being aware of the implications of adoption, that is the child would legally belong to the adoptive parent's family; that the adoption is not induced by any extraneous reasons such as the receipt of money etc.; that the adoptive parents have produced evidence in support of their suitability; and finally that the arrangement would be in the best interest of the child.

The Supreme Court of India has again reiterated the guidelines in case of adoption of children by foreign parents, as originally laid down in the case of *Laxmi Kant Pandey* v. *Union of India (supra, 1984).* While emphatically following these guidelines in *St. Theresa's Tender Loving Care Home* v. *State of Andhra Pradesh,* 2006 (1) HLR 122: AIR 2005 SC 4375: 2005 AIR SCW 5399, the Apex Court pointed in para 10 (at page 128) of the judgment:

"While making the requisite and prescribed exercise it has to be kept in mind that the child is a precious gift and merely because he or she for various reasons is abandoned by the parents cannot be a reason for further neglect by the society...".

As far as the position in UK today is concerned, it is notable that, while India ratified the Hague Convention in 2003, it was not until 2013 that the UK issued the Adoption (Recognition of Overseas Adoptions) Order, 2013, in force with effect from January 03, 2014, revoking and replacing the Adoption (Designation of Overseas Adoptions) Order, 1973. The new order for the first time includes India amongst the countries whose adoptions are now recognised by the UK. However, this does not, unfortunately, mean that adopted children from India will automatically get entry clearance to UK. The other requirements of paragraph 310 of the UK Immigration Rules must still be satisfied. Hence, this does not really help the position on the ground.

II. Brief Overview of Procedure to be followed in Inter-Country Adoption under Revised CARA Guidelines of 2011

CARA guidelines stipulate that every application from a foreigner wishing to adopt a child must be sponsored by a social or child welfare agency recognized or licensed by the Government of the country in which the foreigner is resident. Furthermore, the agency should be recognised by the Central Adoption Resource. Agency (hereafter CARA') set up under the aegis of the Indian Ministry of Welfare. CARA is the principal monitoring agency of the Indian Government handling all affairs connected with national and inter-country adoptions.

No application by a foreigner to adopt a child should be entertained directly by any social or child welfare agency in India working in the areas of inter-country adoption or by any institution or Centre to which the children are committed by the Juvenile Court. The reasons behind this directive have been summed up by M.N. Das in his book *Guardians and Wards Act* (Eastern Law House, 14th Edn, 1995) at pages 80-81:

> 'Firstly, *it will help to reduce, if not eliminate altogether, the possibility of profiteering and trafficking in children, because if a foreigner were allowed to contact directly agencies or individuals in India for the purpose of obtaining a child in adoption, he might, in his anxiety to secure a child for adoption, be induced or persuaded to pay any unconscionable or unreasonable amount which might be demanded by the agency or individual procuring the child.* Secondly, *it would be almost impossible for the court to satisfy itself that the foreigner who wishes to take the child in adoption would be suitable as a parent for the child and whether he would be able to provide a stable and secured family life to the child and would be able to handle trans-racial, trans-cultural and trans-national problems likely to arise from such adoption, because, where the application for adopting a child has not been sponsored by a social or child welfare agency in the country of the foreigner, there would be no proper and satisfactory home study report on which the court can rely.* Thirdly, *in such a case, where the application of a foreigner for taking a child in adoption is made directly without the intervention of social or child welfare agency, there would be no authority or agency in the country of the foreigner who could be made responsible for supervising the progress of the child and ensuring that the child is adopted at the earliest in accordance with law and grows up in an atmosphere of warmth and affection with moral and material security assured to it.'*

III. The Role of Central Adoption Resource Authority

The Central Adoption Resource Authority (hereafter, CARA) is an autonomous body under the Ministry of Women and Child Development, Government of India. Its mandate is to find a loving and caring family for every orphan/destitute/surrendered child in the country. The Central Adoption Resource Authority (CARA) was initially set up in 1990 under the aegis of the Ministry of Welfare in pursuance of Cabinet decision dated 9 May, 1990. Pursuant to a decision of the Union Cabinet dated 2 July, 1998, the then Ministry of Social Justice and Empowerment conferred the autonomous status on CARA with effect from 18 March, 1999 by registering it as a society under the Societies

Registration Act, 1860. It was designated as Central Authority by the Ministry of Social Justice and Empowerment on 17 July, 2003 for the implementation of Hague Convention on Protection of Children & Cooperation in respect of inter-country adoption (1993). The Ministry of Women & Child Development mandated to look after the subject-matters 'Adoption' and 'Juvenile Justice (Care & Protection of Children) Act, 2000' pursuant to 16 February, 2006 notification of Government of India regarding reallocation of the business.

Earlier in-country adoption of Indian children was governed by in-country guidelines 2004 while inter-country adoption procedure was governed by a set of guidelines issued on 14 February, 2006. These guidelines were a follow up of various directions given by the Supreme Court of India in *L.K. Pandey* v. *Union of India* (Supra) and have now been superseded by the 'Guidelines Governing the Adoption of Children, 2011' issued by the Ministry of Women & Child Welfare by a notification on 24 June, 2011.

While being engaged in inter-country adoption as well as in-country adoption of Indian children, the principal aim of CARA is to promote the latter by ensuring that no Indian child is given for inter-country adoption without him/her having been considered by Indian families residing in India. CARA also provides financial assistance to various NGOs and Government-run homes to promote quality child care to such children and place them in domestic adoption.

CARA is ultimately a central nodal adoption authority which governs and have jurisdiction over the other authorities defined and functioning under the CARA guidelines of 2011. The conflict between various such authorities with CARA has been dealt by Bombay High Court in *Varsha Shinde* v. *The Society of the Sassoon Hospital,* Writ Petition No. 9227 of 2013, decided on 18 October, 2013.

In the present case, an inordinate delay was made by SARA and ARC in processing the application for obtaining NOC of the petitioner. While dealing with conflict regarding power of the authorities, to issue such NOC Supreme Court made the following observation:

> *"16. In the Guidelines, the role and functions of each Agency* viz., *CARA, SARA and other Agencies have been clearly defined. However, from the facts which have come on record, it appears that there is some conflict between SARA, ARC on the one side and CARA on the other. It has to be noted that CARA is ultimately a Central Nodal Adoption Agency particularly in case of inter-country adoptions and both, SARA & ARC have to work in coordination with CARA. The ultimate authority to issue No Objection Certificate is given to CARA and the ARC is only supposed to scrutinize the various applications in order to ensure that procedure is properly followed."*

Dealing with general confusion of the authorities over their jurisdiction and as regards to the superiority of CARA, the High Court made its observation in Para 18 of the judgment as follows:

> *"18. In the present case, we are sorry to observe that there appears to be a conflict between SARA, ARC on the one hand and the CARA and RIPA on the other hand and this has resulted in creating bottle-neck in the process of*

adoption. It is possible that SARA and ARC bonafidely *believed that they have power and jurisdiction over CARA Authorities which, unfortunately, is a misconceived perception and have thwarted the smooth functioning of inter-country adoption....*"

Thus, it is clear that CARA being a Central Nodal Adoption Authority has jurisdiction over other authorities functioning under the CARA Guidelines, 2011 including ARC and SARA, which have to work in pursuance to the directions or guidelines issued from time to time by CARA.

IV. Details of Present Procedure to be followed in Inter-Country Adoptions from India under the Revised CARA Guidelines of 2011

Step (I) Authorised Foreign Adoption Agency (AFAA)

- The applicants will have to contact or register with an Authorised Foreign Adoption Agency (AFAA) or Central Authority or Government Department in their country, in which they are resident which shall assist the applicants in obtaining permission of the competent authority for adopting a child.
- Such AFAA or Central Authority or Government Department will conduct a Home Study Report (HSR) of the applicants and the HSR must contain all the documents as specified in Schedule VI.
- All the documents are to be notarised and the signature of the notary is to be apostilled by competent authority of the receiving country. If the documents are in any language other than English, then the originals must be accompanied by attested translations.
- The HSR remains valid for a period of two years and it should also indicate preference of the Prospective Adoptive Parents (PAPs), if any, about the child's age, sex, physical and mental conditions, or location within India.

Step (II) Identification of Recognised Indian Placement Agency (RIPA) by CARA

- The AFAA or Central Authority or Government Department of the country receiving the child will forward one attested or notarized copy of the HSR directly to CARA for identifying a suitable RIPA, where the dossier will be forwarded, after the examination of *prima facie* suitability of the PAPs by the Screening Committee of CARA.
- While deciding to forward the dossier to a particular RIPA, the committee shall keep in mind the preference of PAPs, availability of children, performance of the identified RIPA in in-country adoption, etc. The process of examination of suitability and forwarding the dossier shall be completed preferably within a period of 15 days from its receipt.
- CARA will, then, inform the identified RIPA and will also advice the concerned AFAA or Central Authority or Government Department to send the original dossier to the identified RIPA. The RIPA shall not entertain any application received directly from AFAA or Central Authority or

Government Department or PAPs from out of India for adoption of an Indian child.

- Identification of RIPA does not ensure referral of a child from India and CARA will not be obliged to refer the child.

Step (III) Referral and Acceptance

- The responsibility of assigning, referring and placing the child lies with the RIPA.
- After receiving the original dossier, RIPA will conduct its detailed scrutiny. In case RIPA does not find the PAPs to be suitable, it will inform the CARA about the same along with the reasons thereof, within fifteen days of receipt of original dossier. CARA will have the right to accept or reject such recommendation of the RIPA.
- In case the PAPs are accepted as eligible PAPs, the RIPA will match a child according to the request given by the PAPs as far as possible.
- On such acceptance of PAPs, RIPA will forward the 'Referral' constituting the Child Study Report (CSR) and Medical Examination Report (MER) of the child to the AFAA or Central Authority or Government Department of the receiving country which will transmit the referral to the PAP for acceptance.
- On acceptance of child by the PAPs, the AFAA or Central Authority or concerned Government Department of the receiving country, will send back the original copy of the 'referral' to RIPA, along with the following documents:—
  i. Notarized or attested copy of the CSR and MER duly signed by PAPs;
  ii. Power of Attorney of the PAPs in favour of the official or social worker of the RIPA for filing the case in the court;
  iii. A certificate under Article 5 or agreement under Article 17 of the Hague Convention, as applicable, issued by the Central Authority of the receiving county.
- The process of inter-country adoption of a child shall be completed by the AFAA or Central Authority with a period of forty-five days from date of the referral.

Step (IV) Recommendation by Adoption Recommendation Committee (ARC)

- The State Government will constitute ARC, consisting of Director or Commissioner of the State Government dealing with children in need of care and protection or his representative, Programme Manager (Non-institutional care-SARA) and one external expert or psychologist who has no linkage with any adoption agency, to scrutinize and issue Recommendation Certificate for placement of a child in inter-country adoption.

- On receipt of referral accepted by the PAPs, the RIPA will forward two copies of the dossier (which includes HSR of the PAPs and CSR, including MER, of the child) duly signed by the PAPs to SARA or ARC along with a cheque of Rs. 2500 drawn in favour of SARA or ARC, as the case may be, towards administrative expense. This amount is utilised to meet the expenses in connection with processing the dossiers, payments to external experts and for other adoption promotion activities.
- SARA will receive the dossiers of cases for inter-country adoptions from the RIPA and put up the same before the ARC for issue of Recommendation Certificate. Till SARA becomes operational in a/state, ACA would perform the functions of SARA in that State.
- The SARA or ARC shall ensure that the Recommendation Certificate is issued expeditiously within a period of 15 days from the date of receipt of the dossier. In case of special needs child, such issue shall be made within 5 days from the date of receipt of the dossier.
- In case of medical special needs, the SARA or ARC may ask the RIPA to get a certificate from the reputed medical institution or a Government Medical Officer.
- In case of siblings and older children, the ARC will ensure that there is no waiting Indian PAPs within the region for such child or children.
- The Committee will satisfy itself about the suitability of PAPs for the proposed child and will also verify the documents filed by RIPA and ensure that the procedure has been followed before issuing the Recommendation Certificate.
- If SARA or ARC or ACA is not satisfied with the produced documents for obtaining the certificate, appropriate investigation will be conducted before disposing of the matter.
- The certificate will contain a positive recommendation if the Committee is satisfied that it has no objection to the child being placed with the proposed PAPs in inter-country adoption. The format for the same is in Schedule XII.

Step (V) No Objection Certificate (NOC) by CARA

- After the ARC has issued the Recommendation Certificate, SARA will retain one copy of the dossier with itself and send the second one to CARA along with the recommendation certificate following which, the CARA will constitute a No Objection Certificate (NOC) Committee which will include CARA officials and external experts in the field of child development or psychology or social work or from the medical field.
- The ACA or SARA will send one copy of Recommendation Certificate to the concerned RIPA.
- The NOC Committee will examine the following in order to issue the NOC in each case:—
    i. the relevant documents submitted by the RIPA and verify that due procedure as laid down in the guidelines has been followed.

ii. whether matching and placement of the child with PAPs is in the best interest of the child.

- NOC will be issued in accordance with Article 17 of the Hague Convention and CARA reserves the right to reject any case for inter-country adoption which is not found suitable by the NOC committee by recording reasons for the same.
- The process of issuing NOC is to be completed within a period of fifteen days from the date of receipt of completed dossier in CARA.
- A copy of NOC will be mailed to RIPA, a copy thereof to SARA or ACA, AFAA or Central Authority of the receiving country, as the case may be.

Step (VI) Pre-adoption Foster Care

- Only after issue of NOC by CARA, a child can be given in physical custody to the PAPs in pre-adoption foster care by the RIPA and the adoption agency will inform the PAPs that such foster care will have to continue till the final adoption order is issued. Before physically entrusting the child to PAPs, the Indian adoption agency will also inform them that the process of adoption may take more than the stipulated period so that the PAPs are able to make the informed decision regarding taking the child in foster care.
- The PAPs will be required to produce a certificate from either the Commission in India of the country of the nationality or the central authority of the receiving country permitting them to take the child in foster care.
- The PAPs are required to sign a foster care affidavit stating that they would not leave the country without a valid court order. Also, the PAPs are not allowed to take the child out of the city without the written permission of the concerned Indian adoption agency.

Step (VII) Filing Petition in the Competent Court

- The RIPA will proceed to obtain a Court order for inter-country adoption of the child from the competent court of India, within five days from the receipt of NOC from CARA and the application shall not be filed in the court without the NOC.
- Inter-country adoption of orphan, abandoned and surrendered children will proceed under the Juvenile Justice (Care and Protection of Children) Act, 2000.
- The competent courts are to dispose of the case within a maximum period of two months from the date of its filing, in accordance with the directions of the Honourable Supreme Court of India in *L.K. Pandey* v. *Union of India* (WP no. 1171 of 1982). Since each case for inter-country adoption is processed by Child Welfare Committee and State Government through the ARC and CARA, the court may, to the extent possible, dispose of the case in the first hearing itself in the best interest of the child.

- On the receipt of the Court Order, the CARA will issue a Conformity Certificate (CC) under Article 23 as per the Hague Convention as per Schedule XIII.

Step (VIII) Passport and Visa

- No child adopted in accordance with the JJ Act will be allowed to leave India without a valid NOC from CARA.
- After the Court order is received, RIPA will apply for passport for the adopted child and the application must include the following documents:—
    i. NOC from CARA
    ii. Court order on adoption and the adoption deed; and
    iii. All other documents as stipulated by the passport issuing authority.
- The date of birth of the child would be taken as mentioned in the court order.
- The concerned authority is to issue expeditiously the passport and visa to enable the adopted child to leave India with his or her adoptive parents to their habitual place of residence.
- The adoptive parents will have to come to India and accompany the child to their country.

V. CARA Guidelines 2006 v. CARA Guidelines 2011 — Comparison in Case of Inter-Country Adoption

The draft guidelines that had been pending for so long, put to review and comment by various authorities and stakeholders, having been modified and rectified have now come into existence after notification in the official gazette as 'Guidelines Governing the Adoption of Children, 2011' issued by the Ministry of Women & Child Welfare by a notification on 24 June, 2011.

The new guidelines enacted, have not only consolidated the earlier versions of separately enacted in-country and inter-country adoption guidelines together in a single guideline, but have also modified them to meet the aims and objectives of CARA. The best interest of the child in adoption being the prime object is balanced along with the measures to curb the cumbersome procedures of adoption.

New authorities have been included. Possible scopes of child trafficking and other societal child abuse menaces have been tried to be eliminated *via* various checks of authorities. Several problems that occurred during the cases of adoption *via* previous guidelines have been tried to be eliminated and various Court orders and guidelines adhered to and consolidated in the new CARA Guidelines, 2011.

At the beginning of the procedural aspect, under the CARA Guidelines, 2006 the applicants had to contact or register with an ***Enlisted Foreign Adoption Agency (EFAA)/Central Authority/Government Department in their country,*** in which they were resident, which used to prepare the Home Study Report (HSR) etc. While under CARA Guidelines, 2011, the applicants will now have to contact or register with an ***Authorised Foreign Adoption Agency (AFAA) or Central Authority or Government Department in their country,*** in which they are resident which shall assist the applicants in obtaining permission of the competent authority for adopting a child.

Another major change in the procedure which is a big leap towards securing the welfare of child and not pushing it into child trafficking is eliminating chances of direct contact of foreign adoption agencies with RIPA for adoption. Under CARA Guidelines, 2006 a copy of the application of the prospective adoptive parents along with the copies of the HSR and other documents had to be ***forwarded to RIPA by the Enlisted Foreign Adoption Agency (EFAA) or Central Authority of that country.*** While under CARA Guidelines, 2011 the ***AFAA or Central Authority or Government Department of the country receiving the child will forward one attested or notarized copy of the HSR directly to CARA for identifying a suitable RIPA,*** where the dossier will be forwarded, after the examination of *prima facie* suitability of the PAPs by the Screening Committee of CARA. The ***RIPA shall not entertain any application received directly*** from AFAA or Central Authority or Government Department or PAPs from out of India for adoption of an Indian child. Thus, the role of the central authority CARA is being maintained to check and scrutinize each and every procedure to secure the interest of a child in adoption.

All applications for international adoption, whether from "foreigners" or Indians living abroad, will now be routed through CARA in New Delhi. This seems designed to put an end to foreign adoption agencies developing direct working relationships with specific orphanages, and to ensure that domestic placements take priority. This change also prevents non-resident Indian couples from applying directly to the orphanage of their choice. All prospective parents may request a child from a particular region or express interest in a particular orphanage, but no guarantees. CARA specifically mentions that Indian couples aren't/may not be matched with a child of their same linguistic or ethnic background; they must be willing to accept a child from any region in India.

Once CARA gives preliminary approval to a family, it will route the family's application to a licensed orphanage.

Greater emphasis on placing children with Indian families is given. Past regulations required that 50 percent of children be placed with Indian families. Now CARA says that preference shall be given for placing a child in in-country adoption and the ratio of in-country adoption to inter-country adoption shall be 80 : 20 of total adoptions processed annually, excluding special needs children.

Also, there is change in the procedure of obtaining an NOC; the most important clearance from CARA for adoption. Under CARA Guidelines, 2006, ***RIPA had to make an application for a CARA NOC*** in case of foreign/PIO parents only after ACA Clearance Certificate was obtained. After that *CARA had to issue the 'NOC' within 15 days* from the date of receipt of the adoption dossier, if complete in all respects. While under the CARA Guidelines, 2011 after the ARC has issued the Recommendation Certificate, ***SARA will retain one***

copy of the dossier with itself and send the second one to CARA along with the recommendation certificate following which, the CARA will constitute a No Objection Certificate (NOC) Committee which will include CARA officials and external experts in the field of child development or psychology or social work or from the medical field. The process of issuing NOC is to be *completed within a period of fifteen days* from the date of receipt of completed dossier in CARA. A copy of NOC will be mailed to RIPA, a copy thereof to SARA or ACA, AFAA or Central Authority of the receiving country, as the case may be.

Further the time period for various procedures have been tried to be reduced. Under the CARA Guidelines, 2006 on receipt of the NOC from CARA, the RIPA had to file a petition for adoption/guardianship in the competent court ***within 15 days***. While under CARA Guidelines, 2011, the RIPA will proceed to obtain a Court order for inter-country adoption of the child from the competent Court in India, ***within five days*** from the receipt of NOC from CARA and the application shall not be filed in the court without the NOC. On the receipt of the Court Order, the CARA will issue a Conformity Certificate (CC) under Article 23 as per the Hague Convention as per Schedule XIII. Further in the previous guidelines it was mentioned that the concerned Regional Passport Officer may issue the Passport ***within 10 days***. While the new guidelines do not prescribe any such limit as it says that the concerned authority is to ***issue expeditiously*** the passport and visa to enable the adopted child to leave India with his or her adoptive parents to their habitual place of residence.

The new guideline also gives the adoptive parent a choice to proceed with whichever enactment they prefer *i.e.* either for adoption under Hindu Adoption and Guardianship Act, 1956, for guardianship under the Guardianship and Wards Act, 1890 or for adoption under the secular adoption law of the Juvenile Justice (Care and Protection) Act, 2000, as amended in 2006. However, the guidelines clearly mention that all cases of inter-country adoption are to be dealt by the Juvenile Justice (Care and Protection) Act, 2000.

VI. Critical Analysis of CARA Guidelines, 2011

The Central Adoption Resource Agency (CARA), *i.e.* the federal body in India that oversees adoption, released new guidelines that could substantially improve the process for children in need. Unfortunately, anyone familiar with India's exhaustive bureaucracy is bound to be cynical regarding this ambitious plan.

It has been observed by CARA, in its database as on year 2014, that there has been a decreasing ratio of inter-country adoption although there are several applications still pending. The main reason here is the stringent and cumbersome process of adoption matters especially in cases of inter-country adoptions.

Looking at the various provisions of the new Guidelines of 2011, several flaws are pointed out herewith. There are several problems mentioned below that have already been occurring while dealing with adoption cases while certain provisions are criticized from the perspective of prospective application, keeping in view the ambiguity of these provisions.

The problem occurs on the very outset of the guideline where the guideline defines prospective adoptive parents as the person eligible to adopt as per the Juvenile Justice (Care and Protection) Act, 2000 as amended in 2006 (herein after the JJ Act). Thus, the Act categorizes the adoptive parents in the eligibility criteria of the JJ Act creating confusion among the prospective applicants as the new guidelines were made with a view to give the adoptive parents a choice to proceed with the desired Act (*i.e.*, Hindu Adoption and Maintenance Act, 1956, Guardianship and Wards Act, 1890 or the JJ Act).

The earlier version of 2004 guidelines of in-country adoption under para 1.1.5 Procedure for In-country Adoption, stated under the heading Adoption Act as under:

> *"The child can be legally placed with the parent(s) under HAMA/GAWA/JJ Act, 2000. The prospective parents should be informed about the different Acts available and the ramifications of each one. It would be left to them to decide as to which Act they would like to file their petition under, provided that they are eligible to do so under the chosen Act. As stated above, the prospective parents must be made to fully understand the status of their adoption under each Act."*

The new guidelines make no such clarification making the Prospective Adoptive Parent (PAP) get confused as to which legislation they must opt for.

Further under para 2 clause (zd) of new guidelines a surrendered child is one who is relinquished by parents or guardian and is defined as:

> *(zd) "Surrendered child" means a child, who in the opinion of the Child Welfare Committee, is relinquished on account of physical, emotional and social factors beyond the control of the parent or guardian*

Yet, the further para, in clause 15(9) provides for surrender by person other than biological parents/legal guardians as it says:

> *15.(9) If the surrender is effected by any person other than the biological parent(s), the child shall be treated as abandoned and the same procedure shall be followed as that for an abandoned child.*

Someone may bring a child suggesting that he/she found the child and wishes to surrender the child. But he/she may have procured the child illegally. Thus, promoting surrender by a person not related to the child is legally incorrect. Moreover, it would actually create scope for illegal trafficking by persons who will procure children for the adoption agencies, without the agencies coming under any scanner. Cases filed with various High Courts suggest how the agencies have been involved in getting parents/legal guardians to sign surrender deeds under false pretexts of sending their children to a boarding school or through other ways of fraud and cheating.

Further, CARA Guidelines, 2011, under clause 5(a) mentions that a person is competent to adopt irrespective of his or her marital status:

> *5. Person competent to adopt.—In accordance with the provisions of sub-section (6) of section 41, the Court may allow a child to be given in adoption,—*
>
> *(a) to an individual irrespective of his or her marital status;*

However, clause 5(a) and 6(2) are contradictory where it says:

6.(2) Couples in live-in relationship are not eligible to adopt a child."

If adoption is allowed for any individual irrespective of marital status as stated in clause 5(a) above, why should a live-in relationship matter. Moreover, clause 6(9) says that:

6. (9) An un-married or single male person is not permitted to adopt a girl child.

Here again it means that a male person choosing to adopt a female child under section 7 of HAMA, 1956, where the age difference requirement of 21 years under section 11, clause (iii) of HAMA is maintained is not permitted to adopt from now onwards due to these new CARA Guidelines which also govern in-country adoptions. The scenario is confusing altogether.

In order to increase the cases of inter-country adoption, CARA has taken some irrational measures such as in para 8.(4) where it states:

8. (4) Indian nationals who live in countries which are not signatories to the Hague Convention are also eligible to adopt.

The bigger question now is as to why should countries those who are not signatories to the Hague Convention be allowed to adopt if they have not ratified the Hague Convention. This is because keeping in mind the best interest of the child, how can standards of protection be ensured in these countries. What if the adoption fails? How will the child be brought back etc. are matters that are part of the Hague Convention. Non-ratifying countries may not comply with these, and thus in such matters who will check these adoptions? Thus, the object of best interest and the welfare of the child to be maintained at all cost is completely ignored here.

The CARA Guidelines further show loopholes in para 14(2)(iv) where it states:

14. (2) (iv) In case of biological parents surrendering a child, this process shall be before a two member Child Welfare Committee.

Surrendering implies giving up a right, which only the biological parents/ legal guardians have over a child claimed to be legally theirs. Rule 26(1) of the Juvenile Justice (Care and Protection of Children) Rules, 2007 requires a quorum of at least three members, which may include the Chairperson of the CWC, to hold a meeting or carry on the proceedings. The States can frame their own rules, but the State rules must conform to the Central rules as per rule 96 of the Central Rules of 2007 mentioned above. Reducing the number to two members will render all proceedings *ultra vires*. Surrender is part of the proceedings. It must be remembered that counselling is different from the surrender proceedings. Once the proceedings have been completed, the final order can have signatures of two members, including the Chairperson.

Another error and dichotomy seen in the new guidelines is depicted in para 15.(8) where it states:

15. (8) In case of a child born out of wedlock, only the mother herself can surrender the child and if she is a minor, the signature of an accompanying close relative will be obtained on the surrender document.

Now the question that arises is as to who will ascertain the relation and how, what would be the procedure. Moreover, thumb impression is allowed in case of a child above 7 years of age being given in adoption under para 21(11) of the new CARA Guidelines, but thumb impression is not allowed in case of a minor mother surrendering her child. This is a serious dichotomy and must be removed. Thumb impression of minors should be allowed in both situations.

Moreover, there is conflict of interest and rights of the adopted children and the surrendering parents. As para 15(12) says:

> *15.(12) In all cases of surrender, confidentiality shall be maintained by the authorities and agencies involved in the process.*

It is to be seen that this clause should not interfere with the right of a child to get details about parents who surrendered her/him when the adopted child comes for a root search. The summary of inconsistencies and shortcomings in the new Guidelines of 2011 show that there are serious flaws and drawbacks which need to be addressed suitably in the best interest of the child.

VII. Basic Documentation Needed for Inter-Country Adoption Process

1. Home Study Report

As of now all inter-country adoptions are dealt by 2011 guidelines as it has superseded the 2006 guidelines. Nonetheless, the importance of basic documentation is not undermined even in the present process. As the aim and objective of CARA is to secure the best interest of the child in all cases of adoption, the first step towards looking into the matter is getting a Home Study Report of the PAPs. In fact it is like a clear cut balance sheet of the prospective adoptive parents. It is a very handy document, at the entire stage of adoption process. And also at the time of the visa interview at the concerned Embassy or Consulate to impress upon the visa/consular officer as to the positive aspects of the application, with a view to enhance the chances of the success of the application.

The new guidelines define Home Study Report as follows:

> *2(o) "HSR" means Home Study Report containing details of the Adoptive parents' social and economic status; family background; description of home; standard of living; relationship with spouse, if any, and other family members; health status and the like;*

Further, 20(3) states that *'the Home Study Report shall be based on procedures as laid down at Schedule VI.'*

From the experience of the authors in handling family migration issues, we would recommend compliance of the exhaustive documentation mentioned below for the reasons already mentioned before. According to the new guidelines of 2011 the HSR should have the following information as tabulated below:

(Professional social worker with MSW or MA Psychology background attached to an adoption agency or any competent person identified by the State Government competent to prepare Home Study Report.)

Assessing the ability of a couple to parent a child not born to them is of crucial importance in a successful adoption. Therefore, their suitability to care for an unrelated child is assessed through a home study.

It is important to know the couple's general attitude towards adoption, particularly of an unrelated child, and the motivating force behind their decision to adopt. Their attitude to illegitimacy is an important consideration since a negative attitude may adversely condition their response to a child born out of wedlock. Positive qualities that can be identified are:—an evident enthusiasm to adopt, adjustability and tolerance in their requirements of the child. Negative characteristics can be identified as:—tension in their marital relationship, anticipation of the adoption as a means of alleviating some personal problem, or indecisiveness in their commitment to adoption.

In general, motives those focus on the needs of the child, rather than those of the adoptive parents are acceptable. Some couple may wish to adopt to repair their shaky marriage, to bring in a companion and playmate for their natural born child or to replace an expired child. Combating the loneliness of a mother, creating new interest in the life of a sick and miserable parent, or anticipation of support in old age may be other motives. These are irrational and unrealistic motives and the applicants should be helped to reflect on these areas and even advised to refrain from adopting a child in such cases. They should understand that a child cannot be made a tool in solving the problems of two adults.

It is further important to explore whether both the spouses are equally eager to adopt or if one of them is going along with the plan just to please his or her partner.

(a) Identifying Information: Following information is required for PAPs. (Prospective Adoptive Parents)

- Name:
- Age:
- Years of Marriage:
- Educational Qualifications:
- Financial Situation:
- Occupation:
- Religion:
- Health History

(b) Details of other children and family members

- Name and age of both, biological or adopted children;
- Current relationship between the parents and biological children, if any;
- Development of already adopted children, if any;
- Details of other family members:
- Home and Neighbourhoods:

(c) Description and amenities of the Home

- Standard of living as it appears in the Home;
- Accommodation for the child;

(d) Current relationship between husband and wife

(e) Attitude of grand-parents and relatives towards adoption

(f) Anticipated plans for the adoptive child

(g) Psycho-Social Assessment of the Couple

- Information needs to be collected in several areas to enable the social worker to form a composite psycho-social picture of the adopting couple. Some of the areas are mentioned below:
- General Impression of the Couple:
- Emotional Health:
- Value System:
- Social Status and background of Adopting Couple:
- Quality of Marital Relationship:
- Previous history of divorce or living relationship etc.

(h) Capacity for Parenthood and Expectations of a Child

This includes a capacity to love, accept and offer emotional security to children, a capacity to permit them to grow in their own individuality, a readiness to accept and understand the behavioural problems of children and to be flexible and realistic in their expectations from children.

It is also necessary to explore if the applicants have strong pre-conceived ideas as to what the child should be like. Some parents have a dream image of a child or a desire that the child should become exactly like his or her father or mother in all respects. A child cannot be laden with the burden of futuristic expectations of the adoptive parents. When a relationship is based on such motivations there is an undue emphasis on loyalty. Couples should be helped to understand that a child is a separate entity with his own individuality. Areas which should be explored are a couple's rigidity or otherwise about the background of the child, whether they will be willing to let a child grow in his own way at his own speed while they support him with loving discipline, and their hopes and plans for the child.

If the wife is working the social worker should discuss with her whether she plans to continue to work or to give up her job. If her intention is to continue with her job, it should be ascertained what plans she would be making for the child's care while she is at work.

(i) Attitude of Significant Others

In our traditional cultural set up, next in importance to the applicants themselves, come the members of their extended family. If there are any biological children old enough to have an opinion in the matter, their views regarding the adoption plan and the extent to which their parents have prepared them should be ascertained. If the applicants are living in a joint family, it would be advisable to meet all the family members living in the home. Both sets of prospective adoptive grand parents should be seen where possible. Such contact with significant relatives would give evidence of their degree of support of the adoption plan of the couple, ensure their positive involvement and also help to ascertain if they need support in resolving their own feelings about the idea.

(j) Others Issues

- Plans to Tell the Child of His or Her Adoption;
- Evaluation of Strengths and Weaknesses, and Social Worker's Recommendations;
- Motivation for Adoption;
- *The HSR should also specify Family's Consideration of Possible Medical or Special Needs children.*

2. Documentation needed from foreign adoptive parents and overseas social or child welfare agency for inter-country adoption application

Experience of dealing with CARA and/or the concerned Ministry suggests that the documentation should be complied meticulously in order to avoid bureaucratic delays. The following documents must be submitted by the foreign adoptive parents. It will be noted that the Indian requirements are quite similar to those prescribed in various appendices of RON 117 issued by the British Home Office:

(1) Home Study Report;

(2) Recent photograph of the adoptive family;

(3) Marriage certificate of the foreign adoptive parents;

(4) Declaration concerning the health of the foreign adoptive parents;

(5) Certificate of medical fitness of the foreign adoptive parents duly certified by a medical doctor;

(6) Declaration regarding financial status, together with supporting documents including employer's certificate, wherever applicable;

(7) Employment certificate of the foreign adoptive parents, if applicable;

(8) Income-tax assessment order(s) of the foreign adoptive parents;

(9) Bank reference for the foreign adoptive parents;

(10) Particulars of properties owned by the foreign Prospective Adoptive Parents

(11) Joint declaration tendered by the foreign adoptive parents stating willingness to be appointed guardians of the child;

(12) Undertaking from the social or child welfare enlisted agency sponsoring the foreigner to the effect that the child would be legally adopted by the foreign adoptive parents according to the law of the country within a period not exceeding two years from the time of arrival of the child;

(13) Undertaking from the foreign adoptive parents to the effect that the child would be provided with necessary education and upbringing according to status of the adoptive parents;

(14) Undertaking from recognised foreign social or child welfare agency that the report relating to the progress of the child along with his/her recent photograph would be sent quarterly during first two years and half-yearly for the next three years in the prescribed proforma through the relevant Indian diplomatic post;

(15) Power-of-attorney conferred by the intending parents in favour of social or the child welfare agency in India which will be required to process the case. Such power-of-attorney should also authorise the lawyer in India to handle the case on behalf of the foreign adoptive parents, if they are not in position to come to India;

(16) Certificate from the recognised foreign social or child welfare agency sponsoring the application to the effect that the adoptive parents are permitted to adopt a child according to the laws of their country;

(17) Undertaking from the recognised foreign social or child welfare agency to the effect that, in case of disruption of the adoptive family before the legal adoption has been effected, it will take care of child and find a suitable alternative placement for the child with prior approval of CARA;

(18) Undertaking from the recognised foreign social or child welfare agency that it will reimburse all expenses to the concerned Indian social or child welfare agency as fixed by the competent Court towards maintenance of the child and the processing charge fees.

It is important to reiterate that all the above certificates, declarations and documents in support of the application should be duly notarized by a notary public whose signature should be duly attested either by an officer of the ministry of External Affairs, the Ministry of Justice or the Ministry of Social Welfare of the country of the foreign adoptive parents or by an officer of the Indian Embassy or High Commission or Consulate in that country.

3. List of documents to be filed along with adoption petition in the Court for Inter-country Adoption

(i) Petition for Court Order under relevant Act.

(ii) Copy of the Child Study Report & Medical Examination Report duly signed by the Prospective Adoptive Parents (PAPs).

(iii) Proof of residence.

(iv) Income certificate for the last three years.

(v) Marriage certificate & Photograph.

(vi) Birth certificate of the PAP(s).

(vii) Copy of the HSR, its annexure including reference letters as provided under CARA Guidelines.

(viii) Copy of the license of inter-country adoption (recognition certificate from CARA).

(ix) Copy of the Child Welfare Committee Certificate along with surrender deed wherever applicable.

(x) Copy of the recommendation certificate issued by ARC.

(xi) NOC issued from CARA.

(xii) Power of Attorney from PAPs in favour of the official or social worker of the RIPA.

(No infertility certificate is required for filing in the court)

VIII. CARA Permissions not Necessary in Inter-Country Adoptions, where Families are Known to Each Other—Regional Passport Officer has no Authority to Direct Adoptive Parents/Guardians to Obtain CARA Permission

In the case of *Frank M. Costanzo* v. *The Regional Passport Officer,* Writ Petition Number 14880 of 2011, decided on 17 September, 2010, the petitioners were permitted to take their adopted son to USA by an order of the *Family Court at Puducherry.* This was by virtue of a guardianship order from the Court of competent jurisdiction. And thereafter, they submitted an application to the Regional Passport Officer for the issue of passport to their minor son. But the petitioners received a reply from the Regional Passport Officer stating that, the adoption of Master Praveen Kumar is not in accordance with the extensive procedure laid down by the Government of India, meaning to refer to the CARA Guidelines. Accordingly, they were directed to furnish a no objection certificate from Central Adoption Resource Agency (CARA).

The key issue which arose in this particular case was as follows: whether the condition of CARA clearance imposed by the Regional Passport Officer for the issuance of the passport of the minor child was legally justifiable, where such a child has been taken in guardianship dually supported by guardianship order granted by the Family Court, in a situation where both the families are known to each other?

The Madras High Court in the present case reiterated the law laid down by the Supreme Court of India in the principal judgment of *Lakshmi Kant Pandey* v. *Union of India,* (supra, 1984) and *Smt. Anokha* v. *State of Rajasthan,* (supra), as applicable to the facts and circumstances of the present case.

The Madras High Court in para 10 of the said judgment positively noted the law laid down in the case of *Anokha* (supra), and also noticing the fact that in the case of *Anokha* (supra), the prospective adoptive parents as then they were, had a judicially directed scrutiny of their Home Study Report which culminated into a judgment passed by the Court at Venice. The Supreme Court in effect applied section 13 of the Indian Code of Civil Procedure, 1908. All this has been eloquently reiterated in para 10 of the Madras High Court judgment as hereunder:

> *"10. The Guidelines issued by the Government consequent to the direction of the apex Court would not apply to the voluntary adoption from the biological parents. This view was reiterated by the Apex Court in* Anokha v. State of Rajasthan, *2004 (1) HLR 351: AIR 2004 SC 2820: (2004) 1 SCC 382: 2004 AIR SCW 1363, wherein it has been clearly held that in the case of adoption from biological parents, the Guidelines do not apply. In paragraph 16, it has been held as follows:*
>
> *"16. In the case before us although the Guidelines do not apply, respondents 2 and 3 had produced evidence which fulfilled all the particulars required of a Home Study Report. The appellant has repeatedly affirmed her closeness to respondents 2 and 3 and her conviction that they would nourish and care for baby Alka as if she was their own. Respondents 2 and 3 have produced sufficient*

evidence to justify their suitability to be adoptive parents. There was a judicially directed scrutiny by a local government agency in Venice. The enquiry report has resulted in a judgment passed by the Court at Venice, Italy. That judgment can be accepted by this Court under section 13 of the Code of Civil Procedure, particularly, when the respondents have filed the investigation report and other material on the basis of which the judgment was delivered.""

Furthermore, the Madras High Court categorically turned down the contentions of the Regional Passport Officer, Government of India, Ministry of External Affairs at para 13 of the said judgment in the following terms:

"13.(i). When the Central Adoption Resource Agency (CARA) does not impose such condition in respect of adoption from biological parents, the passport authority cannot raise the same. It has no legal basis;

(ii). The guidelines issued by the passport authorities has no binding force insofar as the petitioners are concerned. It is without authority of law and there is no legal basis for imposing such condition.

(iii). In any event, insisting no objection from Central Adoption Resource Agency (CARA) for issue of passport will run counter to the decisions of the Apex Court cited above."

Finally, the Writ petition of the adoptive parents was allowed by the Madras High Court and the respondents were directed "to issue the passport without any further delay."

In the case of *Tim Cecil* v. *Unknown,* 2011 (5) MLJ 209, the Madras High Court had the occasion to elaborate at length the safeguards in the event of inter-country adoptions made by biological parents directly to foreign nationals. In this particular case, the petitioners were German nationals who did not have any biological child of their own. After coming to India they got acquainted with biological parents of child in question who were willing to give their fourth child to petitioners for being fostered and brought up by them as they already had three daughters.

The two key issues which arose in this case can be summed up as follows: Whether a blanket exemption to biological parents from safeguards prescribed in inter-country adoptions is in the interest of children? Whether the right of biological parents to give their child in adoption absolute and unfettered? The Court before answering these two questions of vital importance first dealt with the operative part of the judgment in such situations in the landmark case of *Lakshmi Kant Pandey* v. *Union of India* (supra 1984), also reiterating the law laid down by the Supreme Court of India in *Anokha* (supra) and finally made substantive references to most of the international instruments and conventions relating to child law. Certainly, the Court with its ingenuity carved out necessary relief, but not without adequately monitored safeguards.

The Court first reiterated the position of law in cases of direct adoptions by biological parents as held by the Supreme Court of India in the primary case of *Lakshmi Kant Pandey* (supra, 1984). Para 11 of the order dated 13 June, 2011 in the case of Cecil stated as follows"

"The Rules relating to Inter Country Adoptions came to be framed in pursuance of the judgment of the Supreme Court in Laxmi Kant Pandey v. Union of India, AIR 1984 SC 469: (1984) 2 SCC 244: 1984 Cri LR (SC) 127. *In paragraph 11 of the said decision, the Supreme Court made it clear that they were not concerned in that case with cases of adoption of children living with their biological parents, since in those cases, the biological parents would be the best persons to decide whether to give their child in adoption to foreign parents or not. It was also clarified in paragraph 11 of the said decision that it is only in cases where the children sought to be adopted are destitute or abandoned and are living in Social or Child Welfare Centres that it was necessary to consider what normative and procedural safeguards should be forged for protecting their interest and promoting their welfare. Therefore, drawing my attention to the observations of the Supreme Court, contained in paragraphs 11, 12 and 13 of the said decision, the learned counsel for the petitioners contended that there is no requirement of sponsorship by an Agency or the production of a Home Study Report."*

The law laid down by the Hon'ble Supreme Court of India in *Lakshmi Kant Pandey* (supra, 1984) was reiterated by the Supreme Court of India in the case of *Smt. Anokha* v. *State of Rajasthan* (supra). It was held by the Court in this judgment that the guidelines do not relate to regulation of adoption procedure in respect of children with biological parents. It is only where there is impersonalized attention of a placement authority that there is a need to closely monitor the process as per the guidelines.

In cases where children are given in adoption by the biological parents, the Court only has to deal with an application under section 7 of the Guardianship and Wards Act, 1890. And the application is to be adjudicated upon after being satisfied that the child is being given in adoption voluntarily by the natural parents after being aware of the implications of their decision to give their child in adoption.

The Madras High Court in the present case of *Cecil* (supra) in para 14 of the order dated 13 June, 2011 distinguished the facts of the case in-hand with the facts of the case of *Anokha* (supra) in the following terms:

"14. But the said decision arose out of a case where the adoptive parents at least produced a Home Study Report, though not sponsored by an Agency. In the case on hand, there is neither a sponsorship by an Agency nor a Home Study Report. In such circumstances, the question that poses a challenge to me is as to whether the right of the biological parents to offer their children in adoption or foster care to foreigners can be said to be unfettered and uncontrolled by any guidelines, as appears to have been suggested in Smt. Anokha."

Clearly, the sensitivity of the Court was pointing out the absence of a Home Study Report in the case in-hand. Furthermore, the court in para 15 of the said order dated 13 June, 2011 noticed the published dissent of CARA in the following terms:

"15. In a book titled "Every Child Deserves a Loving Family" published by the Central Adoption Resource Authority of the Ministry of Women and Child

Development, Government of India, the following observations have been made with regard to the decision of the Apex Court in Smt. Anokha:—

"Under a special situation, one direct case of inter-country adoption was allowed by Honourable Supreme Court of India which was not compatible with Hague Convention on Inter-country Adoption ratified by Government of India. This cannot be used as a precedent since Hague Convention on Inter-country Adoption, 1999, ratified by Government of India does not recognise any case of direct adoption and the receiving country will not issue permission under Article 5/17 to agree to such kind of adoption without involvement of recognised agencies and authorities.""

The Madras High Court order in *Cecil* (supra) in para 16 of the judgment itself furnishes shocking statistics with regard to the miserable plight of the under privileged children in India.

"16. The above observations have to be seen in the context of the statistics about the status of children in India. A recent report contained the following statistics:

(i) There are 18 million street children.

(ii) There are 100 million child labourers.

(iii) Over 59 million children have no access to school.

(iv) One out of two children between the ages of 6 and 14 has no access to primary education.

(v) Out of 27 million children born every year, 2 million do not survive to celebrate their first birthday.

(vi) Every year 27,06,000 children under 5 years die.

(vii) Millions of children are denied even the most basic rights of survival and protection.

(viii) About 60 million children under the age of 6 live below the poverty line.

(ix) Children from 100 million families live without water at home.

(x) 500,000 children are forced into the commercial sex trade every year.

(xi) 1 out of every 3 girls does not live to see her 15th birthday.

(xii) Every sixth girl child's death is due to gender discrimination, 3 lakh more girls than boys die every year.

(xiii) Female mortality exceeds male mortality in 224 out of 402 districts in India.

(xiv) 53% of girls in the age group of 5 to 9 years are illiterate.

(xv) Unrecorded number of girl children are killed within hours of being born.

(xvi) While in 1960 there were 976 girls born for every 1000 boys, in 2001, there are only 927 girls for every 1000 boys.

Even if one does not give undue weightage to these statistics, the social picture presented by it, cannot be ignored in toto."

The Court further expressed serious concern for the view that in cases where children are given in adoption by the biological parents themselves, satisfaction *per se* of the natural parents that the children are voluntarily given for adoption by the parents is simply not enough. The apprehensions of the Court are rightly so very strongly voiced in the following terms in para 17 of the judgment as follows:

> *"17. In a newspaper report published on 14-6-2010 from Karnataka, it was stated that impoverished parents put up their children to sale for a few thousands of rupees. It was reported therein that in a week immediately preceding the date of the report, six families in Tiptur Taluk of Tumkur District of Karnataka sold their children to prosperous families and that adoption procedures were not followed in those cases. Therefore, I think that a blanket exemption of biological parents from the safeguards prescribed in other inter-country adoptions, may not be in the interest of the children, to whom the Court owes an obligation as a Court of Wards. Children are not properties of their parents so as to entitle them to have absolute dominance over them. In a country where abject poverty drives a few families to sell their children for beggary, forced labour or prostitution, it is not safe to rely entirely upon the wisdom of the biological parents, to give their children in adoption or for foster care, to foreigners."*

Going by the above mentioned newspaper report cited in the Madras High Court judgment, it is common knowledge that human trafficking of children as also abuse of children is rampant in our country in alarming proportions. But, it is most respectfully submitted that the view of CARA as stated in the above mentioned publication titled "Every Child Deserves a Loving Family," as also noticed in the Madras High Court order of *Cecil* (supra) as a sequel to the judgment handed down by the Supreme Court of India in *Anokha* (supra) is not correct. The same is not legally sustainable.

Firstly, CARA directives on the administrative side cannot possibly overwrite the law laid down by the Hon'ble Supreme Court of India in the case of *Anokha* in the year 2004.

Secondly, if CARA was aggrieved by the Judgment in the case of *Anokha* (supra) they should have as a nodal institution of the Ministry of Welfare under the aegis of which CARA was set up filed an intervener application or a review application before the Supreme Court of India itself, at the time the judgment was handed down in the case of *Anokha* (supra). The law laid down in the case of *Anokha* (supra) is perfectly correct as it looks directly at genuine *bona fide* adoptions as also advocating the added safe guard of Court scrutiny and possible intervention on guardianship applications, where the parties are known to each other.

Thirdly, CARA has taken shelter of India ratifying the Hague Convention on adoption on 6 June, 2003 in challenging in isolation the correctness of the law laid down by the Hon'ble Supreme Court of India in the case of *Anokha* (supra). As a matter of fact, CARA is yet to come out on any published opinion or material suitably highlighting the advantages of India signing the Hague Convention on adoptions. This of course is much to the disadvantage of the NRI community, who are left in the lurch on account of an unnecessary deep void in this area of law despite India signing the Hague Convention on Adoptions. CARA or the Ministry of Welfare or the Ministry of Women and Child Development possibly in conjunction with Law Ministry of India, should have taken timely and concrete steps in drafting as also implementing and enabling legislation specifically looking at the positive steps of India signing the Hague Convention on adoptions, thereby, giving meaningful interpretation to India signing the Hague Convention on Adoptions.

Further there is discussion in the present order dated 13 June, 2011 itself, on the rights of the biological parents over their children. The court in detail has referred to various international conventions and even reports of the Law Commission of India in order to arrive at a conclusion that the rights of the biological parents to give their children in adoption are not absolute and unfettered. This is by providing a home study report and a guardianship order from a Court of competent jurisdiction. The important international conventions dealing with inter-country adoptions which have been ratified by India include the Convention on the Rights of Child, 20 November, 1989 and the Hague Convention on Protection of Children and Co-operation in respect of inter-country adoptions concluded on 29 May, 1993. And the 153rd Report of Law Commission of India, dated 26 August, 1994 and the Juvenile Justice Act, 2000 are other important national documents discussed in the case on the point of rights of biological parents. The Court has summed up its concern in para 28 of the order dated 13 June, 2011 in the following categorical terms:

> *"28. Therefore, in the light of the mandate contained in the Convention on the Rights of the Child and the Hague Convention, both of which have been ratified by India and also in the light of the provisions of the Juvenile Justice (Care and Protection of Children) Act, 2000 as amended by Act 33 of 2006, the primary responsibility of providing care and protection to children is that of his birth family. Since the child has a fundamental right to be protected against any kind of exploitation, the biological parents cannot be held to have an absolute and unfettered right to give their children in adoption or for foster care to foreign nationals. It is true that the Personal Law of Hindus have always recognised the right of the biological parents to give their child in adoption. But this recognition under the Hindu Law, as pointed out by Sir Henry Maine and other Scholars, was a contrivance to prevent the interruption of succession. The origin of this institution amongst the Hindus was attributed to the religious belief of spiritual efficacy of the possession of a son and a belief that by leaving a male issue in this world, they would save themselves from the torments of the next. Consequently, there was to some extent an element of protection in the form of succession to property. Therefore, the same cannot, as on date, enable the biological parents to contend that their rights to give their children in adoption to foreign nationals is absolute and unfettered. In such circumstances, despite the fact that the parties involved in this case appear to be genuine, I am unable to order the original petition as prayed for unconditionally without even a Home Study Report."*

Hence, it is manifest that the Court logically carved out the necessary relief, as already stated above. According to the Madras High Court the decision of the biological parents, however *bona fide*, need not always be an informed decision. And in view of the detailed reasoning in the order dated 13 June, 2011 the Court issued directions to the Central Adoption Resource Authority,

Ministry of Women and Child Development, Government of India, to engage the services of a recognized and approved agency in Germany and have a home study conducted in respect of the petitioners and submit the same to the Court within a period of three months to enable the Court to allow the above original petition as prayed for, so as to allow the process of adoption without CARA intervention.

However, taking a different opinion from the above stated ruling of the Madras High Court, the Delhi High Court in its recent judgment of *Dr. Jaswinder Singh Bains* v. *Central Adoption Resource Authority*, Writ Petition no. 8775 of 2011, decided on 13 February, 2012, dealt with the issue of application of *Anokha's* case as also the intervention of CARA to obtain NOC in the cases of adoption by the biological parents. It was contended that:

> *"Adoption of Indian children, in the case of adoption of children living with their biological parents were not governed by these guidelines and these guidelines applied only to cases where the child was a destitute or abandoned or living in social or child welfare centres. It is only where there is the impersonalized attention of a placement authority that there is a need to closely monitor the process including obtaining of a no-objection certificate from the Central Adoption Resource Agency (CARA), Ministry of Welfare, the sponsorship of the adoption by a recognized national agency and the scrutiny of the inter-country adoption by a recognized Voluntary Coordinating Agency (VCA). Indeed CARA has been set up under the Guidelines for the purpose of eliminating the malpractices indulged in by some unscrupulous placement agencies, particularly the trafficking in children."*

The High Court, on basis of these, ruled that the NOC is not necessary in such cases where adoption is by the biological parents. The High Court made the following observation:

> *"From the aforesaid, it is clear that No Objection Certificate required by the Canadian authorities from CARA is not called for and it does not fall within the mandate of CARA to grant the No Objection Certificate in the facts of the case, as it is a case of voluntary adoption by the petitioner No.1 of Baby Simran from her biological parents.*
>
> *In the light of the aforesaid discussion, it is declared that there is no requirement for issuance of No Objection Certificate by CARA in relation to the adoption of Baby Simran by petitioner no.1."*

Thus from the above judgments it is clear that there is confusion regarding the position of adoption where biological parents voluntarily give their child in adoption. While the CARA Guidelines are silent on this matter, different courts have presented variant views depending on the facts and circumstances of the case.

On January 24, 2013, the Bombay High Court heard together two petitions, namely *Dr. Abha Agrawal* v. *Central Adoption Resource Authority*, Writ Petition no. 2701 of 2012 and *Promila Ann Massey* v. *Central Adoption Resource Authority*, Writ Petition No. 3279 of 2012 which raised a common question *i.e.*, *"Whether adoptions made directly by the biological parents of a child to another person, without the intervention of the Central Adoption Resource Authority (in short CARA), are valid in the eyes of law?"*

J. Rajiv Shakhder, while framing the issues to be referred to a larger bench, gave his opinion in favour of intervention of CARA in cases of voluntary adoption by the biological parents and stated:

> *"10. In my view, apart from anything else, the court may have to examine whether the State in its capacity parens patriae would need to step-in, to safeguard the rights of the child, who is given in adoption by his biological parents; under Article 21 of the Constitution of India. This is a role which the State adopts to safeguard the interest of the persons who are under legal disability. This is, more particularly true, in case of juveniles. It is a concept by which the State protects its quasi-sovereign interest, which* inter alia *relates to health, comfort and welfare of its citizens.* (See Black's Law Dictionary, *6th Edn. at p. 1114)*
>
> *10.1 Therefore, in my view, even in the absence of any guidelines the court is not disempowered to direct the State to carry out an investigation in the interest of the child, both in the country of his/her origin as well as in foreign country through a recognized agency."*

The aspects referred are:—*(i) Whether the term 'surrendered child' will include those children who are directly taken in adoption from their biological parents without the intercession of any specialized agency or child welfare committee?*

(ii) Whether, in case of direct adoption, the 2011 Guidelines and the provisions of section 41(3) and (4) of the JJ Act are applicable?

(iii) If the answer to issue No. (i) and (ii) is in the affirmative, to what extent the 2011 Guidelines would apply to direct adoptions?

(iv) Can the court direct State to discharge its duty in its capacity as parens patriae to carry out an investigation so as to safeguard the interest and/or rights of the child conferred on him under Article 21 of the Constitution of India?

This case is indeed of great legal importance as to the matter of adoptions directly by the biological parents. The Apex court is hoped to identify these problems and carve out clear cut guidelines and clarify these conflicting position.

IX. Preference to Parents of Indian Origin

Another significant issue in inter-country adoptions, is locating prospective adoptive parents, preferably of Indian origin, the Supreme Court of India, in *Karnataka State Council for Child Welfare* v. *Society of Sisters of Charity St Gerosa Convent,* AIR 1994 SC 658: 1993 AIR SCW 4069: 1994 (1) APLJ 78, held that the rationale behind finding Indian parents or parents of Indian origin is to ensure that the children should grow up in Indian surroundings so that they retain their culture and heritage. This is definitely an issue, which has a bearing on the question of the welfare of the children. The best interest of the children is the main and prime consideration.

The Gujarat High Court in a progressive judgment in *Jayantilal L. Shah* v. *Miss Asha T. Shah,* AIR 1989 Guj 152: (1989) 30 Guj LR 257: (1989) 1 Guj LH 373 upheld the validity of guardianship orders in favor of two Norwegian couples who were appointed as guardians of Hindu children. The Court held in para 12 (at page 156):

> '... *if the biological parents have died rendering the child an orphan then the society owes a duty to the child that at least a semblance of comfort and care which the biological parents could have provided will be provided to the child, if some people from howsoever distant a corner of this planet, come forth to do so. In such a case a petty contention like the change of religion or culture of the child can hardly stand in the way of the court in sanctioning inter-country adoption founded and imaginary apprehensions also are of little consequence and once the court is assured that there is no possibility of the child being abused which assurance can flow from the independent agencies which are ordained for the purpose then nothing can and need to prevent the court from sanctioning an inter-country adoption.*'

Thus, the procedure described above and the supervisory role of the Court serves as a double check on inter-country adoptions. Not only does this dual process ensure a check against suspected child abuse, but at the same time it also removes hyper-technical objections to facilitate the conclusion of the adoption process and to enable the adopted child to leave the country with his or her adoptive parents without further bureaucratic delays.

The Allahabad High Court in *Jagdish Chander Gupta* v. *Dr. Ku Vimla Gupta*, 2004 (1) HLR 282 held that, under section 9 of the Guardian and Wards Act, 1890, the application for guardianship of a minor shall be made to the District Court having jurisdiction in the place where the minor ordinarily resides. The supervisory role of the Court in placing the welfare of the minor as the primary consideration is best reflected in the following words of the Court in para 16 (at page 285):

> '*It should not be lost sight of and must be emphasized that in custody cases, a child has not to be treated as a chattel in which its parents have a proprietary interest. It is a human being to whom the parents owe serious obligations. One's own self-interest sometimes clouds his perception of what is the best for those for whom he or she is responsible. It takes a very high degree of selflessness and maturity-which for most of the people probably is un-attainable degree—for a parent/proposed guardian to acknowledge that it might be better for the child to be brought up by someone else.*'

The Indian parents cannot, however, claim any right over any child to be adopted who has already been referred to and accepted by the parents of foreign origin. In *Varsha Shinde* v. *The Society of the Sassoon Hospital*, Writ Petition No. 9227 of 2011 in the High Court of Bombay, decided on 18 October, 2013, wherein a child was first shown to the parents of foreign origin before showing her to Indian prospective parents due to failure of SARA and ARC to comply with the procedures of the guidelines of 2011, the High Court of Bombay made the following observation:

> "*20. In our view once the child had been shown to Overseas Indians and approved by them on 25-05-2013, the child could not have been shown to the Petitioners or to other Indian parents and, therefore, the Petitioners cannot claim any right*

or priority to get the child in adoption merely because they are Indian parents and that preference should be given to Indian parents over Overseas Indians or foreign couples."

Thus, dealing with the abovementioned problem, the High Court in the instant case issued six guidelines in consonance with the rules of 2011. These are as follows:

1. All the concerned Agencies *viz.*, RIPA, Specialized Adoption Agencies, SARA, ARC, AFAA to scrupulously follow the Guidelines which have been laid down in 2011.
2. RIPA and the Specialized Adoption Agencies are directed to complete the Home Study Report within a stipulated time as prescribed under the Rules and the ratio of 80 : 20 should be adhered to and preference should be given to Indian parents first and if the Indian parents decline to accept the child in adoption only thereafter the child may be shown to foreign parents.
3. Though there is no specific number mentioned in the Guidelines as to the number of Indian parents to whom the child should be shown, we are of the view that within a period of 3/4 weeks, the child should be shown to as many Indian parents as possible and, secondly, at a time, the child should be shown only to one parent and not multiple number of parents as has been done in the present case.
4. Only if the child is not accepted by Indian parents and the Adoption Agencies on account of their experience come to the conclusion that the child is not likely to be taken in adoption by Indian parents then, in that case, it should be shown to foreign parents.
5. When the child is shown to the foreign parents, it should be shown in the list of priorities which are mentioned in the said Guidelines *viz.*, initially it should be shown to NRI then Overseas Indian Parents etc and only thereafter to foreigners.
6. ARC should give Recommendatory Letter within five days in respect of the children with special needs and within 15 days in respect of other children. This should be strictly adhered to. Non-compliance of the said Guideline should be strictly viewed and action if necessary may be taken against the concerned Authorities, ARC or SARA who do not follow the said Schedule. ARC and SARA should work not in conflict but in coordination with CARA, it being the Centralized Nodal Agency.

X. Ratification of the Hague Convention on Inter-Country Adoption by the Government of India on 6 June, 2003

The Government of India has also ratified the Hague Convention on Inter-Country Adoption on 6 June, 2003. Although, the Government of India has ratified the Hague Convention in this regard, but in actual practice the same has not been publicized. And, from the practical point of view not much tangible benefits are forthcoming at all to people residing abroad seeking to adopt children from India. In fact, one of the authors of this article at the Annual

National Meet on Adoption organized in New Delhi on 3-4 May, 2007, by the CARA, now falling under the new created Ministry of Women and Child Development, strongly advocated the emergent need for setting up a committee or a task force to commission a comprehensive report to look at the potential benefits on India signing the Hague Convention on adoptions. If such a report is prepared, it can well be officially circulated to the Foreign Embassies and Missions in India. This is of course, with a view to creating awareness and publicizing the advantages of India signing the Hague Convention on adoptions, to prospective adoptive parents of foreign origin and Persons of Indian Origin domiciled overseas.

Implementation of Hague Convention Recommendations

Indian Government has notified various adoption policies consistent with Hague Convention as shown below.

- ♦ Central Authority (Article 6)
  - Central Adoption Recourse Agency (CARA)
  - Setup as a Wing of the Ministry of Welfare on 28-6-1990
  - Made an autonomous body on 18-3-1999
- ♦ Child is declared adoptable (legally Free for Adoption) by the concerned public authority, such as, Child Welfare Committee, etc. (as required under Article 4.a.)
- ♦ Priority is given to in-country adoption before a child is proposed for inter country adoption (as required under Articles 4.b. & 16.d.)
- ♦ All authorities/agencies including CARA apply the principle of 'Best Interest of the Child' to an adoption case (as required under Article 4.b. & 16.d.)
- ♦ Necessary consents of biological parents, adoptive parents and the older Child are obtained before an adoption is affected. (as required under Article 4.b. & 16.d.)
- ♦ Adoption is permitted only through recognized placement Agencies with Professionally Trained Social Workers. (as required under Article 11)
- ♦ Adoptive parents are required to escort a child from India for the secured transfer of the child (as required under Article 19.2)
- ♦ Any improper financial or other gain is prevented (as required under Articles 8 & 32) through:
  - Fixing adoption costs.
  - Prohibition of direct contact between prospective foreign adoptive parents and Indian Agencies.
  - Prohibition of middlemen.
  - Giving recognition to those Indian Agencies for working under the Convention who work with non-profit motive.
  - Financial Returns furnished by the Inter-country Adoption Agencies to Charity Commissioners, Local State Government & Ministries.

XI. Domestic Law of Adoptions in India under the Provisions of the Hindu Adoption and Maintenance Act, 1956

Having elaborated the law and procedure relating to inter-country adoptions, brief reference is now made to the domestic law governing adoptions by Hindus.

The principal law relating to adoption in India by Hindus only is contained in the Hindu Adoptions and Maintenance Act, 1956 (HAMA, 1956).

(A) Requisites of a Valid Adoption

Section 6 stipulates four conditions for a valid adoption, namely:

(1) the person adopting has the capacity, and also the right, to take in adoption;

(2) the person giving the child in adoption has the capacity to do so;

(3) the person adopted is capable of being taken in adoption; and

(4) the adoption is made in compliance with the other conditions mentioned in Chapter 2 of the HAMA, 1956.

Section 6(iv) requires that the adoption should be made in compliance with other conditions mentioned in Chapter 2 of the HAMA, 1956. In other words, in order that the adoption should be valid, the provisions of sections 7–11 must be satisfied. Section 7 deals with the capacity of a male Hindu to take in adoption; and section 8 with the capacity of a female Hindu to take in adoption. Section 9 qualifies persons capable of giving children in adoption; section 10 categorises those persons who may be adopted; and section 11 enumerates other conditions for a valid adoption. Thereafter, section 12 elaborates the effects of a valid adoption.

(B) Other Conditions for a Valid Adoption

Section 11 of the HAMA, 1956 stipulates other vital conditions for a valid adoption, and is reproduced below.

'11. Other conditions for a valid adoption

In every adoption, the following conditions must be complied with:—

(i) if the adoption is of a son, the adoptive father or mother by whom the adoption is made must not have a Hindu son, son's son or son's son's son (whether by legitimate blood relationship or by adoption) living at the time of adoption;

(ii) if the adoption is of a daughter, the adoptive father or mother by whom the adoption is made must not have a Hindu daughter or son's daughter (whether by legitimate blood relationship or by adoption) living at the time of adoption;

(iii) if the adoption is by a male and the person to be adopted is a female, the adoptive father is at least twenty-one years older than the person to be adopted;

(iv) if the adoption is by a female and the person to be adopted is a male, the adoptive mother is at least twenty-one years older than the person to be adopted;

(v) *the same child may not be adopted simultaneously by two or more persons;*

(vi) *the child to be adopted must be actually given and taken in adoption by the parents or guardian concerned or under their authority with intent to transfer the child from the family of its birth [or in the case of an abandoned child or child whose parentage is not known, from the place or family where it has been brought up] to the family of its adoption:*

Provided that the performance of datta homam *shall not be essential for the validity of adoption'.*

(C) Effects of a Valid Adoption

Section 12 specifically deals with the legal effects of an adoption made in accordance with the provisions of the HAMA, 1956. It can be pointed out that section 12 of the HAMA, 1956 satisfies the requirements of clause (ix) of para 310 of HC 395 of the current British Immigration Rules governing adoption. This clause in very harsh terms states that the adopted child 'has lost or broken his ties with his family of origin'.

As to the legal effects of a valid adoption, it is important to cite certain decisions of the Supreme Court of India. It was held by the Supreme Court of India in *Sitabai* v. *Ramchandra,* 1970 (1) SCJ 476: (1970) 2 SCR 1: AIR 1970 SC 343 (348), para 6 of the judgement:

> *'... The true effect and interpretation of sections 11 and 12 of Act No 78 of 1956 therefore is that when either of the spouses adopts a child, all the ties of the child in the family of his or her birth become completely severed and these are all replaced by those created by the adoption in the adoptive family ...'*

Similarly, it was held by the Supreme Court in *Kartar Singh* v. *Surjan Singh,* (1974) 2 SCC 559: (1975) 1 SCR 742: AIR 1974 SC 2161 (2163), para 7 of the judgment:

> *'... The words in section 11(vi) "with intent to transfer the child from the family of its birth to the family of its adoption" are merely indicative of the result of the actual giving and taking by the parents or guardians concerned referred to in the earlier part of the clause. Where an adoption ceremony is gone through and the giving and taking takes place, there cannot be any other intention ...'*

More recently, the Supreme Court of India in *Chandan Bilasini* v. *Aftabuddin Khan,* (1996) 7 SCC 13: 1996 (2) SCJ 210: (1996) 1 Hindu LR 79 (SC), held at page 81, para 6 of the judgment:

> *'... Section 12 of the Hindu Adoptions and Maintenance Act clearly provides that an adopted child shall be deemed to be the child of his adoptive father or mother for all purposes with effect from the date of the adoption and from such date all ties of the child in the family of his or her birth shall be deemed to be severed and replaced by those created by the adoption in the adoptive family...'*

(D) Section 15 of HAMA, 1956 Provides that a valid adoption not to be cancelled

Finally, section 15 of the HAMA, 1956 underlines the irrevocability of the validly performed adoption by stating that it cannot be cancelled or renounced.

Therefore, under Indian law, once a legitimate adoption is obtained, in accordance with the procedure established by law, the margin for interference is minimal, except in certain exceptional circumstances.

The adoption process once validly effected in terms of HAMA, 1956 is an irrevocable act and the biological parents cannot seek the custody of the child at later point of time. The same principle applies in the interest of the child when children are given in foster care by their parents first voluntarily and later when they seek its return at their whims and pleasure.

The Bombay High Court in a decided case, reported as *Maroti Vithalbhatwalkar* v. *Mahila Vikas Mandal, Chandrapur,* AIR 2007 (NOC) 965 (Bom), has handed down a significant ruling in this regard. In this particular case, the biological parents gave their child to a childless couple, as they stayed away from each other and were not sure whether they would be able to or even wanted to take care of the child properly or not. The foster parents took good care of the child but six and a half years later, the biological parents filed an application with the scrutiny officer, that they wanted the child back with them. They were still living separately and were not sure as to who would keep the child. The matter went to the court and dismissing their claim, the court held that merely because of the report of the scrutiny officer the child cannot be handed over back to the biological parents. Biological parents cannot wait to receive the child indefinitely and leave the fate of the child suspended animation leaving to them the choice of exercising option of claiming child at a later point of time. In the interest of the child, its care and continuity should not be disturbed.

(E) Registered Adoption can be Challenged

Section 16 of the HAMA, 1956 reads as follows:

> ***'16. Presumption as to registered documents relating to adoption***
>
> *Whenever any document registered under any law for the time being in force is produced before any court purporting to record an adoption made and is signed by the person giving and the person taking the child in adoption, the court shall presume that the adoption has been made in compliance with the provisions of this Act unless and until it is disproved.'*

In an important ruling concerning adoption by Hindus, *Jai Singh* v. *Shakuntala,* (2002) 3 SCC 634: AIR 2002 SC 1428: 2002 AIR SCW 1280, the Supreme Court of India has recently held that, though a document registering an adoption should be treated as final proof of adoption, it could still be challenged in a court of law if evidence to the contrary was put forward.

The apex court, in interpreting the statutory intent of section 16 of the HAMA, 1956, said that the presumption about the registered document relating to adoption 'cannot be an irrebuttable presumption'. Justices Umesh C. Banerjee and Brijesh Kumar held at pages 636 and 637, para 2 of the judgment:

> *"2. The section thus envisages a statutory presumption that in the event of there being a registered document pertaining to adoption there would be a presumption that adoption has been made in accordance with law. Mandate of the statute is rather definite since the legislature has used "shall" instead of any other word*

of lesser significance. Incidentally, however, the inclusion of the words "unless and until it is disproved" appearing at the end of the statutory provision has made the situation not that rigid but flexible enough to depend upon the evidence available on record in support of adoption. It is a matter of grave significance by reason of the factum of adoption and displacement of the person adopted from the natural succession — thus onus of proof is rather heavy. Statute has allowed some amount of flexibility, lest it turns out to be solely dependent on a registered adoption deed. The reason for inclusion of the words "unless and until it is disproved" shall have to be ascertained in its proper perspective and as such the presumption cannot but be said to be a rebuttable presumption. Statutory intent thus stands out to be rather expressive depicting therein that the presumption cannot be an irrebuttable presumption by reason of the inclusion of the words just noticed above...."

In the above-mentioned ruling, the Supreme Court also concurred with the similar tenor of law laid down by the Punjab and Haryana High Court in *Modan Singh* v. *Sham Kaur*, AIR 1973 P&H 122: 1972 Cur LJ 210.

Clearly, the ruling in Jai Singh will be of immense help to immigration officers of foreign missions/consulates/embassies in India in weeding out suspect adoption immigration applications lodged from within the applicant's own family designed to circumvent immigration controls.

(F) Case-Law Analysis of Adoptions: Not to be terminated after a Lapse of Long Period of Time.

From the ratio of the case-law handed down by the Supreme Court of India and other High Courts in the country, it emanates that when an adoption ceremony has been performed and the giving and taking of child takes place, there cannot be any other intention other than effecting the adoption.

The catena of case laws also holds that the process of adoption cannot be challenged after a significant lapse of time.

One of the early decisions handed down by the Hon'ble Supreme Court of India in the case of *L. Debi Prasad (dead) by L.Rs* v. *Tribeni Devi*, AIR 1970 SC 1286 (V 57 C 270), is a significant judgment on adoption that cannot be challenged after a significant lapse of time.

Paragraphs 8 and 9 of the said judgment (at pages 1289 and 1290) state as under:

"8. That is also the view expressed in Mayne's Hindu Law wherein it is observed that the giving and receiving are absolutely necessary to the validity of an adoption; they are the operative part of the ceremony, being that part of it which transfers the boy from one family to another; but the Hindu law does not require that there shall be any particular form so far as giving and acceptance are concerned; for a valid, adoption all that the law requires is that the natural father shall be asked by the adoptive parent to give his son in adoption, and that the boy shall be handed over and taken for this purpose.

9. There is no doubt that the burden of proving satisfactorily that he was given by his natural father and received by Gopal Das as his adoptive son is on Shyam

> *Behari Lal. But as observed by the Judicial Committee of the Privy Council in* Rajendrao Nath Holder *v.* Jogendro Nath Benerjee, *(1870-72) 14 Moo Ind App 67 (PC) that although the person who pleads that he had been adopted is bound to prove his title as adopted son, as a fact yet from the long period during which he had been received as an adopted son, every allowance for the absence of evidence to prove such fact was to be favourably entertained, and that the case was analogous to that in which the legitimacy of a person in possession had been acquiesced in for a considerable time, and afterwards impeached by a party, who had a right to question the legitimacy, where the defendant, in order to defend his status, is allowed to invoke against the claimant every presumption which arises from long recognition of his legitimacy by members of his family; that in the case of a Hindu, long recognition as an adopted son, raised even a stronger presumption in favour of the validity of his adoption, arising from the possibility of the loss of his rights in his own family by being adopted in another family. In* Rup Narain *v.* Gopal Devi, *ILR 36 Cal 780: (1990) 36 Ind App 103 (PC), the Judicial Committee observed, that in the absence of direct evidence much value has to be attached to the fact that the alleged adopted son had without controversy succeeded to his adoptive father's estate and enjoyed till his death and that documents during his life and after his death were framed upon the basis of the adoption. A Division Bench of the Orissa High Court in* Balinki Padhano *v.* Gopal Krishna Padhano, *AIR 1964 Ori 117; held that in the case of an ancient adoption evidence showing that the boy was treated for a long time as the adopted son at a time when there was no controversy is sufficient to prove the adoption although evidence of actual giving and taking is not forthcoming. We are in agreement with the views expressed in the decisions referred to above."*

Another High Court ruling in the reported case of *Sauney Majhi* v. *Duli Dei*, AIR 1985 Ori 22, demonstrates the validity of the adoption process in absence of evidence where a significant amount of time has lapsed.

Paragraph 6 (at pages 24 and 25) of the said judgment above reads as under:

> *"6. The law is fairly settled that the evidence in support of an adoption is sufficient to satisfy the very grave and serious onus that rests upon any person who seeks to displace the natural line of succession by alleging an adoption. The fact of adoption must be proved in the same way as any other fact, but where there is a lapse of long period between the date of adoption and the time when it is being questioned, every allowance for the absence of evidence to prove such fact must be favourably entertained, as after the lapse of a long period, direct evidence to prove adoption may not be available."*

The Supreme Court in the case of *L. Debi Prasad* v. *Tribeni Devi* (supra), observed:—

> *"In the case of all ancient transactions, it is but natural that positive oral evidence will be lacking. Passage of time gradually wipes out such evidence. Human affairs often have to be judged on the basis of probabilities. Rendering of justice will become impossible if a particular mode of proof is insisted upon under all*

circumstances. In judging whether an adoption pleaded has been satisfactorily proved or not, we have to bear in mind the lapse of time between the date of the alleged adoption and the date on which the concerned party is required to adduce proof. In the case of an adoption said to have taken place years before the same is questioned, the most important evidence is likely to be that the alleged adoptive father held out the person claiming to have been adopted as his son; the latter treated the former as his father and their relations and friends treated them as father and son. There is no predetermined way of proving any fact. A fact is said to have been proved where after considering the matters before it, the Court either believes it to exist or considers its existence so probable that a prudent man ought, under the circumstances of the particular case, to act upon the supposition that it exists. Hence if after taking an overall view of the evidence adduced in the case, we are satisfied that the adoption pleaded is true, we must necessarily proceed on the basis, in the absence of any evidence to the contrary, that it is a valid adoption as well."

The aforesaid view of the Supreme Court has been followed in a number of cases of this court and other high Courts. The aforesaid principle only regulates the mode of proof of the factum of adoption. In the decision in the case of *Venkata Seetharama Chandra Row* v. *Kanchumarthi Raju*, AIR 1925 PC 201: 89 Ind Cas 817: 53 Mad LJ 858 (PC), which has been approved by the Supreme Court in the case of *Voleti Venkata Ramarao* v. *Kesapragada Bhaskararao*, AIR 1969 SC 1359: (1970) 1 SCR 301, it has been authoritatively said that in the case of an ancient adoption, it stands to reason that after a very long-term of years and a variety of transactions of open life and conduct upon the footing that the adoption was a valid act, the burden must rest heavily upon him who challenges its validity. The appellants in this case rely upon the aforesaid principles and have contended that the date of adoption available from the evidence on record was 1909 and it is not possible to prove the factum of adoption by direct evidence. Thus, according to them the overall view of the evidence on record should lead to the conclusion that there was a valid adoption as alleged by them.

It will be noticed that the aforesaid view of the Supreme Court of India in the matter of *L. Debi Prasad* v. *Tribeni Devi*, AIR 1970 SC 1286, has been followed in the above mentioned-case of *Sauney Majhi* v. *Duli Dei* (supra). The aforesaid principle only regulates the mode of proof of the factum of adoption.

The third ruling in line to support the above-mentioned argument in favour of the validity of the adoption in absence of evidence is the reported case of *Sitaram Nai* v. *Puranmal Sonar*, AIR 1985 Ori 171.

Paragraphs 8 and 9 of the said judgment which are relevant are cited hereunder:

"8. Before examining the correctness of rival contentions and the evidence adduced in this case to find out whether the adoption of defendant No. 2 by late Baluram has been proved in this case or not, it would be profitable to note the law on the point. Under the Hindu law, as it existed prior to the commencement of the Hindu Adoptions and Maintenance Act, the physical act of giving and receiving is absolutely necessary to the validity of an adoption. There is no particular form prescribed for giving and taking but what the law requires is that there

should be some overt act to signify the delivery of the boy from one family to another. The natural parents should hand over the adoptive boy and the adoptive parents should receive him. In case of an old adoption, however, strict proof of the performance of the ceremonies may not be available. An adoption acquiesced in and recognised for a number of years by the person making the adoption and a long course of recognition on the part of the persons who would be expected to know of the fact and who were best acquainted with the circumstances, can give rise to the inference _ that the conditions relating to the adoption' were fulfilled. (See, Mulla's Hindu Law, Section 489). *There is no specific rule as to number of years necessary for the purpose to dub the adoption as an 'old adoption'. By judicial pronouncements, however, the Courts in India have more or less considered adoption, of 25 years and more to be an ancient adoption. In our opinion, no definite formula can be applied as to the number of years to find out whether the adoption is an old adoption or not. But according to us, where on account of lapse of time, it is not possible to give evidence of persons proving the ceremony of giving and taking, then a party can take recourse to the theory of ancient adoption, provided of course, there has been a sufficient lapse of time between the date of alleged adoption and the date on which the same is challenged. But if the evidence discloses that the persons who attended the adoption ceremony are available to give evidence, then in such a case one cannot discharge his burden of proving the factum of giving and taking merely by taking recourse to the fact that the adoption had taken place 25 or 30 years before the same is challenged. In our opinion, it depends upon the facts and circumstances of each case.*

9...... In the case of Gouranga Sahu *v.* Bhaga Sahu, AIR 1976 Ori 43, *S.K. Ray, J. (as he then was) was considering the case of an old adoption and also the burden of proof and the mode of appreciation of evidence thereto. In that case, the adoption was 36 year old. In paragraph 6 of the judgment, his lordship held:—*

".... So even though the normal rule is that one who seeks to deflect the natural line of succession to property by alleging adoption must discharge that heavy burden, in cases of ancient adoption every allowance for the absence of evidence to prove such fact must be favourably entertained. Where there is a long lapse of years between the adoption and the time when it is being questioned and during that period of interregnum a variety of transactions of open life and conduct upon the footing that the adoption was a valid act have taken place, the initial burden necessarily shifts to the person who challenges its validity....."

After applying the law to the facts of that case, his lordship held:—

".... Considering the entire evidence on record, both documentary and oral, and the variety of transactions of open life and conduct upon the fooling of adoption coupled with the weakness of the defence evidence, and absence of any casteman or relative coming forward in support of the defence case, it is impossible to say that the plaintiff is the adopted son of Mohana is erroneous....."

From the said judgment, it is not quite clear as to what was the evidence which, his Lordship has considered in coming to the aforesaid conclusion.

A conspectus of aforesaid authorities unequivocally lays down the rule that a person who claims title on the basis of adoption must prove the adoption and it has to be established that the essential ceremony of giving and taking did take place. That burden, however shifts to the person who challenges the adoption to disprove when on account of long lapse of years, direct evidence of giving and taking has disappeared. But if direct evidence is available, then the burden would not shift and the person who claims title on the basis of adoption must discharge that burden.

Another recent example in support of the validity of adoption where a significant amount of time has lapsed is the case of *Muniven Katappa* v. *Dodamuniyappa*, 2008 (2) HLR 308.

Para 13 (at page 311) of the judgment read as under:

> *"13. ...It is also to be noticed that under the Hindu Law giving and receiving of a boy are absolutely necessary to the validity of adoption. They are the operative part of ceremony, which converts the boy of one family to another family. But however, it is to be noticed that the Hindu Law does not require giving and receiving of a boy, so far as acceptance is concerned. For a valid adoption all that the law requires is that the parent in adoption and that the boy shall be handed over and taken over by the parties. It is to be noticed that the case of a long recognition of an adoption raises a strong presumption in favour of the validity of the adoption arising from the loss of his rights from his own family and adopt the right of another family. In ancient adoptions, where the evidence by lapse of time is not available and there are documents evidencing the adoption, then in such circumstances, it is for them who challenge the adoption to prove that the said adoption has not taken place, as there is no circumstance sufficient to prove adoption is forthcoming."*

In light of the above-mentioned rulings, it is noticed that even though grave and serious onus lies on the person who seeks to deflect from the natural line of succession, a clear exception has been made by the Hon'ble Supreme Court of India and various High Courts in the country in a number of cases dealing with the issue of ancient adoptions. A strong presumption is raised in favour of the validity of adoption in such cases. Meaning thereby, that where due to long lapse of years, it is not possible to get the evidence to prove the adoption, it is to be presumed that the adoption is valid and the burden to prove that the adoption did not take place actually and consequently shifts on the person challenging the said adoption in question. However, if direct evidence is available in such cases, the burden to prove the adoption does not shift in such a situation and the person claiming the title on the basis of the adoption has to prove the adoption satisfactorily.

(G) Position of customary adoption before and after the commencement of the Hindu Adoptions and Maintenance Act, 1956.

Brief case-law analysis on the position of Recognition of Customary Adoptions before and after the commencement of the Hindu Adoptions and Maintenance Act, 1956.

In the case of *Mohinder Singh* v. *Gurbax Singh,* 2004 (138) PLR 154, the Punjab and Haryana High Court has analysed the position of law relating to customary adoptions specifically before and after the commencement of the Hindu Adoption and Maintenance Act, 1956 (Hereinafter referred to as the HAMA, 1956).

The key issue in the present case was to analyse as to what was the effect of the provisions of the HAMA, 1956, after the commencement of the HAMA, 1956 on 21 December, 1956 on customary adoptions made before the enactment of the said legislation.

Both the trial Court as well as the first appellate Court held that the adoption in the present case was valid under the customary rules and the same cannot be cancelled or set aside. Therefore, the Hon'ble High Court upheld in appeal the customary adoption made on 3 February, 1946.

The issue in hand was discussed at length before the Hon'ble High Court by both the parties in the present case. The legal point of the difference in the position of customary adoptions before and after the enactment of the HAMA, 1956 was noticed and analyzed by the Hon'ble High Court in paragraphs 14 (at pages 158 and 159) in the following terms:

> "14. *While referring to section 30 of the Adoptions and Maintenance Act, learned counsel for the defendant further submitted that in this case, the alleged adoption was made in the year 1946* i.e., *much prior to the commencement of the Adoptions and Maintenance Act, therefore, the validity and the effect of such an adoption has to be determined in accordance with the position existing prior to the Adoptions and Maintenance Act. He submitted that the adoption in question was customary, which was nothing but appointment of a legal heir. Though, such adoption has been abolished now under section 4 of the Adoptions and Maintenance Act, but the nature of the adoption in the instant case would not change, in view of section 30 of the Adoptions and Maintenance Act as the provisions of sections 4 and 12 of the said Act will not be applicable in the instant case. Section 12 of the Adoptions and Maintenance Act provides that an adopted child shall be deemed to be the child of his adoptive father or mother for all purposes with effect from the date of the adoption and from such date all the ties of the child in the family of his or her birth shall be deemed to be severed and replaced by those created by the adoption in the adoptive family. In view of this Section, now there is no scope for customary adoption i.e. appointment of legal heirs. But sections 4 and 12 of the Adoptions and Maintenance Act will not be applicable on an adoption, which was made prior to coming into force of this Act. The validity and effect of such adoption will be determined on the basis of law or custom prevailing at that lime. In the instant case, the adoption was made in the year 1946 under the custom. The said adoption was nothing but the appointment of a legal heir. Thus, the status of the plaintiff will not change after coming into force of the Adoptions and Maintenance Act and the validity and effect of the adoption of the plaintiff by Dasondha Singh has to be analysed according to the position existing prior to the Adoptions and Maintenance Act. In nutshell, the contention of learned counsel for the defendant is that under*

the customary law of Punjab, the adoption of the plaintiff was nothing but an appointment of a legal heir and by such appointment, he was not transplanted to the family of the appointor or conversely he did not become grandson of Rur Singh, father of Dasondha Singh. Therefore, he could not form a coparcenary with Dasondha Singh, and without being a coparcener, he did not have any right to challenge any alienation made by his appointor i.e. Dasondha Singh. In support of his contention, learned counsel for the defendant relied upon a decision of the Hon'ble Apex Court in Daniraiji Vrajlalji, Junagadh *v.* Maharaj Shri Chandraprabha, *AIR 1975 SC 784: (1975) 1 SCC 612: (1975) 3 SCR 32, wherein it was held that an adoption in 'Goda Datta' form made before the passing of the Adoptions and Maintenance Act can be cancelled or revoked even after coming into force of that Act. Neither section 4 nor section 15 of the Adoptions and Maintenance Act is retrospective in its operation. Any custom or usage as part of the Hindu Law in force prior to the commencement of the Act has ceased to have effect in regard to any matter for which provision has been made in Chapter II, except what has been expressly provided in the Adcptions and Maintenance Act, which prohibits cancellation of adoption, applies to an adoption which has been validly made in accordance with the provisions contained in Chapter II of the Adoptions and Maintenance Act and after its commencement. It does not do away with the incident and characteristic of revocability of the custom of Goda Datta. Validity of an adoption made before the commencement of the Adoptions and Maintenance Act and also its effect has to be examined and determined with reference to the law or the custom as it stood prior to the coming into force of the Adoptions and Maintenance Act and not in accordance with it. Thus, on the basis of the aforesaid, learned counsel for the defendant submitted that the plaintiff being only an appointed heir under the customary law was having no* locus standi *to contest the alienation made by Dasondha Singh. By such an adoption, he did not become the member of the family of his adoptive father and thus, he did not acquire the status of a coparcener. Therefore, neither he has any right in the coparcenary property being a coparcener nor he has right to challenge the alienation of the ancestral coparcenary property made by Dasondha Singh during his life time."*

The Hon'ble High Court has given a detailed analysis of adoptions under the customary law of Punjab in paragraphs 20 and 21 (at pages 162 and 163) of the said judgment in the following terms:

"20. Under the customary law of Punjab, there was distinction between customary formal adoption and adoption by way of customary appointment of heirs. Under the Hindu Law or in case of customary formal adoption, the adoption is primarily a religious act intended to confer spiritual benefit on the adopter, and under the Customary Law in Punjab, adoption was a secular act the object of which was to appoint a legal heir. The formal adoption by customary method confers on the adopted son the status of a son in the adoptive family with a right of collateral succession in the family of the adoptive father. The formal adoption may be made in accordance with custom and by observing the customary forms. It is not necessary to comply with the rules of Hindu Law in the matter of ritual or otherwise. In case of customary adoption the adoption was no more than a

mere appointment of a legal heir creating a personal relationship between the adoptive father and the appointed heir only. There is no tie of kinship between the appointed heir and the collaterals of the adoptive father. The appointed heir does not acquire the right to succeed collaterally in the adoptive father's family. He acquires the right to succeed the property which his adoptive father leaves for him at the time of his death. He has no right to challenge any alienation made by the adoptive father during his life time. The status of the appointed heir is, thus, materially different from that of a son adopted under the Hindu Law or formal adoption under custom.

21. The adoption is formal if the parties manifest a clear intention that there should be a complete change of the family of the adopted son, so that he ceases to be a member of his natural family and loses his right of collateral succession in that family and at the same time becomes a member of the adoptive father's family and acquires a right of collateral succession in the family. This distinction has been clearly recognised by the Hon'ble Supreme Court in Kehar Singh *v.* Dewan Singh, AIR 1966 SC 1555: 1966 (2) SCJ 363: (1966) 3 SCR 393 *wherein it was held as under:—*

"A customary adoption in Punjab is ordinarily no more than a mere appointment of an heir creating a personal relationship between the adoptive father and the appointed heir only, see Mela Singh *v.* Gurdas, *ILR 3 Lah 362: AIR 1922 Lah 433 (FB). There is no tie of kinship between the appointed heir and the collaterals of the adoptive father. The appointed heir does not acquire the right to succeed collaterally in the adoptive father's family. The status of the appointed heir is thus materially different from that of a son adopted under the Hindu law."*

The general custom negating the right of the appointed heir to succeed collaterally in the adoptive father's family is stated in article 49 of ***Rattigan's Digest of Customary Law,*** **13th Edn., D 572 thus:—**

"49. Nor, on the other hand, does the heir acquire a right to succeed to the collateral relatives of the person who appoints him, where no formal adoption has taken place, in as much as the relationship established between him and the appointer is a purely personal one."

The rule in article 49 does not apply to a formal adoption by the customary method. The customary formal adoption completely severs the connection of the adopted son with his natural family and transplants him from his natural family to the adoptive family. Such an adoption confers on the adopted son the right of collateral succession in the adoptive father's family and takes away the right of collateral succession in the natural family. The formal adoption may be made in accordance with custom and by observing the customary forms, and it is not necessary to comply with the rules of Hindu law in the matter of ritual or otherwise. See Abdur Rehman *v.* Raghubir Singh, *(1949) 51 PLR 119;* Waryaman *v.* Kanshi Ram, *ILR 3 Lah 17: AIR 1922 Lah 105."*

Further it was also held in *Mukand Singh* v. *Wazir Singh,* (1972) 4 SCC 178 that a Hindu governed by customary law in Punjab was not disentitled to make a formal adoption according to customary adoption or according to Hindu rites and ceremonies."

In effect in this particular judgment, the Hon'ble High Court has categorically held that customary adoption in the State of Punjab before the commencement of the HAMA, 1956 was no more than a mere appointment of a legal heir creating a personal relationship between the adoptive father and the adopted heir only. But in paragraph 24 (at page 164) of the said judgment it has been upheld that the customary adoption in the present case was not a mere appointment of a legal heir but it was a formal adoption as well having the effect of the adopted child becoming a member of the family of the adoptive father.

In the case of *S.T. Krishanappa* v. *Shivkumar*, JT 2007 (6) SC 641, the Apex Court has dealt with the application of the "*Dvyamushyayana*" form of adoption, which was the main question in the appeal proceedings before the Supreme Court of India. The said deed of adoption admittedly did not contain any form of evidence at all as to whether the adoption was in "*Dvyamushyayana*" form or in any other form. The Hon'ble Supreme Court rejected the said appeal purely on the ground that there was no evidence on record to sustain the fact that the said adoption was in "*Dvyamushyayana*" form.

The Apex Court cited with approval, some of its earlier decisions directly on the subject in para 11 of the judgment in the following terms:

> "11. *What are the requisite ingredients of adoption in the said form came up for consideration in* Rajgopal (Dead) by LRs v. Krishna Gopal, *(2003) 10 SCC 653: AIR 2003 SC 4319: 2003 AIR SCW 4986, wherein a Division Bench of this Court upon taking into consideration a large number of decisions stated the law thus;*
>
> "18. *In every case of absolute Dvyamushyayana form of adoption, there must be an agreement to the effect that the person given in adoption shall be the son of both i.e. the natural father as well as the adoptive father and such an agreement must be proved like any other fact by the party alleging the same. See* Laxminathrao Shrinivas Deshpande *v.* Venkatesh Tirmal Deshpande *and* Mohna Mal *v.* Mula Mal".

The adoption deed in question in the above-mentioned case was executed on 15 February, 1945 prior to the commencement of HAMA, 1956 on 21 December, 1956. This judgment in the year 2007 reiterates the earlier law laid by the Hon'ble Supreme Court in *Kartar Singh (Minor) through Guardian Bachan Singh* v. *Surjan Singh (Dead)*, (1974) 2 SCC 559: (1975) 1 SCR 742: AIR 1974 SC 2161 (2163), wherein it was categorically held that adoptions according to custom stood abolished upon the commencement of HAMA, 1956.

(H) Customary Adoption and Supporting Proof thereof.

In the case of *Salekh Chand (Dead) thr. Lrs.* v. *Satya Gupta*, (2008) 13 SCC 119: AIR 2009 SC (Supp) 418: 2008 AIR SCW 4211, the Hon'ble Supreme Court of India elaborated in an analytical and chronological manner the catalogue of evidence required for proving and establishing custom followed by customary adoptions in India, as applicable to various communities, more so before the commencement of the HAMA, 1956. The said judgment also elaborates in detail the Hindu mythological belief and age old tradition in effectuating adoptions.

The analysis of Apex Court is contained in paragraphs 20 at sub-paras (13) to (20) (at pages 128 to 130) of the judgment in the following terms:

"13. Custom must be ancient, certain and reasonable as is generally said. It will be noticed that in the definition in clause (a) of section 3 of the Act, the expression 'ancient' is not used, but what is intended is observance of custom or usage for a long time. The English rule that ' a custom, in order that it may be legal and binding, must have been used so long that the memory of man runneth not to the contrary' has not been strictly applied to Indian conditions. All that is necessary to prove is that the custom or usage has been acted upon in practice for such a long period and with such invariability and continuity as to show that it has by common consent been submitted to as the established governing rule in any local area, tribe, community, group or family. Certainty and reasonableness are indispensable elements of the rule. For determination of the question whether there is a valid custom or not, it has been emphasized that it must not be opposed to public policy. I shall deal with the question of public policy later on.

14. The origin of custom of adoption assumes great importance. The origin of custom of adoption is lost in antiquity. The ancient Hindu Law recognized twelve kinds of sons of whom five were adopted. The five kinds of adopted sons in early times must have been of very secondary importance, for, on the whole, they were, relegated to an inferior rank in the order of sons. Out of the five kinds of adopted sons, only two survive today; namely, the. Dattaka form prevalent throughout India and the Kritrima form confined to Mithila and adjoining districts. The primary object of adoption was to gratify the means of the ancestors' by annual offerings and therefore it was considered necessary that the offerer should be as much as possible a reflection of a real descendant and had to look as much like a real son as possible and certainly not be one who would never have been a son. Therefore, the body of rules was evolved out of a phrase of Saunaka that he must be 'the reflection of a son'. The restrictions flowing from this maxim had the effect of eliminating most of the forms of adoption. (See Hindu Law by S.V. Gupte, *3rd Edn., at pp. 899-906).*

15. The whole law of Dattaka adoption is evolved from two important texts and a metaphor. The texts are of Manu and Vasistha, and the metaphor that of Saunaka. Manu provided for the identity of an adopted son with the family into which he was adopted. (See: Manu.Chapter IX, pages 141-142, as translated by Sir W. Jones). The object of an adoption is mixed, being religious and secular. According to Mayne, the recognition of the institution of adoption in early times had been more due to secular reasons than to any religious necessity, and the religious motive was only secondary; but although the secular motive was dominant, the religious motive was deniable. The religious motive for adoption never altogether excluded the secular motive. (See Mayne's Hindu Law and Usage, *12th Edn., p. 329).*

16. As held by this Court in V.T.S. Chandrasekhar Mudaliar v. *Kulandaivelu Mudaliar,* AIR 1963 SC 185: (1963) 2 SCR 440, *substitution of a son for spiritual reasons is the essence of adoption; and consequent devolution of property is mere accessory to it; the validity of an adoption has to be judged by spiritual rather than temporal considerations; and, devolution of property is only of secondary importance.*

17. In Hem Singh *v.* Harnam Singh, *AIR 1954 SC 581: 1954 SCJ 566: 1955 SCR 44, it was observed by this Court that under the Hindu Law adoption is primarily a religious act intended to confer spiritual benefit on the adopter and some of the rules have therefore been held to be mandatory, and compliance with them regarded as a condition of the validity of the adoption. The first important case on the question of adoption was decided by the Privy Council in the case of Amarendra Mansingh* v. *Sanatan Singh, AIR 1933 PC 155: 60 Ind App 242: 12 Pat 642 (PC). The Privy Council said "Among the Hindus, a peculiar religious significance has attached to the son, through Brahminical influence, although in its origin the custom of adoption was perhaps purely secular. The texts of the Hindus are themselves instinct with this doctrine of religious significance. The foundation of the Brahminical doctrine of adoption is the duty which every Hindu owes to his ancestors to provide for the continuance of the line and the solemnization of the necessary rites."*

18. With these observations it decided the question before it, viz., *that of setting the limits to the exercise of the power of a widow to adopt, having regard to the well established doctrine as to the religious efficacy of sonship. In fact the Privy Council in that case regarded the religious motive as dominant and the secular motive as only secondary.*

19. This object is further amplified by certain observations of this Court. It has been held that an adoption results in changing the course of succession, depriving wife and daughters of their rights, and transferring the properties to comparative strangers or more remote relations. [See: Kishori Lal *v.* Chaltibai, *AIR 1959 SC 504: 1959 SCJ 560: 1959 SCR Supp (1) 698]. Though undeniably in most of the cases motive is religious, the secular motive is also dominantly present. We are not concerned much with this controversy, and as observed by Mayne it is unsafe to embark upon an enquiry in each case as to whether the motives for a particular adoption were religious or secular and an intermediate view is possible that while an adoption may be a proper act, inspired in many cases by religious motives, courts are concerned with an adoption, only as the exercise of a legal right by certain persons.*

20. The Privy Council's decision in Amarendra Mansingh's *case (supra), has reiterated the well established doctrine as to the religious efficacy of sonship, as the foundation of adoption. The emphasis has been on the absence of a male issue. An adoption may either be made by a man himself or by his widow on his behalf. The adoption is to the male and it is obvious that an unmarried woman cannot adopt. For the purpose of adoption is to ensure spiritual benefit for a man after his death by offering of oblations and rice and libations of water to the manes periodically. Woman having no spiritual needs to be satisfied, was not allowed to adopt for herself. But in either it is a condition precedent for a valid adoption that he should be without any male issue living at the time of adoption.""*

Clearly, the Hon'ble Supreme Court of India has outlined the origin of customary law of adoptions and the law on the subject as it existed before the enactment of HAMA, 1956.

Further, the Court has emphasized on the proof of existence of customs in cases of adoptions. The Hon'ble Supreme Court has reiterated the earlier existing case-law insofar as relating to proving the validity of the customs so advanced, in paras 21 to 23 and 25 to 29 (at pages 130 to 132) of the judgment in the following terms:

> *"21. In* Mookka Kone *v.* Ammakutti Ammal, *AIR 1928 Mad 299 (FB), it was held that where custom is set up to prove that it is at variance with the ordinary law, it has to be proved that it is not opposed to public policy and that it is ancient, invariable, continuous, notorious, not expressly forbidden by the legislature and not opposed to morality or public policy. It is not disputed that even under the old Hindu law, adoption during the lifetime of a male issue was specifically prohibited. In addition, I have observed that such an adoption even if made would be contrary to the concept of adoption and the purpose thereof, and unreasonable. Without entering into the arena of controversy whether there was such a custom, it can be said that even if there was such a custom, the same was not a valid custom."*
>
> *22. It is incumbent on party setting up a custom to allege and prove the custom on which he relies. Custom cannot be extended by analogy. It must be established inductively and not by a priori methods. Custom cannot be a matter of theory but must always be a matter of fact and one custom cannot be deduced from another. It is a well established law that custom cannot be enlarged by parity of reasoning.*
>
> *23. Where the proof of a custom rests upon a limited number of instances of a comparatively recent date, the court may hold the custom proved so as to bind the parties to the suit and those claiming through and under them; but the decision would not in that case be a satisfactory precedent if in any future suit between other parties fuller evidence with regard to the alleged custom should be forthcoming. A judgment relating to the existence of a custom is admissible to corroborate the evidence adduced to prove such custom in another case. Where, however a custom is repeatedly brought to the notice of the courts, the courts, may hold that the custom was introduced into law without the necessity of proof in each individual case.*
>
> *25. ... All that is necessary to prove is that usage has been acted upon in practice for such a long period with such invariability as to show that it has, by consent, been submitted so as to establish governing rules of a particular locality or community.*
>
> *26. A custom, in order to be binding must derive its force from the fact that by long usage it has obtained the force of law, but the English rule that "a custom in order that it may be legal and binding, must have been used so long that the memory of man runneth not to the contrary" should not be strictly applied to Indian conditions. All that is necessary to prove is that the usage has been acted upon in practice for such a long period and with such invariability as to show that it has, by common consent, been submitted to as the established governing rule of a particular locality.*

> *27. A custom may be proved by general evidence as to its existence by members of the tribe or family who would naturally be cognizant of its existence, and its exercise without controversy, and such evidence may be safely acted on when it is supported by a public record of custom such as the Riwaj-i-am or Manual of Customary Law.*
>
> *28. In yet another decision* Hem Singh v. Harnam Singh, *AIR 1954 SC 581: 1954 SCJ 566: 1955 SCR 44, this Court observed that the custom recorded in the 'Riwaj-i-am' is in derogation of the general custom and those who set up such a custom must prove it by clear and unequivocal language. Similarly, when a custom is against the written texts of the Hindu Law then, one who sets up such a custom must prove it by a clear and unequivocal language. It may also be pointed out that the settled law is that for a valid adoption, not only the person adopting should be capable of lawfully taking in adoption; but the person giving must be capable of lawfully giving in adoption and the person adopted must be capable of being lawfully taken in adoption. It is necessary that all these three conditions should be satisfied and that it is not sufficient that one of them be satisfied.*
>
> *29. In the case of* Hem Singh *(supra) this court quoted with approval of some of the observations in* Mulla's Principles of Hindu Law, *11th Edn., p. 541 with such observations in paragraph 434 to the following effect:*
>
> *"It has similarly been held that the texts which prohibit the adoption of an only son, and those which prohibit the adoption of an only son, those which enjoin the adoption of a relation in preference to a stranger, are only directory; therefore, the adoption of an only son, or a stranger in preference to a relation, if completed, is not invalid; that in cases such as the above, where the texts are merely directory, the principle of* factum valet *applies, and the act done is valid and binding."*

But just thereafter the following observations occurred in the same paragraph:

> *"But the texts relating to the capacity to give, the capacity to take, and the capacity to be the subject of adoption are mandatory. Hence the principle of* factum valet *is ineffectual in the case of an adoption in contravention of the provisions of those texts.""*

Therefore, the Court has given a detailed analysis of the ways in which the person alleging the existence of the custom may prove it.

Hence, in the present case the Hon'ble Supreme Court has laid down the guidelines on which it can be decided whether a particular act is a custom or not and has further, mentioned the ways in which a customary adoption may be proved by persons alleging its existence.

In the case of *Atluri Brahmanandam* v. *Anne Sai Bapuji,* JT 2010 (12) SC 441: AIR 2011 SC 545: (2010) 12 SCALE 157, the issue for consideration before the Hon'ble Supreme Court of India was whether the plaintiff was the adopted son of the auction-purchaser under the customary law, as he was adopted when he was more than 15 years of age and whether the said adoption was prohibited under section 10(iv) of the HAMA, 1956. The Supreme Court upheld the adoption to be valid in terms of the saving clause contained in section 10(iv) of the HAMA, 1956. The reasoning of the Apex Court supported by the statute law as also, earlier precedent of the Andhra Pradesh High Court judicially recognizing the prevalence of the said "Kamma" custom in the community of Andhra Pradesh has been summed up in paras 12 to 16 of the judgment in the following terms:

> "*12. We are concerned for the purpose of this case with clause (iv) of section 10 which provides that a person to be adopted should not have completed the age of 15 years. But there is also an exception provided therein to the aforesaid required qualification which provides that if there is a custom or usage applicable to the parties permitting persons who have completed the age of 15 years being taken in adoption, such a person could also be validly adopted. On the other hand, the effect and the implication of section 16 of the Act is that if there is any document purporting to record an adoption made and is signed by the person giving as well the person taking the child in adoption is registered under any law for the time being in force and if it is produced in any Court, the Court would presume that the adoption has been made in compliance of the provisions of the Act unless and until it is disproved.*
>
> *13. There is no denial of the fact in the present case that the respondent was more than 15 years of age at the time of his adoption. But the respondent has relied upon the exception provided in section 10(iv) and has proved by leading cogent and reliable evidence like Ex. A-8 that there is a custom in the "Kamma" community of Andhra Pradesh for adoption of a boy even above the age of 15 years. Therefore, the aforesaid exception which is engrafted in the same part of the provision of section 10 of the Act was satisfied. Since the aforesaid custom and aforesaid adoption was also recorded in a registered deed of adoption, the Court has to presume that the adoption has been made in compliance with the provisions of the Act, since the respondent has utterly failed to challenge the said evidence and also to disprove the aforesaid adoption.*
>
> *14. Reference has also been made to a Division Bench decision of the Andhra Pradesh High Court reported in 1964 AWR 156. In the said decision, the Division Bench has recognized that there is a custom among the members of the "Kamma" caste to adopt a boy of more than 15 years old and that such custom is valid. The said decision rendered by a Division Bench in 1964 has stood the test of time and has remained binding till date.*
>
> *15. In the case of* Ujagar Singh *v.* Mst. Jeo, *AIR 1959 SC 1041: 1959 SCJ 16: 1959 SCR Supp (2) 781, this Court has held that the ordinary rule is that all customs general or otherwise have to be proved, but under section 57 of the Evidence Act, 1872 nothing need to be proved of which the Court can take judicial notice. It was also held that when a custom has been repeatedly recognized by Courts, it is blended into the law of land and proof of the same would become unnecessary under section 57 of Evidence Act, 1872.*
>
> *16. The aforesaid decision is squarely applicable to the facts and circumstances of the present case. The Andhra Pradesh High Court has recognized such a custom among the "Kamma" community of Andhra Pradesh of taking in adoption of a person even above the age of 15 years of age and has held the same to be legal and valid.*"

Hence, in light of the legal position as enunciated above, the said over aged customary adoption was held to be valid

Summing-up the position of law insofar as relating to customary adoptions under the provisions of the HAMA, 1956, section 4 of the HAMA, 1956, expressly prohibits customary adoption after the commencement of the HAMA, 1956 on 21 December, 1956. Whilst, section 5 of HAMA, 1956 categorically states that all the adoptions made after the enactment of the HAMA, 1956 have to be made in accordance with compliance of the provisions of the HAMA, 1956. Furthermore, under section 10(iv) of the HAMA, 1956 a limited relaxation had been made allowing customary adoptions in cases of persons who are above the age of fifteen years, provided that there is existing ongoing established custom in support thereof. The above mentioned Supreme Court judgment in the case of *Atluri Brahmanandam* (supra) is a recent example of an adoption upheld under section 10(iv) of the HAMA, 1956.

XII. Directions by Supreme Court of India to CARA to Constitute Expert Committee Including Medical Experts in Cases of Adoption of Children with Special Needs

The 153rd Law Commission Report on inter-country adoption recommended in 1994 itself the need for the concern and involvement of children with special needs in inter-country adoptions. It reported in the following terms:

> *"Although adoption by Indian parents is growing in number yet the families normally go around selecting babies of their choice. As such, babies who are ill-nourished, very dark in complexion, handicapped, having medical problems or special need do not find homes in India. If we cannot find the family life for these children in our country, it is suggested, we must not hesitate to select foreign families for them."*

In the recent case of *Craig Allen Coates* v. *State*, (2010) 8 SCC 794, the Hon'ble Supreme Court of India, adopted a very humane approach with a view to evaluate and facilitate the adoption of a mentally challenged child.

In this particular case, Ms. Coates from USA, having an extended experience in home based nursing filed a petition for adopting minor child Anil who had developmental delays and difficulties with respect to learning and expressing and required special care for learning needs. But, both the District Court as well as the High Court rejected the petition. An appeal was then filed in Supreme Court of India to get permission and clearance for adoption process.

The main issue that arose in the case can be summed up as follows: Whether the adoption of a child with special needs is in the best interest of the child? What procedure should be adopted in such cases?

Keeping in mind the circumstances of the case, the Supreme Court of India requested the learned Solicitor-General, who has appeared as *amicus curiae* in this case, to get the matter examined by an expert committee as to whether the adoption of the child Anil by Ms. Coates would be in the interest of the child. According to the opinion of the Board such a child will benefit from family based care and nurturance rather than institutional care.

The Board went through the adoption home studies made by Lutheran Social Services Wisconsin, USA which gave a detailed analysis of the adoptive parents and the family. The Board further examined Ms. Coates, her intentions, her professional experience and her proposed education of the child. She has had extended experience in home based nursing and in a respite home where she has given personal care to patients with neuro-muscular disorders, cognitive impairments and other handicaps. Her experience in home health and her sensitivity towards multi-cultural issues was evident in her interactions. She presented a clear vision of the family, school and community resources she needs to mobilize in order to make the adoption successful. She is committed to providing physical therapy, occupational therapy, speech therapy and special education to her adopted child.

From the records made available to the board it seemed that she had adequate financial and emotional resources to provide for the adopted child. The board also viewed the recorded video made with the child's current setup where the child's interaction within the group was observed. The reciprocity in the relationship between Ms. Coates and the child became apparent during the boards interview. Thus in the opinion of the board the petitioners should be allowed to adopt the minor male child.

After considering the report of the expert committee the Supreme Court of India allowed the appeal and directed formalities regarding adoption as per the procedure prescribed to be completed as expeditiously as possible.

The Supreme Court of India disposed the appeal with some directions for such future cases of adoption of children with special needs. The positive and meaningful directions as laid down in para 5 (at page 796) of the said judgment which state as follows:

> *"We further direct that for inter-country adoptions the procedure followed heretofore could include a reference to an expert committee on the lines constituted in the present case to ensure that inter-country adoption are allowed only after full and proper satisfaction is recorded by all the agencies including a committee of experts wherever reference to such a committee is considered necessary. We are told that Central Adoption Resource Agency (CARA) has the power to make references but no expert committee as such has been constituted or identified for that purpose. In our opinion, it would be appropriate if Central Adoption Resource Agency requests the Director, All India Institute of Medical Sciences to constitute a committee of experts to be headed by Professor and Head of the Department of psychiatry, AIIMS.*

CARA may have similar expert committees constituted in other States also to facilitate references to them in regard to children who may be living at distant places from Delhi."

Certainly, the above-mentioned judgment is a good precedent for the future as well, where genuine and *bona fide* prospective foreign applicants who have the will power, resources and determination to look after handicapped children are outrightly not denied an opportunity of a prospective inter-country adoption from India.

XIII. New Dimensions for the Better—The Juvenile Justice (Care and Protection of Children) Amendment Act, 2006

The Ministry of Women and Child Development has of late been mandated to look after the subject-matters 'Adoption & Juvenile Justice (Care and Protection of Children) Act, 2000' pursuant to 16 February, 2006 notification of Government of India regarding reallocation of the business.

Also, the Government enacted the Juvenile Justice (Care and Protection of Children) Act, 2000 and further amended it in the year 2006 to ensure adequate protection and rehabilitation measures for children in need of care and protection.

It is important to advert to the historical perspective leading to the enactment of the above-mentioned legislation and the need to fill in the void on account of secular perspectives from the point of view of potential adoptive parents which are not just confined to Hindus. This has been very eloquently elaborated in para 3 of the judgment handed down by the High Court of Kerala in the matter of *Andrew Mendez* v. *State of Kerala*, 2008 (1) KLT 1000. Para 3 of the said judgment reads as under:

> *"Then came the enactment of The Juvenile Justice (Care and Protection of Children) Act, 2000. It contained provisions relating to adoption. Adoption as a legal concept was available only among the members of the Hindu community except where custom permits such adoption for any sections of the polity. But in Chapter 6 of the Act dealing with rehabilitation and social re-integration of children we find the legislature accepting the concept of secular adoption whereby without any reference to the community or the religious persuasions of the parents or the child concerned, a right appears to have been granted to all citizens to adopt and all children to be adopted. The history of the attempt to bring in the concept of secular adoption into our system of laws narrates a sad tale of inaction and action without conviction on the part of the legislature. It is perhaps unfortunate that even now the republic of India does not have a codified law of adoption applicable to all Indians. The attempts of the Indian Parliament in this direction did not bear fruit. The history of the Adoption of Children's Bill, 1972 and Adoption of Children's Bill, 1980 do not, of course, bring credit to the secular credentials of the Indian polity. Let us accept the reality. Awareness and acceptance of failure can be stepping stones to eventual success. We have not been able to bring in a secular law of adoption applicable to all Indians so far. It is in this context that a laudable attempt is undertaken by the Legislature by the stipulations which have been made in Chapter IV of the Juvenile Justice (Care and Protection of Children) Act, 2000. There was still confusion as the concept of adoption was not defined in the Act. The provisions were criticized to be inadequate as the legal status of the adopted child has not by law been declared to be equal to that of a biological legitimate child. It is in this context that Act 33 of 2006 was introduced under which the concept of adoption was defined by enacting section 2(aa) of the Act which reads as follows:*
>
> *"Adoption" means the process through which the adopted child is permanently separated from his biological parents and become the legitimate child of his*

adoptive parents with all the rights, privileges and responsibilities that are attached to the relationship....

4. After the amendment by Act 33 of 2006, section 41 reads as follows:

"41. Adoption.—(1) The primary responsibility for providing care and protection to children shall be that of his family.

(2) Adoption shall be resorted to for the rehabilitation of the children who are orphan, abandoned or surrendered through such mechanism as may be prescribed.

(3) In keeping with the provisions of the various guidelines for adoption issued from time to time, by the State Government, children may be given in adoption by a court after satisfying itself regarding the investigations having been carried out as are required for giving such children in adoption.

(4) The State Government shall recognise one or more of its institutions or voluntary organisations in each district as specialized adoption agencies in such manner as may be prescribed for the placement of orphan, abandoned or surrendered children for adoption in accordance with the guidelines notified under sub-section (3):

Provided that the children's homes and the institutions run by the State Government or a voluntary organisation for children in need of care and protection, who are orphan, abandoned or surrendered, shall ensure that these children are declared free for adoption by the Committee and all such cases shall be referred to the adoption agency in that district for placement of such children in adoption in accordance with the guidelines notified under sub-section (3).

(5) No child shall be offered for adoption.

- *(a) until two members of the Committee declare the child legally free for placement in the case of abandoned children.*
- *(b) till the two months period for reconsideration by the parents is over in the case of surrendered children, and*
- *(c) without his consent in the case of a child who can understand and express his consent.*

(6) The Court may allow a child to be given in adoption-

- *(a) to a person irrespective of marital status or;*
- *(b) to parents to adopt a child of same sex irrespective of the number of living biological sons or daughters; or*
- *(c) to childless couples."*

The Supreme Court in, *Stephanie Joan Becker v. State*, AIR 2013 SC 3495: 2013 AIR SCW 4668: (2013) 2 SCALE 312, has acknowledged the significant changes made in the JJ Act, 2006 with regard to inter-country adoption, while concluding the importance of section 41 in the said Act. The concerned Para of the judgment reads as follows:

"8. Two significant developments in the law governing adoptions may now be taken note of. Section 41 of the Juvenile Justice (Care and Protection of Children) Act, 2000 (hereinafter for short the "JJ Act") was amended by Act

33 of 2006 by substituting sub-sections 2, 3 and 4 by the present provisions contained in the aforesaid sub-sections of section 41. The aforesaid amendment which was made effective from 22-8-2006 is significant in as much as under sub-section 3 power has been conferred in the Court to give a child in adoption upon satisfaction that the various guidelines issued from time to time, either by the State Government or the CARA and notified by the Central Government have been followed in the given case. The second significant development in this regard is the enactment of the Juvenile Justice (Care and Protection of Children) Rules, 2007 by repeal of the 2001 Rules in force. Rule 33(2) makes it clear that "for all matters relating to adoption, the guidelines issued by the Central Adoption Resource Agency and notified by the Central Government under sub-section (3) of section 41 of the Act, shall apply." Rule 33(3) in the various sub-clauses (a) to (g) lays down an elaborate procedure for certifying an abandoned child to be free for adoption. Similarly, sub-rule (4) of rule 33 deals with the procedure to be adopted for declaring a surrendered child to be legally free for adoption. Once such a declaration is made, the various steps in the process of adoption spelt out by the Guidelines of 2006, details of which have been extracted here in above, would apply finally leading to departure of the child from the country to his/her new home for completion of the process of adoption in accordance with the laws of the country to which the child had been taken. In this regard the order of the courts in the country under section 41(3) of the JJ Act would be a step in facilitating the adoption of the child in the foreign country."

The Juvenile Justice (Care and Protection of Children) Amendment Act, 2006 applies to all children as well as parents irrespective of their religion and gender. All adoptable children under the category of children in need of care and protection (as defined under JJ Act), shall be processed under this specific legislation by district Courts, city civil Courts, Family Court and other appropriate courts as may be defined under State JJ Rules to be framed based on the above Act. The legislation being child focused legislation, guarantees all rights to an adopted child and it is also recognized under international obligations by all Hague member countries.

On implementation of JJ Amendment Act, 2006 and its State rules, all cases of orphan, abandoned and surrendered children have to be processed under the Act so that unrelated children have adequate safeguards in their placements.

In an editorial article titled "Adopting New Guidelines," dated 19 November, 2007, published in The Hindustan Times of India, it has been analyzed "..... *In a bid to put adoptive parents of all faiths on the same platform, amendments to the Juvenile Justice (Care and Protection) Act (JJ Act) have now been notified and guidelines framed. One of the most important amendments to the Act made clear that adoption under legislation would allow an adopted child to become the "legitimate child of his adoptive parents, with the rights, privileges and responsibilities attached to the relationship." This is a significant move considering till now, adoption by non-Hindus has been guided by the Guardian and Wards Act (GAWA), 1890, which gives them the status of 'guardians', a relationship that becomes void when the child enters adulthood. Conversely, it doesn't give the 'ward' legal right due to a biological child. "*

In effect, non-Hindu parents can now claim full parenthood instead of just the interim "guardian" status that they were allowed until recently. That prior to the enactment of JJ Act, 2006 only Hindu couples who adopted children could claim to be parents. Non-Hindus were just guardians to their adopted children. This of course, also led to children being denied rights to inherited property and besides also creating day-to-day problems for parents at the time of school admissions and such like matters.

Another major upshot of the JJ Act, 2006 is that inter-country adoptions are permissible under the same. The point to be noted is as to how would the Embassies and Foreign Missions in India view adoption orders granted to Hindus and non-Hindus as well as foreigners. This is the moot point.

All opinions are not positive. The JJ Act had initially drawn some amount of criticism as well. In an article titled "Time to Unscramble the Adoption Tangle," dated 20 November, 2007, published in the Times of India, Swati Deshpande came out with some very valid criticisms as follows.

> *"….Activists emphasise that there is no clarity on the provisions for adoption in the Juvenile Justice (Care and Protection) Act. "There is a lot of confusion on the issue of adoption under the Juvenile Justice (JJ) Act," said child-rights activist Sangeeta Punalekar. She noted that adoption was provided for under the JJ Act in 2000 itself to aid the rehabilitation and social integration of orphaned, abandoned or neglected children. "But even then it met with hardly any response," Punalekar said. To date, there are no known cases of adoption under the JJ Act in Maharashtra, though there have been a few cases in Delhi. Punalekar said the law stipulates that instead of getting the approval of higher courts—like district courts and High Courts (in the case of inter-country adoption)—adoption should be done locally by child welfare committees and juvenile justice boards. However, she and other activists said there seem to be no rules or infrastructure in place nor is there clarity on related issues, like if the law will apply to Muslims. As it stands, the amendment to the JJ Act defines adoption as the "process through which the adopted child is permanently separated from his biological parents and becomes the legitimate child of his adoptive parents with all the rights, privileges and responsibilities attached to the relationship". In other words, the Act would apply to all Indians. ….It is not clear how this law would override the provisions of other personal laws. The Muslim Personal Law, for instance, does not permit adoption, she noted. The government can't try and plug loopholes in one Act by amending another…."*

In the above-mentioned judgment of Kerala High Court in *Andrew Mendez* v. *State of Kerala*, (supra) it was tersely held that only the District Court can have jurisdiction to entertain an application under section 41(6) of the Juvenile Justice Act read with rule 33(5) of the Central Rules. Initially, it was stipulated that the Juvenile Justice Board may allow the child to be adopted. It was also explicitly held in this judgment that the 'Court' and not the Board has powers under section 46 of the Act to allow adoptions. Also, this judgment is laudable for the fact, that it reiterates the provisions with regard to the time scales for adjudicating upon such applications, as laid down initially by the Supreme Court of India in the case of *Lakshmi Kant Pandey* in the year 1984. The concluding portion of para 27 of this judgment held:

> "... *that such applications must be disposed of within a period of two months from the date of presentation. The courts have to sympathetically consider the plight of guardians yearning for an order for adoption and the need of children being given in adoption with expedition.*"

XIV. Provisions of the Juvenile Justice Act, 2000 to Prevail Over the Provisions of the Hindu Adoption and Maintenance Act, 1956

The JJ Act is a secular law, it has wider objective. It's a law with an object to do welfare to the juveniles. One may also refer to the Judgment of the Supreme Court in *Pratap Singh* v. *State of Jharkhand,* AIR 2005 SC 2731: 2005 Cr LJ 3091: (2005) 3 SCC 551 wherein the Court while dealing with the question of the purpose and object of the Juvenile Justice Act, 1986 and the Act, noted as under:

> '10. *Thus, the whole object of the Act is to provide for the care, protection, treatment, development and rehabilitation of neglected or delinquent juveniles. It is a beneficial legislation aimed at making available the benefit of the Act to the neglected or delinquent juveniles. It is settled law that the interpretation of the statute of beneficial legislation must be to advance the cause of legislation for the benefit of whom it is made and not to frustrate the intendment of the legislation.*'

Thus, it is to be kept in mind that the object of this legislation is not violated. In case of conflict, where the provisions cannot be harmoniously constructed, it is the JJ Act that would prevail due to the wider object of this legislation to benefit the juveniles.

In the case of, (In Re:) *Adoption of Payal @ Sharinee Vinay Pathak and his wife Sonika Sahay @ Pathak,* 2010 (1) AIR Bom R 327, the Bombay High Court gave a very lucid and meaningful interpretation to the provisions of the Juvenile Justice Act, 2000 (hereinafter referred to as JJ Act, 2000) especially with regard to the conflict of legal position in so far relating to same sex adoptions as envisaged under the provisions of the Hindu Adoption and Maintenance Act, 1956 (hereinafter referred to as HAMA, 1956).

The main issue in the petition revolved around the interpretation of HAMA, 1956 and the JJ Act, 2000 on the point as to whether a Hindu couple governed by the provisions of the HAMA, 1956 with a natural biological child of their own could possibly adopt a child of the same gender under the provisions of JJ Act, 2000? And in case of conflict between the provisions of the HAMA, 1956 and the JJ Act, 2000, which act would prevail?

In the above-mentioned case, both the petitioners were Hindus and married on June, 2001. They were blessed with a daughter on 4 February, 2003. In the present petition, the petitioners sought an order appointing them as the guardians of a female child subsequently born on 12 November, 2004. The biological parents of the child executed a declaration on 16 November, 2004, four days after the child was born, recording the circumstances in which they had decided to surrender the child at the nursing home where the child was born. The declaration explicitly stated that the mother and the spouse had been counseled by a placement agency duly recognized by the Government of India and that they had voluntarily agreed to surrender their newly born child in adoption. The child was not claimed by the parents within the stipulated two months period of reconsideration. By an order of Justice A.M. Khanwilkar, dated 8 June, 2005 of the Bombay High Court itself, the petitioners were appointed the guardians of the minor child and the child has since then lived with them for over four years. In the present case, a petition was filed seeking a declaration that the petitioners were the adoptive parents of the child with all the consequential rights.

Justice D.Y. Chandrachud while dealing with the issue of the declaration in the said appeal petition, first dealt with the key issue of the interpretation of the relevant legislations enacted by the Parliament of India, comparing the contradicting provisions of the two enactments in question. The provisions of the said two relevant enactments are summed up as follows:

> *'The HAMA, 1956 amends and codifies the law relating to adoptions and maintenance among Hindus and specifies conditions for valid adoption. One of them is that if the adoption is of a daughter, the father or mother who wishes to adopt the child must not have a Hindu daughter (or a son's daughter) living at the time of adoption'.*

The Hon'ble Court stated whilst, the JJ Act, 2000, enacted to provide for the rehabilitation and social integration of orphaned, abandoned or surrendered children. Adoption is one of the techniques recognized by Parliament to facilitate the object of rehabilitation. The JJ Act, 2000 does not incorporate a restrictive condition foreclosing the right of parents who have a child to adopt another child of the same gender. The JJ Act, 2000 specifically recognizes the right of parents to adopt children irrespective of the number of living biological sons or daughters.

In the light of the provisions of the above-mentioned enactments, the key point of consideration was as to whether a Hindu couple with a child of their own, can adopt another child of the same gender. The Hon'ble High Court has dealt with the relevant provisions of both the said enactments in a remarkable manner with crystal clear clarity, leaving no room for ambiguity at all before arriving at a perfectly workable solution.

Section 11 of the HAMA, 1956 provides certain conditions that must be complied with in every case of adoption. Since, section 11 of the HAMA, 1956 has already been reproduced in the earlier portion of this article the same is not being repeated again. Basically, section 11 of the HAMA, 1956 prohibits same sex adoption by the same couple.

The High Court on the appellant side in the present case proceedings gave a logical interpretation of section 11 of the HAMA, 1956 in para 7 of the judgment as follows:

> *"7. What these clauses stipulate is a prohibition on the adoption of a child of the same gender where the adoptive father or mother already have a child living*

at the time of the adoption. If the adoption is of a daughter, the adoptive father or mother must not have a Hindu daughter or a son's daughter living at the time of adoption. Where the adoption is of a son, the condition is more stringent because the adoptive father or mother should not have a Hindu son, son's son or son's son's son living."

The Court in the above-mentioned paragraph highlighted the restrictions and prohibitions on the adoption of a minor child of Hindus.

Further, in para 8 of the judgment the Court has reminded us of the Constitutional obligation warranted by the Constitution of India insofar as relating to the safety of health, welfare and education of the minor children. The Constitutional provisions in this regard as summed-up in para 8 and 9 of the judgment are as follows:

"8. Article 15 of the Constitution empowers the State, in clause (3), to make special provisions for women and children. Article 39 is part of the Directive Principles of State policy. Clause (e) of article 39 directs the State in framing its policies to secure that the tender age of children is not abused. In clause (f) the State has to ensure that children are given opportunities and facilities to develop in a healthy manner and in conditions of freedom and dignity so as to ensure that childhood and youth are protected against exploitation and against moral and material abandonment. By Article 45 the State has to endeavour to provide early childhood care and education for all children until they complete the age of six. Article 47 requires the State to raise levels of nutrition. Under article 51A it is the fundamental duty of every citizen who is a parent or guardian to provide opportunities for education to his or her child or, as the case may be, ward between the age of six and fourteen.

9. Fundamental as they are in the governance of the country, these provisions are part of a sensitive vision of the founding fathers. The human tragedy of the exploitation of children, of child abuse and of malnutrition among children was in contemplation as these provisions were drafted. Those provisions are a composite part of our constitutional ethos which places freedom and dignity as one of the foremost values of governance in civil society. Freedom and dignity of the young must count above all. The young are amongst the most vulnerable to disease and deprivation which follow upon abandonment and isolation. Poverty has no religion."

Furthermore, the Court has also emphasized on the Convention of the Rights of the Child, ratified by India on 11 December, 1992. Some of the provisions of the Convention mentioned in para 10 of the judgment are as follows:

"10. India ratified the Convention on the Rights of the Child on 11th December, 1992. Article 3 of the Convention provides that in all actions concerning children, whether undertaken by public or private social welfare institutions, Courts of law, administrative authorities or legislative bodies, the best interests of the child shall be a primary consideration. All States have undertaken to ensure to children such protection and care as is necessary for their well being and to take all appropriate legislative and administrative measures. Article 20 of the Convention provides that a child temporarily or permanently deprived of his or her family environment

shall be entitled to special protection and assistance provided by the State. Such care could include foster placement and adoption amongst other alternatives. Under Article 21 States who are parties to the Convention recognized that the system of adoption shall ensure that the best interests of the child shall be the paramount consideration."

Certainly, the Court has laid emphasis on the safeguards and the measures for the protection of children that need to be kept in mind by the State while dealing with matters relating to delicate and sensitive subject of adoptions, which is all the more important in a country like India, where there is large scale abuse of under privileged children.

The Court has further discussed the provisions and the object of the JJ Act, 2000. The Court in paras 11 and 12 of the said judgment has elaborated the object with which the Parliament of India had enacted the JJ Act, 2000 in the following terms:

> *"11. The Juvenile Justice (Care and Protection of Children) Act was enacted in 2000, "to consolidate and amend the law relating to juveniles in conflict with law and children in need of care and protection". The object of the Act is to provide for "care, protection and treatment by catering to their development needs and by adopting a child friendly approach in the adjudication and disposition of matters in the best interest of children and for their ultimate rehabilitation". The Preamble to the Act makes reference to several constitutional provisions which have a bearing on the welfare of children and to the obligation assumed by India as a responsible member of the international community.*
>
> *12. Parliament enacted the Juvenile Justice (Care and Protection of Children) Act, 2000 to effectuate constitutional provisions and fulfill India's international obligations. The Act as now enacted is intended to provide effective provisions and various alternatives for rehabilitation and social reintegration such as adoption, foster care, sponsorship and aftercare of abandoned, destitute, neglected and delinquent juveniles and children. The Act was amended in 2006 in order to effectuate the beneficial objects of the legislation and in order to remove the anomalies which had arisen in the implementation of the Act."*

The Hon'ble Court has further examined the provisions of the JJ Act, 2000 which are contradictory and in contrast to the provisions of HAMA, 1956. Few important provisions of the JJ Act, 2000 in this regard elaborated by the Hon'ble Court are as follows:

> *"13. Chapter IV of the Juvenile Justice Act is entitled "Rehabilitation and Social Reintegration". Section 40 of the Act provides that rehabilitation and social reintegration of a child shall be carried out alternatively by (i) adoption, (ii) foster care, (iii) sponsorship and (iv) sending the child to an after care organisation. Sub-section (1) of section 41 provides that the primary responsibility for providing care and protection to a child is to be that of his or her family. By sub-section (2) adoption is to be resorted "for the rehabilitation of children who are orphaned, abandoned or surrendered" through such mechanism as may be prescribed. Sub-section (3) of section 41 empowers the Court to give children in adoption subject to satisfaction of investigations having been carried out, as are required*

for giving children in adoption. Sub-section (4) empowers the State Government to recognize one or more of its institutions or voluntary organizations in each district as specialized adoption agencies for the placement of orphaned, abandoned or surrendered children for adoption. Sub-section (5) of section 41 contains the following stipulations for offering children in adoption: "(5) No child shall be offered for adoption—

(a) until two members of the Committee declare the child legally free for placement in the case of abandoned children,

(b) till the two months period for reconsideration by the parents is over in the case of surrendered children, and

(c) without his consent in the case of a child who can understand and express his consent.

14. Sub-section (6) emphasizes that the Court may allow a child to be given in adoption (a) to a person irrespective of marital status; or (b) to parents to adopt a child of the same sex irrespective of the number of living biological sons or daughters; or (c) to childless couples. These provisions of the Juvenile Justice Act must be read in the context of some of the definitions. The expression "adoption" is defined by clause (aa) of section 2 as follows:

(aa) 'adoption' means the process through which the adopted child is permanently separated from his biological parents and becomes the legitimate child of his adoptive parents with all the rights, privileges and responsibilities that are attached to the relationship.

15. Section 2(d) defines the expression "child in need of care and protection". Clause (v) includes within this category a child who does not have a parent and whom no one is willing to take care of or whose parents have abandoned or surrendered the child.

16. Rules have been framed under the Act and rule 33 provides for rules for implementing Chapter IV which deals with rehabilitation and social integration."

In para 17 of the said judgment, the Court has drawn-up a crisp comparison as to the ethos and objective behind the above-mentioned two child-related Central legislations, the subject-matter of discussion in the present case *i.e.*, the provisions of HAMA, 1956 and the JJ Act, 2000. The said analysis reads as follows:

"17. The Hindu Adoptions and Maintenance Act, 1956 regulates adoptions by or to a Hindu. The Act spells out requisites of valid adoptions, defines capacities for men and women professing the Hindu religion to take in adoption and to give in adoption, for persons who may be adopted and the conditions for adoption. The Act enunciates consequences or effects of a valid adoption in law. The Act establishes rules of general applicability to Hindus in specific areas of family law - adoption and maintenance. The Juvenile Justice (Care and Protection of Children) Act, 2000 is beneficent secular legislation. The Act makes special provisions for a limited sub class of children - those juveniles in conflict with law and children in need of care and protection. Adoption under the Act of 2000 is an instrument of legislative policy to rehabilitate and provide social integration to children who

are in need of care and protection. The Preamble to the Act emphasizes that the legislation was enacted to consolidate and amend the law relating to juveniles in conflict with law and children in need of care and protection. Rehabilitation and social integration of orphaned, abandoned and surrendered children is a matter of legislative regulation by the Juvenile Justice Act. Adoption is a technique contemplated by the law in order to facilitate rehabilitation and reintegration of children of a particular class governed by Chapter IV. The mission of the law is to provide special rules to govern the adoption of a narrow sub class of children namely, those who are orphaned, surrendered or abandoned. In construing the provisions of the Juvenile Justice Act the effort of the Court must be to ensure that the beneficent object with which the legislation was enacted must be facilitated and furthered. Beneficial legislation, it is a trite principle of interpretation, must be construed liberally."

The Hon'ble Court in para 18 of the said judgment has touched upon the constitutionality of the JJ Act, 2000 being approved by the Supreme Court of India, in the following terms:

> *"18. The provisions of the Juvenile Justice Act came up for consideration before a Constitution bench of the Supreme Court in* Pratap Singh v. State of Jharkhand, *AIR 2005 SC 2731: 2005 Cr LJ 3091: (2005) 3 SCC 551. The Supreme Court held that the Act was not only beneficial legislation but that it was also remedial in character. The Constitution bench held that the statute must be construed in a manner that would make it effective and operative on the principle of* ut res magis valet quam pereat. *A similar approach had been adopted by a Bench of three Learned Judges of the Supreme Court in* Umesh Chandra v. State of Rajasthan, (1982) 2 SCC 202: 1982 Cr LJ 994: AIR 1982 SC 1057. *The Rajasthan Children Act, 1970 was regarded as a piece of social legislation which the Court held, would have to be "liberally and meaningfully construed."*

It is ought to mention that the Hon'ble Court has observed in para 19 of the said judgment that adoption is a facet of the right to life under article 21 of the Constitution of India.

Further, para 20 of the judgment demonstrates the creativity of the Court in finding an alternative solution, where a same sex adoption of a child, does not fit within the traditionally acceptable mould within the provisions of the HAMA, 1956 and emphasizes that in practice the Courts will have to go to great lengths to protect the welfare of the abandoned, orphaned or surrendered children as envisaged within the provisions of the JJ Act, 2000. Para 20 of the said judgment reads as under:

> *"20. The Hindu Adoptions and Maintenance Act, 1956 and the Juvenile Justice Act, 2000 must be harmoniously construed. The Hindu Adoptions and Maintenance Act, 1956 deals with conditions requisite for adoption by Hindus. The Juvenile Justice Act of 2000 is a special enactment dealing with children in conflict with law and children in need of care and protection. While enacting the Juvenile Justice Act, 2000 the legislature has taken care to ensure that its provisions are secular in character and that the benefit of adoption is not*

restricted to any religious or social group. The focus of the legislation is on the condition of the child taken in adoption. If the child is orphaned, abandoned or surrendered, that condition is what triggers the beneficial provisions for adoption. The legislation seeks to ensure social integration of such children and adoption is one method to achieve that object. The religious identity of the child or of the parents who adopt is not a precondition to the applicability of the law. The law is secular and deals with conditions of social destitution which cut across religious identities. The legislature in its wisdom clarified in sub-section (6) of section 41 that the Court may allow a child to be given in adoption to parents to adopt a child of the same sex irrespective of the number of living biological sons or daughters. This provision is intended to facilitate the rehabilitation of orphaned, abandoned or surrendered children. The condition must apply to all persons irrespective of religious affiliation who seek to adopt children of that description. The object of rehabilitation and providing for social reintegration to orphaned, abandoned or surrendered children is a matter of high legislative policy. It is in effectuation of that policy that the legislature has stipulated that adoption of such a child must proceed irrespective of the marital status of a person taking in adoption and irrespective of the number of living biological children of the parents seeking adoption. Consequently, where the child which is sought to be adopted falls within the description of an orphaned, abandoned or surrendered child within the meaning of sub-section (2) of section 41 or a child in need of care and protection under clause (d) of section 2, the provisions of the Juvenile Justice (Care and Protection of Children) Act, 2000 must prevail. In such a case the embargo that is imposed on adopting a child of the same sex by a Hindu under clauses (i) and (ii) of section 11 of the Hindu Adoptions and Maintenance Act, 1956 must give way to the salutary provisions made by the Juvenile Justice Act. Where, however, the child is not of a description falling under the purview of Chapter IV of the Juvenile Justice Act, 2000, a Hindu desirous of adopting a child continues to be under the embargo imposed by clauses (i) and (ii) of section 11 of the Act of 1956. If the two pieces of legislation, both of which are enacted by Parliament are harmoniously construed, there is no conflict of interpretation."

By analogy and judicial reasoning, the Court has skillfully navigated a conclusion that both the above pieces of central legislation enacted by the Parliament of India upon harmonious construction have no conflict of interpretation at all.

However, in an alternative argument the Court has also dealt with a situation where both the enactments are in conflict with each other. The Hon'ble Court in such a situation has also provided a solution in para 21 of the said judgment as follows:

"21. Alternatively, even if there were to be a conflict between the provisions of the Hindu Adoptions and Maintenance Act, 1956 and the Juvenile Justice Act of 2000, it is the latter Act which would prevail. This is on the well settled principle that when there are two special Acts dealing with the same subject matter, the legislation which has been enacted subsequently should prevail. The Supreme Court applied this principle in the context of a conflict between the Companies Act, 1956 and the Recovery of Debts Due to Banks and Financial Institutions

> *Act, 1993 in its decision in* Allahabad Bank *v.* Canara Bank, *(2000) 4 SCC 406: AIR 2000 SC 1535: 2000 AIR SCW 1347. Where a later enactment does not expressly amend (whether textually or indirectly) an earlier enactment which it has power to override, but the provisions of the later enactment are inconsistent with those of the earlier, the later by implication amends the earlier so far as is necessary to remove the inconsistency between them."*

Hence, in terms of the law laid down by the Hon'ble Court, it is manifest that the provisions of the JJ Act, 2000 would prevail in the event of any conflict with the provisions of the HAMA, 1956.

The petition was, therefore, disposed of in terms of the reliefs sought by the appellants. The petitioners were declared to be adoptive parents of the minor child in question with all the rights, privileges, responsibilities and consequences under the law.

There is no shadow of doubt that this beautifully carved out judgment has harmoniously blended the supremacy of the provisions of the JJ Act, 2000 over the provisions of the HAMA, 1956 with a view to a positive meaningful interpretation in the given circumstances of the case, as also taking into account Article 21 of the Constitution of India and the Convention on the Rights of the Child with the ultimate relief standing out like a pyramid.

But, it is a matter of deep regret that the above-mentioned judgment has not been taken due note of by the CARA authorities. One would have expected that the CARA authorities would have issued some sort of clarification stating that provisions of the JJ Act, 2000 coupled with the added safeguard of guardianship orders from the Court of competent jurisdiction, would be applicable to the large Non-resident Indians fraternity, Overseas Citizens of India and Persons of Indian Origin. Also, any such addition in the existing guidelines should adequately clarify that foreign Missions and Embassies in India should recognise same sex adoptions within the ambit, scope and provisions of the JJ Act, 2000.

After a detailed analysis of the judgment in appeal proceedings relating to *In Re: Adoption of Payal* (supra), it is strongly felt that we need an immediate review of our existing adoption legislation and the creation of new adoption law, which acknowledges in reality the problems of our NRI community, who are sadly childless. Also, the new legislation needs to be realistic with a pragmatic international perspective and of course to provide support as also succor to that Section of the childless NRI community, in an increasingly globalized world without borders.

Having elaborated on the wide sweeps of the enlarged ambit of the provisions of the Juvenile Justice (Care and Protection of Children) Act, 2000 as amended by Act no. 23 of 2006, it is now equally important to advert to the position of law relating to surrogacy, which is a new order of the day.

Surrogacy has indeed arrived in India. In our day-to-day practice; we are confronted with queries from foreign lawyers as to the legal position relating to surrogacy arrangements. Here, it would be pertinent to briefly elaborate as to the legal position in this regard.

XV. The Law as Applicable in India as to the Legal Parentage of Children Born in that Jurisdiction as a Result of a Surrogacy Arrangement

There are a lot of legal and social impediments to this issue. It is not easy for a mother to nurture a child in her womb, and then in the end of it hand it over to someone strange. The most derogatory part is the consideration for it. Can anyone ever estimate a price for this sacrifice? It seems to be a mockery of emotions. But, turning our mind to the ugly side of it we come to know that India is known to be a reproductive tourism destination. Since, it is happening it has to be regulated under the shield of law.

It was in *Baby Manji Yamada* v. *Union of India*, AIR 2009 SC 84: 2008 AIR SCW 6964: (2008) 13 SCC 518, the Supreme Court of India held that commercial surrogacy was legal in India. The legal issues mainly pertain to the rights of the genetic parents and the surrogate mother, the identity of the child. Jurisdictions in various countries have held different views regarding the legalization of surrogacy.

In UK, the surrogate mother is the legal mother; *vide* section 27(1) of the Human Fertilization and Embryology Act, 1990. Section 30 of the said Act at the same time provides that if the surrogate mother consents to the child to be treated as the child of the commissioning parents the court may make a parental order to that effect. This section also prohibits giving or taking of money or other benefit (other than expenses reasonably incurred) in consideration of the making of the order or handing over of the child. In India, according to the National Guidelines for Accreditation, Supervision and Regulation of ART Clinics, evolved in 2005 by the Indian Council of Medical Research (ICMR) and the National Academy of Medical Sciences (NAMS), the surrogate mother is not considered to be the legal mother. The birth certificate is made in the name of the genetic parents. The US position as per the Gestational Surrogacy Act, 2004 is quiet similar to that of India.

In India at the moment, we do not have any legislation on legal parentage as a result of surrogacy arrangements. At the moment, in India we have the Registration of the Births and Deaths Act, 1969 which does not contain any provision regarding parentage as a result of a surrogacy arrangement. The said enactment laid down by the Parliament of India came into force on 31 May, 1969. Surrogacy parentage was not an issue at the time the said legislation came into being. Neither, have there been any amendments or additions with regard to any surrogacy issues in the said enactment pertaining to the registration of births and deaths in the Indian jurisdiction.

As far as legislation on surrogacy is concerned draft surrogacy proposals were going through the Parliament at some stage. The current position in this regard is not very clear. Guidelines dealing with Artificial Reproductive Technologies (ART) have been prepared by an expert committee of the Indian Council of Medical Research in association with the National Academy of Medical Sciences (India), which could in the future become a part of the final draft of a proposed legislation. The *Introduction in Chapter 1* of the Guidelines as circulated, specifically points out that:

"At present here are neither guidelines nor legislation in regard to the practice of ART in India. This document aims to fill this lacuna. It has been prepared after extensive consultations held at both the ICMR and other national institutions, with scientists, medical practitioners, lawyers, social scientists and activists.

The present guidelines are meant to ensure that ART clinics in India are accredited, regulated and supervised to assure the patients as well as the public that our ART clinics offer services that are at par with those available anywhere in the world. Medical malpractice now comes under the purview of the legal redressal machinery of the country; this makes it all the more necessary to have national guidelines for the practice of ART."

For this purpose the National Guidelines for accreditation, supervision and Regulation of ART Clinics in India have been framed in 2005. These Guidelines provide a foundation for the proposed legislation relating to this field of law. These guidelines state that the surrogate mother is under no circumstances considered to be the legal mother.

Para 3.5.4 of the said Guidelines provides that in cases where the surrogate mother is biologically unrelated to the child, the birth certificate shall have the name of the genetic parents. Therefore, if the genetic parents are the Commissioning parents, who have contributed their genetic material for the unborn child, they shall be automatically recorded as the legal parents, if DNA tests prove the same. No adoption procedure needs to be followed by the genetic parents under such circumstances. Para 3.5.4 of the said Guidelines reads as under:

"3.5.4 - A surrogate mother carrying a child biologically unrelated to her must register as a patient in her own name. *While registering she must mention that she is a surrogate mother and provide all the necessary information about the genetic parents such as names, addresses, etc. She must not use/register in the name of the person for whom she is carrying the child, as this would pose legal issues, particularly in the untoward event of maternal death (in whose names will the hospital certify this death?).* ***The birth certificate shall be in the name of the genetic parents.*** *The clinic, however, must also provide a certificate to the genetic parents giving the name and address of the surrogate mother. All the expenses of the surrogate mother during the period of pregnancy and post-natal care relating to pregnancy should be borne by the couple seeking surrogacy. The surrogate mother would also be entitled to a monetary compensation from the couple for agreeing to act as a surrogate; the exact value of this compensation should be decided by discussion between the couple and the proposed surrogate mother. An oocyte donor can act as a surrogate mother." However, an oocyte donor cannot act as a surrogate mother for the couple to whom the oocyte is being donated.*

Para 3.10.1 *A child born through surrogacy must be adopted by the genetic (biological) parents unless they can establish through genetic (DNA) fingerprinting (of which the records will be maintained in the clinic) that the child is not theirs."*

However, in terms of the above mentioned Guidelines, in cases where the surrogate mother also donates her egg, the commissioning parents (infertile couple) will have to legally adopt the child, and it is only after this legal procedure has been complied with, then the infertile couple become the legal parents of the child born through such an arrangement. This fact will also have to be recorded in the birth certificate issued to such a child.

Furthermore, where the genetic material is supplied by third party donors, in such cases the birth certificate issued to the child will initially have the names of the genetic parents. Here, it would become mandatory for the infertile couple to legally adopt the child so born, before they can be referred to as the legal parents of such a child.

In order to avoid conflicts at a later stage, the said Guidelines categorically state that once the child has been legally adopted by the infertile couple, then the third party donor and the surrogate mother shall relinquish all parental rights connected with the child. Para 3.5.5 of the said Guidelines mandates as under:

> "**3.5.5** - *A third-party donor and a surrogate mother must relinquish in writing all parental rights concerning the offspring and vice versa.*"
>
> Guidelines dealing with legitimacy of the child born through ART state that the child shall be presumed to be the legitimate child of the married/unmarried couple/single parent with all the attendant rights of parentage, support, and inheritance.
>
> **3.12.1** A child born through ART shall be presumed to be the legitimate child of the couple, having been born in wedlock and with the consent of both the spouses. Therefore, the child shall have a legal right to parental support, inheritance, and all other privileges of a child born to a couple through sexual intercourse.
>
> **3.12.4** *In the case of a divorce during the gestation period, if the offspring is of a donor programme – be it sperm or ova – the law of the land as pertaining to a normal conception would apply"*.

The cross border surrogacy leads to problems in citizenship, nationality, motherhood, parentage, and rights of a child. There are occasions where children are denied nationality of the country of intended parents and this results in either a long legal battle like *in case of the German couple with twin surrogate children or the Israeli gay couple who had to undergo DNA testing to establish parentage* or have a bleak future in orphanage for the child. There are incidences where the child given to couple after surrogacy is not genetically related to them and in turn, is disowned by the intended parent and has to spend his life in an orphanage.

However, it is submitted that the law relating to surrogacy in India is in its prenatal stage and unfortunately at the moment there is no legislation in existence prescribing a code of practice governing the moral, ethical and legal aspects of such surrogate arrangements. Hence, the said Guidelines only have persuasive value at this moment in time.

It seems ironical that people are engaging in the practice of surrogacy when nearly 12 million Indian children are orphans. Adoption of a child in India is a complicated and a lengthy procedure for those childless couples who want to give a home to these children. Even 60 years of Independence have not given a comprehensive adoption law applicable to all its citizens, irrespective of the religion or the country they live in as Non-Resident Indians (NRIs), Persons of Indian Origin (PIOs) or Overseas Citizens of India (OCIs). As a result, they resort to the options of IVF or surrogacy. The Guardian and Wards Act, 1890 permits Guardianship and not adoption. The Hindu Adoption and Maintenance Act, 1956 does not permit non-Hindus to adopt a Hindu child, and requirements of immigration after adoption have further hurdles.

There is a strong need to modify and make the adoption procedure simple for all. This will bring down the rates of surrogacy. Altruistic and not commercial surrogacy should be promoted. Laws should be framed and implemented to cover the grey areas and to protect the rights of women and children in cases where there is scope for exploitation in commercial surrogacy.

In a very unique proceeding before Supreme Court of India, keeping in view the peculiar facts of the case, the Apex Court directed the concerned authorities of CARA to consider and process the case of adoption of two minor children born out of a surrogacy arrangement commissioned by their German parents. Twin baby boys were born to a German couple with the aid of Assisted Reproductive Technology after fertilized embryo was transplanted in the womb of a surrogate mother in India. Upon the failure of the parents to get any travel documents for the two baby boys to enable their journey to Germany, they petitioned the Gujarat High Court and ultimately by a Judgment dated November 11, 2009 reported as *Jan Balaz* v. *Anand Municipality,* AIR 2010 Guj 21: 2010 AIHC 407 (NOC): 2010 (3) Rec Civ R 635, it was directed that the Passport authorities should release Indian passports for the two minor children for their return to Germany with their German parents. The Government of India challenged this judgment in an appeal before the Supreme Court of India and on November 25, 2009 in *Special Leave to Appeal (Civil) 31639 of 2009,* the operation of the impugned judgment dated November 11, 2009 was stayed. Subsequently, on January 18, 2010, a proposal was mooted that the German couple explore the modalities of adopting the children born through surrogacy. Thereafter, on January 20, 2010, it was stated that the Government of India will take all possible measures to expedite the inter-country adoption of these children. Thereafter, on February 25, 2010, it was stated that the procedure for temporary adoption was under process by CARA, even though a surrogate child is not subjected to adoption. The court directed that CARA may consider the case sympathetically. Ultimately, on March 17, 2010, the court directed CARA to consider and process the case of the two minor children for adoption and take appropriate action in consultation with the Government of India and the German Embassy keeping in view the peculiar facts of the case. It was reported to the court on May 5, 2010 that all steps which could facilitate inter-country adoption had been taken by CARA and no objection certificate would be issued as soon as the willingness of the concerned agency of Germany is received in this regard. By this process, upon the intervention of the Apex Court, inter-country adoption procedure processed through CARA, the exit of the two minor children to Germany was facilitated on humanitarian grounds, without it being quoted as a precedent. Thereafter, the appeal of the Government of India on the issue of granting Indian citizenship to surrogate children born in India, is still pending final adjudication. The decision on the issue whether Indian Passports can be given to children born to foreigners through surrogacy will be important to determine future cases and hence the issue is important. However, regardless, inter-country adoption process assisted by CARA facilitated the twin German children born out of surrogacy in the present case to leave India.

The new Assisted Reproductive Technologies (Regulation) Bill, 2013 or the so called the Surrogacy Bill too is still pending. The legislation in the pipeline is still to be passed and enacted. Thus, presently we do not have any proper legislation to regulate surrogacy in India.

XVI. Conflict of Laws in Inter-Country Adoptions

From 3 January, 2014 the **Adoption (Recognition of Overseas Adoptions) Order, 2013** revoked and replaced the **Adoption (Designation of Overseas Adoptions) Order, 1973**. Under the latter, adoptions affected by the law of most Commonwealth countries were recognized by the United Kingdom, with notable exceptions, such as India, wherein India was specifically a 'Non-designated country'.

Under the 1973 Order, we, during our time as counsel dealing with adoption applications at the British High Commission and other major Embassies at New Delhi, had quite frequently encountered conflict of laws situation where Non-Resident Indians, who had been residing abroad for several decades, adopt child from within their own family. The preference for adoption by immediate blood relatives is a common South Asian phenomenon.

The unsuspecting parents duly complied with the requirements of the HAMA, 1956 for taking the child in adoption. The adoption deed was proudly presented to the immigration authorities; and this was where the trouble began. The UK immigration authorities completely disregarded the Indian adoption deed, and they were legally justified in doing so under the 1973 Order, SI 1973/19.

If the child has not been legally adopted from a 'designated' country or the adoption is from a country whose adoption orders are not recognized as valid in UK law, that is the child from 'non-designated' country, entry clearance will have to be obtained for the child to travel to the United Kingdom for adoption through English Courts. *India is now specified to be a 'designated' country under the Adoption (Recognition of Overseas Adoption) Order, 2013 and has joined ranks with the countries whose adoption orders are recognized. India's recognition is due to its having signed up to the Hague Convention on Inter-country Adoptions.*

Even so, the Court of Appeal in its judgment upheld a judgment under the provisions of HAMA, 1956. But, the central plank to uphold the validity of such an adoption is on the basis of right to family life. This judgment of immense significance has been analysed by our co-author Rambert De Mello in our book titled *"Acting for Non-resident Indian Clients,"* (Jordan Publishing Limited, 1st Edn., 2004) at pp. 221-222. His analysis is as follows:

"Recently, the Court held that the bias against Indian adoption custom was wrong and that it was a breach of the right to family life and discriminatory to refuse an adopted child entry clearance to the United Kingdom by giving less weight to an adoption effected by customary law in India and which was recognised as valid there, on the ground that it was not a recognised practice in English law: Singh *v.* ECO Delhi, [2004] EWCA Civ 1075.

(1) The main principle arising for consideration in Singh was whether an adoption which does not meet the requirements of relevant international instruments should invariably be a reason for according little weight to it in determining whether family life exists or not. The adoption of the boy in the case of Singh was valid in India but not recognised in the United Kingdom.

(2) The Court concluded that such a rigid and formulaic approach is not justified and that the failure to satisfy the requirement of relevant international instruments will vary from case to case, and that of considerable importance will be the nature of the departure from the provisions of a relevant instrument. If the departure is one of substance rather than procedure and goes to the heart of the safeguards that the instrument is intended to promote, then it may well be appropriate to give the adoption order little weight ([2004] EWCA Civ 1075 at [33]).

(3) In this case much might be said of the fact that the children had not been adopted and that their biological link with their natural parents was fluid, continuing and developing.

(4) The principles enunciated in Singh *which are relevant in determining whether family life exists between an adopted child and adoptive parents are equally applicable in a situation which needs to resolve whether there is family life existing between a child and his natural parents who are separated from each other.*

(5) The best interests of the child will be relevant and may well be determinative at the stage at which the court has to decide the extent to which respect should be given to family life or whether interference with family life is justified under article 8.2 [2004] EWCA Civ 1075 at [34] per Dyson LJ, at [68] per Munby J.

(6) The potential for development of family life is relevant in determining whether family life already exists and this is not confined to cases involving children and their natural parents; unless some degree of family life is already established, the claim to family life will fail and will not be saved by the fact that at some time in the future it could flower into a full-blown family life or that the applicants have a genuine wish to bring this about [2004] EWCA Civ 1075 at [38].

(7) The fact is that many adults and children, whether through choice or circumstance, live in families more or less removed from what until comparatively recently would have been recognised as the typical nuclear family – the Convention is a living instrument [2004] EWCA Civ 1075 at [63]–[64] per Munby J). The law must adapt itself to these realities (at [65]. There is no bright line test that the law can set. The infinite variety of the human condition precludes arbitrary defining.

(8) The existence or non-existence of family life is a question of fact depending upon the real existence in practice of close personal ties – a close personal relationship which has sufficient constancy and substance to create de facto *family ties – the parents' cohabitation with the child will often be highly significant but this is not decisive [2004] EWCA Civ 1075 at [79].*

(9) The fact that the parents do not see their children frequently is not fatal to establishing family life; one must be cautious before setting too high a benchmark for the existence of family life certainly where there is the constancy and commitment which a parent has shown towards his child [2004] EWCA Civ 1075 at [90]."

Likewise, the American Embassy and numerous European Embassies at New Delhi also outrightly refused to accept the above-mentioned adoption deeds under the provisions of HAMA, 1956. Hence, only guardianship orders are acceptable. These can be obtained only by lodging guardianship petitions under the provisions of the Hindu Minority and Guardianship Act, 1956 in the Court of the Guardian Judge, in whose jurisdiction the minor child is residing. It is like a full blown trial. It is very difficult to obtain guardianship orders. These petitions have to be supported by exhaustive documentation as to the background and standing of the proposed overseas adoptive parents. Sometimes, it can be a time consuming exercise, and it is very difficult in such a situation for the foreign couple to spend long periods of time in India awaiting custody orders. With these custody orders, the adoption ultimately takes place in the foreign country of habitual residence of the adoptive parents.

Furthermore, adoptions within the family fold are not encouraged, while adoption applications by foreigners seeking to adopt children from orphanages and welfare homes are likely to receive positive treatment.

The noose of British immigration law has been tightened by changes to HC 395, which were given effect by HC 538, and came into force on 1 April, 2003. Reference in this regard is drawn to the observations of Richard McKee, a prominent Immigration Appeals Adjudicator:

'Now HC 538 has not only lifted the restriction on third party support, but it has introduced a provision for de facto *adoption. For all adopted children coming from countries whose adoption orders (if they have such things) are not recognised in the UK, the adoptive parents must have been living abroad, having assumed the role of the child's parents, for at least 18 months, of which the last 12 must have been spent living together with the child. This is to show a genuine transfer of parental responsibility. The expectation that the adoptive parents be married has now been dropped.'* [For details *see Richard McKee 'New Immigration Rules' [2003] 17.2 IA & NL 127–129*].

The most worrying issue about these changes is that it is next to impossible for Non-Resident Indian couples to come and spend one complete calendar year with the adoptive child in India. Certainly, no UK employer or any other overseas employer would grant such long leave to any employee. However, more positively, senior level expatriates posted in India could possibly comply with the time requirement stipulated by the provisions of HC 538.

Furthermore, there has been a European Court of Human Rights decision on the basis of a friendly settlement having very wide ramifications. This case was the fallout of the immigration officer's denial to permit an Indian couple to bring their adopted child to UK, which resulted in the Government of United Kingdom paying costs and damages totalling to more than £ 42,000 before the European Court of Human Rights. This was a friendly settlement in the case of *Singh* v. *The United Kingdom,* application number 60148/00 which was disposed of on 8-6-2006. The said application was lodged before the ECHR on 24 May, 2000 and admitted for hearing thereafter, upon preliminary submissions and arguments.

Earlier on 11 March, 1997 the immigration authorities had refused permission to the adoptive parents to bring the child into the UK. This was because adoptions from India are not recognised for the purpose of entry clearance. Thus, the child fell out of the rules for entry clearance as he was not adopted because of any inability on the part of his parents to care for him. But, there was a genuine transfer of parental responsibility. Incidentally, this adoption application was lodged by us at the British High Commission, New Delhi. This judgment has not received much publicity and academic analysis at this moment in time. This case was reported in the London Times on 21 June, 2006.

Recent relevant case-law on the ever expanding ambit of article 8 of the ECHR as possibly applicable to inter-country adoptions handed down by the House of Lords as then it was, the Supreme Court of England and Wales and the European Court of Human Rights is analysed hereunder.

XVII. House of Lords Judgment in the Case of *Huang (FC)* v. *Secretary of State for the Home Department and Kashmiri (FC)* v. *Secretary of State for the Home Department (Conjoined Appeals)* Session 2006-07, 19th Report, ([2007) UKHL 11], on Appeal from: [2005] EWCA Civ 105, on Application of Article 8 of the ECHR

The above mentioned case is being cited with a view to draw support on the interpretation of article 8 of the ECHR in inter-country adoption cases, especially from India. It is common knowledge that it is a South Asian phenomena to adopt within the family fold, rather than going in for adoptions from orphanages and social organisations in the voluntary sector. The point to be conveyed is that there is potentially a genuine semblance of some form of established family life from the time the formal adoption process or the guardianship applications are lodged in the Court of competent jurisdiction, as the case may be until the time the adoptive parents or the prospective adoptive parents are entangled in the immigration hoops.

In the event of any appeal proceedings initiated post refusal, the issue of family life also assumes added significance, among other crucial factors. In these circumstances, law on the right to family life has to be canvassed vigorously as well to demonstrate established family life, which in turn is likely to considerably enhance the chances of the success of the appeal proceedings. Hence, there is brief analysis below of the above-mentioned judgment by the erstwhile House of Lords in the case of *Huang* (supra).

In *Huang (FC)* v. *Secretary of State for the Home Department and Kashmiri (FC)* v. *Secretary of State for the Home Department (Conjoined Appeals): House of Lords: Session 2006-07, 19th Report, ([2007] UKHL 11)*, an appeal from: [2005] EWCA Civ 105, two appeals had been heard together as they raised a common question on the decision-making role or function of appellate immigration authorities (adjudicators, the Immigration Appeal Tribunal, immigration judges) when deciding appeals, on Convention grounds, against refusal of leave to enter or remain, under section 65 of the Immigration and Asylum Act, 1999 and Part III of Schedule 4 to the said legislation. *First*, the facts are being set out, before adverting to the relevant legislation that is the Human Rights Act, 1998 and the case-law analysis in particular reference to article 8 of the ECHR.

Mrs. Huang was a Chinese citizen born on 29 March, 1942. Her husband (from whom she was separated), daughter, son-in-law and two grandsons were British citizens living in the UK. Mr Kashmiri was an Iranian citizen born on 4 July, 1981. His parents and two siblings came to the UK in 2000 and were in due course granted indefinite leave to remain as refugees, but Mr Kashmiri's claim to asylum has been refused. As stated in the judgment, neither of the applicants qualified for the grant of leave to remain in the UK under the immigration rules and administrative directions promulgated at that time. Both of them claimed that their refusal of leave to remain was unlawful because it was incompatible by their Convention rights to respect for their family guaranteed by sections 2, 3 and 6 of and Article 8 in Schedule 1 to the Human Rights Act, 1998.

It is important to advert to the relevant UK legislation in this regard. That in terms of the UK Human Rights Act, 1998 the public authorities as also the British Courts are duty bound to follow the provisions of the ECHR as set out in schedule 1 of the Human Rights Act, 1998, as also held by the Court in para 8 of the said judgment of *Huang* (supra). Para 8 of the said judgment reads as follows:

> *"8. In the Human Rights Act, 1998 Parliament not only enabled but required the Convention rights set out in Schedule 1 to the Act (including article 8) to be given effect as a matter of domestic law in this country. It did so (section 2) by requiring courts or tribunals determining a question which had arisen in connection with a Convention right to take into account any relevant Strasbourg jurisprudence, by requiring legislation, where possible, to be read compatibly with Convention rights (section 3) and, most importantly, by declaring it unlawful (section 6) for a public authority to act in a way incompatible with a Convention right. Thus immigration officers, the appellate immigration authority and the courts, as public authorities (section 6(3)), act unlawfully if they do not (save in specified circumstances) act compatibly with a person's Convention right under article 8. The object is to ensure that public authorities should act to avert or rectify any violation of a Convention right, with the result that such rights would be effectively protected at home, thus (it was hoped) obviating or reducing the need for recourse to Strasbourg."*

Para 9 of the said judgment talks of provisions relating to compliance of convention rights in terms of the above-mentioned domestic legislation in the UK in the following terms:

"9. Two important steps were taken to ensure compliance with this new domestic legal obligation. The first was to amend (Cm 4851, September 2000) the then current Immigration rules so as to require immigration officers, entry clearance officers and all staff of the Home Office Immigration and Nationality Directorate to carry out their duties in compliance with the provisions of the Human Rights Act, 1998. It is these officers who ordinarily decide, in the first instance, whether leave to enter or remain in the country should be granted."

By virtue of the above-mentioned domestic legislation in the UK, as also incorporated in the British immigration rules, it can well possibly be argued even at the time of lodging the adoptions entry clearance applications at any of the British posts in India, the entry clearance officers to take into account article 8 of the ECHR, as also incorporated in the Human Rights Act, 1998. This argument of course, will depend on the facts and circumstances of each individual case.

Further, para 18 of the said judgment gives a brief overview of the convention jurisprudence *i.e.,* the ECHR and more than that emphatically dwells on the sensitivity factor, while dealing and adjudicating upon family reunion issues in the following terms:

"18. The authority must of course take account, as enjoined by section 2 of the 1998 Act, of Strasbourg jurisprudence on the meaning and effect of article 8. While the case law of the Strasbourg court is not strictly binding, it has been held that domestic courts and tribunals should, in the absence of special circumstances, follow the clear and constant jurisprudence of that court: R (Alconbury Developments Ltd.) *v.* Secretary of State for the Environment, Transport and the Regions, *[2001] UKHL 23; [2003] 2 AC 295, para 26;* R (Ullah) *v.* Special Adjudicator, *[2004] UKHL 26: [2004] 2 AC 323, para 20. It is unnecessary for present purpose to attempt to summarise the Convention jurisprudence on article 8, save to record that the article imposes on member states not only a negative duty to refrain from unjustified interference with a person's right to respect for his or her family but also a positive duty to show respect for it. The reported cases are of value in showing where, in many different factual situations, the Strasbourg court, as the ultimate guardian of Convention rights, has drawn the line, thus guiding national authorities in making their own decisions. But the main importance of the case law is in illuminating the core value which article 8 exists to protect. This is not, perhaps, hard to recognise. Human beings are social animals. They depend on others. Their family, or extended family, is the group on which many people most heavily depend, socially, emotionally and often financially. There comes a point at which, for some, prolonged and unavoidable separation from this group seriously inhibits their ability to live full and fulfilling lives. Matters such as the age, health and vulnerability of the applicant, the closeness and previous history of the family, the applicant's dependence on the financial and emotional support of the family, the prevailing cultural tradition and conditions in the country of origin and many other factors may all be relevant. The Strasbourg court has repeatedly recognised the general right of states to control the entry and residence of non-nationals, and repeatedly acknowledged that the Convention confers no right on individuals or families to choose where they prefer to live. In most cases where the applicants*

complain of a violation of their article 8 rights, in a case where the impugned decision is authorized by law for a legitimate object and the interference (or lack of respect) is of sufficient seriousness to engage the operation of article 8, the crucial question is likely to be whether the interference (or lack of respect) complained of is proportionate to the legitimate end sought to be achieved. Proportionality is a subject of such importance as to require separate treatment."

Para 19 of the said judgment reminds adjudicators, now designated as immigration Judges to take into account the issue of proportionality, while adjudicating upon convention questions by referring to its earlier judgment, as follows:

"19. ....The House is recognised as much in R (Razgar) *v.* Secretary of State for the Home Department, *[2004] UKHL 27: [2004] 2 AC 368, paras 17-20, 26, 27, 60, 77, when, having suggested a series of questions which an adjudicator would have to ask and answer in deciding a Convention question, it said that the judgment on proportionality "must always involve the striking of a fair balance between the rights of the individual and the interests of the community which is inherent in the whole of the Convention. The severity and consequences of the interference will call for careful assessment at this stage.*

If, as counsel suggest, insufficient attention has been paid to this requirement, the failure should be made good."

Para 20, the penultimate part of the judgment is of utmost significance in international family migration matters. Para 20 in categorical terms provides as follows:

"20. In an article 8 case where this question is reached, the ultimate question for the appellate immigration authority is whether the refusal of leave to enter or remain, in circumstances where the life of the family cannot reasonably be expected to be enjoyed elsewhere, taking full account of all considerations weighing in favour of the refusal, prejudices the family life of the applicant in a manner sufficiently serious to amount to a breach of the fundamental right protected by article 8. If the answer to this question is affirmative, the refusal is unlawful and the authority must so decide. It is not necessary that the appellate immigration authority, directing itself along the lines indicated in this opinion, need ask in addition whether the case meets a test of exceptionality. The suggestion that it should is based on an observation of Lord Bingham in Razgar above, para 20. He was there expressing an expectation, shared with the Immigration Appeal Tribunal, that the number of claimants not covered by the Rules and supplementary directions but entitled to succeed under article 8 would be a very small minority. That is still his expectation. But he was not purporting to lay down a legal test."

Two recent developments in the UK, apart from coming into force of the 2013 Orders, are of relevance in the context of inter-country adoptions. *First,* section 55 of the Borders, Citizenship and Immigration Act, 2009 imposes a duty on all public authorities to safeguard and promote the welfare of children. The term public authorities of course includes, entry clearance officers at the British Posts/ Missions dealing with settlement applications including adoption applications.

Secondly, the Supreme Court of England and Wales in *ZH (Tanzania)*, [2011] UKSC 4 has held that in article 8 cases where children are involved, the best interests of the child must be "a primary consideration," which can only be outweighed by very serious countervailing factors. This emphasis on the welfare and best interests of children will strengthen the argument of couples who have adopted children in countries whose adoption orders are not recognised in the UK. Hence, if genuine 'family life' has been established between the children and their adoptive parents, which of course is well documented by credible evidence on record, it will generally be a breach of article 8 if the children are not granted entry clearance.

Section 55 of the Borders, Citizenship and Immigration Act, 2009 mandates as follows:

> *'55 Duty regarding the welfare of children.—(1) The Secretary of State must make arrangements for ensuring that—*
>
> *(a) the functions mentioned in sub-section (2) are discharged having regard to the need to safeguard and promote the welfare of children who are in the United Kingdom, and*
>
> *(b) any services provided by another person pursuant to arrangements which are made by the Secretary of State and relate to the discharge of a function mentioned in sub-section (2) are provided having regard to that need.*
>
> *(2) The functions referred to in sub-section (1) are—*
>
> *(a) any function of the Secretary of State in relation to immigration, asylum or nationality;*
>
> *(b) any function conferred by or by virtue of the Immigration Acts on an immigration officer;*
>
> *(c) any general customs function of the Secretary of State;*
>
> *(d) any customs function conferred on a designated customs official.*
>
> *(3) A person exercising any of those functions must, in exercising the function, have regard to any guidance given to the person by the Secretary of State for the purpose of sub-section (1).*
>
> *(4) The Director of Border Revenue must make arrangements for ensuring that—*
>
> *(a) the Director's functions are discharged having regard to the need to safeguard and promote the welfare of children who are in the United Kingdom, and*
>
> *(b) any services provided by another person pursuant to arrangements made by the Director in the discharge of such a function are provided having regard to that need.*
>
> *(5) A person exercising a function of the Director of Border Revenue must, in exercising the function, have regard to any guidance given to the person by the Secretary of State for the purpose of sub-section (4).*
>
> *(6) In this section—*

"children" means persons who are under the age of 18; "customs function", "designated customs official" and "general customs function" have the meanings given by Part 1.

(7) A reference in an enactment (other than this Act) to the Immigration Acts includes a reference to this section.

(8) Section 21 of the UK Borders Act, 2007 (c. 30) (children) ceases to have effect."

As far as the position in UK today is concerned, it is notable that, while India ratified the Hague Convention in 2003, it was not until 2013 that the UK issued the Adoption (Recognition of Overseas Adoptions) Order, 2013, in force with effect from January 03, 2014, revoking and replacing the Adoption (Designation of Overseas Adoptions) Order, 1973. The new order for the first time includes India amongst the countries whose adoptions are now recognised by the UK. However, this does not, unfortunately, mean that adopted children from India will automatically get entry clearance to UK. The other requirements of paragraph 310 of the UK Immigration Rules must still be satisfied. Hence, this does not really help the position on the ground.

XVIII. Recent Judgment of the Supreme Court of England and Wales in the Case of *ZH (Tanzania) (FC)* v. *Secretary of State for the Home Department* Reported as [2011] UKSC 4 on appeal from: [2009] EWCA CIV 691 Amplifying the Scope of Article of the ECHR

The judgment of the Supreme Court of England and Wales in the case of *ZH (Tanzania) (FC)* v. *Secretary of State for the Home Department,* [2011] UKSC 4 on appeal from: [2009] EWCA Civ 691 has amplified the scope of article 8 of the ECHR, especially with regard to the best interests of the children. The same is discussed hereunder:

Basically, the crucial issue involved in the case has been summed-up in para 1 of the judgment in the following terms:

> *"1. The over-arching issue in this case is the weight to be given to the best interests of children who are affected by the decision to remove or deport one or both of their parents from this country. Within this, however, is a much more specific question: in what circumstances is it permissible to remove or deport a non-citizen parent where the effect will be that a child who is a citizen of the United Kingdom will also have to leave? There is, of course, no power to remove or deport a person who is a United Kingdom citizen: see Immigration Act, 1971, section 3(5) and (6). They have a right of abode in this country, which means that they are free to live in, and to come and go into and from the United Kingdom without let or hindrance: see 1971 Act, sections 1 and 2. The consistent stance of the Secretary of State is that UK citizens are not compulsorily removed from this country (e.g., Phil Woolas, Hansard, Written Answers, 15 June, 2009). However if a non-citizen parent is compulsorily removed and agrees to take her children with her, the effect is that the children have little or no choice in the matter. There is no machinery for consulting them or giving independent consideration to their views."*

But, the present ruling takes into account the Strasbourg jurisprudence, as also the May 2008 UNHCR guidelines in determining the best interests of the child which also includes within its wide sweep adoption cases. The purpose of citing this judgment is to demonstrate as to how right to family life under Article 8 of the ECHR, helps in supporting the case of genuine inter-country adoption cases from India, where there is strong and compelling established family life.

Basically, this case is central to the fact of the mother's deportation and the fate of her UK-born children if they were to be left behind in the UK or alternatively to accompany the mother to her country of origin, as stated in start of para 14 (at page 5) of the judgment as follows:

> *"14. This is the mother's appeal on the ground that her removal will constitute a disproportionate interference with her right to respect for her private and family life, guaranteed by article 8 of the European Convention on Human Rights..."*

The ruling in the present case also reiterates the right to respect family life in para 14 (at page 6) of the judgment as follows:

> *"14. .... However, in* Beoku-Betts *v.* Secretary of State for the Home Department, *[2008] UKHL 39, [2009] AC 115, the House of Lords held that both the Secretary of State and the immigration appellate authorities had to consider the rights to respect for their family life of all the family members who might be affected by the decision and not just those of the claimant or appellant in question. Lord Brown of Eaton-under-Heywood summarised the argument which the House accepted thus, at para 20:*
>
> *"Together these members enjoy a single family life and whether or not the removal would interfere disproportionately with it has to be looked at by reference to the family unit as a whole and the impact of removal upon each member. If overall the removal would be disproportionate, all affected family members are to be regarded as victims...""*

Quite often in adoption and marriage refusal cases, the arguments raised by Entry Clearance Officers in refusal cases is that Article 8 of the ECHR does not recognise the choice of the country with regard to the right to family reunion. The present judgment at para 19 (page 9) has reiterated the law in this regard as follows:

> *"19. It was long ago established that mixed nationality couples have no right to set up home in whichever country they choose: see* Abdulaziz *v.* United Kingdom, (1985) 7 EHRR 471. *Once they have done so, however, the factors relevant to judging the proportionality of any interference with their right to respect for their family lives have quite recently been rehearsed in the case of* Rodrigues da Silva, Hoogkamer *v.* Netherlands, (2007) 44 EHRR 729, *at para 39:*
>
> *". . . Article 8 does not entail a general obligation for a state to respect immigrants' choice of the country of their residence and to authorise family reunion in its territory. Nevertheless, in a case which concerns family life as well as immigration, the extent of a state's obligations to admit to its territory relatives of persons residing there will vary according to the particular circumstances of the*

> *person involved and the general interest [the reference is to* Gûl *v.* Switzerland, *(1996) 22 EHRR 93 at [38]]. Factors to be taken into account in this context are the extent to which family life is effectively ruptured, the extent of the ties in the contracting state, whether there are insurmountable obstacles in the way of the family living in the country of origin of one or more of them, whether there are factors of immigration control (e.g. a history of breaches of immigration law) or considerations of public order weighing in favour of exclusion [the reference is to* Solomon *v.* The Netherlands, *App. No. 44328/98, 5 September, 2000]. Another important consideration will also be whether family life was created at a time when the persons involved were aware that the immigration status of one of them was such that the persistence of that family life within the host state would from the outset be precarious. The Court has previously held that where this is the case it is likely only to be in the most exceptional circumstances that the removal of the non-national family member will constitute a violation of article 8 [the reference is to* Mitchell *v.* United Kingdom, App. No. 40447/98, 24 November, 1998; Ajayi *v.* United Kingdom, App. No. 27663/95, 22 June, 1999].""

The judgment above in the case of *ZH (Tanzania)* (supra) sufficiently takes into account the UNCRC and the best interests of the child. Paras 21 to 23 (at pages 11 and 12) are a terse reminder as follows:

> *"21. It is not difficult to understand why the Strasbourg Court has become more sensitive to the welfare of the children who are innocent victims of their parents choices. For example, in* Neulinger *v.* Switzerland, (2010) 28 BHRC 706, *para 131, the Court observed that "the Convention cannot be interpreted in a vacuum but must be interpreted in harmony with the general principles of international law. Account should be taken . . . of 'any relevant rules of international law applicable in the relations between the parties' and in particular the rules concerning the international protection of human rights."*

The Court went on to note, at para 135, that "there is currently a broad consensus – *including in international law – in support of the idea that in all decisions concerning children, their best interests must be paramount"*

> *22. The Court had earlier, in paras 49 to 56, collected references in support of this proposition from several international human rights instruments: from the second principle of the United Nations Declaration on the Rights of the Child, 1959; from article 3(1) of the Convention on the Rights of the Child, 1989 (UNCRC); from articles 5(b) and 16(d) of the Convention on the Elimination of All Forms of Discrimination against Women, 1979; from General Comments 17 and 19 of the Human Rights Committee in relation to the International Covenant on Civil and Political Rights, 1966; and from article 24 of the European Union's Charter of Fundamental Rights. All of these refer to the best interests of the child, variously describing these as "paramount", or "primordial", or "a primary consideration". To a United Kingdom lawyer, however, these do not mean the same thing.*
>
> *23. For our purposes the most relevant national and international obligation of the United Kingdom is contained in article 3(1) of the UNCRC:*

"In all actions concerning children, whether undertaken by public or private social welfare institutions, courts of law, administrative authorities or legislative bodies, the best interests of the child shall be a primary consideration.""

Furthermore, para 23 of the said judgment also takes into account the import of section 55 of the Borders, Citizenship and Immigration Act, 2009, as follows:

"23. .... This is a binding obligation in international law, and the spirit, if not the precise language, has also been translated into our national law. Section 11 of the Children Act, 2004 places a duty upon a wide range of public bodies to carry out their functions having regard to the need to safeguard and promote the welfare of children. The immigration authorities were at first excused from this duty, because the United Kingdom had entered a general reservation to the UNCRC concerning immigration matters. But that reservation was lifted in 2008 and, as a result, section 55 of the Borders, Citizenship and Immigration Act, 2009 now provides that, in relation among other things to immigration, asylum or nationality, the Secretary of State must make arrangements for ensuring that those functions "are discharged having regard to the need to safeguard and promote the welfare of children who are in the United Kingdom"

Para 25 of the said judgment dwells upon the legitimate expectation of the Supreme Court emanating from the recent Strasbourg Court jurisprudence for the national authorities to apply the relevant provisions of UNCRC in the following terms:

"25. Further, it is clear from the recent jurisprudence that the Strasbourg Court will expect national authorities to apply article 3(1) of UNCRC and treat the best interests of a child as "a primary consideration". Of course, despite the looseness with which these terms are sometimes used, "a primary consideration" is not the same as "the primary consideration", still less as "the paramount consideration". Miss Joanna Dodson QC, to whom we are grateful for representing the separate interests of the children in this case, boldly argued that immigration and removal decisions might be covered by section 1(1) of the Children Act, 1989:

"When a court determines any question with respect to—(a) the upbringing of a child; or

(b) the administration of a child's property or the application of any income arising from it, the child's welfare shall be the court's paramount consideration."

However, questions with respect to the upbringing of a child must be distinguished from other decisions which may affect them. The UNHCR, in its Guidelines on Determining the Best Interests of the Child (May 2008), explains the matter neatly, at para 1.1:

"The term 'best interests' broadly describes the well-being of a child.... The CRC neither offers a precise definition, nor explicitly outlines common factors of the best interests of the child, but stipulates that:

the best interests must be the determining factor for specific actions, notably adoption (Article 21) and separation of a child from parents against their will (Article 9);

the best interests must be a primary (but not the sole) consideration for all other actions affecting children, whether undertaken by public or private social welfare institutions, courts of law, administrative authorities or legislative bodies (Article 3)."

This seems to me accurately to distinguish between decisions which directly affect the child's upbringing, such as the parent or other person with whom she is to live, and decisions which may affect her more indirectly, such as decisions about where one or both of her parents are to live. Article 9 of UNCRC, for example, draws a distinction between the compulsory separation of a child from her parents, which must be necessary in her best interests, and the separation of a parent from his child, for example, by detention, imprisonment, exile, deportation or even death."

But, from the context of the present article, it is immensely significant to note that adoptions are covered in the ambit of Article 21, UNCRC which of course can also be pleaded as part of consular representation at the time of lodging of the entry clearance application at the British High Commission at New Delhi or the concerned British Deputy High Commissions in other parts of the country or in the appeal grounds in the event of refusal.

Further, Lord Hope in the concurring portion of his judgment while agreeing with the principle judgment handed down by Lady Hale has concluded that the precarious immigration status of the mother cannot be held against the children. This is in para 44 (at page 20) of the judgment in the following terms:

"44. There is an obvious tension between the need to maintain a proper and efficient system of immigration control and the principle that, where children are involved, the best interests of the children must be a primary consideration. The proper approach, as was explained in Wan *v.* Minister for Immigration and Multicultural Affairs, [2001] FCA 568, para 32, *is, having taken this as the starting point, to assess whether their best interests are outweighed by the strength of any other considerations. The fact that the mother's immigration status was precarious when they were conceived may lead to a suspicion that the parents saw this as a way of strengthening her case for being allowed to remain here. But considerations of that kind cannot be held against the children in this assessment. It would be wrong in principle to devalue what was in their best interests by something for which they could in no way be held to be responsible."*

Finally, Lord Kerr in the penultimate part of the judgment has yet again highlighted in eloquent terms the primacy of the best interest of the child in para 46 (at page 20) of the judgment as follows:

"46. It is a universal theme of the various international and domestic instruments to which Lady Hale has referred that, in reaching decisions that will affect a child, a primacy of importance must be accorded to his or her best interests. This is not, it is agreed, a factor of limitless importance in the sense that it will prevail over all other considerations. It is a factor, however, that must rank higher than any other. It is not merely one consideration that weighs in the balance alongside other competing factors. Where the best interests of the child clearly favour a certain course, that course should be followed unless countervailing reasons of

> *considerable force displace them. It is not necessary to express this in terms of a presumption but the primacy of this consideration needs to be made clear in emphatic terms. What is determined to be in a child's best interests should customarily dictate the outcome of cases such as the present, therefore, and it will require considerations of substantial moment to permit a different result."*

Clearly, in light of the analysis on the case-law relating to Article 8 of the ECHR, the importance of the same cannot be overstated, in cases of family migration. But, the stumbling block even in genuine and *bona fide* cases, especially in marriage cases is the argument put forward by the entry clearance officers that the family life can exist even in the habitual country of residence and domicile, of the applicant wanting to join his/her spouse or adoptive parents in the UK, as the case may be. Further, the stumbling block encountered is that such an intending immigrant, cannot choose the country of his/her choice where family life is further sought to be pursued in the future. This of course creates further serious problems. Either the existing relationship is put to serious disrepair forcing split family life in different countries, or if it is a marriage case, the spouse settled in the UK is left with no choice but to relocate to India more out of compulsion than choice.

XIX. Conclusion

There has been a growing demand for a general law of adoption enabling any person, irrespective of his religion, race or caste, to adopt a child. There is now a clear case for overhauling the existing adoption law in India. The new CARA Guidelines of 2011 that are enacted are just a guideline to be adhered to while there is absence of any proper legislation by the Parliament. These guidelines too have several flaws that are already critically elaborated in the main body of the article.

As far as the mechanics of inter-country adoption are concerned, all the major Embassies in India are more than stringent in dealing with adoption applications. The refusal rates are very high. There is no room at all for compassion. The hurdles are almost insurmountable, causing lot of hardship to childless Non-Resident Indian couples.

The question that remained to be answered was as to how successful the revised 2006 Guidelines. Sadly, the answer can be found in a very recent Andhra Pradesh High Court judgment, *John Clements* v. *All Concerned,* 2003 (2) HLR 331 (AP). The Court lamented in paras 59-61, page 331 of the judgment as follows:

> *'59. Para 2.14 of the guidelines envisages that no application by foreigner for taking a child in adoption should be entertained directly by any social child welfare agency in India working in the areas of inter-country adoption or by any institution or centre or Home to which children are committed by the Juvenile Court. The very next paragraph says "the original application along with original documents as prescribed by the Supreme Court of India would be forwarded by the foreign enlisted agency to a recognized placement agency in India".*
>
> *60. Taking advantage of the inconsistency in the guidelines and ignoring the judgment of the Supreme Court the foreign enlisted agencies started directly*

approaching the placement agencies in India and are trying to take the Indian children in adoption with their connivance and active support of VCA and CARA officials, who are simply putting their seal of approval on these adoptions without bothering whether the procedure prescribed for inter-country adoption of a child is followed or not. With the result, trafficking in female children is going on unabated in violation of the guidelines given by the Supreme Court.

61. After the present scam came to light, the Government of Andhra Pradesh issued the Andhra Pradesh Orphanages and other Charitable Homes (Supervision and Control) Rules in G.O. Ms. No. 16, dated 18-4-2001. In para 11 (VII) of the said G.O. it is stated that "relinquishment" of child by "biological parents" on family grounds of poverty, number of children, unwanted girl child will not be permitted. Such children should not be admitted in Homes or "Orphanages" and, if admitted, the license and recognition of Home or Orphanage shall be cancelled or withdrawn.'

The finalisation of the 2007 Guidelines that was eagerly awaited have been enacted as 2011 Guidelines yet after consuming so much of time in the pipelining, these guidelines have done hopelessly. The consolidated comprehensive guidelines that were to carve out clear cut and precise uniformity in areas and legal issues of concern as pointed out in the article and not provide piecemeal reforms and solutions have failed to do so. The prospective failure of the guideline creating several confusing cases of adoption is demonstrated by the flaws, the conflict and confusions depicted in various provisions of the guideline in the main body of the article.

Furthermore, it could have been hoped that the new guidelines of 2011 would not only make the stringent and cumbersome process a bit easier but would also secure the best interest of the child to a greater extent. Yet, all this hope have gone futile.

Therefore, it can be concluded that, although there is no doubt that CARA is doing good work in its policing role, the negative media feedback has definitely not escaped judicial notice.

While the Government has been grappling on an *ad hoc* basis with lacunas arising out of the guidelines, which have been revised from time to time, in the interim, new issues have cropped-up and can be summarized as hereunder:

Firstly, there are legal issues connected with surrogacy. There is no legislation in India pertaining to surrogacy as yet.

Secondly, no practical tangible useful benefits are forthcoming at all to prospective NRI adoptive parents and persons of foreign origin arising out of India signing The Hague Convention Adoptions.

India has ratified the Hague Convention on Protection of Children and Cooperation in respect of inter-country adoptions on 6 June, 2003. Sadly enough, this significant development in the area of child law has gone completely unnoticed. However, the CARA authorities in their existing guidelines are yet to recognise in any form the ratification of Hague Convention on adoptions by India. It is suggested that the CARA authorities working in tandem conjointly with the Law Ministry of India, the Ministry of Women and Child Development, the Ministry of External Affairs, the Ministry of Overseas Indians Affairs as also the Legal and Treaties Division should take concrete steps in drafting as also implementing enabling legislation specifically looking at the positive steps of India signing the Hague convention on adoptions. In actual practice and interface with the abovementioned Government agencies during seminars and conferences of national importance, it appears that there is little co-ordination and interaction *inter se* within these important Government departments and ministries. Alternatively, if it is too late in the day to enact new enabling legislation with a view to seeking implementation of the Hague Convention on adoptions in the Indian jurisdiction, then in such a situation either of the ministries as mentioned above could well come out with a notification on the lines mentioned above. But, more importantly any such notification or directive should carry a specific direction to all the Embassies and Foreign Missions in India, to the effect that all Hague Convention adoptions made by the NRI community, subject to compliance of the due provisions of law, should be given due recognition. Also, any such notification or directive should clearly aim to define the concept of the "sending country," and the "receiving country," leaving little room for ambiguity.

Thirdly, there needs to be a categorical attempt to provide a clear cut direction in no uncertain terms to all major Embassies, High Commissions and Consulates in India, that all adoptions under the provision of the Juvenile Justice (Care and Protection of Children) Amendment Act, 2006 by Non-Resident Indians, Persons of Indian Origin and foreigners as well, should be duly acknowledged and their validity accepted as well to facilitate movement of the adopted children in the country of the habitual residence of the adopting parents. This of course has to be hedged with safeguards and compliance of due process of law, both in India and abroad. But, the core issue is the recognition of adoption orders handed down by the designated Courts in India under the provisions of the above mentioned amended provisions of the JJ Act of 2006. It is very important that these three new major issues also receive the due attention they warrant in the present day and age.

It was suggested in the earlier version of this book that the concept of gender free adoptions as provided under the provisions of the JJ Act, 2006 should well be taken into account in the CARA Guidelines which were under revision while the earlier version of this book was published. It was also suggested that the CARA authorities should take into account the provisions of the JJ Act, 2006 as also to specifically support the concept of gender free inter-country adoptions bearing in mind the plight of that particular section of NRI community, who are actually childless or even those who are willing to adopt children from India even though they have a child from an existing matrimonial relationship. The concept of gender free adoption however inculcated in the new Guideline of 2011 is confusing. The confusing position that has already been mentioned in the critical analysis of the new Guidelines clearly demonstrate how the language as well as the stand taken by the guidelines is sure to create conflict of law. Furthermore, the invoking of CARA Guidelines in the case of surrogacy, as was done in the case of *Jan Balaz (supra)*, though under the direction of the Supreme Court also requires examination to see if the 2011 Guidelines can accommodate cases arising out of discrepancies in surrogacy arrangements.

It is further suggested that the stand of adoption by gay, lesbian, bisexual and transgender (LGBT) section of the society too needs to be defined as the CARA Guidelines lack in this matter. The new CARA Guidelines of 2011 are secular; implementing every scope of effective and maximum adoptions in it. The scope of definition of Prospective Adoptive Parents (PAPs) is far and wide, including single parent, parent with previous children as well, etc. Adoption is allowed irrespective of marital status. However, the position of LGBT as usual is still undefined in these Indian guidelines/rules too. As usual the government and the ministry is silent and do not want to take a stand on the position of this section of the society. However, the recent judgment of the Apex Court in *National Legal Service Authority* v. *Union of India*, 2014 STPL (Web) 271 SC, proposing transgender legal rights as available to other genders will require serious introspection by CARA to confirm similar rights of adoption for transgenders (TG).

The position of adoption, although very much prevalent in the Indian society is not defined in any code and is unregulated for TG. The CARA Guidelines too have not mentioned anything for TG people while the new Surrogacy Bill which is still to be passed completely disqualify LGBTs, homosexual couples, foreign single individuals and couples in live-in relationships from having children through surrogate mothers in India. Thus, getting a child either by adoption or by surrogacy legally, is not possible for LGBT section of society. In the recent case of *National Legal Service Authority v. Union of India*, 2014 STPL (Web) 271 SC, the Bench of two Supreme Court judges, K.S. Radha Krishnan and A.K. Sikri emphasized on the UNDP report recommendations for the need to make legislations for Hijra/TG in para number 45, UNDP recommendation number 6 as follows:

> *"45. Transgender people, as a whole, face multiple forms of oppression in this country. Discrimination is so large and pronounced, especially in the field of health care, employment, education, leave aside social exclusion. A detailed study was conducted by the United Nations Development Programme (UNDP – India) and submitted a report in December, 2010 on Hijras/Transgenders in India:*
>
> *The UNDP in its report has made the following recommendations, which are as under:*
>
> *"...6. Develop action step towards taking a position on legal recognition of gender identity of Hijras/TG need to be taken in consultation with Hijras/TG and other key stakeholders. Getting legal recognition and avoiding ambiguities in the current procedures that issue identity documents to Hijras/TGs are required as they are connected to basic civil rights such as access to health and public services, right to vote, right to contest elections, right to education, inheritance rights, and marriage and* ***child adoption.""***

Thus, it is suggested that these recommendations need to be considered seriously and solutions need to be inculcated in CARA Guidelines to regulate the adoption by this section of society too.

Lastly, the authors' experience reveals that Guardian Judges, especially in small towns and cities in India, who deal with such cases, are not particularly conversant with the interpretation of the Inter-country Adoption Guidelines discussed in this chapter. Therefore, in sum and substance it can be stated that a uniform but strict procedure must be evolved which can be easily followed and adhered to both in letter and spirit. No doubt procedural hurdles and legal formalities are necessary to prevent abuse of the process but separate and intricate adoption and immigration procedures often leave foreign adoptive parents in confusion over differing interpretations. Therefore, if the adoption process and procedures are overhauled so that they conform to a uniform pattern, it may make the process more convenient, less cumbersome and easier to follow. All of this would be in the best interests of the child, which is undoubtedly the paramount consideration, and at the same time would allow both the letter and spirit of law to be adhered to. Considerable changes are thus urgently required in the field of inter-country adoption from India. Time has also come to enact legislation dealing with legal parentage issues of children born out of surrogacy arrangements.

POSTSCRIPT – EASIER ADOPTION LAW FOR NRIs ON THE CARDS, BUT NOT YET A LAW

The Government is contemplating re-enacting a new JJ Act, 2014 to replace the JJ Act, 2000. In this process, the salient suggested changes concerning inter country adoptions in the draft of The Juvenile Justice (Care and Protection of Children) Bill, 2014 can be briefly summarized as hereunder for purpose of ready reference:

i. The Government is planning to do away with the multiple layers of checks and balances for adoption of orphan children by Non-Resident Indians (NRIs) who are defined as persons holding an Indian Passport and residing abroad for more than one year. Overseas citizens of India and Persons of Indian Origin too have been defined.

ii. It is proposed that a Principal Magistrate shall allow a child to be given in adoption to a person irrespective of marital status, to parents to adopt a child of the same sex irrespective of the number of living biological sons or daughters and to childless couples.

iii. It is proposed to treat the NRI prospective adoptive parents at par with resident Indians. However, there is no proposal to ease the norms for foreigners. However, both Indian and foreign citizens shall be eligible to adopt.

iv. Another major hurdle obstructing adoptions is that there is a 80:20 adoption ratio criteria stipulated by the Government which provides preference for in country adoptions at 80 percent against only 20 percent to NRIs for overseas adoptions. Hence, only a restricted one fifth number of children are available for overseas adoption. This means that a child cannot be given away in adoption to foreigners until the 80 percent domestic adoptions were accomplished. That hardly ever happened and a child for overseas adoption kept waiting to get a home. The proposed bill scraps the above ratio of restrictive adoption by NRIs.

v. The Draft JJ Bill incorporates the principles of the Hague Convention on Protection of Children and Cooperation in Respect of Inter-Country Adoption (1993) which was absent in the original JJ Act, 2000.

vi. Section 58 of the draft Bill lays down special emphasis on inter-country adoptions. It states that all applications for adoption by prospective adoptive parents shall be filed before a Principal Magistrate of the concerned jurisdiction where the specialised and registered adoption agency is located.

vii. Speeding up the adoption process would be another focus area. The new proposed law suggests that no child should remain in an adoption home for more than 100 days after being declared legally free for adoption by the district child welfare committee.

viii. There is a proposal that adoption agencies would be blacklisted if they fail to update and upload information on the children with them on CARINGS, the national database for adoption on the Women and Child Development Ministry website.

ix. It is proposed that adoption agencies that work on the ground as intermediaries between the applicant couples and the adoption homes that shelter the children can function only if they have a certificate from CARA.

x. It is proposed to give CARA the status of a statutory body in line with the National Commission for Women and the National Commission for the Protection of Child Rights, which were formed by Acts of Parliament.

xi It is proposed that CARA upon being made a statutory body, CARA should be vested with functions of in-country and inter-country adoptions besides issuing guidelines on adoption as also carrying out the functions under the Hague Convention on protection of children.

However, it may be stated that till the coming of the present book, the above proposed law has not been enacted.

Divorce Nullity and Related Matters under the Hindu Marriage Act, 1955

The HMA, 1955 recognises nine fault grounds of divorce which are available to both the spouses, as provided in section 13(1) of the HMA, 1955. Additionally, a further four fault grounds of divorce are available to the wife alone in terms of section 13(2) of the HMA, 1955. Sections 13(1) and (2) of the HMA, 1955 are briefly stated hereunder:

*"**13. Divorce.**—(1) Any marriage solemnized, whether before or after the commencement of the Act, may, on a petition presented by either the husband or the wife, be dissolved by a decree of divorce on the ground that the other party—*

(i) has, after the solemnization of the marriage had voluntary sexual intercourse with any person other than his or her spouse; or

(ia) has, after the solemnization of the marriage, treated the petitioner with cruelty; or

(ib) has deserted the petitioner for a continuous period of not less than two years immediately preceding the presentation of the petition; or

(ii) has ceased to be a Hindu by conversion to another religion; or

(iii) has been incurably of unsound mind, or has suffering continuously or intermittently from mental disorder of such a kind and to such an extent that the petitioner cannot reasonably be expected to live with the respondent.

Explanation.—In this clause—

(a) the expression "mental disorder" means mental illness, arrested or incomplete development of mind, psychopathic disorder or any other disorder or disability of mind and include schizophrenia;

(b) the expression "psychopathic disorder" means a persistent disorder or disability of mind (whether or not including sub-normality of intelligence) which results in abnormally aggressive or seriously irresponsible conduct on the part of the other party and whether or not it requires or is susceptible to medical treatment; or

(iv) has been suffering from a virulent and incurable form of leprosy; or

(v) *has been suffering from venereal disease in a communicable form; or*

(vi) *has renounced the world by entering any religious order; or*

(vii) *has not been heard of as being alive for a period of seven years or more by those persons who would naturally have heard of it, had that party been alive;*

Explanation.—In this sub-section, the expression "desertion" means the desertion of the petitioner by the other party to the marriage without reasonable cause and without the consent or against the wish of such party, and includes the willful neglect of the petitioner by the other party to the marriage, and its grammatical variations and cognate expression shall be construed accordingly."

NON-COMPLIANCE OF A DECREE OF JUDICIAL SEPARATION OR RESTITUTION OF CONJUGAL RIGHTS

Furthermore, section 13(1A) of the HMA, 1955 provides that either spouse may file a petition for divorce on the ground that there has been no resumption of cohabitation for one year or more after the decree of judicial separation or the decree for restitution of conjugal rights has been passed.

ADDITIONAL GROUNDS AVAILABLE TO THE WIFE

"(2) A wife may also present a petition for the dissolution of her marriage by a decree of divorce on the ground—

(i) *in the case of any marriage solemnized before the commencement of this Act, that the husband had married again before the commencement or that any other wife of the husband married before such commencement was alive at the time of the solemnization of the marriage of the petitioner:*

Provided that in either case the other wife is alive at the time of the presentation of the petition;

(ii) *that the husband has, since the solemnization of the marriage, been guilty of rape, sodomy or bestiality; or*

(iii) *that in a suit under section 18 of the Hindu Adoptions and Maintenance Act (78 of 1956), or in a proceeding under section 125 of the Code of Criminal Procedure, 1973 (Act 2 of 1974) or under corresponding section 488 of the Code of Criminal Procedure (5 of 1898), a decree or order, as the case may be, has been passed against the husband awarding maintenance to the wife notwithstanding that she was living apart and that since the passing of such decree or order, cohabitation between the parties has not been resumed for one year or upwards; or*

(iv) *that her marriage (whether consummated or not) was solemnized before she attained the age of fifteen years and she has repudiated the marriage after attaining that age but before attaining the age of eighteen years.*

Explanation.—This clause applies whether the marriage was solemnized before or after the commencement of the Marriage Law (Amendment) Act, 1976."

DIVORCE BY MUTUAL CONSENT – UNDER SECTION 13B, HMA, 1955

Section 13B(1) provides that, subject to the provisions of the HMA, 1955, a petition for dissolution of marriage by a decree of divorce may be presented to the district court by both the parties to a marriage together, whether such marriage was solemnised before or after the commencement of the Marriage Laws (Amendment) Act, 1976, on the ground that they have been living separately for a period of one year or more, that they have not been able to live together and that they have mutually agreed that the marriage should be dissolved.

Section 13B(2) provides that after a joint petition has been presented by both the parties to the marriage, there is a waiting period of six to eighteen months during which the petition is heard by the Court for passing a decree of divorce. This is subject to the condition that the petition is not withdrawn in the meantime, and the court shall, on being satisfied, after hearing the parties and after making such inquiry as it thinks fit, that a marriage has been solemnised and that the averments in the petition are true, pass a decree of divorce declaring the marriage is to be dissolved with effect from the date of the decree.

NO PETITION FOR DIVORCE TO BE PRESENTED WITHIN ONE YEAR OF MARRIAGE

Section 14 of the HMA, 1955 provides that it shall be not competent for any Court to entertain any petition for dissolution of a marriage within one year of marriage with an exception in cases of exceptional hardship or exceptional depravity.

In a recent case of *Sankapl Singh* v. *Prathana Chandra*, 2013 (2) HLR 619, a matter came up before the Delhi High Court as to whether section 14 applies to divorces filed under section 13B, by mutual consent and whether section 13B shall be construed to be an exception under the proviso of section 14. It was also contended in the case that since in a petition for divorce by mutual consent no allegations are made out against each other by the parties to the marriage, it will be difficult to prove the case of exceptional hardship or exceptional depravity. While emphasizing on the three conditions to be fulfilled in order to obtain a divorce under section 13B, the court dismissed the petition and the contentions thereof and held:

> *"28. It is not in dispute or doubt that before the proviso to sub-section (1) of section 14 of the said Act can be invoked, a case of exceptional hardship or exceptional depravity has to be made out. Those are the essential ingredients of the proviso. A mutual consent divorce petition envisages no allegation against each other. In fact, the settlement arrived at inter se the parties in the mediation proceedings also emphasized this aspect. However, in our view this cannot exclude the parties to jointly set forth the exceptional hardship even if they do not want to make allegations against each other. Exceptional hardships can be set out either in the application filed under the proviso to sub-section (1) of section 14 of the said Act or the same can be enclosed in a sealed cover by the parties for the benefit of the Court and the Court would have to satisfy itself whether the parameters of such exceptional hardship are satisfied for invoking the provisions of proviso of sub-section (1) of section 14 of the said Act before such an application can be entertained.*
>
> *29. Let us suppose that the trial court/Family Court is satisfied about a case of exceptional hardships, what would be the sequitur. We have already held that there is an element of essential ingredient of there being a lapse of separation*

of one (1) year for entertaining a petition under sub-section (1) of section 13B of the said Act. There is also an essential ingredient of six (6) months period between the first motion and the second motion under sub-section (2) of section 13B of the said Act. We are also conscious of the objective of introduction of section 13B of the said Act which was to permit divorce by mutual consent rather than throw mud on each other irrespective of who is at fault. If we apply the strict parameters the result would be that a party by making an allegation against the other would be able to present a petition before the expiry of one (1) year of the marriage but if a mutual consent divorce is sought, it would not be permissible.

30. A more liberal construction can envisage the application of the proviso to section 14(1) of the said Act without compromising on the essential ingredients of section 13B(1) of the said Act. This is possible by ensuring that none of the three essential ingredients are compromised. Thus, parties should have been living separately for one (1) year or more, that they have not been able to live together and have mutually agreed that the marriage should be dissolved. However, the dissolution of marriage has to take effect only after the hiatus period of six (6) to eighteen (18) months, on the second motion being filed. Thus, before such a decree of divorce is passed post second motion the period of one (1) year of separation ought to have elapsed but in order to present the first motion, the requirement of one (1) year separation would not apply provided it meets the parameters of proviso to section 14 (1) of the said Act. This view would not compromise on the essential ingredients of any part of section 13B of the said Act and simultaneously respect the wisdom of the legislature which enacted section 13B of the said Act and incorporated it by insertion with sub-section (1) beginning with "Subject to the provisions of this Act" which would include section 14. Not only that section 14 of the said Act itself begins with a "Notwithstanding" clause. This would, thus, be the harmonious construction of the provisions of the said Act which would enable to give meaning to all the relevant provisions of the said Act without compromising the ingredients of any. Such a course of action is possible especially because there will not be a waiver of minimum six (6) months hiatus period between the grant of first motion and the second motion being presented with the additional condition under section 13B (1) of the said Act that even if the first motion is presented within the first year of marriage as per the satisfaction of proviso to section 14(1) of the said Act, the decree of divorce would only be granted once the period of one (1) year has elapsed from the separation."

Hence, the bar of section 14 applies even in cases of divorce by mutual consent under section 13B of the Hindu Marriage Act, 1955.

JURISDICTION AND PROCEDURE FOR OBTAINING DIVORCE – COURT TO WHICH THE PETITION SHALL BE PRESENTED

Section 19 of the HMA, 1955 stipulates that every petition under the Act shall be presented to the district court within the local limits of its ordinary original civil jurisdiction where—

'(i) the marriage was solemnised, or

(ii) the respondent, at the time of the presentation of the petition, resides, or

(iii) the parties to the marriage last resided together, or

(iv) the petitioner is residing at the time of the presentation of the petition, in a case where the respondent is, at that time, residing outside the territories to which this Act extends, or has not been heard of as being alive for a period of seven years or more by those persons who would naturally have heard of him if he were alive.'

CONTENTS AND VERIFICATION OF PETITIONS

Section 20(1) stipulates that every petition presented under this Act shall state as distinctly as the nature of the case permits, the facts on which the claim to relief is founded [except in a petition for a void marriage] and that there is no collusion between the petitioner and the other party to the marriage.

Section 20(2) of the HMA, 1955 further states that the statements contained in every petition under this Act shall be verified by the petitioner or some other competent person, in the manner required by law for the verification of plaints, and may at the hearing, be referred to as evidence.

Divorce proceedings are governed by the Indian Code of Civil Procedure (see section 21 of the HMA, 1955).

CONSIDERATIONS TO BE FOLLOWED BY THE COURT BEFORE GRANTING THE DIVORCE DECREE

In terms of section 23 of the HMA, 1955 the Court is duty bound to consider the following issues before granting the decree of divorce:

(1) that the petitioner is not taking advantage of his or her own wrong or disability;

(2) that the petitioner has not connived at or condoned the acts complained of or where the ground of the petition is cruelty, the petitioner has not in any manner condoned the cruelty;

(bb) when a divorce is being sought on the ground of mutual consent, such consent has not been obtained by force, fraud or undue influence;

(2) that there is no collusion between the parties;

(3) that there is no unnecessary or improper delay in presenting the petition;

(4) that there is no legal ground as to why relief should not be granted.

In terms of section 23(2) the court must endeavour to bring about a reconciliation between the parties before granting divorce. The court may order the respondent to make maintenance *pendente lite* and expenses of the proceedings (section 24) or subsequently permanent alimony and maintenance (section 25). The court may make any order regarding custody, maintenance and education of the minor children, consistent with their wishes (section 26). The court may make such provisions in the decree as it deems just and proper with respect to any property presented, at or about the time of marriage, which may belong jointly to both the husband and the wife (section 27). Section 28 of the Act states that all decrees made by the District or the High Court under the Act, shall be appealable as decrees of the court made in the exercise of its original civil jurisdiction on all points except costs to the parties. Section 28(A) of the Act provides that all decrees and orders made by the court in any proceeding under this Act shall be enforced like any other decree or order made by the court in the exercise of its original civil jurisdiction.

In *Ashok Kumar Jain* v. *Sumati Jain,* AIR 2013 SC 2916, it was held by the Apex Court that it is always open to the Court to examine whether the person seeking divorce *"is not in anyway taking advantage of his or her own wrong or disability for the purpose of such relief."* On such examination, if it is so found that the person is taking advantage of his or her own wrong or disability, it is open to the Court to refuse to grant relief. In the case at hand, the Supreme Court upheld the findings of the Courts below that the husband was not only cruel to the wife, but also brought the situation to a point where the wife had no option but to leave the matrimonial home. Thus, the Apex Court upheld the findings that the husband was taking advantage of his own wrong and was not entitled to the relief of divorce sought by him.

DUTY OF COURT TO ENCOURAGE GENUINE SETTLEMENT OF MATRIMONIAL DISPUTES

In a remarkable judgment, *B.S. Joshi* v. *State of Haryana,* 2003 (4) SCC 675, the apex court emphasised the need of the hour, *i.e.,* the inherent duty of the court to encourage genuine settlements of matrimonial disputes. Justice Y.K. Sabharwal tersely conveyed this message in paragraphs 2, 12 and 13 respectively, at pages 678 and 682 of the judgment as follows:

'2. *The question that falls for determination in the instant case is about the ambit of the inherent powers of the High Courts under section 482 of the Code of Criminal Procedure (the Code) read with articles 226 and 227 of the Constitution of India to quash criminal proceedings. The scope and ambit of power under section 482 has been examined by this Court in a catena of earlier decisions but in the present case that is required to be considered in relation to matrimonial disputes. The matrimonial disputes of the kind in the present case have been on considerable increase in recent times resulting in filing of complaints by the wife under sections 498A and 406, IPC not only against the husband but his other family members also. When such matters are resolved either by the wife agreeing to rejoin the matrimonial home or mutual separation of husband and wife and also mutual settlement of other pending disputes as a result whereof both sides approach the High Court and jointly pray for quashing of the criminal proceedings or the first information report or complaint filed by the wife under sections 498A and 406, IPC, can the prayer be declined on the ground that since the offences are non-compoundable under section 320 of the Code, therefore, it is not permissible for the court to quash the criminal proceedings or FIR or complaint ...*

12. *The special features in such matrimonial matters are evident. It becomes the duty of the court to encourage genuine settlements of matrimonial disputes.*

13. *The observations made by this Court, though in a slightly different context, in* G.V. Rao *v.* L.H.V. Prasad, *(2000) 3 SCC 693 are very apt for determining the approach required to be kept in view in a matrimonial dispute by the courts. It was said that there has been an outburst of matrimonial disputes in recent times. Marriage is a sacred ceremony, the main purpose of which is to enable the young couple to settle down in life and live peacefully. But little matrimonial skirmishes suddenly erupt which often assume serious proportions resulting in commission of heinous crimes in which elders of the family are also involved with the result that those who could have counselled and brought about rapprochement are rendered helpless on their being arrayed as accused in the criminal case. There are many other reasons which need not be mentioned here for not encouraging matrimonial litigation so that the parties may ponder over their defaults and terminate their disputes amicably by mutual agreement instead of fighting it out in a court of law where it takes years and years to conclude and in that process the parties lose their 'young' days in chasing their 'cases' in different courts.'*

Noticeably, the court has itself highlighted the problem of delays in fighting bitter legal matrimonial battles in District Courts, where the couples literally waste the best years of their life. This is especially the situation where adamant parties to the litigation contest divorce proceedings on the fault grounds. This is also a true acceptance of undue delays in Indian courts where matrimonial cases are known to linger on because of different reasons responsible for the same.

In a recent decision on July 2, 2014, in Criminal Appeal No. 1277 of 2014, *Arnesh Kumar* v. *State of Bihar*, the Supreme Court issued comprehensive directions in a measure to check the misuse of the provisions of section 498A, IPC and the provisions of the Dowry Prohibition Act, 1961, by holding as follows:

"(1) *All the State Governments to instruct its police officers not to automatically arrest when a case under section 498A of the IPC is registered but to satisfy themselves about the necessity for arrest under the parameters laid down above flowing from section 41, Cr.PC;*

(2) *All police officers be provided with a check list containing specified sub-clauses under section 41(1)(b)(ii);*

(3) *The police officer shall forward the check list duly filed and furnish the reasons and materials which necessitated the arrest, while forwarding/producing the accused before the Magistrate for further detention;*

(4) *The Magistrate while authorising detention of the accused shall peruse the report furnished by the police officer in terms aforesaid and only after recording its satisfaction, the Magistrate will authorise detention;*

(5) *The decision not to arrest an accused, be forwarded to the Magistrate within two weeks from the date of the institution of the case with a copy to the Magistrate which may be extended by the Superintendent of police of the district for the reasons to be recorded in writing;*

(6) *Notice of appearance in terms of section 41A of Cr.PC be served on the accused within two weeks from the date of institution of the case, which may be extended by the Superintendent of Police of the District for the reasons to be recorded in writing;*

(7) *Failure to comply with the directions aforesaid shall apart from rendering the police officers concerned liable for departmental action, they shall also be liable to be punished for contempt of court to be instituted before High Court having territorial jurisdiction.*

(8) *Authorising detention without recording reasons as aforesaid by the judicial Magistrate concerned shall be liable for departmental action by the appropriate High Court.*

We hasten to add that the directions aforesaid shall not only apply to the cases under section 498A of the I.P.C. or section 4 of the Dowry Prohibition Act, the case in hand, but also such cases where offence is punishable with imprisonment for a term which may be less than seven years or which may extend to seven years; whether with or without fine."

It is hoped and anticipated that in true and effective implementation of the above mandate, both Courts and Police officers will make a serious endeavor to prevent the wrongful use of the above provisions so that marital harmony can be preserved and spouses or extended family members are not dragged into undesirable use of process of criminal law.

In *K. Srinivas Rao* v. *D.A. Deepa*, AIR 2013 SC 2176, the Apex Court had also issued comprehensive directions for resolution of matrimonial disputes and amicable settlement which may be reproduced as hereunder for ready reference:

(a) *"In terms of section 9 of the Family Courts Act, the Family Court shall make all efforts to settle the matrimonial disputes through mediation. Even if the Counsellors submit a failure report, the Family Courts shall, with the consent of the parties, refer the matter to the mediation centre. In such a case, however, the Family Court shall set a reasonable time limit for mediation centre to complete the process of mediation because otherwise the resolution of the disputes by the Family Court may get delayed. In a given case, if there is good chance of settlement, the Family Court in its discretion, can always extend the time limit.*

(b) *The criminal courts dealing with the complaint under section 498A of the Indian Penal Code should, at any stage and particularly, before they take up the complaint for hearing, refer the parties to mediation centre if they feel that there exist elements of settlement and both the parties are willing. However, they should take care to see that in this exercise, rigour, purport and efficacy of section 498A of the Indian Penal Code is not diluted. Needless to say that the discretion to grant or not to grant bail is not in any way curtailed by this direction. It will be for the concerned court to work out the modalities taking into consideration the facts of each case.*

(c) *All mediation centres shall set up pre-litigation desks/clinics; give them wide publicity and make efforts to settle matrimonial disputes at pre-litigation stage."*

It may be stated that the above laudable guidelines will serve a very effective purpose in resolving matrimonial disputes and in putting an end to offences punishable under section 498A, IPC if in appropriate cases parties settle their matters through mediation. Moreover, putting together broken homes will help children and families to be saved from living apart and being raised without the love, affection of both parents together jointly.

SAVINGS AND REPEALS

Chapter VI primarily comprises the savings clause, which is very important as besides other things it gives statutory recognition to customary marriages and divorces. This aspect of the matter is very important as far as a certain category of Indian immigrants are concerned, who have migrated abroad from parts of rural India, and have subsequently remarried after divorcing their Indian wives by pleading customary divorce. Before permanent settlement can be obtained by the Indian immigrant, who has subsequently remarried a girl of foreign origin and extraction, the immigration authorities want to be satisfied about the legal validity of the customary divorce obtained in India. There are certain principles regarding the validity of the custom, before it can be applied. The custom must be ancient, certain and reasonable. It is very important to note that custom has to be pleaded and proved and must be a settled practice in the community of the parties pleading the same.

Section 29 of the HMA, 1955, is reproduced hereunder for ready reference:

> '29. *Savings.*—(1) A marriage solemnised between Hindus before the commencement of this Act, which is otherwise valid, shall not be deemed to be invalid or ever to have been invalid by reason only of the fact that the parties thereto belonged to the same gotra or pravara or belonged to different religions, castes or sub-divisions of the same caste.
>
> (2) Nothing contained in this Act shall be deemed to affect any right recognised by custom or conferred by any special enactment to obtain the dissolution of a Hindu marriage, whether solemnised before or after the commencement of this Act.
>
> (3) Nothing contained in this Act shall affect any proceeding under any law for the time being in force for declaring any marriage to be null and void or for annulling or dissolving any marriage or for judicial separation pending at the commencement of this Act, and any such proceeding may be continued and determined as if this Act had not been passed.
>
> (4) Nothing contained in this Act shall be deemed to affect the provisions contained in the Special Marriage Act, 1954 (43 of 1954) with respect to marriages between Hindus solemnised under that Act, whether before or after the commencement of this Act.'

CUSTOMARY DIVORCE

Section 29 of the HMA, 1955 gives statutory recognition to customary divorce. But the party relying on a custom needs to prove the existence of such a custom. Also, such a custom should be ancient, certain, reasonable and not opposed to public policy. The Madras High Court in *P. Mariamonia* v. *Padmanabham,* AIR 2001 Mad 350, overruled the trial court finding that there cannot be customary divorce after the HMA, 1955 came into force. It was categorically held that customary divorce was recognised both before and after passing of the HMA,

1955 and the courts also uphold such a custom if it is not opposed to public policy. It was further held that since such customs are saved under section 29(1) of the HMA, 1955, it is not necessary for the parties in such a case to go to court to obtain divorce on grounds recognised by custom.

COURTS CAN TAKE JUDICIAL NOTICE OF GENERAL CUSTOMS

The Punjab and Haryana High Court in *Ranbir Kaur* alias *Harjit Kaur* v. *Gurnam Singh*, 1996 (2) HLR 71, held that the courts can take judicial notice of general customs. The court elaborated that the term 'general custom' is used in the sense that it has by repeated recognition by courts over a period of time become entitled to judicial notice. Paragraph 8 at page 74 of this judgment crystallizes the law on judicial notice of general customs by consolidating the earlier case-law as follows:

> *'8. Whoever sets up a custom must prove the same. Sometimes the custom is recognised by Courts and it passes into the law of the land. This question was considered by the Supreme Court in the case of* Ujagar Singh *v.* Mst. Jeo, *AIR 1959 SC 1041. In paragraph 14 it was held:—*
>
> > *"14. It therefore appears to us that the ordinary rule is that all customs, general or otherwise, have to be proved. Under section 57 of the Evidence Act however nothing need to be proved of which courts can take judicial notice. Therefore, it is said that if there is a custom of which the courts can take judicial notice, it need not be proved. The circumstances in which the courts can take judicial notice of a custom were stated by Lord Dunedin in* Raja Ram Rao *v.* Raja of Pittapur, *45 Ind App 148 (154, 155): AIR 1918 PC 81 (83), in the following words, 'When a custom or usage, whether in regard to a tenure or a contract or a family right, is repeatedly brought to the notice of the Courts of a country, the Courts may hold that custom or usage to be introduced into the law without necessity of proof in each individual case.' When a custom has been so recognised by the courts, it passes into the law of the land and the proof of it then becomes unnecessary under section 57(1) of the Evidence Act. It appears to us that in the courts in the Punjab the expression 'general custom' has really been used in this sense, namely, that a custom has by repeated recognition by courts, become entitled to judicial notice as was said in* Bawa Singh *v.* Mt. Taro, *AIR 1951 Punj 239; and* Sukhwant Kaur *v.* Balwant Singh, *AIR 1951 Punj 242."'*

Emphasizing that Karewa form of marriage is *"a social response to bring respectability to a widow through remarriage for which elaborate ceremonies are unnecessary"*, the Punjab and Haryana High Court in a erudite verdict rendered by Justice K. Kannan in *Darbara Singh* v. *Jaswant Kaur*, 2014 (1) RCR (Civil) 1004, with the aid of diligent research, very ably expounded the background and concept of Karewa marriage, which can be best relied upon by quoting the relevant extract from the judgment itself reading as follows:

> *"6. Any customary rite as spoken to by witnesses shall be taken as sufficient proof of marriage. We should indeed push for an agenda that approves of minimum formalities so long as the society recognizes them as sufficient. If*

after the ceremonies, however informal and modest they were, the man and woman lived together as husband and wife that itself ought to be taken as sufficient. Every State has responded in its own way to approve of expression of intentions as sufficient to supplant elaborate ceremonies. In Tamil Nadhu, the suya mariyada *(self-respect) was statutorily recognized by an amendment to the Hindu Marriage Act in 1967. In Punjab, it is* karewa *form which is the approved form of remarriage of a widow. Even a legislation legitimizing remarriage of widows will obtain its full value only if it approves of minimal ceremonies accompanying such functions as sufficient to validate the marriage. It will be abominable to look for ceremonies like* saptapati, *a la brahminical form, to legitimise a customary form of marriage prevalent among jat sikhs. Section 7(2) shall be construed to include any minimal ceremony, sans religiosity, so long as it is acceptable to the community. Available literature on the subject suggests that Widow re-marriage in the* karewa *form prevalent in Punjab is known 'as a marriage by a widow with the brother or some other male relative of her deceased husband and requires no religious ceremonies and confers all the rights of a valid marriage' (underlining mine; see 38 P.R. 1879; 316 of 1879; 26 P.R. 1880; 36 P.R. 1881; 48 P.R. 1890; 98 P.R. 1890; 54 P.R. 1900 - reproduced from punjabrevenue.nic.in). In the book Haryana: Past and Present by Suresh K. Sharma (Mittal Publications, 2006), it is stated (at page 45) "Karewa or a widow marrying one of the brothers of her deceased husband is known among the Jats, Ahirs, Gujars and Harijans is un-accompanied by ceremonies of any kind. The woman merely resumes her jewels and coloured clothes which, he had ceased to wear on her husband's death. Sometimes, there is a public ceremony to give it a sanctimonious touch; generally living together is held to constitute karewa." In Women and Social Reform in Modern India: A Reader by Sumit Sarkar, and Tanika Sarkar, (Indiana University Press, 2008), the authors state: "The agrarian needs which allowed bride price also sanctified widow-remarriage. Like the former, this was also a feature which the agriculturist castes shared in common with the lower castes. However, the custom of widow-remarriage as followed here had special features of its own. Known as* karewa, karao, *or* chaddal andazi, *the custom was a throw back to the old Rig-vedic niyog (levirate marriage) which was prevalent in the geographical region of Haryana-Punjab and associated with the early vedic Aryan settlements.* Karewa, *a white sheet coloured at the corners, was thrown by the man over the widow's head signifying his acceptance of her as his wife. This custom represented social consent for cohabitation. There could be certain variations. For example, it could take the form of placing* churis *(glass bangles) on the widow's wrist in full assembly and sometimes even a gold* nath *(nose ring) in her nose and a red sheet over her head with a rupee tied in one of its corners. This could be followed by the distribution of* gur *(jaggery) or sweets. Significantly, this form of marriage was not accompanied by any kind of religious ceremony, as no woman could be customarily married twice, that is, go through the ceremony of* biah *(religious wedding). After* Karewa *the widow merely resumed her jewels and coloured clothes which she had ceased to wear on her husband's death. So much so sometimes mere cohabitation was considered sufficient to legitmize the relationship and it conferred all the rights of a valid marriage. [(underlining mine). Reference sourced to C.I. Tupper, The Punjab Customary Law (Calcutta: Government Printing 1881) Vol. 2, pp. 93, 123) See also E. Joseph, Customary Law of the Rohtak District, 1910 (Lahore: Govt. Printing, 1911), p. 45]. If witnesses have spoken about the ceremonies, we shall not be looking towards elaborate forms to render invalid a lawful relationship. In this case, there was enough evidence of such customary practices as government texts and Punjabi (and Haryanvi as well) literature admit of."*

It is further pertinent to mention that Karewa marriage is just one of the many forms of customary marriages, but as a matter of fact customary marriages in India vary within different communities and regionally as well. *Karewa* marriage was defined way back by Sir W.H. Rattigan [in W.H. Rattigan *A Digest of Customary Law* (Allahabad: University Book Agency, 15th Edn., revised by Prakash Aggarawala, with a foreword by Dr. Bakshi Tek Chand, 1989) para 75 of Chapter 5], before the partition of India took place, as follows:

'A "Karewa" *marriage with the brother or some other male relative of the deceased husband requires no religious ceremonies, and confers all the rights of a valid marriage.'*

Thus, to sum up, it can be stated that the onus of proving and establishing a custom would lie on the party who claims its benefit. Whether it is to be taken judicial notice of or it is to be proved separately, would depend upon the facts and circumstances of each case. It may be added that in the northern Indian State of Punjab, customary divorce and subsequent re-marriage is an acceptable customary practice in some local communities. A Digest of Customary Law (in Punjab) (*supra*) authored by Sir W.H. Rattigan way back in 1880 and reprinted subsequently by other authors, discusses in great detail customary law practices prevalent in the Punjab in all walks of life. The now available reprinted edition (1995) in Chapter V specifically reports and discusses known prevalent customary practices of Marriage and Divorce in different classes and communities in the State of Punjab.

RESTITUTION OF CONJUGAL RIGHTS AND JUDICIAL SEPARATION

Section 9 of the HMA, 1955 provides for restitution of conjugal rights. Section 9 states that when either the husband or the wife has, without reasonable excuse, withdrawn from the society of the other, the aggrieved party may apply, by petition to the district court, for restitution of conjugal rights and the court, on being satisfied of the truth of the statements made in such petition and that there is no legal ground why the application should not be granted, may decree restitution of conjugal rights accordingly.

Section 10 of the HMA, 1955 talks of judicial separation. It states that either party to a marriage, whether solemnised before or after the commencement of this Act, may present a petition praying for a decree for judicial separation on any of the grounds specified in section 13(1) of the HMA, 1955, as reproduced above and in the case of a wife also on any of the grounds specified in section 13(2) thereof, as grounds on which a petition for divorce might have been presented.

Section 10(2) further states that where a decree for judicial separation has been passed, it shall no longer be obligatory for the petitioner to cohabit with the respondent, but the court may, on the application by petition of either party and on being satisfied of the truth of the statements made in such petition, rescind the decree if it considers it just and reasonable to do so.

NULLITY OF MARRIAGE

A void marriage is one which cannot be enforced by either of the parties to the marriage. A voidable marriage is one which can be avoided at the option of either of the parties to the marriage and, until it is done so, it remains a valid marriage for all purposes. Section 11 of the HMA, 1955 provides the grounds for void marriages. Section 12 of the Act lays down grounds for voidable marriages. Both the sections are reproduced hereunder for ready reference:

VOID MARRIAGES

Section 11 of the Act states that any marriage solemnised after the commencement of the Act shall be null and void and may, on a petition presented by either party thereto against the other party, be so declared by a decree of nullity if it contravenes any one of the conditions specified in clauses (i), (iv) and (v) of section 5 of the HMA, 1955.

VOIDABLE MARRIAGES

Section 12(1) of the HMA, 1955 states that any marriage solemnised, whether before or after the commencement of the Act, shall be voidable and may be annulled by a decree of nullity on any of the following grounds, namely:

'*(a) that the marriage has not been consummated owing to the impotence of the respondent; or*

(b) that the marriage is in contravention of the condition specified in clause (ii) of section 5 of the HMA, 1955; or

(c) that the consent of the petitioner, or the consent of the guardian in marriage of the petitioner was obtained by fraud. Consent of the guardian was required under section 5 as it stood immediately before the commencement of the Child Marriage Restraint (Amendment) Act, 1978 (2 of 1978).

(d) that the respondent was at the time of the marriage pregnant by some person other than the petitioner.'

TIME-LIMITS FOR PRESENTING A NULLITY PETITION

Section 12(2) of the HMA, 1955 imposes time-limits for instituting a nullity petition, which reads as follows:

> '*12(2) Notwithstanding anything contained in sub-section (1), no petition for annulling a marriage—*
>
> *(a) on the ground specified in clause (c) of sub-section (1) shall be entertained if—*
>
> *(i) the petition is presented more than one year after the force had ceased to operate or, as the case may be, the fraud had been discovered; or*
>
> *(ii) the petitioner has, with his or her full consent, lived with the other party to the marriage as husband or wife after the force had ceased to operate or, as the case may be, the fraud had been discovered;*

(b) on the ground specified in clause 12(1)(d) shall be entertained unless the court is satisfied—

(i) that the petitioner was at the time of the marriage ignorant of the facts alleged;

(ii) that proceedings have been instituted in the case of a marriage solemnised before the commencement of this Act within one year of such commencement and in the case of marriages solemnised after such commencement within one year from the date of the marriage; and

(iii) that marital intercourse with the consent of the petitioner has not taken place since the discovery by the petitioner of the existence of the said ground.'

Sections 11 and 12 came up for interpretation by the Supreme Court of India in *Yamunabai* v. *Anantrao,* AIR 1988 SC 644. In this case, the apex Court also elaborated upon the distinction between void and voidable marriages. Paragraph 3 of the judgment at page 647 in this regard is reproduced below:

'... *The marriages covered by section 11 are* void ipso jure, *that is, void from the very inception, and have to be ignored as not existing in law at all if and when such a question arises. Although the section permits a formal declaration to be made on the presentation of a petition, it is not essential to obtain in advance such a formal declaration from a court in a proceeding specifically commenced for the purpose. The provisions of section 16, which is quoted below, also throw light on this aspect:*

"16. Legitimacy of children of void and voidable marriages.—

Notwithstanding that a marriage is null and void under section 11, any child of such marriage who would have been legitimate if the marriage had been valid, shall be legitimate, whether such child is born before or after the commencement of the Marriage Laws (Amendment) Act, 1976 (68 of 1976), and whether or not a decree of nullity is granted in respect of that marriage under this Act and whether or not the marriage is held to be void otherwise than on a petition under this Act.

(2) Where a decree of nullity is granted in respect of a voidable marriage under section 12, any child begotten or conceived before the decree is made, who would have been the legitimate child of the parties to the marriage if at the date of the decree it had been dissolved instead of being annulled, shall be deemed to be their legitimate child notwithstanding the decree of nullity.

(3) Nothing contained in sub-section (1) or sub-section (2) shall be construed as conferring upon any child of a marriage which is null and void or which is annulled by a decree of nullity under section 12, any rights in or to the property of any person, other than the parents, in any case where but for the passing of this Act, such child would have been incapable of possessing or acquiring any such rights by reason of his not being the legitimate child of his parents."' (Emphasis added).

Sub-section (1), by using the words italicised above, clearly implies that a void marriage can be held to be so without a prior formal declaration by a court in a proceeding. While dealing with cases covered by section 12, sub-section (2) refers to a decree of nullity as an essential condition and sub-section (3) prominently brings out the basic difference in the character of void and voidable marriages as covered respectively by sections 11 and 12. It is also to be seen that while the legislature has considered it advisable to uphold the legitimacy of the paternity of a child born out of a void marriage, it has not extended a similar protection in respect of the mother of the child. The marriage of the appellant must, therefore, be treated as null and void from its very inception.

However, it may be added that in *Deoki Panjhiyara* v. *Shashi Bhushan Narayan Azad*, AIR 2013 SC 346, it has been held that *"though the law specifically does not cast obligation on either party to seek declaration of nullity of marriage and it may be open to the parties even without recourse to the Court to treat the marriage as a nullity, such a course is neither prudent nor intended and a declaration in terms of section 11 of the Hindu Marriage Act, 1955 will have to be asked for, for the purpose of precaution and /or record. Therefore, until the declaration contemplated by section 11 of the Hindu Marriage Act, 1955 is made by a competent Court, the woman with whom the second marriage is solemnized continues to be the wife within the meaning of section 494, Indian Penal Code and would be entitled to maintain a complaint against her husband."*

Therefore, it may be stated that seeking a declaration of nullity of marriage, both in a void or voidable marriage, may not only be advisable but would also be a legal necessity to settle the rights of parties. Particularly when a second marriage is contracted during the validity of a first marriage which may be stated to be a void or a voidable marriage. In the above case, the Apex Court had accordingly held that *"until the invalidation of the marriage between the Appellant and the Respondent is made by a competent Court, it would only be correct to proceed on the basis that the Appellant continues to be the wife of the Respondent so as to entitle her to claim all benefits and protection available under the Protection of Women from Domestic Violence Act, 2005."*

LEGITIMACY OF CHILDREN OF VOID AND VOIDABLE MARRIAGES

Section 16 of the HMA, 1955 above lays down the provisions for legitimacy of children of void and voidable marriages. These provisions confer legitimacy and all succession rights even on children of void marriages. In this regard, the law laid down by the Supreme Court of India in *Rameshwari Devi* v. *State of Bihar*, (2000) 2 SCC 431 may be quoted in support. In this particular case a Hindu government employee had contracted a second marriage during the subsistence of his first marriage. There were children born out of the second marriage. Although, the second marriage itself was void, the children born out of the second marriage were held to be legitimate and also entitled to family pension.

It may further be added that the Supreme Court of India in *P.E.K. Kalliani Amma* v. *K. Devi*, AIR 1996 SC 1963, clearly laid down that the provisions of section 16(1) which intend to confer legitimacy on children born of void marriages will operate with full vigor in spite of section 11 which nullifies only those marriages which are concluded after the enforcement of the Act and in the performance of which section 5 is contravened. Therefore, Indian law does not discriminate against children and by a legal fiction they are treated as legitimate notwithstanding that the marriage was void or voidable.

In the case of *General Manager, Southern Railway, Chennai* v. *R. Thangaraja*, 2012 (2) MLJ 720, where the lower courts had held such son to be legitimate under section 16(1), the question which arose in an appeal before the Madras High Court was *whether under section 16(l) of the Hindu Marriage Act, 1955, a Court can legitimize a son, born before the marriage of his parents, when the first marriage of the father of the child with another person, was subsisting, when the child was born.* Setting aside the judgments and decrees of the lower courts, the High Court held that such status of "legitimate children" under the said section is conferred only in the case where there is void or voidable marriage and not in the case where there is no marriage, at all. Confirming the same to be in accordance with the intention of the legislation, the court observed:

> *"49. In* **Jinia Keotin v. Kumar Sitaram Manjhi,** *(supra), while considering the interpretation to section 16 of the Hindu Marriage Act, 1955 and having regard to the Court's limited power, at paragraph 5, the Supreme Court held that under the guise of interpretation, the Court cannot re-legislate on the subject against the will expressed in the enactment. As stated supra, the intention of the legislature in engrafting a rule of legal fiction in ordaining the children, though illegitimate, to be treated as legitimate, is confined only to a case, where there is a void or voidable marriage and not in the case, where there is no marriage at all. It is also settled legal position, while interpreting a provision, the Court cannot re-legislate on the subject against the will expressed in the enactment.*
>
> *50. In the light of the discussion and decisions stated supra, this Court, on the facts and circumstances of this case, is of the view that both the Courts below have erred in applying section 16(1) of the Hindu Marriage Act, 1955, in declaring the legitimacy of the child born to the plaintiff and K. Mohanambal, not through a wedlock and during the subsistence of the first marriage of the plaintiff. Both the substantial questions of law are decided in favour of the appellant. The judgments and decrees of the lower Courts are set aside and the second appeal is allowed. No costs."*

In the recent case of *Revanasiddappa* v. *Mallikarjun*, (2011) 11 SCC 1, a matter came up before the Apex Court to examine whether the illegitimate children are entitled to a share in the coparcenary property or whether their share is limited only to the self-acquired property of their parents under section 16(3) of the Hindu Marriage Act, 1955. In the present appeal, the court has referred the said matter to a larger bench due to its view different from that of the earlier cases of *Jinia Keotin* v. *Kumar Sitaram Manjhi*, (2003) 1 SCC 730; *Neelamma* v. *Sarojamma*, (2006) 9 SCC 612; and *Bharatha Matha* v. *R. Vijaya Renganathan*, AIR 2010 SC 2685. All these cases held that where an illegitimate child is entitled to a share of his parents, such share must relate to the self-acquired properties and not the ancestral ones.

The Court is of the opinion that these cases represent a narrow view of section 16(3). Also, such entitlement of the illegitimate children in the coparcenary property as well, is in conformity with the article 37 of the Constitution of India and the same is stated below:

"35. In our view, in the case of joint family property such children will be entitled only to a share in their parents' property but they cannot claim it on their own right. Logically, on the partition of an ancestral property, the property falling in the share of the parents of such children is regarded as their self acquired and absolute property. In view of the amendment, we see no reason why such children will have no share in such property since such children are equated under the amended law with legitimate offspring of valid marriage. The only limitation even after the amendment seems to be that during the life time of their parents such children cannot ask for partition but they can exercise this right only after the death of their parents.

36. We are constrained to differ from the interpretation of section 16(3) rendered by this Court in Jinia Keotin *(supra) and, thereafter, in* Neelamma *(supra) and* Bharatha Matha (supra) *in view of the constitutional values enshrined in the preamble of our Constitution which focuses on the concept of equality of status and opportunity and also on individual dignity. The Court has to remember that relationship between the parents may not be sanctioned by law but the birth of a child in such relationship has to be viewed independently of the relationship of the parents. A child born in such relationship is innocent and is entitled to all the rights which are given to other children born in valid marriage. This is the crux of the amendment in section 16(3). However, some limitation on the property rights of such children is still there in the sense their right is confined to the property of their parents. Such rights cannot be further restricted in view of the preexisting common law view discussed above. It is well known that this Court cannot interpret a socially beneficial legislation on the basis as if the words therein are cast in stone. Such legislation must be given a purposive interpretation to further and not to frustrate the eminently desirable social purpose of removing the stigma on such children. In doing so, the Court must have regard to the equity of the Statute and the principles voiced under Part IV of the Constitution, namely, the Directive Principles of State Policy. In our view this flows from the mandate of article 37 which provides that it is the duty of the State to apply the principles enshrined in Chapter IV in making laws. It is no longer in dispute that today State would include the higher judiciary in this country. Considering article 37 in the context of the duty of judiciary, Justice Mathew in* **Kesavananda Bharati Sripadagalvaru** ***v.*** **State of Kerala, *(1973)* 4 *SCC* 225** *held:*

"I can see no incongruity in holding, when article 37 says in its latter part "it shall be the duty of the State to apply these principles in making laws", that judicial process is 'State action' and that the judiciary is bound to apply the Directive Principles in making its judgment."

Hence, the view that when an illegitimate child is entitled to a share of his parents' properties, such share must relate to the self-acquired properties and not the ancestral ones, is now to be adjudicated by a larger Bench of the Apex Court. However, till then the settled view prevails and children will have a right to whatever becomes the property of their parents whether self acquired or ancestral.

PROBLEMS FACED IN CROSS-BORDER MARRIAGES

There are three specific areas in this realm of divorce law which are of main concern to non-resident Indians and their foreign lawyers, *i.e.*, irretrievable breakdown of marriage, divorce by mutual consent and recognition of divorce decrees passed by foreign courts. Validity of foreign divorce decrees is of immense concern to Indian spouses married to NRIs, which issue is discussed in detail in the subsequent portion of this chapter. Only these three areas are being elaborated upon while the rest of the fault grounds, as elaborated above are not being discussed. Of course, desertion and cruelty are also serious major issues in cross-border marriages.

IRRETRIEVABLE BREAKDOWN OF MARRIAGE

A marriage under the provisions of the SMA, 1954 or the HMA, 1955 cannot be dissolved by a decree of divorce on the ground of irretrievable breakdown of marriage. It is not a ground of dissolution of marriage either in section 13 of the HMA, 1955 or section 27 of the SMA, 1954, respectively. Recent Supreme Court judgments are seriously addressing this issue, which has become very relevant because of changing social conditions especially in urban India and metropolitan cities. The irretrievable breakdown ground could be of immense help where either of the spouses is a non-resident Indian or a foreign national and the marriage has not worked out. Obviously, this will depend upon the facts and circumstances of each case. One has to tread with caution. This weapon in the armoury of divorce law, can work as a double-edged sword, facilitating the dumping of spouses from India married to NRIs. One has also to bear in mind that it is very difficult to access social welfare measures in India. Neither are state run pensions disbursed to unemployed or deserted spouses.

The Supreme Court of India has held in *Chetan Dass* v. *Kamla Devi,* (2001) 4 SCC 250, that it is not appropriate to apply the irretrievable breakdown as a straight jacket formula for the grant of relief of divorce. *Chetan Dass* is one of the leading decisions highlighting the legal position in Indian law that breakdown of marriage is not in itself a ground for divorce. It may be a governing factor to be borne in mind at the time of adjudication by the Court. From the catena of leading cases discussed on this issue, it emerges that the irretrievable breakdown principle is a cautious import of judge-made law into family law jurisprudence. But, the rider *'in facts and circumstances of each case'*, firmly continues to be in place.

A few excerpts from the Seventy-first Report of the Law Commission of India on the Hindu Marriage Act, 1955, 'Irretrievable breakdown of marriage', dated 7 April, 1978, have been boldly highlighted in a Supreme Court of India decision, *Ashok Hurra* v. *Rupa Bipin Zaveri*, AIR 1997 SC 1266. The relevant extracts of this Law Commission Report appear in paragraph 23 at pp. 1273–1274 of this judgment and are reproduced below:

> *'Irretrievable breakdown of marriage is now considered, in the laws of a number of countries, good ground of dissolving the marriage by granting a decree of divorce ...*

> *Proof of such a breakdown would be that the husband and wife have separated and have been living apart for, say, a period of five or ten years and it has become impossible to resurrect the marriage or to reunite the parties. It is stated that once it is known that there are no prospects of the success of the marriage, to drag the legal tie acts as cruelty to the spouse and gives rise to crime and even abuse of religion to obtain annulment of marriage ...*
>
> *The theoretical basis for introducing irretrievable breakdown as a ground of divorce is one with which, by now, lawyers and others have become familiar. Restricting the ground of divorce to a particular offence or matrimonial disability, it is urged, causes injustice in those cases where the situation is such that although none of the parties is at fault, or the fault is of such a nature that the parties to the marriage do not want to divulge it, yet there has arisen a situation in which the marriage cannot be worked. The marriage has all the external appearances of marriage, but none of the reality. As is often put pithily, the marriage is merely a shell out of which the substance is gone. In such circumstances, it is stated, there is hardly any utility in maintaining the marriage as a facade, when the emotional and other bounds which are of the essence of marriage have disappeared.*
>
> *After the marriage has ceased to exist in substance and in reality, there is no reason for denying divorce. The parties alone can decide whether their mutual relationship provides the fulfillment which they seek. Divorce should be seen as a solution and an escape route out of a difficult situation. Such divorce is unconcerned with the wrongs of the past, but is concerned with bringing the parties and the children to terms with the new situation and developments by working out the most satisfactory basis upon which they may regulate their relationship in the changed circumstances ...*
>
> *Moreover, the essence of marriage is a sharing of common life, a sharing of all the happiness that life has to offer and all the misery that has to be faced in life, an experience of the joy that comes from enjoying, in common, things of the matter and of the spirit and from showering love and affection on one's offspring. Living together is a symbol of such sharing in all its aspects. Living apart is a symbol indicating the negation of such sharing. It is indicative of a disruption of the essence of marriage "breakdown" and if it continues for a fairly long period, it would indicate destruction of the essence of marriage "irretrievable breakdown".'*

The Supreme Court of India way back in 1985 in *Ms Jorden Diengdeh* v. *S.S. Chopra,* 1985 (2) HLR 199, forcefully made a judicial recommendation for a complete reform of the law of marriage and also for introducing irretrievable breakdown of marriage as a ground for divorce. Justice O. Chinnappa Reddy lamented in the penultimate paragraph of the judgment at p. 207:

> *'It appears to be necessary to introduce irretrievable breakdown of marriage and mutual consent as grounds of divorce in all cases. The case before us is an illustration of a case where the parties are bound together by a marital tie which is better untied. There is no point or purpose to be served by the continuance of a marriage which has so completely and signally broken down. We suggest that the time has come for the intervention of the legislature in these matters to provide*

for a uniform code of marriage and divorce and to provide by law for a way out of the unhappy situations in which couples like the present find themselves in. We direct that a copy of this order may be forwarded to the Ministry of Law and Justice for such action as they may deem fit to take. In the meanwhile, let notice go to the respondents.'

In *Bhagat* v. *Bhagat*, AIR 1994 SC 710, the court held in no uncertain terms in paragraph 23 of the judgment at pp. 720–721:

'... Merely because there are allegations and counter-allegations, a decree of divorce cannot follow. Nor is mere delay in disposal of the divorce proceedings by itself a ground. There must be really some extraordinary features to warrant grant of divorce on the basis of pleadings (and other admitted material) without a full trial. Irretrievable breakdown of the marriage is not a ground by itself. But while scrutinising the evidence on record to determine whether the ground(s) alleged is made out and in determining the relief to be granted, the said circumstance can certainly be borne in mind. The unusual step as the one taken by us herein can be resorted to only to clear up an insoluble mess, when the Court finds it in the interest of both the parties.'

The Supreme Court of India while exercising its inherent powers under article 142 of the Constitution of India in several cases has held that, where the marriage is dead and there is no chance of its retrieval, it is better to bring it to an end. This was also the mandate of law laid down in *Chanderkala Trivedi* v. *Dr. S.P. Trivedi*, 1993 (4) SCC 232.

A similar situation warranting exercise of the apex court's inherent powers arose in *Romesh Chander* v. *Savitri*, AIR 1995 SC 851. In this case the husband and the wife had been litigating for 25 years. The court held in paragraphs 3 and 4 of the judgment at p. 852:

"... In this case the marriage is dead both emotionally and practically. Continuance of marital alliance for name-sake is prolonging the agony and affliction. It cannot be disputed that the husband has not been dutiful and conscious of his responsibilities either towards his wife or his son. He did not contribute any thing towards upbringing of the child. Yet the marriage being dead, the continuance of it would be cruelty, specially when the child born out of the wedlock of the appellant and the respondent as far back as 1968 having now grown and being in service. The appellant has expressed remorse for his conduct and is willing to compensate for his past mistakes by transferring the only house in his name in favour of his wife.

4. Considering the facts and circumstances of this case we, in exercise of power under article 142 of the Constitution of India, direct that the marriage between appellant and the respondent shall stand dissolved subject to the appellant transferring the house in the name of his wife. The house shall be transferred within four months from today. The dissolution shall come into effect from the date the house is transferred and possession is handed over to the respondent."

Similarly, in *Sneh Prabha* v. *Ravinder Kumar*, AIR 1995 SC 2170, the apex court while exercising its powers under article 142 of the Constitution of India, tersely held that where in an appeal against an order confirming the decree of restitution of conjugal rights, despite conciliation and much efforts by the Supreme Court itself, it felt that the marriage of the parties had irretrievably broken down and there were no chances of the husband and wife living together, divorce should be granted. Hence, the Supreme Court granted the divorce.

Furthermore, in *Chetan Dass* v. *Kamla Devi,* (2001) 4 SCC 250, the Supreme Court came down very heavily on an erring adulterous husband. In this case the husband wanted to dump his wife on the ground of desertion. The wife's contention of adultery and the illegitimate relationship of the husband with another woman stood proved before the trial court. The high court upheld these findings and held that, given the circumstances of the case, a decree of divorce on the ground of irretrievable breakdown of marriage could not be granted. The husband contended before the Supreme Court that the marriage had broken down irretrievably and no purpose would be served by prolonging the agony of the parties. The wife was still ready to live with the husband provided he discontinued the adulterous relationship. The court held that the appellant husband alone was to be blamed for such an unhappy and unfortunate situation.

In paragraph 19 at pages 260 and 261 Brijesh Kumar, J. said:

> *'19. In the present case, the allegations of adulterous conduct of the appellant have been found to be correct and the courts below have recorded a finding to the same effect. In such circumstances, in our view, the provisions contained under section 23 of the Hindu Marriage Act, 1955 would be attracted and the appellant would not be allowed to take advantage of his own wrong. Let the things be not misunderstood nor any permissiveness under the law be inferred, allowing an erring party who has been found to be so by recording of a finding of fact in judicial proceedings, that it would be quite easy to push and drive the spouse to a corner and then brazenly take a plea of desertion on the part of the party suffering so long at the hands of the wrongdoer and walk away out of the matrimonial alliance on the ground that the marriage has broken down. Lest the institution of marriage and the matrimonial bonds get fragile easily to be broken which may serve the purpose most welcome to the wrongdoer who, by heart, wished such an outcome by passing on the burden of his wrongdoing to the other party alleging her to be the deserter leading to the breaking point.'*

Brijesh Kumar, J. also distinguished the three earlier Supreme Court cases cited by counsel for the appellant husband. The court was of the considered opinion that the facts of the case in *Chanderkala Trivedi (SMT)* v. *Dr. S.P. Trivedi,* (1993) 4 SCC 232, were peculiar in nature. The court remarked that the factual position in this case was entirely different and hence it had no application to the present case.

Coming to the second case of *Romesh Chander* v. *Savitri,* AIR 1995 SC 851, the court observed that the order in this case was passed considering the facts and circumstances of the case *'in exercise of inherent powers of the Supreme Court under article 142 of the Constitution of India'.*

The third case *Saroj Rani* v. *Sudarshan Kumar Chadha,* (1984) 4 SCC 90, was also found to be inapplicable to the present case. In this case the husband did not obey the decree of restitution of conjugal rights obtained by his wife to which he had initially not objected. But later on, he filed a petition for divorce under section 13(1A)(ii) of the HMA, 1955, on the ground that one year had passed from the date of decree of restitution of conjugal rights but no actual cohabitation had taken place between the parties. The wife raised a plea that the husband was taking advantage of his own wrong in terms of section 23(1)(a) of the HMA, 1955, as he had not resumed his matrimonial relationship even after the decree of restitution of conjugal rights was passed. The court held that the conduct of the husband did not attract section 23(1)(a) of the HMA, 1955. The wife had also alleged maltreatment both by the husband as well as her in-laws. The court observed in paragraph 9 of the judgment in *Saroj Rani's* case:

> '... Furthermore we reach this conclusion without any mental compunction because it is evident that for whatever be the reasons this marriage has broken down and the parties can no longer live together as husband and wife, if such is the situation it is better to close the chapter.'

Hence, the observations in Saroj Rani were not accepted simpliciter as affording divorce on the ground of irretrievable breakdown in the present case of *Chetan Dass* v. *Kamla Devi,* AIR 2001 SC 1709.

In *Savitri Pandey* v. *Prem Chandra Pandey,* (2002) 2 SCC 73, the wife was initially granted divorce by the Family Judge. Cross appeals were filed by both the parties. The high court disposed of both the appeals by setting aside the decree and holding that the appellant wife herself was the guilty party and that she had been unable to prove the allegations of cruelty and desertion. Before the Supreme Court it was argued that the appellant wife had remarried after the decree of divorce was granted by the Family Judge and also a child was born from the subsequent remarriage; the marriage ought to be dissolved in the interest of justice. The court did not sympathise at all with her conduct. The appellant wife was disentitled from claiming divorce on the ground of desertion. The court held that granting divorce to her would result in allowing her to take advantage of her own wrong. The court came down with a heavy hand and held in paragraphs 17 and 18 at pp. 84 and 85 of the judgment as follows:

> *'17. The marriage between the parties cannot be dissolved only on the averments made by one of the parties that as the marriage between them has broken down, no useful purpose would be served to keep it alive. The legislature, in its wisdom, despite observation of this Court has not thought it proper to provide for dissolution of the marriage on such averments. There may be cases where, on facts, it is found that as the marriage has become dead on account of contributory acts of commission and omission of the parties, no useful purpose would be served by keeping such marriage alive. The sanctity of marriage cannot be left at the whims of one of the annoying spouses. This Court in* V. Bhagat *v.* D. Bhagat *held that irretrievable breakdown of the marriage is not a ground by itself to dissolve it.*
>
> *18. As already held, the appellant herself is trying to take advantage of her own wrong and in the circumstances of the case, the marriage between the parties cannot be held to have become dead for invoking the jurisdiction of this Court under article 142 of the Constitution for dissolving the marriage.'*

Hence, it is clear from the enunciation of law laid down by the apex Court above, that under the guise of irretrievable breakdown of marriage, the Supreme Court cannot be asked to invoke its powers under article 142 of the Constitution. Besides, the bar of section 23(1)(a) HMA, 1955 obstructs the grant of such relief. Moreover, in some cases, the policy of law does not seem to be to confer judicial recognition on the principle of irretrievable breakdown of marriage where the Court is of the opinion that it is an abuse or misuse of the due process of law.

The apex Court in this ruling of *Savitri Pandey* v. *Prem Chandra Pandey,* (2002) 2 SCC 73 also distinguished the earlier cases from the facts of the present case in hand. Counsel for the appellant cited the following authorities: *Anita Sabharwal* v. *Anil Sabharwal,* (1997) 1 SCC 490; *Shashi Garg* v. *Arun Garg,* (1997) 7 SCC 565; *Ashok Hurra* v. *Rupa Bipin Zaveri,* (1997) 4 SCC 226; *Madhuri Mehta* v. *Meet Verma,* (1997) 11 SCC 81. The court opined in paragraph 15 at page 84 of the judgment:

> '... *In all the cases relied upon by the appellant and referred to hereinabove, the marriage between the parties was dissolved by a decree of divorce by mutual consent in terms of application under section 13B of the Act. This Court while allowing the applications filed under section 13B took into consideration the circumstances of each case and granted the relief on the basis of compromise. Almost in all cases the other side was duly compensated by the grant of lump sum amount and permanent provision regarding maintenance.*'

The earlier observations of the apex Court in *Jorden Deingdeh* v. *S.S. Chopra,* AIR 1985 SC 935 regarding complete reform of the law of marriage, to make a uniform law applicable to all people irrespective of religion or caste and for introduction of the irretrievable breakdown theory, also finds mention in paragraph16 at page 84 of *Pandey's* judgment.

Another very important issue that arises in this case is that the husband's appeal against the divorce decree was instituted 4 months after the limitation period had expired. Meanwhile, during the pendency of the appeal in the Supreme Court, the wife solemnised a second marriage. The Apex Court declared the second marriage of the appellant wife to be invalid as the same was solemnised during the pendency of appeal. The facts and circumstances of the case are not clear as to whether the wife had received the notice of the appeal before her remarriage. However, the issue that emanates is the time frame to which the parties need to keep a check on the appellate legal recourse. After the divorce decree is granted and the limitation stands expired, before they get remarried, would the parties be required to wait still further? The Apex Court in *Savitri Pandey's* case has recommended to the Ministry of Law and Justice for appropriate changes in the legislation to increase the period of limitation from 30 days to 90 days since 30 days has been held to be insufficient and inadequate for filing the appeal.

In *G.V.N. Kameswara Rao* v. *G. Jabilli,* (2002) 2 SCC 296, the Supreme Court came to the rescue of a highly educated couple who had been unsuccessfully litigating for the last 15 years. The court held that because of the non-cooperation and the hostile attitude of the respondent wife, the appellant husband had been subjected to a serious traumatic experience which could safely be termed as cruelty within the purview of section 13(1)(i-a) of the HMA, 1955. From the evidence on record, the court came to the conclusion that the relationship between the parties had irretrievably broken down. In this case, the main issue was that of mental cruelty inflicted upon the husband, while the court *suo moto* applied the breakdown theory in the facts and circumstances of the case.

Parveen Mehta v. *Inderjit Mehta,* (2002) 5 SCC 706, is another case of a high degree of cruelty inflicted upon the husband. In this case the parties had been living separately for the last 10 years. The marriage took place in the year 1986, while the divorce petition was filed in the year 1996. All frantic compromise efforts failed to calm down the appellant wife. There was a long period of separation between the husband and the wife. The court inferred from the circumstances of the case that the marriage had broken down irretrievably without any fault of the respondent husband. The court concluded that on this ground the decision of the high court in favour of the respondent for the dissolution of the marriage should not be disturbed. Also, a very high degree of cruelty had been inflicted upon the respondent husband by his wife.

Another case where the Supreme Court refused to apply the irretrievable breakdown theory is *Vishnu Dutt Sharma* v. *Manju Sharma,* AIR 2009 SC 2254, where the appellant-husband was proved to have inflicted cruelty upon the respondent-wife. The appeal was preferred to the High court and consequently to the Supreme Court, where it was dismissed. The High court held that it would not be doing justice to the respondent if divorce is granted to the appellant despite his cruelty only on the ground of irretrievable breakdown. The Apex Court, further rejected applying the irretrievable breakdown theory on the ground that section 13 does not provide the same and it is not the function of court to make or amend laws. The concluding paragraphs are as hereunder:

> *"9. In this connection it may be noted that in section 13 of the Hindu Marriage Act, 1955 (for short 'the Act') there are several grounds for granting divorce e.g. cruelty, adultery, desertion etc. but no such ground of irretrievable breakdown of the marriage has been mentioned for granting divorce. Section 13 of the Act reads as under:*
>
> *"13. Divorce.—(1) Any marriage solemnized, whether before or after the commencement of this Act, may, on a petition presented by either the husband or the wife, be dissolved by a decree of divorce on the ground that the other party—*
>
> *(i) has, after the solemnization of the marriage, had voluntary sexual intercourse with any person other than his or her spouse; or*
>
> *(i-a) has, after the solemnization of the marriage, treated the petitioner with cruelty; or*
>
> *(i-b) has deserted the petitioner for a continuous period of not less than two years immediately preceding the presentation of the petition; or*
>
> *(ii) has ceased to be a Hindu by conversion to another religion; or*

(iii) has been incurably of unsound mind, or has been suffering continuously or intermittently from mental disorder of such a kind and to such an extent that the petitioner cannot reasonably be expected to live with the respondent.
xx xx xx
xx xx xx

(iv) has been suffering from a virulent and incurable form of leprosy; or

(v) has been suffering from venereal disease in a communicable form; or

(vi) has renounced the world by entering any religious order; or

(vii) has not been heard of as being alive for a period of seven years or more by those persons who would naturally have heard of it, had that party been alive."

10. On a bare reading of section 13 of the Act, reproduced above, it is crystal clear that no such ground of irretrievable breakdown of the marriage is provided by the legislature for granting a decree of divorce. This Court cannot add such a ground to section 13 of the Act as that would be amending the Act, which is a function of the legislature.

11. Learned counsel for the appellant has stated that this Court in some cases has dissolved a marriage on the ground of irretrievable breakdown. In our opinion, those cases have not taken into consideration the legal position which we have mentioned above, and hence they are not precedents. A mere direction of the Court without considering the legal position is not a precedent. If we grant divorce on the ground of irretrievable breakdown, then we shall by judicial verdict be adding a clause to section 13 of the Act to the effect that irretrievable breakdown of the marriage is also a ground for divorce. In our opinion, this can only be done by the legislature and not by the Court. It is for the Parliament to enact or amend the law and not for the Courts. Hence, we do not find force in the submission of the learned counsel for the appellant."

In a more recent case, *Smt. Seema Kumari* v. *Suniul Kumar Jha,* AIR 2014 Pat 44, the Family court allowed a divorce filed by the respondent in the present case on the ground of irretrievable breakdown of marriage coupled with desertion. The appellant appealed against the said order of the family court on the grounds that the family court had abruptly arrived at the conclusion of desertion by the appellant, without any evidence in its support, and also that irretrievable breakdown of marriage is not a ground for divorce under the Hindu Marriage Act, 1955. On the basis of these, the Patna High Court in present appeal set aside the impugned order. It held that the power to grant divorce on the ground of irretrievable breakdown of marriage lies with the Supreme Court under article 142 of the Constitution and the same is not available to the High Court or the Family Court.

In *Hitesh Bhatnagar* v. *Deepa Bhatnagar,* (2011) 3 SCC 234, when the Apex Court was examining a matrimonial dispute for divorce by mutual consent where the second motion was not made by both the parties, it was held that no Court can pass a decree in violation of section 13B of the HMA, 1955. The Apex Court also declined to use its power under article 142 of the Constitution to hold that the marriage had broken down irretrievably and held that the Apex Court grants a decree of divorce only in those situations in which the Court is convinced beyond any doubt that there is absolutely no chance of the marriage surviving and it is beyond repair. The Court held that *"even if the chances are infinitesimal for the marriage to survive, it is not for this Court to use its power under article 142 to dissolve the marriage as having broken down irretrievably."* Clearly, the Apex Court has propounded a view to rule out use of its powers when not called for.

In *Darshan Gupta* v. *Radhika Gupta,* (2013) 9 SCC 1, the Apex Court was pleased to hold that the claim for divorce cannot be maintained under the HMA, 1955 and the Court declined to exercise its jurisdiction under article 142 of the Constitution as entertaining the plea of irretrievable breakdown of marriage would not constitute and serve the ends of justice. The Apex Court dismissed the appeal of the husband and upheld the decisions declining divorce to him.

In *U. Sree* v. *U. Srinivas,* (2013) 2 SCC 114, the Apex Court affirmed the finding of the Family Court and the High Court relating to mental cruelty as the foundation for grant of divorce. Fixing the permanent alimony at Rs. 50 lacs, the Apex Court affirmed the decree for dissolution of marriage on the ground of mental cruelty.

In *Kollam Chandra Sekhar* v. *Kollam Padma Latha,* (2014) 1 SCC 225, the Apex Court came to be conclusion that even if the wife did suffer from Schizophrenia, the Court cannot grant the dissolution of marriage on the basis of one spouse's illness since mental disorder as alleged had not been proved. Accordingly, the judgment of the High Court in not granting a decree of divorce was upheld and the petition of the wife for grant of a decree for restitution of conjugal rights under section 9 of the HMA, 1955 was allowed.

However, in *Malathi Ravi* v. *B.V. Ravi,* (2014) 7 SCC 640, the Apex Court noticing extreme incompatibility between the parties perpetuated by mental cruelty led the Court to conclude that the marriage has become illusory and that the decree of divorce granted by the High Court deserves to be affirmed. Likewise, in *Vimi V. Chopra v. Vinod G. Chopra,* 2014 (3) RCR (Civil) 959 (SC), where husband and wife had been litigating for long and had arrived at a settlement, were permitted by the Supreme Court to be granted a decree of divorce under section 13B HMA, 1955 by waving the statutory period in order to do complete justice under Article 142 of the Constitution.

From the above stated cases of *G.V.N. Kameswara Rao,* (2002) 2 SCC 296; *Parveen Mehta,* (2002) 5 SCC 706; *U. Sree* v. *U. Srinivas,* (2013) 2 SCC 114, *Malathi Ravi* (2014) 7 SCC 640 and *Vimi V. Chopra* 2014 (3) RCR (Civil) 959, it will be noticed that a high degree of proved inflicted mental cruelty among other attendant circumstances prompted the apex Court to apply the irretrievable breakdown principle. These five judgments, in addition to other cited cases, canvass the fact that the breakdown principle is not applied simpliciter in a mechanical fashion. There is an extreme degree of reluctance on the part of the courts to apply the same. *Chetan Dass,* (2001) 4 SCC 250; *Hitesh Bhatnagar,* (2011) 5 SCC 234; *Darshan Gupta,* (2013) 9 SCC 1, and *Kollam Chandra,* (2014) 1 SCC 225, as discussed above, is a glaring example in this regard. What then is required to be done? The breakdown theory which finds judicial recognition under section 13(1A), HMA, 1955 as an additional ground for divorce on non-resumption of cohabitation after one year of the passing of the decree of judicial separation or restitution of conjugal rights, does not seem to serve the purpose anymore in the current situation. The trend of some recent judgments of the apex Court clearly demonstrates that irretrievable breakdown of marriage itself directly needs to be brought on to the statute book as an additional independent ground for obtaining divorce. This however should be limited only to cases where one or both parties of Hindu religion are non resident Indians. Undoubtedly, it will have to be hedged about with all necessary safeguards and precautionary conditions to prevent hasty divorces and other abrupt attempts at misuse. But, all the same, the time has now come to make it available separately as a ground for divorce in Indian matrimonial law to discourage overseas litigation. This will greatly facilitate parties to settle amicably their matrimonial disputes on Indian soil and prevent them from entering into protracted litigation where allegations and insinuations are hurled freely for achieving a matrimonial victory. Such a legislative change will thus bring relief not only to litigating spouses but also to members of extended families who are invariably involved in the litigation process as a common Indian practice.

The proposal for including *"irretrievable breakdown of marriage"* as a ground for divorce was first made almost three decades ago in the Seventy-first Report of the Law Commission of India and has been included in the grounds for divorce under section 13 of Hindu Marriage Act, 1955 along with the Special Marriage Act, 1954 in the Marriage Laws (Amendment) Bill, 2013, which has not yet been accepted. As per the Report, "the Hindu marriage should be allowed to be dissolved if the husband and wife have lived apart for a period of say five to ten years and the marriage is irretrievably broken down due to incompatibility, clash of personality or similar other reasons, as is permissible under many systems of law of advanced countries." A fresh look is now warranted in the above limited area as suggested by the authors.

FOREIGN MARRIAGE DIVORCE DECREE ON GROUNDS OF IRRETRIEVABLE BREAK DOWN OF MARRIAGE.

Another case relating to the applicability of the irretrievable breakdown theory while granting a decree for divorce is the case of *Rupak Rathi* v. *Anita Chaudhary,* 2014 (2) RCR (Civil) 697. Justice Rajiv Narain Raina of the Punjab and Haryana High court, in an illuminating judgement in this case, extensively dealt with the jurisdiction of the foreign courts regarding the dissolution of a Hindu marriage. The facts of the case are that Rupak Rathi, appellant, instituted divorce proceedings against his wife, Anita Chaudhary, in UK on March 17, 2011. During the pendency of these proceedings, Anita Chaudhary instituted the proceedings for divorce in Panchkula on May 17, 2011 and the UK proceedings were acknowledged before the court in Panchkula. Both the proceedings ran parallel. Proceedings in the English Court were concluded absolutely on January 31, 2012 and the divorce was granted in favour of the husband on the ground of irretrievable breakdown of marriage. In response to the divorce petition by the wife at Panchkula, on July 18, 2012, the husband responded before the Matrimonial Court in Panchkula for rejecting the divorce proceedings against him on the ground that the divorce decree of the English Court is binding on both the parties and hence, the divorce petition by wife was barred on the principles of *res judicata* and *estoppel*. However, the wife contended that the English Courts have no jurisdiction to pass a decree on an unavailable ground of irretrievable breakdown of marriage under the Hindu Marriage Act, 1955 and since both the parties were domiciled in India, they were to be governed by the Hindu Law. The High Court finally held that the English court cannot grant such divorce decree as irretrievable breakdown of marriage was not a ground of divorce in the Hindu Marriage Act, 1955 itself, which governs the parties in the present case. The High Court accordingly held:

> *" 17. A close analysis of para. 20 leaves no manner of doubt that the major premise or what we may call the rule which is clearly statutory in nature with reference to both section 13, CPC and section 13, HMA, 1955, that if a foreign Court enters upon a matrimonial action brought by a Hindu husband against a Hindu wife married under the Hindu Law, then both the jurisdiction and grounds have deservedly to be in accordance with HMA, 1955. Here, the word jurisdiction refers to the right, power, as well as authority to interpret and implement the law, or simply put in a nut shell, the authority and power to decide a* lis. *Court jurisdictions are limited by physical boundaries as well as by subject* matter. *The original jurisdictional court in the present case by all means is the court of the District Judge exercising territorial jurisdiction in India and the grounds on which the action can be brought, must be one which are mentioned in section 13 of HMA, 1955. But that is not the end of the matter. There can be cases where parties confer jurisdiction on the foreign Court and the said Court will assume jurisdiction available to the Matrimonial Court in India but would remain confined to adjudicate the action in accordance with the matrimonial law of the parties* i.e. *HMA, 1955 and the grounds available therein. The legal principle being that when a Hindu couple tied by the nuptial knot according to Hindu rites travel abroad with intention to settle down and reside there to set up matrimonial home, they carry their personal laws on their back, off loading it in a foreign court for adjudication in the event parties intend to litigate for dissolving the marriage, mutually or by contest on one or more of HMA, 1955 recognized principles. A foreign Court can then grant a valid decree of dissolution of marriage but the adjudication must be upon one of the available grounds in the Indian law. Since* ***irretrievable breakdown*** *of marriage is not available in HMA, 1955, the twin test of forum jurisdiction and relief based grounds would remain unsatisfied and the foreign Court decree would not be binding in India nor recognized..."*

Thus, the court in *Rupak Rathi's* case upheld the order passed by the learned District Judge, Panchkula by which the Court at Panchkula had declined the application of the husband under Order VII, rule 11, CPC for accepting the decree of the English Court and dismissing the divorce petition of the wife as not maintainable. The land mark view has brought explicit clarity and has given a clear precedent to be followed wherever foreign matrimonial decrees fall for interpretation before a Family Court before whom a matrimonial cause is pending and a foreign verdict is cited as a *fait accompli*.

DIVORCE BY MUTUAL CONSENT: REQUIREMENTS

Section 13B of the HMA, 1955, came up for interpretation by the Bombay High Court in *Leela Mahadeo Joshi* v. *Mahadeo Sitaram Joshi*, AIR 1991 Bom 105.

The Court held that the three ingredients with regard to which the Court must satisfy itself before granting divorce by mutual consent are, first that the petition must be a joint petition presented by both the parties praying for a divorce by mutual consent. *Secondly*, that they have been living separately for a period of one year or more prior to the presentation of the petition. *Lastly*, they have not been able to live together and have mutually agreed that the marriage should be dissolved. The safeguards as enumerated in section 23 of the HMA, 1955 must undoubtedly be borne in mind, namely that the consent of the parties has not been obtained by force, fraud or undue influence and this aspect must necessarily be ascertained by the trial Court.

Furthermore, the court held in paragraph 13 at page 108 of the above mentioned judgment:

> *'It is material to note that section 13B, sub-section (2) makes it mandatory on the part of the Court to pass a decree once the above ingredients are satisfied and it is, therefore, not open to the Court to refuse to pass a decree in such circumstances. Such refusal would be contrary not only to the provisions of law but the very purpose of the amendment and would frustrate the basic objective of providing an honourable and effective dissolution of marriage in cases of matrimonial break-down without having to go through the exercise of an adversary litigation involving allegations against each other ...'*

MERE COMPROMISE NOT SUFFICIENT

Section 13B stipulates specific conditions and circumstances for grant of divorce by mutual consent, only upon satisfaction of the court. In *Munesh* v. *Anasuyamma,* AIR 2001 Kant 355, the husband's petition for divorce on the grounds of desertion was dismissed. This was on account of the failure of the husband to prove the desertion against the wife. The husband appealed against the decision. Pending the institution of the appeal, the husband recorded a compromise under Order XXIII, rule 3 of the Code of Civil Procedure, 1908, which was placed on record in the pending family appeal in the High Court. The compromise petition did not contain any averment or admission to show that the wife had deserted her husband without any justifiable cause. The court doubted the compromise petition. The said petition only recited that the litigation had been continuing for more than 15 years, the marriage itself was dead, and both the parties were agreeable to judicial separation. The court frowned upon such an agreement. The court held that such an agreement is not a lawful agreement. It was further held that no decree for divorce can be granted on the basis of such a compromise. The court observed that such compromise is against the scheme of the provisions of section 13 and section 13B of the HMA, 1955 and renders nugatory these provisions of the Act. According to the court, such a divorce petition should have been presented before the original competent court, *i.e.,* the District Court or the Family Court.

SUPREME COURT'S PURPORTED EXERCISE OF INHERENT POWERS UNDER ARTICLE 142 OF THE CONSTITUTION TO GRANT DIVORCE BY MUTUAL CONSENT

In *Shashi Garg* v. *Arun Garg,* (1997) 7 SCC 565, the Supreme Court in an application under section 25 of the Code of Civil Procedure (Power of the Supreme

Court to transfer suits, etc. from one jurisdiction to another) substantially altered the relief available to the parties.

In this case, initially a petition for dissolution of the marriage had been filed by the respondent husband on the grounds of cruelty. The wife moved the apex Court seeking to transfer the proceedings from the Court of the District Judge, Delhi to the Court of competent jurisdiction at Rewari, Haryana. Notice of the transfer petition was issued to the respondent husband.

When the transfer petition came up for hearing, the parties settled outside the court and filed a memorandum of agreement in the Supreme Court. In the light of the agreement, the Supreme Court took the matter on board. The apex Court scrutinised the agreement. The parties to the marriage prayed to the Court that their marriage be dissolved by mutual consent which was otherwise emotionally dead and for all other practical reasons. The Court concluded as follows in paragraph 8 of the judgment at page 566:

> *'The requirements of section 13B of the Act have been satisfied and there is no impediment in granting the decree for divorce by mutual consent by altering the relief in HMA, 1955 Case No. 221 of 1996, as one available under section 13B of the Act with a view to do complete justice between the parties and avoid unnecessary further litigation. We are also satisfied that the interest of the minor daughter has been safe guarded ...'*

In the ruling above, the apex Court seems to have exercised its powers under article 142 of the Constitution of India, without expressly referring to the same. The Court was more than particular in protecting the pecuniary interest of the minor daughter. The use of the phrase 'to do complete justice between the parties and avoid unnecessary further litigation' is indicative of this fact. Under article 142 of the Constitution, the Supreme Court in the exercise of its jurisdiction may pass any decree or order as is necessary for doing 'complete justice' in any matter pending before it. Section 25, CPC only empowered the Supreme Court to transfer the case from one Civil Court to another. Perhaps, in its wisdom, the apex Court to prevent any further ordeal to the parties of relegating them for further relief to another Court, took upon itself the task of doing substantial justice by there and then terminating a dead marriage, hence rendering substantial justice to all the parties to the litigation.

In *Madhuri Mehta* v. *Meet Verma,* (1997) 11 SCC 81, during the course of the hearing of the transfer petition, the parties to the marriage made an application for dissolution of their marriage under section 13B of the HMA, 1955. The Court also conferred visitation rights on the husband to meet their only child from the marriage. The court noticed that the parties had been estranged and had been living apart since January 1996. The court entertained the joint plea of the parties to the marriage. The ruling concluded in no uncertain terms, that divorce by mutual consent was being granted in exercise of powers under article 142 of the Constitution of India, for which there is ample authority reflective from the past decisions of the apex court itself.

In a third transfer petition case, reported at the same time as *Maduri Mehta's* case, (1997) 11 SCC 81 the apex Court gave a yet more liberal interpretation to the mutual consent provisions. This is the case of *Anita Sabharwal* v. *Anil Sabharwal*, (1997) 11 SCC 490.

In this case the respondent husband's divorce petition was pending in the court of the Additional District Judge, Delhi. The wife moved the transfer petition seeking transfer of the said case to Mumbai. During the pendency of the transfer petition, the parties as well as the Counsel put on the record of the court a compromise deed wherein they had agreed to get divorce by mutual consent.

The Judges observed that the petition had not been filed under section 13B of the HMA, 1955 and that the statutory period of 6 months had not even commenced. The apex Court summoned the trial court record and noticed that the parties had been married for 14 years. The court noticed that sadly enough, they had spent the prime of their life in acrimony and litigation. The court held that it was time that their mutuality bore some fruit in putting them apart. The court concluded in this short but liberal judgment reported as (1997) 11 SCC 490, where at page 491, it held as follows:

> *'... We, therefore, in the spirit of section 13B of the Act, and in view of the fact that all hopes to unite them together have gone, hereby grant to the parties divorce by a decree of dissolution by mutual consent to end their prolonged unhappiness. Ordered accordingly. The transfer petition stands disposed of.'*

The remarkable feature of this judgment is that the court was not bogged down by the technicalities of law while interpreting section 13B of the HMA, 1955. Also, the Court adequately satisfied itself as to the financial arrangements for the education of the children. The estranged father tendered in Court a sum of seven lacs by way of bank drafts. He was also given visitation rights to visit his children. The decision of the Court to do substantial justice to the parties was unfettered. The spouses parted amicably. Due provision was made for the future and welfare of the children's rights. Hence, the Court rendered complete justice to the parties.

MERELY LIVING SEPARATELY IS NO GROUND FOR SECTION 13B PETITION

Mere agreement of the parties to live separately, and the fact of living separately, is not a ground for granting divorce under section 13B of the HMA, 1955. A decree for divorce can be granted only when all of the statutory conditions mentioned in the HMA, 1955 for the grant of relief are found to exist and not merely on the ground that the parties had agreed to the grant of such a decree. This was the mandate of law laid down in *Surinder Kaur* v. *Amarjit Singh*, 1986 (2) HLR 120, and *Apurba Mohan Ghosh* v. *Manashi Ghosh*, 1989 (1) HLR 247.

The Delhi High Court in the case of *Gaurav Kapoor* v. *Komal Babbar*, 2014 (206) DLT 637, reiterated the explanation of the term "living separately" under section 13B, given by the Apex Court in the case of *Smt. Sureshta Devi* v. *Om Prakash*, (1991) 2 SCC 25, and in paragraph 6 of 2014 (206) DLT 637, it was held as follows:

"6. .... The similar question came up before the Apex Court in the case of **Smt. Sureshta Devi *v.* Om Prakash,** ***(1991)*** **2** ***SCC*** **25**. *In paragraph 9 of the said judgment, it was observed:*

"9. The 'living separately' for a period of one year should be immediately preceding the presentation of the petition. It is necessary that immediately preceding the presentation of petition, the parties must have been living separately. The expression 'living separately' connotes to our mind not living like husband and wife. It has no reference to the place of living. The parties may live under the same roof by force of circumstances, and yet they may not be living as husband and wife. The parties may be living in different houses and yet they have no desire to perform marital obligations and with that mental attitude they have been living separately for a period of one year immediately preceding the presentation of the petition. The second requirement that they 'have not been able to live together' seems to indicate the concept of broken down marriage and it would not be possible to reconcile themselves. The third requirement is that they have mutually agreed that the marriage should be dissolved.""

Hence, besides living separately, the Court clarified the requirements of not having been able to live together and mutual agreement to dissolve the marriage, as the three necessary and mandatory ingredients of a mutual consent divorce petition under section 13B of the Hindu Marriage Act, 1955, which cannot be relaxed or waived.

MUTUAL CONSENT SHOULD CONTINUE UNTIL THE DIVORCE DECREE

There has been conflict of legal situation as to whether consent of both the parties to the marriage should continue up to the date of the final decree. This issue was resolved by the Supreme Court of India in 1992 but the correctness of this decision has been doubted by the apex court itself in the year 1997. The law at this moment in time appears to be that mutual consent of both the parties should continue until the decree is passed by the court. The law on this issue is analysed briefly hereunder.

The Punjab and Haryana High Court in *Harcharan Kaur* v. *Nachhatar Singh*, AIR 1988 P&H 27, held that either party to the marriage is at liberty to revoke its consent any time before the petition is finally disposed of. The court held in paragraph11 of the judgment at p. 30:

'... In our view, unless the parties to the petition under section 13B of the Act, who have mutually consented to have the marriage dissolved, continued to signify their mutual consent for the dissolution of the marriage right up to the date of the decree, the marriage cannot be dissolved under sub-section (2) of section 13B of the Act merely on the basis that six months earlier the parties had together presented the petition for dissolution of marriage by mutual consent. Either of the parties to the petition under section 13B, that is, husband or wife, is at liberty to revoke its consent any time before the petition is finally disposed of; and if the other party is still keen to have the marriage dissolved, the other provisions of the Hindu Marriage Act, 1955 are still available for the grant of necessary relief if a case is made out for the same. The object of section 13B is to provide an

additional speedy remedy to the husband and wife to have the marriage dissolved if even after sufficient efflux of time both of them find, that it is not possible for them to continue as husband and wife any further. Obviously, if both the parties agree, the decree of divorce can be granted by mutual consent under section 13B and if one of them fails to agree and does not want to oblige the other party by extending the requisite consent to the divorce, decree of divorce cannot be passed under section 13B of the Act. For that, other provisions of the Act would have to be resorted to.'

The Delhi High Court in a contradictory view to the above mentioned decision of the Punjab and Haryana High Court in *Chander Kanta* v. *Hans Kumar*, AIR 1989 Del 73, held that a petition presented under section 13B of HMA, 1955 cannot be withdrawn by one party unilaterally. Of course, if the court is satisfied that the consent was not a free consent and it was the result of force, fraud or undue influence then it is a different situation because the court in such a case is empowered to refuse to grant the decree of divorce.

The Kerala High Court, like the Punjab and Haryana High Court in *K.I. Mohanan* v. *Jeejabai*, AIR 1988 Ker 28, held that it is open to one of the spouses to withdraw the consent given to the petition at any time before the Court passes a final decree for divorce.

In *Sureshta Devi* v. *Om Prakash*, AIR 1992 SC 1904, the apex Court had the occasion to deal in detail with the conflicting views of different High Courts on the question of withdrawal of consent by either party to the marriage before the passing of the divorce decree. The law laid down in this ruling was that a party to a 13B petition for divorce by mutual consent can unilaterally withdraw the consent. It is not irrevocable. Mutual consent must continue till the time a final divorce decree is passed. Therefore, if in the interregnum period of 6 to 18 months waiting, the mutual consent is withdrawn, no divorce by mutual consent can be granted. The apex Court upheld the interpretation given by the High Courts of Kerala, Punjab & Haryana and Rajasthan and overruled the views of the High Courts of Bombay, Delhi and Madhya Pradesh as not laying down good law.

The court while supporting the above views held in paragraph 13 of the judgment at pp. 1907–1908;

> *'13. From the analysis of the section, it will be apparent that the filing of the petition with mutual consent does not authorise the court to make a decree for divorce. There is a period of waiting from 6 to 18 months. This interregnum was obviously intended to give time and opportunity to the parties to reflect on their move and seek advice from relations and friends. In this transitional period one of the parties may have a second thought and change the mind not to proceed with the petition. The spouse may not be a party to the joint motion under sub-section (2). There is nothing in the section which prevents such course. The section does not provide that if there is a change of mind it should not be by one party alone, but by both. The High Courts of Bombay and Delhi have proceeded on the ground that the crucial time for giving mutual consent for divorce is the time of filing the petition and not the time when they subsequently move for*

divorce decree. This approach appears to be untenable. At the time of the petition by mutual consent, the parties are not unaware that their petition does not by itself snap marital ties. They know that they have to take a further step to snap marital ties. Sub-section (2) of section 13B is clear on this point. It provides that "on the motion of both the parties ... if the petition is not withdrawn in the meantime, the Court shall ... pass a decree of divorce ..." What is significant in this provision is that there should also be mutual consent when they move the Court with a request to pass a decree of divorce. Secondly, the Court shall be satisfied about the bona fides and the consent of the parties. If there is no mutual consent at the time of the enquiry, the Court gets no jurisdiction to make a decree for divorce. If the view is otherwise, the Court could make an enquiry and pass a divorce decree even at the instance of one of the parties and against the consent of the other. Such a decree cannot be regarded as decree by mutual consent.'

The court in paragraph 14 of the judgment at p. 1908 also relied on *Halsbury's Laws* by stating that:

> *'... The consent must continue to decree nisi and must be valid subsisting consent when the case is heard.' [See* Halsbury's Laws of England, *4th Edn., Vol. 13, paragraph 645;* Rayden on Divorce, *12th Edn., Vol. 1, p. 291; and* Beales v. Beales, *(1972) 2 All ER 667.]*

The Supreme Court in *Ashok Hurra's* case *(AIR 1997 SC 1266)* has doubted the correctness of the above mentioned decision. It has been held that for mutual consent to continue till the divorce decree is passed after a passage of 6 to 18 months appears to be too wide and does not logically accord with section 13B(2) of the HMA, 1955. The Supreme Court in this later decision has held that the observations made in *Sureshta Devi's* case, to the effect that mutual consent should continue till the divorce decree is passed, even if the petition is not withdrawn by either of the parties within the period of 18 months, appears to be too wide and is not in consonance with section 13B(2) of the HMA, 1955. The court felt that this issue would require reconsideration in an appropriate case. The Judges did not deliberate further on this issue. Since in this case the wife had withdrawn her consent for divorce before the passing of the final decree and the Supreme Court felt that the marriage was dead and that it warranted the exercise of jurisdiction under article 142 of the Constitution to grant a decree of divorce by mutual consent under section 13B of the Act, the Supreme Court dissolved the marriage between the parties in order to meet the ends of justice. The Court held that ground realities cannot deter it to take a total and broad view of the situation when dealing with adjustment of human relationships. Subject to the financial settlement between the parties, the Court dissolved the marriage by mutual consent under section 13B, HMA, 1955. This judgment seems to be an eye-opener where the Court brushed aside the technical interpretation of continuing consent till the passing of the final decree and for rendering complete substantial justice between parties clearly differed from the earlier view of the Supreme Court. The judgment is thus indeed salutary in nature.

Furthermore, once any party has withdrawn its consent for a petition under section 13B, it is not the duty of the court to find into the *bona fides* or reasonableness of withdrawal of consent. Once consent is withdrawn, the only option available to the Court is to close the matter at that stage and dismiss the petition without going into the merits or demerits of the matter. This has been held in a judgment in *Rajesh R. Nair* v. *Meera Babu,* 2014 (1) HLR 263. A similar view has been settled by the Apex Court in *Hitesh Bhatnagar* v. *Deepa Bhatnagar,* (2011) 5 SCC 234 clearly holding that if a second motion is not made in a petition for divorce by mutual consent, no Court can pass a decree of divorce by mutual consent.

SIX MONTHS STATUTORY WAIVER PERIOD

The tenor of several High Court decisions lays down that the statutory requirement of the waiting period of 6 to 18 months after filing the mutual consent divorce petition, can be waived, in instances where the parties have been litigating for a long time or where the marriage has lasted for a sufficient period of time and the spouses have been living apart. The period of 6 to 18 months is given in divorce by mutual consent so as to give time and opportunity to the parties to reflect on their move and seek advice from relations and friends if there is any hope of reconciliation between the parties.

The Punjab and Haryana High Court in *Mohinder Pal Kaur* v. *Gurmit Singh,* 2002 (1) HLR 537, held that the 6 months waiting period under section 13B of the HMA, 1955, can be reduced in cases where the divorce petition is already pending on some other fault ground for more than 6 months and the reconciliation efforts have been unsuccessful. The court also added a rider that this period cannot be curtailed altogether in freshly instituted petitions.

The same court in *Vinod Kumar* v. *Kamlesh,* 2002 (1) HLR 270, has held that the statutory period of 6 months as provided under section 13B(2) of the HMA, 1955 can be waived if the marriage has broken down completely and the parties are living separately. This Punjab and Haryana High Court ruling places reliance on an earlier Andhra Pradesh High Court decision in

Re Grandhi Venkata Chitti Abbai, AIR 1999 AP 91. In the instant case, criminal proceedings and maintenance proceedings were already pending. On the intervention of village elders and friends the parties agreed to obtain a divorce by consent. Under the terms of the compromise the maintenance settled was payable to the wife only after the divorce. She, therefore, filed an application before the senior sub-judge for preponement of the divorce. The same was rejected, hence the appeal was instituted in the High Court. The court held that there was no possibility of revival of marriage in this case. The court held in paragraph 5 at p. 92 of the judgment as follows:

> *'... When once such a situation is ruled out having liberalised the process of divorce by mutual consent which was not there prior to the amendment it will not serve any purpose in directing the parties to continue the agony for six more months. Hence, in a case of this nature, I feel that the statutory period of six months prescribed under the statute for taking divorce by mutual consent can be waived and the parties can be given liberty to part their company without waiting for the statutory period.'*

Likewise in *Paresh Shah* v. *Vyjayanthimala,* AIR 1999 AP 186, in a case pertaining to a well-educated couple, where the marriage had lasted for several years, the court granted a divorce decree by consent. Paragraph 4 at p. 188 of the judgment takes cognizance of the agony of the parties in such a situation. Paragraph 4 reads as follows:

> *'From the above compromise memos, filed by both the parties, it is clear that both are educated and in a position to understand the concept of marriage and their responsibility towards each of them as husband and wife. But their feelings, mal-adjustment and temperament, made their lives miserable and to pull on as husband and wife an impossibility. For them, divorce is a blessing than to continue as husband and wife in miserable circumstances ...'*

In *Bijal Chandreshbhai Bhatt* v. *Chandreshbhai Sahdevbhai Bhatt*, AIR 1999 Guj 203, the parties to the marriage had irreconcilable differences which also culminated in criminal litigation between them. The parties were not at all willing to reunite. The court while dispensing with the requirement of 6 months waiting period, highlighted the need to shorten litigation in such matters.

In one of the recent case of *Devinder Singh Narula* v. *Meenakshi Nangia*, 2013 (3) DMC (SC), the Apex court granted divorce, after 4 months of cooling period, to the parties who had been living separately for more than 1 year by invoking the powers of the Supreme Court under article 142 of the Constitution of India. In this case, the Apex Court was pleased to hold:

> *"13. In the above circumstances, in our view, this is one of those cases where we may invoke and exercise the powers vested in the Supreme Court under article 142 of the Constitution. The marriage is subsisting by a tenuous thread on account of the statutory cooling off period, out of which four months have already expired. When it has not been possible for the parties to live together and to discharge their marital obligations towards each other for more than one year, we see no reason to continue the agony of the parties for another two months."*

In conclusion it can be inferred that only the Supreme Court can exercise its discretion to waive the statutory 6 to 18 months waiting period in suitable cases as an exception wherever the need is felt to do so in exercise of its powers under article 142 of the Constitution of India for doing complete justice to parties in any cause or matter pending before it. This power is not vested with the High Courts or any other court. Therefore, as a normal rule, the statutory 6 to 18 months waiting period has to be adhered to necessarily. This time gap is a safeguard which prevents hasty divorces and helps parties to think over and decide on their intentions to divorce by mutual consent.

GUIDELINES LAID DOWN BY THE SUPREME COURT OF INDIA ON RECOGNITION OF FOREIGN MATRIMONIAL JUDGMENTS

Section 13 of the Indian Code of Civil Procedure is the general provision of law relating to conclusiveness of judgments by foreign courts. There is no separate provision of law prescribed in the HMA, 1955 or SMA, 1954 relating to recognition of foreign matrimonial judgments. Hence, the general provisions of law laid down in section 13, CPC are also applicable to matrimonial matters decided by foreign courts.

The Supreme Court of India in 1991 laid down comprehensive fresh guidelines to recognise foreign matrimonial judgments by the Courts in India.

The apex Court in *Y. Narasimha Rao* v. *Y. Venkata Lakshmi*, JT 1991 (3) SC 33, made it clear that Indian courts would not recognise a foreign judgment if it has been obtained by fraud which need not be only in relation to the merits of the matter but may also be in relation to jurisdictional facts. The ruling declared a divorce decree passed by a US court as 'unenforceable.'

In this case a decree for dissolution of marriage had been passed by the Circuit Court of St Louis County Missouri, USA. Three important factors were noteworthy in the case. In the first instance, the Court assumed jurisdiction over the matter on the ground that the first appellant had been a resident of the State of Missouri for 90 days preceding the commencement of the action and hence the petition could be filed in that Court. Secondly, the decree had been passed on the only ground of irretrievable breakdown of marriage. Thirdly, the respondent wife had not submitted to the jurisdiction of the Court. The Supreme Court of India observed from the record, that the wife had filed two replies of the same date. Both were identical in nature except that one of the replies began with an additional averment as follows:

> *'... without prejudice to the contention that this respondent is not submitting to the jurisdiction of this Hon'ble court, this respondent submits as follows ...'*

This observation is found in paragraph 5 at page 37 of the judgment. The wife raised several objections in her defence along with other issues. She stated that they both were Hindus, were governed by Hindu law and got married at Tirupati in India under Hindu law. She further contended that she was an Indian citizen and was not governed by the laws in force in the State of Missouri. Hence, the foreign court had no jurisdiction to entertain the petition.

The Supreme Court held that in terms of section 19 of the HMA, 1955, (section 19 lays down the Court to which the divorce petition shall be presented), the Circuit Court of St Louis County, Missouri had no jurisdiction to entertain the petition, in terms of which admittedly the parties were not married. Secondly, irretrievable breakdown of marriage is not one of the grounds recognised by the HMA, 1955 for dissolution of the marriage. Hence, the decree of divorce passed by the foreign court was on a ground which was not available under the HMA, 1955.

The Court interpreted section 13 of the Indian Code of Civil Procedure, 1908 (hereafter CPC 1908) with special reference to validity of foreign divorce decrees. Section 13 of the CPC, 1908 states that a foreign judgment is not conclusive as to any matter directly adjudicated upon between the parties if:

(a) it has not been pronounced by a Court of competent jurisdiction;

(b) it has not been given on the merits of the case;

(c) it is founded on an incorrect view of international law or a refusal to recognise the law of India in cases in which such law is applicable;

(d) the proceedings are opposed to natural justice;

(e) it is obtained by fraud;

(f) it sustains a claim founded on a breach of any law in force in India.

Justice P.B. Sawant analyzed and consolidated the reasons for framing the guidelines in terms of section 13 of the CPC, 1908. The reasons are advanced in paragraphs 11 and 13 at pp. 39 and 40 respectively of the judgment which are reproduced hereunder:

> *'11. The rules of Private International Law in this country are not codified and are scattered in different enactments such as the Civil Procedure Code, the Contract Act, the Indian Succession Act, the Indian Divorce Act, the Special Marriage Act, 1954 etc. In addition, some rules have also been evolved by judicial decisions ...*
>
> *13. We cannot also lose sight of the fact that today more than ever in the past, the need for definitive rules for recognition of foreign judgments in personal and family matters, and particularly in matrimonial disputes has surged to the surface. Many a man and woman of this land with different personal laws have migrated and are migrating to different countries either to make their permanent abode there or for temporary residence. Likewise there is also immigration of the nationals of other countries. The advancement in communication and transportation has also made it easier for individuals to hop from one country to another. It is also not unusual to come across cases where citizens of this country have been contracting marriages either in this country or abroad with nationals of the other countries or among themselves, or having married here, either both or one of them migrate to other countries. There are also cases where parties having married here have been either domiciled or residing separately in different foreign countries. This migration, temporary or permanent, has also been giving rise to various kinds of matrimonial disputes destroying in its turn the family and its peace. A large number of foreign decrees in matrimonial matters is becoming the order of the day. A time has, therefore, come to ensure certainty in the recognition of the foreign judgments in these matters ...'*

The Apex Court laid down the following broad principles in the interpretation of section 13 of the CPC, 1908, with special emphasis on foreign matrimonial judgments.

(i) Clause (a) of section 13 states that a foreign judgment shall not be recognised if it has not been pronounced by a court of competent jurisdiction. The court was of the view that this clause should be interpreted to mean that only such court will be a court of competent jurisdiction, which the HMA, 1955 or the law under which the parties are married, recognises as a court of competent jurisdiction to entertain the matrimonial dispute.

(ii) Clause (b) of section 13 states that if a foreign judgment has not been given on the merits of the case, the courts in this country will not recognise such a judgment. This clause should be interpreted to mean (a) that the decision of the foreign court should be on a ground available under the law under which the parties are married, and (b) that the decision should be a result of the contest between the parties. The latter requirement is fulfilled only when the respondent is duly served and voluntarily and unconditionally submits himself/herself to the jurisdiction of the court and contests the claim, or agrees to the passing of the decree with or without appearance. A mere filing of the reply to the claim under protest and without submitting to the jurisdiction of the court, or an appearance in the Court either in person or through a representative for objecting to the jurisdiction of the Court, should not be considered as a decision on the merits of the case.

(iii) The marriages which take place in India can only be under either the customary or the statutory law in force in India. Hence, the only law that can be applicable to the matrimonial disputes is the one under which the parties are married, and not any other law. When a foreign judgment is founded on a jurisdiction or on a ground not recognised by such law, it is a judgment which is in defiance of the law in India. Hence, it is not conclusive of the matters adjudicated therein and, therefore, unenforceable in India.

(iv) Section 13(d) of the CPC, 1908 which makes a foreign judgment unenforceable on the ground that the proceedings in which it is obtained are opposed to natural justice. The court held that in the realm of family law such as matrimonial disputes, this principle has to be extended to mean something more than mere compliance with the technical rules of procedure. Therefore, it is necessary for the court to ascertain whether the respondent was in a position to represent himself/herself and effectively contest the said proceedings.

(v) Section 13(e) of the CPC, 1908 stipulates that the courts in India will not recognise a foreign judgment, which is *prima facie* obtained by fraudulent means. The court here placed reliance on its earlier decision in *Satya* v. *Teja Singh*, 1975 (2) SCR 197. In this case it was held that the fraud need not be only in relation to the merits of the matter but may also be in relation to jurisdictional facts.

The Apex Court ruled in paragraph 20 at page 43 of the judgment that the jurisdiction assumed by the foreign court as well as the grounds on which the relief was granted must be in accordance with the matrimonial law under which the parties were married. The court also elaborated upon the exceptions to this rule, which are as follows:

(a) where the matrimonial action is filed in the forum where the respondent is domiciled or habitually and permanently resides and the relief is granted on a ground available in the matrimonial law under which the parties are married;

(b) where the respondent voluntarily and effectively submits to the jurisdiction of the forum and contests the claim which is based on a ground available under the matrimonial law under which the parties are married;

(c) where the respondent consents to the grant of the relief although the jurisdiction of the forum is not in accordance with the provisions of the matrimonial law of the parties.

Therefore, the Indian Apex Court has given clear guidelines in accordance with the general law of the land for enforcement of foreign matrimonial judgments in India to prevent erring spouses from taking advantage of liberal matrimonial laws of foreign jurisdiction which permit quick divorce on easier grounds not available in the Indian Jurisdiction. The necessity to do so arose on account of a large number of foreign divorce decrees mostly obtained in default, being sought to be enforced on Indian soil and which gave no choice to a helpless spouse invariably deserted and pitted on Indian land much against his or her wishes.

In the case of *Rupak Rathi* v. *Anita Chaudhary*, 2014 (2) RCR (Civil) 697 (Supra), the Punjab and Haryana High Court gave its opinion with respect to applicability, as also interpretation of exception (ii) in paragraph 20 of *Y. Narasimha Rao* (Supra) and interpretation of Order VII, rule 11, CPC in the following terms. The court held as follows:

> *"In exceptions (i) and (ii) the words "grounds" or "ground" have been used in the rule and also in exceptions (i) and (ii) but not in exception (iii). The word, "relief" has been used in the rule and in exceptions (i) and (iii) but not in exception (ii). The first exception talks of 'forum' where the respondent is domiciled or habitually and permanently resides and this is clarified by the conjunction "and" to mean that the "relief" is granted on a ground available under HMA, 1955.*
>
> *Exception (iii) applies in cases which are not contested and are based on consent. It follows that when 'contest' and 'consent/s' are referable to grounds available under HMA, 1955, only then can relief flow. This is for the reason that there is no estoppel against the statute. What is meant by consent to the grant of relief even though the English Court's jurisdiction is contrary to HMA, 1955 is the moot point presenting some difficulty. The rule in para. 20 confers and recognizes jurisdiction by assumption conferred on a foreign Court to act in accordance with the mandate of Indian matrimonial law. The Supreme Court chose not to use the word "grounds" in exception (iii) and this is how some ambiguity is felt after the heated debate on the interpretation of exception (iii) vehemently argued by the respective counsel and the learned amicus from many angles and prisms or points of view. It is, however, well settled that the words used in a judgment cannot be read as one would read words used by the legislature in enactments which latter have to be given their ordinary and plain meaning. In cases of ambiguity in the statutory rule and of the words used by the Parliament, then the court can step in to harmonize the provisions in a way which is in consonance with the objects and reasons for which the Act was passed and to further the intention of the law.*
>
> *There is a difference between the words "relief" and "jurisdiction" of the "forum" in exception (iii). Even in the rule, the forum has no jurisdiction but is assumed to have one when it acts on a principle permitted by section 13, HMA, 1955 to be the grounds for dissolution of marriage by a decree of divorce. It is for this reason the Supreme Court used the word "may" when it observed while carving out the three exceptions that the "exceptions to this rule may be as follows". To my mind, if any other interpretation is placed on the word 'relief" in exception*

(iii), it may result in grant of an illegal decree of dissolution of marriage made available to a party on the ground of irretrievable breakdown of marriage which is an impermissible ground of divorce not so far heralded into the Hindu law of marriage.

Exception (iii) is consent based for relief to the respondent but not to the petitioner in forum conveniens; "although the jurisdiction of the forum is not in accordance with the provisions of the matrimonial law of the parties". When the Supreme Court carved out this last exception it avoided introducing the word 'grounds'. If it were employed, the meaning then would have admitted no further debate and full effect would have to be given to the declaration under article 141 of the Constitution of India and for this Court to act in aid. However, since an exception cannot be seen to obliterate the rule itself or to rewrite it, then what the Supreme Court, in my humble view, in fact meant was a consent based decree obtained on foreign soil on HMA, 1955 grounds and not otherwise. Therefore, HMA, 1955 law would have to be read into exception (iii) to align it with the rule and not create a new rule since then it would not qualify as an exception to a rule. Reading the exception in isolation, will, in my considered view, be in violation of the rule itself. Thus, in cases of contested and consented decrees both would suffer HMA, 1955 standards, failing which, the foreign court will be overstepping Parliamentary mandates in India and the decrees so obtained cannot be recognized in India unless falling in exceptions (i) and (ii). This is more so, as I see, when exception (i) talks neither of contest nor consent. Otherwise, there would hardly be any visible distinction between exception (i) and exception (iii) because even in exception (i) the assumed jurisdiction of the foreign court was not in accordance with the provisions of the matrimonial law of the parties or the relief granted was not in accordance with the matrimonial law under which the parties are married. This would be the 'just and equitable' rule to follow for the protection of women who are the most vulnerable sections of society as observed in para 21 of Y. Narasimha Rao itself. Besides, consent to a foreign decree not questioned or litigated in court by parties makes no lis *and remains good till it lasts. However, this is not a matter of law but of personal choice where the arms of law may not reach. But consent itself is a question of evidence if the mode and manner in which it was given is taken to a court of law for determination."*

Further, the High Court laid down seven guidelines for the Matrimonial Courts functioning under its jurisdiction for dealing with applications under Order VII, rule 11, CPC in the context of HMA, 1955 and section 13, CPC. These are as follows:

"*(i) If the spouse aggrieved by the foreign matrimonial decree has not submitted to the jurisdiction of the foreign court or consented to the passing of the foreign Court judgment, it ought not to be recognised being unenforceable under section 13, CPC. This position of law ought to be applied to the facts of the individual case.*

(ii) There may be occasions that a spouse relying upon the judgment of a foreign matrimonial court, upon receipt of a summon or notice from a court of competent jurisdiction under the HMA, 1955, may not choose to file a written statement in response to a petition seeking a matrimonial cause under HMA, 1955 in Punjab, Haryana or Chandigarh. Instead, the contesting spouse may prefer to

move an application under Order VII, rule 11, CPC seeking to rely upon or invoke the provisions of section 13, CPC. Thus, it may be contended before the court of competent jurisdiction under the HMA, 1955 that since the matrimonial action between the parties has already been decided and concluded by a Court in the foreign jurisdiction, the adjudication in the matter in issue between the same spouses based on the same matrimonial cause of action is barred by the principle of res judicata *and spouses are estopped in law from agitating the same again.*

(iii) *It is respectfully contended that wherever both or any spouse arrayed in a matrimonial cause in a matrimonial action under HMA, 1955 contest, dispute, question or oppose any above such application under Order VII, rule 11, CPC involving interpretation of the principles laid down under section 13, CPC thereby necessitating requirement of detailed pleadings and evidence of spouses, no summary decision may seem possible to decide the matter in the preliminary stage.*

(iv) *In the above situation, there may also be circumstances involving application of issues of domicile as also applicability of sections 1 and 2 of the HMA, 1955 regarding extra territorial application of the provisions of HMA, 1955. Determination of these issues may also require parties to put their pleadings and testimony as well on the record of the Court of competent jurisdiction under the HMA, 1955.*

(v) *The application of the provisions of the CPC finding mention under section 21, HMA, 1955, the Court of Competent jurisdiction under the HMA, 1955 in Punjab, Haryana or Chandigarh may then be guided by the procedural law of pleadings contained in the Orders and Rules of the CPC and Punjab & Haryana High Court amendments, if any, for further proceedings in the matter. Accordingly, filing of a written statement, counter claim, rejoinder and/or other pleadings may be necessitated for having the factual matrix on record leading to the settlement of issues under Order XIV, CPC which can only be framed upon allegations made by parties to be read along with the contents of documents produced by spouses. Hence, this procedure may be necessary to be adopted to decide upon the warring claims of spouses relying on averments in support or against the judgment of the foreign matrimonial court between the parties.*

(vi) *Based on the above procedural requirements, the Court of competent jurisdiction under the HMA, 1955 may then examine the process, pleadings, grounds and other details in the passing of the judgment/decree of the matrimonial court of foreign jurisdiction to test it on the anvil of section 13, CPC and based on the principles laid down by the Apex Court in* Y. Narasimha Rao *v.* Y. Venkata Lakshmi, *(1991) 3 SCC 451 and exception (iii) as understood in the present opinion. Hence, in the event of a contest, dispute, opposition to the applicability of the foreign matrimonial judgment in the Indian jurisdiction, a summary disposal may not be possible. To do complete justice to both the spouses and to ensure that prejudice has not been caused to either of them as also that issues of maintenance, settlement of matrimonial property, child custody etc. arising in India have been completely settled between spouses based on provisions of HMA, 1955, the Court of competent jurisdiction under the HMA, 1955 may examine the matter on the lines suggested above.*

(vii) Thereafter, if the issue relating to the jurisdiction of Competent Court under the HMA, 1955 as also any bar to the matrimonial cause created by any existing law appears to be established, the matrimonial court in Punjab, Haryana or Chandigarh may upon the facts and circumstances of the case take an appropriate decision under Order XIV, rule 2, CPC whether it needs to pronounce judgment on all issues or decide the issue of jurisdiction or maintainability as a preliminary issue. In such circumstances, the Competent Court under the HMA, 1955 may after forming an opinion take an appropriate decision on the facts of the case as to whether the issue of jurisdiction or maintainability is to be decided as a preliminary issue or pronounce judgment together on all the issues. Accordingly, based on the individual facts and circumstances, the Court ought to take a decision whether to decide the preliminary issue of jurisdiction or maintainability or postpone the settlement of other issues after such preliminary issues has been determined."

Smt. Neeraja Saraph v. *Jayant V. Saraph*, JT 1994 (6) SC 488, is another case of wife dumping by a foreign husband. The apex Court rightly so, came down heavily on the erring husband by upholding an interim order for compensation payable to the helpless wife. The facts of this case are as follows. The appellant was a post-graduate daughter of a senior Air Force Officer. She was serving as a teacher and drawing a salary of Rs. 3000. She was married to respondent number 1, a doctor in computer sciences who was employed in the USA. The marriage took place at the behest of her father-in-law who approached through a common family friend. The marriage was performed on 6 August, 1989 and the appellant was taken on a honeymoon to Goa for a few days. Respondent number 1 returned to the USA on 24 August, 1989, wrote letters to the appellant on 15 September, 20 October and 14 November, 1989 persuading her to give up her job and suggesting the various avenues for her career in the US. The appellant was lured, she tried to obtain a visa and ultimately resigned from her job in November 1989. But from December things started getting cold. Ultimately, in June 1990 the respondent's brother came to Delhi and handed over a petition for annulment of marriage presented in an American Court and the father-in-law had sent a sentimental letter owning moral responsibility only. The wife filed a suit in India for damages against the husband and the father-in-law for ruining her life in *forma pauperis*. The suit was decreed *ex parte* for rupees 22 lacs.

The court held in paragraphs 4 and 5 at pages 490 and 491 of the judgment respectively;

> *'... Various submissions have been advanced on behalf of the father-in-law to support the order of the High Court including his helplessness financially. Is it a case of any sympathy for the father-in-law at this stage? In our opinion not. True the decree is* ex-parte. *Yet it is a money decree. However, no opinion is expressed on this aspect as the appeal is pending in the High Court. But the order of the High Court is modified by directing that the execution of the decree shall remain stayed if the respondents deposit a sum of Rs. 3,00,000 including Rs. 1,00,000 directed by the High Court within a period of two months from today, with the Registrar of the High court...*
>
> *5. Why the facts of this case have been narrated in brief with little background is to impress upon readers the need and necessity for appropriate steps to be*

taken in this direction to safeguard the interest of women. Although it is a problem of private International Law and is not easy to be resolved, with change in social structure and rise of marriages with NRI, the Union of India may consider enacting a law like the Foreign Judgments (Reciprocal Enforcement) Act, 1933 enacted by the British Parliament under section (1) in pursuance of which the Government of the United Kingdom issued the Reciprocal Enforcement of Judgments (India) Order, 1958. Apart from it there are other enactments such as the Indian and Colonial Divorce Jurisdiction Act, 1940 which safeguard the interest so far as the United Kingdom is concerned. But the rule of domicile replacing the nationality rule in most of the countries, for assumption of jurisdiction and granting relief in matrimonial matters, has resulted in conflict of laws. This domicile rule is not necessary to be discussed. But feasibility of legislation safeguarding the interests of women may be examined by incorporating such provisions as the following—

(1) no marriage between a NRI and an Indian woman which has taken place in India may be annulled by a foreign court;

(2) provision may be made for adequate alimony to the wife in the property of the husband both in India and abroad.

(3) the decree granted by Indian courts may be made executable in foreign courts both on the principle of comity and by entering into reciprocal agreements like section 44A of the Civil Procedure Code which makes a foreign decree executable as it would have been a decree passed by that court.'

It will be noticed that the proposed guidelines in both the above mentioned Supreme Court and High Court rulings are meaningful and, if implemented, can mitigate the plight of wives dumped in India by foreign husbands. Though the Apex Court has clearly stated that there is need for suitable legislation on the subject, until now no comprehensive Indian law has been enacted to protect the rights of deserted and abandoned spouses in India. In essence, therefore, judicial verdicts of the Courts of Law are the only available law in India to come to the rescue of helpless Indian spouses who protest against the uncontested foreign divorce decrees invariably obtained in default by spouses from overseas jurisdictions. Some codified laws on the subject are undoubtedly now an absolute necessity in India today to cope with the need for interpretation and enforcement of foreign matrimonial judgments of overseas courts.

FOREIGN COURT JUDGMENTS ON CHILD CUSTODY – ISSUES AND CONSIDERATIONS BEFORE COURTS

India not being a signatory to the Hague Convention on Civil Aspects of International Child Abduction, 1980, foreign Court orders requiring return of children to the country of their habitual residence are not mechanically implemented by Indian Courts which examine the best interest and the welfare of the child in an independent adjudication before Indian Courts. As an update of the latest position reflected by some recent precedents, a short summary is drawn up as under:

(i) In *Ruchi Majoo* v. *Sanjeev Majoo* AIR 2011 SC 1952, where the husband and wife were American citizens of Indian origin, a child born to them in America was the subject of a custody battle between them. The wife came to India alongwith the child and filed a petition claiming exclusive custody of her child. The interim custody was granted to the mother. The husband filed a petition in a US Court, which granted custody of child to the father which was sought to be enforced in India. The Supreme Court held that the principle of comity of Courts ensures that foreign Judgments and orders are unconditionally conclusive of the matters in controversy, but in the matter of custody of child interest and welfare of the minor being paramount, a competent court in this country is entitled and indeed duty bound to examine the matter independently, taking the foreign judgment, if any, only as an input for its final adjudication. In the facts of the instant case, the repatriation of child to America could not be allowed on the principle of comity of Courts as the interest of the minor shall be better served if he continued in the custody of his mother, especially when the father had contracted a second marriage as also had consented to the bringing of the child from USA to India by the mother.

(ii) In *Shilpa Aggarwal* v. *Aviral Mittal,* decided on 9 December, 2009, (2010) 1 SCC 591, a three and a half year old girl child, who was a British citizen born in UK to Indian parents, was removed to India from UK by the mother in contravention of British Court orders. The mother was directed by the Supreme Court of India to return with child to UK as the matter to determine, which parent was best suited to have the custody in the interest and welfare of the minor child, was pending adjudication before a British Court.

(iii) In *Dr. V. Ravi Chandaran* v. *Union of India,* decided on 17 November, 2009, (2010) 1 SCC 174, a seven year old boy, who was a US citizen and was born in USA to Indian Parents, who had become US citizens, was removed to India from USA by the mother contrary to US Court orders. The mother was directed by the Supreme Court to return to USA with the child failing which the father would be entitled to do so of his own.

(iv) In *Vikramvir Vohra* v. *Shalini Bhalla,* decided on 25 March, 2010, JT 2010 (3) SC 213, it was held by the Supreme Court of India that child custody orders are interlocutory in nature and can be altered for the welfare of the child. Consequently, the Supreme Court permitted the mother to take her minor son aged about ten years to Australia as per the wishes of the child to stay with the mother upholding the welfare of the child as a paramount consideration.

(v) In *Philip David Dexter* v. *State NCT of Delhi,* 2013 (3) DMC 45, the Delhi High Court directed the wife to return the custody of child to the father before the Registrar of The Delhi High Court as the wife had abducted the child and brought her to India violating the joint custody order and had no evidence to prima facie justify that there was risk of grave danger to the life of the child on return to the Republic of South Africa. The matter is now pending appeal before the Supreme Court and the operation of the High Court judgment has been stayed till the final decision by the Apex Court.

(vi) In *Arathi Bandi* v. *Bandi Jagadrakshaka Rao,* AIR 2014 SC 918, a decree of dissolution of marriage was obtained from a US Court. The custody of the child was given to the husband. The wife thereafter travelled to India alongwith child in defiance of Court order. The husband then came to India and filed a habeas corpus petition before the High Court seeking production of child and permitting him to take custody of the minor in compliance with the order passed by US Court. The High Court directed the wife to submit to the jurisdiction of the US Courts. The appeal by the wife was dismissed by the Supreme Court holding that a parent committing a wrong by removing children out of the country does not gain any advantage by his or her wrongdoing; and that the contention that the American court, which passed the order/decree has no jurisdiction and the same being inconsistent in Indian Law cannot be executed in India, is not tenable.

From a collective reading of the above recent judgments, it can be stated that in matters of child custody foreign court orders do not find mechanical application in India and the Indians Courts decide custody issues in the best interest of the child in which process, the foreign court order is only one consideration for adjudicating upon the matter on merits alone.

ACCEPTING MAINTENANCE UNDER FOREIGN COURT JUDGMENT DOES NOT BAR FILING OF DIVORCE PETITION IN INDIA

The above mentioned case of *Y. Narasimha Rao* v. *Y. Venkata Lakshmi,* (1991) 3 SCC 451, was followed by the Delhi High Court in *Veena Kalia* v. *Jatinder Nath Kalia,* AIR 1996 Del 55. The husband in this case had filed divorce proceedings in the Supreme Court of Nova Scotia in Canada on the ground of irretrievable breakdown. The court held that, since the wife had not contested the proceedings in Canada, it would not mean that she had conceded to the jurisdiction of the Canadian Court. The court further held that the decree of divorce granted by the Canadian Court was violative of the principles of natural justice and was as such a nullity. The subsequent petition for divorce by the wife in India on the ground of adultery, cruelty and desertion was not barred by the principles of estoppel or from *res judicata* simply because she had accepted maintenance under the foreign judgment.

MAINTENANCE, DISPOSAL OF PROPERTY AND CUSTODY OF CHILDREN UNDER HINDU LAW

The Hindu husband has a statutory liability to maintain his wife under the provisions of the HMA, 1955, HAMA, 1956 and the Indian Code of Criminal Procedure, 1973 (hereafter CrPC, 1973). The crucial distinction is that under sections 24 and 25 of the HMA, 1955, the wife is entitled to ask for maintenance only in the event of any matrimonial litigation. But, there is no such contingency or embargo imposed by the provisions of the CrPC, 1973. The wife, while invoking the jurisdiction under CrPC, 1973, can claim maintenance if she is living separately in the absence of any matrimonial litigation, provided she meets the conditions stipulated in section 125 of the CrPC, 1973. Additionally, the Hindu wife can also claim maintenance under section 18 of the HAMA, 1956, under certain circumstances in the absence of any matrimonial proceedings.

Section 26 of the HMA, 1955 deals with the provision for custody of children. Section 27 of the HMA, 1955 provides for disposal of the property of the parties to the litigation. The relevant maintenance provisions under the HMA, 1955, CrPC, 1973, HAMA, 1956 and the custody and the disposal of property provisions under the HMA, 1955 are reproduced hereunder:

MAINTENANCE UNDER THE PROVISIONS OF THE HINDU MARRIAGE ACT 1955

'24. *Maintenance* pendente lite *and expenses of proceedings.—Where in any proceeding under this Act it appears to the court that either the wife or the husband, as the case may be, has no independent income sufficient for her or his support* and *the necessary expenses of the proceeding, it may, on the application of the wife or the husband, order the respondent to pay to the petitioner the expenses of the proceeding, and monthly during the proceeding such sum as, having regard to the petitioner's own income and the income of the respondent, it may seem to the court to be reasonable.*

[Provided that the application for the payment of the expenses of the proceeding and such monthly sum during the proceeding, shall, as far as possible, be disposed of within 60 days from the date of service of notice on the wife or the husband, as the case may be.]

25. Permanent alimony and maintenance.—(1) Any court exercising jurisdiction under this Act may, at the time of passing any decree or at any time subsequent thereto, on application made to it for the purpose by either the wife or the husband as the case may be, order that the respondent shall pay to the applicant for her or his maintenance and support such gross sum or such monthly or periodical sum for a term not exceeding the life of the applicant as, having regard to the respondent's own income and other property, if any, the income and other property of the applicant , the conduct of the parties and other circumstances of the case, it may seem to the court to be just, and any such payment may be secured, if necessary, by a charge on the immovable property of the respondent.

(2) If the court is satisfied that there is a change in the circumstances of either party at any time after it has made an order under sub-section (1), it may at the instance of either party, vary, modify or rescind any such order in such manner as the court may deem just.

(3) If the court is satisfied that the party in whose favour an order has been made under this section has re-married or, if such party is the wife, that she has not remained chaste, or, if such party is the husband, that he has had sexual intercourse with any woman outside wedlock, it may at the instance of the other party vary, modify or rescind any such order in such manner as the court may deem just.'

MAINTENANCE UNDER SECTION 125 OF THE INDIAN CODE OF CRIMINAL PROCEDURE, 1973

Significantly it will be noticed that the ambit of section 125 of the CrPC, 1973, also extends to maintenance of children and parents. The relevant extract of section 125 reads as follows:

> *'125. Order for maintenance of wives, children and parents.—(1) If any person having sufficient means neglects or refuses to maintain—*
>
> *(a) his wife, unable to maintain herself, or*
>
> *(b) his legitimate or illegitimate minor child, whether married or not, unable to maintain itself, or*
>
> *(c) his legitimate or illegitimate child (not being a married daughter) who has attained majority, where such child is, by reason of any physical or mental abnormality or injury unable to maintain itself, or*
>
> *(d) his father or mother, unable to maintain himself or herself,*
>
> *a Magistrate of the first class may, upon proof of such neglect or refusal, order such person to make a monthly allowance for the maintenance of his wife or such child, father or mother, at such monthly rate, as such magistrate thinks fit, and to pay the same to such person as the magistrate may from time to time direct...'*

In *Saygo Bai* v. *Chueeru Bajrangi*, (2010) 13 SCC 762, the Apex Court held that all the three Courts below have completely misunderstood the true import of section 125, CrPC by showing scant disregard to the provisions of section 125(3), CrPC. Accordingly, the Supreme Court came to the conclusion that *"firstly, the Courts below erred in holding that the wife had left the matrimonial house for 4-5 years and refused to join the company of her husband and, secondly, the Courts are totally in error in holding that on that count she has lost the rights of maintenance."* In a true interpretation of the intent and meaning of providing maintenance under section 125, CrPC for survival to ameliorate the agony, anguish and financial suffering of a woman who had left her matrimonial home, the Apex Court instead of remanding the matter for deciding the amount of maintenance and considering that the wife is in a state of penury, awarded her maintenance at the rate of Rs. 1500 per month from the date of her application under section 125, CrPC after setting aside all the three orders of the Courts below.

In *Shabano Bano* v. *Imran Khan*, AIR 2010 SC 305, the Supreme Court held that cumulative reading of the judgments of the Apex Court in *Danial Latifi* v. *Union of India*, (2001) 7 SCC 740 and *Iqbal Bano* v. *State of Uttar Pradesh*, (2007) 6 SCC 785 would *"make it crystal clear that even a divorced Muslim women would be entitled to claim maintenance from her divorce husband, as long as she does not remarry. This being a beneficial piece of legislation, the benefit thereof must accrue to the divorced Muslim women."* The Apex Court reiterated the law laid down in *Mohd. Ahmed Khan* v. *Shah Bano Begum*, (1985) 2 SCC 556 as the starting point with regard to Muslim divorced women's rights and *"held that even if a Muslim woman has been divorced, she would be entitled to claim maintenance from her husband under section 125 of the CrPC after the expiry of period of Iddat also, as long as she does not remarry."* Further, interpreting section 20 of the Family Courts Act, 1984 as having overriding effect on all other enactments, the Apex Court upheld the jurisdiction of the Family Court to disposed off the matter on merits.

In *Shamim Bano* v. *Asraf Khan*, 2014 (5) SCALE 299, following the law laid down in *Shabano Bano* v. *Imran Khan*, AIR 2010 SC 305, the Supreme Court held that *"as the Magistrate still retains the power of granting maintenance Under section 125 of the Code to a divorced Muslim woman and the proceeding was continuing without any objection and the ultimate result would be the same, there was no justification on the part of the High Court to hold that the proceeding after the divorce took place was not maintainable."* Setting aside the impugned orders, the matter was remitted to the Magistrate for readjudication of the controversy leaving it open to the wife to file a fresh application for grant of interim maintenance, if so advised.

Similarly, in *Poongodi* v. *Thangavel*, (2013) 10 SCC 618, it was decided by the Supreme Court that the liability to pay maintenance under section 125, CrPC is in the nature of a continuing liability. The Court also upheld the remedy to approach the Court by means of successive application under section 125(3), CrPC highlighting the subsequent defaults in payment of maintenance. In a salutary interpretation, the Court held that the liability to pay maintenance cannot be taken to have been discharged by sending the person liable to pay the monthly allowance, to jail, since it is only a mode or method of recovery and not a substitute for recovery.

Lamenting on the delay in deciding a maintenance application under section 125, CrPC, In Criminal Appeal No. 1331 of 2014 *Bhuwan Mohan Singh* v. *Meena*, 2014 STPL (Web) 467 SC decided on 15 July, 2014, the Supreme Court held:

> *"13. The Family Courts have been established for adopting and facilitating the conciliation procedure and to deal with family disputes in a speedy and expeditious manner. A three-Judge Bench in* K.A. Abdul Jaleel v. T.A. Shahida, *(2003) 4 SCC 166, while highlighting on the purpose of bringing in the Family Courts Act by the legislature, opined thus:—*
>
> *The Family Courts Act was enacted to provide for the establishment of Family Courts with a view to promote conciliation in, and secure speedy settlement of, disputes relating to marriage and family affairs and for matters connected therewith.*
>
> *14. The purpose of highlighting this aspect is that in the case at hand the proceeding before the Family Court was conducted without being alive to the objects and reasons of the Act and the spirit of the provisions under section 125 of the Code. It is unfortunate that the case continued for nine years before the Family Court. It has come to the notice of the Court that on certain occasions the Family Courts have been granting adjournments in a routine manner as a consequence of which both the parties suffer or, on certain occasions, the wife becomes the worst victim. When such a situation occurs, the purpose of the law gets totally atrophied. The Family Judge is expected to be sensitive to the issues, for he is dealing with extremely delicate and sensitive issues pertaining to the marriage and issues ancillary thereto. When we say this, we do not mean that the Family Courts should show undue haste or impatience, but there is a distinction*

between impatience and to be wisely anxious and conscious about dealing with a situation. A Family Court Judge should remember that the procrastination is the greatest assassin of the lis *before it. It not only gives rise to more family problems but also gradually builds unthinkable and Everestine bitterness. It leads to the cold refrigeration of the hidden feelings, if still left. The delineation of the* lis *by the Family Judge must reveal the awareness and balance. Dilatory tactics by any of the parties has to be sternly dealt with, for the Family Court Judge has to be alive to the fact that the* lis *before him pertains to emotional fragmentation and delay can feed it to grow. We hope and trust that the Family Court Judges shall remain alert to this and decide the matters as expeditiously as possible keeping in view the objects and reasons of the Act and the scheme of various provisions pertaining to grant of maintenance, divorce, custody of child, property disputes, etc."*

In the above matter the Supreme Court held that while deciding an application under section 125, CrPC, a "*Magistrate is required to record reasons for granting or refusing to grant maintenance to wives, children or parents. Such maintenance can be awarded from the date of the order, or, if so ordered from the date of the application for maintenance, as the case may be. For awarding maintenance from the date of the application, express order is necessary. No special reasons, however, are required to be recorded by the Court.*" Considering the enormous delay of nine years in disposal of the application under section 125, CrPC, the Supreme Court ordered grant of maintenance to the wife from the date of application and allowed the husband to pay the arrears along with the maintenance awarded at present in a phased manner.

From a collective reading of the recent pronouncements authoritatively made by the Supreme Court recently, it is crystal clear that no laxity or delay would be permitted to pay maintenance under section 125, CrPC as a continuing liability, even if required to be paid after divorce, if the circumstances and financial situation so requires and warrants.

MAINTENANCE OF THE WIFE UNDER THE PROVISIONS OF THE HINDU ADOPTIONS AND MAINTENANCE ACT 1956

Section 18 of the HAMA, 1956, is reproduced hereunder for ready reference:

'18. Maintenance of wife.—(1) Subject to the provisions of this section, a Hindu wife, whether married before or after the commencement of this Act, shall be entitled to be maintained by her husband during her life time.

(2) A Hindu wife shall be entitled to live separately from her husband without forfeiting her claim to maintenance—

(a) if he is guilty of desertion, that is to say, of abandoning her without reasonable cause and without her consent or against her wish or willfully neglecting her;

(b) if he has treated her with such cruelty as to cause a reasonable apprehension in her mind that it will be harmful or injurious to live with her husband;

(c) if he is suffering from a virulent form of leprosy;

(d) if he has any other wife living;

(e) if he keeps a concubine in the same house in which his wife is living or habitually resides with a concubine elsewhere;

(f) if he has ceased to be a Hindu by conversion to another religion;

(g) if there is any other cause justifying living separately.

(3) A Hindu wife shall not be entitled to separate residence and maintenance from her husband if she is unchaste or ceases to be a Hindu by conversion to another religion.'

The Delhi High Court in *Neelam Malhotra* v. *Rajinder Malhotra,* AIR 1994 Del 234, held that after considering the status of the husband, the wife should be awarded maintenance *pendente lite,* even though there is no separate provision in HAMA, 1956, for grant of maintenance *pendente lite.* The obligation to maintain the wife remains on the husband even though the wife might be living separately. The court was conscious of the fact that the suit for maintenance under section 18 of the Act may take a long time before it is decided, hence, the wife in the first instance cannot be subjected to starvation and then subsequently granted maintenance from the date of filing of suit. The court was of the opinion that such a restrictive view would be against the letter and spirit of section 18 of the Act.

Section 19 of the HAMA, 1956, provides for maintenance of the widowed daughter-in-law and is reproduced hereunder for ready reference:

'19. Maintenance of widowed daughter-in-law.—(1) A Hindu wife, whether married before or after the commencement of this Act, shall be entitled to be maintained after the death of her husband by her father-in-law:

Provided and to the extent that she is unable to maintain herself out of her own earnings or other property or, where she has no property of her own, is unable to obtain maintenance—

(a) from the estate of her husband or her father or mother, or

(b) from her son or daughter, if any, or his or her estate.

(2) Any obligation under sub-section (1) shall not be enforceable if the father-in-law has not the means to do so from any coparcenary property in his possession out of which the daughter-in-law has not obtained any share, and any such obligation shall cease on the re-marriage of the daughter-in-law.'

FACTORS GOVERNING QUANTUM OF MAINTENANCE

Section 23 provides that it shall be at the discretion of the Court to determine the amount of maintenance, if any, payable at all and in doing so the Court shall be guided by the considerations set out in section 23(2) or (3) of the HAMA, 1956, which are stated hereunder:

'23(2) In determining the amount of maintenance, if any, to be awarded to a wife, children or aged or infirm parents under this Act, the following factors shall be taken into account—

(a) the position and status of the parties;

(b) the reasonable wants of the claimant;

(c) if the claimant is living separately, whether the claimant is justified in doing so;

(d) the value of the claimant's property and any income derived from such property, or from the claimant's own earnings or from any other source;

(e) the number of persons entitled to maintenance under this Act.

(3) In determining the amount of maintenance, if any, to be awarded to a dependant under this Act, regard shall be had to—

(a) the net value of the estate of the deceased after providing for the payment of his debts;

(b) the provision, if any, made under a will of the deceased in respect of the dependant;

(c) the degree of relationship between the two;

(d) the reasonable wants of the dependant;

(e) the past relations between the dependant and the deceased;

(f) the value of the property of the dependant and any income derived from such property, or from his or her earnings or from any other source;

(g) the number of dependants entitled to maintenance under this Act.

Section 25 of the HAMA, 1956 also provides that the amount of maintenance may be altered on change of circumstances. The comprehensive position of law on factors governing award of quantum of maintenance are as below:

The needs of the wife and the status and standards she was used to in her husband's house is to be kept in mind while awarding maintenance. In *Jasbir Kaur Sehgal* v. *District Judge*, AIR 1997 SC 3397, the court held that the amount fixed should be such as she can live in reasonable comfort considering her status and the mode of life she was used to when she lived with her husband and also that she does not feel handicapped in the prosecution of her case.

S.R. Batra v. *Tarun Batra*, AIR 2009 SC 1118, was a case where a wife sought to enforce her right of residence in the alleged matrimonial home and 'shared-household', where the property belonged to the mother-in-law. While the Delhi High Court conceded her right, the same was rejected by the Supreme Court on the ground that the shared household was not owned by the husband and being a property belonging to the mother in law, the wife had no right of residence in it.

Komalam Amma v. *Kumara Pillai Raghavan Pillai*, AIR 2009 SC 636, the Supreme Court of India endorsed the right of a woman to a residence as included in the general term 'maintenance.' The Apex Court elaborated on the concept of maintenance in AIR 2009 SC 636 para 9 at page 637 of the judgment as follows:

> *"9. Maintenance, as we see it, necessarily must encompass a provision for residence. Maintenance is given so that the lady can live in the manner, more or less, to which she was accustomed. The concept of maintenance must, therefore, include provision for food and clothing and the like and take into account the basic need of a roof over the head. Provision for residence may be made either by*

giving a lump sum in money, or property in lieu thereof. It may also be made by providing, for the course of the lady's life, a residence and money for other necessary expenditure. Where provision is made in this manner, by giving a life interest in property for the purposes of residence, that provision is made in lieu of a pre-existing right to maintenance and the Hindu lady acquires far more than the vestige of title which is deemed sufficient to attract section 14(1)."

In *Sarla Singh* v. *Kr. Ajay Partap Singh*, 2011 (2) Marri LJ 372, the High Court of Punjab and Haryana held as follows:

> *"It is settled law, that in estimating the amount of permanent alimony or permanent maintenance, the Court, while dealing with the fact of income, is not to focus its attention only on the disposable income of a spouse in the year of proceedings but would also normally have regard to the earnings in the previous years and probable earnings in the future. The Court is also to look into the position and the status of parties and in absence of any reliable data on the point of income, the Court is to take into consideration overall financial position of the spouses and their necessities having regard not merely to their income but their properties, debts and liabilities. It is well settled that the wife besides maintenance is now also entitled to right of residence with the equal status as that of husband. Even a flat of two rooms is worth more than Rs. 80 lacs (Rupees eighty lac only). However, the right of residence along with right to maintenance is assessed at Rs. 1,00,000,00 (Rupees one crore only), if paid in lump sum. For the reasons stated, this appeal is allowed, the permanent alimony payable is enhanced to Rs. 40,000 (Rupees forty thousand only) per month with right of residence or in the alternative a sum of Rs. 1,00,000,00 (Rupees one crore only) as one time alimony which would not represent even 1/10th of the property owned by the respondent."*

In *Vinny Parmvir Parmar* v. *Parmvir Parmar*, AIR 2011 SC 2748, was pleased to hold as follow in a case to determine as to what would be the reasonable amount the wife is entitled by way of maintenance from the husband under section 25, HMA, 1955. The Court held

> *"12. As per section 25, while considering the claim for permanent alimony and maintenance of either spouse, the respondent's own income and other property, and the income and other property of the applicant are all relevant material in addition to the conduct of the parties and other circumstances of the case. It is further seen that the court considering such claim has to consider all the above relevant material and determine the amount which is to be just for living standard. No fixed formula can be laid for fixing the amount of maintenance. It has to be in the nature of things which depend on various facts and circumstances of each case. The court has to consider the status of the parties, their respective needs, the capacity of the husband to pay, having regard to reasonable expenses for his own maintenance and others whom he is obliged to maintain under the law and statute. The courts also have to take note of the fact that the amount of maintenance fixed for the wife should be such as she can live in reasonable comfort considering her status and mode of life she was used to live when she lived with her husband. At the same time, the amount so fixed cannot be excessive or affect the living condition of the other party. These are all the broad principles*

courts have to be keep in mind while determining maintenance or permanent alimony.

In *Vishwanath* v. *Sau Sarla Vishwanath Agrawal*, (2012) 7 SCC 288, while deciding permanent alimony, it was held:

"41. Presently, we shall deal with the aspect pertaining to the grant of permanent alimony. The court of first instance has rejected the application filed by the respondent-wife as no decree for divorce was granted and there was no severance of marital status. We refrain from commenting on the said view as we have opined that the husband is entitled to a decree for divorce. Permanent alimony is to be granted taking into consideration the social status, the conduct of the parties, the way of living of the spouse and such other ancillary aspects. During the course of hearing of the matter, we have heard the learned counsel for the parties on this aspect. After taking instructions from the respective parties, they have addressed us. The learned senior counsel for the appellant has submitted that till 21-2-2012, an amount of Rs. 17,60,000 has been paid towards maintenance to the wife as directed by the courts below and hence, that should be deducted from the amount to be fixed. He has further submitted that the permanent alimony should be fixed at Rs. 25 lacs. The learned counsel for the respondent, while insisting for affirmance of the decisions of the High Court as well as by the courts below, has submitted that the amount that has already been paid should not be taken into consideration as the same has been paid within a span of number of years and the deduction would affect the future sustenance. He has emphasised on the income of the husband, the progress in the business, the inflation in the cost of living and the way of life the respondent is expected to lead. He has also canvassed that the age factor and the medical aid and assistance that are likely to be needed should be considered and the permanent alimony should be fixed at Rs. 75 lacs.

42. In our considered opinion, the amount that has already been paid to the respondent-wife towards alimony is to be ignored as the same had been paid by virtue of the interim orders passed by the courts. It is not expected that the respondent-wife has sustained herself without spending the said money. Keeping in view the totality of the circumstances and the social strata from which the parties come from and regard being had to the business prospects of the appellant, permanent alimony of Rs. 50 lacs (rupees fifty lacs only) should be fixed and, accordingly, we so do. The said amount of Rs. 50 lacs (rupees fifty lacs only) shall be deposited by way of bank draft before the trial court within a period of four months and the same shall be handed over to the respondent-wife on proper identification."

In *U. Sree* v. *U. Srinivas*, AIR 2013 SC 415, the Apex Court holding that no arithmetic formula was possible to be devised in calculating permanent maintenance, was pleased to hold as follows:

"33. We have reproduced the aforesaid orders to highlight that the husband had agreed to buy a flat at Hyderabad. However, when the matter was listed thereafter, there was disagreement with regard to the locality of the flat arranged by the husband and, therefore, the matter was heard on merits. We have already

> *opined that the husband has made out a case for divorce by proving mental cruelty. As a decree is passed, the wife is entitled to permanent alimony for her sustenance. Be it stated, while granting permanent alimony, no arithmetic formula can be adopted as there cannot be mathematical exactitude. It shall depend upon the status of the parties, their respective social needs, the financial capacity of the husband and other obligations. In* Vinny Parmvir Parmar *v.* Parmvir Parmar, *2011 (3) RCR (Civil) 900: 2011 (4) RAJ 357: (2011) 13 SCC 112, while dealing with the concept of permanent alimony, this Court has observed that while granting permanent alimony, the Court is required to take note of the fact that the amount of maintenance fixed for the wife should be such as she can live in reasonable comfort considering her status and the mode of life she was used to when she lived with her husband. At the same time, the amount so fixed cannot be excessive or affect the living condition of the other party.*
>
> *34. Keeping in mind the aforesaid broad principles, we may proceed to address the issue. The respondent himself has asserted that he has earned name and fame in the world of music and has been performing concerts in various parts of India and abroad. He had agreed to buy a flat in Hyderabad though it did not materialise because of the demand of the wife to have a flat in a different locality where the price of the flat is extremely high. Be that as it may, it is the duty of the Court to see that the wife lives with dignity and comfort and not in penury. The living need not be luxurious but simultaneously she should not be left to live in discomfort. The Court has to act with pragmatic sensibility to such an issue so that the wife does not meet any kind of man-made misfortune. Regard being had to the status of the husband, the social strata to which the parties belong and further taking note of the orders of this Court on earlier occasions, we think it appropriate to fix the permanent alimony at Rs 50 lacs which shall be deposited before the learned Family Judge within a period of four months out of which Rs 20 lacs shall be kept in a fixed deposit in the name of the son in a nationalized bank which would be utilised for his benefit. The deposit shall be made in such a manner so that the respondent wife would be in a position to draw maximum quarterly interest. We may want to clarify that any amount deposited earlier shall stand excluded."*

In *Vishwanath Sitaram Agrawal* v. *Sau. Sarla Vishwanath Agrawal*, AIR 2012 SC 2586 the apex Court while granting permanent alimony has observed that the amount that has already been paid to the respondent-wife towards alimony is to be ignored as the same had been paid by virtue of the interim orders passed by the courts. It is not expected that the respondent-wife has sustained herself without spending the said money.

In *U. Sree* v. *U. Srinivas*, AIR 2013 SC 415, the apex Court while dealing with section 25 of the Act has observed as follows:—

> *".. while granting permanent alimony, no arithmetic formula can be adopted as there can not be mathematical exactitude. It shall depend upon the status of the parties their respective social needs, the financial capacity of the husband and other obligations."*
>
> *In the said judgment the apex Court has also observed that ".. it is the duty of the court to see that the wife lives with dignity and comfort and not in penury.*

The living need not be luxurious but simultaneously she should not be left to live in discomfort. The court has to act with pragmatic sensibility to such an issue so that the wife does not meet any kind of man made misfortune"

Clearly, there is no mathematical or universal formula in granting need based maintenance to a spouse upon termination of marriage. However, all factors relating to sustenance, right to live in a residential property, upkeep of children, and other benefits due to a spouse are all quantified in a lumpsum amount of alimony which may be paid in one instalment or may be spread over to a number of instalments depending on the facts and circumstances of a given case.

PRACTICAL PROBLEMS IN REALISING MAINTENANCE

As a brief observation to actually realizing maintenance in practical terms, it may be submitted that even though sufficient legislation exists in India for providing maintenance and settlement of other ancillary relief, in reality the implementation and enforcement of this beneficial legislation needs attention. The quantum of maintenance awarded by the courts is generally quite low and procedural delays of the process do not provide much succour to a spouse in distress.

Issues of settlement of matrimonial property and custody of children are often overtaken by bitter matrimonial wrangling between the contesting spouses and the benevolent purpose of beneficial legislation for settling the aftermath is clouded and overshadowed in courts where the focus is on the divorce proceedings only. The priorities in the courts need to change. Sufficient maintenance in need must be awarded and the rights of children need to be settled more vigorously and placed on a higher pedestal. This is perhaps one area where the courts of law need to pursue the above propositions with more vehemence and more generously to expedite the settlement of adequate maintenance and matrimonial property besides providing quicker justice to the children of a broken marriage. Furthermore, the mechanism of Alternative Dispute Resolution, Mediation and Conciliation in Family law matters needs to be developed in a big way at the grass roots level in the Trial Courts so that parties can settle their disputes amicably without getting into bitter matrimonial battles. There is sufficient legislation in various existing enactments to support these conciliatory steps, but, in actual practice the implementation and strict application of these benevolent provisions is seriously lacking.

CUSTODY OF CHILDREN UNDER SECTION 26 OF THE HMA, 1955

Section 26 of the HMA, 1955 provides for custody of children of the parties to the litigation and is reproduced hereunder:

'26. Custody of Children.—In any proceeding under this Act, the court may, from time to time, pass such interim orders and make such provisions in the decree as it may deem just and proper with respect to the custody, maintenance and education of minor children, consistently with their wishes, wherever possible, and may, after the decree, upon application by petition for the purpose, make from time to time, all such orders and provisions with respect to the custody, maintenance and education of such children as might have been made by such

decree or interim orders in case the proceeding for obtaining such decree were still pending, and the court may also from time to time revoke, suspend or vary any such orders and provisions previously made:

Provided that the application with respect to the maintenance and education of the minor children, pending the proceeding for obtaining such decree, shall, as far as possible, be disposed of within 60 days from the date of service of notice on the respondent.'

DISPOSAL OF PROPERTY UNDER SECTION 27 OF THE HMA, 1955

Section 27 of the HMA, 1955, empowers the court to adjudicate upon the division and distribution of the properties of the divorced couple at the time of the passing of the decree, and is reproduced hereunder for ready reference:

'27. Disposal of property.– In any proceeding under this Act, the court may make such provisions in the decree as it deems just and proper with respect to any property presented, at or about the time of marriage, which may belong jointly to both the husband and the wife.'

The Delhi High Court held in *Subhash Lata* v. *V.N. Khanna,* AIR 1992 Del 14, that section 27 of the Act concerns only the properties presented at or about the time of marriage, which are alleged to belong jointly to both the spouses. Section 27 can only relate to a limited class of property that is owned jointly by the spouses which has been presented at or about the time of marriage. The pre-condition for getting relief is that such property must belong jointly to both the spouses.

CONCLUSION

The Supreme Court of India's concern in its judgments directing the Government of India to consider enacting a uniform civil code has gone completely unheeded. Such directions have been necessitated on account of legal inequities that exist between men and women in India. It will be noted that customary divorce, subject to certain conditions, is given statutory recognition under the provisions of the HMA, 1955. Further, children of void and voidable marriages are recognised as legitimate in the eyes of the law. The issue of the stigma attached to divorced women in India, especially those hailing from rural areas, married to NRIs becomes an important issue, in the event of broken marriages, where they may be on the verge of deportation from foreign countries. Even personal family laws of all communities need to be suitably looked into for bringing in need based and current circumstances oriented changes which are necessitated with the advent of time. Inter parental cross border child custody issues also need to be resolved by enacting suitable legislation.

DOES DIVORCE LAW IN INDIA NEED AN OVERHAUL?

In brief conclusion to this chapter, after analysing the divorce, maintenance and child custody options and its interpretations by Indian courts, a lurking thought arises. Does the divorce law in India need an overhaul? Keeping in mind that the institution of marriage under HMA, 1955 in India is sacramental and not contractual, any major overhaul may be counter-productive to the very concept of Hindu marriage. The answer therefore is that the existing three-tier divorce structure in India under the HMA, 1955 and SMA, 1954, *i.e.*, the fault grounds, mutual consent principle and stated breakdown theory, seems to provide sufficient options in the existing societal structure within India.. Therefore, no major changes are called for domestically. However, an additional ground to a limited category of non resident Indians only is suggested as an amendment to the existing grounds for divorce in India. It is proposed that for a civilised parting of spouses before Indian Courts, only when both or either of the spouses are non resident Hindus domiciled in a foreign jurisdiction and whose marriage has broken down, irretrievable breakdown needs to be incorporated in the statute book as an additional ground for divorce, which should be hedged with protections and safeguards for the spouse at a disadvantage in a broken relationship. This will have an immediate three-fold benefit. *Firstly*, where parties, one or both, who reside abroad, have irreconcilable differences and want to part amicably, an option will be available to such Hindu spouses to legally and logically part in observance of the sanctity of their personal law, without resorting to a protracted time-consuming legal battle on trumped up charges either in India or abroad at prohibitive legal costs. The minimum six month waiting after filing of a petition for divorce by mutual consent, and one year prior period of living apart can thus be obviated. *Secondly*, resort to divorces in foreign jurisdictions may reduce once a proper legal option of irretrievable breakdown is available on Indian soil to spouses of a dead marriage. Irretrievable breakdown can thus serve as an additional ground for divorce in the HMA, 1955 and SMA, 1954 only for non resident spouses of Hindu religion to prevent hasty divorces abroad on unfriendly terms. However, to prevent misuse, sufficient statutory safeguards can be incorporated to arm the Indian judiciary to stall any abuse of the process of law. *Thirdly*, inter parental child custody conflicts across international borders can be avoided if suitable redressal forums are available in India and children will be saved from the agony of living apart deprived of the love and affection of joint rearing of both their parents. Beyond that, domestically, no change is advocated by the authors for in-country residents in India as the existing three tier divorce structure meets the requirements sufficiently for local purposes. Keeping the Hindu ceremonial and sacramental concept of marriage intact must be adhered to at least domestically. Erosion of values in matrimonial life must be checked. Marriage in its traditional form must be protected. Hindu divorce law does not need an overhaul. It only needs some amendments. The Hindu institution of a family, a home and children of the marriage as they exist today under Hindu law needs protection.

Hindu Law and Uniform Civil Code – The Indian Experience

I. INTRODUCTION – THE INDIAN BACKGROUND

The Constitution of India enacted on 26 November, 1949 resolved to constitute India as a Union of States and a Sovereign, Socialist, Secular, Democratic Republic. Today, a population of over 1.2 billion Indians lives in 29 States and seven Union Territories within India, besides about 30 million Indians who reside in foreign jurisdictions - called non-resident Indians. Within the territory of India - spread over an area of 3.28 million sq. km, the large Indian population - comprised of multicultural societies professing and practicing different religions and speaking different local languages, coexist in harmony in one of the largest democracies in the world.

The Indian Parliament at the helm of affairs legislates on central subjects in the Union and Concurrent lists and State legislatures enact laws pertaining to State subjects as listed in the Constitution of India. Likewise, pertaining to the Judiciary, under article 214 of the Indian Constitution there shall be a High Court for each State and under article 124 there shall be a Supreme Court of India. Under article 141 of the Constitution, the law declared by the Supreme Court shall be binding on all Courts within the territory of India. However, the Supreme Court may not be bound by its own earlier views and can render new decisions.

Part III of the Constitution of India secures to its citizens 'Fundamental Rights' which can be enforced directly in the respective High Courts of the States or directly in the Supreme Court of India by issue of prerogative writs under articles 226 and 32 respectively of the Constitution of India. Under the Constitutional scheme, among others, Freedom of Religion and the right to freely profess, practice and propagate religion are sacrosanct and are thus enforceable by a writ.

Simultaneously, Part IV of the Indian Constitution lays down 'Directive Principles of State Policy' which are not enforceable by any Court but are nevertheless fundamental in the governance of the country and it shall be the duty of the State to apply these principles while making laws. Under article 44 of the Constitution in this Part, the State shall endeavour to secure for the citizens a Uniform Civil Code throughout the territory of India. However, realistically speaking, to date a Uniform Civil Code remains an aspiration which India has yet to achieve and enact.

How does the system of law and society work in India? Against the background of an enforceable Fundamental Right of Religion in a multicultural and diverse society professing different religions, how does a Uniform Civil Code fit in? How do Indian Courts harmonize law and religion in a Democratic, Secular, Sovereign, Socialist Republic? What are the views expressed by Courts in judgments on such issues? Do religious Courts and extra judicial forums find acceptance in the Indian judicial system? Is a Uniform Civil Code an illusion? Does family law in India need reform? Does judicial activism in India trigger off an impetus for making changes in family laws? How are the clashes on issues of personal family laws resolved? Does custom override statutory family laws? Does child removal as fallout of broken marriages need to be curbed by legislation? Do non-resident Indians bring in foreign judgments contrary to Indian family law which Indian Courts do not implement mechanically? These are only some conflict areas which will be dealt with in this chapter along with supporting case-law in some areas of family law to see how best the current system seeks to handle them.

Against the backdrop of the brief description above, this chapter is a modest attempt to put together possible answers to the above questions and issues raised to examine the harmonious coexistence of law and religion in the Indian democracy in the light of the different family law legislation enacted by the Indian Parliament and the views of the Indian Supreme Court expressed on the issues posed above.

II. EXISTING FAMILY LAW LEGISLATION PREVALENT IN INDIA

India is a land of diversities with several religions. The oldest part of the Indian legal system is the personal laws governing the Hindus and the Muslims. The Hindu personal law has undergone changes by a continuous process of codification. The process of change in society has brought changes in law reflecting the changed social conditions and attempting to solve social problems by new methods in the light of experience of legislation in other countries of the world. The Muslim personal law has been comparatively left untouched by legislations.

The Indian legal system is basically a common law system. The Indian Parliament has enacted the following family laws which are applicable to the religious communities defined in the respective enactments themselves. A brief description of each of these separate enactments is given hereunder.

(a) The main marriage law legislation in India applicable to the majority population constituted of Hindus is known as the Hindu Marriage Act, 1955, which is an Act to amend and codify the law relating to marriage among Hindus. Ceremonial marriage is essential under this Act and registration is optional. It applies to any person who is a Hindu, Buddhist, Jaina or Sikh by religion and to any other person who is not a Muslim, Christian, Parsi or Jew by religion. The Act also applies to Hindus resident outside the territory of India. Nothing contained in this Act shall be deemed to affect any right recognised by custom or conferred by any special enactment. Likewise, in other personal law matters, Hindus are governed by the Hindu Succession Act, 1956, which is an Act to amend and codify the law relating to intestate succession among Hindus. The Hindu Minority and Guardianship Act, 1956 is an Act to amend and codify certain parts of the law relating to minority and guardianship among Hindus and the Hindu Adoptions and Maintenance Act, 1956 is an Act to amend and codify the law relating to adoptions and maintenance among Hindus. It may be pertinent to point out that the Indian Succession Act, 1925 is an Act to consolidate the law applicable to intestate and testamentary succession in India unless parties opt and choose to be governed by their respective codified law otherwise applicable to them. In respect of issues relating to guardianship, the Guardian and Wards Act, 1890 would apply to non-Hindus. Interestingly, section 125 of the Code of Criminal Procedure, 1973 provides that irrespective of religion, any person belonging to any religion can approach a magistrate to be provided with maintenance. Therefore, apart from personal family law legislations, both Hindus and non-Hindus have an independent right of maintenance under the general law of the land, if he or she is otherwise entitled to maintenance under this Code.

(b) The Indian Parliament also enacted the Special Marriage Act, 1954 as an Act to provide a special form of marriage in certain cases, for the registration of such and certain other marriages and for divorces under this Act. This enactment of solemnising marriage by registration is resorted to by Hindus, non-Hindus and foreigners marrying in India who opt out of the ceremonial marriage under their respective personal laws. Registration is compulsory under this enactment. Divorce can also be obtained by non-Hindus under this Act. This legislation governs people of all religions and communities in India, irrespective of their personal faith. Likewise, under the Foreign Marriage Act 1969, a person has only to be a citizen of India to have a marriage solemnised under this Act outside the territorial limits of India.

(c) The Parsi Marriage and Divorce Act 1936, as amended in 1988, is an Act to amend the law relating to marriage and divorce among the Parsis in India.

(d) The Christian Marriage Act, 1872 was enacted as an Act to consolidate and amend the law relating to the solemnisation of the marriages of Christians in India and the Divorce Act, 1869, as amended in 2001, is an Act to amend the law relating to divorce and matrimonial causes relating to Christians in India.

(e) The Muslim Personal Law (Shariat) Application Act, 1937, Dissolution of Muslim Marriages Act, 1939, Muslim Women (Protection of Rights on Divorce) Act, 1986 and Muslim Women (Protection of Rights on Divorce Rules, 1986, apply to Muslims living in India.

For enforcement and adjudication of all matrimonial and other related disputes of any person in any of the different religious or non-religious communities under the respective legislation mentioned above, the designated judicial forum or court where such petition is to be lodged is prescribed in the respective enactments themselves. There is an organised system of designated civil and criminal judicial courts within every State in India which works under the overall jurisdiction of the respective High Court in the State. It is in the hierarchy of these courts that all family and matrimonial cases are lodged and decided by the aggrieved party. In addition, the Indian Parliament has enacted the Family Courts Act, 1984 to provide for the establishment of Family Courts with a view to promote conciliation in and to secure speedy settlement of disputes relating to marriage and family affairs. Despite the existence of an organised, well regulated and established hierarchy of judicial courts in India, there are still unrecognised parallel community and religious courts in existence whose interference has been deprecated by the judicial courts since such unauthorised and unwarranted bodies work without the authority of law and are not parts of the judicial system.

III. CONFLICT AREAS IN INDIAN FAMILY LAW

To assess, evaluate, analyse and examine how different codified Indian family laws actually work in the Indian societal set up and how Courts interpret them and also to construe what are the lacunas involved in these individual family causes, it would be appropriate to deal with the individual subjects hereunder.

(a) Marriage laws

Societal conflicts, law and realities

All the codified marriage legislation in India stipulates conditions of a valid marriage. The bone of contention in these stipulations hovers around two harsh realities, *i.e.*, age of marriage and registration of marriages. The principal family law legislation in India, *i.e.*, the Hindu Marriage Act, 1955, does not render a marriage void or voidable in the event that the boy has not reached the age of 21 years or the girl has not reached the age of 18 years. Child marriages are performed even though the Child Marriage Restraint Act, 1929 provides punishment for solemnising child marriages of boys below 20 years of age and girls below 18 years of age. To add to the problem, India to date does not have a compulsory requirement by law for registration of marriages. This practice is in harmony with reality. Child marriages in practically all religious communities in India are accepted practices, which obviously cannot be registered due to non-fulfilment of the minimum age of marriage. Therefore, the violation of the condition of the minimum age of marriage does not entail nullity of the marriage since registration is optional and not compulsory.

However, the lack of will on the part of the Indian legislature to enact a compulsory law for registration of marriages has not gone unnoticed by the courts. The Supreme Court of India in *Seema* v. *Ashwani Kumar,* AIR 2006 SC 1158 has directed all States in India to notify rules for compulsory registration of marriages irrespective of religion, in a time bound period. This reform, which has been spearheaded by the National Commission for Women, has struck a progressive blow to check child marriages, prevent marriages without consent of the parties, check bigamy/polygamy, enable women's rights of maintenance, inheritance and residence, deter men from deserting women and check young girls being sold in the garb of marriage. The Supreme Court of India in another unreported decision dated 27 March, 2006 has stayed the legal validity of the marriages of minor girls below 18 years of age, which had been earlier upheld by the two High Court orders being appealed against in the Supreme Court. At least seven States in India have high incidence of child brides and the law does not take care of the anomaly by banning child marriages.

The orders of the Indian Apex Court may open a Pandora's box. Besides Hindus, the problem will also be with the other minority religious communities. Even among Muslims mere non-registration of a marriage will not make it invalid. Codification of some personal laws among some religious communities in India is itself a very debatable issue. Besides, consequences of non-registration of marriages has created a large number of abandoned spouses in India deserted by non-resident Indians who habitually reside abroad. Times have changed, laws have not. Education, economic prosperity, agricultural improvements, cross border migration and Western influences have changed practices and lifestyles in urban India while rural set-ups are still struggling with adherence to customary practices in family law matters. Will society catch up with law or will the legislature enact a law on the request of the Courts to change societal practices? This remains to be seen. However, the fact remains that until the rural masses in India are educated and motivated to change for the better, any change in laws will not really help. Reality must dawn that the unhealthy social edifices of child marriage must be dismantled and the exploitation of married women must cease. Awareness must come from within the people and cannot be enforced by any law.

Inter caste marriages: a national interest

The Constitution of India guarantees the Fundamental Rights to equality, freedom and protection of life and personal liberty. Equality of laws and equal protection of laws are the touchstone and the spirit of these rights. Additionally, the Directive Principles of State Policy endeavour to get the State to strive to promote the welfare of the people in a social order in which justice, social, economic and political, shall inform all the institutions of national life. However, the fact remains that in India when young men and women marry outside their castes or community, it evokes strong sentiments and even honour killings, although there is no bar to inter caste marriages under any codified marriage law. In one such decision rendered by the Indian Supreme Court in *Lata Singh* v. *State of Uttar Pradesh,* (2006) 5 SCC 475, it was held that the caste system is a curse on the nation and needs to be destroyed for the better. Acts of violence and threats against such inter caste couples are wholly illegal and those who commit them should be severely punished. The administration and police authorities all over the country were directed by the Supreme Court to ensure that no inter caste couple is harassed by anyone or subjected to any threat or acts of violence. Truly, the message of the Court is clear, India of the 21st century cannot be built on the basis of casteism. To amalgamate as a nation, inter caste and inter religious marriages among communities in India must be accepted by society. Barbaric practices of honour killings must be obliterated. But how far can Court decisions achieve this? The government must enforce the law of the land and uphold the citizen's fundamental rights. A heavy hand is required to check this menace. The realisation must dawn on citizens that in the path to development such archaic practices retard growth, reverse progress and kill the spirit of equality. Therefore, law and society must be in tandem to root out such prejudicial practices.

Unconstitutional extra judicial courts: a blow to codified laws

Community practices in certain States in India in certain religious denominations have led to the creation of Community or Religious Courts which do not have the legitimate backing of the system of law and have no sanctity in the official legal system. It is in the matter of inter caste or inter religious marriages or divorces that such self-styled extra-constitutional authorities take upon themselves the power of Courts of law to issue community mandates to people within the community. Such religious edicts result from summary hearings often in violation of Fundamental Rights guaranteed by the Constitution of India. In this regard, the Supreme Court of India on 27 March, 2006 in *Vishwa Lochan Madan* v. *Union of India*, issued notices to the Central Government, State Governments, All India Muslim Personal Law Board (AIMPLB) and Darul Uloom, an Islamic seminary, in the matter of the existence of parallel Islamic and Shariat Courts in the country, which are posing a challenge to the Indian judicial system. In this petition filed as a Public Interest Litigation petition in the Supreme Court of India, Advocate Vishwa Lochan Madan was seeking immediate dissolution of all Islamic and Shariat Courts in India. Earlier, on 16 August, 2005, in *Vishwa Lochan Madan* v. *Union of India*, the Supreme Court of India had also issued notices to the Indian States of Uttar Pradesh, Haryana, Assam, Madhya Pradesh, Rajasthan, West Bengal and Delhi, where, according to the petition, Islamic courts have been formed and were posing a challenge to the judicial system of the country. Shariat law refers to a set of canonical Islamic laws derived from the Quran, the Muslim holy book, and Hadith, which refers to the sayings and examples from the Prophet's life as interpreted by the founders of four ancient schools of Islamic law. Shariat law is variously applied in different countries.

The Petitioner in the above case sought an immediate dissolution of all Islamic and Shariat courts in India, alleging that the AIMPLB had established *Darul Qaza* (Muslim Courts) in India at Thane (Maharashtra), Akola Dholiya (Rajasthan), Indore (Madhya Pradesh), South and East Delhi, Asansol and Purulia (West Bengal), Lucknow and at Sitapur (Uttar Pradesh). Citing the *fatwa* (a religious decree) issued by the Deoband-based seminary in the State of Uttar Pradesh known as *Darul Uloom* in an earlier rape case and the supporting stand of AIMPLB, the above named petitioner pointed out that the criminal law was not allowed to have its natural course as the entire issue was said to be hijacked by the Muslim clerics. The petitioner sought a ban on the establishment of such Islamic courts, along with a declaration that these fatwas have no legal sanctity and requested the Court to direct the Central and the State Governments to take effective steps to dissolve all *Darul Qazas* and Shariat Courts in India. In this direct petition before the Supreme Court, it was acting on a Public Interest Litigation filed by Advocate Vishwa Lochan Madan, after a 2005 *fatwa* from the State of Uttar Pradesh had annulled the marriage of a 28 year old mother of five children and asked her to stay with her father-in-law who had allegedly raped her.

The petitioner further sought a direction from the Court to the AIMPLB and Darul Uloom, Deoband, other seminaries and Muslim organisations asking them to refrain from establishing a parallel Muslim Judicial System (*Nizam-e-Qaza*). A direction from the Court was also sought to restrain these organisations from interfering with the marital status of Indian Muslim citizens and passing any judgment, remarks or fatwas as well as deciding matrimonial disputes amongst Muslims. This petition no doubt raises a crucial issue as to whether there could be two parallel legal systems in operation, one legal and the other religious, particularly when the Constitution of India prohibits discrimination on grounds of caste or religion, and whether the right to freedom of religion could be extended to the establishment of a parallel judicial system. By a epic and historical judgment in WP (C) No. 386 of 2005, *Vishwa Lochan Madan* v. *Union of India,* decided on July 7, 2014, the Supreme Court whilst deciding the above matter, for the first time, has spelt out the status of the Shariat Courts by giving a verdict summarized hereunder as per the following conclusions:

- *Dar-ul-Qazas* (Islamic Courts) have no constitutional or legal basis.
- *Fatwas,* or edicts, issued by such Islamic Courts have no force of law and cannot be enforced. They are not binding and can be ignored by the parties.
- *Dar-ul-Qazas* (Islamic Courts) cannot issue fatwas concerning an individual unless asked for by the person or persons having a direct interest in the matter before the Islamic Courts.
- No religion is allowed to curb Fundamental Rights of Indian citizens. *Qazis* or *Muftis* who man the Islamic Courts cannot impose their opinion through coercion or other methods.
- People in the Islamic community are free to voluntarily consult Islamic Courts for arbitration in personal matters.
- Supreme Court has refused to disband *Dar-ul-Qazas* by stating that they are part of the informal justice delivery system.

The import of the thoughtful Supreme Court ruling on Shariat based forums established to adjudicate disputes amongst Muslims in India is far fetched. The Court has authoritatively ruled that personal laws ought to be administered by the regular law Courts and personal laws cannot be enforced in derogation of fundamental rights by religious Courts that lack such legal sanctity. The above landmark judgment has been hailed as a positive step towards a uniform civil code. However, the fact remains, that the actual implementation and the enforcement of the milestone verdict will largely depend on its acceptance by the members of the Islamic community themselves. Regardless, the fact remains that India being a sovereign, socialist, secular, democratic Republic, the aim and goal set in article 44 of the Constitution of India as part of the Directive Principles of State Policy is that *"the State shall endeavour to secure for the citizens a uniform civil code throughout the territory of India."* Hence, to strive towards reaching this objective as part of the aspirations of the founders of the Constitution, all affirmative steps in this direction must be hailed as an accomplishment.

On similar lines exist the caste khap panchayats (village councils) especially in the State of Haryana in India. These caste panchayats throw several lives into turmoil, often by declaring marriages invalid, and invariably their victims belong to the weakest sections of society. Traditionally, caste panchayats have played a powerful role at the village level in several other States of the country also. However, *khap panchayats* (caste-based village councils) are not elected bodies and their decisions are not enforceable by law as such extra-constitutional bodies have no sanctity or recognition in law. They, however, derive support from community recognition.

Khap panchayats are so powerful because of their ability to mobilise a large number of people that they appear to be democratic from the outside, but they are not. They exclude women, the young people as well as the groups who are lower down in the caste hierarchy in the village.

In response to a public interest litigation (PIL) filed by the Haryana unit of the People's Union for Civil Liberties (PUCL), the State's High Court directed the government to protect the life and liberty at all costs of a couple who had entered into an inter-caste wedlock. The High Court also directed the authorities to ensure that nobody coerced the couple to change the status of their marriage. A similar situation had arisen when the Punjab and Haryana High Court heard a number of writ petitions challenging the fatwas issued by the self-styled caste-based *khap panchayats* in the State of Haryana ordering married couples to dissolve their marriages and live separately and ordering their expulsion from the villages on their refusal to do so. Another recent village panchayat dictated that a divorced Muslim woman could remarry her husband only if she marries and divorces her brother-in-law first – this has also been reported in the *Indian Express* dated 6 August, 2006. Other such decisions are also glaring and abound. The positive decisions by the courts of law are no doubt a setback to the caste panchayats of Haryana which have a powerful influence in its socially and culturally backward villages. A positive step has been taken by the Court but there cannot be a constructive outcome until society as a whole decides to fight back to demolish this age-old obsolete system. The executive authorities have done little to check the extra-judicial activities of these unauthorised courts which are a blatant interference with the Fundamental Rights of citizens. The responsibility of the State cannot be abdicated. If this be so, judicial courts in India seem to be the best recourse in giving relief in individual matters involving blatant violation of Fundamental Rights of the citizens by community councils enforcing their edicts by force and extra-judicial means on alleged moral grounds. But then, should courts grant relief as an alternative to ailing legislation? Courts may not legislate but must vindicate human rights. Clearly, the duty of the State also to enforce the law of the land is the need of the day. The courts unhesitatingly should strike down any mandate of any such extra-judicial bodies which have no legal sanctity in a civilised society.

(b) Divorce: customs, practice and law

The two principal family law pieces of legislation in India, *i.e.,* the Hindu Marriage Act, 1955 and the Special Marriage Act, 1954, contain three sets of separate grounds in a three-tier divorce structure. These are the fault grounds, breakdown grounds on non-compliance with judicial separation or restitution of conjugal rights and grounds of mutual consent. Irretrievable breakdown of marriage *simpliciter* is not a ground for divorce under any codified Indian family law. The Parsi Marriage and Divorce Act, 1936 (as amended) and the Divorce Act, 1869 (as amended) follow suit. The Dissolution of Muslim Marriages Act, 1939 lays down the grounds for a decree for dissolution of marriage of Muslims.

Custom and the effect of codified law

Section 29 of the Hindu Marriage Act, 1955 gives statutory recognition to customary divorces. This in effect means that parties relying on a custom need not go to Court and obtain a decree for divorce. However, the onus on the party who relies on a custom is indeed weighty and the custom should be ancient, certain, reasonable and not opposed to public policy. Even though Courts take judicial notice of customs, the validity of a deed of dissolution of marriage under a customary practice has to be established by leading cogent evidence by the person propounding such custom. In *Subramani* v. *M. Chandralekha,* JT 2005 (11) SC 562, the Apex Court, following well-settled earlier principles of law, held that, since there was no custom prevalent in the community to which the parties belonged for dissolution of marriage by mutual consent, the alleged deed of dissolution of marriage could not be executed.

It is common for parties in India to set up customary divorce practices as a short cut to statutory procedures but with the vigilant judiciary such abuse of the process of law does not succeed. Regardless, multiple marriages are often solemnised in contravention of codified law by taking advantage of non-existent customs. To this extent neither law nor the Courts come to the rescue of such parties. However, section 16 of the Hindu Marriage Act, 1955 clearly provides that, notwithstanding that such marriage is null and void, any child of such marriage who would have been legitimate if the marriage had been valid shall be legitimate. Consequently, even though spouses may not gain, the statute protects and provides property and other inheritance rights to children of such unions. Conferring such rights upon children has been reiterated by the Supreme Court of India in *Bhogadi* v. *Vuggina,* (2006) 5 SCC 532. The policy of law is therefore clear to provide beneficial effects to the offspring without condoning the contravention and violation of marriage laws. Customs will not die but their misuse must be prevented and curtailed.

Divorce by irretrievable breakdown of marriage: is it now a necessity?

Keeping in mind that the institution of marriage in Indian society is largely still a sacrament and not a contract, especially under the Hindu Marriage Act, 1955, any major overhaul may be counter-productive to the very concept of Hindu Marriage. The existing three-tier divorce structure in India, largely applicable to all communities, *i.e.,* fault grounds, breakdown theory and the mutual consent principle, provide the codified and statutory grounds for divorce in Indian Courts. Two different High Court decisions, i.e. *Yudhister Singh* v. *Sarita,* HLR 2004 (1) 228; *Kakali Dass* v. *Dr Asish Kumar,* HLR 2004 (1) 448, and a Supreme Court of India decision in *Sham Sunder* v. *Sushma,* AIR 2004 SC 5111, give a clear indication that the ground of irretrievable breakdown of marriage should be rarely used.

Another recent case where the Supreme Court refused to apply the irretrievable breakdown theory is *Vishnu Dutt Sharma* v. *Manju Sharma,* AIR 2009 SC 2254, where the appellant-husband was proved to have inflicted cruelty upon the respondent-wife. The appeal was preferred to the High court and consequently to the Supreme Court, where it was dismissed. The High court held that it would not be doing justice to the respondent if divorce is granted to the appellant despite his cruelty only on the ground of irretrievable breakdown. The Apex Court, further rejected applying the irretrievable breakdown theory on the ground that section 13 does not provide the same and it is not the function of court to make or amend laws. The concluding paragraphs are as hereunder:

> *"9. In this connection it may be noted that in section 13 of the Hindu Marriage Act, 1955 (for short 'the Act') there are several grounds for granting divorce e.g. cruelty, adultery, desertion etc. but no such ground of irretrievable breakdown of the marriage has been mentioned for granting divorce. Section 13 of the Act reads as under:*
>
> *"13. Divorce.—(1) Any marriage solemnized, whether before or after the commencement of this Act, may, on a petition presented by either the husband or the wife, be dissolved by a decree of divorce on the ground that the other party—*
>
> *(i) has, after the solemnization of the marriage, had voluntary sexual intercourse with any person other than his or her spouse; or*
>
> *(i-a) has, after the solemnization of the marriage, treated the petitioner with cruelty; or*
>
> *(i-b) has deserted the petitioner for a continuous period of not less than two years immediately preceding the presentation of the petition; or*
>
> *(ii) has ceased to be a Hindu by conversion to another religion; or*
>
> *(iii) has been incurably of unsound mind, or has been suffering continuously or intermittently from mental disorder of such a kind and to such an extent that the petitioner cannot reasonably be expected to live with the respondent.*
>
> *xx xx xx*
>
> *xx xx xx*
>
> *(iv) has been suffering from a virulent and incurable form of leprosy; or*
>
> *(v) has been suffering from venereal disease in a communicable form; or*
>
> *(vi) has renounced the world by entering any religious order; or*
>
> *(vii) has not been heard of as being alive for a period of seven years or more by those persons who would naturally have heard of it, had that party been alive."*
>
> *10. On a bare reading of section 13 of the Act, reproduced above, it is crystal clear that no such ground of irretrievable breakdown of the marriage is provided by the legislature for granting a decree of divorce. This Court cannot add such a ground to section 13 of the Act as that would be amending the Act, which is a function of the legislature.*

11. Learned counsel for the appellant has stated that this Court in some cases has dissolved a marriage on the ground of irretrievable breakdown. In our opinion, those cases have not taken into consideration the legal position which we have mentioned above, and hence they are not precedents. A mere direction of the Court without considering the legal position is not a precedent. If we grant divorce on the ground of irretrievable breakdown, then we shall by judicial verdict be adding a clause to section 13 of the Act to the effect that irretrievable breakdown of the marriage is also a ground for divorce. In our opinion, this can only be done by the legislature and not by the Court. It is for the Parliament to enact or amend the law and not for the Courts. Hence, we do not find force in the submission of the learned counsel for the appellant."

In *Hitesh Bhatnagar* v. *Deepa Bhatnagar,* (2011) 3 SCC 234, when the Apex Court was examining a matrimonial dispute for divorce by mutual consent where the second motion was not made by both the parties, it was held that no Court can pass a decree in violation of section 13B of the HMA, 1955. The Apex Court also declined to use its power under article 142 of the Constitution to hold that the marriage had broken down irretrievably and held that the Apex Court grants a decree of divorce only in those situations in which the Court is convinced beyond any doubt that there is absolutely no chance of the marriage surviving and it is beyond repair. The Court held that *"even if the chances are infinitesimal for the marriage to survive, it is not for this Court to use its power under article 142 to dissolve the marriage as having broken down irretrievably."* Clearly, the Apex Court has propounded a view to rule out use of its powers when not called for.

In *Darshan Gupta* v. *Radhika Gupta,* (2013) 9 SCC 1, the Apex Court was pleased to hold that the claim for divorce cannot be maintained under the HMA, 1955 and the Court declined to exercise its jurisdiction under article 142 of the Constitution as entertaining the plea of irretrievable breakdown of marriage would not constitute and serve the ends of justice. The Apex Court dismissed the appeal of the husband and upheld the decisions declining divorce to him.

However, some decisions of the Supreme Court of India indicate that the Apex Court has recommended that 'irretrievable breakdown of marriage' should be added as a ground for divorce on the statute book. The Supreme Court in *Naveen Kohli* v. *Neelu Kohli,* AIR 2006 SC 1675, has recommended to the Union of India to seriously consider bringing an amendment in the Hindu Marriage Act, 1955 to incorporate irretrievable breakdown of marriage as a ground for divorce. It is not uncommon for the Apex Court to apply this principle in dissolving marriages as was recently done in *Durga Prasanna* v. *Arundhati,* AIR 2005 SC 3297, following five earlier precedents of the Apex Court rendered in the last 5 years by invoking its powers under article 142 of the Constitution of India available to the Supreme Court only.

In a more recent case, *Smt. Seema Kumari* v. *Suniul Kumar Jha,* AIR 2014 Pat 44, the Family court allowed a divorce filed by the respondent in the present case on the ground of irretrievable breakdown of marriage coupled with desertion. The appellant appealed against the said order of the family Court on the grounds that the family court had abruptly arrived at the conclusion of desertion by the appellant, without any evidence in its support, and also that irretrievable breakdown of marriage is not a ground for divorce under the Hindu Marriage Act, 1955. On the basis of these, the Patna High Court in the present appeal set aside the impugned order. It held that the power to grant divorce on the ground of irretrievable breakdown of marriage lies with the Supreme Court under article 142 of the Constitution & the same is not available to it.

In *U. Sree* v. *U. Srinivas,* (2013) 2 SCC 114, the Apex Court affirmed the finding of the Family Court and the High Court relating to mental cruelty as the foundation for grant of divorce. Fixing the permanent alimony at Rs. 50 lacs, the Apex Court affirmed the decree for dissolution of marriage on the ground of mental cruelty.

In *Kollam Chandra Sekhar* v. *Kollam Padma Latha,* (2014) 1 SCC 225, the Apex Court came to be conclusion that even if the wife did suffer from Schizophrenia, the Court cannot grant the dissolution of marriage on the basis of one spouse's illness since mental disorder as alleged had not been proved. Accordingly, the judgment of the High Court in not granting a decree of divorce was upheld and the petition of the wife for grant of a decree for restitution of conjugal rights under section 9 of the HMA, 1955 was allowed.

However, in Civil Appeal No. 5862 of 2014, *Malathi Ravi* v. *B.V. Ravi,* (2014) 7 SCC 640, the Apex Court noticing extreme incompatibility between the parties perpetuated by mental cruelty led the Court to conclude that the marriage has become illusory and that the decree of divorce granted by the High Court deserves to be affirmed. Matter was sent to the mediation centre where parties entered into a memorandum of settlement by payment of Rs. 3 lacs in name of the minor child of the parties.

Another case relating to the applicability of the irretrievable breakdown theory while granting a decree for divorce is the case of *Rupak Rathi* v. *Anita Chaudhary,* 2014 (2) RCR (Civil) 697. The Punjab and Haryana High court, in this case, extensively dealt with the jurisdiction of the foreign courts regarding the dissolution of marriage. The facts of the case are that Rupak Rathi, appellant, instituted divorce proceedings against his wife, Anita Chaudhary, in UK on 17 March, 2011. During the pendency of these proceedings, Anita Chaudhary instituted the proceedings for divorce in Panchkula on 17 May, 2011 and the UK proceedings were acknowledged before the court in Panchkula. Both the proceedings ran parallel. Proceedings in the English Court were concluded absolutely on 31 January, 2012 and the divorce was granted in favour of the husband on the ground of irretrievable breakdown of marriage. In response to the divorce petition by the wife at Panchkula, on 18 July, 2012, the husband responded before the Matrimonial Court in Panchkula for rejecting the divorce proceedings against him on the ground that the divorce decree of the English Court is binding on both the parties and hence, the divorce petition by wife was barred on the principles of *res judicata* and *estoppel.* However, the wife contended that the English Courts have no jurisdiction to pass a decree on an unavailable ground of irretrievable breakdown of marriage under the Hindu Marriage Act, 1955 and since both the parties were domiciled in India, they were to be governed by the

Hindu Law. The High Court finally held that the English court cannot grant such divorce decree as irretrievable breakdown of marriage was not a ground of divorce in the Hindu Marriage Act, 1955 itself, which governs the parties in the present case. The High Court accordingly held:

> *"17. A close analysis of para. 20 leaves no manner of doubt that the major premise or what we may call the rule which is clearly statutory in nature with reference to both section 13, CPC and section 13, HMA, 1955, that if a foreign Court enters upon a matrimonial action brought by a Hindu husband against a Hindu wife married under the Hindu Law, then both the jurisdiction and grounds have deservedly to be in accordance with HMA, 1955. Here, the word jurisdiction refers to the right, power, as well as authority to interpret and implement the law, or simply put in a nut shell, the authority and power to decide a* lis. *Court jurisdictions are limited by physical boundaries as well as by subject matter. The original jurisdictional court in the present case by all means is the court of the District Judge exercising territorial jurisdiction in India and the grounds on which the action can be brought, must be one which are mentioned in section 13 of HMA, 1955. But that is not the end of the matter. There can be cases where parties confer jurisdiction on the foreign Court and the said Court will assume jurisdiction available to the Matrimonial Court in India but would remain confined to adjudicate the action in accordance with the matrimonial law of the parties* i.e., *HMA, 1955 and the grounds available therein. The legal principle being that when a Hindu couple tied by the nuptial knot according to Hindu rites travel abroad with intention to settle down and reside there to set up matrimonial home, they carry their personal laws on their back, off loading it in a foreign court for adjudication in the event parties intend to litigate for dissolving the marriage, mutually or by contest on one or more of HMA, 1955 recognized principles. A foreign Court can then grant a valid decree of dissolution of marriage but the adjudication must be upon one of the available grounds in the Indian law. Since* ***irretrievable breakdown*** *of marriage is not available in HMA, 1955, the twin test of forum jurisdiction and relief based grounds would remain unsatisfied and the foreign Court decree would not be binding in India nor recognized..."*

Thus, the court in *Rupak Rathi's* case upheld the order passed by the learned District Judge, Panchkula by which the Court at Panchkula had declined the application of the husband under Order VII, rule 11, CPC for accepting the decree of the English Court and dismissing the divorce petition of the wife as not maintainable.

The proposal for including "irretrievable breakdown of marriage" as a ground for divorce was first made almost three decades ago in the Seventy-first Report of the Law Commission of India and has been included in the grounds for divorce under section 13 of Hindu Marriage Act, 1955 along with the Special Marriage Act, 1954 in the Marriage Laws (Amendment) Bill, 2013, which has not yet been accepted. As per the Report, "the Hindu marriage should be allowed to be dissolved if the husband and wife have lived apart for a period of say five to ten years and the marriage is irretrievably broken down due to incompatibility, clash of personality or similar other reasons, as is permissible under many systems of law of advanced countries."

It is proposed that for a civilised parting of spouses before Indian Courts, only when both or either of the spouses are non resident Hindus domiciled in a foreign jurisdiction and whose marriage has broken down, irretrievable breakdown needs to be incorporated in the statute book as an additional ground for divorce, which should be hedged with protections and safeguards for the spouse at a disadvantage in a broken relationship. This will have an immediate three-fold benefit. *Firstly,* where parties, one or both, who reside abroad, have irreconcilable differences and want to part amicably, an option will be available to such Hindu spouses to legally and logically part in observance of the sanctity of their personal law, without resorting to a protracted time-consuming legal battle on trumped up charges either in India or abroad at prohibitive legal costs. The minimum six month waiting after filing of a petition for divorce by mutual consent, and one year prior period of living apart can thus be obviated. *Secondly,* resort to divorces in foreign jurisdictions may reduce once a proper legal option of irretrievable breakdown is available on Indian soil to spouses of a dead marriage. Irretrievable breakdown can thus serve as an additional ground for divorce in the HMA, 1955 and SMA, 1954 only for non resident spouses of Hindu religion to prevent hasty divorces abroad on unfriendly terms. However, to prevent misuse, sufficient statutory safeguards can be incorporated to arm the Indian judiciary to stall any abuse of the process of law. *Thirdly,* inter parental child custody conflicts across international borders can be avoided if suitable redressal forums are available in India and children will be saved from the agony of living apart deprived of the love and affection of joint rearing of both their parents. Beyond that, domestically, no change is advocated by the authors for in- country residents in India as the existing three tier divorce structure meets the requirements sufficiently for local purposes. Keeping the Hindu ceremonial and sacramental concept of marriage intact must be adhered to at least domestically. Erosion of values in matrimonial life must be checked. Marriage in its traditional form must be protected. Hindu divorce law does not need an overhaul. It only needs some amendments. The Hindu institution of a family, a home and children of the marriage as they exist today under Hindu law needs protection.

Child removal – a fallout of broken marriages

The world is a far smaller place now than it was a decade ago. Inter-country and inter-continental travel is easier and more affordable than it has ever been. The corollary to this is an increase in relationships between individuals of different nationalities and from different cultural backgrounds. Caught in the crossfire of broken relationships with ensuing disputes over custody and relocation, the hazards of international abduction loom large over the chronic problems of maintaining access or contact internationally with the uphill struggle of securing cross-frontier child support. In a population of over a billion Indians, 25 million are non-resident Indians who by migrating to different jurisdictions have generated a new crop of spousal and family disputes.

Cross-border family relationships arising from such exchange have carved out a new niche in the jurisdiction of family law disputes. Such problems have no ready-made solutions in the conventional legislation prevailing within the legal system in India. The net result: the innovative judicial system in India with its dynamic jurisprudence when invoked provides a tailor-made answer for every individual case. But then, this does not provide a consistent, uniform and universal remedy to be adhered to in an international perspective. What then is the answer in the highly sensitive area of family law disputes involving conflict of jurisdictions in inter-parental child custody cases when children are removed to India in violation of inter-parental rights or infringement of foreign court orders?

In a decision dated 3 March, 2006 of the High Court of Bombay at Goa, between a 62-year-old American father and 39-year-old British mother resident in Ireland litigating over the custody of their 8-year-old daughter said to be illegally detained in Goa by the father, the Court declining the issuance of a writ of habeas corpus held that the parties could pursue their remedies in normal civil proceedings in Goa. The Court dismissing the mother's plea for custody concluded that the question of permitting the child to be taken to Ireland without first adjudicating upon the rival contentions of the parents in normal civil proceedings in Goa is not possible and directed that the status quo be observed. The mother's appeal to the Supreme Court of India against the above High Court decision was dismissed on 21 August, 2006, with a direction that, if a custody petition was filed in the appropriate forum, it would be decided within 3 months and until then the status quo would be observed regarding the custody and visitation rights as held by the High Court. This in effect means that the 8-year-old girl continues to live in Goa without her mother or any other female family member in the father's house. This case is reported as *Mandy Jane Collins* v. *James Michael Collins*, 2006 (2) HLR (Bom) 446.

The Hague Convention on Civil Aspects of International Child Abduction came into force on 1 December, 1983 and has now 80 contracting nations to it. The Convention secures the prompt return of children wrongfully removed to or retained in any Contracting State and ensures the rights of custody and access under the laws of such Contracting States. India unfortunately to date is not a signatory to the Hague Convention and from practical experience it can be stated that the principles laid down in the Convention are not applicable in India. However, India is now actively considering accession to the said Convention due to the fact that its 30 million non-resident Indian population, spread out over 130 countries of the globe, seriously require such an initiative from an international perspective.

India not being a signatory to the Hague Convention on Civil Aspects of International Child Abduction, 1980, foreign Court orders requiring return of children to the country of their habitual residence are not mechanically implemented by Indian Courts which examine the best interest and the welfare of the child in an independent adjudication before Indian Courts. As an update of the latest position reflected by some recent precedents, a short summary is drawn up as under:

(i) In *Ruchi Majoo* v. *Sanjeev Majoo* AIR 2011 SC 1952, where the husband and wife were American citizens of Indian origin, a child born to them in America was the subject of a custody battle between them. The wife came to India alongwith the child and filed a petition claiming exclusive custody of her child. The interim custody was granted to the mother. The husband filed a petition in a US Court, which granted custody of child to the father which was sought to be enforced in India. The Supreme Court held that the principle of comity of Courts ensures that foreign Judgments and orders are unconditionally conclusive of the matters in controversy, but in the matter of custody of child interest and welfare of the minor being paramount, a competent court in this country is entitled and indeed duty bound to examine the matter independently, taking the foreign judgment, if any, only as an input for its final adjudication. In the facts of the instant case, the repatriation of child to America could not be allowed on the principle of comity of Courts as the interest of the minor shall be better served if he continued in the custody of his mother, especially when the father had contracted a second marriage as also had consented to the bringing of the child from USA to India by the mother.

(ii) In *Shilpa Aggarwal* v. *Aviral Mittal*, decided on 9 December, 2009, (2010) 1 SCC 591, a three and a half year old girl child, who was a British citizen born in UK to Indian parents, was removed to India from UK by the mother in contravention of British Court orders. The mother was directed by the Supreme Court of India to return with child to UK as the matter to determine, which parent was best suited to have the custody in the interest and welfare of the minor child, was pending adjudication before a British Court.

(iii) In *Dr. V. Ravi Chandaran* v. *Union of India*, decided on 17 November, 2009, (2010) 1 SCC 174, a seven year old boy, who was a US citizen and was born in USA to Indian Parents, who had become US citizens, was removed to India from USA by the mother contrary to US Court orders. The mother was directed by the Supreme Court to return to USA with the child failing which the father would be entitled to do so of his own.

(iv) In *Vikramvir Vohra* v. *Shalini Bhalla*, decided on 25 March, 2010, JT 2010 (3) SC 213, it was held by the Supreme Court of India that child custody orders are interlocutory in nature and can be altered for the welfare of the child. Consequently, the Supreme Court permitted the mother to take her minor son aged about ten years to Australia as per the wishes of the child to stay with the mother upholding the welfare of the child as a paramount consideration.

(v) In *Philip David Dexter* v. *State NCT of Delhi*, 2013 (3) DMC 45, the Delhi High Court directed the wife to return the custody of child to the father before the Registrar of The Delhi High Court as the wife had abducted the child and brought her to India violating the joint custody order and had no evidence to *prima facie* justify that there was risk of grave danger to the life of the child on return to the Republic of South Africa. The matter is now pending appeal before the Supreme Court and the operation of the High Court judgment has been stayed till the final decision by the Apex Court.

(vi) In *Arathi Bandi* v. *Bandi Jagadrakshaka Rao*, AIR 2014 SC 918, a decree of dissolution of marriage was obtained from a US Court. The custody of the child was given to the husband. The wife thereafter travelled to India alongwith child in defiance of Court order. The husband then came to India and filed a *habeas corpus* petition before the High Court seeking production of child and permitting him to take custody of the minor in compliance with the order passed by US Court. The High Court directed the wife to submit to the jurisdiction of the US Courts. The appeal by the wife was dismissed by the Supreme Court holding that a parent committing a wrong by removing children out of the country does not gain any advantage by his or her wrongdoing; and that the contention that the American court, which passed the order/decree has no jurisdiction and the same being inconsistent in Indian Law cannot be executed in India, is not tenable.

From a collective reading of the above recent judgments, it can be stated that in matters of child custody foreign court orders do not find mechanical application in India and the Indians Courts decide custody issues in the best interest of the child in which process, the foreign court order is only one consideration for adjudicating upon the matter on merits alone.

The above situation promotes and encourages child removal to India by an offending parent and deprives the child's custody rights from being determined by the laws of the country where the child was normally resident. It also diverts the best interest of the child as the litigation in India gets converted into a fight of superior rights of parents whereas the real issue of the welfare of the child becomes subservient and subordinate. Practical experience also shows that foreign courts now largely disallow children from overseas jurisdictions to be brought to India, apprehending that children will not be returned to the country of their residence.

In the totality of the emerging scenario, it is now practically seen that, in the absence of any Indian legislation on the subject, there is no uniform pattern of decisions to resolve issues of custody and contact which arise when parents are separated and live in different countries. The recent decision quoted above and another child custody dispute in the Supreme Court of India where a US Court declined the return of children to India despite the Supreme Court's directions show that the time has now come for some international perspective in this regard. In January 2005, the British Government appointed Lord Justice Thorpe as then Head of International Family Law in the UK judicial system for promoting development of international instruments and conventions in the field of family law with greater international judicial collaboration. Pakistan has signed a judicial protocol between the President of the Family Division of the High Court of London and the Chief Justice of the Supreme Court of Pakistan for co-operation between judicial authorities of the two countries on such issues. In the larger interest of children at risk, the conflict of jurisdiction of Courts must take a back seat. It is, therefore, the need of the hour that the Indian Legislature consider enacting some legislation to protect the rights of the abducted child to resolve the clash between the rule of domicile and the nationality rule. Maybe, until this is done, the Supreme Court of India could well lay down some uniform guidelines to be consistently followed in inter-parental child abduction from foreign jurisdictions. India cannot be promoted as a haven for parking removed children.

Enforcement of judgments and orders of foreign courts in India arising in family and matrimonial matters in overseas jurisdictions

With the ever-increasing multifold population of Indians migrating and settling in foreign jurisdictions, the link with their home country does not sever. Family ties, connections of property and movable assets, and the invariable link with some Indian end for any reason whatsoever often lead to cross-border litigation in human relationship matters. Situations abound when a non-resident Indian invokes the jurisdiction of the foreign Court where he is resident and convinces the overseas Court to pass favourable orders in such matters which are thereafter sought to be executed in the Indian jurisdiction through the Courts of law in India.

Indian law reports contain a number of judgments on matters relating to marriage, divorce, maintenance, succession, settlement of matrimonial property, child custody, parental abduction of children from foreign jurisdictions in matrimonial disputes and cases relating to adoption. These foreign court orders, once passed, are sought to be enforced or executed in India through the medium of the Courts. Since there exists no separate provision for recognition of foreign matrimonial judgments or other foreign decisions in related matters in the Hindu Marriage Act, 1955, Special Marriage Act, 1954, Hindu Succession Act, 1956, Hindu Adoption and Maintenance Act, 1956, Hindu Minority and Guardianship Act, 1956 or in any other Indian legislation relating to family matters, the only recourse lies in section 13 of the Indian Code of Civil Procedure (CPC) which is the general provision of law relating to conclusiveness of judgments by foreign Courts.

In view of the aforestated position, the provisions of section 13, CPC are also fully applicable to matrimonial matters decided by foreign Courts. In such a situation, the precedents giving instances of such reported matters are therefore available only in the shape of judicial pronouncements of Indian Courts which have from time to time rendered a laudable service in interpreting foreign court orders in the best interests of human relationships rather than executing them *simpliciter* in letter and spirit. The Indian judiciary in such a pivotal role is extremely humane and considerate in family matters by implementing the foreign court orders in a practical way rather than a mechanical execution of the order or judgment of the overseas Court. Perhaps this openness and fluidity are possible since the Indian Courts are not strictly bound by a foreign court order in family matters but when asked to implement or enforce the same, the Indian Courts apply principles of good conscience, natural justice, equity and fair play, thereby rendering substantial justice to parties in litigation. This can be best seen in decisions of some Indian Courts which have resulted from the Court being asked to implement or execute a court order or judgment arising from a foreign jurisdiction.

A very commonly arising issue pertains to recognition and indirect implementation of divorce decrees of foreign Courts produced in India by spouses residing in foreign jurisdictions. In this regard, different views have been expressed by different Indian Courts at different points of time. Consequently, the Supreme Court of India in 1991 laid down fresh comprehensive guidelines for the recognition of foreign matrimonial judgments by the Courts in India. It may be pertinent to point out that under article 141 of the Constitution of India, the law declared by the Supreme Court shall be binding on all Courts within the territory of India. The Apex Court in *Y. Narasimha Rao* v. *Y. Venkata Lakshmi*, (1991) 3 SCC 451, made it clear that Indian Courts would not recognise a foreign judgment if it had been obtained by fraud, which need be not only in relation to the merits of the matter but also in relation to jurisdictional facts. By this ruling, the Supreme Court on the facts of the case declared a divorce decree passed by a US Court to be unenforceable in India. Interpreting section 13, CPC the Court laid down broad principles to be followed by Indian Courts with special emphasis on matrimonial judgments.

Likewise in *Neeraja Saraph* v. *Jayant Saraph*, (1994) 6 SC 461, on the facts of the case, the Apex Court came down heavily on the erring non-resident husband residing in a foreign jurisdiction who had abandoned his Indian wife without providing for any maintenance to her.

In the case of *Rupak Rathi* v. *Anita Chaudhary*, 2014 (2) RCR (Civil) 697 *(Supra)*, the Punjab and Haryana High Court gave its opinion with respect to applicability, as also interpretation of exception (ii) in paragraph 20 of *Y. Narasimha Rao* (Supra) and interpretation of Order VII, rule 11, CPC. The court held:

> *"In* Exceptions *(i) and (ii) the words "grounds" or "ground" have been used in the rule and also in exceptions (i) and (ii) but not in* Exception *(iii). The word, "relief" has been used in the rule and in exceptions (i) and (iii) but not in* Exception *(ii). The first* Exception *talks of 'forum' where the respondent is domiciled or habitually and permanently resides and this is clarified by the conjunction "and" to mean that the "relief" is granted on a ground available under HMA, 1955.*
>
> Exception *(iii) applies in cases which are not contested and are based on consent. It follows that when 'contest' and 'consent/s' are referable to grounds available under HMA, 1955, only then can relief flow. This is for the reason that there is no estoppel against the statute. What is meant by consent to the grant of relief even though the English Court's jurisdiction is contrary to HMA, 1955 is the moot point presenting some difficulty. The rule in para. 20 confers and recognizes jurisdiction by assumption conferred on a foreign Court to act in accordance with the mandate of Indian matrimonial law. The Supreme Court chose not to use the word "grounds" in exception (iii) and this is how some ambiguity is felt after the heated debate on the interpretation of exception (iii) vehemently argued by the respective counsel and the learned amicus from many angles and prisms or points of view. It is, however, well settled that the words used in a judgment cannot be read as one would read words used by the legislature in enactments which latter have to be given their ordinary and plain meaning. In cases of ambiguity in the statutory rule and of the words used by the Parliament, then the court*

can step in to harmonize the provisions in a way which is in consonance with the objects and reasons for which the Act was passed and to further the intention of the law.

There is a difference between the words "relief" and "jurisdiction" of the "forum" in Exception *(iii). Even in the rule, the forum has no jurisdiction but is assumed to have one when it acts on a principle permitted by section 13, HMA, 1955 to be the grounds for dissolution of marriage by a decree of divorce. It is for this reason the Supreme Court used the word "may" when it observed while carving out the three exceptions that the "*Exceptions *to this rule may be as follows". To my mind, if any other interpretation is placed on the word 'relief' in* Exception *(iii), it may result in grant of an illegal decree of dissolution of marriage made available to a party on the ground of irretrievable breakdown of marriage which is an impermissible ground of divorce not so far heralded into the Hindu law of marriage.*

Exception *(iii) is consent based for relief to the respondent but not to the petitioner in forum conveniens; "although the jurisdiction of the forum is not in accordance with the provisions of the matrimonial law of the parties". When the Supreme Court carved out this last exception it avoided introducing the word 'grounds'. If it were employed, the meaning then would have admitted no further debate and full effect would have to be given to the declaration under article 141 of the Constitution of India and for this Court to act in aid. However, since an* Exception *cannot be seen to obliterate the rule itself or to rewrite it, then what the Supreme Court, in my humble view, in fact meant was a consent based decree obtained on foreign soil on HMA, 1955 grounds and not otherwise. Therefore, HMA, 1955 law would have to be read into* Exception *(iii) to align it with the rule and not create a new rule since then it would not qualify as an* Exception *to a rule. Reading the exception in isolation, will, in my considered view, be in violation of the rule itself. Thus, in cases of contested and consented decrees both would suffer HMA, 1955 standards, failing which, the foreign court will be overstepping Parliamentary mandates in India and the decrees so obtained cannot be recognized in India unless falling in* Exceptions *(i) and (ii). This is more so, as I see, when* Exception *(i) talks neither of contest nor consent. Otherwise, there would hardly be any visible distinction between* Exception *(i) and* Exception *(iii) because even in* Exception *(i) the assumed jurisdiction of the foreign court was not in accordance with the provisions of the matrimonial law of the parties or the relief granted was not in accordance with the matrimonial law under which the parties are married. This would be the 'just and equitable' rule to follow for the protection of women who are the most vulnerable sections of society as observed in para 21 of* Y. Narasimha Rao *itself. Besides, consent to a foreign decree not questioned or litigated in court by parties makes no* lis *and remains good till it lasts. However, this is not a matter of law but of personal choice where the arms of law may not reach. But consent itself is a question of evidence if the mode and manner in which it was given is taken to a court of law for determination."*

Further, the High Court laid down seven guidelines for the Matrimonial Courts functioning under its jurisdiction for dealing with applications under

Order VII, rule 11, CPC in the context of HMA, 1955 and section 13, CPC. These are as follows:

"*(i) If the spouse aggrieved by the foreign matrimonial decree has not submitted to the jurisdiction of the foreign court or consented to the passing of the foreign Court judgment, it ought not to be recognised being unenforceable under section 13, CPC. This position of law ought to be applied to the facts of the individual case.*

(ii) There may be occasions that a spouse relying upon the judgment of a foreign matrimonial court, upon receipt of a summon or notice from a court of competent jurisdiction under the HMA, 1955, may not choose to file a written statement in response to a petition seeking a matrimonial cause under HMA, 1955 in Punjab, Haryana or Chandigarh. Instead, the contesting spouse may prefer to move an application under Order VII, rule 11, CPC seeking to rely upon or invoke the provisions of section 13, CPC. Thus, it may be contended before the court of competent jurisdiction under the HMA, 1955 that since the matrimonial action between the parties has already been decided and concluded by a Court in the foreign jurisdiction, the adjudication in the matter in issue between the same spouses based on the same matrimonial cause of action is barred by the principle of res judicata *and spouses are estopped in law from agitating the same again.*

(iii) It is respectfully contended that wherever both or any spouse arrayed in a matrimonial cause in a matrimonial action under HMA, 1955 contest, dispute, question or oppose any above such application under Order VII, rule 11, CPC involving interpretation of the principles laid down under section 13, CPC thereby necessitating requirement of detailed pleadings and evidence of spouses, no summary decision may seem possible to decide the matter in the preliminary stage.

(iv) In the above situation, there may also be circumstances involving application of issues of domicile as also applicability of sections 1 and 2 of the HMA, 1955 regarding extra territorial application of the provisions of HMA, 1955. Determination of these issues may also require parties to put their pleadings and testimony as well on the record of the Court of competent jurisdiction under the HMA, 1955.

(v) The application of the provisions of the CPC finding mention under section 21 HMA, 1955, the Court of Competent jurisdiction under the HMA, 1955 in Punjab, Haryana or Chandigarh may then be guided by the procedural law of pleadings contained in the Orders and Rules of the CPC and Punjab & Haryana High Court amendments, if any, for further proceedings in the matter. Accordingly, filing of a written statement, counter claim, rejoinder and/or other pleadings may be necessitated for having the factual matrix on record leading to the settlement of issues under Order XIV, CPC which can only be framed upon allegations made by parties to be read along with the contents of documents produced by spouses. Hence, this procedure may be necessary to be adopted to decide upon the warring claims of spouses relying on averments in support or against the judgment of the foreign matrimonial court between the parties.

(vi) Based on the above procedural requirements, the Court of competent jurisdiction under the HMA, 1955 may then examine the process, pleadings, grounds and other details in the passing of the judgment/decree of the matrimonial court of

foreign jurisdiction to test it on the anvil of section 13, CPC and based on the principles laid down by the Apex Court in Y. Narasimha Rao v. Y. Venkata Lakshmi, (1991) 3 SCC 451 *and exception (iii) as understood in the present opinion. Hence, in the event of a contest, dispute, opposition to the applicability of the foreign matrimonial judgment in the Indian jurisdiction, a summary disposal may not be possible. To do complete justice to both the spouses and to ensure that prejudice has not been caused to either of them as also that issues of maintenance, settlement of matrimonial property, child custody etc., arising in India have been completely settled between spouses based on provisions of HMA, 1955, the Court of competent jurisdiction under the HMA, 1955 may examine the matter on the lines suggested above.*

(vii) Thereafter, if the issue relating to the jurisdiction of Competent Court under the HMA, 1955 as also any bar to the matrimonial cause created by any existing law appears to be established, the matrimonial court in Punjab, Haryana or Chandigarh may upon the facts and circumstances of the case take an appropriate decision under Order XIV, rule 2, CPC whether it needs to pronounce judgment on all issues or decide the issue of jurisdiction or maintainability as a preliminary issue. In such circumstances, the Competent Court under the HMA, 1955 may after forming an opinion take an appropriate decision on the facts of the case as to whether the issue of jurisdiction or maintainability is to be decided as a preliminary issue or pronounce judgment together on all the issues. Accordingly, based on the individual facts and circumstances, the Court ought to take a decision whether to decide the preliminary issue of jurisdiction or maintainability or postpone the settlement of other issues after such preliminary issues has been determined."

It will be noted that the proposed guidelines in the above-mentioned Supreme Court and High Court rulings are meaningful and if implemented can mitigate the plight of wives dumped in India by foreign husbands. Although the Apex Court has clearly stated the need for suitable legislation on the subject, as yet no Indian law has been enacted to protect the rights of deserted and abandoned spouses in India. In essence, therefore, the judicial verdicts of courts of law are the only available law in India to come to the rescue of hapless Indian spouses who protest against the uncontested foreign divorce decrees invariably obtained in default by spouses from overseas jurisdictions. Thus, some codified law in India on the subject is undoubtedly now an absolute necessity.

A reading in totality of the matters in the overseas family law jurisdiction gives an indication that in such affairs, it is the judicial precedents which provide the best available guidance and judicial legislation on the subject. With the large number of non-resident Indians now permanently living in overseas jurisdictions, it has now become important that some composite legislation is enacted to deal with the problems of non-resident Indians to prevent them from importing judgments from foreign Courts to India for implementation of their rights. The answer therefore lies in giving them a law applicable to them as Indians rather than letting them invade the Indian system with judgments of foreign jurisdictions which do not find applicability in the Indian system. Hence, it is the Indian legislature which now seriously needs to review this issue and come out with composite legislation for non-resident Indians in family law matters. Until this is done, foreign Court judgments in domestic matters will keep cropping up and Courts in India will continue with their salutary efforts in interpreting them in harmony with the Indian laws and doing substantial justice to parties in the most fair and equitable way. However, in this process, the Indian judiciary has made one thing very clear: the Indian Courts would not simply mechanically enforce judgments and decrees of foreign Courts in family matters. The Indian Courts have now started looking into the merits of the matters and deciding them on the consideration of Indian law and the best interest of the parties rather than simply implementing the orders without examining them. Fortunately, we can hail the Indian judiciary for these laudable efforts and until such time when the Indian Legislature comes to the rescue with appropriate legislation, we seek solace with our unimpeachable and unstainted faith in the Indian Judiciary which is rendering a yeoman service.

(c) Dowry and the law: a social menace

The evil of dowry, *i.e.*, any property or valuable security given or agreed to be given by parties to the marriage or to their parents and given before or at any time after the marriage in connection with or in consideration of the marriage, is widely rampant in India. The Dowry Prohibition Act, 1961 was enacted to prohibit the giving and taking of dowry, but this social menace in the institution of marriage is a deep-rooted community practice which continues despite stringent court verdicts. The practice by which dowry seekers attempt to justify it by quoting examples from Hindu scriptures has percolated to all religions in India though it has no customary or religious sanctity attached to it. Both the Dowry Prohibition Act and section 498A of the Indian Penal Code (IPC) deal with dowry-related harassment of a married woman. Unfortunately, sometimes dowry leads to death by hanging or burning of a helpless girl tortured for the greed of money. Dowry deaths by burning or suicide have become a ponderous point. Section 304B was introduced in IPC by the Dowry Prohibition Amendment Act, 1986 and section 113B of the Indian Evidence Act, 1872 was also amended in 1986 to reinforce the statutory presumptions of dowry deaths. The decisions of the Supreme Court of India in *Vidhya Devi* v. *State of Haryana,* AIR 2004 SC 1757; *Surinder Kaur* v. *State of Haryana,* AIR 2004 SC 1747, and *Kunhiabdulla* v. *State of Kerala,* AIR 2004 SC 1731, show that dowry deaths by suicide result in conviction of only one person whereas dowry deaths by burning result in convictions of all concerned. This anomaly of law does not mitigate the crime. Therefore, if a married woman commits suicide on account of the dowry menace, the law and the law courts ought to be sensitised to the crime of the silent sufferer. In societal terms, the menace of dowry cannot be uprooted until the masses are educated in the ills of this malpractice and awareness comes from within. At the same time, the law must come down with a heavy hand on dowry seekers and provide deterrent punishment as an example for others who follow it. Harsher and more stringent penalties in law must be further advocated. The Supreme Court of India In Criminal Appeal No. 1277 of 2014 *Arnesh Kumar* v. *State of Bihar*, decided on July 2, 2014, the following directions were issued by Supreme Court:

"(1) All the State Governments to instruct its police officers not to automatically arrest when a case under section 498A of the IPC is registered but to satisfy themselves about the necessity for arrest under the parameters laid down above flowing from section 41, Cr.PC;

(2) All police officers be provided with a check list containing specified sub-clauses under section 41(1)(b)(ii);

(3) The police officer shall forward the check list duly filed and furnish the reasons and materials which necessitated the arrest, while forwarding/producing the accused before the Magistrate for further detention;

(4) The Magistrate while authorising detention of the accused shall peruse the report furnished by the police officer in terms aforesaid and only after recording its satisfaction, the Magistrate will authorise detention;

(5) The decision not to arrest an accused, be forwarded to the Magistrate within two weeks from the date of the institution of the case with a copy to the Magistrate which may be extended by the Superintendent of police of the district for the reasons to be recorded in writing;

(6) Notice of appearance in terms of section 41A of Cr.PC be served on the accused within two weeks from the date of institution of the case, which may be extended by the Superintendent of Police of the District for the reasons to be recorded in writing;

(7) Failure to comply with the directions aforesaid shall apart from rendering the police officers concerned liable for departmental action, they shall also be liable to be punished for contempt of court to be instituted before High Court having territorial jurisdiction.

(8) Authorising detention without recording reasons as aforesaid by the judicial Magistrate concerned shall be liable for departmental action by the appropriate High Court."

The Supreme Court added "we hasten to add that the directions aforesaid shall not only apply to the cases under section 498A of the I.P.C. or section 4 of the Dowry Prohibition Act, the case in hand, but also such cases where offence is punishable with imprisonment for a term which may be less than seven years or which may extend to seven years; whether with or without fine."

It is hoped that the above recent decision will help to check the misuse of this provision of law.

(d) Uniform Civil Code – an aspiration or an illusion?

Article 44 of the Constitution of India requires the State to secure for the citizens of India a Uniform Civil Code throughout the territory of India. As has been noticed above, India is a unique blend and merger of codified personal laws of Hindus, Christians, Parsis and, to some extent, of Muslims. However, there exists no uniform family related law in a single statutory book for all Indians which are universally acceptable to all religious communities in India.

Indian case-law: directions to enact a code

The Supreme Court of India for the first time directed the Indian Parliament to frame a Uniform Civil Code in 1985 in the case of *Mohammad Ahmed Khan* v. *Shah Bano Begum*, AIR 1985 SC 945. In this case a penurious Muslim woman claimed maintenance from her husband under section 125 of the Code of Criminal Procedure after her husband pronounced triple Talaq (divorce by announcing the word 'Talaq' three times). The Apex Court held that the Muslim woman had a right to receive maintenance under section 125 of the Code and also held that article 44 of the Constitution had remained a dead letter. To undo the above decision, the Muslim Women (Right to Protection on Divorce) Act, 1986, which curtailed the right of a Muslim Woman to maintenance under section 125 of the Code, was enacted by the Indian Parliament.

Thereafter, in the case of *Sarla Mudgal* v. *Union of India,* AIR 1995 SC 1531, the question which was raised was whether a Hindu husband married under Hindu Law can, by embracing the Islamic religion, solemnise a second marriage. The Supreme Court held that a Hindu marriage solemnised under Hindu Law can only be dissolved under the Hindu Marriage Act, 1955 and conversion to Islam, as also marrying again, would not by itself dissolve the Hindu marriage. Further, it was held that a second marriage solemnised after converting to Islam would be an offence of bigamy under section 494 of the Indian Penal Code. In this context, the views of Mr. Justice Kuldip Singh as follows are pertinent:

> *'Where more than 80 percent of the citizens have already been brought under the codified personal law there is no justification whatsoever to keep in abeyance, any more, the introduction of the "Uniform Civil Code" for all the citizens in the territory of India.'*

Thus, the Supreme Court reiterated the need for Parliament to frame a Common Civil Code which will help the cause of national integration by removing contradictions based on ideologies. Thus, the Directive Principle of enacting a Uniform Civil Code has been urged by the Apex Court repeatedly in a number of decisions as a matter of urgency. Unfortunately, in a subsequent decision reported as *Lily Thomas* v. *Union of India,* (2000) 6 SCC 224, the Apex Court, dealing with the validity of a second marriage contracted by a Hindu husband after his conversion to Islam, clarified that the Court had not issued any directions for the codification of a common civil code and that the Judges constituting the different Benches had only expressed their views on the facts and the circumstances of those cases. Even the lack of will to do so by the Indian Government can be deciphered from the recent stand stated in the Indian press. It has been reported in the *Asian Age,* dated 5 August, 2006, by the Press Trust of India (the Official Government News Agency) that the Indian Government does not intend to bring legislation to ensure a Uniform Civil Code because it does not want to initiate changes in the personal laws of minority communities. However, this ought not to deter the efforts of the Supreme Court of India in issuing mandatory directions to the Central Government to bring a Common Civil Code applicable to all communities irrespective of their religion and practices in a secular India. Hopefully, the Apex Court may review its findings in some other case and issue mandatory directions to the Central Government to bring a Common Civil Code applicable to all communities irrespective of their religion.

Secularism and the Uniform Civil Code

The preamble of the Indian Constitution resolves to constitute a 'secular' Democratic Republic. This means that there is no State religion and that the State shall not discriminate on the ground of religion. Articles 25 and 26 of the Constitution of India as enforceable fundamental rights guarantee freedom of religion and freedom to manage religious affairs. At the same time article 44 which is not enforceable in a Court of Law states that the State shall endeavour to secure a Uniform Civil Code in India. How are they to be reconciled? What will be the ingredients of a Uniform Civil Code? Since the personal laws of each religion contain separate ingredients, the Uniform Civil Code will need to strike a balance between protection of fundamental rights and religious principles of different communities. Marriage, divorce, succession, inheritance and maintenance can be matters of a secular nature and the law can regulate them. India needs a codified law which will cover all religions in relation to the personal laws of different communities.

Critics of the Uniform Civil Code think that the true principles of Muslim Law remain eclipsed by its extensive alleged misreading over the years. It is suggested by Tahir Mahmood (*'Muslim Personal Law: Clearing the Cobwebs'* The Hindu, 30 July, 2006), an eminent scholar, that 'an Indian Code of Muslim Law based on an eclectic selection of principles from the various schools of Shariat is the ideal solution to all the contemporary problems of Muslim Law'. In another report dated 11 May, 2006 in *The Hindu*, it has been reported that the Supreme Court of India dismissed a Public Interest Litigation Petition challenging the legality of the customs of polygamy, talaq and divorce practised by Muslims under personal laws. The plea for a direction to the Central Government to make Uniform Marriage Laws for all communities was rejected on the ground that it is for Parliament to change or amend the law. Thus, the debate is endless and the issue remains unresolved.

To sum up, it can be concluded that for citizens belonging to different religions and denominations, it is imperative that for promotion of national unity and solidarity a Unified Code is an absolute necessity on which there can be no compromise. Different streams of religion have to merge to a common destination and some unified principles must emerge in the true spirit of secularism. India needs a unified Code of Family Laws under an umbrella of all its constituent religions. Whether it is the endeavour of the State, the mandate of the Court or the will of the people is an issue which only time will decide for a true Indian Secular Democratic Republic.

(e) Judicial activism in family laws: a turning point

A series of decisions by the Supreme Court of India in the areas of family laws in the recent past has gone to show that the Apex Court is motivating a lot of positive and well meaning reforms which have become necessary over a period of time. Three recent decisions of the apex Court can be cited in support of this proposition:

(a) In *Re: Enforcement and Implementation of Dowry Prohibition Act, 1961*, 2005 (5) SC 71 the Apex Court directed the Indian Central and State Governments to implement all the interim directions issued by the Supreme Court earlier and take effective measures to frame rules and enforce the provisions of the Dowry Prohibition Act 1961 by devising measures to create honest, efficient and committed machinery for the purpose of the implementation of this Act meant to eradicate the social evil of dowry.

(b) In *Sushil Kumar Sharma* v. *Union of India,* 2005 (6) SC 266, the Apex Court upholding the constitutional validity of section 498A of the Indian Penal Code held that the object of section 498A is prevention of dowry menace and to check cruelty and harassment of women and therefore, the provision does not offend the Constitution of India.

(c) In *St Theresa's Tender Loving Care Home* v. *State of Andhra Pradesh,* (2005) 9 SC 11: AIR 2005 SC 4375: 2005 AIR SCW 539, it was held that the working of the homes run by State Governments for abandoned and destitute children offering them for adoption needs to be seriously improved and the Central and State Governments would do well to look at these problems with the humanitarian approach and concern they deserve.

(d) In *Shabnam Hashmi* v. *Union of India,* (2014) 4 SCC 1, the Supreme Court had held that prospective parents, irrespective of their religious background are free to adopt children after following the prescribed procedure. The Court in its Judgment said that '*personal beliefs and faiths, though must be honoured, cannot dictate the operation of the provisions of an enabling statute*". The Supreme Court of India declared that the right to adopt a child by a person as per the provisions of the Juvenile Justice Act, 2000, would prevail over all personal laws and religious codes in the country. Personal laws, though, would continue to govern any person who chooses to submit himself until such time that the vision of a uniform civil code is achieved.

However, the Supreme Court has also tested various aspects of personal laws on the touchstone of fundamental rights. In *Gita Hariharan* v. *Reserve Bank of India,* (1999) 2 SCC 228, the Supreme Court read down section 6 of the Hindu Minority and Guardianship Act, 1956 to mean that the mother is also a natural guardian, and irrespective of whether the father was unfit or not, the mother should also be given equal rights as a natural guardian. In *John Vallamattom* v. *Union of India,* AIR 2003 SC 2902, section 118 of the Indian Succession Act was struck down as unconstitutional as it was held to be discriminatory against Christians in imposing unreasonable restrictions on the donation of their property for religious or charitable purposes by will. In *Danial Latifi* v. *Union of India,* (2001) 7 SCC 740, a Constitutional Bench of the Supreme Court gave a categorical finding that, in view of their interpretation of the Muslim Women (Protection of Rights on Divorce) Act, 1986, the provisions of the Act were not in violation of articles 14 and 21 of the Constitution, the Fundamental Rights of which guarantee equality of law and right to life and personal liberty.

The views of the Indian Apex Court on the issue of registration of marriages, inter-caste marriages, child marriages, Dowry Prohibition Act, irretrievable breakdown of marriage, Uniform Civil Code and a secular approach have already been referred to earlier. A legislative setup which is slow to respond to societal changes and a proactive judiciary which is keen to motivate reforms in law is therefore clearly visible on the Indian horizon. Even in matters affecting the environment, pollution and the health of people, the role of the judiciary in India has been very constructive. The vibrant, dynamic and open jurisprudential system in India is amenable and flexible to the changing needs of people. We could therefore well have reform in family law through the views of the court even if there is opposition from religious communities in respect of personal laws. If a Uniform Civil Code does not come as a result of legislation, decisions of Courts will always suggest reforms to improve the plight of children and women who are affected the most. The Indian judiciary indeed deserves to be hailed in this regard for its yeoman efforts for the welfare of Indians.

IV. CONCLUSION

A net analysis of the various propositions and viewpoints discussed above drives home the ideal solution that for Indians there is needed one indigenous Indian law applicable to all its communities which coexist democratically. Analytically speaking, the answers to the social issues examined above are within the system. Codification of a Uniform Civil Code may be the ultimate solution. Other measures will only tide over time. Judicial verdicts will keep the momentum going. Accommodating personal laws of all religions under such a Code is an uphill task. It may take time. The Legislature will ultimately have to perform this onerous duty of compiling the Code. Religion will have to keep pace with the law. Unity in India exists in its diversity. Times have moved ahead, but personal laws have not kept pace. The Courts in India perform a herculean task in carving out solutions on a case-by-case basis. The Executive and the Legislature in India however now need to contribute to provide the much needed solutions. In the e-age today, the path to progress must be chartered with harmony at home. India itself is a confluence and not a clash of civilisations. Indians are vibrant, amenable to change and have an astonishing ability to adapt to their environment. As the largest democracy in the world, India projects a role model in various aspects of family laws. Maybe with further changes and amendments in some aspects, a better role model to emulate may emerge in the Indian subcontinent.

Analysis of the Law of Marriage from an International Perspective, under Hindu Law

I. INTRODUCTION

The present India chapter principally analyses recent significant judgments and the position of law in the realm of marriage under the provisions of the Hindu Marriage Act, 1955. The discussion starts with the Supreme Court of India's interpretation in the year 2003 of the right to marry in the case of those persons affected by HIV. The positive interpretation of the issue of bigamous marriages has time and again triggered a vigorous debate for enacting a uniform civil code in India. This is much more so in the light of a judgment, handed down by a bench headed by the Chief Justice of India, in a succession of property case i.e. *John Vallamattam* v. *Union of India,* (2003) 6 SCC 611. The trail of judgments of the highest court of the land stressing the need for enacting a Uniform Civil Code in polygamy cases has been suitably highlighted. The root cause of the need for a uniform civil code in India is that of the legal inequalities between men and women. These are also discussed in this chapter.

II. SUPREME COURT OF INDIA'S RECENT INTERPRETATION OF THE RIGHT TO MARRY

In a first judgment of its kind on the right of a patient suffering from contagious venereal disease to marry, the Supreme Court of India has ruled that, so long as the person is not cured of the disease or impotency, his right to marry cannot be enforced through a court of law. The judgment is reported as *Mr 'X'* v. *Hospital 'Z',* (1998) 8 SCC 296.

The Supreme Court firmly held that if the man's marriage has been cancelled due to his being an AIDS patient, his right to marry will remain a 'suspended right'. Furthermore, he is not entitled to claim any compensation from the hospital which has disclosed his medical condition to the would-be bride's family.

The judgment came in the wake of a doctor's petition seeking compensation from Apollo Hospital in Chennai. The hospital had detected that he was an HIV-positive patient. This fact was also disclosed to his would-be bride's family. The marriage was called off immediately. The doctor contended that the hospital had violated medical ethics by disclosing his medical condition to the bride's family. This led to his social ostracisation.

The issue in the above-mentioned case went a step further. A subsequent petition was filed in the Supreme Court of India, seeking clarification of the above-mentioned judgment to facilitate marriage of an HIV-positive person after 'full, free and informed consent is taken for the marriage' *('SC seeks opinion on AIDS patients' right to marry', The Times of India, New Delhi, 8 February 2000).*

The same Supreme Court Bench comprising Justice B.N. Kirpal and Justice S. Sagir Ahmad, which had earlier handed down the above-mentioned judgment, issued notices in the subsequent petition to the Union of India and the Medical Council of India to ascertain their views. The second petition on this subject was filed by Sahara, a centre for residential care and rehabilitation of HIV-positive persons under the AIDS care project and is discussed below.

The original judgment in *X* v. *Hospital Z* (1998) again came up for reinterpretation and reconsideration before a different bench of the Supreme Court of India. The subsequent rollover judgment is reported as *Mr 'X'* v. *Hospital 'Z'*, (2003) 1 SCC 500. The author of the subsequent judgment, Justice Rajendra Babu, is clearly in disagreement with the findings given in the earlier judgment in 1998.

The court in para 3 at page 502 explained the reasons for reopening of the case as follows:

> *'3. A special leave petition was filed before this court. This court made an order on 21 September, 1998 (1998) 8 SCC 296 dismissing the said petition. However, in the course of the order several findings have been given, particularly those relating to "suspend right to marry". In that proceeding, this court heard only the appellant and there was no issue of notice to any other person nor had this court occasion to hear any of the persons representing the HIV or AIDS infected persons or their rights, much less any of the non-government organisations which are doing work in the field were heard. In those circumstances, a writ petition was filed under article 32 of the Constitution before this court for setting aside the said judgment. However, in the proceedings dated 7 February, 2000 it was noted that prayer was deleted and the other prayer which indirectly concerned the correctness of the judgment already passed was also deleted. However, the petition was ordered to be treated as an application for clarification or directions in the case already decided by this court ...'*

Accordingly, the court directed that the fresh writ petition filed under article 32 of the Constitution of India be registered separately as an interlocutory application for clarification/directions in the earlier original judgment reported as (1998) 8 SCC 296. Notices were also issued to the National Aids Control Organisation, Union of India, Indian Medical Association and the Medical Council of India.

The Supreme Court clarified in paras 4-7 at p. 503 of the judgment reported as (2003) 1 SCC 500 and held as follows:

> *'4. By an order dated 2 September, 2001, it has been further directed that the IAs should be listed before a three-Judge Bench.*

5. In IA No. 2 of 1999 filed by the impleaded petitioner, the petitioner has raised the question whether a person suffering from HIV(+) contracting marriage with a willing partner after disclosing the factum of disease to that partner will be committing an offence within the meaning of sections 269 and 270, IPC. In substance, the petitioner wants the court to clarify that there is no bar for the marriage, if the healthy spouse consents to marry in spite of being made aware of the fact that the other spouse is suffering from the said disease.

6. The various organisations to which the notice was issued have also entered their appearance before this court and filed a plethora of material giving their respective stands. The practical difficulties in ensuring disclosure to the person proposed to be married or in monitoring such cases are pointed out. It is not necessary to examine these matters in any detail in as much as in our view this court has rested its decision on the facts of the case that it was open to the hospital or the doctor concerned to reveal such information to persons related to the girl whom he intended to marry and she had a right to know about the HIV-positive status of the appellant. If that was so, there was no need for this court to go further and declare in general as to what rights and obligations arise in such context as to right to privacy or confidentiality or whether such persons are entitled to be married or not or in the event such persons marry they would commit an offence under law or whether such right is suspended during the period of illness. Therefore, all those observations made by this court in the aforesaid matter were unnecessary, particularly when there was no consideration of the matter after notice to all the parties concerned.

7. In that view of the matter, we hold that the observations made by this court, except to the extent of holding as stated earlier that the appellant's right was not affected in any manner in revealing his HIV-positive status to the relatives of his fiancée, are uncalled for. We dispose of these applications with these observations.'

Analysing the above two judgments, it seems that the subsequent judgment in 2003 takes away what the earlier judgment in 1998 gave. In the 1998 decision, the Supreme Court, while laying down that the infringement of the suspended right to marry cannot be legally compensated by damages either in torts or common law, expounded the rights of persons suffering from a communicable disease like AIDS. The latter judgment by the Supreme Court in 2003, instead of further delving into the concepts, cut short the matter by stating that even the earlier observations of the court were unnecessary, particularly when there was no consideration of the matter. Thus, the rights of persons suffering from diseases like AIDS or who are HIV-positive, which could have been further gone into, were abruptly cut short. There is no specific legislation in India which takes care of rights of such persons. Therefore, in some appropriate case, the judiciary itself will be faced with the task of interpreting the rights of such persons by expounding the benefit of existing legislation. Whether the rights will be extended or curtailed remains to be seen. But certainly, the Supreme Court which lays down the law of the land under article 141 of the Constitution, and which can under article 142 of the Constitution pass such orders as are necessary for doing complete justice in any cause or matter pending before it, may have to address the above issue sooner or later given the gravity of the matter. Avoiding answering the questions may not serve the purpose. Thus, with all humility, it may be argued that the earlier judgment in 1998 was better law in the making. It would have been immensely helpful had the subsequent judgment in 2003 laid down some sort of criterion regarding obligations, duties and liabilities of HIV or AIDS-affected persons embarking upon matrimony, both in the event of wilful and non-wilful disclosure, which may have shed some more light on the subject.

III. MODERN HINDU LAW PROHIBITS POLYGAMY, AND SUPREME COURT OF INDIA'S CONCERN FOR ENACTING UNIFORM CIVIL CODE

It is important to refer to sections 11 and 15 of the 1955 Act and section 494 of the Indian Penal Code which prohibit polygamy. Sections 11 and 15 of the 1955 Act read as follows:

> '***11. Void marriages.***—*Any marriage solemnized after the commencement of this Act shall be null and void and may, on a petition presented by either party thereto against the other party, be so declared by a decree of nullity if it contravenes any one of the conditions specified in clauses (i), (iv) and (v) of section 5.*
>
> ***15. Divorced persons when may marry again.***—*When a marriage has been dissolved by a decree of divorce and either there is no right of appeal against the decree or, if there is such a right of appeal, the time for appealing has expired without an appeal having been presented or an appeal has been presented but has been dismissed, it shall be lawful for either party to the marriage to marry again.*'

Section 494 of the Indian Penal Code reads as follows:

> '***494. Marrying again during lifetime of husband or wife.***—*Whoever, having a husband or wife living, marries in any case in which such marriage is void by reason of it taking place during the life of such husband or wife, shall be punished with imprisonment of either description for a term which may extend to 7 years, and shall also be liable to fine.*
>
> *Exception.—This section does not extend to any person whose marriage with such husband or wife has been declared void by a court of competent jurisdiction, nor to any person who contracts a marriage during the life of a former husband or wife, if such husband or wife, at the time of the subsequent marriage, shall have been continually absent from such person for the space of seven years, and shall not have been heard of by such person as being alive within that time provided the person contracting such subsequent marriage shall, before such marriage takes place, inform the person with whom such marriage is contracted of the real state of facts so far as the same are within his or her knowledge.*'

In *Smt. Sarla Mudgal, President, Kalyani* v. *Union of India*, JT 1995 (4) SC 331 the Supreme Court of India dealt in depth with the issue of bigamy. In para 2 of the judgment at p. 336, the following questions were formulated for consideration:

> *'2. The questions for our consideration are whether a Hindu husband, married under Hindu Law, by embracing Islam, can soleminise a second marriage? Whether such a marriage without having the first marriage dissolved under law, would be a valid marriage qua the first wife who continues to be Hindu? Whether the apostate husband would be guilty of the offence under section 494 of the Indian Penal Code (IPC)?'*

Justice Kuldip Singh after eloquently analysing the case-law on bigamy way back from 1891, held in para 14 at p. 341 of the judgment:

> *'14. It is thus, obvious from the catena of case-law that a marriage celebrated under a particular personal law cannot be dissolved by the application of another personal law to which one of the spouses converts and the other refuses to do so. Where a marriage takes place under Hindu Law the parties acquire a status and certain rights by the marriage itself under the law governing the Hindu Marriage and if one of the parties is allowed to dissolve the marriage by adopting and enforcing a new personal law, it would be tantamount to destroying the existing rights of the other spouse who continues to be Hindu. We, therefore, hold that under the Hindu Personal Law as it existed prior to its codification in 1955, a Hindu marriage continued to subsist even after one of the spouses converted to Islam. There was no automatic dissolution of the marriage.'*

Paragraph 17 of the above-mentioned judgment tersely lays down that Modern Hindu Law strictly enforces monogamy. A marriage performed under the 1955 Act cannot be dissolved except on the grounds available under section 13 of the 1955 Act. The grounds of divorce are discussed in a separate chapter. One of the grounds under section 13(I)(ii) is that *'the other party has ceased to be a Hindu by conversion to another religion'*.

Apart from crystallising and consolidating the law on bigamy, the main thrust of the judgment at the end of the day was to propose to the Government of India that it should enact a Uniform Civil Code, as envisaged in article 44 of the Constitution of India.

In a recent case, *Lily Thomas* v. *Union of India*, JT 2000 (5) SC 617, the identical issue of conversion as in *Sarla Mudgal's* case again arose for consideration before the Supreme Court of India. This was a collection of six cases decided by the apex court involving the same legal point.

In one of the cases before the Supreme Court, in civil writ petition number 509 of 1992, the respondent husband adopted the Muslim religion and became a convert to that religion for the sole purpose of having a second wife which is strictly forbidden under Hindu law. The court noticed that the 34-year-old unemployed petitioner wife was undergoing great mental trauma.

The court was at pains to observe in para 21 of the judgment (supra) at page 624:

> *'That in the past several years, it has become very common amongst the Hindu males who cannot get a divorce from their first wife, that they convert to Muslim religion solely for the purpose of marriage. This practice is invariably adopted by those erring husbands who embrace Islam for the purpose of second marriage*

but again become reconvert so as to retain their rights in the properties etc and continue their service and all other business in their old name and religion.'

The court strongly deprecated this practice in para 37 of the judgment at page 636 by observing as hereunder:

'... Looked at from this angle, a person who mockingly adopts another religion where plurality of marriage is permitted so as to renounce the previous marriage and desert the wife, he cannot be permitted to take advantage of his exploitation as religion is not a commodity to be exploited. The institution of marriage under every personal law is a sacred institution. Under Hindu Law, Marriage is a sacrament. Both have to be preserved.'

The earlier mandate of law as in *Sarla Mudgal's* case was reiterated in para 34 of the judgment at page 634:

'From the above, it would be seen that mere conversion does not bring to an end the marital ties unless a decree for divorce on that ground is obtained from the court. Till a decree is passed, the marriage subsists. Any other marriage, during the subsistence of first marriage would constitute an offence under section 494 read with section 17 of the Hindu Marriage Act, 1955 and the person, in spite of his conversion to some other religion, would be liable to be prosecuted for the offence of bigamy. It also follows that if the first marriage was solemnised under the Hindu Marriage Act, 1955, the "husband" or the "wife", by mere conversion to another religion, cannot bring to an end the marital ties already established on account of a valid marriage having been performed between them. So long as that marriage subsists, another marriage cannot be performed, not even under any other personal law, and on such marriage being performed, the person would be liable to be prosecuted for the offence under section 494, IPC.'

In this judgment, the apex court has differed on the issue of direction given by the Supreme Court itself in *Sarla Mudgal's* case. Justices R.P. Sethi and Sagir Ahmad held that any direction for the enforcement of article 44 of the Constitution of India could not have been issued by only one of the judges in *Sarla Mudgal's* case.

Furthermore, this judgment has additionally touched on two very important issues. First, reliance has been placed on *Sayeda Khatoon and A.M. Obadiah* v. *M Obadiah*, (1944–45) 49 CWN 745 wherein it was held that a marriage solemnised in India according to one personal law cannot be dissolved according to another personal law simply because one of the parties has changed his or her religion.

Secondly, the court made a distinction under Mohammedan law regarding conversion. It was held in para 35 at page 635 of the judgment reported as JT 2000 (5) SC 617 that:

'The position under the Mohammedan Law would be different as, in spite of the first marriage, a second marriage can be contracted by the husband, subject to such religious restrictions as have been spelled out by Brother Sethi J in his separate judgment, with which I concur on this point also. This is the vital difference between Mohammedan Law and other personal laws. Prosecution under section 494 in respect of a second marriage under Mohammedan Law

can be avoided only if the first marriage was also under the Mohammedan Law and not if the first marriage was under any other personal law where there was a prohibition on contracting a second marriage in the life-time of the spouse.'

It emanates from these two recent judgments of the Supreme Court of India that the interpretation of the law of bigamy is crystal clear. The judgments in *Sarla Mudgal* (supra) and *Lily Thomas* (supra) plug the legal loophole and put an end to the popular notion that a Hindu man can circumvent the punishment for bigamy if he remarries after conversion to the Muslim faith as he professes that he ceases to be a Hindu.

It is important to advert to the most recent judgment handed down by the Supreme Court of India on 21 July, 2003. The then Chief Justice of India VN Khare's observation while heading a bench in *John Vallamattam* v. *Union of India*, (2003) 6 SCC 611 that article 44 of the Constitution of India has not been given effect to and that the Parliament of India is still to step in for framing a common civil code, has triggered off a vigorous debate.

Chief Justice Khare lamented in para 44 at page 627 of the judgment:

'Before I part with the case, I would like to state that article 44 provides that the State shall endeavour to secure for the citizens a uniform civil code throughout the territory of India. The aforesaid provision is based on the premise that there is no necessary connection between religious and personal law in a civilized society. Article 25 of the Constitution confers freedom of conscience and free profession, practice and propagation of religion. The aforesaid two provisions viz *articles 25 and 44 show that the former guarantees religious freedom whereas the latter divests religion from social relations and personal law. It is no matter of doubt that marriage, succession and the like matters of a secular character cannot be brought within the guarantee enshrined under articles 25 and 26 of the Constitution. Any legislation which brings succession and the like matters of secular character within the ambit of articles 25 and 26 is a suspect legislation, although it is doubtful whether the American doctrine of suspect legislation is followed in this country. In* Sarla Mudgal v. Union of India, *(1995) 3 SCC 635 it was held that marriage, succession and like matters of secular character cannot be brought within the guarantee enshrined under articles 25 and 26 of the Constitution. It is a matter of regret that article 44 of the Constitution has not been given effect to. Parliament is still to step in for framing a Common Civil Code in the country. A Common Civil Code will help the cause of national integration by removing the contradictions based on ideologies.'*

The three-judge Bench in *John Vallamattam* (supra) struck down the legality of section 118 of the Indian Succession Act, 1925. Justice Khare in penultimate para 45 of his judgment declared section 118 to be unconstitutional, being violative of article 14 of the Constitution of India. Section 118 reads as follows:

*'**118. Bequest to religious or charitable uses.**—No man having a nephew or niece or any nearer relative shall have power to bequeath any property to religious or charitable uses, except by a will executed not less than 12 months before his death, and deposited within six months from its execution in some place provided by law for the safe custody of the will of the living person:*
Provided that nothing in this section shall apply to a Parsi.'

It has also been held in para 26 of the judgment above that under section 118 the testator who lives beyond the statutory period of 12 months is not able to execute his wishes in relation to his property; the impugned provision defeats the object of the will. Such a provision is unreasonable and arbitrary.

Dr. Justice AR. Lakshmanan in his concurring judgment (supra) ruled in para 67 at p. 632:

> *'The Indian Succession Act though is claimed to be a universal law of testamentary disposition, but in effect, crucial sections apply only to Christians. There is no acceptable answer from the other side as to why section 118 of the Act is made applicable to Christians alone and not to others.'*

Both *Sarla Mudgal* (1995) and *Lily Thomas* (2000) thus highlight the focus of the apex judiciary and the real concern to stem the rampant exploitation of Indian women, through misuse of personal laws, especially in the lower strata of the society. Instances also abound of women not enjoying equal legal rights on a par with men. Some such instances are discussed below.

IV. THE HINDU MARRIAGE ACT 1955

The principal law of marriage and divorce relating to Hindus is contained in the Hindu Marriage Act, 1955 (HMA, 1955), which came into force on 8 May, 1955. The HMA, 1955 also governs validity of marriages of those Indian spouses who are permanently resident overseas. It is an Act to amend and codify the law relating to marriage among Hindus.

Extent and jurisdiction of the HMA, 1955

Section 1 of the HMA, 1955 states that the said Act extends to the whole of India except the State of Jammu and Kashmir, and applies also to Hindus domiciled in the territories to which this Act extends who are outside the said territories. In effect, the Act has extra-territorial application, because a Hindu carries with him the personal law of marriage.

Application of the HMA, 1955

In terms of section 2 of the HMA, 1955, Hindu law applies to the following three categories:

(a) any person who is a Hindu, Jain, Sikh or Buddhist by religion;

(b) any person who is born of Hindu parents; and

(c) any other person domiciled in the territories to which this act extends who is not a Muslim, Christian, Parsi or Jew.

V. SOME INSTANCES OF LEGAL INEQUALITIES BETWEEN MEN AND WOMEN IN INDIA

Personal laws in India govern the institution of marriage, divorce, succession, inheritance, child custody, alimony and maintenance. It is a matter of fact that personal laws of different religions discriminate in varying degrees as to women's right to equality as guaranteed by the Constitution of India. Although, as explained above, Hindu law prohibits bigamy, the practice continues unabated among Hindu men. This is more common among men from the rural areas, men who migrate abroad and remarry, leaving their women in the lurch. Such Hindu women who seek divorce or maintenance have the insurmountable task of proving the factum of the second marriage. Since registration of marriages is not compulsory under the provisions of the HMA, 1955, it becomes all the more difficult to prove the remarriage of the erring spouse. Desertion of wives in the State of Punjab by husbands residing abroad is a very common phenomenon. This multiplies their woes. According to a study conducted by the Indian Council of Social Welfare Punjab, as in 2003, the State is home to as many as 8000 women who have been deserted by their non-resident Indian husbands. The results of this survey were published in the Chandigarh edition of the *Indian Express* dated 9 March, 2003 ('Women's day: NRI marriages revisited, 8000 women in Punjab deserted by NRIs: Study'). Regrettably, even in the twenty-first century of cyber vision, female infanticide, bride burning, torture, cruelty and domestic violence are common among Hindus.

The Hindu Succession Act, 1956 (hereafter HSA, 1956) provides for an equal right to parental property for Hindu women in the case of intestate succession. But the prevalent practice is that women relinquish their right to parental property. The trade off is at the time of marriage. The marriage expenses and the dowry in lieu thereof are construed and actually taken to be the share of the woman from inheritance of the property left behind by the parents. Most of the women do not protest at all, for the fear of spoiling relations with their family.

Likewise, the HSA, 1956 has a provision for a Hindu Undivided Family to ensure that the property remains within the male line of descent. A son gets a share corresponding to his father's share. On the other hand, regressively, a daughter gets only a share in her father's share of the property. Furthermore, a daughter cannot reside in the family home unless she is single or divorced, and also cannot claim her share of the property as long as the men of the family continue to live in the family household. These are some glaring instances of discrimination against Hindu women in Indian society. However, with the amendment of Section 6 of the HSA, 1956 the position has changed after September 9, 2005

A Hindu woman or girl will have equal property rights along with other male relatives for any partition made in intestate succession after September 2005 under the Hindu Succession (Amendment) Act, 2005, the daughters are entitled to equal inheritance rights along with other male siblings, which was not available to them prior to the amendment. The female inheritors would not only have the succession rights but also the same liabilities fastened on the property along with the male members.

In *Ganduri Koteshwaramma* v. *Chakiri Yanadi,* AIR 2012 SC 169, the Apex Court in a judgment said that under the Hindu Succession (Amendment) Act, 2005, the daughters are entitled to equal inheritance rights along with other male siblings, which was not available to them prior to the amendment. The Court held that:

"The new section 6 provides for parity of rights in the coparcenary property among male and female members of a joint Hindu family on and from September 9, 2005. The legislature has now conferred substantive right in favour of the daughters."

"According to the new section 6, the daughter of a coparcener becomes a coparcener by birth in her own rights and liabilities in the same manner as the son. The declaration in section 6 that the daughter of the coparcener shall have same rights and liabilities in the coparcenary property as she would have been a son is unambiguous and unequivocal".

The term coparcener refers to the equal inheritance right of a person in a property. The apex court passed the ruling while upholding the appeal filed by Ganduri Koteshwaramma, daughter of late Chakiri Venkata Swamy, challenging the Andhra Pradesh High Court's decision not to recognise equal property rights of women along with their male siblings.

Some Muslim laws have been codified as the Shariat Act, 1937, the Dissolution of Muslim Marriages Act, 1939, and the Muslim Women (Protection of Rights on Divorce) Act, 1986. The Shariat Act states that Muslim personal law shall govern Muslims and that law has priority over custom. Muslim personal law is mostly based on the interpretations from the holy book of Quran. In terms of the 1939 Act, Muslim women can seek divorce on grounds of cruelty and impotence, which of course are very difficult to prove. On the other hand, a Muslim man is armed with the right to unilateral divorce on the basis of triple *talaq*. Furthermore, the 1937 Act outrightly denies the right for women to hold any agricultural land.

As far as the Christians are concerned, their personal laws are contained in the Indian Christian Marriage Act, 1872, and the Divorce Act, 1869 (DA, 1989). The Divorce Act has recently been amended by the Indian Divorce (Amendment) Act, 2001 providing comprehensive grounds of divorce both to the husband and the wife including divorce by mutual consent. Under the Divorce Act, 1869, couples wanting to seek divorce on the basis of mutual consent have to wait for a two-year separation. The analogous provision under the HMA, 1955 mandates a one-year waiting period for couples desirous of seeking divorce on the basis of mutual consent.

These are some of the intense inequalities among Hindus, Muslims and Christians. The degree of stigma attached to divorced women in India is intimately connected with the issue of inequalities between men and women as discussed. The status of divorced women in India is of immense concern to foreign lawyers, especially when they are acting on behalf of battered and separated spouses whose immigration status is at stake. They may be on the verge of deportation. The overseas immigration lawyers in such a situation plead gender persecution in the event of deportation to India, depending upon the facts and circumstances of each case. Quite often the authors are called upon to prepare expert reports on this branch of law.

VI. STIGMA ATTACHED TO DIVORCED WOMEN IN INDIA

A. Attitude in rural areas

It is common knowledge that divorce in rural areas, semi-rural areas and small towns in India is considered to be a taboo and a social stigma. Divorced women in such areas encounter negative peer pressure, and pressure from the society as a whole. Social considerations in such situations and in certain communities in some geographical areas lead to ill-treatment of divorced women.

Divorced women in rural areas are treated very shabbily. They can be ill treated and condemned to a life of misery. In Indian metropolitan cities, divorce may not be a taboo, which again depends upon the standing and the education of the spouses.

Divorced women remarrying in India, especially in rural and semi-rural areas, have to make many compromises. This can be on account of the age gap and economic considerations. Quite often, in a situation where the divorced girl is young and is not from an economically privileged background, she may be compelled to marry a much older man of means. This is a case where the girl is at the higher end of the scale. Both the girl and her family have to compromise severely, only with a view to rehabilitation. Reported instances abound in the media, where divorced spouses, who have remarried or are single, and also separated spouses are subject to domestic violence. This is a big issue of grave concern to the judiciary, lawyers, academics, jurists and social organisations in India.

B. Acceptance in metropolitan cities and big towns

With a growing number of divorces, second marriages are no longer considered to be a taboo, especially in metropolitan cities and big towns. In the present day's fast changing socio-economic conditions, many parents want their daughters to remarry and settle down. This is more prominent in cases where their daughters have been divorced at a relatively young age. Social pressures in the upwardly mobile milieu are not a hair-raising issue. Young educated people remarry because they feel that they have an entire life ahead of them. This obviously precipitates the desire to get married again. The loneliness in such situations is also the motivating factor. The joint family system is somewhat disintegrating in the present day and age. This is on account of individualism, better education and career prospects and a shrinking world without borders. A broken marriage may no longer be tolerated by a working woman. Relationships formed by working spouses at places of work influence younger people to form new unions. New work avenues and increasing job opportunities with good career prospects have changed the culture and lifestyle in big Indian cities for modern Indian young men and women.

Many women also take the plunge to get remarried simply because they do not want to end up as a liability to their ageing parents. Winds of change are blowing fast. Times have changed. Quite often, mutual incompatibility may be the main reason for divorce between couples who are high up on the social ladder. Unlike in the past, a large number of men and women may have clung to a dead marriage for the sake of children, which however is not the case any more. People today prefer walking out of a bad marriage and optimistically taking the plunge the second time. Changing attitudes in a new ethos, economic independence and increasing freedom to choose partners are some of the factors responsible for forming new matrimonial unions when the wear and tear of old liaisons takes its toll. Although this may be the case in big Indian cities and metropolitan areas it is not in rural areas and small towns, where the age-old concept of relationships for ever is still traditionally adhered to, observed and followed. Therefore, the changes are limited to the areas stated above.

Alternative Dispute Resolution in Indian Family Law – Realities, Practicalities and Necessities

I. INTRODUCTION: THE INDIAN BACKGROUND

The Constitution of India enacted on the 26 November, 1949 resolved to constitute India as a Union of States and a sovereign, socialist, secular, democratic republic. Today, a population of about 1.2 billion Indians live in 29 states and 7 union territories within India besides about 30 million non-resident Indians who reside in foreign jurisdictions all over the world. Within the territory of India spread over an area of 3.28 million sq. kms, the large Indian population comprises of multicultural societies professing and practising different religions and speaking different local languages, all coexisting in harmony in one of the largest democracies in the world.

The Indian Parliament, at the helm of affairs, legislates on central subjects in the union and concurrent lists and state legislatures enact laws pertaining to state subjects as per the state and concurrent lists with regard to the subjects enumerated in the Constitution of India. Likewise, pertaining to the judiciary, under article 214 of the Indian Constitution there shall be a High Court for each state and under article 124 there shall be a Supreme Court of India. Under article 141 of the Constitution, the law declared by the Supreme Court shall be binding on all courts within the territory of India. However, the Supreme Court may not be bound by its own earlier views and can render new decisions.

Part III of the Constitution of India secures 'Fundamental Rights' to its citizens which can be enforced directly in the respective High Courts of the states or directly in the Supreme Court of India by issue of prerogative writs under articles 226 and 32 respectively of the Constitution of India. Under the constitutional scheme, amongst others, 'Freedom of Religion' and the right to freely profess, practise and propagate it is sacrosanct and is thus enforceable by a prerogative writ issued by the superior courts.

Simultaneously, Part IV of the Indian Constitution lays down 'Directive Principles of State Policy' which are not enforceable by any court but are nevertheless fundamental in the governance of the country and it shall be the duty of the state to apply these principles while making laws. Under article 44 of the Constitution in this Part, the state shall endeavour to secure a uniform civil code for citizens throughout the territory of India. However, realistically speaking, to date a uniform civil code remains an aspiration which India has yet to achieve and enact.

It is seen that the Indian legal system has grown and evolved with the lives and aspirations of its people and its varied cultures, religious practices and personal laws. The Indian legal system is founded and fortified by age-old concepts and precepts of justice, equity and good conscience, which are, indeed, the hallmarks of the common law.

The Constitution of India is the fundamental authority of law in India. The Constitution gives due recognition to statutes, case-law and customary law consistent with its dispensations. A single unified judicial system is the unique feature of the Indian judiciary system. The Supreme Court at the apex of the entire judicial system is followed by High Courts in each state or group of states. Under the High Courts exists a hierarchy of Civil and Criminal Subordinate Courts. Panchayat Courts also function in some states under various names like Nyaya Panchayat, Panchayat Adalat and Gram Kachheri (Village level Courts), to decide civil and criminal disputes of petty and local nature. These are grassroot level petty courts meant to decide small disputes at the lowest level.

II. EXISTING FAMILY LAW LEGISLATION PREVAILING IN INDIA

India is a land of diversities with several religions. The oldest part of the Indian legal system is the personal laws governing Hindus and Muslims. The Hindu personal law has undergone changes by a continuous process of codification. The process of change in society has brought changes in law reflecting the changed social conditions and attempts the solution of social problems by new methods in the light of experience of legislation in other countries of the world. The Muslim personal law has been comparatively left untouched by legislation.

The Indian legal system is basically a common law system. The Indian Parliament has enacted the following family laws which are applicable to the religious communities defined in the respective enactments themselves. A brief description of each of these separate enactments is given below.

The main marriage law legislation in India applicable to the majority population constituted of Hindus is known as The Hindu Marriage Act, 1955, which is an Act to amend and codify the law relating to marriage among Hindus. Ceremonial marriage is essential under this Act and registration is optional. It applies to any person who is a Hindu, Buddhist, Jaina or Sikh by religion and to any other person who is not a Muslim, Christian, Parsi or Jew by religion. The Act also applies to Hindus resident outside the territory of India. Nothing contained in this Act shall be deemed to affect any right recognised by custom or conferred by any special enactment. Likewise, in other personal law matters, Hindus are governed by the Hindu Succession Act, 1956, which is an Act to amend and codify the law relating to intestate succession among Hindus. The Hindu Minority and Guardianship Act, 1956 is an Act to amend and codify certain parts of the law relating to minority and guardianship among Hindus and the Hindu Adoptions and Maintenance Act, 1956 is an Act to amend and codify the law relating to adoptions and maintenance among Hindus.

It may be pertinent to point out that the Indian Succession Act, 1925, is an Act to consolidate the law applicable to intestate and testamentary succession in India unless parties opt and choose to be governed by their respective codified law otherwise applicable to them. In respect of issues relating to guardianship, the Guardian and Wards Act, 1890 would apply to non-Hindus. Interestingly, section 125 of the Code of Criminal Procedure, 1973 provides that, irrespective of religion, any person belonging to any religion can approach a magistrate seeking maintenance. Therefore, apart from personal family law legislation, both Hindus and non-Hindus have an independent right of maintenance under the general law of the land, if he or she is otherwise entitled to maintenance under this Code.

The Indian Parliament also enacted the Special Marriage Act, 1954, as an Act to provide a special form of marriage in certain cases, for the registration of such and certain other marriages and for divorces under this Act. This enactment of solemnising marriage by registration is resorted to by Hindus, non-Hindus and foreigners marrying in India who opt out of the ceremonial marriage under their respective personal laws. Registration is compulsory under this enactment. Divorce can also be obtained by non-Hindus under this Act. This legislation governs people of all religions and communities in India, irrespective of their personal faith. Likewise, under the Foreign Marriage Act, 1969, a person has only to be a citizen of India to have a marriage solemnised under this Act outside the territorial limits of India.

The Parsi Marriage and Divorce Act, 1936 as amended in 1988, is an Act to amend the law relating to marriage and divorce among the Parsis in India.

The Indian Christian Marriage Act, 1872, was enacted as an Act to consolidate and amend the law relating to the solemnisation of the marriages of Christians in India and the Divorce Act, 1869, as amended in 2001, is an Act to amend the law relating to divorce and matrimonial causes relating to Christians in India.

The Muslim Personal Law (Shariat) Application Act, 1937, the Dissolution of Muslim Marriages Act, 1939, the Muslim Women (Protection of Rights on Divorce) Act, 1986 and the Muslim Women (Protection of Rights on Divorce) Rules, 1986, apply to Muslims living in India.

For enforcement and adjudication of all matrimonial and other related disputes of any person in any of the different religious or non-religious communities under the respective legislation mentioned above, the designated judicial forum or court where such petition is to be lodged is prescribed in the respective enactments themselves. There is an organised system of designated civil and criminal judicial courts within every state in India which works under the overall jurisdiction of the respective High Court in the state. It is in the hierarchy of these courts that all family and matrimonial causes are lodged and decided. In addition, the Indian Parliament has enacted the Family Courts Act, 1984 to provide for the establishment of Family Courts with a view to promote conciliation in and to secure speedy settlement of disputes relating to marriage and family affairs. Despite the existence of an organised, well regulated and established hierarchy of judicial courts in India, there are still unrecognised parallel community and religious courts in existence whose interference has been deprecated by the judicial courts since such unauthorised and unwarranted bodies work without the authority of law and are not part of the judicial system.

III. BACKGROUND NOTE TO ALTERNATIVE DISPUTE RESOLUTION IN INDIA

It is believed that the development of the country can be also understood from the capability of its legal system in rendering effective justice. The practice of amicable resolution of disputes can be traced back to historic times, when the villages' disputes were resolved between members of a particular relationship or occupation or between members of a particular locality. In rural India, the 'panchayats' (assembly of elders and respected inhabitants of the village) decided almost all disputes between residents of the village, while disputes between members of a clan continued to be decided by the elders of the clan. These methods of amicable dispute resolution were recognised methods of administration of justice and not just an 'alternative' to the formal justice system formed by the sovereigns, feudal lords or the adalat systems initiated by the British and the formal court system. The two systems continued to function analogous to each other. The process followed by the traditional institutions was that of arbitration and conciliation, depending on the character of dispute.

In India there is a massive legal system comprising nearly 15,000 courts across the country. It is the constitutional obligation of the judiciary to exercise its jurisdiction to reaffirm the faith of the people in the judicial set up. Therefore, evolution of new juristic principles for dispute resolution is not only important but imperative. In India the need to evolve alternative mechanisms simultaneously with the revival and strengthening of traditional systems of dispute resolution has been reiterated in reports of expert bodies (Report of the Committee on Legal Aid (1971), Report of the Expert Committee on Legal Aid: Processual Justice to the People (Government of India, Ministry of Law, Justice and Company Affairs, 1973), Report on National Juridicare Equal Justice – Social Justice (Ministry of Law, Justice and Company Affairs, 1977). Each of these reports saw the process of improving access to justice through legal aid mechanisms and alternative dispute resolution (ADR) as a part of the systematic reform of the institution of the judiciary coupled with substantive reforms of laws and processes.

IV. EXISTING STATUTORY PROVISIONS FOR ADR IN LAW IN INDIA

The sensitivity of the legislature towards providing speedy and efficacious justice in India is mainly reflected in several enactments which are enumerated as follows:

- arbitration under the Arbitration and Conciliation Act, 1996;
- settlement under Order XXXIIA of the Indian Code of Civil Procedure, 1908;

- the incorporation (w.e.f. the 2002 amendment of the CPC) of section 89 in the traditional Civil Procedure Code (CPC) read with Order X, rules IA, IB, and IC for settlement of disputes outside court;
- the establishment of Lok Adalat under the Legal Services Authority Act, 1987 looks to mediation, conciliation and informal settlement of disputes in litigation;
- reconciliation under section 23(2) and (3) of the Hindu Marriage Act, 1955 as also under section 34(3) of the Special Marriage Act, 1954;
- duty of the Family Court to make efforts for settlement under the Family Courts Act, 1984.

(a) The Constitutional Mandate

Article 21 of the Constitution of India declares in a mandatory tone that no person shall be deprived of his life or his personal liberty except according to procedure established by law. The words 'life and liberty' are not to be read narrowly in the sense monotonously dictated by dictionaries; they are organic terms which are to be construed meaningfully.

The right to speedy trial has been rightly held to be a part of the right to life or personal liberty by the Supreme Court of India *[Hussainara Khatoon (1)* v. *Home Secretary, State of Bihar,* (1980) 1 SCC 81*]*. The Supreme Court has allowed article 21 to stretch its arms as wide as it legitimately can *(article 21 is a Fundamental Right that can be directly enforced in the Supreme Court under article 32 of the Constitution of India. Fundamental Rights, as incorporated in Part III of the Constitution, are different from Constitutional Rights that cannot be directly enforced under article 32. All Fundamental Rights are Constitutional Rights but not* vice-versa*)*. The reason is very simple. This liberal interpretation of article 21 is to redress that mental agony, expense and strain which a person proceeded against in litigation has to undergo and which, coupled with delay, may result in impairing the capability or ability of the accused to defend himself effectively. Thus, the Supreme Court has held:

> "the right to speedy trial a manifestation of fair, just and reasonable procedure enshrined in article 21. A speedy trial encompasses within its sweep all its stages including investigation, inquiry, trial, appeal, revision and re-trial. In other words, everything commencing with an accusation and expiring with the final verdict falls within its ambit. The same has got recognition from the 'legislature' as well in the form of the introduction of 'Alternative Dispute Resolution Mechanism' (ADRM) through various statutes *(The Culture of ADR in India by Praveen Dalal' available at: www. odr. info/ THE CULTURE OF ADR IN INDIA.doc)*."

(b) The Indian Arbitration and Conciliation Act, 1996

The above is a generalised list of statutory enactments which govern the arena of Indian dispute resolution by finding expression in different words under separate laws. Arbitration generally is now a prevalent practice in the Indian civil jurisdiction. Due to mounting arrears of cases in courts in India, there was a dire need for effective means of alternative dispute resolution. India's first enactment on arbitration was the Arbitration Act, 1940. Other supporting legislation in existence was the Arbitration [Protocol and Convention] Act of 1937 and the Foreign Awards Act of 1961. Arbitration under these laws was never effective and led to further litigation as a result of rampant challenge of the awards rendered under these laws. The Indian legislature thus enacted the existing current Arbitration and Conciliation Act, 1996 to make arbitration, both domestic and international, more effective in India. The Act is based on the UNCITRAL Model Law (as recommended by the UN General Assembly) and facilitates international commercial arbitration as well as domestic arbitration and conciliation. Under the above 1996 Act, an arbitral award can be challenged only in the manner prescribed and on limited grounds. The 1996 Act also restricts court's intervention in arbitration proceedings to minimal interference. India is party to the New York Convention of 1958 on the Recognition and Enforcement of Foreign Arbitral Awards. As the name of the Act suggests, it also covers conciliation, which is a form of mediation. Accordingly, arbitration is a popular mode of dispute resolution in civil disputes and commercial agreements invariably contain an arbitration clause.

(c) Provisions for ADR under the Code of Civil Procedure, 1908

The Code of Civil Procedure, 1908 (CPC), as amended from time to time is an Act to consolidate and amend the laws relating to the procedure of the Courts of Civil Judicature in India. All litigation of a civil nature in India is essentially governed by the substantive provisions of law, contained in the various sections of the CPC and the corresponding implementing provisions are contained in various orders and rules of the CPC. There are three substantive and procedural provisions contained in the CPC which provide for settlement of disputes outside the court. These can be identified briefly as the following before quoting the details of the respective provisions:

- Section 89 of the Code of Civil Procedure: Settlement of disputes outside the Court;
- Order X of the Code of Civil Procedure, 1908: Examination of Parties by the Court; and
- Order XXXIIA *(Order XXXIIA inserted by section 80 of Act No. 104 of 1976 (with effect from 1 February, 1977)* of the Code of Civil Procedure, 1908: Suits Relating to Matters Concerning the Family.

It may now be useful to quote the details of all the three provisions of the CPC mentioned above. They are extracted hereunder in the order given above.

(i) Section 89 of the Code of Civil Procedure: Settlement of disputes outside the Court

(Inserted by CPC (Amendment) Act, 1999 with effect from 1 July, 2002. The earlier section 89 of the CPC was repealed by the Arbitration Act, 1940. There is now an independent Arbitration and Conciliation Act, 1996. The law has been consolidated in that Act and hence the present parallel amendment was necessitated in the CPC in 1999)

With a view to implementing the 129th Report of the Law Commission of India, it was made obligatory for courts to refer disputes after the issues were framed for settlement either by way of arbitration, conciliation, mediation, judicial settlement or through Lok Adalat (a settlement court). It was felt that only after the parties failed to get their disputes settled through any one of the alternate dispute resolution methods should the litigation proceed further in the court in which it was filed. Accordingly, section 89 of the CPC reads as follows:

> ***"89. Settlement of disputes outside the Court.***—*(1) Where it appears to the court that there exist elements of a settlement which may be acceptable to the parties, the court shall formulate the terms of settlement and give them to the parties for their observations and after receiving the observation of the parties, the court may reformulate the terms of a possible settlement and refer the same for—*
>
> *(a) arbitration;*
>
> *(b) conciliation;*
>
> *(c) judicial settlement including settlement through Lok Adalat; or*
>
> *(d) mediation.*
>
> *(2) Where a dispute had been referred–*

for arbitration or conciliation, the provisions of the Arbitration and Conciliation Act, 1996 (26 of 1996) shall apply as if the proceedings for arbitration or conciliation were referred for settlement under the provisions of that Act;

to Lok Adalat, the court shall refer the same to the Lok Adalat in accordance with the provisions of sub-section (1) of section 20 of the Legal Services Authority Act, 1987 (39 of 1987) and all other provisions of that Act shall apply in respect of the dispute so referred to the Lok Adalat;

> *(a) for judicial settlement, the court shall refer the same to a suitable institution or person and such institution or person shall be deemed to be a Lok Adalat and all the provisions of the Legal Services Authority Act, 1987 (39 of 1987) shall apply as if the dispute were referred to a Lok Adalat under the provisions of that Act;*
>
> *(b) for mediation, the court shall effect a compromise between the parties and shall follow such procedure as may be prescribed."*

A perusal of section 89 of the CPC quoted above clearly spells out the statutory modes, mechanisms, machinery and procedure provided and stipulated for alternative modes of dispute redressal in all matters of civil litigation in India. These substantive provisions are procedurally supported by Order X, rules 1A, 1B and 1C as below.

(ii) Order X of the Code of Civil Procedure, 1908: Examination of Parties by the Court

Rules 1A, 1B and 1C were inserted in Order X by the CPC (Amendment) Act, 1999. This was consequential to the insertion of section 89(1) of the CPC, making it obligatory upon the courts to refer the dispute for settlement by way of arbitration, conciliation, judicial settlement including settlement through Lok Adalat or mediation. A settlement can thus be made by adopting any of the said modes specified in the amended section 89. Order X of the CPC along with rules 1, 1A, 1B and 1C read in the following terms:

> ***'Order X: Examination of Parties by the Court.***
>
> *1. Ascertainment whether allegations in pleadings are admitted or denied – At the first hearing of the suit the court shall ascertain from each party or his pleader whether he admits or denies such allegations of fact as are made in the plaint or written statement (if any) of the opposite party, and as are not expressly or by the necessary implication admitted or denied by the party against whom they are made. The court shall record such admissions and denials.*
>
> *1A. Direction of the court to opt for any one mode of alternative dispute resolution (Added by Act No 46 of 1999, section 20 (with effect from 1 July, 2002).*
>
> *After recording the admissions and denials, the court shall direct the parties to the suit to opt either mode of the settlement outside the court as specified in sub-section (1) of section 89. On the option of the parties, the court shall fix the date of appearance before such forum or authority as may be opted by the parties.*
>
> *1B. Appearance before the conciliatory forum or authority*
>
> *Where a suit is referred under rule 1A, the parties shall appear before such forum or authority for conciliation of the suit.*
>
> *1C. Appearance before the court consequent to the failure of efforts of conciliation*
>
> *Where a suit is referred under rule 1A and the presiding officer of conciliation forum or authority is satisfied that it would not be proper in the interest of justice to proceed with the matter further, then, it shall refer the matter again to the Court and direct the parties to appear before the court on the date fixed by it.'*

As per the rule 1A above, the parties to the suit are given an option for settlement of the dispute outside court. When the parties have exercised their option, it shall fix the date of appearance before such forum or authority as may be opted by the parties for settlement. As per rule 1B, the parties are required to appear before such forum or authority opted by them. Rule 1C provides for the presiding officer of the forum or authority to refer the matter again to the court in case it feels that, in the interest of justice, the forum or authority should not proceed with the matter.

(iii) Order XXXIIA of the Code of Civil Procedure, 1908

(Order XXXIIA inserted by section 80 of Act No 104 of 1976 (w.e.f. 1 February, 1977))

It may be pertinent to point out that all proceedings under the Hindu Marriage Act, 1955 and the Special Marriage Act, 1954 in India are regulated by the provisions contained in the CPC. Accordingly, insofar as suits relating to matters concerning the family are concerned, by an amendment made in 1976, the Indian Parliament in its wisdom added Order XXXIIA to the Code of Civil Procedure to provide for mandatory settlement procedures in all matrimonial proceedings specifically. Order XXXIIA of the CPC which is relevant to the present context is quoted below for reference:

"Order XXXIIA: Suits Relating to Matters Concerning the Family:

1. Application of the Order

(1) The provisions of this Order shall apply to suits or proceedings relating to matters concerning the family.

(2) In particular, and without prejudice to the generality of the provisions of sub-rule (1), the provisions of this Order shall apply to the following suits or proceedings concerning the family, namely:—

(a) a suit or proceeding for matrimonial relief, including a suit or proceeding for declaration as to the validity of a marriage or as to the matrimonial status of any person;

(b) a suit or proceeding for a declaration as to legitimacy of any person;

(c) a suit or proceeding in relation to the guardianship of the person or the custody of any minor or other member of the family, under a disability;

(d) a suit or proceeding for maintenance;

(e) a suit or proceeding as to the validity or effect of an adoption;

(f) a suit or proceeding, instituted by a member of the family relating to wills, intestacy and succession;

(g) a suit or proceeding relating to any other matter concerning the family in respect of which the parties are subject to their personal law.

(3) So much of this Order as relates to a matter provided for by a special law in respect of any suit or proceeding shall not apply to that suit or proceeding.

***2. Proceedings to be held* in camera**

In every suit or proceeding to which this Order applies, the proceeding may be held in camera *if the Court so desires and shall be so held if either party so desires.*

3. Duty of Court to make efforts for settlement

(1) In every suit or proceeding to which this Order applies, an endeavour shall be made by the Court in the first instance, where it is possible to do so consistent with the nature and circumstances of the case, to assist the parties in arriving at a settlement in respect of the subject-matter of the suit.

(2) If, in any such suit or proceeding, at any stage it appears to the Court that there is a reasonable possibility of a settlement between the parties, the Court may adjourn the proceeding for such period as it thinks fit to enable attempts to be made to effect such a settlement.

(3) The power conferred by sub-rule (2) sholl be in addition to, and not in derogation of, any other power of the Court to adjourn the proceedings.

4. Assistance of welfare expert

In every suit or proceeding to which this Order applies, it shall be open to the Court to secure the services of such person (preferably a woman where available), whether related to the parties or not, including a person professionally engaged in promoting the welfare of the family as the Court may think fit, for the purpose of assisting the Court in discharging the functions imposed by rule 3 or this Order.

5. Duty to inquire into facts

In every suit or proceeding to which this Order applies, it shall be the duty of the Court to inquire, so far it [sic] reasonably can, into the facts alleged by the plaintiff and into any facts alleged by the defendant.

6. "Family" – meaning of

For the purposes of this Order, each of the following shall be treated as constituting a family, namely:—

(a) (i) a man and his wife living together,

(ii) any child or children being issue of theirs; or of such man or such wife,

(iii) any child or children being maintained by such man and wife;

(b) a man not having a wife or not living together with his wife, any child or children, being issue of his, and any child or children being maintained by him;

(c) a woman not having a husband or not living together with her husband any child or children being issue of hers, and any child or children being maintained by her

(d) a man or woman and his or her brother, sister, ancestor or lineal descendant living with him or her; and

(e) any combination of one or more of the groups specified in clause (a), clause (b), clause (c) or clause (d) of this rule.

Explanation.—For the avoidance of doubts, it is hereby declared that the provisions of rule 6 shall be without any prejudice to the concept of "family" in any personal law or in any other law for the time being in force.'

A reading of the above clearly establishes the statutory mandate laid down by the CPC to make an endeavour in the first instance to assist the parties in arriving at a settlement in a matrimonial cause in any matrimonial proceeding before a court of competent jurisdiction. Hence, in any suit or proceeding for matrimonial, ancillary or other relief in matters concerning the family, there is a separate and independent statutory provision providing for mandatory settlement proceedings. This is over and above the other statutory provisions applicable.

(d) Lok Adalat system under the Legal Services Authority Act, 1987

The Legal Services Authorities Act, 1987, as per its preamble, was enacted as:

'An Act to constitute legal services authorities to provide free and competent legal services to the weaker sections of the society to ensure that opportunities for securing justice are not denied to any citizen by reason of economic or other disabilities, and to organise Lok Adalats to secure that the operation of the legal system promotes justice on a basis of equal opportunity.'

Under Chapter VI of the Act, authorities may organise Lok Adalats (Settlement Courts) at such intervals and places and for exercising such jurisdiction and for such areas as it thinks fit. Generally, the Lok Adalat consists of serving or retired judicial officers and other persons of eminence, specified by the respective government in consultation with the judiciary. Over the passage of time, such Lok Adalats have become a popular mode for informal settlement of civil disputes of all nature. Written compromises, settlements and negotiated conclusions drawn up in Lok Adalats are returned to the court of competent jurisdiction for passing an appropriate judicial award, decision, decree or compromise as the case may be. Even matrimonial matters are settled in Lok Adalats and thereafter such negotiated settlements are affirmed by the respective matrimonial courts by appropriate orders or consent decrees/judgments so drawn up.

Lok Adalat generally means 'People's Court'. India has had a long history of resolving disputes through the mediation of village elders. The system of Lok Adalats is an improvement on that and is based on Gandhian principles. This is a non-adversarial system, where mock courts (called Lok Adalats) are held by the State Authority, District Authority, Supreme Court Legal Services Committee, High Court Legal Services Committee, or Taluk Legal Services Committee, periodically for exercising such jurisdiction as they think fit. These are usually presided by retired judges, social activists, or members of the legal profession. Lok Adalats do not have jurisdiction on matters pertaining to non-compoundable offences.

There is no court fee and no rigid procedural requirement (*i.e.* no need to follow mandatory process laid down by the CPC or Evidence Act), which makes the process very fast. Parties can directly interact with the Lok Adalat judges in vernacular language, which feature is not possible in regular courts.

Cases that are pending in regular courts can be transferred to a Lok Adalat if both the parties agree and consent to it. A case can also be transferred to a Lok Adalat if one party applies to the court in writing where the matter is pending. If the court sees some chances of settlement after giving an opportunity of being heard to the other party, the matter can be transferred to the Lok Adalat for settlement.

The focus in Lok Adalats is on compromise and settlement. When no compromise is reached, the matter goes back to the regular court. However, if a compromise is reached, an award is made by consent and is binding on the parties. It is enforced as a decree of a civil court after it is affirmed as such by the regular court. An important aspect is that the award is final and cannot be appealed, not even under article 226 of the Constitution of India, because it is a judgment by consent and consent orders are not appealable.

All proceedings of a Lok Adalat are deemed to be judicial proceedings and every Lok Adalat is deemed to be a civil court under the Legal Services Authorities Act, 1987.

The Law Commission of India in its 129th Report recommended that the alternate modes of dispute redressal be obligatory on the courts after framing of issues. It is only after the parties fail to get their disputes settled through any one of the alternate dispute resolution methods that the suit shall proceed further in the court where it was filed and where the matter was pending before settlement was attempted.

(e) Settlement under Indian Family Law Statutes

Reconciliation is mandatory under the Hindu Marriage Act, 1955 (HMA) and the Special Marriage Act, 1954 (SMA). However, other Indian matrimonial statutes do not provide for it and there is therefore no statutory mandate to attempt settlement in other cases.

(i) Reconciliation under section 23(2) and (3) of the Hindu Marriage Act, 1955

Section 23(2) of the HMA, 1955 states that, before proceeding to grant any relief under it, there shall be a duty on the Court in the first instance, in every case to make every endeavour to bring about reconciliation between the parties where relief is sought on most of the fault grounds for divorce specified in section 13 of the HMA, 1955. Section 23(3) of the HMA, 1955 makes a provision empowering the court on the request of parties or if the court thinks it just and proper to adjourn the proceedings for a reasonable period not exceeding 15 days to bring about reconciliation. It must be borne in mind that a Hindu marriage is a sacrament and not a contract. Even if divorce is sought by mutual consent, it is the duty of the court to attempt reconciliation in the first instance. Accordingly, Hindu law advocates rapprochement and reconciliation before dissolving a Hindu marriage. Section 23(2) and (3) of the HMA, 1955, relevant for the present context, are reproduced below:

"23. Decree in Proceedings—

(1) ...

(2) Before proceeding to grant any relief under this Act, it shall be the duty of the court in the first instance, in every case where it is possible so to do consistently with the nature and circumstances of the case, to make every endeavour to bring about a reconciliation between the parties:

[Provided that nothing contained in this sub-section shall apply to any proceeding wherein relief is sought on any of the grounds specified in clause (ii), clause (iii), clause (iv), clause (v), clause (vi) or clause (vii) of sub-section (1) of section 13.

(3) For the purpose of aiding the court in bringing about such reconciliation, the court may, if the parties so desire or if the court thinks it just and proper so to do, adjourn the proceedings for a reasonable period not exceeding fifteen days and refer the matter to any person named by the parties in this behalf or to any person nominated by the court if the parties fail to name any person, with directions to report to the court as to whether reconciliation can be and

has been, effected and the court shall in disposing of the proceeding have due regard to report.]' (Inserted by Act 68 of 1976, section 16 (with effect from 27 May, 1976)"

(ii) section 34 of the Special Marriage Act, 1954

The provisions of section 34(2) and (3) of the SMA, 1954 are *pari materia* to the provisions contained in section 23(2) and (3) of the HMA, 1955. Even though the marriage contracted under the SMA, 1954 does not have the same sacramental sanctity as marriage solemnised under the HMA, 1955, the Indian Parliament in its wisdom has retained the provisions for reconciliation of marriages in the same terms in the SMA, 1954 as they exist in the HMA, 1955. The mandatory duty on the court is thus in similar terms. For reference, section 34(2) and (3) of the SMA, 1954 are quoted below:

"34. Duty of Court in passing decrees-

(1) xx xx xx xx

(2) Before proceeding to grant any relief under this Act it shall be the duty of the court in the first instance, in every case where it is possible so to do consistently with the nature and circumstances of the case, to make every endeavour to bring about a reconciliation between the parties:

[Provided that nothing contained in this sub-section shall apply to any proceeding wherein relief is sought on any of the grounds specified in clause (c), clause (e), clause (f), clause (g) or clause (h) of sub-section (1) of section 27 of the Special Marriage Act, 1954.

(3) For the purpose of aiding the court in bringing about such reconciliation, the court may, if the parties so desire or if the court thinks it just and proper so to do, adjourn the proceedings for a reasonable period not exceeding fifteen days and refer the matter to any person named by the parties in this behalf or to any person nominated by the court if the parties fail to name any person, with directions to report to the court as to whether reconciliation can be and has been, effected and the court shall in disposing of the proceeding have due regard to the report.]' (Inserted by Act 68 of 1976, section 34 (with effect from 27 May, 1976)"

It may be noticed that the provisions under both the statutes are almost identical and accordingly every endeavour to bring about reconciliation is mandatory.

(iii) Other pre-emptive measures under the Hindu Marriage Act, 1955

Section 14 of the HMA, 1955 is another pre-emptive measure provided by the said Act, which was presumably designed with the object of preventing hasty recourse to legal proceedings by the spouses without making a real effort to reconcile and save their marriage from being dissolved. In this context, it may be useful to quote section 14(1) of the HMA, 1955 which states that:

"Notwithstanding anything contained in this Act, it shall not be competent for any court to entertain any petition for dissolution of marriage by a decree of divorce, (Substituted by Act 68 of 1976, section 9) [unless at the date of presentation of the petition one year has elapsed] since the date of marriage"

Thus, section 14 of the HMA, 1955 provides a deterrent from initiating divorce proceedings in the first year of marriage. The logic again is to advocate settlement and reconciliation between parties and avoid hasty divorces.

However, under the proviso to section 14 of the HMA, 1955, the court is conferred a discretionary power to entertain a petition before the expiry of one year, if it finds on the allegation in the affidavit filed in support of the petition that *prima facie* there is exceptional hardship to the petitioner or depravity on the part of the respondent [*Gulzar Singh* v. *State of Punjab*, 1998 (2) HLR 204 (P&H)]. It presupposes an application for leave of court to present a petition for divorce before the expiry of one year from the date of marriage. Hence, the statute provides discretion to the court in entertaining a petition of divorce in the first year of marriage on the ground of exceptional hardship or exceptional depravity.

Section 14(2) of the HMA, 1955 further states that:

> *"In disposing of any application under this section for leave to present a petition for divorce before the [expiration of one year] (Substituted by Act 68 of 1976, section 9, for 'expiration of three years' (w.e.f. 27 May, 1976)) from the date of marriage, the court shall have regard to the interests of any children of the marriage and to the question whether there is a reasonable probability of a reconciliation between the parties before the expiration of the [said one year]"*
>
> *[Substituted by Act 68 of 1976, section 9, for 'said three years' (with effect from 27 May, 1976)]*

Section 29 of the SMA, 1954 contains similar provisions with similar bars.

(iv) Petition for divorce by mutual consent

Under section 13B of the HMA, 1955 and section 28 of the SMA, 1954, divorce by mutual consent is available. However, it is not granted instantly and a joint motion made by both parties in the first instance has to wait for 6 months but not longer than 18 months to be confirmed for granting a divorce by mutual consent in the second motion. It is evident that reconciliation may be out of the question in a petition for divorce by mutual consent. But there is an inbuilt opportunity for reconciliation if parties wish to avail of it. When a joint petition is presented, it is adjourned for a minimum period of 6 months. This period is to enable them to think over the matter of divorce and, if the parties want to prolong their consideration of reconciliation, they can do so for another year (total period is 18 months, within which they can move the motion of a decree of divorce). Section 28 of the SMA, 1954 contains similar provisions with similar bars. The logic in these enactments is again to provide for reconciliation in a thinking period between the first and the second motion.

Some precedents settled by Indian courts may be cited in support. In *Hitesh Narendra Doshi* v. *Jesal Hitesh Doshi*, 2000 (2) HLR (AP) (DB) 45: AIR 2000 AP 362 the minimum 6-month waiting period from the date of the presentation of the petition for snapping the marital ties between the parties by mutual consent under section 13B(2) of the HMA, 1955 was held to be mandatory and it was held that the court has no power to relax the said compulsory time wait of 6 months and cannot pass a decree of divorce forthwith.

However, in *Mohinder Pal Kaur* v. *Gurmeet Singh,* 2002 (1) Hindu LR (P&H) 537 it was held that the 6-month waiting period can be brought down in cases where an existing divorce petition is already pending for more than 6 months and efforts for reconciliation have been made earlier but without any success. Thus, the waiting period can be curtailed in a freshly instituted petition for divorce by mutual consent if, in an earlier petition on fault or other grounds, the parties have already been litigating for more than 6 months and reconciliation between them has been of no avail.

(v) Matters to which reconciliation does not apply: petition on certain fault grounds

When a petition for divorce under the HMA, 1955 is presented on the ground of change of religion [section 13(1)(ii)], unsoundness of mind [section 13(1)(iii)], leprosy [section 13(1)(iv)], venereal disease [section 13(1)(v)], renunciation of world [section 13(1)(vi)], or presumption of death [section 13(1)(vii)] reconciliation efforts need not be made, that is to say, the provisions of section 23(2) do not apply. The proviso to section 23(2) of the HMA, 1955 exempts the mandatory requirement of attempting reconciliation between the parties when divorce is sought on any of the grounds in HMA, 1955 above.

Similarly, when a petition for divorce is made under the SMA, 1954 on the ground of 7 years sentence of imprisonment [section 27(1)(c)], unsoundness of mind [section 27(1)(e)], venereal disease (section 27(1)(f)), leprosy [section 27(1)(g)], or presumption of death [section 27(1)(h)], no efforts at reconciliation need be made. The proviso to section 34(2) of the SMA, 1954 exempts the mandatory requirement of attempting reconciliation between the parties when divorce is sought on any of the grounds in SMA, 1954 stipulated above.

However, it may be added out of abundant clarification that on all other grounds of divorce, both under the HMA, 1955 and SMA, 1954, the court has an obligation to make efforts at reconciliation [*Pramila* v. *Ajit,* AIR 1989 Pat 163: (1989) 2 DMC 466]. This mandatory and statutory duty of the court cannot be waived.

(vi) Reconciliation by the court

Section 23(2) of the HMA, 1955 and section 34(2) of the SMA, 1954 lay down that at first instance it is the duty of the court to make every effort to bring about reconciliation between the parties where it is possible to do so consistently with the nature and circumstances of the case. The words are *'before proceeding to grant relief'*. At one time a view was propounded that the reconciliation endeavour should be made towards the end of the proceedings when the court comes to a conclusion that it is going to grant 'relief'. But then the provision also states 'at the first instance' and this has been interpreted to mean that before the court takes up the case for hearing, it should make an effort at reconciliation. Presently, the latter is the prevalent view and hence reconciliation is to be attempted in the first instance.

(f) Family Courts Act, 1984

The Preamble to the Family Courts Act, 1984 enacted by the Indian Parliament states that it is:

'An Act to provide for the establishment of Family Courts with a view to promote conciliation in, and secure speedy settlement of disputes relating to marriage and family affairs and for matters connected therewith.'

In the Statement of Objects and Reasons of the Family Courts Act, five essential requirements were pinpointed in the context of providing reconciliatory efforts to litigating parties and these can be summarised as follows:

(a) make it obligatory on the part of the Family Court to endeavour, in the first instance to effect a reconciliation or a settlement between the parties to a family dispute. During this stage, the proceedings will be informal and rigid rules of procedure shall not apply;

(b) provide for the association of social welfare agencies, counsellors, etc, during conciliation stage and also to secure the service of medical and welfare experts;

(c) provide that the parties to a dispute before a Family Court shall not be entitled, as of right, to be represented by legal practitioners. However, the court may, in the interest of justice, seek assistance of a legal experts as *amicus curiae* in the case;

(d) simplify the rules of evidence and procedure so as to enable a Family Court to deal effectively with a dispute; and

(e) provide for only one right of appeal which shall lie to the High Court.

In seeking to achieve the above objects, the endeavour of the Family Courts Act was to adopt a friendly, conciliatory and informal dispute resolution atmosphere which would enable parties to amicably settle their differences without the shackles of the technical rules of the law of procedure and evidence. These objects find expression in the Constitution of the Family Courts Act, its jurisdiction and procedure. The necessary provisions for reconciliation in the Family Courts Act, 1984 are dealt with under section 9 of the Act which reads as follows:

"9. Duty of Family Court to make efforts for settlement:

(2) In every suit or proceeding, endeavour shall be made by the Family Court in the first instance, where it is possible to do so consistent with the nature and circumstances of the case, to assist and persuade the parties in arriving at a settlement in respect of the subject-matter of the suit or proceeding and for this purpose a Family Court may, subject to any rules made by the High Court, follow such procedure as it may deem fit.

(3) If, in any suit or proceeding, at any stage, it appears to the Family Court that there is a reasonable possibility of a settlement between the parties, the Family Court may adjourn the proceedings for such period as it think fit to enable attempts to be made to effect such a settlement.

(4) The power conferred by sub-section (2) shall be in addition to, and not in derogation of any other power of the Family Court to adjourn the proceedings."

The Act also makes it open to the Family Courts under section 12:

> '. . . *to secure the services of a medical expert or such person (preferably a woman where available), whether related to the parties or not, including a person professionally engaged in promoting the welfare of the family as the court may think fit, for the purposes of assisting the Family Court in discharging the functions imposed by this Act.*'

Clearly, the thought, logic and motive in the Act in making available services of professional experts is to provide counselling, expert help and assistance of trained mediators. Therefore, this enactment is wholesome legislation on reconciliatory modes in family law disputes in the Indian matrimonial jurisdiction.

V. ANALYSIS OF THE STATUS OF ADR IN FAMILY LAW IN INDIA

The duty of making or amending laws is on the legislature but to develop it and to interpret it to suit the needs and circumstances of society is the call of the judiciary. Hence, unless and until the beneficial provisions of the matrimonial legislation promoting and advocating reconciliation in matrimonial disputes in India are favourably interpreted and strictly implemented by the courts, the letter of law may be an illusory mirage which remains on the statute book only. It is therefore the solemn duty of the matrimonial courts in India to ensure that the mandatory settlement efforts are actually put into practice and parties are encouraged to actually utilise them for out-of-court settlements. Thus, there is a heavy burden on the courts to discharge this duty failing which it will be neither possible nor useful to enforce reconciliatory measure in matrimonial disputes in the Indian jurisdiction. Accordingly, it would be most useful to cite and quote some recent prominent verdicts of superior Indian courts which have stressed and highlighted the dire necessity of the beneficial provisions of Indian legislation which provide mandatory reconciliation procedures.

Section 23 of the HMA, 1955 and Order XXXIIA of the CPC and the duty enjoined upon the court came up for interpretation before the Supreme Court recently in the case *Jagraj Singh* v. *Bir Pal Kaur*, JT 2007 (3) SC 389. The Supreme Court upheld the order of the High Court summoning the respondent husband by non-bailable warrants and held as follows:

> *"26 From the above case law in our judgment, it is clear that that a court is expected, nay, bound, to make all attempts and section (2) of section 23 is a salutary provision exhibiting the intention of the parliament requiring the court 'in the first instance' to make every endeavour to bring about a reconciliation between the parties. If in the light of the above mentioned intention and paramount consideration of the legislature in enacting such provision, an order is passed by a Matrimonial Court asking a party to the proceeding (husband or wife) to remain personally present, it cannot successfully be contended that the court has no such power and in case a party to a proceeding does not remain present, at most, the court can proceed to decide the case* ex parte *against him/her. Upholding of such argument would virtually make the benevolent provision nugatory, ineffective and unworkable, defeating the laudable object of reconciliation in matrimonial*

disputes. The contention of the learned counsel for the appellant therefore cannot be upheld.'

Hence, the order of the Apex Indian Court upholding the directions of the High Court summoning the respondent – husband in the above case – through non-bailable warrants clearly reflects the legislative intent of attempting mandatory reconciliation procedures. This judgment of the Supreme Court clearly confirms that settlement efforts in matrimonial matters are not an empty meaningless ritual to be performed by the matrimonial court. The verdict clearly reflects the benevolent legislative purpose.

A novel question came up for decision before the High Court of Kerala in *Bini* v. *K.V. Sundaran,* AIR 2008 Ker 84, *i.e.* as to whether conciliation is mandatory after the introduction of the Family Courts Act, 1984, even on the excepted grounds of conversion to another religion, renunciation of the world, mental disorder, venereal disease and leprosy. Calling the Family Courts Act, 1984 a special statute, and its provisions to make attempt at reconciliation mandatory at the first instance, the High Court in the aforesaid case held:

> *'The parties can disagree on matters of faith and still lead a happy marital life if they could be convinced that matters of faith should not stand in the way of union of hearts. Thus though under the Hindu Marriage Act, 1955, no endeavour for reconciliation need be made in a petition for divorce on the ground of conversion to another religion, or other grounds excepted under section 13(1) of the Hindu Marriage Act, 1955 or on similar or other grounds available under any other law also, after the introduction of the Family Courts Act, 1984, the Family Court is bound to make an endeavour for reconciliation and settlement. The requirement is mandatory. That is the conceptual change brought out by the Family Courts Act, 1984 which is a special statute.'*

The court further says that *'the primary object is to promote and preserve the sacred union of parties to marriage. Only if the attempts for reconciliation are not fruitful, the further attempt on agreement or disagreement be made by way of settlement' (Paragraphs 3 and 7 of the judgment).*

Hence, from a reading of the above judgment it is clear that the duty cast upon the matrimonial courts to attempt mandatory reconciliation cannot be avoided and cannot be circumvented even when divorce is sought on certain exceptional grounds which under the HMA, 1955 and SMA, 1954 do not provide compulsory settlement action.

Still further, stressing the need to treat the cases pertaining to family matters in a humanitarian way, the Supreme Court of India in the case *Balwinder Kaur* v. *Hardeep Singh,* AIR 1998 SC 764 laid down in paragraph 9 of the judgment as follows:

> *' . . . stress should always be on preserving the institution of marriage. That is the requirement of law. One may refer to the Objects and Reasons which lead to setting up of Family Courts under the Family Courts Act, 1984. For the purpose of settlement of family disputes emphasis is 'laid on conciliation and achieving socially desirable results' and elimination of adherence to rigid rules of procedure and evidence.'*

The Supreme Court further held in paragraphs 10 and 11 of the judgment as follows:

> '... *it is now obligatory on the part of the Family Court to endeavour, in the first instance to effect a reconciliation or settlement between the parties to a family dispute. Even where the Family Courts are not functioning, the objects and principles underlying the constitution of these courts can be kept in view by the Civil Courts trying matrimonial causes.*'

The Supreme Court held in paragraph 9 of the above judgment that the objectives and principles of section 23 of the HMA, 1955 govern all courts trying matrimonial matters.

Deciding on the importance of making an attempt at reconciliation at the first instance, a Division Bench of the Calcutta High Court in *Shiv Kumar Gupta* v. *Lakshmi Devi Gupta*, 2005 (1) HLR 483 felt that the compliance with section 23(2) of the HMA, 1955 is a statutory duty of the judge trying matrimonial cases. The court in this case relied upon the decision of the Supreme Court in *Balwinder Kaur* v. *Hardeep Singh* (which has been dealt with in preceding paragraphs) and held in paragraph 8 of the judgment as follows:

> '... *on a reading of section 23(2) of the Act and on the perusal of the judgment in Balwinder Kaur on the interpretation of section 23(2) this Court held that the decree, which was passed without complying with section 23(2) of the said Act, cannot be sustained.*'

In another perspective, in *Love Kumar* v. *Sunita Puri*, AIR 1997 P&H 189: 1997 (1) HLR 179 it was held that the matrimonial court had acted in haste to pass a decree of divorce against the husband for his non-appearance at the time of reconciliation proceedings. The High Court accordingly set aside the divorce decree and remanded the matter back to the matrimonial court to be decided on its merits. The object of section 23(2) of the HMA, 1955 was explained in paras 19 and 21 of this judgment as follows:

> *'19. Under section 23(2) of the Act it is incumbent on the matrimonial Court, to endeavour to bring about reconciliation between the parties, a great responsibility is cast on the Court. A Hindu marriage is not contractual but sacrosanct, it is not easy to create such ties but more difficult to break them; once annulled, it cannot be restored. A Judge should actively stimulate rapprochement process. It is fundamental that reconciliation of a ruptured marriage is the first duty of the Judge. The sanctity of marriage is the corner stone of civilization. The object and purpose of this provision is obvious. The State is interested in the security and preservation of the institution of marriage and for this the Court is required to make attempt to bring about a reconciliation between the parties. However, omission to make attempts at reconciliation will not take away the jurisdiction of the Court to pass any decree under the Act. This is not correct to say that in a divorce case reconciliation efforts have to be timed immediately preceding the grant of decree and not at any other stage of the proceedings of the trial. Such an attempt can be and should be made at any stage. The matrimonial Court is required to call parties and make a genuine effort for their reconciliation, there is*

not even a whisper in this provision that the matrimonial Court has the power to strike off the defence of that spouse, who after being given opportunities for reconciliation fails to appear.

...

21. But under section 23(2) of the Act neither such a liability is cast on the one spouse nor such a right is given to the other spouse. Reconciliation is a mutual dialogue to bury their differences. A duty is cast on the Court to call the party at the initial stage for reconciliation. Even before delivering judgment and decree, the Court can make effort for reconciliation. Thus, the stage of trial for calling the parties for reconciliation is left to the discretion of the Court.'

From a reading of the above judgments, it can clearly be spelt out that, though reconciliation is a mandatory process, the timing and stage at which it is to be implemented may vary depending on the facts and circumstances of each case. At the same time causing prejudice to the rights of one party by striking off the defence or dismissing the petition may actually work injustice to the rights of such party. Therefore, the matrimonial court in its wisdom may fashion and design the stage of attempting matrimonial reconciliation depending on the facts of each case without causing prejudice to the substantive rights of the parties. However, at the same time, the matrimonial court ought not to give the mandatory settlement procedure a go by.

In another case, High Court of Allahabad called it the bounded duty of the Family Court to make an attempt at conciliation before proceeding with the trial of the case [*Rajesh Kumar Saxena* v. *Nidhi Saxena*, 1995 (1) HLR 472]. In the recent case of *Aviral Bhatla* v. *Bhavana Bhatla*, (2009) 3 SCC 448, the Supreme Court has upheld the settlement of the Delhi mediation centre, appreciating the effective manner in which the mediation centre of the Delhi High Court helped the parties to arrive at a settlement.

In a unique unreported case decided by the Supreme Court of India on 15 July, 2013 in the matter of **Pamela Sharda *v.* Rama Sharda,** a petition for Special Leave to Appeal (Civil) No. 11714 of 2012, preferred against a Judgment of the High Court of Delhi, the Apex Court was pleased to uphold a settlement arrived at between the parties at the Supreme Court Mediation Centre. It may be mentioned that this Centre assists parties for resolution of disputes through process of mediation. Clauses 2, 5, 7 and 9 of the Settlement between parties read as follows:

"2. That the First Party shall pay a sum of Rs. 45,00,000 (Rupees Forty-five Lakhs only) to the Third Party in full and final settlement of her claims towards Istridhan, maintenance pendente lite, *alimony temporary and permanent and pursuant to the receipt of Rs. 45,00,000 (Rupees Forty-five Lakhs only) the Third Party shall have no claim whatsoever against the First Party. The Third Party shall also make no claim in future qua the rights of residence as envisaged under section 19 of the Domestic Violence Act, Hindu Adoption and Maintenance Act, 1956 and Hindu Marriage Act, 1955 or under any other statutory enactment and all her statutory rights, claims qua the First Party shall stand extinguished upon the payment of Rs. 45,00,000 (Rupees Forty-five Lakhs only).*

5. That it has been agreed between the First Party and the Third Party that the amount received by the Third Party from the First Party shall not be considered as an amount towards dissolution of marriage as permanent alimony. Further the First Party had assured the Third Party that he shall not file any proceedings for obtaining divorce on any ground and in lieu of that assurance the Third Party has undertaken that she will not claim any maintenance past, present or future or permanent alimony or expenses of the proceedings, costs, etc., from the First Party in any form whatsoever or under any statutory enactment.

7. That pursuant to the receipt of Rs. 45,00,000 (Rupees Forty-Five Lakhs only) from the First Party the Third Party shall cease to have any right to reside with the First Party nor shall claim any right of residence from the First Party nor claim any restitution of conjugal rights or any form of matrimonial relationship with the First Party before any Court, Tribunal or Forum. The Third Party shall have no right to stay with the First and the Second Parties and shall not cause any disturbance in the normal day to day life of the First and the Second Parties and in the event the Third Party tries to invade the privacy of the First and the Second Party, then in that event, the First and the Second Party shall be entitled to seek injunction against the third party. However, it is agreed that for the three months i.e. *August, September and October, 2013 the first party shall pay maintenance of Rs. 15,000 per month to the third party and thereafter all the rights of the third party to claim any maintenance, permanent alimony, istridhan shall stand extinguished in law, against the first party.*

9. That pursuant to the receipt of the amount of Rs. 45,00,000 (Rupees Forty-Five Lakhs only) the Third Party shall have no right, title or interest in the said property or any other property belonging to the First and the Second Parties and further undertakes that she shall not file any claim, case or action against the First and the Second Parties nor shall stake any claim qua the movable and immovable properties of the First and the Second Parties and even upon the demise of the first and second party, the third party shall not claim any right, title or interest over the said property or over any movable or immovable properties of the first and the second party, including the said property."

In this inimitable decision rendered on 15 July, 2013, the Supreme Court, accepting the tripartite settlement deed executed between the wife, husband and his mother through mediation, permitted parties to part ways upon a onetime payment of Indian Rupees 45,00,000 (Rs. 45 lacs) to the wife with the condition that both would not seek divorce on any ground. The couple married for 30 years agreed to withdraw all their pending litigations and the wife agreed not to cause any disturbance or invade the privacy of her husband and his 83 year old mother living in their household property. The sum of Indian Rupees 45,00,000 (Rs. 45 lacs) paid in full and final settlement to the wife was towards all her financial claims. Both parties living separately since 2009, agreed that they shall have nothing to do with each other's lives and will not undergo any divorce proceedings. The wife would also not claim restitution of conjugal rights or rights of residence in the household. However, in the event of remarriage of the husband, the agreement shall stand terminated and the wife would be entitled to revive her claim maintenance or alimony for the present and future, since the sum of Indian Rupees 45,00,000 (Rs. 45 lacs) shall not be considered as an amount towards dissolution of marriage and payment of permanent alimony. The Apex Court by its Judgment of 15 July, 2013 accepting the *Settlement Deed* and the *Undertakings* of the parties, disposed off the matter and permitted parties to file the same before all Courts where litigations were pending with liberty to invoke the provisions of the Contempt of Courts Act, 1971 upon breach if any. Hence, prior to divorce or at the time of settlement of permanent alimony upon divorce, the wife can claim her right of residence in a property owned by the husband or demand an equivalent share to compensate her for her right to residence so that the wife and her children can have suitable living accommodation as per the standards they were living in when the parties were married and were enjoying residential facilities jointly.

Lamenting on the delay in deciding a maintenance application under section 125, CrPC. In Criminal Appeal No. 1331 of 2014 *Bhuwan Mohan Singh* v. *Meena*, 2014 STPL (Web) 467 SC decided on 15 July, 2014, the Supreme Court held:

> *"13. The Family Courts have been established for adopting and facilitating the conciliation procedure and to deal with family disputes in a speedy and expeditious manner. A three-Judge Bench in* K.A. Abdul Jaleel *v.* T.A. Shahida, *(2003) 4 SCC 166, while highlighting on the purpose of bringing in the Family Courts Act by the legislature, opined thus:—*
>
> > *The Family Courts Act was enacted to provide for the establishment of Family Courts with a view to promote conciliation in, and secure speedy settlement of, disputes relating to marriage and family affairs and for matters connected therewith."*

In *K. Srinivas Rao* v. *D.A. Deepa*, AIR 2013 SC 2176, the Apex Court had also issued comprehensive directions for resolution of matrimonial disputes and amicable settlement which may be reproduced as hereunder for ready reference:

> *"In terms of section 9 of the Family Courts Act, the Family Court shall make all efforts to settle the matrimonial disputes through mediation. Even if the Counsellors submit a failure report, the Family Courts shall, with the consent of the parties, refer the matter to the mediation centre. In such a case, however, the Family Court shall set a reasonable time limit for mediation centre to complete the process of mediation because otherwise the resolution of the disputes by the Family Court may get delayed. In a given case, if there is good chance of settlement, the Family Court in its discretion, can always extend the time limit."*

From a reading of the recent pronouncements of law discussed above, it is apt to conclude that there is a growing emphasis on the need for attempting mandatory reconciliatory measures and wherever matrimonial courts have been lacking in their duties to do so, superior Indian courts have stepped in, to set the records straight. Therefore, there is a growing jurisprudence to adapt to out-of-court settlement and reconciliation rather than litigating in matrimonial courts. However, the performance of this mandatory exercise ought not to be reduced to an empty ritual or a meaningless exercise. Otherwise, the utility of the beneficial provision will be lost.

VI. CONCLUSIONS: NEED FOR REFORM AND SOME SUGGESTIONS

The philosophy of alternate dispute resolution systems is well illustrated by Abraham Lincoln's famous words: 'discourage litigation, persuade your neighbours to compromise whenever you can. Point out to them how the normal winner is often a loser in fees, expense, cost and time.' These words spell out grim reality and truth.

Litigation in respect of any matter concerning the family, whether divorce, maintenance and alimony or custody, trial of juvenile offenders or any other matrimonial cause, should not be viewed in terms of failure or success of legal action but as a social therapeutic problem. It should not be viewed as a prestigious dispute in which parties and their counsel are engaged in winning or defeating, but as a societal problem needing resolution. The amicable settlement of family conflict requires special procedures designed to help people in conflict and in trouble, to reconcile their differences, and where necessary to obtain professional assistance. Family disputes need to be seen with a humanitarian approach and hence attempts should be made to reconcile the differences so as to not disrupt the family structure. Adjudication of family disputes is an entirely different matter from conventional civil or criminal proceedings, it is a different culture and has a different jurisprudence altogether *(Paras Diwan Law of Marriage and Divorce (Preface to the 1st Edn.)* (Universal Law Publishing, Delhi, 5th Edn., 2008). The whole of society feels the reverberations of a family dispute.

Whereas there already exist some provisions for the conduct of arbitration, conciliation and Lok Adalat in different statutes, the need for a framework to regulate the ADR process as a whole and mediation in particular has been sought to be fulfilled by the Supreme Court of India. It has done so by providing the final version of the Model Rules of ADR and the Model Rules of Mediation, both framed by the Law Commission of India, in its orders passed in the case of *Salem Bar Association* v. *Union of India*, (2003) 1 SCC 49 with a direction that all High Courts should adopt these with such modifications as they may consider necessary.

The Supreme Court has also made an observation regarding the disturbing phenomena of the large number of cases flooding the courts pertaining to divorce or judicial separation. Recently, in 2009, in *Gaurav Nagpal* v. *Sumedha Nagpal*, AIR 2009 SC 557, in paragraph 50 the Supreme Court observed as hereunder:

> *'It is a very disturbing phenomenon that large numbers of cases are flooding the courts relating to divorce or judicial separation. An apprehension is gaining ground that the provisions relating to divorce in the Hindu Marriage Act, 1955 (in short the 'Marriage Act') has led to such a situation. In other words, the feeling is that the statute is facilitating breaking of homes rather than saving them, this may be too wide a view because actions are suspect. But that does not make the section invalid. Actions may be bad, but not the section. The provisions relating to divorce categorise situations in which a decree for divorce can be*

sought for. Merely because such a course is available to be adopted, should not normally provide incentive to persons to seek divorce, unless the marriage has irretrievably broken. Efforts should be to bring about conciliation to bridge the communication gap which lead to such undesirable proceedings. People rushing to courts for breaking up of marriages should come as a last resort, and unless it has an inevitable result, courts should try to bring about conciliation. The emphasis should be on saving of marriage and not breaking it. As noted above it is more important in cases where the children bear the brunt of dissolution of marriage.'

However, we cannot remain oblivious to the fact that India with its population of 1.2 billion Indians has over 30 million non-resident Indians who live in 180 countries abroad. Some of these former Indian citizens are foreign nationals with overseas spouses. But, the fact remains that their personal family law still governs them due to extra territorial application. Resolution of marital disputes of such citizens of Indian origin creates conflicts since India does not have on its statute book irretrievable breakdown of marriage as a ground for divorce in India. Therefore, foreign divorce decrees on the breakdown ground with no prior mandatory reconciliation procedures do not find favour either in Indian courts or in the domestic societal set up. How does one resolve such emerging dimensions of family law disputes where marriages solemnised in India are sought to be dissolved abroad in countries of foreign residence? The authors have advocated a solution (Anil Malhotra and Ranjit Malhotra Acting for Non-Resident Indian Clients (Jordan Publishing Limited, 2004) Chapter 3, pages 76-77) penned as follows:

'The answer therefore is that the existing three-tier divorce structure in India under the HMA, 1955 and the SMA, 1954, i.e. *fault grounds, mutual consent principle and break down theory, seems to provide sufficient options in the existing societal structure. Therefore, no major changes are called for. However, a civilized parting of spouses where a marriage has irretrievably broken down needs to be incorporated in the statute book as an additional ground for divorce, but only in cases where both the parties to the marriage jointly petition the court for such relief. This, in the opinion of the authors, will have an immediate two-fold benefit. First, where parties have irreconcilable differences and want to part amicably, an option will be available to them to part legally and logically without resorting to a protracted time-consuming legal battle on "trumped-up" grounds. Secondly, recourse to divorce in foreign jurisdictions may decline once a proper legal option of irretrievable break down is available on Indian soil. Irretrievable breakdown can thus serve as an additional ground for divorce in the HMA, 1955 and the SMA, 1954, and to prevent hasty divorces or misuse, sufficient statutory safeguards can be incorporated to arm the judiciary to prevent any abuse of the process of law. Keeping the Hindu ceremonial and sacramental concept of marriage intact is essential. Erosion of values in matrimonial life must be checked, and traditional marriage protected. The institutions of family, home and children of the marriage, as they exist today under Hindu law, need protection. Hindu law therefore does not need any major overhaul. It is self-sufficient, but does need some immediate amendment.'*

The above views of the authors clearly depict the inbuilt conciliatory settlement theory embedded in Indian family law to save the marriage by in-house settlement. But, marriages solemnised in India according to personal laws of non-resident Indians who have permanently migrated abroad need to find resolution in the existing statutory family laws either by suitable amendments or a brand new legislation which will incorporate corresponding mandatory conciliatory procedures. For this problem, the authors have advocated their suggestions in this regard in the following words [Malhotra India, NRIs and the Law (Universal, New Delhi, 2009) at pp. 271–272]:

> *'A reading in totality of the matters in the overseas family law jurisdiction gives an indication that in such affairs, it is the judicial precedents which provide the much available guidance and judicial legislation on the subject. With the large number of non-resident Indians now permanently living in overseas jurisdictions, it has now become important that some composite legislation is enacted to deal with the problems of non-resident Indians to avoid them from importing judgments from foreign Courts to India for implementation of their rights. The answer therefore, lies in giving them law applicable to them as Indians rather than letting them invade the Indian system with judgments of foreign jurisdictions which do not find applicability in the Indian system. Hence, it is the Indian legislature which now seriously needs to review this issue and come out with a composite legislation for non-resident Indians in family law matters. Till this is done, foreign Court judgments in domestic matters will keep cropping up and Courts in India will continue with their salutary efforts in interpreting them in harmony with the Indian laws and doing substantial justice to parties in the most fair and equitable way. However, in this process, the Indian judiciary has made one thing very clear* i.e. *the Indian Courts would not simply mechanically enforce judgments and decrees of foreign Courts in family matters. The Indian Courts have now started looking into the merits of the matters and deciding them on the considerations of Indian law and the best interest of the parties rather than simply implementing the orders without examining them. Fortunately, we can hail the Indian judiciary for these laudable efforts and till such time when the Indian Legislature comes to rescue with appropriate legislation, we seek solace with our unimpeachable and unstinted faith in the Indian Judiciary, which is rendering a yeoman service.'*

Therefore, the dire pressing need of the day in the current social milieu, where 30 million Indians now live outside India, is to create a law and infrastructural machinery for ADR mechanisms in resolving marriages solemnised in India but which have been fractured or broken abroad. For the lack of resolution, they lead to interparental child removal custody conflicts, disputes of maintenance and differences over settlement of matrimonial property. It is these limping marriages which need reconciliatory formulas in India to prevent them from being split abroad on grounds and reasons which do not find favour with the personal family laws of the parties in India. These cross border marital conflicts should not stem into or branch out into other ancillary issues multiplying the problem. This, in the opinion of the authors, ought to be the focus of the legislative intent today in creating, harmonising and balancing the societal structure of Indians, non-resident Indians and all those who form relationships with them to build families abroad. ADR needs to be developed in a big way for resolving limping unions.

Some suggestions can be mooted by the authors to improve the situation and to make ADR a reality in the structure of the current Indian family law.

(1) Participation of citizens

Alternative dispute resolution cannot see the light of the day unless citizens also 'participate' in that movement. The citizens can help in the achievements of these benign objectives by restraining themselves while invoking jurisdictions of the 'traditional courts' where the matter in dispute can be conveniently and economically taken care of by ADR mechanisms. The right to speedy trial is not a fact or fiction but a 'constitutional reality' and it has to be given its due respect. The courts and the legislature have already accepted it as one of the media of reducing the increasing workloads on the courts. The same is also gaining popularity among the masses due to its advantages. We need 'private initiatives' for not only the establishment of ADR facilities in India but equally a 'liberal use' of the same by its citizens. This initiative needs awakening by self consciousness and not by implementation of laws. Spouses, parents and couples need to realise the advantages of reconciliation, mediation and alternative dispute resolution methods in the family structure. Matrimonial relief carved out by settlement will serve better than results obtained by adversary litigation involving time, effort, finances and above all by breaking up a family.

(2) More authority should be given to the Family Courts

Family matters should not be litigated in any court unless it is of an extraordinarily grave nature; it should be amicably resolved. Family disputes such as divorce, matrimonial property division, custody of children and maintenance should not come into the higher courts and they should be resolved mutually and conclusively in the Family Court itself. It would save the time of the superior courts where other matters could be resolved in the time which would have been consumed for settling matrimonial disputes. Family disputes are disputes that can be resolved even in the home itself by a unanimous consensus. Mandatory reconciliatory procedures should assume finality so that matters can be put to rest conclusively without any further challenge.

(3) Creation of more Family Courts

The necessity and urgency of creating more Family Courts under the Family Courts Act, 1984 in India is a very important factor which will contribute to the resolution of family law disputes by ADR. The current handling of matrimonial litigation by conventional courts in jurisdictions where there are no Family Courts is a poignant reminder of the situation created by lack of Family Courts in such jurisdictions. The availability of trained counsellors, mediators, professionally trained persons and above all specialist family law judges would all form part of a well organised team in a Family Court which in turn would itself create a mechanism and structure for alternative disputes resolution of family law disputes. This would therefore give a new dimension to the existing matrimonial scenario in the Indian jurisdiction.

India has the laws to promote ADR modes in the existing litigation setup but the infrastructure, professional assistance and the medium through which these beneficial reconciliatory mediation procedures are to be implemented are lacking within India. Therefore, creating the via media by which the beneficial ADR laws can be implemented in family law disputes is what is required today. Additionally, legislative changes are required for providing reconciliatory methods of marriages of non-resident Indians. The package is wholesome. The need is dire. The numbers are huge. The sooner we begin, the sooner reform will start.

Law and Surrogacy Arrangements in India

I. POSITION OF INDIAN LAW FOR SURROGACY ARRANGEMENTS

Surrogacy in India is as of now considered legitimate because no Indian law prohibits surrogacy, but then, as a retort, no law to date permits surrogacy either. Hence, surrogacy agreements in India are governed by ordinary contract law, *i.e.*, the Indian Contract Act, 1872, to determine the legality of any such contract or agreements executed in India for different forms of surrogacy arrangements. The enforceability of any such agreement is within the domain of Indian civil procedural laws and the main component of this is in the Indian Code of Civil Procedure.

In the absence of any law to govern surrogacy, the Indian Council of Medical Research (ICMR) had issued guidelines in 2005 to check the malpractices in India but these guidelines being non statutory are not mandatory, do not have any compulsive force and are not enforceable or justiciable in a court of law in India.

The recent case [*Baby Manji Yamada* v. *Union of India*, JT 2008 (11) SC 150] of a Japanese baby born of an Indian surrogate mother has triggered a debate as to the natural/genetic father's rights, since, after divorce, he could not claim custody according to Indian laws on the facts of that case. The Supreme Court of India had in the case dealt with the matter upon the grandmother's claim to custody and had made observations regarding commercial and other forms of surrogacy since the Union of India had pleaded before it as follows:

> *'that there is no law governing surrogation in India and in the name of surrogation, a lot of irregularities are being committed. According to it, in the name of surrogacy, a money making racket is being perpetuated. It is also the stand of the said respondent that the Union of India should enforce stringent laws relating to surrogacy.'*

However, it may be added that the Supreme Court of India stated that:

> *'Surrogates may be relatives, friends or previous strangers. Many surrogate arrangements are made through agencies that help match up intended parents with women who want to be surrogates for a fee. The agencies often help manage the complex medical and legal aspects involved. Surrogacy arrangements can also be made independently. In compensated surrogacies, the amount a surrogate*

receives varies widely from almost nothing above expenses to over $30,000. Careful screening is needed to assure their health as the gestational carrier incurs potential obstetrical risks.'

It may further be added that the Supreme Court of India, fully realising the existing surrogacy practices prevalent in India, observed:

> *'5. Surrogacy is a well known method of reproduction whereby a woman agrees to become pregnant for the purpose of gestating and giving birth to a child she will not raise but hand over to a contracted party. She may be the child's genetic mother (the more traditional form for surrogacy) or she may ... as a gestational carrier carry the pregnancy to delivery after having been implanted with an embryo. In some cases, surrogacy is the only available option for parents who wish to have a child that is biologically related to them. The word "surrogate", from Latin "subrogare", means "appointed to act in the place of". The intended parent(s) is the individual or couple who intends to rear the child after its birth.*
>
> *6. In "traditional surrogacy" (also known as the Straight method) the surrogate is pregnant with her own biological child, but this child was conceived with the intention of relinquishing the child to be raised by others; by the biological father and possibly his spouse or partner, either male or female. The child may be conceived via home artificial insemination using fresh or frozen sperm or impregnated via IUI (intrauterine insemination), or ICI (inter-cervical insemination) which is performed at a fertility clinic.*
>
> *7. In "gestational surrogacy" (also known as the Host method) the surrogate becomes pregnant via embryo transfer with a child of which she is not the biological mother. She may have made an arrangement to relinquish it to the biological mother or father to raise, or to a parent who is themselves unrelated to the child (e.g. because the child was conceived using egg donation, germ donation or is the result of a donated embryo). The surrogate mother may be called the gestational carrier.*
>
> *8. "Altruistic surrogacy" is a situation where the surrogate receives no financial reward for her pregnancy or the relinquishment of her child (although usually all expenses related to the pregnancy and birth are paid by the intended parents such as medical expenses, maternity clothing and other related expenses).*
>
> *9. "Commercial surrogacy" is a form of surrogacy in which a gestational carrier is paid to carry a child to maturity in her womb and is usually resorted to by well off infertile couples who can afford the cost involved or people who save and borrow in order to complete their dream of being parents. This medical procedure is legal in several countries including in India where due to excellent medical infrastructure, high international demand and ready availability of poor surrogates it is reaching industry proportions. Commercial surrogacy is sometimes referred to by the emotionally charged and potentially offensive terms "wombs for rent", "outsourced pregnancies" or "baby farms".*
>
> *10. Intended parents may arrange a surrogate pregnancy because a woman who intends to parent is infertile in such a way that she cannot carry a pregnancy to term. Examples include a woman who has had a hysterectomy, has a uterine*

malformation, has had recurrent pregnancy loss or has a health condition that makes it dangerous for her to be pregnant. A female intending parent may also be fertile and healthy, but unwilling to undergo pregnancy.

11. Alternatively, the intended parent may be a single male or a male homosexual couple.'

From a reading of the above, it is apparent that 'commercial surrogacy' is a medical procedure which is considered to be legal in India due to the factors mentioned in para 9 of the judgment above. However, the fact remains that there is no statutory codified law governing commercial surrogacy and other arrangements.

It may be noticed here that a Draft Bill called the 'Assisted Reproductive Technology (Regulation) Bill & Rules, 2010' which has been prepared by a 12-member committee including experts from Indian Council for Medical Research and from the Ministry of Health and Family Welfare, as well as medical specialists and other experts, has been circulated for comment and posted online recently for feedback. The new Assisted Reproductive Technology (Regulation) Bill & Rules, 2010, propose to legalise commercial surrogacy and its salient points are:

- The surrogacy agreement will be legally enforceable.
- The surrogate mother may receive monetary compensation for carrying the child in addition to health care and treatment expenses during pregnancy.
- The surrogate mother will relinquish all parental rights over the child once the amount is transferred and birth certificates will be in the name of genetic parents.
- The prescribed age limit for a surrogate mother is between 21 and 45 years. The proposed Bill also states that no surrogate mother can undergo an embryo transfer more than three times.
- Single parents can also have children using a surrogate mother.
- All foreigners seeking infertility treatment in India will first have to register with their embassy. Their notarised statement will then have to be handed over to the treating doctor. The foreign couple will also state whom the child should be entrusted to in case of an eventuality such as a genetic parent's death.

The Bill is still being debated and has not yet become law in India. Hence, anything quoted above is only a proposed law. Therefore, in the absence of any codified law as the situation exists today, in respect of surrogacy arrangements, the ordinary civil law of the land is applicable in respect of surrogacy also since there is no specific law on the subject to govern such arrangements. The Code of Civil Procedure, 1908, is an Act made by the Indian Parliament for the entire territorial jurisdiction of India as a federal law to consolidate and amend the laws relating to the procedure of the Courts of Civil Judicature. Section 9 of this Code permits courts to try all civil suits unless barred:

'9. Courts to try all civil suits unless barred.—The Courts shall subject to the provisions herein contained have jurisdiction to try all suits of a civil nature excepting suits of which their cognizance is either expressly or impliedly barred.'

As a result, in the law as it exists in India today, both the validity and enforceability of any surrogacy arrangement or agreement can be achieved in a civil court by a civil suit under section 9 of the Code, seeking appropriate relief as is admissible to parties under Indian law. However, the touchstone of the validity of a civil suit would have to be tested under contract law.

Against this backdrop, it may thus be necessary to also see the position of surrogacy arrangements or agreements under the Indian law of contract. It is first be pertinent to quote section 10 of the Indian Contract Act, 1872:

'10. What agreements are contracts.—All agreements are contracts if they are made by the free consent of parties competent to contract, for a lawful consideration and with a lawful object, and are not hereby expressly declared to be void.'

For the present context, any surrogacy arrangement or agreement, which is arrived at by the free consent of the parties who are competent to contract and who have entered into the arrangement or agreement for a lawful consideration as also with a lawful object which is not expressly declared to be void, would be a contract. It may be added that since under the prevalent law in India, commercial surrogacy procedures are legal in India, subject to the fulfilment of other conditions of section 10 of the Contract Act a surrogacy arrangement or agreement would be a contract. In the face of this conclusion, a surrogacy agreement or arrangement would be a contract enforceable by civil suit under section 9 of the Code of Civil Procedure.

For the present purposes, it may be helpful to note certain observations of the Supreme Court of India interpreting section 9 of the Code of Civil Procedure. The Supreme Court of India in the case of *E Achuthan Nair* v. *P Narayanan Nair*, AIR 1987 SC 2137, held as follows:

'In India, the question whether a suit is cognizable by a civil court is to be decided with reference to section 9 of the Civil Procedure Code. If the suit is of a civil nature, the court will have jurisdiction to try the suit unless it is either expressly or impliedly barred.'

Further, the Supreme Court of India in another case, *P.M.A. Metropolitian* v. *Marthoma*, AIR 1995 SC 2001 (2022-23), held:

'The expansive nature of the section 9 is demonstrated by use of phraseology with positive and negative. The earlier part opens the door widely and later debars entry to only those, which are expressly or impliedly barred. The two explanations, one existing from inception and latter added in 1976 bring out clearly the legislative intention of extending operation of the section to such religious matters where right to property or office is involved irrespective of whether any fee is attached to the office or not. The language used is simple but explicit and clear. It is structured on the basic principle of a civilized jurisprudence that absence of

> *machinery for enforcement of right renders it nugatory. The heading which is normally key to the section brings out unequivocally that all civil suits are cognizable unless barred. What is meant by it is explained further by widening the ambit of the section by use of the word "shall" and the expression, "all suits of a civil nature" unless "expressly or impliedly barred". Each word and expression casts an obligation on the Court to exercise jurisdiction for enforcement or right. The word "shall" makes it mandatory. No Court can refuse to entertain a suit if it is of description mentioned in the section. That is amplified by use of expression, "all suits of civil nature". The word "civil nature" is wider than the word "civil proceeding". The section would, therefore, be available in every case where the dispute has the characteristic of affecting one's rights which are not only civil but of civil nature.'*

In the face of the above interpretations of section 9 of the Code of Civil Procedure by the Supreme Court of India, it is safe to conclude that surrogacy agreements or arrangements which satisfy the ingredients of section 10 of the Indian Contract Act would be contracts which are enforceable in a civil Court since the cognizance of such a civil suit would neither be expressly or impliedly barred.

There also exists in India another piece of federal legislation applicable throughout the territory of India called 'The Guardian and Wards Act, 1890', which is an Act to consolidate and amend the law relating to guardians and wards prevalent in India. Section 4 of the Act specifies the persons entitled to apply for a guardianship order and section 9 prescribes the court as having jurisdiction to entertain the guardianship application. Section 10 lays down the form of the application and section 11 prescribes the procedure on admission of the application. Section 13 lays down the requirement of hearing of evidence before making of an order under the Act and section 26 permits the removal of a ward from the jurisdiction of the court. This is the second possible option which can be availed of by the biological father in the present case for enforcement of his rights arising from the surrogacy arrangement or agreement existing in the present case.

II. FACTS AND LAW RELATING TO JAPANESE BABY MANJI YAMADA BORN IN INDIA ON 25 JULY, 2008 BY SURROGACY ARRANGEMENT

Since there is no statutory codified law governing surrogacy in India, there is only a 126-page document regulating the technologies used in surrogacy. The Indian Council of Medical Research (ICMR) issued the National Guidelines for Accreditation, Supervision and Regulation of ART Clinics in India in 2005, but the guidelines being non-statutory have no legal sanctity and are not binding. They are hazy on issues like the right of the surrogate, the minimum age of the surrogate, details about the contracts, informed consent, adoption requirements etc. The issue of legal parentage has been particularly contentious in the absence of any law.

Dr. Ikufumi Yamada (45), an orthopaedic surgeon attached to a Tokyo hospital and his former wife Dr. Yuki Yamada came to India in 2007 and had chosen a surrogate mother in Anand, Gujarat. When Dr. Yuki Yamada could not conceive, the couple had chosen the surrogate mother in Ahmedabad to carry the child. They signed an agreement of surrogacy with Dr. Nayanaben Patel of Akansha IVF Centre, an Ahmedabad Hospital on 22 November, 2007.

The surrogacy agreement was entered into between the biological father and biological mother on one side and the surrogate mother on the other side. Pritiben Mehta, wife of Brijeshbhai Mehta also from Ahmedabad, signed the agreement to serve as the surrogate mother. The fertilisation process of Yuki's eggs with Ikufumi's sperm was completed in Tokyo and the embryo was brought to Ahmedabad to be implanted in the surrogate mother. The embryo transfer was done at Dr. Nayanaben's Hospital on 22 November, 2007 in the presence of the Japanese couple. After that they left for Tokyo and the child was born on 25 July, 2008 in Anand, Gujarat. However, a month before that Yuki divorced her husband Ikufumi Yamada and she subsequently disowned the child.

On 3 August, 2008, the child was moved to Arya Hospital in Jaipur following a law and order situation in Gujarat and she was provided with much needed care including being breast-fed by a woman who had given birth to a baby girl as the surrogate mother had also abandoned the baby. A friend of Ikufumi, Mr. Kamal Vijayvargiya, a jeweller from Jaipur and settled in Tokyo, was instrumental in getting the baby shifted to Arya Hospital in Jaipur and also to get Ikufumi's mother to come down and take care of the child.

It transpired that the biological father Ikufumi had come to take custody but had to return to Japan before his visa expired. Custody was denied even to the grandmother (Ikufumi's mother) after a *habeas corpus* petition was filed in the Jaipur Bench of the Rajasthan High Court by an NGO, Satya, who claimed that in the absence of surrogacy laws in India, the custody of the child should not be given to the grandmother. To complicate things further, before the Rajasthan High Court, neither the biological father nor the surrogate mother had moved an application seeking custody of the child. The Municipal Council at Anand in Gujarat had issued a birth certificate to the baby indicating the name of the genetic father.

Against the directions of the Rajasthan High Court, the grandmother, Emiko Yamada filed a writ petition in the Supreme Court. It was contended in the Supreme Court that under the National Guidelines for Accreditation, Supervision and Regulation of ART Clinics in India, 2005 ('the ICMR, 2005 Guidelines') the surrogate child is the legitimate child of its genetic parents. Paragraph 3.16.1 of the ICMR, 2005 Guidelines in Chapter 3 entitled Code of Practice, Ethical Considerations and Legal Issues states:

> ***'3.16 Legal Issues***
>
> ***3.16.1 Legitimacy of the child born through ART***
>
> *A child born through ART shall be presumed to be the legitimate child of the couple, born within wedlock, with consent of both the spouses, and with all the attendant rights of parentage, support and inheritance. Sperm/oocyte donors shall have no parental right or duties in relation to the child, and their anonymity shall be protected except in regard to what is mentioned under item 3.12.3.'*

In accordance with the pleadings before the Supreme Court of India, when the matter first came before it on 14 August, 2008, the Court by an interim order allowed the grandmother to take care of the baby until the legal wrangles were sorted out by the Court.

Ultimately, on 29 September, 2008, the Supreme Court of India disposed of the writ petition filed by the grandmother with directions that, if any person has any grievance or complaint relating to the child, it can be vented in accordance with the Commission for Protection of Child Rights Act, 2005. This was with regard to the allegations of the Jaipur NGO 'Satya' that the child was abandoned as neither the natural parents nor the surrogate mother were taking care of the child.

In relation to the grievance of the grandmother that the permission to travel to Japan including issuance of a passport to the child was under consideration of the central government and that no orders had been passed in that regard, the Supreme Court directed that if a comprehensive application as required under law is filed, it was to be disposed of expeditiously. All proceedings pending in the High Court relating to the matter which had been dealt with stood disposed of by the Supreme Court order of 29 September.

Following the directions of the Supreme Court, the Regional Passport Office in Jaipur on 17 October, 2008 issued an 'Identity Certificate' to the baby allowing her to travel to Japan to meet her father Ikufumi Yamada. However, the baby's citizenship status still remained unclear. Reportedly, the baby Manji Yamada and her Japanese grandmother Emkio Yamada, who had been looking after her, left India for Japan on 1 November, 2008.

The ICMR Guidelines say that the child born through surrogacy must be adopted by genetic (biological) parents unless they can establish through genetic (DNA) fingerprinting that the child is not theirs. This is a legal parenthood option arising out of surrogacy arrangements. Paragraph 3.10.1 of the ICMR, 2005 Guidelines in Chapter 3 entitled Code of Practice, Ethical Considerations and Legal Issues states:

> ***'3.10 Surrogacy: General Considerations***
>
> *3.10.1 A child born through surrogacy must be adopted by the genetic (biological) parents unless they can establish through genetic (DNA) fingerprinting (of which the records will be maintained in the clinic) that the child is not theirs.'*

However, it may be clarified that the legal process of adoption in India by any foreign parents is itself not possible since the Guardian and Wards Act 1890 permits guardianship orders only and adoption processes have to follow in the respective countries of the nationality or permanent residence of the proposed adoptive parents. Hence, no legal adoption can take place in India by foreign parents except those who are Hindus by religion and are governed by Hindu laws in this regard.

It may also be pointed out that the Indian law on the subject of adoption, entitled 'the Hindu Adoption and Maintenance Act, 1956', is an Act to amend and codify the law relating to adoptions and maintenance among Hindus only. Likewise, 'the Hindu Minority and Guardianship Act, 1956', is an Act to amend and codify certain parts of the laws relating to minority and guardianship among Hindus. These personal laws governing Hindus permit adoption as laid down in the said laws.

III. VALIDITY OF GUARDIANSHIP PROCEEDINGS

The Indian law applicable in the present case is the Guardians and Wards Act, 1890 (GWA) which is the legislation meant to consolidate and amend the law relating to guardians and wards in India. This is because under the Hindu Minority and Guardianship Act, 1956 (HMGA) and under the Hindu Adoptions and Maintenance Act, 1956 (HAMA) only those persons in India who are Hindu by religion can adopt or be appointed as guardians of Hindu minor children.

In the case of normal inter-country adoptions, to enable any foreign adoptive parents to take a Hindu child in adoption from India, such parents would be required to obtain a guardianship order from the Court of the Guardian Judge in the appropriate jurisdiction within India and thereafter obtain adoption orders in accordance with the law applicable to such foreign parents in the country of their nationality. The position therefore in this regard can be summed up as follows:

(a) In so far as the law in India is concerned, only persons who are Hindus by religion can adopt children in India since section 2 of the HAMA and section 3 of HMGA make it explicitly clear that the respective Acts are applicable only to those persons who are Hindus by religion.

(b) As per the provisions of the GWA applicable to all persons in India, the adoptive parents are permitted to be appointed as guardians of minor children in India and are thereafter free to adopt them in the country of their nationality to which they are allowed to take the children for adoption by the Guardian Judge in India.

(c) It is relevant to quote and extract sections 7, 8, 9, 10, 11, 13, 17 and 26 of the GWA which are relevant in the present case as follows:

'***7. Power of the Court to make order as to guardianship.***

(1) Where the Court is satisfied that it is for the welfare of a minor that an order should be made—

(a) appointing a guardian of his person or property, or both, or

(b) declaring a person to be such a guardian, the Court may make an order accordingly.

(2) An order under this section shall imply the removal of any guardian who has not been appointed by will or other instrument or appointed or declared by the Court.

(3) Where a guardian has been appointed by will or other instrument or appointed or declared by the Court, an order under this section appointing or declaring another person to be guardian in his stead shall not be made until the powers of the guardian appointed or declared as aforesaid have ceased under the provisions of this Act.

8. Persons entitled to apply for order.

An order shall not be made under the last foregoing section except on the application of—

(a) the person desirous of being, or claiming to be, the guardian of the minor, or

(b) any relative or friend of the minor, or

(c) the Collector of the district or other local area within which the minor ordinarily resides or in which he has property, or

(d) the Collector having authority with respect to the class to which the minor belongs.

9. Court having jurisdiction to entertain application.

(1) If the application is with respect to the guardianship of the person of the minor, it shall be made to the District Court having jurisdiction in the place where the minor ordinarily resides.

(2) If the application is with respect to the guardianship of the property of the minor, it may be made either to the District Court having jurisdiction in the place where the minor ordinarily resides or to a District Court having jurisdiction in a place where he has property.

(3) If an application with respect to the guardianship of the property of a minor is made to a District Court other than that having jurisdiction in the place where the minor ordinarily resides, the Court may return the application if in its opinion the application would be disposed of more justly or conveniently by any other District Court having jurisdiction.

10. Form of application.

(1) If the application is not made by the Collector, it shall be by petition signed and verified in manner prescribed by the 1 Code of Civil Procedure (14 of 1882), for the signing and verification of a plaint, and stating, so far as can be ascertained—*

(a) the name, sex, religion, date of birth and ordinary residence of the minor;

(b) where the minor is a female, whether she is married, and, if so, the name and age of her husband;

(c) the nature, situation and approximate value of the property, if any, of the minor;

(d) the name and residence of the person having the custody or possession of the person or property of the minor;

(e) what near relations the minor has, and where they reside;

(f) whether a guardian of the person or property, or both, of the minor has been appointed by any person entitled or claiming to be entitled by the law to which the minor is subject to make such an appointment;

(g) whether an application has at any time been made to the Court or to any other Court with respect to the guardianship of the person or property, or both, of the minor, and, if so, when, to what Court and with what result;

(h) whether the application is for the appointment or declaration of a guardian of the person of the minor, or of his property, or of both;

(i) where the application is to appoint a guardian, the qualifications of the proposed guardian;

(j) where the application is to declare a person to be a guardian, the grounds on which that person claims;

(k) the causes which have led to the making of the applications; and

(l) such other particulars, if any, as may be prescribed or as the nature of the application renders it necessary to state.

(2) If the application is made by the Collector, it shall be by letter addressed to the Court and forwarded by post or in such other manner as may be found convenient, and shall state as far as possible the particulars mentioned in sub-section (1).

(3) The application must be accompanied by a declaration of the willingness of the proposed guardian to act and the declaration must be signed by him and attested by at least two witnesses.

11. Procedure on admission of application.

(1) If the Court is satisfied that there is ground for proceeding on the application, it shall fix a day for the hearing thereof, and cause notice of the application and of the date fixed for the hearing—

(a) to be served in the manner directed in the Code of Civil Procedure (14 of 882) on—

(i) the parents of the minor if they are residing in any State to which this Act extends,

(ii) the person, if any, named in the petition or letter as having the custody or possession of the person or property of the minor,

(iii) the person proposed in the application or letter to be appointed or declared guardian, unless that person is himself the applicant, and

(iv) any other person to whom, in the opinion of the Court, special notice of the application should be given; and

(b) to be posted on some conspicuous part of the courthouse, and of the residence of the minor, and otherwise published in such manner as the Court, subject to any rules made by the High Court under this Act, thinks fit.

(2) The State Government may, by general or special order, require that, when any part of the property described in a petition under section 10, sub-section (1), is land of which a Court of Wards could assume the superintendence, the Court shall also cause a notice as aforesaid to be served on the Collector in whose district the minor ordinarily resides, and on every Collector in whose district any portion of the land is situate, and the Collector may cause the notice to be published in any manner he deems fit.

(3) No charge shall be made by the Court or the Collector for the service or publication of any notice served or published under sub-section (2).

13. Hearing of evidence before making of order.

On the day fixed for the hearing of the application, or as soon afterwards as may be, the Court shall hear such evidence as may be adduced in support of or in opposition to the application.

17. Matters to be considered by the Court in appointing guardian.

(1) In appointing or declaring the guardian of a minor, the Court shall, subject to the provisions of this section, be guided by what, consistently with the law to which the minor is subject, appears in the circumstances to be for the welfare of the minor.

(2) In considering what will be for the welfare of the minor, the Court shall have regard to the age, sex and religion of the minor, the character and capacity of the proposed guardian and his nearness of kin to the minor, the wishes, if any, of a deceased parent, and any existing or previous relations of the proposed guardian with the minor or his property.

(3) If the minor is old enough to form an intelligent preference, the Court may consider that preference.

(4) Omitted

(5) The Court shall not appoint or declare any person to be a guardian against his will.

26. Removal of ward from jurisdiction.

(1) A guardian of the person appointed or declared by the Court unless he is the Collector or is a guardian appointed by will or other instrument, shall not, without the leave of the Court by which he was appointed or declared, remove the ward from the limits of its jurisdiction except for such purposes as may be prescribed.

(2) The leave granted by the Court under sub-section (1) may be special or general, and may be defined by the order granting it.'

A reading of the above provisions specifies the persons who are entitled to apply for guardianship, powers of the court to make an order for guardianship, the court having the jurisdiction to entertain the application, procedure on admission of application, leading of evidence before making of an order for guardianship and matters to be considered by the court in appointing a guardian. Likewise, the Guardian Court can permit the removal of the ward from its jurisdiction under sections 26 of the GWA.

In relation to conventional inter-country adoption proceedings in India and following the landmark judgment of the Supreme Court of India in *Lakshmi Kant Pandey* v. *Union of India,* AIR 1984 SC 469, the Central Adoption Resource Agency (CARA) was established by the Ministry of Social Justice and Empowerment, Government of India, and guidelines were issued for adoption of children and for providing a uniform mechanism for processing cases of inter-country adoptions. With the Hague Convention on inter-country adoptions of 1993 coming into force in India with effect from 1 October, 2003, it has been obligatory for CARA to produce guidelines on family adoptions. The process of inter-country adoptions in the CARA Guidelines was streamlined in accordance with the requirements of the Hague Convention. Revised guidelines were accordingly laid down by CARA in 1995 which were again revised in 2006, 2007, 2008 and 2010.

However, in so far as the provisions of the GWA are concerned there is no change and the same provisions are still applicable. However, in view of the mandate of the Supreme Court of India in the above decision, adherence to the provisions of the CARA Guidelines is compulsory in conventional inter-country adoptions from India. Hence, all clearances and permissions which have to be obtained under CARA besides adherence to the procedure for conventional inter-country adoptions must be followed strictly.

In so far as the guardianship proceedings are concerned, the Guardian Judge under the GWA is competent to make a decision on the guardianship application presented to him. Detailed provisions in this regard have been quoted above. Once permission has been granted by the Guardian Judge to take the child out of the country under section 26 of the GWA, and the guardianship order has been made by the Guardian Judge under the GWA in India, thereafter, the competent foreign court would be empowered to make a decision in the adoption case before such court. This is because there can be no adoption application or order for adoption in India in respect of the foreign adoptive father. Hence, the courts in India in the present case will confine themselves to the guardianship proceedings only.

IV. RIGHTS OF SAME-SEX COUPLES SEEKING PARENTHOOD IN INDIA

Israeli gay couple Yonatan and Omer Gher became parents in India on 12 October, 2008 when their child was conceived with the help of a Mumbai-based surrogate mother in a fertility clinic in Bandra. It is reported that a 3.8 kg baby boy was born to them at Hiranandani Hospital in Powai (Mumbai).

Reportedly, Yonatan and Omer had been together for 7 years and had decided to start a family. But since Israel does not allow same-sex couples to adopt or have a surrogate child, India became their choice to find a surrogate mother. Yonatan and Omer first came to Mumbai in January 2008 for an IVF cycle when Yonatan is stated to have donated his sperm. Thereafter, they selected an anonymous 'mother'. Accordingly, the child was conceived with the help of a Mumbai-based surrogate mother in a fertility clinic in Bandra. After the child was born, the gay couple left for Israel with the child on 17 November 2008.

Even though homosexuality is an 'unnatural offence' under section 377 of the Indian Penal Code as Indian law criminalises homosexuality, there is no bar to gay couples hiring a surrogate mother to deliver children for them in India. Thus, there are reports in the media that there are numerous gay couples coming to India to look for surrogate mothers as India does not disallow such surrogacy arrangements.

V. FACTUAL AND LEGAL POSITION FOR SINGLE OR GAY FOREIGN CITIZENS IN INDIA

One conclusion that can be made is that a single or a homosexual man can be considered to be the custodial parent of a child by virtue of being the genetic or biological father of the surrogate child born out of a surrogacy arrangement.

The *Japanese baby's* case and relevant rules are relied upon in the following submissions which are made in support of this answer.

The answer above is straightaway supported by two recent examples of a single/homosexual parent (in both cases it was the father) in which the children were born by surrogate arrangements. In the case of *Baby Manji Yamada,* the Municipal Council at Anand in Gujarat had issued a birth certificate to the baby indicating the name of the genetic father. In the case of the Israeli gay couple mentioned above, India permitted the surrogacy arrangement which was fathered with the sperm of Yonatan, the genetic or biological father of the child. These two instances, in which after their birth the babies were allowed to be taken away to Japan and Israel respectively, show that in India a single or a homosexual man can be considered as the custodian parent of the surrogate child by virtue of being the genetic or biological father of the child fathered by him and mothered by a surrogate mother through a surrogacy arrangement.

It may also be added that the Supreme Court of India, in its judgment in *Baby Manji Yamada* v. *Union of India,* JT 2008 (11) SC 150, after discussing various forms of surrogacy arrangements held:

> *'11. Alternatively, the intended male parent may be a single male or a male homosexual couple.'*

A reading of the above and an analysis of the complete judgment of the Supreme Court of India, support the answer given above and confirms that a single or a homosexual man can be considered to be the custodial parent of a surrogate child.

The above conclusion is also supported by the ICMR, 2005 Guidelines where in para 3.16.1 dealing with legitimacy of the child born through ART, it is stated that:

> *'A child born through ART shall be presumed to be the legitimate child of the couple, born within wedlock, with consent of both the spouses, and with all the attendant rights of parentage, support and inheritance. Sperm/oocyte donors shall have no parental right or duties in relation to the child, and their anonymity shall be protected except in regard to what is mentioned under item 3.12.3.'*

Even though these guidelines are non statutory, but all the same they were the basis of the claim in the Supreme Court of India in *Baby Manji Yamada's* case. Hence, even under the prevalent guidelines, the claim can be made by the biological father to be considered as the custodial parent of the surrogate child as in the case of single male parent there will be no other spouse to stake any joint claim.

It is further important to supplement the above proposition with the draft Assisted Reproductive Technology (Regulation) Bill & Rules, 2010, as in Chapter VII dealing with Rights and Duties of Patients, Donors, Surrogates and Children, in para 35(3), it is stipulated as follows:

> *'35. Determination of status of the child—*
>
> *(3) In the case of a single woman the child will be the legitimate child of the woman, and in the case of a single man the child will be the legitimate child of the man.'*

From this, it is clear that a single parent or gay or lesbian parents who have contributed either the egg or the sperm in the birth of a surrogate child can stake their claim for custody on the basis of the legitimacy of their offspring born by surrogacy arrangements. Even though this law is still in the Bill stages, the fact remains that the Supreme Court of India in *Baby Manji Yamada's* case opined that commercial surrogacy medical procedures are legal in India and that the intended male parent may be a single male or a male homosexual couple. Hence, the above provision will have persuasive value even though it is still not declared to be statutory law. Thus, a single male can be the custodial parent of a surrogate child.

However, the issue of exclusive custodial rights of a foreign single parent in India may require a judicial verdict for determination of the parties' rights in a surrogacy arrangement. Hence, only in a petition for guardianship under the GWA and/or in a suit for a declaration in an Indian civil court can the exclusive custodial rights be adjudicated by a court of competent jurisdiction upon appreciation of the evidence and considering claims, if any, of other parties to such surrogacy arrangements.

The above process of adjudication by a court of competent jurisdiction in either or both of the two processes is in no way a bar for a single male or homosexual parent to be recognised as the biological or genetic father of the surrogate child. The Supreme Court of India in its judgment in *Baby Manji Yamada* v. *Union of India*, JT 2008 (11) SC 150 at para 5, pp. 152 and 153, held that the medical procedure of surrogacy is legal in India. Hence, it can be safely concluded that a single male or homosexual parent who is the biological or genetic father has clear rights to be recognised in such a capacity.

As a note of caution it may also be clarified here that any single male or homosexual foreign parent who has fathered a child in India by virtue of a surrogacy arrangement can only claim guardianship of such a child under the GWA. The adoption process can only take place in the foreign parent's country of nationality or permanent residence as the case may be. This is because the HMGA and HAMA do not allow any adoption proceedings to non-Hindus and any foreign parent who is a non-Hindu cannot invoke the above personal laws for carrying out adoption proceedings in India. Therefore, any single male or homosexual foreign parent can by virtue of having been appointed a guardian under the GWA claim exclusive custody and leave of the Court to remove the ward to the country of his nationality or his permanent residence for adoption in accordance with the laws of such country by virtue of being the biological/genetic father.

The ultimate right of a single male or a homosexual biological or a genetic parent of adopting a child born from a surrogacy arrangement will have to be determined in accordance with the adoption laws of the country of the nationality or the permanent residence of such single parent. Also, the weight which the foreign court will give to a guardianship order and exclusive custody rights granted in India under GWA will have to be determined in accordance with the laws and procedures of the foreign country.

In case of Japanese baby Manji Yamada, from a reading of the judgment of the Supreme Court of India, it appears that no custody proceedings were taken out either by the biological father or the surrogate mother. On the contrary the NGO by the name of Satya had invoked the jurisdiction of the High Court of Rajasthan by claiming that the child was abandoned as neither the natural parents nor the surrogate mother were taking care of the child. However, the Supreme Court of India observed that no complaint had been made by anybody relating to the child and permission was granted to any person with a grievance to vent it before the Commission for Protection of Child Rights. The grandmother who had petitioned the Supreme Court of India challenging the orders of the Rajasthan High Court was granted interim custody and liberty to approach the central government for issuance of a passport and permission for the child to travel with her to Japan. These having been granted, the Regional Passport Officer in Jaipur issued an 'Identity Certificate' to the baby allowing her to travel to Japan with the grandmother.

An examination of the available documents and the judgment of the Supreme Court of India in *Baby Manji Yamada's* case shows that there was no court order by which the biological father was declined the custody of his daughter born out of the surrogacy arrangement. In fact it is borne out from the available information that the biological father returned to Japan before his visa expired. There is no record of any court proceeding by which the custody of his biological daughter was denied to him. Moreover, from what is seen from the available information, the fertilisation process by the biological parents was done in Tokyo and the fertilised embryo was brought to Ahmedabad to be implanted in the surrogate mother. Therefore, there must have been an agreement between the parties for some possible joint custody arrangement which was perhaps not possible to be executed since the biological parents had divorced when the child was born and the biological mother had disowned the child. In these circumstances it is difficult to comment as to why the Japanese father could not get the custody as there is no record available in the Supreme Court order of the father claiming or being declined the custody rights of the baby.

In *Baby Manji Yamada's* case, the custody ended up with the grandmother Emiko Yamada because she approached the Supreme Court of India to challenge the directions given by the Rajasthan High Court relating to production and custody of the baby. It is borne out from the judgment of the Supreme Court of India that the genetic father Dr. Ikufumi Yamada had to return to Japan due to expiration of his visa. It is perhaps this situation which had prompted the NGO 'Satya' to file a habeas corpus petition in the High Court of Rajasthan seeking custody of the baby on the alleged ground that neither the biological parents nor the surrogate mother were allegedly taking care of the child. However, the Supreme Court of India did not accept any of these allegations and granted interim custody of Baby Manji Yamada to the grandmother Emiko Yamada by an interim order on 14 August, 2008. This position continued until the conclusion of the case on 29 September, 2008 and until 1 November, 2008 when the baby and the grandmother left the country for Japan after being permitted to do so.

Hence, if a single or a homosexual man who is the genetic father of the surrogate baby petitions the Guardian Judge under the GWA, then, upon presentation of relevant evidence to prove the genetic material, the father can stake his claim for guardianship of the surrogate child. The surrogate mother who can be arrayed as a respondent can certify this claim which can be established by genetic evidence. The surrogate mother can concede her custodial claim in favour of the genetic father and, if desired, this can also be done by the ovum donor. Upon a presentation of the total facts, the single male or homosexual parent can plead before the Guardian Judge that he should be appointed the custodial parent as a guardian of the child and be able to take the child out of the country for adoption in accordance with the laws of the nationality of his country or permanent residence as the case may be. Therefore, the above custodial rights can be enforced in a petition under GWA by the single male or homosexual parent in respect of his surrogate child.

A second conclusion that can be made is that the biological father is considered the legal parent of the children under Indian law by virtue of the surrogacy agreement executed between the parties. The following submissions are made in support of this conclusion.

The surrogacy agreement is a contract in terms of section 10 of the Indian Contract Act. Therefore, the surrogacy agreement dated 18 July, 2008 is an enforceable and valid contract under Indian law. The validity of a surrogacy agreement in India has already been commented upon at length and hence it can be safely concluded that the terms and conditions of the said agreement between the parties legally confers all rights vested upon the parties as stated in the agreement. Therefore, the biological father as per the agreement is the legal parent of the proposed surrogate children as their genetic father.

An agreement between the parties and its terms and conditions are governed by Indian laws and the parties can agree to submit to the exclusive jurisdiction of the appropriate courts in India. Under Indian law the biological father would be entitled to enforce his rights as a legal parent of the children by virtue of the agreement between the parties.

An agreement between the parties can in no uncertain terms set out the stipulation that the surrogate mother agrees and undertakes cooperation before the government offices/authorities/local bodies and also appear before appropriate judicial authorities to give full effect to the agreement and to ensure that the intending father gets legal custody and rights of parentage of the child. This unequivocal statement by the surrogate mother is an admission of rights of the biological father. If this is in any way retracted, changed, modified, withdrawn or resiled from by the surrogate mother, the biological father has a clear remedy in law by filing a suit for declaration and permanent injunction to enforce his rights as legal parent of the children.

An agreement between the parties can also contain clauses as follows:

- It is clearly understood and unequivocally confirmed that neither the surrogate mother nor her husband shall have any physical or legal custody of or any parental rights or duties with respect to the child born out of this surrogacy process and that the Intended father shall exclusively have such custody and all parental rights and duties from the moment of the child's birth.

- The surrogate mother will relinquish physical custody of the child to intended father upon birth. The surrogate mother will, however, cooperate in all proceedings, if so required, for legal custody of the child by intended father and getting her surrogate motherhood perpetually severed from and disassociated with the child. This will include but not be limited to legal agreements/documents that need to be presented to the court, legal bodies/official, and/or hospital prior to/after the delivery of the child.
- Notwithstanding the foregoing or any other provision of this agreement, it is expressly understood and agreed that this agreement does not warrant or condition payment of any compensation or any valuables to the surrogate mother for her handing over the child to the intended father together with relinquishment of her parental right, if any, over the child unto the intended father, since it is clearly understood and agreed by the surrogate mother pursuant to this agreement that the child genetically and contractually belongs to the intended father, who has the physical and legal custody of the child and it is in the best interests of the child that the child be brought up by the intended father only.
- The surrogate mother and/or her husband shall never assert any right over the child nor shall they or any one of them claim the custody of the child in any manner whatsoever nor make any attempt to form any parental relationship with the child.
- The intended father will take full custody of the child as soon as it is medically practicable following the child's birth and will bring up the child without any kind of interference from the surrogate mother and/or her husband. The surrogate mother and/or her husband shall be bound to take any further lawful action, if and as may be necessary, to enable the Intended father to become the physical and legal custodian and natural guardian of the child.
- The surrogate mother shall have no right and waives the right to make any medical or other decisions regarding the child after birth. Medical or other decisions regarding the child after birth will be made by the intended father or his designated representative.
- The birth certificate of the child given birth pursuant to this agreement shall bear the names of the intended father as the legal parent and natural guardian of the child. The surrogate mother and/or her husband shall have no say nor shall make any objection whatsoever to the issuing of birth certificate of the child carrying the name of the intended father as the parent of the child. In order to ensure issuance of the birth certificate of the child in the aforesaid manner, the surrogate mother will take whatever steps necessary to have the names of the intended father recorded as legal parents and natural guardian of the child.

In view of what is stated above, it is established beyond doubt that the surrogate mother will relinquish, surrender, give up, waive and not assert any rights in respect of the surrogate child as also that the exclusive parental rights of care custody and control will vest in the biological father for all intents and purposes. Hence, in terms of the conclusive contract between the parties, there is no doubt that the biological father would be the legal parent of the child in terms of the surrogacy agreement between the parties.

At the cost of repetition, it may be stated that, if any terms, conditions or stipulations between the parties are violated, infringed or contravened, the biological father has clear legal remedies to seek necessary relief. Additionally or optionally, the biological father is at liberty to invoke the provisions of the GWA through a guardianship petition for being appointed as the sole legal guardian of the child and for being granted permission to take the child out of India for the purposes of adoption in the country of his nationality of permanent residence. Therefore, in any eventuality, the biological father under Indian law can exercise his legal rights as the sole parent of the child born to him by surrogacy.

An agreement can also be duly supported by an affidavit of the husband of the surrogate mother by which he fully agrees that since he is not the biological father of the children, he shall not assert any parental or custody rights whatsoever in respect of the said child and that he will assist his wife in fully implementing in terms of the agreement. This fortifies the agreement made by the parties and reinforces the rights of the biological father as the sole legal parent of the surrogate children.

In addition to the contractual terms and agreement between the parties, under the permissible medical legal procedure of commercial surrogacy, the biological father has full legal rights over his surrogate child. In the judgment of the Supreme Court of India in *Baby Manji Yamada's* case, the legality of the medical procedure of commercial surrogacy is accepted and, alternatively, the intended parent may be a single male or a male homosexual couple. This shows that, even otherwise, the biological father under Indian law would be considered to be the legal parent of the children.

Both under the ICMR, 2005 Guidelines and under the draft Assisted Reproductive Technology (Regulation) Bill & Rules, 2010, the fact of the legal rights of the biological father as the legal parent of the child born out of surrogacy arrangement are recognised irrespective of whether the father is a single or a homosexual man. In practice, the case of Japanese Baby Manji Yamada born on 25 July, 2008 and the child born to the Israeli gay couple on 12 October, 2008 bear testimony to the fact that in such instances parental rights have been enforced in relation to children born out of surrogacy arrangements.

Thus, under Indian Law, be it the law of contract or the GWA, the biological father has clear remedies in law to enforce the contract, seek a declaration of his rights as a single parent and obtain guardianship orders in this regard. Hence, under the existing legal position, the father has clear and unequivocal rights which can be established by invoking the judicial machinery in India.

In enforcing the biological rights as a father, reliance can be placed upon genetic evidence to establish the rights of the biological father. Aided and abetted by relevant medical data and genetic details, the father can establish his biological rights as the father. This is permissible under the medical procedures of legal surrogacy in India. Hence, viewed from any angle, the biological father has clear rights as a legal parent of his unborn child which he can establish upon their birth in India.

VI. SPEED BREAKERS ON THE ROAD TO SURROGACY

(a) Burgeoning surrogacy industry is propelled by absence of cohesive legislation and mushrooming IVF and ART clinics wantonly advertising services for providing wombs for rent

The unregulated reproductive tourism industry procreating surrogacy is booming, with India being the first country proposing to legalise commercial surrogacy. Whilst, the new Assisted Reproductive Technology (Regulation) Bill & Rules, 2010, are still in the womb, the non-statutory ICMR, 2005 Guidelines rule the roost. The Indian entrepreneurial industry spirit has catapulted the business of providing 'wombs for rent' to a whopping trade valued at rupees 25,000 crores. Despite legal, moral and social complexities that shroud surrogacy, economic necessity stimulates women to shake off their inhibition and fear of social ostracism to be lured by agents or corporate surrogacy consultants for international markets. Free availability of a large pool of women willing to be surrogates, a good medical infrastructure, fractional costs, less waiting time, close monitoring of surrogate mothers by over 200,000 in vitro fertilization (IVF) clinics and no check of any law restricting single, gay or unmarried couples becoming parents by surrogacy, has made this unethical trade in India skyrocket to spiraling heights.

(b) New Indian medical visa regulations will cap surrogacy but need legislation

However, soon, the business of surrogacy will plummet and boomerang. Under the latest and new Indian visa regulations, effective 15 November, 2012, onwards, all foreigners visiting India for commissioning surrogacy will be required to apply for 'medical visas' and cannot avail of simple tourist visas for surrogacy purposes. The Ministry of Home Affairs, by a letter of 9 July, 2012, has stipulated mandatory conditions for such medical visas, which, if not fulfilled, will lead to visa rejection. These new medical visa regulations stipulate that a letter from the embassy of the foreign country in India or its foreign ministry should be enclosed with the visa application stating clearly that such country recognises surrogacy and that the child to be born to the commissioning couple through the Indian surrogate mother will be permitted entry into their country as a biological child of the couple commissioning surrogacy who will undertake to take care of their surrogate child. The treatment will be done only at registered ART Clinics in India recognised by the ICMR and the foreign commissioning couple must produce a duly notarised agreement between them and the prospective surrogate Indian mother. Further, surrogacy has been restricted only to foreign couples, *i.e.*, men and women with at least two years of a sustained marriage.

After the surrogate baby is born, an exit permission for a commissioning couple before leaving India will be required from the Indian Foreigners Regional Registration Office (FRRO) to verify issuance of a certificate from the ART Clinic confirming discharge of liabilities of the Indian surrogate mother and ensuring custody of the child with the commissioning parents. Clearly, the safeguards, checks and balances besides moral and ethical dimensions, which to date remain unaddressed through any legislation, have been administratively put in place to regulate the surrogacy industry. The dam built with the strong bricks of the conditions of medical visas will temporarily prevent the gushing flow of unrestricted, pouring and muddled surrogate waters which had polluted India by becoming a bane for women's health, their basic dignity and human fundamental rights. However, it has created a situation of administratively encroaching upon rights of legitimate single parents.

Thus, this temporary solution is not the answer as proper legislation is required on the subject. Moreover, the stipulation on disallowing single parent surrogacy is contradictory to adoption rules prevalent in India which allow single parent adoptions. There cannot be inconsistent stands on adoptions and surrogacy by foreigners in India. This conflict should be curbed by appropriate legislation and not by administrative processes. Further, administratively, right of single parents for surrogacy cannot be taken away, except by a due process of law. The latest view of the Indian Ministry of Home Affairs in restricting surrogacy only to infertile Indian married couples will further prejudice the rights of foreigners and other non-resident Indians, who have acquired foreign nationality. Therefore, it would be desirable if surrogacy is restricted by proper rules through checks and balances before it is commissioned by foreign parents as banning foreigners from surrogacy altogether may not be a constitutionally valid proposition in the eyes of law. Hence, rather than closing the door altogether for surrogacy for foreigners, is not an appropriate or a desirable approach. Providing safeguards and mechanisms, as in the case of inter-country adoptions, would be the correct method to control and regulate surrogacy. The 2005 ICMR Guidelines and the 2008 as also the 2010 ART Regulation Bill which have culminated in a 2013 ART Regulation Bill must be discussed in public domain. The 2013 ART Regulation Bill which is reported to be part of a Cabinet note as of now, to be put up before the Cabinet of Ministers of the Central Government, before it is taken to Parliament, is as per official procedure, *'A Top Secret Document'*. This cannot be the case for long. The matter cannot rest unless it is put for discussion publically for soliciting views and opinions of all stake holders. Hence, any such proposal may need debate and discussion before it is deliberated in Parliament.

(c) Medical visa regulations will harmonise with existing Indian and foreign law of countries of commissioning parents

Commercial surrogacy is illegal in the United Kingdom, though permissible under British law, on payment of reasonable expenses to the surrogate mother. In most US states, compensated surrogacy agreements are either illegal or unenforceable. In some Australian states, arranging commercial surrogacy is a criminal offence and surrogacy agreements giving custody to others are void. In New Zealand and Canada, commercial surrogacy is illegal, although altruistic surrogacy is allowed. In Italy, Germany and France, commercial or other surrogacy is unlawful, in Israel, commercial surrogacy is illegal and the law only accepts the surrogate mother as the real mother. India, in total contrast, accepts commercial surrogacy and no law declares it illegal. The Supreme Court on 29 September, 2008, in *Baby Manji Yamada* v. *Union of India,* AIR 2009 SC 84, observed that 'Commercial Surrogacy [reaching] industry proportions is sometimes referred to by the emotionally charged and potentially offensive terms: wombs for rent, outsourced pregnancies or baby farms.' However, the new Indian Medical Visa Regulations by disallowing Indian visas to foreigners whose countries prohibit surrogacy will ensure that we also harmonise and fall in tandem internationally with those foreign nations whose overseas citizens wish to wrongfully patronise surrogacy in India. But, the appropriate method to do so would be by proper legislation and not through piecemeal administrative circulars which are inconsistent with prevailing laws allowing adoptions to foreigners through a well guided mechanism made by Parliament after due deliberations and Court interventions.

(d) Reactions and responses of foreign governments

Most foreign embassies have indicated on their websites that the Indian government now requires medical visas for foreigners coming to India for surrogacy. Besides, stringent DNA tests are already in place to establish genetic connections for parentage and foreign nationality. Indian consulates overseas and Visa Facilitation Services (VFS) have also notified that foreign nationals must ascertain beforehand whether their country permits surrogacy and that they cannot enter India for surrogacy purposes by tourist visas. The British High Commission, New Delhi, in advance preparation, by its letter of 30 October, 2012 to the Indian High Commission, London, states that the British government recognises surrogacy and makes provisions for commissioning couples for children born overseas through surrogacy. The UK Human Fertilization and Embryology Act, 1990 is cited in support. It allows surrogacy if one parent is genetically related to the surrogate child and no money other than reasonable expenses is paid in respect of the surrogacy arrangement. Alternatively, the letter uses the UK Human Fertilization and Embryology Act 1990 for providing parental orders to commissioning parents. This letter is stated to be a request for entertaining applications for medical visas for purposes of surrogacy in India as per the requirements of the new Indian Medical Visa Regulations.

VII. CONCLUSION

Rather than the Indian Parliament catching up to make a law to regulate the unscrupulous surrogacy trade, the new Medical Visa Regulations have stepped in temporarily to do what the law ought to have done. But, they also infringe on the rights of single foreign parents. Instead of permitting surrogate children to be born in India with the risk of being stateless persons and being denied entry into foreign countries where their commissioning parents reside, it is apt and necessary that such unethical practices leading to such disastrous situations must be pre-empted and prevented. Recent instances of surrogate children from Germany, Japan and Israel born in India and leaving upon court intervention should well make legislators think of enacting a strict surrogacy monitoring law. The Assisted Reproductive Technology (Regulation) Bill & Rules, 2010 itself has legal lacuna, lacks creation of a specialist legal authority for determination and adjudication of legal rights of parties, in addition to falling in conflict with existing family laws. These pitfalls should not become a graveyard for a law which is yet to be born. Surrogacy needs to be checked and regulated by a proper statutory law. Piecemeal administrative decisions cannot substitute legislation to override settled statutory rights conferred by laws made for inter-country adoptions to foreigners and non-resident Indians who have acquired foreign nationalities. The law makers must enact a law to put checks, controls and regulatory steps in place through a legislative mechanism. Surrogacy should be controlled by proper legislative methods as existing in the case of inter-country adoptions. The Assisted Reproductive Technology (Regulation) Bill & Rules, 2010 must be overhauled for providing mechanisms to regulate, check and control unethical practices as also to grant protection to rights of parties who are at a disadvantage. Hence, the proper course would be a statutory law which looks at all perspectives and protects the rights of all parties without infringing on the claims of others.

Surrogacy for Single & Unmarried Foreign Persons – A Challenge under Indian Law

I. INTRODUCTION

At a time when the World's first Test-tube baby Louise Brown born in 1978 in UK has now herself become a mother and high profile international adoptions by celebrities like Madonna and Angelina Jolie are glorifying international adoption, India does not lag behind. Noted Indian film actress Sushmita Sen inspires single women both in India and abroad to adopt children breaking conventional taboos and age-old practices. Resultantly, orphan girls are finding mothers in India and abroad. However, genuine adoptive foreign and Non-Resident would be parents too are pitted against an insurmountable wall. Child adoption in India is a complicated issue. It is over burdened with knotty legal processes and complicated lengthy procedures for those who want to give a new home and a new life to reported 12 million Indian orphans. Even though the Indian Constitution ordains it to be a sovereign, socialist, secular, democratic republic, 65 years of Independence have not given a comprehensive adoption law applicable to all its citizens, irrespective of the religion they profess or the country they live in as Non-Resident Indians (NRIs), Persons of Indian Origin (PIOs) or Overseas Citizens of India (OCIs). Resultantly, those who cannot by law adopt and can be appointed only as guardians under personal Indian laws, turn to options of IVF clinics or rent surrogate wombs. It is in this perspective that India now needs to adopt another law to turn to actual reality, the dreams of those who live abroad rather than turning to unhappy and sometimes unethical practices.

A silent revolutionary change is fast heralding a new dawn in matter of inter-country adoptions. However, the plethora of Indian laws, does not improve the plight of 12 million orphaned children in India who need adoptive parents. The Guardian and Wards Act (GWA), 1890 permits guardianship and not adoption. The Hindu Adoption and Maintenance Act (HAMA), 1956 does not permit non-Hindus to adopt a Hindu child. Requirements of immigration have further hurdles even after adoption. May be the urge to be a parent has now taken over in the form of "embryo adoption" wherein fertilized sperms and eggs developed into an embryo are successfully implanted in Indian clinics and nurtured by foreign mothers in their homeland ensuring hassle free adoption of Indian embryos without complicated procedures. Technology has overtaken law.

As a background to the practice of surrogacy today, mythological surrogate mothers in the past are well known in India. Yashoda played mother to Krishna though Devki and Vasudeva were biological parents. Likewise, in Indian mythology Gandhari made Dhritarashtra the proud father of 100 children though he had no biological relation with them. The primordial urge to have a biological child of one's own flesh, blood and DNA aided with technology and the purchasing power of money coupled with the Indian entrepreneurial spirit has generated the "reproductive tourism industry". This comes as a boon to childless couples all round the world. Clinically called "Assisted Reproductive Technology" (ART), it has been in vogue in India since 1978 and today an estimated 200, 000 clinics across the country offer artificial insemination, In-Vitero Fertilization (IVF) and surrogacy.

II. RECENT CASES:

- In the decision of the Supreme Court on 29 September, 2008 in **Baby *Manji Yamada* v. *Union of India*, AIR 2009 SC 84**, Japanese baby Manji born on 25 July, 2008 to an Indian surrogate mother with IVF technology upon fertilization of her Japanese parents eggs and sperms in Tokyo and the embryo being implanted in Ahmedabad, triggered off complex, knotty issues. The Japanese biological parents got divorced and the mother disowned the infant upon its birth in India. The grandmother of the infant petitioned the Supreme Court challenging the directions given by the Rajasthan High Court relating to production and custody of baby Manji Yamada. The grandmother's request to the Apex Court for permission for the infant to travel with her and for issuance of a passport under consideration with the Central Government was directed to be disposed off expeditiously. Following the directions of the Supreme Court, the Regional Passport Office in Jaipur issued an "Identity Certificate" to the baby. Hence, there was an implied recognition of the status of single parent since the divorced father as a single parent got custody of the child where after he flew to Japan.
- In another separate case, Israeli gay couple Yonatan and Omer Gher became parents in India on 12 October, 2008, when their child was conceived with the help of a Mumbai based surrogate mother in a fertility clinic in Bandra. It is reported that a 3.8 kilo baby boy was born to them at Hiranandani Hospital in Powai (Mumbai). Reportedly, Yonatan and Omer had been together for the past seven years and had decided to start a family. But since Israel reportedly does not allow same sex couples to adopt or have a surrogate child, India became their choice to find a surrogate mother. Yonatan and Omer reportedly first came to Mumbai in January 2008 for an IVF cycle when Yonatan is stated to have donated his sperm. Thereafter, they selected an anonymous "mother". Accordingly, the child was conceived with the help of a Mumbai based surrogate

mother in a fertility clinic in Bandra. After the child was born, the gay couple left for Israel with the child. In this case, a same sex couple was able to achieve surrogacy arrangements in India without any objections.

- Subsequently, in the year 2010, another gay couple, Dan Goldberg and Arnon Angel from Israel to whom twin baby boys were born in Mumbai from an Indian surrogate mother, were stranded in India after the refusal of The Jerusalem Family Court to allow a paternity test to initiate the process for Israeli citizenship for the twins. The issue was debated in The Knesset (Israeli Parliament) where Prime Minister Benjamin Netanyahu had to intervene so that the infants could be brought to Israel following legal procedures. Ultimately, in appeal, the Jerusalem District Court, accepted the claim that it was in the best interest to hold a DNA paternity test to establish that Dan Goldberg was the father of the twin baby boys Itai and Liron. The DNA samples of Goldberg and the twins were brought to the Sheeba Medical Centre in Israel which established Goldberg as the father of the infants. After being stranded in Mumbai for over 3 months, Goldberg and his twin baby boys returned to Israel in May 2010 after being granted Israeli passports.
- After a frustrating two year legal battle in India on behalf of their surrogate sons – Nikolas and Leonard – German couple Jan Balaz and Susan Anna Lohald got to go to Germany after the Supreme Court of India intervened and in a Court hearing on 26 May, 2010, the Indian Government agreed to provide them exit permits. The twin babies were born in the State of Gujarat in January 2008 and registered as children born of a foreign couple through an Indian surrogate mother. Upon being declined birth certificates, Jan Balaz moved the Gujarat High Court which ruled that since the surrogate mother is an Indian national, therefore, the children will also be treated as Indian nationals and will be entitled to Indian passports. However, the Government of India challenged this decision stating that the toddlers being surrogate children, they could not be granted Indian citizenship, which rendered the twins stateless as they got neither German nor Indian citizenship. The German authorities had also refused visas to the twins on the ground that German law did not recognize surrogacy as a means to parenthood. Ultimately, Jan Balaz and Susan Lohald went through an inter-country adoption process in India, upon which the Indian Government granted exit permits to the German surrogate twins to enable their journey back home to Germany.

III. PREVAILING LEGAL POSITION

- In the absence of any law to govern surrogacy the Indian Council of Medical Research (ICMR) issued *National Guidelines for Accreditation, Supervision and Regulation of ART Clinics in India, 2005 (Guidelines)*, to check the malpractices of Assisted Reproductive Technology (ART). The preface of these guidelines clearly state that in the Indian context, where barrenness is looked down upon, infertile parents look up to ART as the last resort to parenthood. These Guidelines are said to be widely publicized, discussed and debated by experts and practitioners of ART involving over 4000 participants. Para 3.5.2 of these Guidelines stating Desirable Practices/Prohibited Scenarios states that there would be no bar to use of ART by single women and the child thus born will have all the legal rights on the woman or the man, as follows:

> *"3.5.2 There would be no bar to the use of ART by a single women who wishes to have a child, and no ART clinic may refuse to offer its services to the above, provided other criteria mentioned in this document are satisfied. The child thus born will have all the legal rights on the women or the man."*

A reading of the above clearly indicates that these guidelines clearly permit single parents to commission surrogacy and prescribe that no ART clinic may refuse to offer it services to single women/men. These Guidelines are still prevalent till date.

- In a phenomenal exercise to legalise commercial surrogacy, The Assisted Reproductive Technology (Regulation) Bill & Rules, 2010 (ART Bill), a draft bill prepared by a 12 member committee including experts from ICMR, medical specialists and other experts from the Ministry of Health and Family Welfare, Government of India has been posted online for feedback. Also earlier floated in 2008 for comment, the ART Bill is stated to be an Act to provide for a national frame work for the Regulation and Supervision of Assisted Reproductive Technology and matters connected therewith or incidental thereto as a unique proposed law to be put before the Indian Parliament. Abetting surrogacy, it legalizes commercial surrogacy stating that the surrogate mother may receive monetary compensation and will relinquish all parental rights. Single parents can also have children using a surrogate mother. Foreigners, upon registration with their Embassy can seek surrogate arrangements. It also legalizes commercial surrogacy for single persons, married or unmarried couples stating that the surrogate mother shall enter into a legally enforceable surrogacy agreement. The 2010 draft bill states that foreigners or NRIs coming to India to rent a womb shall have to submit documentation confirming that their country of residence recognizes surrogacy as legal and that it will give citizenship to the child born through the surrogacy agreement from an Indian mother.

The proposed Bill which is called an Act *"to provide for a national framework for the regulation and supervision of assisted reproductive technology and matters connected therewith or incidental thereto"* provides for the constitution of a National Advisory Board for Assisted Reproductive Technology, comprising of members not exceeding 21, whose functions are confined to promoting the cause of reproductive technology. The salient details are:

- The new Assisted Reproductive Technology (Regulation) Bill & Rules, 2010, legalises commercial surrogacy, stating that the surrogate mother may receive monetary compensation for carrying the child in addition to health-care and treatment expenses during pregnancy.

- Both the couple or individual seeking surrogacy through the use of Assisted Reproductive Technology, and the surrogate mother shall enter into a surrogacy agreement which shall be legally enforceable.
- The surrogate mother will relinquish all parental rights over the child once the amount is transferred and birth certificates will be in the name of commissioning parent/s.
- The prescribed age-limit for a surrogate mother is between 21-35 years. The proposed Bill also states that no women shall act as a surrogate mother for more than five children including her own.
- Single persons, men or women or single parents, unmarried couples can also have children using a surrogate mother. In case of a single man or a woman, the baby will be his/her legitimate child. A child born to an unmarried couple using a surrogate mother and with the consent of both the parties shall be their legitimate child.
- All foreigners seeking infertility treatment in India will first have to register with their embassy. Their notarised statement will then have to be handed over to the treating doctor. The foreign couple will also state whom the child should be entrusted to in case of an eventuality such as a genetic parent's death.
- A foreigner or foreign couple not resident in India or an NRI individual or couple seeking surrogacy in India shall appoint the local guardian legally responsible for taking care of the surrogate child during and after pregnancy.
- The party seeking surrogacy must ensure and establish to the ART clinic that the party would be able to take the child born through surrogacy outside India to the country of the party's origin or residence as the case may be.
- A child born out of surrogacy shall be the legitimate child of both the parties or of the single man or woman as the case may be. The birth certificate will contain the name or names of the genetic parent or parents (as the case may be) who sought such use. If parties get divorced or separated, the child shall be the legitimate child of the couple. The birth certificate of a child born through the use of Assisted Reproductive Technology shall contain the name or names of the parent or parents, as the case may be, who sought such use.
- If a foreigner or a foreign couple seeks sperm or egg donation, or surrogacy, in India, and a child is born as a consequence, the child, even though born in India, shall not be an Indian citizen.
- Foreigners or NRIs coming to India seeking surrogacy in India shall appoint a local guardian who will be legally responsible for taking care of the surrogate during and after pregnancy till the child is delivered to the foreigner or foreign couple or the local guardian. Further, the party seeking surrogacy must ensure and establish through proper documentation that the country of their origin permits surrogacy and

that the child born through surrogacy in India will be permitted entry in the country of their origin as a biological child of the commissioning couple/individual. If the foreign party seeking surrogacy fails to take delivery of the child born to the surrogate mother, the local guardian will be legally obliged to take the child and be free to hand over the child to an adoption agency. In case of adoption or the legal guardian having to bring up the child in India, the child will be given Indian citizenship.

- Surrogacy be recommended for patients for whom it is medically impossible/undesirable to carry a baby to term.
- ART clinic must not advertise surrogacy arrangements. The responsibility should rest with the couple or a semen bank.
- ART clinic must ensure that the surrogate woman satisfies all the testable criteria (sexually transmitted or communicable disease that may endanger the pregnancy).
- A prospective surrogate mother must be tested for HIV and shown to be a seronegative for this virus just before embryo transfer.

➢ A reading of the above Bill which recognises the rights of individuals as well as couples to commission surrogacy by approaching ART clinics identifies even unmarried couples and individuals besides married couples as prospective parent/s. The ART Bill in Chapter IV dealing with duties of an ART Clinic clearly stipulates that individuals or couples will be provided professional counselling, knowledge about choices of treatment and other information to create awareness about ART. Likewise, Chapter VII dealing with Rights and Duties of Patients, Donors, Surrogates & Children in section 32 states as follows:

"32. ***Rights and duties of patients***—

Subject to the provisions of this Act and the rules and regulations made thereunder, assisted reproductive technology shall be available to all persons including single persons, married couples and unmarried couples."

It is abundantly clear that the competent authority in the matter have clearly spelt out the legislative intent of making available ART to all persons including single persons, married couples and unmarried couples. This policy decision is already clearly in vogue today in the shape of the ICMR Guidelines. Hence, surrogacy and ART, which is a subject matter to be dealt with as a portfolio has been appropriately dealt with by the Ministry of Health and Family Welfare who is competent to take decisions with respect to issues pertaining to them.

➢ It may also be pertinent to point out that The Law Commission of India in Report No. 228 of August 2009 titled *"Need for legislation to regulate assisted reproductive technology clinics as well as rights and obligations of parties to a surrogacy"*, has given its views on surrogacy achieved through ART. After examining all the issues and various view points besides discussing actual cases of foreign nationals who have utilised ART for commissioning surrogacy in India, various recommendations have been made by the Law Commission of India in its said Report and in Chapter IV of said Report dealing with conclusions and recommendations, para 4.2[4] reads in the following terms:

> *"4.2 The draft Bill prepared by the ICMR is full of lacunae, nay, it is incomplete. However, it is a beacon to move forward in the direction of preparing legislation to regulate not only ART clinics but rights and obligations of all the parties to a surrogacy including rights of the surrogate child. Most important points in regard to the rights and obligations of the parties to a surrogacy and rights of the surrogate child the proposed legislation should include may be stated as under:*
>
> *[1] to [3] xxxxxx*
>
> *[4] One of the intended parents should be a donor as well, because the bond of love and affection with a child primarily emanates from biological relationship. Also, the chances of various children of child-abuse, which have been noticed in case of adoption, will be reduced. In case the intended parent is single, he or she should be a donor to be able to have a surrogacy child. Otherwise, adoption is the way to have a child which is resorted to if biological (natural) parents and adoptive parents are different."*

Clearly, the Law Commission of India which recommends that a pragmatic approach should be adopted by legalising altruistic surrogacy arrangements recommends and approves of surrogacy arrangements for single parents as well. Hence, there is no move indicated by the Law Commission to propose that single parents should not be allowed use of ART for surrogacy & position is to contrary.

IV. LAW FOR ENTRY OF FOREIGNERS IN INDIA

The entry, stay and exit of foreigners into India is governed by The Passport (Entry into India) Act, 1920, the Passport (Entry into India) Rules, 1950, Foreigners Act, 1946, and the Registration of Foreigners Rules, 1992. The Policies, Acts and Rules relating to entry of foreigners into India are framed by the Ministry of Home Affairs, Government of India. To facilitate an easy understanding of purposes of the above Acts, a tabulated account is as below:

1	The Passport (Entry into India) Act, 1920 and the Passport (Entry into India) Rules, 1950	It prescribes specific authorization of foreigner nationals on their valid travel documents/ passports for allowing entry into the country. Under this Act and the Rules made there under, the foreigners coming to India are required to get visa from Indian Missions/Posts
2	The Foreigners Act, 1946 and the Foreigners Order, 1948.	It regulates the entry of foreigners into India, their presence therein and their departure therefrom.
3.	The Registration of Foreigners Act, 1939 and the Registration of Foreigners Rules, 1992.	It mandates that certain categories of foreigners whose intended stay in India is more than the specified period, or as provided in their visa authorization, are required to get themselves registered with the Registration Officer.

From a reading of the above, it is evident that under the above provisions, the Ministry of Home Affairs can make provisions for prohibiting, regulating or restricting the entry, departure and presence of foreigners into India by enacting justifiable and legitimate Visa Rules and Regulations with a classification for different purposes. The basic principles of the visa policy is non discrimination. Though the decision to grant a visa in a particular category may depend upon requisite conditions, but it cannot create an unjust classification by debarring any category of persons from being ineligible to apply for a particular category of a specific visa in violation of articles 14 & 21 of The Constitution of India which provides equality of laws besides protection of life and personal liberty to all persons including foreign nationals.

V. BAR ON SINGLE AND UNMARRIED PERSONS

Even though the Ministry of Health and Family Welfare do not prohibit or debar single persons or unmarried couples from commissioning surrogacy through ART in India, the Ministry of Home Affairs by administrative guidelines dated 9 July, 2012, has stipulated that only married foreign men and women whose marriage has sustained for atleast two years would be eligible to apply for medical visas for purposes of surrogacy in India. Consequently, all single persons and unmarried couples have been declared ineligible from even applying for a visa in any category whatsoever for coming to India for the purposes of surrogacy. This unreasonable classification violative of articles 14 and 21 of the Constitution has no nexus with the object sought to be achieved and directly curtails/ interferes with *"the right of reproductive autonomy"* which is a facet of the *"right of privacy"* under article 21 of the Constitution. No reasons, justification, logic or explanation is forthcoming as to why single persons or unmarried couples have been debarred and excluded from commissioning surrogacy in India. None of the grounds made out in the impugned Guidelines justify or validate this arbitrary exclusion and unfounded ineglibility of single persons/ unmarried couples who have been debarred from even applying for visas to India even though the ICMR Guidelines, ART Bill, and Law Commission Report do not contemplate any such restrictions.

VI. INDIAN LAW ON SURROGACY

(i) Surrogacy in India is legitimate for married couples/unmarried couples/ single persons because no Indian law prohibits surrogacy. To determine the legality of surrogacy agreements, the Indian Contract Act would apply and thereafter the enforceability of any such agreement would be within the domain of section 9 of The Indian Code of Civil Procedure (CPC). Alternatively, the biological parent/s can also move an application under the Guardian and Wards Act for seeking an order of appointment for a declaration to be declared as the Guardian of the surrogate children.

(ii) In the absence of any law to govern surrogacy, the 2005 ICMR Guidelines apply to all couples/single persons. Under para 3.10.1 a child born through surrogacy must be adopted by the genetic (biological parents). However, this may not be possible in case of non-Hindu foreign parents who cannot adopt in India but can be appointed as guardians under the Guardians and Wards Act. Under para 3.5.2 of the ICMR Guidelines, there would no bar to the use of ART by single women and a child born will have all the legal rights on the woman or man as the case may be.

(iii) Under section 10 of the Indian Contract Act, 1872 all agreements are contracts, if they are made by free consent of parties competent to contract, are for a lawful consideration, are with a lawful object, and are not expressly declared to be void. Therefore, if any surrogacy agreement of a married/unmarried couple/single parent satisfies these conditions, it is an enforceable contract. Thereafter, under section 9 of the Code of Civil Procedure, 1908 prescribing that the Courts may try all civil suits unless barred, it can be the subject of a civil suit before a Civil Court to establish all/any issues relating to the surrogacy agreement and for a declaration/injunction for the reliefs prayed for.

(iv) Other issues, which have now cropped up for opinion are as to whether a single parent or unmarried couple can be considered to be the custodial parent of a surrogate child. As of today, it may be stated that a single parent or unmarried couple can be considered to be the custodial parent by virtue of being the genetic or biological father of the surrogate child born out of a surrogacy arrangement. Japanese baby *Manji Yamada's* case, JT 2008 (11) SC 150 and the Israel gay couples case who fathered the child in India are clear examples to establish that this is possible. Under paras 3.16.1 and 3.5.2 of the 2005 ICMR Guidelines dealing with legitimacy of children born through ART (which were the basis of the claim in the Japanese baby's case in the Supreme Court), this claim can be made. However, only in a petition for guardianship under GWA and/or in a suit for declaration in a Civil Court, the exclusive custodial rights can be adjudicated by a court of competent jurisdiction upon appreciation of evidence and considering all claims made in this regard.

(v) What would be the status of divorced biological parents in respect of the custody of a surrogate child. Essentially, this is a question which will require determination in accordance with the surrogacy agreement between the parties. There would be apparently no bar to either of the divorced parents claiming custody of a surrogate child if the other parent does not claim the same. However, if the custody is contested, it may require adjudication by a court of competent jurisdiction as per provisions of Civil Procedure Code.

(vi) Would biological parent/s be considered the legal parent of the children? In answer to this question it can be stated that the biological parents would be considered to be the legal parents of the children by virtue of the surrogacy agreement executed between the parties and the surrogate mother. Under para 3.16.1 of the 2005 ICMR Guidelines dealing with legitimacy of the child born through ART, it is stated that "*a child born through ART shall be presumed to be the legitimate child of the couple, born within wedlock, with consent of both the spouses, and with all the attendant rights of parentage, support and inheritance.*" Under para 3.5.2 of the ICMR Guidelines a single man/woman can have a child by ART through surrogacy. Even in the 2010 Draft Bill and Rules, a child born to a married couple, an unmarried couple, a single parent or a single man or woman shall be the legitimate child of the couple man or woman as the case may be.

(vii) That as per the Law Commission of India Report, in its conclusions and recommendations in para 4.2(4), it has been stated that in case the intended parent is single, he or she should be a donor to be able to have a child through surrogacy. Clearly, in the views of the Law Commission, there is clear recommendation to the Government of India to permit surrogacy for single parents.

(viii) POSITION OF LAW UNDER THE 2010 BILL

- Under the ART Regulation Bill 2010, Assisted Reproductive Technology, Surrogacy, "gamete", and Surrogacy agreement have been defined as follows:

  "Assisted Reproductive Technology", with its grammatical variations and cognate expressions, means all techniques that attempt to obtain a pregnancy by handling or manipulating the sperm or the oocyte outside the human body, and transferring the gamete or the embryo into the reproductive tract;

  "Surrogacy", means an arrangement in which a woman agrees to a pregnancy, achieved through assisted reproductive technology, in which neither of the gametes belong to her or her husband, with the intention to carry it and hand over the child to the person or persons for whom she is acting as a surrogate;

  "Gamete", means sperm and oocyte (that is egg);

  "Surrogacy Agreement", means a contract between the person(s) availing of assisted reproductive technology and the surrogate mother;

- Chapter 2 of the Bill describes the constitution of authorities to regulate Assisted Reproductive Technology. A 21-Member National Advisory Board comprising of various experts is sought to be created with functions to promote Assisted Reproductive Technology related issues. State Boards are recommended in States and State Registration authorities are sought to be created for procedural purposes. Proceedings before the National and State Boards are deemed to be Civil Court Proceedings for limited purposes & are sought to be treated as Judicial Proceedings even though the constitution of the National or State Advisory Board have no Judicial Officers, Judges or Designated Courts as constituents.

- Chapter 3 of the Bill talks for procedures for registration and complaints in respect of Assisted Reproductive Technology Clinics. Chapter 4 talks of the duties of such clinics. Chapter 5 talks of Sourcing, Storage, handling and record keeping for Gametes, Embryos and Surrogates. Chapter 6 relates to Regulation on Research on Embryos.

- Chapter 7 discusses Rights and Duties of Patients, Donors, Surrogates and Children in extensor. The Rights and Duties are well defined and determination of the status of the child is laid out in detail irrespective of the status of parties as a couple, as an unmarried couple, as single parents, gay parents or otherwise. The duty to take children born through surrogacy from India to the country of origin or residence of the biological parents or residence is spelt out.

- Chapter 8 talks of Offences and Penalties for contravening the provisions of the Act and Chapter 9 in the Miscellaneous section talks of maintenance of records, power to search and seize, power to make regulation and rules. The Act is stated to be in addition to and not in derogation with any other law for the time being in force.
- The National and State Advisory Boards are only authorities who will promote ART Technology, Surrogacy Arrangements and related procedures. The proceedings of these Boards have been deemed to be "Judicial Proceedings" before Civil Courts for limited purposes.
- Chapter 3 talks of complaints, Chapter 4 talks of duties, Chapters 5 and 6 talks of more ART related issues. Chapter 7 talks of duties. Chapter 8 talks of offences and penalties which carry serious consequences.

VII. CHALLENGES TO RESTRICTION ON SURROGACY BY SINGLE AND UNMARRIED FOREIGN PERSONS

In the face of the above position of fact and law enunciated by the ICMR Guidelines, ART Bill, 2010 and the Law Commission Report, which reflect the policies, decisions and the mandate of the Ministry of Health and Family Welfare, who are competent and authorised to opine and decide such matters, there is no bar on surrogacy in India for foreign single persons or foreign unmarried couples. In fact, there is no statutory law made or policy decision taken by the Ministry of Health and Family Welfare, whereby surrogacy by single persons or unmarried couples of foreign nationality has been prohibited or banned. In the face of such a factual situation, the Ministry of Home Affairs have no authority under law to lay down the Guidelines restricting surrogacy only to married foreign couples with two years of marriage. Hence, the Guidelines to this extent are illegal, without any authority of law and are beyond the competence of the Ministry of Home Affairs. Therefore, para 2(i) restricting surrogacy only to married foreign men and women is illegal without sanction of law and it is beyond the competence to make such guidelines.

(a) That under the 1920 Act read with the 1950 Rules, the Foreigners Act, 1946, read with The Foreigners Order, 1948 and the provisions of The Registration of Foreigners Act, 1939 read with the Registration of Foreigners Rules, 1992, it is beyond the competence, authority and power of the Ministry of Home Affairs to debar, prohibit and exclude single persons and unmarried couples from commissioning surrogacy agreements through ART. Under the above provisions of law the entry of foreigners into India can be regulated and conditions can be prescribed for their stay in India on valid travel documents thereby restricting the entry, departure and presence of foreigners into India by making justifiable and legitimate visa regulations. This however cannot empower the Ministry of Home Affairs to restrict the entry of single persons or unmarried couples into India for surrogacy purposes. It is beyond the competence and authority of the Ministry of Home Affairs to lay down any guidelines to impose any such restriction debarring single persons or unmarried couples from coming to India for surrogacy. No such power or authority is vested in law under the enactments/rules whereby such a bar can be imposed by the Ministry of Home Affairs. Therefore, para 2(i) of the Guidelines are illegal and ultra vires the provisions of article 14 and 21 of the Constitution of India since they take away the protection of law and invade the right of privacy guaranteed to the petitioner and thus deserve to be struck down.

(b) That the Ministry of Home Affairs cannot interfere and abrogate to themselves functions and powers which cannot be attributed to them. The Ministry of Health and Family Welfare, are the competent authorities who are duly empowered under the Rules of Business of The Government of India to enact laws and make policies which are within the domain of their appropriate functions dealing with subjects under the portfolio of Health and Family Welfare. The Ministry of Home Affairs cannot take over the functions of the Ministry of Health and Family Welfare as also the Indian Council of Medical Research. A team of dedicated experts has enacted the Guidelines and a similar team of experts has made the ART Bill. The Law Commission itself through its members appointed by the Government of India has given its recommendations to the Government in its Report. The Ministry of Home Affairs therefore cannot start taking decisions beyond their competence and start dictating policies which run contrary to the mandate of the Ministry of Health and Family Welfare. Therefore, para 2(i) of the Guidelines are illegal, beyond the authority of law and are ultra vires the provisions of the Constitution of India since the Ministry of Home Affairs cannot usurp powers and functions of the Ministry of Health and Family Welfare, to make contradictory policies in contravention of article 14 and 21 of the Constitution of India.

(c) That para 2(i) of the Guidelines infringe upon the right of privacy guaranteed to the petitioner under article 21 of the Constitution of India as a foreign national. The right of privacy of the petitioner is a facet of article 21 of the Constitution. The Apex Court in *Govind* v. *State of Madhya Pradesh,* AIR 1975 SC 1378, and *Kharak Singh* v. *State of Uttar Pradesh,* AIR 1963 SC 1295 *have identified the right of privacy as a constitutionally protected right as a facet of article 21 of the Constitution.* The personal decision of the petitioner as a single person about the birth of a baby through surrogacy called "the right of reproductive autonomy" is a facet of the right of privacy guaranteed under article 21 of the Constitution. Thus, the right of privacy of the petitioner as a single person to be free from unwarranted Governmental intrusion into matters fundamentally affecting the petitioners and his decision to bear or beget a child through surrogacy cannot be taken away by the Ministry of Home Affairs, particularly when the Ministry of Health and Family Welfare, do not bar or restrict any such right whereby surrogacy is permissible to single persons or unmarried couples. Therefore, this discriminative policy advocated by the Ministry of Home Affairs infringes the right of privacy under article 21 of the Constitution, has no nexus with the objects sought to be achieved and is invading the protection of article 14 of the Constitution. Para 2(i) of the

Guidelines directly curtails and interferes with the right of the petitioner to take a decision in the matter of procreation by banning his entry into India for the purposes of Surrogacy as a single person. Such a restriction is constitutionally impermissible in the context of facet of the rights guaranteed under article 21 of the Constitution. Hence, para 2(i) of the Guidelines are ultra vires the provisions of article 21 of the Constitution and deserve to be struck down since they create unreasonable classification on the right of the petitioner of procreation by surrogacy as a single parent in India.

(d) That para 2(i) of the Guidelines create an unjust and arbitrary classification by meting out unequal treatment to equals. In effect, para 2(i) of the Guidelines, discriminate between Indian nationals and foreign citizens by debarring only foreign single men/women and unmarried couples from commissioning surrogacy through ART in India. Single Indian men/women or unmarried Indian couples can commission surrogacy arrangements in India through ART since the Ministry of Health and Family Welfare, do not impose any bar or embargo on surrogacy for single Indian nationals or unmarried Indian Couples. Hence, the ban by the Ministry of Home Affairs on foreign single persons or foreign unmarried couples from commissioning surrogacy in India through ART is wholly unjustified, illegal, arbitrary, discriminatory and is a wholly unjust/whimsical classification unwarranted or authorised by any law. The Ministry of Home Affairs who have no competence to take a policy decision on the subject of surrogacy within the domain and portfolio of Health and Family Welfare have thus made a policy decision which is illegal, beyond law, wholly tenable and totally contradictory. This unreasonable and unjust classification treats equals unequally thereby violating equality of law and equal protection of laws. Foreign nationals, overseas citizens of India, and person of Indian Origin cannot be discriminated in the matter of surrogacy upon comparison with Indian nationals. Therefore, imposing a ban on surrogacy by foreign single persons or foreign unmarried couples under para 2(i) of the Guidelines amounts to an unreasonable, unjust and arbitrary classification which has no nexus with the object sought to be achieved. The purpose if any of protection and beneficial factors suggested are adequately taken care of by the other conditions contained in para 2 of the Guidelines. Therefore there is no logic, justification, ground, reason or objective in imposing restrictions on foreign single persons or unmarried couples in commissioning surrogacy in India.

(e) That it is not within the domain or authority of the Ministry of Home Affairs to enact Rules, make policies or issue guidelines which impinge upon the functions, duties, portfolios and subjects of the Ministry of Health and Family Welfare. At the most, the Ministry of Home Affairs can issue Guidelines restricting all foreign applicants to apply for a medical visa if they want to visit India for purposes of surrogacy through ART. However, it is not within the domain or authority of the Ministry of Home Affairs to issue guidelines to state that single foreign persons or unmarried couples will not be granted medical visas for purposes of surrogacy in India. Such a guideline contained in para 2(i) of the Guidelines is unjustified, beyond the authority of law and violates article 14 of the Constitution. This unjust, unreasonable and unwarranted classification is wholly illegal and beyond the scope of power of the Ministry of Home Affairs. Therefore, the Guidelines are wholly unwarranted and are not authorised by virtue of the powers conferred upon the Ministry of Home Affairs under the Enactments, Orders and Rules.

(f) That para 2(i) of the Guidelines clearly militate against the position of law stated by the Apex Court in Baby Manji Yamda, the judgment in which a single divorced parent was allowed to take a surrogate baby to Japan.

From a reading of the above, it is evident that under the above provisions, the Ministry of Home Affairs can make provisions for prohibiting, regulating or restricting the entry, departure and presence of foreigners into India by enacting justifiable and legitimate Visa Rules and Regulations with a classification for different purposes. The basic principles of the visa policy is non discrimination. Though the decision to grant a visa in a particular category may depend upon requisite conditions, but it cannot create an unjust classification by debarring any category of persons from being ineligible to apply for a particular category of a specific visa in violation of articles 14 & 21 of The Constitution of India which provides equality of laws besides protection of life and personal liberty to all persons including foreign nationals.

CONCLUSION: AN UNJUSTIFIED BAR ON SINGLE AND UNMARRIED PERSONS

Even though the Ministry of Health and Family Welfare do not prohibit or debar single persons or unmarried couples from commissioning surrogacy through ART in India, the Ministry of Home Affairs by administrative guidelines dated 9 July, 2012, has stipulated that only married foreign men and women whose marriage has sustained for atleast two years would eligible to apply for medical visas for purposes of surrogacy in India. Consequently, all single persons and unmarried couples have been declared ineligible from even applying for a visa in any category whatsoever for coming to India for the purposes of surrogacy. This unreasonable classification violative of articles 14 and 21 of the Constitution has no nexus with the object sought to be achieved and directly curtails/interferes with *"the right of reproductive autonomy"* which is a facet of the *"right of privacy"* under article 21 of the Constitution. No reasons, justification, logic or explanation is forthcoming as to why single persons or unmarried couples have been debarred and excluded from commissioning surrogacy in India. None of the grounds made out in the impugned Guidelines justify or validate this arbitrary exclusion and unfounded ineglibility of single persons/ unmarried couples who have been debarred from even applying for visas to India even though the ICMR Guidelines, ART Bill, and Law Commission Report do not contemplate any such restrictions.

Inter-Country Parental Child Removal and the Law

I INTRODUCTION

The world is a far smaller place now than it was a decade ago. Inter-country and inter-continental travel is easier and more affordable than it has ever been. The corollary to this is an increase in relationships between individuals of different nationalities and from different cultural backgrounds. Logically, the world in which we and our children live has grown immensely complex. It is filled with opportunities and risks. International mobility, opening up of borders, cross-border migration and dismantling of inter-cultural taboos are all positive developments but are nevertheless fraught with a new set of risks for children caught up in cross-border situations. Caught in the crossfire of broken relationships with ensuing disputes over custody and relocation, the hazards of international abduction loom large over the chronic problems of maintaining access or contact internationally with the uphill struggle of securing cross-frontier child support. In a population of over 1.2 billion Indians, 30 million are non-resident Indians who, by migrating to different jurisdictions, have generated a new crop of spousal and family disputes.

(a) Definition of child removal

Families with connections to more than one country face unique problems if their relationship breaks down. The human reaction in this already difficult time is often to return to one's family and country of origin with the children of the relationship. If this is done without the approval of the other parent or permission from a court, a parent taking children from one country to another may, whether inadvertently or not, be committing child removal or inter-parental child abduction. This concept is not clearly defined in any relevant legislation. As a matter of convention, it has come to mean the removal of a child from the care of the person with whom the child normally lives.

A broader definition encompasses the removal of a child from his or her environment, where the removal interferes with parental rights or right to contact. Removal in this context refers to removal by parents or members of the extended family. It does not include independent removal by strangers. The Convention on the Civil Aspects of International Child Abduction signed at The Hague on 25 October, 1980, with 80 contracting countries today as parties, however, defines removal or detention wrongful in the following words:

'Article 3

The removal or the retention of a child is to be considered wrongful where:

(a) it is in breach of rights of custody attributed to a person, an institution or any other body, either jointly or alone, under the law of the State in which the child was habitually resident immediately before the removal or retention; and

(b) at the time of removal or retention those rights were actually exercised, either jointly or alone, or would have been so exercised but for the removal or retention.

The rights of custody mentioned in sub-paragraph (a) above may arise in particular by operation of law or by reason of a judicial or administrative decision, or by reason of an agreement having legal effect under the law of that State.'

Child removal does not find any specific definition in the Indian statute books and, since India is not a signatory to the Hague Convention, there is no parallel Indian legislation enacted to give the force of law to the Hague Convention. Hence, in India, all interpretations of the concept of child removal are based on judicial innovation in precedents of case-law decided by Indian courts in disputes between litigating parents of Indian and/or foreign origin.

(b) Global solutions and remedies

The Hague Convention on Civil Aspects of International Child Abduction came into force on 1 December, 1983 and now has 80 contracting nations. The objects of the Convention were:

(a) to secure the prompt return of children wrongfully removed to or retained in any contracting state; and

(b) to ensure that rights of custody and of access under the law of one contracting state are effectively respected in the other contracting states.

It operates as an effective deterrent providing a real and practical means of restoring the status quo prior to the abduction, prevents abductors from reaping the benefits of an act opposed to the interests of children, upholds the right of the child to maintain contact with both parents and introduces harmony where previously chaos prevailed. The Permanent Bureau of the Hague Conference on Private International Law at The Hague, Netherlands, renders a superb service by monitoring and helping the development of services to support effective implementation and consistent operation of the Hague Conventions and review their operations. Since there is no centralised system of enforcement or interpretation, the Secretariat of the Hague Conferences guides nations in post-Convention services. In terms of the Hague Convention on Civil Aspects of International Child Abduction, the Secretariat has published guides to good practice in three parts, namely Central Authority Practice, Implementing Measures and Preventing Measures which are all approved by contracting states. The Secretariat thus helps to create an international medium of consenting states who contract with each other to return children who are wrongfully removed.

(c) Why should India be interested in joining the 1980 Convention?

The Hague Convention on the Civil Aspects of International Child Abduction is a remarkable document, which has had significant impact on child protection policies in much of the world. In a civilised society, where globalisation and free interaction is part of a rapidly changing set up, India is emerging as a major destination in the developing world. Non-resident Indians have achieved laurels in all walks of life. But, back home, the problems on the family law front are largely unresolved. Times have changed but laws are still the same. Marriage, divorce, custody, maintenance and adoption laws in India are in need of reform. Child removal is often treated as a custody dispute between parents for agitating and adjudicating rights of spouses while spontaneously extinguishing the rights of the child. Therefore, from an international perspective, four major reasons can be identified to establish and support the necessity of India's signing the Convention.

First, India is no longer impervious to international inter-parental child removal. In the absence of the Convention principles, the Indian courts determine the child's best interest by dealing with any child removal like any custody dispute. In this process, the litigation is a fight of superior rights of parties and the real issue of the welfare of the child becomes subservient and subordinate. Clash of parental interests and rights of spouses determine the question of custody. The overpowering parent wins by establishing his rights and the resultant determination of the best interest of the child is a misnomer and a misconception. Such a settlement is not truly in the best interest of the removed child.

Secondly, such a determination in India plays into the hands of the abducting parent and usurps the role of the court which is best placed to determine the long-term interests of the child, namely the court of the country where the child had his or her home before the wrongful removal or retention took place. By contrast, the advantage of the Hague Convention approach is that it quickly restores the position to what it was prior to when the wrongful removal or retention took place and supports the proper role played by the court in the country of the child's habitual residence. The correct law to be applied to the child would be that of the country of the child's origin and so would be the court of that country. In India, determination of rights as per the Indian law of a foreign child removed to India by an offending parent may often be clouded, may not be in the best interest of the child and ought to be determined by the law and the court of the child's origin.

Thirdly, the fact that India is not a party to the Hague Convention may have a negative influence on a foreign judge who is deciding whether a child living with a parent in a foreign country should be permitted to spend time in India to enjoy contact with an Indian parent and extended family. Without the guarantee afforded by the Hague Convention to the effect that the child will be swiftly returned to the country of origin, the foreign judge may be reluctant to give permission for the child to travel to India. As a logical corollary of this principle, membership of the Hague Convention will bring the prospect of achieving the return to India of children who have their homes in India but have been abducted to one of the 80 states that are parties to the Convention.

Fourthly, the Convention provides a structure for the resolution of issues of custody and contact which may arise when parents are separated and living in different countries. The Convention avoids the problems that may arise in courts of different countries who are equally competent to decide such issues. The recognition and enforcement provisions of the Convention avoid the need for re-litigating custody and contact issues and ensure that decisions are taken by the authorities of the country where the child was habitually resident before removal.

It is thus hoped that India will give a serious consideration to joining the 1980 Hague Convention due to the convincing grounds cited above.

(d) The UK judicial initiative

In January 2005, Lord Justice Thorpe at the Royal Courts of Justice, London was appointed Head of International Family Law for England and Wales (a newly created title within the UK judicial system). The appointment confirms the increasing importance attached to the development of international instruments and conventions in a field of family law and to the value of international judicial collaboration, particularly in the extension of the global network of liaison judges specialising in family law. This may prompt some other jurisdictions in the world, whether or not they are signatories to the Hague Convention on Civil Aspects of International Child Abduction, 1980, to make similar appointments. In relation to wrongful removal or retention of children, as between the UK and Pakistan, a protocol has been agreed between the President of the Family Division of the High Court of London and the Chief Justice of the Supreme Court of Pakistan for co-operation between the judicial authorities of the two countries and providing agreed procedures for dealing with such cases. India, however, has not taken any steps in such regard.

II. GENERAL POSITION OF INDIAN LAW ON THE PROPOSITION OF INTER-PARENTAL AND INTER-COUNTRY CHILD REMOVAL

(a) Introduction

International child abduction law in India stands substantially modified as a result of the Supreme Court judgment in *Dhanwanti Joshi* v. *Madhav Unde,* (1997) 8 SC 720 handed down on 4 November 1997. It deals with the provisions and case-law analysis relating to the Hindu Minority and Guardianship Act, 1956, read with the Guardian and Wards Act, 1890. The two enactments principally govern the law relating to child custody in India.

Under Indian law, the prime consideration is the welfare of the child, though section 6(a) of the Guardian and Wards Act, 1890 says that the custody of a minor who has not attained the age of 5 shall ordinarily be with the mother.

The Court held:

> *'So far as non-Convention countries are concerned, or where the removal related to a period before adopting the Convention, the law is that the Court to which the child is removed will consider the question on merits bearing the welfare of*

the child as of paramount importance and consider the order of the foreign Court as only a factor to be taken into consideration as stated in McKee v. McKee, *[1951] AC 352, unless the Court thinks it fit to exercise summary jurisdiction in the interests of the child and its prompt return is for its welfare, as explained in* Re L, *[1974] 1 All ER 913 (CA). As recently as 1996–1997, it has been held* in Re P (A minor) (Child Abduction: Non-Convention Country), *[1996] 3 FCR 233 (CA) by Ward, LJ, 1996 (Current Law) (Year Book) 165–166) that in deciding whether to order the return of a child who has been abducted from his or her country of habitual residence – which was not a party to the Hague Convention, 1980 – the Courts' overriding consideration must be the child's welfare. There is no need for the Judge to attempt to apply the provisions of article 13 of the Convention by ordering the child's return unless a grave risk of harm was established ...'*

From the above mandate of law, it is clear that courts in India now would not exercise a summary jurisdiction only to return the children to the foreign country of their habitual residence.

It was also held (at para 21) that orders relating to the custody of children are by their very nature not final, but interlocutory in nature, and subject to modification at any future time upon proof of a change of circumstances requiring change of custody; but such change in custody must be proved to be in the paramount interests of the child. This was the position of law laid down by the Supreme Court of India in *Rosy Jacob* v. *Jacob A Chakramakkal,* (1973) 1 SCC 840, which has since been explicitly reaffirmed in the above-mentioned 1997 ruling.

It was further held that the custody order of a foreign court is only one of the factors which will be taken into consideration by a court of law in India. The court will draw up an independent judgment on the merits of the matter with regard to the welfare of the children. Lastly, superior financial capacity cannot be a sole ground for removing children from their mother's custody.

(b) Further case-law

The tenor of law laid down in the above-mentioned judgment of *Dhanwanti Joshi,* 1997 (8) SC 720 has more recently been reaffirmed by the Supreme Court of India in *Sarita Sharma* v. *Sushil Sharma,* 2000 (2) SC 258. The facts of this case are outlined in brief below.

The parents of the children were living in the United States. The children were placed in the custody of their father, while their mother was given visiting rights. In exercise of her visiting rights, on 7 May, 1997 the mother picked up the children from the father's residence. She was to return the children next morning. The next morning, the father discovered that the children had not been brought back to school. Eventually, the mother, without obtaining any US court order, flew to India with the children. The father filed a petition for the issue of a writ of *habeas corpus* at the Delhi High Court on 9 September, 1997. To seek the release of any individual in illegal custody, a *habeas corpus* petition can be filed in any High Court in India under article 226, or under article 32 of the Constitution of India if the jurisdiction of the Supreme Court of India is to be invoked directly. The wife's contention was that, by virtue of the orders dated 5 February, 1996 and 2 April, 1997 passed by the courts in the United States, both she and the father were appointed as possessory conservators. Hence, both the children were in her lawful custody.

The Delhi High Court held that, in view of the interim orders passed by the United States Court, the wife had committed a wrong in not informing that Court and not seeking its permission to remove the children from the jurisdiction of that Court. The Delhi High Court took note of the fact that a competent court having territorial jurisdiction had passed a decree of divorce and had ordered that only the father should have the custody of the children. The Delhi High Court allowed the petition and directed the wife to restore the custody of the two children to the father. It was also declared that it was open to the father to take the children to the United States without any hindrance. The wife appealed to the Supreme Court of India.

The Supreme Court (at 263, para 4) noted from the record that there were serious differences between the two warring spouses. The husband was an alcoholic and had been violent towards the wife. The conduct of the wife was also not very satisfactory. The Court framed the following issues:

> *'The question is whether the custody became illegal, as she had committed a breach of the order of the American Court directing her not to remove the children from the jurisdiction of that Court without its permission. After she came to India a decree of divorce and the order for the custody of the children have been passed. Therefore, it is also required to be considered whether the mother's custody became illegal thereafter.'*

The Court held (at 264 and 265, para 6):

> *'Therefore, it will not be proper to be guided entirely by the fact that the appellant Sarita had removed the children from [the] USA despite the order of the Court of that country. So also, in view of the facts and circumstances of the case, the decree passed by the American Court though a relevant factor, cannot override the consideration of welfare of the minor children. We have already stated earlier that in [the] USA respondent Sushil is staying along with his mother aged about 80 years. There is no one else in the family. The respondent appears to be in the habit of taking excessive alcohol. Though it is true that both the children have the American citizenship and there is a possibility that in [the] USA they may be able to get better education, it is doubtful if the respondent will be in a position to take proper care of the children when they are so young. Out of them one is a female child. She is aged about five years. Ordinarily, a female child should be allowed to remain with the mother so that she can be properly looked after. It is also not desirable that two children are separated from each other. If a female child has to stay with the mother, it will be in the interest of both the children that they both stay with the mother. Here in India also proper care of the children is taken and they are at present studying in good schools. We have not found the appellant wanting in taking proper care of the children. Both the children have a desire to stay with the mother. At the same time it must be said that the son, who is elder than the daughter, has good feelings for his father also. Considering all the aspects relating to the welfare of the children, we are of the*

opinion that in spite of the order passed by the Court in [the] USA it was not proper for the High Court to have allowed the Habeas Corpus writ petition and directed the appellant to hand over custody of the children to the respondent and permit him to take them away to [the] USA. What would be in the interest of the children requires a full and thorough inquiry and, therefore, the High Court should have directed the respondent to initiate appropriate proceedings in which such an inquiry can be held ...'

Furthermore, the Supreme Court (at 264, para 5) reaffirmed para 31 of the judgment in *Dhanwanti Joshi's* case, 1997 (8) SC 720 (reproduced above). *Sarita Sharma's* case is the second ruling of its kind handed down by the Supreme Court of India altering the earlier dicta on child abduction law.

In another case, the Supreme Court of India dismissed a *habeas corpus* petition instituted by a mother seeking custody of her two minor children, where earlier contested custody orders had been passed by the Family Court awarding custody to the paternal grandmother of the minor children in question. In this particular case, *Saihba Ali* v. *State of Maharashtra,* JT 2003 (6) SC 79, the wife directly filed the *habeas corpus* petition in the Supreme Court of India under article 32 of the Constitution of India. The facts of the case are as follows.

The father of the minor children was serving a jail term in the United States. The mother contended that, under the terms of an order of a competent court of the United States, she being the mother and natural guardian had been granted the custody of her two minor children. Consequently, the mother petitioned for custody of her minor children along with their passports and travel documents.

The fourth respondent, the paternal grandmother of the children, by virtue of her defence, brought to the apex court's notice that the children were in her custody under the terms of an order passed by the competent Family Court in Nagpur. The Court also noted the fact that the writ petitioner, *i.e.* the mother, was a party to the said Family Court proceedings. Subsequently, the mother preferred an appeal before the Nagpur Bench of the Bombay High Court, which was later withdrawn. Counsel for the respondent grandmother contended that the Family Court order had assumed finality as to the custody of the children. Hence, the *habeas corpus* petition was not maintainable. She also contended that the Family Court, while granting the custody of minor children to her, had held the US custody order to be one without jurisdiction and not a decree; due notice of it should have been taken by the Indian courts under section 13 of the Civil Procedure Code, 1908.

The court accepted the submissions of the respondent paternal grandmother. The apex court held that the Indian Family Court order was an order passed by a competent court of jurisdiction. The apex court further held that the children were in legal custody, until the order was set aside by the superior courts. The court firmly concluded that the *habeas corpus* petition was not maintainable. The court was sympathetic to the mother, who had led a 5-year sustained campaign to reaffirm the visiting rights initially given to her by the Nagpur Family Court. But it also recognised the fact that the petitioner mother had remarried, and had had another child from the remarriage.

However, the Supreme Court, in order to carry out complete justice, passed orders in the interest and welfare of the minor children by liberalising the visitation rights of the petitioner mother earlier granted to her by the Court, to enable her to take her children out for an extended period of time on every weekday and at weekends. The tenor of the law laid down in this ruling is identical to that laid down in the above-mentioned cases of *Dhanwanti Joshi,* JT 1997 (8) SC 720 and *Sarita Sharma,* JT 2000 (2) SC 258. Though there is no mention at all of these two judgments or the earlier position of relevant case-law, in essence, the welfare of the minor children seems to be the paramount consideration in deciding custody rights of children in cases of broken marriages.

Clearly, in the above case, scant regard has been given to the foreign court custody order obtained by the mother, as it was held to be without jurisdiction. This ruling yet again fortifies the view that the courts in India will independently come to their own judgment in the given circumstances of the case, irrespective of foreign court child custody orders.

Before the above-mentioned 1997, 1999 and 2003 rulings were handed down by the Supreme Court of India, there was case-law to the contrary allowing enforcement of foreign court custody orders on the principle of comity on a case-by-case basis. Such orders were normally enforced by initiating *habeas corpus* proceedings in the High Court under article 226 of the Constitution of India where the child was located within the territorial jurisdiction of the High Court or directly in the Supreme Court of India under article 32 of the Constitution of India.

It is pertinent to mention that article 137 of the Constitution of India provides for review of judgments or orders made by the Supreme Court of India. Further, article 141 of the Constitution of India mandates that the law declared by the Supreme Court of India shall be final and binding on all courts within the territory of India.

Hence, the Supreme Court of India from time to time may change the law on any aspect of judicial interpretation, and this will bind all other courts in India. Therefore, the above recent views of the apex court lay down the current position of applicable law in matters of enforcement of foreign court child custody orders when sought to be implemented in India.

(c) Earlier contrary case-law

There is ample earlier case-law contrary to the law recently laid down in *Dhanwanti Joshi* and *Sarita Sharma*. One such Supreme Court of India ruling, *Surinder Kaur Sandhu* v. *Harbax Singh Sandhu,* AIR 1984 SC 1224, as noted in *Sarita Sharma* (262, para 5), read:

> *'We may add that the spouses had set up their matrimonial home in England where the wife was working as a clerk and the husband as a bus driver. The boy is a British citizen, having been born in England, and he holds a British passport. It cannot be controverted that, in these circumstances, the English Court had jurisdiction to decide the question of his custody. The modern theory of conflict of Laws recognises and, in any event, prefers the jurisdiction of the State which has the most intimate contact with the issues arising in the case. Jurisdiction is*

not attracted by the operation or creation of fortuitous circumstances such as the circumstance as to where the child, whose custody is in issue, is brought or for the time being lodged. To allow the assumption of jurisdiction by another State in such circumstances will only result in encouraging forum-shopping. Ordinarily, jurisdiction must follow upon functional lines. That is to say, for example, that in matters relating to matrimony and custody, the law of that place must govern which has the closest concern with the well-being of the spouses and the welfare of the offsprings of marriage. The spouses in this case had made England their home where this boy was born to them. The father cannot deprive the English Court of its jurisdiction to decide upon his custody by removing him to India, not in the normal movement of the matrimonial home but, by an act which was gravely detrimental to the peace of that home. The fact that the matrimonial home of the spouses was in England, establishes sufficient contacts or ties with that State in order to make it reasonable and just for the Courts of that State to assume jurisdiction to enforce obligations which were incurred therein by the spouses. [See International Shoe Company v. State of Washington, *90 L Ed 95 (1945): 326 US 310] which was not a matrimonial case but which is regarded as the fountainhead of the subsequent developments of jurisdictional issues like the one involved in the instant case). It is our duty and function to protect the wife against the burden of litigating in an inconvenient forum which she and her husband had left voluntarily in order to make their living in England, where they gave birth to this unfortunate boy.'*

In *Sarita Sharma* the Supreme Court also noted the earlier law laid down in *Elizabeth Dinshaw* v. *Arvand M. Dinshaw,* AIR 1987 SC 3. In this ruling the apex court had exercised summary jurisdiction regarding the return of the minor child. In *Dinshaw* it was also stressed that the interest and the welfare of the minor child is the predominant criterion in child custody matters. The earlier law laid down in *Surinder Kaur Sandhu* v. *Harbaksh Singh Sandhu,* AIR 1984 SC 1224 and *Dinshaw,* AIR 1987 SC 3 stands substantially modified with the recent mandate of law in *Dhanwanti Joshi,* 1997 (8) SC 720; *Sarita Sharma,* JT 2000 (2) SC 258 and *Sahiba Ali,* JT 2003 (6) SC 79.

Thus, it can be safely concluded that the exclusive emphasis of the apex court's verdict now is to safeguard the welfare of the children. Mere mechanical implementation of an order of the foreign court is no longer the final response of the court. Hence, irrespective of the dictate of a court of overseas jurisdiction, the Supreme Court of India still rightly insists on a proper evaluation of the best interests of the children of a broken marriage.

(d) Visiting rights cannot be denied

The Supreme Court of India, in a recent ruling in *N. Nirmala* v. *Nelson Jeyakumar,* JT 1999 (5) SC 223, held that depriving a mother of visiting rights was not justified.

This appeal was about the custody of a minor daughter. The respondent father was permitted to retain custody as legal guardian. A single judge of the High Court confirmed the custody of the minor daughter with the father but gave visiting rights to the appellant mother.

Against this order, passed by the Single Bench of the High Court, the appellant mother, in search of an order of custody, went on a further appeal before a Division Bench of the High Court, which by the impugned judgment dismissed the appeal and deprived the appellant mother of her visiting rights, to which there were no cross-objections on the part of the husband respondent. The matter went on further appeal to the Supreme Court on this judgment being questioned by the mother.

The apex court held in the above-mentioned judgment (at 223–224, para 3) as follows:

> *'In our opinion, such a further adverse order against the appellant was not justified. The interest of justice will be served if the order of the learned Single Judge continuing the custody of the minor child with the respondent and as confirmed by the Division Bench is maintained subject to the modification that visiting right which was denied to the appellant by the Division Bench be continued ....'*

Consequently, the apex court held that depriving the mother of her visiting rights was not justified. Hence, the spirit of the final judicial view is again in the best interest of the child, who was held entitled to receive the love and care of both parents.

(e) Orders relating to custody of children are interlocutory in nature

Justice Mukul Mudgal of the Delhi High Court, in the case of *Leeladhar Kachroo* v. *Umang Bhatt Kachroo*, 2005 (2) HLR 449 (457) para 21, reiterated the earlier position of law as follows:

> *'In* Jaiprakash Khadria v. Shyam Sunder Agarwalla, *II (2000) CLT 212 (SC): (2000) 6 SCC 598, it was held as under:*
>
> *"Orders relating to custody of children are by their very nature not final but are interlocutory in nature and subject to modification at any future time upon proof of change of circumstances requiring change of custody but such change in custody must be proved to be in the paramount interest of the child."'*

(f) *Habeas corpus* can also be issued by a person who is not a citizen of India

It is well established that a writ of *habeas corpus* can be issued to secure the custody of a minor child. This can be sought even by a person who is not a citizen of India, as was recently held in *Atya Shamim (Miss)* v. *Deputy Commissioner/Collector, Delhi (Prescribed Authority under Citizenship Act)*, AIR 1999 J&K 140. The Jammu and Kashmir High Court in this ruling reaffirmed *Dinshaw*, AIR 1987 SC 3 where the Supreme Court of India had issued a writ at the instance of a person who was not an Indian citizen.

(g) Welfare of the children is the paramount consideration in deciding custody matters

It may be stated that whether issues of child removal are domestic or international across borders, the underlining principle in determining their rights of care and custody is universal *i.e.*, the best interest and the welfare of the child. In doing so and adjudicating child custody matters, Courts, formulate an independent opinion after hearing both the parties and interviewing children, wherever possible. Ultimately, irrespective of the superior financial capacity of a parent or other preferential rights claimed by a parent, Courts always decide the matter after ascertaining the wishes of the children, wherever and whenever possible, and upon determining the best interest of the child. The welfare of the child is a paramount consideration and a foreign court order granting custody to a parent is only one of the factors which will weigh before the Court in determining who gets the custody of the child. It may further be added that in such a process, the Court may even grant custody to a grand parent, in preference to a natural parent, if the Court forms an opinion that the welfare of the child will be prejudiced upon the custody remaining with a natural parent. In doing so, the Courts also jump the statutory hurdle requiring a natural parent, when alive, to be declared unfit, before granting custody to a person who is not the natural parent of the child. This universal formula has been reiterated in the following decisions stretching over a span of about 50 years as can be noticed from a tabulated list of decisions which are set down as hereunder. The relevant paragraphs and pages of the judgments where this discussion and decision to adjudicate on the best interest of a child finds mention is quoted in the following judgments tabulated hereunder for purpose of ready reference..

1.	*Harbans Singh* v. *Vidya Wanti,* AIR 1960 Pun 372 at para 6 page 35
2.	*Captain Rattan Amol Singh* v. *Smt. Kamaljit Kaur,* AIR 1961 Punj 51 (DB) at paras 13, 17 & 21, pages 41-43
3.	*Shanti Devi* v. *Rattan Chand,* AIR 1962 Punj 367 at para 2 page 45
4.	*Rosy Jacob* v. *Jacob A. Chakramakkal,* AIR 1973 SC 2090 at para 14 pages 9, 10 & 11
5.	*Shri Babu Ram* v. *Shri Keshwa Chand Joshi,* AIR 1978 Punj 174 at paras 5 & 6 pages 50, 51
6.	*Sawarn Singh* v. *Narinder Singh,* 1983 HLR 79 at paras 3 and 5 page 53
7.	*Bharat Bhushan* v. *Smt. Kaushalya,* 1991 (2) HLR 226 at para 6, page 60
8.	*Kirti Kumar Joshi* v. *Pradipkumar Joshi,* (1992) 3 SCC 573, at para 7 page 14
9.	*Shantabai Sonu* v. *Gautam Vishnu,* 1995 (1) HLR 107 Bom (DB) at paras 5, 7, 10, pages 66-68
10.	*Gian Chand* v. *Sudha,* AIR 2000 Punj 208 at paras 6 & 7, pages 62, 63
11.	*Nil Ratan Kundu* v. *Abhijit Kundu,* (2008) 9 SCC 413 at paras 56, 62 63, 74 & 83, pages 28, 29, 30, 31 & 32
12.	*Sarbati* v. *Phoolwati,* 2009 (1) ILR Punj 488 at paras 10, 20 & 22, pages 56-58

Therefore, the universal principle of the best interest of the child is the prevailing mandate in all matters of inter-parental child custody, be it domestic or inter-country issues. For this process, the Court may adopt any suitable method for such adjudication of child rights.

III. RELEVANT LEGISLATION AND FORUM FOR CUSTODY PROCEEDINGS

As far as the forum for securing the return of the children is concerned, it is important to mention that India is not a signatory to the Hague Convention on the Civil Aspects of International Child Abduction, 1980. Under article 226 of the Constitution of India, a parent whose child has been abducted can petition the State High Court to issue a writ of *habeas corpus* against the abducting spouse for the return of the child. Alternatively, a *habeas corpus* petition seeking recovery of the abducted child can be directly filed in the Supreme Court of India under article 32 of the Constitution of India.

With respect to the relevant legislation, the mother could well seek recourse to the provisions of the Hindu Minority and Guardianship Act, 1956 (HMGA, 1956), which is an Act to amend and codify certain parts of the law relating to minority and guardianship among Hindus. The provisions of HMGA, 1956 are supplemental to the earlier Guardians and Wards Act, 1890. HMGA, 1956, like the Hindu Minority Act, 1955, has extra-territorial application. It extends to the whole of India except the State of Jammu and Kashmir. Under section 4(a) of the HMGA, 1956, 'minor' means a person who has not reached the age of 18 years. A 'guardian' in section 4(b) is defined as a person having the care of the person of the minor or of his property or both and includes a natural guardian, a guardian appointed by will of the minor's natural parents, a guardian appointed or declared by a court and a person empowered to act as such under any enactment.

(a) India and the Hague Convention on Civil Aspects of International Child Abduction, 1980

Currently, India is not a party to the Hague Convention on Civil Aspects of International Child Abduction, 1980. Other than the statutory provisions of law quoted above in which matters of child custody are argued in different courts in different proceedings, the principles of the Hague Convention cannot be enforced in Indian courts. Different recent decisions indicate a trend that Indian courts generally tend to decide the inter-parental child custody disputes on the paramount consideration of the welfare of the child and the best interest of the child. A foreign court custody order is only one of the considerations in adjudicating any such child custody dispute between parents. Foreign court orders of child custody are no longer mechanically enforced and normally the courts go into the merits of the matter to decide the best interest of the child irrespective of any foreign court custody order. Hence, the position of law in India varies from case to case and there is no uniform precedent which can be quoted or cited as a universal rule.

(b) The position of Indian law on child abduction

Under article 214 of the Constitution of India, there shall be a High Court for each state in India and under article 124 there shall be a Supreme Court of India. Under article 141, the law declared by the Supreme Court shall be binding on all courts within India. However, the Supreme Court may not be bound by its own earlier views and can render new decisions. Part III of the Constitution secures 'fundamental rights' to citizens, which can be enforced directly in the respective High Courts of the states or directly in the Supreme Court of India by issue of prerogative writs under articles 226 and 32 respectively of the Constitution of India.

The High Courts and the Supreme Court in India entertain petitions for issuance of a writ of *habeas corpus* for securing the custody of the minor at the behest of a parent who lands on Indian soil alleging violation of a foreign court custody order or seeks the return of children to the country of their parent jurisdiction. Invoking of this judicial remedy provides the quickest and most effective solution.

Different High Courts within India have from time to time expressed different views in matters of inter-parental child custody petitions when their jurisdiction has been invoked by an aggrieved parent seeking to enforce a foreign court custody order or implementation of their parental rights upon removal of the child to India without parental consent. The Supreme Court of India too has rendered different decisions with different viewpoints on the subject in the past three decades. A quick summary of Indian law laying down this position is as follows:

(1) In *Marggarate* v. *Chacko,* AIR 1970 Ker 1, in deciding if custody and care of a child could be entrusted to a parent who was living outside the country and outside the Court's jurisdiction, it was held that where the welfare of the child so demands, the Court can also permit the child to be taken out of the country by one of the parents, with proper safeguards laid down by the court.

(2) In *Marilynn Anita Dhillon Gilmore* v. *Margaret Nijjar,* 1984 (1) ILR (P&H) 1, in a *Habaes Corpus* Petition, it was held that respecting the order of the foreign court, the custody of the children who were US nationals and who were brought to India from USA, should be returned to the mother as per the US court order, subject to the safeguards of this Court.

(3) In *Surinder Kaur* v. *Harbax Singh Sandhu,* 1984 HLR 780 (SC), it was held that the provisions of HMGA, 1956 cannot supersede the paramount consideration as what is conducive to the welfare of the child while exercising summary jurisdiction in returning the minor children to the foreign country of their origin.

In *Elizabeth Dinshaw* v. *Arvand M. Dinshaw,* AIR 1987 SC 3, the Court again exercising summary return of a removed child upheld the right of a foreigner mother to directly invoke the jurisdiction of the Supreme Court to seek the custody of a minor child from his father on the principle that the matter is to be decided not on the considerations of the legal rights of the parties but on the sole and predominant criterion of the best interest of the minor child.

(3) In *Kuldeep Sidhu* v. *Chanan Singh,* AIR 1989 P&H 103, in a criminal writ petition exercising summary return, it was held that the welfare of the children who were Canadian citizens would override any consented custody arrangement and the children have a right to be brought up in the culture and environment of the country of their birth.

(4) In *Amita Gautam* v. *Ramesh Gautam,* 1989 (2) HLR P&H 385, following the above decisions, it was held that the orders of the Canadian Court granting interim custody to the mother must be honoured by restoring forthwith the custody of the minor to the mother who had been removed from Canada to India by the father without authorisation.

(5) In *Sarvajeet Kaur Mehmi* v. *State of Rajasthan,* (1987 (2) HLR Raj 607 the custody of the minor child was given to the mother without hearing the father in view of the orders passed by the High Court of Justice (Family Division), UK, requesting the courts in India to pass necessary orders and issue directions seeking the return of the minor back from India to the UK.

(6) In *Kala Aggarwal* v. *Suraj Prakash Aggarwal,* 1993 (1) HLR Del 145, despite the children being brought to India from the United States in violation of US Court custody orders, the Court upholding the petition only granted access but declined to grant custody to the mother by concluding that the children's welfare was with the father until they attained majority.

(7) In *Jacqueline Kapoor* v. *Surinder Pal Kapoor,* 1994 (2) HLR P&H 97, following earlier precedents, the Court upheld the mother's petition seeking custody of her minor daughter in accordance with the orders of the competent court in Germany and directed that the child be handed over to the mother as the judgment of the German Court was binding on the father who had removed the child to India by deceitful means.

(8) In *Atya Shamim* v. *Deputy Commissioner/Collector Delhi,* AIR 1999 J&K 140, a *habeas corpus* petition by a person who was not a citizen of India was held to be maintainable to secure the custody of a minor.

(9) In *Dhanwanti Joshi* v. *Madhav Unde,* (1998) 1 SCC 112, the Supreme Court observed that the order of the foreign court will only be one of the facts which must be taken into consideration while dealing with child custody matters and India being a country which is not a signatory to the Hague Convention, the law is that the court within whose jurisdiction the child is removed will consider the question on its merits bearing the welfare of the child as of paramount importance. It is in this case that the Supreme Court changed the earlier view and did not exercise summary jurisdiction in returning the removed children to their parent country.

(10) The above observations by the Supreme Court of India were followed in its later decision in *Sarita Sharma* v. *Sushil Sharma,* JT 2000 (2) SC 258. Thereafter, in *Sahiba Ali* v. *State of Maharashtra,* 2004 (1) HLR 212, the Supreme Court declined to grant the custody of her children to the mother but at the same time issued directions for the grant of visitation rights in the interest and welfare of the minor children.

(11) In *Paul Mohinder Gahum* v. *State of NCT of Delhi,* 2005 (1) HLR 428, upholding a *habeas corpus* petition, the High Court held that the orders passed by foreign courts granting custody take a back seat in preference to what lies in the best interest of the minor rather than what a foreign court has directed.

(12) In *Eugenia Archetti Abdullah* v. *State of Kerala,* HLR 2005 (1) (Ker) 34, upholding the right of the US citizen, *i.e.,* the petitioner mother before the Court in a *habeas corpus* petition, the custody of the children was handed over to the mother after holding that the High Court can exercise such jurisdiction under article 226 of the Constitution of India.

(13) In *Leeladhar Kachroo* v. *Umang Bhat Kachroo,* 2005 (2) HLR Del 449, upholding the order of a Canadian Court granting custody to the mother of her younger son and allowing him to go back to Canada, the Court held that it has the jurisdiction to order the travel out of the country of the minor child with one of the parents and the mere possibility of losing jurisdiction would not dissuade the Court from permitting the departure of the child with the parent in the interest of the child. Hence, the Court held that it was empowered to entrust the custody of a child to a parent who resides outside its jurisdiction, if it is conducive to the welfare of the child.

(14) In *Paul Mohinder Gahun* v. *Selina Gahun,* 2007 (1) RCR (Civil) 129, it was held that, where the wife, husband and the minor girl child were all Canadian citizens and where the wife had stealthily come to India with the minor daughter, the Indian Guardian Court at Delhi had no jurisdiction to try and decide the petition of the mother for a guardianship order as their matrimonial home was in Canada where the child was ordinarily resident.

(15) In a judgment dated 3 March, 2006 of the High Court of Bombay at Goa, reported as *Mandy Jane Collins* v. *James Michael Collins,* 2006 (2) HLR Bom 446, between a 62-year-old American father and 39-year-old British mother resident in Ireland litigating over the custody of their 8-year-old minor daughter said to be illegally detained in Goa by the father, the Court declining to issue a writ of *habeas corpus* held that the parties could pursue their remedies in normal civil proceedings in Goa. The Court dismissing the mother's plea for custody concluded that the question of permitting the child to be taken to Ireland without first adjudicating upon the rival contentions of the parents in normal civil proceedings in Goa was not possible and directed that the status quo be observed. This in effect meant that the 8-year-old minor girl must continue to live in Goa without her mother or any other female family member in the father's house. In a challenge to this decision by the mother before the Supreme Court of India, the appeal was dismissed on 21 August, 2006, leaving it open to the parties to move the appropriate forum for the custody of the child, which if done, was directed by the Supreme Court to be decided within a period of 3 months with earlier visitation rights continuing for the mother.

(16) In another matter reported as *Ranbir Singh* v. *Satinder Kaur Mann,* 2006 (3) Punj LR 571, the Punjab and Haryana High Court declined to issue a writ of *habeas corpus* to the petitioner father residing in Malaysia who was seeking release of his 5-year-old son and 3-year-old daughter from their mother's custody in India. The High Court of Malaya at Kuala Lumpur had held that the petitioner was entitled to the legal guardianship of the said minor children. However, the High Court in India, declining to enforce the foreign judgment of the Malaysian High Court, held that the matter could be re-argued before the appropriate forum with regard to the custody of the children on the basis of evidence to be adduced by

parties. The *habeas corpus* petition was dismissed with the observation that it would be open to either party to move for custody of the minor children under appropriate law before an appropriate forum

(17) In *Kulwinder Dhaliwal* v. *State of Punjab,* ILR 2008 (2) P&H 730, decided by the Punjab and Haryana High Court on July 21, 2008, in a writ of Habeas Corpus, it was held that the orders of the Foreign Court giving custody of the minors to the petitioner deserves to be respected and the children were directed to be handed over to the petitioner with liberty to take them to Canada. The children were citizens of Canada and by an order passed by the Ontario Superior Court of Justice; the custody of the minors was given to the petitioner.

(18) In Criminal Writ Petition No. 1076 of 2008, *Paramjeet Kaur Toor* v. *Santosh Kaur,* decided by the Punjab and Haryana High Court on November 19, 2008, in a writ of *Habeas Corpus* it was directed that the custody of the minor children, who were British nationals and who were detained by the grand parents in India, be handed over to the mother along with their passports to enable them to return to England and that any contentions sought to be made can be thereafter agitated before the High Court of Justice, Family Division, London, which at that point of time was already hearing the matter and had passed orders for the return of the children.

(19) In Criminal Writ Petition No. 608 of 2008, *Manjit Kaur* v. *State of Punjab,* decided by the Punjab and Haryana High Court on August 14, 2008, where a minor child of 9 months was taken away by his grandparents when their non-resident Indian daughter-in-law had come from abroad for a short period, the High Court held that the *Habeas Corpus* Petition filed by her was maintainable as the child had been illegally snatched away from the mother. The custody of the minor child was handed over to the mother leaving the parties to avail other remedies in accordance with law.

(20) In Criminal Writ Petition No. 543 of 2008, *Gippy Arora* v. *State of Punjab,* decided by the Punjab and Haryana High Court on November 25, 2008, reported as 2012 (4) RCR (Civil) 397, the court after examining the entire law on the subject held in a case of domestic child abduction that a writ of *Habeas Corpus* should not be dismissed merely because it is for the Court of the Guardian Judge to determine the question of welfare of the minor child in custody of another person. Consequently, the minor child was directed to be handed over to the mother till the matter was finally decided by the Family Court or the Guardian Judge.

(21) In *Gurmeet Kaur Batth* v. *State of Punjab,* 2009 (2) Punj LR 250 (P&H) the High Court held that it can exercise jurisdiction vested in it under article 226 of the Constitution of India by issuance of the writ of *Habeas Corpus* when the custody of the child had been taken away by one of the natural guardians by playing a fraud upon the other. Relying on the Canadian Court Order in favour of the petitioner mother, the Court held that since

the court of competent jurisdiction in Canada had held that the mother is entitled to the custody of the child, she will be permitted to take the child with travel documents to Canada.

(22) In *Shilpa Aggarwal* v. *Aviral Mittal*, decided on 9 December, 2009, (2010) 1 SCC 591, a three and a half year old girl child, who was a British citizen born in USA to Indian parents was removed to India from USA by the mother in contravention of British Court orders. The mother was directed by the Supreme Court of India to return with the child to USA.

(23) In *Dr. V. Ravi Chandaran* v. *Union of India decided* on 17 November, 2009 (2010) 1 SCC 174, a seven year old boy, who was a US citizen and was born in USA to Indian Parents (who had become US citizens) was removed to India from USA by the mother contrary to US Court orders. The mother was directed by the Supreme Court of India to return to USA with the child failing which the father would be entitled to do so to take the child to USA.

(24) In *Vikramvir Vohra* v. *Shalini Bhalla*, decided on 25 March 2010, JT 2010 (3) SC 213, it was held by the Supreme Court of India that child custody orders are interlocutory in nature and can be altered for the welfare of the child. Consequently, the Supreme Court permitted the mother to take her minor son aged about ten years to Australia as per the wishes of the child to stay with the mother upholding the welfare of the child as a paramount consideration.

(25) In *Ruchi Majoo* v. *Sanjeev Majoo*, AIR 2011 SC 1952 the husband and wife were American citizens of India origin, and a child was born to them in America. They came to India on a vacation, along with the child. With mutual consent of parties, their plan to return to America changed and a decision was taken by them that the wife will stay back in India to explore career options. The minor son was allowed to stay back and was admitted to a school in Delhi. The husband filed a petition in the US Court, seeking divorce and also custody of the minor child, leveling allegations of child abduction against the mother and the US Court issued a red corner notice. The mother took refuge in a petition filed before the Guardian Judge, Delhi, under the Guardian and Wards Act, 1890, claiming custody of the child and the interim custody was granted to the mother. The father impugned this in appeal before the High Court at Delhi which dismissed the custody case before the Guardian Judge, Delhi, holding that the Guardian Judge Delhi had no jurisdiction as the child was not resident at Delhi. In further appeal by the mother, the Supreme Court reversed the order of the Delhi High Court and ordered that the proceedings before the Guardian Judge will be disposed off on merits as expeditiously as possible. Interim custody was restored to the mother with visitation rights to the father. The Supreme Court held that *"(i) Principle of Comity of Courts ensures that foreign Judgments and orders are unconditionally conclusive of the matters in controversy, but in the matter of custody of child interest and welfare of the minor being paramount, a competent*

court in this country is entitled and indeed duty bound to examine the matter independently, taking the foreign judgment, if any, only as an input for its final adjudication. (ii) In the facts of the case instant repatriation of child to America could not be allowed on principle of comity of Courts as interest of the minor shall be better served if he continued in the custody of his mother especially when father contracted a second marriage."

(26) In *Chandrashekar Mungerveli Puttappa* v. *Commissioner of Police, Chennai Suburban,* 2011 (3) MLJ (Cri) 289, the matter related to the custody of a minor child born to Indian parents who were settled in America. Differences arose between husband and wife and the wife left USA with child aged 2 years. It was held by the Madras High Court that the wife was not guilty of the illegal act of abduction, as there was no order of U.S. Court regarding custody of minor child. The husband, having obtained a decree of divorce from a Court in USA, would not entitle him to obtain custody of child. The High Court observed that the question of custody of the minor has to be decided considering paramount interest and welfare of child. It further said that the presence of minor in India is not illegal. The custody of the child was given to the mother as the return of the minor child to USA was not regarded to be in favour of the interest of the child.

(27) In *Philip David Dexter* v. *State NCT of Delhi,* 2013 (3) DMC 45, the wife obtained an *ex-parte* interim custody order from the Guardian Judge, Delhi. The husband contested the proceedings contending that the divorce and custody petition had been settled in South Africa by a consent arrangement and the child had been removed in violation of the South African Court orders. Thereupon, the Guardian Judge, Delhi held that it had no jurisdiction to try the matter as the child was not resident in Delhi. In a Habeas Corpus petition by the father, and in an appeal by the wife, both heard jointly by the Delhi High Court, it was directed that the wife should return the custody of child to the father before the Registrar of High Court since the wife had abducted the child and brought her to India, violating the joint custody order and had no evidence to *prima facie* justify that there was risk of grave danger to the life of child on return to the Republic of South Africa. The wife's appeal is still pending before the Supreme Court.

(28) In *Arathi Bandi* v. *Bandi Jagadrakshaka Rao,* AIR 2014 SC 918, a decree of dissolution of marriage was obtained from a US Court. The custody of child was given to husband. The wife thereafter travelled to India along with child in defiance of the US Court order. The husband then came to India and filed a *Habeas Corpus* petition before the High Court seeking production of the child and permitting him to take custody of the minor in compliance with the order passed by the US Court. The High Court directed the wife to submit to the jurisdiction of the US Courts. An appeal by the wife was dismissed by Supreme Court which held that: *"(i) A parent doing wrong by removing children out of the country does not gain any advantage by his or her wrongdoing; and (ii) Contention that the American*

court, which passed the order/decree has no jurisdiction and being inconsistent in Indian Laws cannot be executed in India is not tenable"

The above is the consolidated case-law summary on inter-parental removal of children from foreign jurisdictions to India and the decisions in different courts in India as a non-Convention country.

(c) Position of foreign court orders in India

The principles governing the validity of foreign court orders are laid down in section 13 of the Indian Code of Civil Procedure (CPC). The CPC is an Act to consolidate and amend the laws relating to the procedure of the Courts of Civil Judicature in India. The principles in section 13 of the CPC have been affirmed in relation to the guidelines laid down by the Supreme Court of India on recognition of foreign matrimonial judgments.

It is reiterated, as discussed above, that Indian courts would not exercise summary jurisdiction to return the children to the country of habitual residence. The courts consider the question on the merits of the matter, with the welfare of the children being of paramount importance.

Section 14 of the CPC talks of presumption as to foreign judgments. It provides that the court shall presume, upon the production of any document purporting to be a certified copy of a foreign judgment, that such judgment was pronounced by a court of competent jurisdiction, unless the contrary appears on the record; but such presumption may be displaced by proving want of jurisdiction.

(d) The position of Indian law on shared residence orders

Under the relevant Indian statute law pertaining to child custody matters, that is HMGA, 1956 supplemented with the provisions of the Guardians and Wards Act 1890, there exists no concept of shared residence orders. However, there is one recent judgment of the Kerala High Court, reported as *Eugenia Archetti Abdullah* v. *State of Kerala,* 2005 (1) HLR (Ker) 34, where on the facts and circumstances of the case the Court handed down an order, which was close to a shared custody order. This was in a case where divorce and custody proceedings were pending in the United States and the mother was held to be entitled to custody of the children until a final decision was announced by the courts in the United States. The facts of the case are outlined below.

The petitioner wife, the respondent husband and the children were all US citizens. The petitioner wife had approached the Court with a *habeas corpus* petition seeking a direction that the respondents numbers 2 to 4 produce two infants named Roshan and Nishant before the Court and to hand over their custody with their passports to the petitioner, their mother. The two infant twins were less than 3 years old.

The petitioner and the respondent got married while in the United States after which they moved to Bahrain where the petitioner gave birth to the two children. Because of the shift of employment they went back to the state of Texas in the United States and settled there. According to the petitioner, their married life was not happy which led to domestic violence by the second respondent (the husband). This resulted in a criminal case. Finally, the matter was settled. The respondent lost his employment in Texas and both of them with their children visited India and came to Kozhikode in the state of Kerala where the second respondent had his roots. While there, according to the petitioner, there was again ill-treatment by the second respondent and the petitioner was thrown out of the residential house and was forced to fly back to the United States without the children. According to her, the custody of the children by the respondent was an act of illegal custody and hence they were illegally detained. The petitioner wife had already moved a petition for custody of the children as well as for the dissolution of the marriage with the second respondent, in accordance with the family law applicable in the state of Texas in the United States.

In light of the facts and circumstances of the case, the Court, while granting custody of the children to the petitioner wife, laid down rigorous conditions, one of which was shared custody/visitation rights for a period of 7 days from the time of the court order to the time the petitioner wife left India. In this regard it is necessary to refer to para (e) of the guidelines, mentioned below, laid down in the judgment. *Secondly,* the judgment is relevant to the facts of the case in hand, because it allowed continued access/visitation rights to the respondent spouse to meet up with his minor children for 3 hours everyday, although quite limited and laying down contingency measures in the event of violation of the said conditions by the petitioner wife.

Paragraph 24 at 41 of the judgment above, stipulating the guidelines, reads as follows:

'(a) *The petitioner shall furnish a bank guarantee for 7,500 US dollars before she takes the children to the United States. The bank guarantee shall be in the name of the Registrar of the Court.*

(b) *She shall also execute a bond for another amount of 7,500 dollars, undertaking to produce the children before this Court as and when ordered.*

(c) *The petitioner shall also obtain an undertaking from the US Embassy or US Consulate in Madras that whenever this Court requires, with a notice of 15 days, she shall be present and shall produce the children at her own expenditure, and that in case of her failure, the Texas/US Administration including the Embassy will see that the directions of this Court in this regard are complied with and the children be produced before this Court.*

(d) *She can take the children to Texas only on fulfillment of the aforesaid conditions and on expiry of the period mentioned (1) below.*

(e) *The petitioner, shall, from tomorrow onwards, for 7 days, stay in Kozhikode so that the 2nd respondent shall have frequent visit to the children between 10 a.m. and 1.00 p.m. during the said seven days. Until she leaves India, the children shall be regarded as in the joint custody of both, so that the 2nd respondent shall have visitorial rights on the children.*

(f) *The 2nd respondent shall entrust the passport of the children and their birth certificates with the Registrar of this Court within a week from today and the Registrar shall give appropriate receipt to him.*

(g) *The petitioner shall send bi-monthly reports about the health of the children from the Senior Pediatrician of at least 20 years of practice, duly attested by a notary or the Indian Embassy/Consulate in US.*

(h) *The petitioner shall not remove herself or the children from her present address shown in this petition, i.e.:*

[address deleted by authors for confidentiality]

(i) *She shall not, except to take the children to India as per the order, if any, to be passed by this Court, take them beyond the State of Texas.*

(j) *In case of any default or violation of any of the conditions in this judgment by the petitioner, or in case of any emergency in respect of the children the second respondent is free to fly to Texas and for that he can obtain sufficient amount from out of the bank guarantee provided by the petitioner.*

(k) *Whenever the second respondent goes to Texas, the petitioner shall provide him the visitorial rights always to see the children and shall put them in his company.*

(l) *Even if the petitioner complies with all the conditions, we make it clear that she shall not take the children out of India for a period of three weeks from today.*

(m) *A copy of the passport of the petitioner and the children, duly attested by the Registrar of this Court with the seal of this Court, shall be regarded as a duly original passport for the purpose of their travel inside India.*

(n) *If the petitioner doesn't comply with the aforesaid conditions, the petitioner's passport as well as the passports and the birth certificate given to her as mentioned in direction (m) shall be returned to the Registrar.*

(o) *If the petitioner happens to leave without complying with the above directions, necessarily, she shall leave the custody of the children to the 2nd respondent.*

(p) *The petitioner shall not, except for going to Calicut and Chennai, leave her present address in Ernakulam.*

(q) *This arrangement in terms of this judgment will be in force until the Family Court at Texas, where the petitioner has instituted a* lis, *passes any interim or final order, as the case may be, regarding the custody of the children. We make it clear that any such order passed by the Court at Texas will override the directions contained in this judgment.*

Writ petition is disposed of as above.'

In another reported case of the Delhi High Court, *Leeladhar Kachroo* v. *Umang Bhat Kachroo*, 2005 (2) HLR Del 449, upholding the order of a Canadian Court granting custody to the mother of her younger son and allowing him to go back to Canada, the Court upheld the contention that it has jurisdiction to order travel out of the country of the minor child with one of the parents and the mere possibility of losing jurisdiction would not dissuade the Court from permitting the departure of the child with the parent in the interest of the child. Hence, the Court held that it was empowered to entrust the custody of a child to a parent who resides outside its jurisdiction, if it is conducive to the welfare of the child.

In the above mentioned case, the custody of the older son, who was residing with the father, was not in question and the case was confined to determining the custody of the younger son. However, it must be noted here that this is a particular reported case, looking in the round at the custody of two children, between the husband and the wife in two different countries. But, it does not talk of a situation looking at shared custody with respect to the same child.

In view of the fact that there is no statutory concept of a 'shared residence order' under Indian legislation, the Indian courts would view interpreting any such order of a foreign court in the light of the principle of the best interest of the child, maintaining the welfare of the child as of paramount consideration. Undoubtedly, access rights of the father can be enforced on the basis of a shared residence order and if such rights are violated, they can be enforced in an Indian court of law. However, this would be viewed as an enforcement of a private contractual arrangement between the parents. The court would still go into the welfare of the child to determine the rights of the child. Hence, the position would vary from case to case and there is no uniform principle which can be quoted as a universal rule.

(e) Value attached by the court to the wishes of the child

The court shall certainly consider the wishes of the parents and the minor child, but it is at the discretion of the court. As is evident from the case-law analysis, the paramount consideration is the welfare of the minor child.

Justice Mukul Mudgal of the Delhi High Court in the case of *Leeladhar Kachroo* v. *Umang Bhatt Kachroo,* 2005 (2) HLR 449 analysed some of the decided cases taking into consideration the wishes of the children in child custody matters. At 454, para 14 of the judgment, he reiterated the earlier position of law as follows:

> *'(b) In* Indira Khurana v. Prem Prakash, *60 (1995) DLT 633, the learned Single Judge of this Court held as under:—*
>
> *"10 . . . It goes without saying that when the grant of custody is concerned, ascertainment of wishes of the children, especially when they are at an age to make an intelligent preference is a relevant and germane consideration. In none of the cited cases, the question of visitation rights only was involved. In the cited cases, the Court was considering the grant of custody and while doing so, had also made provision for visitation rights. It is also significant that in these cases visitation rights were granted to the spouse who did not have the custody. This is because there should be very strong reasons to deny visitation rights to any of the spouse. These could be cases say where the grant of visitation rights could be injurious to the mental and physical health of the children.*
>
> *11. The Guardian Judge while exercising his judicious discretion in granting visitation rights can ascertain the wishes of the children by meeting them. In fact, it would be desirable to do so. However, omission to do so in case of visitation rights cannot be fatal especially when there is sufficient material on record available otherwise, supporting grant of visitation rights. This is so in the instant case. The memorandum of understanding had been entered into on the 6th day of December, 1993. The petitioner has not pointed out anything attributable*

to respondent after 6-12-1993, which would render grant of visitation rights to the respondent injurious to the mental and physical health of the children. The petitioner in terms of memorandum was willing to share the vacation and visitation rights to the respondent. Moreover the expression of wishes of children is very often conditioned by the persuasion of the party in whose exclusive custody the children have been. The Court, therefore, while ascertaining the mind of the children, has to be conscious of the fact that what the children say could be the reflection of the views of the estranged spouse induced by him/her."

(c) In Shyam Sunder Trikha v. Sunita, *67 (1997) DLT 619; 1997 IV AD (Del) 198, a learned Single judge of this Court held as under:—*

" ... The Court can only reiterate that the Guardian-Judge, while ascertaining mind of the child during a meeting has been conscious and cautious of the fact that what the child is saying could be reflection of the views of the estranged spouse and as induced by him/her."

The above judgments in the cases of *Indira Khurana* (supra) and *Shyam Sunder Trikha* (supra), in fact refer to the desirability of ascertaining the wishes of the children, I have also not discounted the possibility of the child being influenced by the parent he last stayed with. But even then in view of the overall circumstances of the case and taking into account the factors discussed hereinabove the impugned order has to be sustained except in relation to the enhancement of the amount of personal bond from Rs. 2 lakhs to Rs. 3 lakhs.'

In view of the position of the law quoted above, it is significant to note that the Indian courts would definitely ascertain the wishes and the feelings of the child before deciding on the issue of the custody of the child.

(f) No provision for mirror orders in India

In light of the prevailing child abduction law in India discussed above, it is not possible to obtain mirror orders, as this is only a concept known to the English and not to the Indian legal system. Since foreign court custody orders cannot now be mechanically enforced, it is suggested that, in the event of any litigation in the foreign country of habitual residence, a letter of request be obtained from the foreign court in which litigation is pending for incorporating safeguards and conditions to ensure the return of the minor child to the country of normal residence.

This letter of request should be addressed by the foreign court to the Registrar General of the High Court within whose jurisdiction the estranged spouse is residing with the minor child. It should also be specifically mentioned that the passports of both the parent and the child should be deposited with the Registrar General of the State High Court to ensure that the child is not taken away from the jurisdiction of the court where he or she is confined. However, despite the best of assurances, documentation, paperwork, affidavits and legal remedies adopted, none of the methods offer an iron clad guarantee for the return of the child to its parent Country upon coming to India.

(g) A possible solution

With the increasing number of non-resident Indians abroad and multiple problems leading to family conflicts, inter-parental child removal to India now needs to be resolved on an international platform. It is no longer a local problem. The phenomenon is global. Steps have to be taken by joining hands globally to resolve these conflicts through the medium of courts interacting with each other. Until India becomes a signatory to the Hague Convention, this may not be possible. It is no longer possible for the Indian courts to adapt to different foreign court orders arising in different jurisdictions. It is equally important that, in order to create a uniform policy of law, some clear, authentic and universal child custody law is enacted in India by adhering to the principles laid down in the Hague Convention. Divergent views emerging at different times may not be able to cope with the rising number of such cases, which appear from time to time for interpretation. We in India require an expeditious acceptance and implementation of the international principles of inter-parental child removal which are couched in the Hague Convention. Let us not delay the resolution of these disputes.

IV. LAW IN THE MAKING: AN AFTERMATH

Borders divide jurisdictions but families reunite them. The chain to this link is the global citizen. However, this inter-nation cross-flow has, with the passage of time, generated a new crop of legal issues in the realm of private international law which comprises rules a court would apply whenever there is a case involving a foreign element. Such legal dilemmas of the diaspora baffle systems of law but do not defy solutions if nations make conscious efforts to resolve such complications. Even in surrogacy matters, a statutory codified law is the need of the hour.

A fugitive non-resident Indian (NRI) parent, declared a proclaimed offender in matrimonial proceedings in India, cannot even see or talk to his children removed to India. A foreign court refuses to permit NRI children to be taken to India and likewise local courts decline to implement foreign court orders directing the return of NRI children. These occurrences find daily mention but no straightforward resolution for the NRI in any Indian law. International parental child abduction, defined as the removal or retention of a child across international borders by one parent which is either in contravention of court orders or is without the consent of the other parent, is sadly an increasing phenomenon which causes acute emotional distress to the abducted child.

The Indian diaspora is 30 million and swelling. The acute problems associated with this have fortunately led the Government to begin the process of acceding to the Convention. However, before that is done and India becomes a member of about 80 contracting Convention nations, appropriate Indian legislation will have to be enacted for its implementation. In this way children removed to and from India will be reunited with their aggrieved parent and India will no longer be a sought-after destination for placing removed NRI children from foreign jurisdictions. Also, foreign courts will be encouraged to permit NRI children to freely visit India without fear of abduction.

The draft of the Indian Civil Aspects of International Child Abduction Bill, 2007, meant to secure the prompt return of children wrongfully retained or removed to India, proposes to ensure that the rights of custody and access under laws of contracting states are respected by providing for prompt removal of wrongfully removed children. The salient and salutary features of this proposed law are as follows.

- The proposed law seeks to create a Central Authority for performance of duties under the Hague Convention for securing the return of removed children by instituting judicial proceedings in the relevant High Court.
- The appropriate authority or a person of a contracting country may apply to the Central Authority for the return of a removed child to the country of habitual residence.
- The High Court may order the return of a removed child to the country of habitual residence but may refuse to make such an order if there is grave risk of harm or if it would put the child in an intolerable situation. Consent or acquiescence may also lead to refusal for the return of a child by the Court.
- The High Court may refuse to return a child if the child objects to being returned upon the Court being satisfied that the child has attained an age and degree of maturity to take into account his views.
- The High Court before making an order of return may request the Central Authority to obtain from the relevant authorities of the country of habitual residence a decision or determination as to whether the removal or retention of the child in India is wrongful.
- The High Court upon making an order of return may direct that the person who has removed the child to India pay the expenses and costs incurred in returning the child to the country of habitual residence.

The creditable sacrosanct feature in recognising and retaining the jurisdiction of the High Court to protect the paramount consideration, *i.e.* the best interest and the welfare of the child, by carving out exceptions for grounds of refusal has upheld the majesty of law vested in the Indian courts. But at the same time, this proposed law will be a big relief to the children who have been removed from their parents. The temptation to wrongfully remove will also be deterred. The cruel abduction of NRI children for the purposes of forced marriages will also be checked.

Missing Children in India – Suggestions, Remedies and Solutions

I. INTRODUCTION

The Constitution of India enacted on the 26 November, 1949 resolved to constitute India as a Union of States and a sovereign, socialist, secular, democratic republic. Today, a population of over 1.2 billion Indians live in 29 States and 7 Union Territories within India besides about 30 million Indians who reside in foreign jurisdictions and are called non-resident Indians. Within the territory of India spread over an area of 3.28 million sq kms, the large Indian population comprised of multicultural societies professing and practising different religions and speaking different local languages coexist in harmony in one of the largest democracies in the world.

The Indian Parliament at the helm of affairs legislates on central subjects in the Union and concurrent lists, and state legislatures enact laws pertaining to state subjects as per the state and concurrent lists with regard to the subjects enumerated in the Constitution of India. Likewise, pertaining to the judiciary, under article 214 of the Indian Constitution there is a High Court for each state and under article 124 there is a Supreme Court of India. Under article 141 of the Constitution, the law declared by the Supreme Court is binding on all courts within the territory of India. However, the Supreme Court may not be bound by its own earlier views and can render new decisions.

Part III of the Constitution of India secures for its citizens 'Fundamental Rights' which can be enforced directly in the respective High Courts of the states or directly in the Supreme Court of India by issue of prerogative writs under articles 226 and 32 respectively of the Constitution of India. Under the constitutional scheme, amongst others, freedom of religion and the right to freely profess, practise and propagate religion is sacrosanct and is thus enforceable in the extraordinary writ jurisdiction.

Simultaneously Part IV of the Indian Constitution lays down 'Directive Principles of State Policy' which are not enforceable by any court but are nevertheless fundamental in the governance of the country and it is the duty of the state to apply these principles while making laws. Under article 44 of the Constitution in this Part ,the state shall endeavour to secure for the citizens a Uniform Civil Code throughout the territory of India. However, realistically speaking, to date a Uniform Civil Code remains an aspiration which India has yet to achieve and enact.

The Indian Penal Code, 1860 is a general penal code for India and extends to the whole of India. Chapter XVI of the Indian Penal Code (IPC) relates to 'Offences Affecting the Human Body' which include not merely culpable homicide (including one amounting to murder) but also 'hurt' (simple or grievous) and involves within its sweep cases of wrongful restraint, wrongful confinement, use of criminal force, assault simpliciter, kidnapping or abduction or trafficking in human beings and sexual offences including rape and unnatural offence. It is plain that the expression 'hurt', as defined in section 319 of the IPC includes causing of 'bodily pain, disease or infirmity' to any person. The offence of dowry death (section 304B) was added in 1986, along with the offence of cruelty by husband or relatives of husband (section 498A) in the wake of outrage felt by the civil society due to increased incidents of cases where women had been subjected to domestic violence and harassment soon after marriage.

The increase in the number of missing children in India and the need for a proper investigation in such cases of missing children, who due to their age and gender are more vulnerable to crimes, has become an alarming and a startling issue at the present time in India. A number of petitions have been filed before different High Courts in the country seeking formation of separate investigation cells for the search of missing children, involving officers having special knowledge and expertise in the matter. A news item appeared on 25 December, 2011 in the *Indian Express* (*Chandigarh Newsline*) titled, '943 missing since 2000, no sign of 54 abducted'. The news item was based on the data furnished by the police department of the union territory of Chandigarh. The statistics reveal that 943 persons from Chandigarh have been missing since 2000 and 54 persons who have been kidnapped since 2000 are yet to be traced. It has become a prime concern for the entire country that certain guidelines and measures are laid down in order to trace the missing children and to prevent an increase in the number of children missing or abducted in future. Before doing so, it may be useful to quote relevant extracts from synopsis of the book entitled *Missing Children of India [Bachpan Bachao Andolan Missing Children of India (Delhi: Vitasta Publishing Pvt. Ltd., 2011)]*, a pioneering study by the Bachpan Bachao Andolan (BBA) which is a leading child rights organisation in New Delhi. This book was released in December 2011 by BBA. Furthermore, the National Human Rights Commission report on missing children [*Report of the NHRC Committee on Missing Children (New Delhi: National Human Rights Commission, 2007)]* released in 2007 is also an authentic, detailed and wholesome study on the subject of missing children all over India. Both these studies are the basis of the present chapter to suggest remedies and solutions which can possibly be utilised and implemented as a measure for resolving this malady.

II. CRIMINAL OFFENCES AND PROCESS IN CRIMINAL MATTERS IN INDIA

The substantive law of crimes in India is contained in the Indian Penal Code (Act XLV of 1860) (IPC) which is governed by the procedure enacted in the Code of Criminal Procedure, 1973 (CrPC). Both are federal laws and apply uniformly throughout the territory of India.

Section 2(c) of the CrPC defines a 'cognizable offence' as an offence for which, and defines a 'cognizable case' as a case in which, a police officer may, in accordance with the First Schedule or under any other law for the time being in force, arrest without warrant.

Section 2(l) of the CrPC defines a 'non-cognizable offence' as an offence for which, and defines a 'non-cognizable case' as a case in which, a police officer has no authority to arrest without warrant.

An aggrieved person can approach a police station which falls in the jurisdiction of the area where the offence has been allegedly committed and can get his or her grievance recorded. The police are under a duty to record the complaint in the form of a Daily Diary Report (DDR).

(i) If upon inquiry, the police are of the opinion that a cognizable offence is made out in terms of the Indian Penal Code or any other law in force in India, then the DDR can be converted to a First Information Report (hereinafter referred to as FIR) under section 154 of the CrPC. An FIR is recorded by the police officer on duty upon information given either by the aggrieved person or any other person about the commission of an alleged offence and is followed by an investigation into the offence.

(ii) If, upon inquiry, the police are of the opinion that a non-cognizable offence is made out in terms of the IPC or any other law in force in India, then according to section 155 of the CrPC, the police officer shall enter or cause to be entered the substance of the information in a book to be kept by such officer in such form as may be prescribed by the state government from time to time (DDR). He shall then refer the informant to the magistrate.

(iii) According to section 155(2) of the CrPC, a police officer does not have the power to investigate a non-cognizable case without an order of a magistrate having power to try such a case or commit the case for trial.

Therefore, any person who is aggrieved on account of a criminal wrong having been committed against her or him on account of any offence having been made out in terms of the IPC or any other law in force in India has an option of making a grievance in three possible ways which are briefly explained here:

First, the aggrieved person can give the information relating to the commission of a cognizable/non-cognizable offence to an officer in charge of a police station as mentioned under sections 154 and 155 of the CrPC.

Section 154 of the CrPC is reproduced here for ready reference:

'154. Information in cognizable cases.

(1) *Every information relating to the commission of a cognizable offence, if given orally to an officer in charge of a police station, shall be reduced to*

writing by him or under his direction, and be read over to the informant; and every such information, whether given in writing or reduced to writing as aforesaid, shall be signed by the person giving it, and the substance thereof shall be entered in a book to be kept by such officer in such form as the State Government may prescribe in this behalf.

(2) A copy of the information as recorded under sub-section (1) shall be given forthwith, free of cost, to the informant.

(3) Any person, aggrieved by a refusal on the part of an officer in charge of a police station to record the information referred to in sub-section (1) may send the substance of such information, in writing and by post, to the Superintendent of Police concerned who, if satisfied that such information discloses the commission of a cognizable offence, shall either investigate the case himself or direct an investigation to be made by any police officer subordinate to him, in the manner provided by this Code, and such officer shall have all the powers of an officer in charge of the police station in relation to that offence.'

Secondly, if a person has a grievance that the police station is not registering the FIR under section 154 of CrPC, then that person can approach the superintendent of police under section 154(3) of the CrPC by an application in writing as stated above.

Thirdly, if the FIR is not registered in any way as mentioned above, then it is open to the aggrieved person to file an application under section 156(3) of the CrPC before the magistrate concerned. If such an application under section 156(3) is filed, the magistrate can direct the FIR to be registered.

The Supreme Court of India in *Sakiri Vasu* v. *State of Uttar Pradesh,* AIR 2008 SC 907 (908), para 11 has ruled at page 908 as follows:

'... if a person has a grievance that the police station is not registering his FIR under section 154, CrPC, then he can approach the Superintendent of Police under section 154(3), CrPC, by an application in writing. Even if that does not yield any satisfactory result in the sense that either the FIR is still not registered, or that even after registering it no proper investigation is held, it is open to the aggrieved person to file an application under section 156(3), CrPC before the learned Magistrate concerned. If such an application under section 156(3) is filed before the Magistrate, the Magistrate can direct the FIR to be registered and also can direct a proper investigation to be made, in a case where, according to the aggrieved person, no proper investigation was made. The Magistrate can also under the same provision monitor the investigation to ensure a proper investigation.'

Once the FIR has been registered, the investigation in the case commences. Investigation includes all the proceedings of the collection of evidence conducted by a police officer or by any person who is authorised by the magistrate on his behalf.

Section 156 of the CrPC in this regard which gives the powers to the police to investigate the cognizable offences is reproduced here:

'156. Police officer's power to investigate cognizable cases

(1) *Any officer in charge of a police station may, without the order of a Magistrate, investigate any cognizable case which a Court having jurisdiction over the local area within the limits of such station would have power to inquire into or try under the provisions of Chapter XIII.*

(2) *No proceeding of a police officer in any such case shall at any stage be called in question on the ground that the case was one which such officer was not empowered under this section to investigate.*

(3) *Any Magistrate empowered under section 190 may order such an investigation as above-mentioned.'*

According to the judgment of the Indian Supreme Court (above), even if after registering the FIR no proper investigation is conducted, it is open to the aggrieved person to file an application under section 156(3) of the CrPC before the magistrate concerned. If such an application under section 156(3) is filed before the magistrate, the magistrate can direct a proper investigation to be made. It may be added here that the magistrate can also under the same provision monitor the investigation to ensure a proper investigation.

The police while conducting the investigation of the case records the statements of the witnesses under section 161 of the CrPC. Section 157 of the CrPC casts a duty upon the investigating police officer to forthwith send the report of the cognizable offence, prepared under section 173 of the CrPC, to the concerned magistrate. The police officer is also under a duty to follow the procedure laid down in section 157 of the CrPC as follows:

'157. Procedure for investigation.

(1) If, from information received or otherwise, an officer in charge of a police station has reason to suspect the commission of an offence which he is empowered under section 156 to investigate, he shall forthwith send a report of the same to a Magistrate empowered to take cognizance of such offence upon a police report and shall proceed in person, or shall depute one of his subordinate officers not being below such rank as the State Government may, by general or special order, prescribe in this behalf, to proceed, to the spot, to investigate the facts and circumstances of the case, and, if necessary, to take measures for the discovery and arrest of the offender:

Provided that—

(a) *when information as to the commission of any such offence is given against any person by name and the case is not of a serious nature, the officer in charge of a police station need not proceed in person or depute a subordinate officer to make an investigation on the spot;*

(b) *if it appears to the officer in charge of a police station that there is no sufficient ground for entering on an investigation, he shall not investigate the case.*

(2) In each of the cases mentioned in clauses (a) and (b) of the proviso to sub-section (1), the officer in charge of the police station shall state in his report his reasons for not fully complying with the requirements to that sub-section,

and, in the case mentioned in clause (b) of the said proviso, the officer shall also forthwith notify to the informant, if any, in such manner as may be prescribed by the State Government, the fact that he will not investigate the case or cause it to be investigated.'

Thereupon, after all the evidence has been collected by the police, a report (called 'Challan') is filed in the court before a competent magistrate and thereafter, as prescribed in the CrPC, charges are framed by the court against the accused under section 211 of the CrPC. The court under section 211 of the CrPC has the power to alter the charges at any time during the trial but before the judgment.

Besides the procedural provisions quoted above, section 482 of the CrPC is also reproduced for ready reference:

'482. Saving of inherent power of High Court

Nothing in this Code shall be deemed to limit or affect the inherent powers of the High Court to make such orders as may be necessary to give effect to any order under this Code, or to prevent abuse of the process of any Court or otherwise to secure the ends of justice.'

It may be commented that, if there is any lacuna in the criminal process or there is failure to comply with the provisions of law or there is any apprehension to any part in any criminal litigation of any threat to life or personal liberty, the person can invoke the jurisdiction of the High Court directly in a petition under section 482 of the CrPC for seeking appropriate orders to secure the ends of justice.

In *Shankar Kisanrao Khade* v. *State of Maharashtra*, (2013) 5 SCC 546, deciding appeals concerned with the gruesome murder of a minor girl with intellectual disability, the Apex Court analyising in detail crime against children issued various directions to stake holders for compliance to prevent abuse of children as provided in Protection of Children against Sexual Offences Act, 2012, which are reproduced as hereunder for ready reference.

"55. I my opinion, the case in hand calls for issuing the following directions to various stake-holders for due compliance:

(1) *The persons in-charge of the schools/educational institutions, special homes, children homes, shelter homes, hostels, remand homes, jails etc. or wherever children are housed, if they come across instances of sexual abuse or assault on a minor child which they believe to have committed or come to know that they are being sexually molested or assaulted are directed to report those facts keeping upmost secrecy to the nearest S.J.P.U. or local police, and they, depending upon the gravity of the complaint and its genuineness, take appropriate follow up action casting no stigma to the child or to the family members.*

(2) *Media personals, persons in charge of Hotel, lodge, hospital, clubs, studios, photograph facilities have to duly comply with the provision of section 20 of the Act 32 of 2012 and provide information to the S.J.P.U., or local police. Media has to strictly comply with section 23 of the Act as well.*

(3) *Children with intellectual disability are more vulnerable to physical, sexual and emotional abuse. Institutions which house them or persons in care and protection, come across any act of sexual abuse, have a duty to bring to the notice of the J.J. Board/S.J.P.U. or local police and they in turn be in touch with the competent authority and take appropriate action.*

(4) *Further, it is made clear that if the perpetrator of the crime is a family member himself, then utmost care be taken and further action be taken in consultation with the mother or other female members of the family of the child, bearing in mind the fact that best interest of the child is of paramount consideration.*

(5) *Hospitals, whether Government or privately owned or medical institutions where children are being treated come to know that children admitted are subjected to sexual abuse, the same will immediately be reported to the nearest J.J. Board/ SJPU and the JJ Board, in consultation with SJPU, should take appropriate steps in accordance with the law safeguarding the interest of child.*

(6) *The non-reporting of the crime by anybody, after having come to know that a minor child below the age of 18 years was subjected to any sexual assault, is a serious crime and by not reporting they are screening offenders from legal punishment and hence be held liable under the ordinary criminal law and prompt action be taken against them, in accordance with law.*

(7) *Complaints, if any, received by NCPCR, S.C.P.C.R. Child Welfare Committee (CWC) and Child Helpline, NGO's or Women's Organizations etc., they may take further follow up action in consultation with the nearest J.J. Board, S.J.P.U. or local police in accordance with law.*

(8) *The Central Government and the State Governments are directed to constitute SJPUs in all the Districts, if not already constituted and they have to take prompt and effective action in consultation with J. J. Board to take care of child and protect the child and also take appropriate steps against the perpetrator of the crime.*

(9) *The Central Government and every State Government should take all measures as provided under section 43 of the Act 32/2012 to give wide publicity of the provisions of the Act through media including television, radio and print media, at regular intervals, to make the general public, children as well as their parents and guardians, aware of the provisions of the Act."*

In *Bachpan Bachao Andolan* v. *Union of India*, (2013) (7) SCALE 509, the Apex Court gave valuable directions to Government agencies for helping the cause of missing and abused children. In *Childline India Foundation* v. *Allan John Waters*, (2011) 6 SCC 261, deciding appeals against the common final judgment of the High Court of Bombay acquitting all the accused under the IPC, Cr.P.C and the Juvenile Justice Act, 2000 or child abuse, the Apex Court elaborating on constitutional provisions relating to protection of children, set aside the impugned High Court judgment and restored the conviction of all the accused as decided by the Trial Judge. The Apex Court held as follows:

"..30. The above analysis shows our Constitution provides several measures to protect our children. It obligates both Central, State and Union Territories

to protect them from the evils, provide free and good education and make them good citizens of this country. Several legislations and directions of this Court are there to safeguard their interest. But these are to be properly implemented and monitored. We hope and trust that all the authorities concerned through various responsible NGOs implement the same for better future of these children."

Earlier, in *Sakshi* v. *Union of India*, AIR 2004 SC 3566, deciding a public interest litigation to provide assistance to victims of sexual abuse and other atrocities, the Apex Court passed comprehensive directions for providing protection to children particularly in matters of criminal trials. However, now, with the enactment of Protection of Children against Sexual Offences Act, 2012, the call of the Court has been heeded in making a benevolent legislation.

In *State of Rajasthan* v. *Vinod Kumar*, AIR 2012 SC 2301, the Apex Court hearing appeals against award of conviction under section 376, IPC held that no reasons have been assigned by the High Court for reducing punishment less than the minimum sentence of 7 years. Therefore, the Court held that, *"Such an order is violative of the mandatory requirement of law and has defeated the legislative mandate. Deciding the case in such a casual manner reduces the criminal justice delivery system to mockery."* The Apex Court accordingly, restored the seven years rigorous imprisonment awarded by the Trial Court.

In *Shyam Narain* v. *The State of NCT of Delhi*, AIR 2013 SC 2209, the Apex Court hearing an appeal against conviction under section 376(2), IPC lamented that the victim, an eight years old girl had been *"deprived of the dreams of "Spring of life" and might be psychologically compelled to remain the "Torment of Winter."* The Supreme Court in its judicial discretion maintain the sentence of rigorous imprisonment for life for the heinous crime.

In Criminal Appeal Nos. 1278-1279 of 2013, *Shimbhu* v. *State of Haryana*, decided on August 27, 2013, while deciding appeals against the final judgment passed by the Punjab and Haryana High Court affirming the conviction by the Trial Court in matters of rape and sexual abuse, the Apex Court held that, *"This is yet another opportunity to inform the subordinate courts that despite stringent provisions for rape under section 376, IPC, many Courts in the past have taken a softer view while awarding sentence for such a heinous crime. This Court has in the past notice that few subordinate and High Courts have reduced the sentence of the accused to the period already undergone to suffice as the punishment by taking aid of the proviso to section 376(2), IPC. The above trend exhibits stark insensitivity to the need for proportionate punishments to be imposed in such cases."*

In *Medha Kotwal Lele* v. *Union of India*, AIR 2013 SC 93, considering the issue of sexual harassment in work places, the Apex Court has reiterated the need of the legislature to enact suitable legislation and till such time, guidelines have been provided to ensure protection to women at work place to prevent sexual harassment.

Likewise, in W.P (Crl.) No.129 of 2006 *Laxmi* v. *Union of India* decided on July 18, 2013, the Apex Court has on the lines of existing schemes, suggested that States and Union Territories who have not already done so, should make schemes under section 357A, Cr.P.C for providing funds for purposes of compensation to acid attack victims. The Court directed that acid attack victims shall be paid compensation of atleast Rs. 3 lacs by the concerned State Government/Union Territory as after care and rehabilitation cost.

An analysis of the judgments of the Apex Court rendered recently shows the acute sensitivity of the Court in matters pertaining to women and children, more particularly in the light of the heinous crimes committed to this vulnerable section of society where children at risk are subjected to grave dangers. The alarming sense of concern shown by the Supreme Court are extremely beneficial guidelines for trial courts to observe and implement child welfare laws strictly and seriously whilst making sure that no person who is guilty of heinous crimes against children goes free or unpunished.

III. EXTRACT FROM BACHPAN BACHAO ANDOLAN'S SYNOPSIS OF THE BOOK TITLED *MISSING CHILDREN OF INDIA* (2011)

The book *Missing Children of India (Bachpan Bachao Andolan Missing Children of India (Delhi: Vitasta Publishing Pvt Ltd, 2011))* is a compilation of information collected on missing children by Bachpan Bachao Andolan during the period from January 2008 to January 2010. This book gives the following findings and figures which are extracted for ready reference.

'The recent official figures (of Census 2011) related to children are yet to be published, but, figures regarding missing children (as per RTI, *i.e.* Right to information under the Right to Information Act, 2000, applications) show that 117,480 children were reported missing, 74,209 were traced and 41,546 remained untraced in two years between 2008 and 2010.'

A tabulated extract of the numbers of missing children state/union territory wise in the country for the period January 2008 to January 2010 follows:

Status of missing children (national)

Jan 2008–Jan 2010

S No	State/UTs	Reported	Traced	Untraced	NCRB* (200820010)
1	A&N	115	112	3	22
2	Andhra Pradesh	3,555	2,939	616	1,146
3	Arunachal Pradesh	243	152	91	30
4	Assam	2,686	551	410	12
5	Bihar	3,345	1,752	1,593	1,321
6	Chandigarh	156	116	40	63
7	Chhattisgarh	5,594	4,252	1342	226
8	Dadra & Nagar Haveli	48	39	9	19
9	Delhi	13,570	11,870	1,700	3,459
10	Goa	238	206	32	45
11	Haryana	185	146	39	253
12	HP	113	72	41	158
13	Jharkhand	320	178	142	45
14	Karnataka	9,956	6,522	3,434	175

S No	State/UTs	Reported	Traced	Untraced	NCRB* (200820010)
15	Kerala	2116	1900	216	197
16	MP	12,777	9,537	3,240	713
17	Maharashtra	26,211	18,706	7,505	1,244
18	Meghalaya	178	112	66	33
19	Mizoram	0	0	0	3
20	Nagaland	457	226	231	3
21	Sikkim	342	279	63	9
22	Uttar Pradesh	9,482	7,586	1,896	3,759
23	Uttarakhand	380	303	77	36
24	West Bengal	25,413	6,653	18,760	583
	TOTAL	117,480	74,209	41,546	13,554

*NCRB is National Crimes Record Bureau

In the synopsis of the book, the following findings have been attributed to the large number of missing children:

'Findings:

Some of the most significant findings of this study are:

- *No clear-cut definition of missing children as per legal system, which leads to confusion as to how the cases should be treated.*
- *No provision on addressing the issue of missing children in the Indian legal system.*
- *No comprehensive SOPs/Protocol for addressing the issue of missing children at the national level, involving all states/UTs and other stakeholders. (SOP – Standing Operations Procedure)*
- *No proper mechanism to document and update the database and information on the number of registered, traced and untraced cases of missing children.*
- *Lack of coordination between the agencies dealing with the missing children for example police, NCRB/SCRB/DCRB and NGOs/CSOs. (NCRB – National Crime Records Bureau, SCRB – State Crime Records Bureau, DCRB – District Crime Records Bureau, NGOs – Non-Government Organisations, CSOs – Civil Society Organisations)*
- *Urban centres have high number of children reported missing.*
- *Areas with better connectivity and facility of transport and communications have high number of missing children.*
- *States and districts with international borders also have large number of children registered missing.*
- *Regions with migratory population, including slums, are registering more missing children.*
- *Children and families from socially and economically poorer background formed the majority of victims.'*

In the light of the findings given in the book, Bachpan Bachao Andolan has made its recommendations and suggests a plan of action that needs to be followed in order to deal with the disturbing issue of the rise in the cases of the missing children all over the country.

IV. EXTRACT FROM THE NHRC REPORT (2007)

It is further pertinent to analyse the approximate number of missing children complaints that are increasing over the years. For this purpose, the National Human Rights Commission (NHRC) Report (*Report of the NHRC Committee on Missing Children (New Delhi: National Human Rights Commission, 2007))* may be the most relevant document. The NHRC was constituted in India under the protection of Human Rights Act, 1993, for better protection of human rights and for matters connected therewith or incidental thereto. The NHRC Report is based on an exhaustive study on the subject of missing children in India. For purposes of ready reference, an extract from Executive Summary of the NHRC Report follows:

> *'India is home to more than 400 million children below the age of 18 years, and is considered one of the countries in which youth and children comprise more than 55% of the population. These children represent diverse cultures, religions, castes, communities & social and economic groups. The Government is undoubtedly committed to doing its best for children. However, despite its best efforts, there are innumerable children who are subjected to exploitation and atrocities of various kinds. Moreover, countless children go "missing" every year. These cases of missing children represent a conglomeration of a number of problems, including abductions/kidnappings by family members, abductions/kidnappings carried out by non-family members or strangers, children who run away on their own or are forced to run away due to compelling circumstances in their families and extended surroundings, children who face unfriendly and hostile environment and are asked to leave home or who are abandoned, children who are trafficked or smuggled or exploited for various purposes, and children who are lost or injured. Undoubtedly, each of these groups of children exemplifies different social problems. Since, as a group, missing children – are so heterogeneous, there is no adequate data or consistently applied set of definitions to describe them. In addition, many cases of missing children are not reported to the police at all for various reasons, and police involvement in the resolution of different kinds of cases varies widely across the country. All this poses a serious problem. The NHRC Action Research on Trafficking, published by Orient Longman in 2005, has shown that in any given year, an average of 44000 children are reported missing; of them, as many as 11000 remain untraced.*
>
> *The revelations at Nithari exemplify that missing children may end up in a variety of places and situations – killed and buried in a neighbour's backyard, working as cheap forced labour in illegal factories/establishments/homes, exploited as sex slaves or forced into the child porn industry, as camel jockeys in the Gulf countries, as child beggars in begging rackets, as victims of illegal adoptions or forced marriages, or perhaps worse than any of these as victims of organ trade and even grotesque cannibalism as reported at Nithari.*

The Committee observed that there are some studies conducted by both governmental and non-governmental organizations which bear testimony to the fact that a large number of girls and boys who run away from their homes or are said to have run away from their homes are mainly school dropouts or children get fed up with domestic conditions. The glamour and lure of big cities often make them blind to the stark realities of urban life. Being vulnerable, they often fall prey to promises of jobs or careers in films or modeling and eventually end up as sex workers or as domestic help/labourers in homes, small hotels/restaurants, tea shops/stalls and unorganized establishments, many of them hazardous. Many of the run away boys and girls become victims of the organized begging rackets or pickpocketing/drug peddling racket etc. Most of these children are also trafficked and further abused, physically or sexually, and their cases are not even brought to the knowledge of the police. Many of these children come from indigent families who either do not have access to authorities or whose complaints are not treated with due diligence.

The Action Research Study on Trafficking by NHRC has brought out several case studies to establish this linkage between "trafficking" and "persons reported missing".

The Committee observed that the juvenile justice system too has failed to provide due care and protection to children. Despite the specific provisions made in the Juvenile Justice (Care and Protection of Children) Act, 2000, many State Governments/Union Territories are yet to frame Rules under the principal Act. In a majority of places, Special Juvenile Police Units had not been set up. All this has eroded the confidence of the people in the system.

When a child goes missing, nobody, except the perpetrator, knows the real intent behind it. It could be quite possible that the child for various reasons has run away on his or her own from home, a relative's home, or an institution which the child's parents/caretakers construe as "missing". On the other hand, it is also possible that the child may have gone missing from the scene for a different reason altogether, which could be sexual gratification, sexual exploitation, labour exploitation, profit-making, or personal vengeance etc. In these cases the person(s) directly or indirectly involved in the incident may resort to crimes of various kinds ranging from kidnapping, abduction, grievous hurt, assault, rape, unnatural offences, and even murder of the child. In fact, even a child who has run away on purpose is also susceptible to being kidnapped, abducted, abused or assaulted. This raises the question as to why reports of missing children are not treated as cognizable offence.'

Later the Report states:

'The NCRB, under the TALASH Information System, maintains a national level database of missing persons under the following broad categories – "missing", "kidnapped", "arrested", "deserted", "escaped", "proclaimed offender", "wanted", "unidentified dead body", "unidentified person" and "traced/found". Earlier, data on missing children under the broad category of "missing" was not available. However, this is now available for both the sexes under the age group 0–12 and 13–18. The NCRB, by and large, functions as a "Documentation Centre" or at best a "Transfer Desk"' because as of today the NCRB neither investigates, nor

does it monitor or facilitates the recovery of missing children as a pro-active organization. The Police Stations, too, generally do not give any feed back to the NCRB when the missing child is rescued, traced or returned. Hence the data lacks accuracy. Thus, despite being the national repository of "crime data", the NCRB is unaware both of children who are traced or of those who remain untraced.

Interestingly enough, though the category of missing children has come to be reflected in the TALASH Information System, there is no mention or analysis of it to date in the Crime in India Report being published by the NCRB. This is in spite of the fact that Chapter Six therein titled "Crime Against Children" categorically affirms that "Generally, the offences committed against children or the crimes in which children are the victims are considered as Crime Against Children". It then goes on to highlight crimes committed against children that are punishable under the Indian Penal Code 1860 and crimes committed against children that are punishable under the Special and Local Laws.

As per the latest Crime in India Report – 2005, a total of 14,975 cases of crimes against children were reported in the country during 2005 as compared to 14,423 cases during 2004, signifying an increase of 3.8 per cent. The highest crime rate was reported from Delhi (6.5) followed by Chandigarh (5.7) and Madhya Pradesh (5.6) as compared to the national average of 1.4. A total of 4026 cases of child rape were reported in the country during 2005 as compared to 3542 in 2004 accounting for a significant increase of 13.7 % during the year. The State of Madhya Pradesh reported the highest number of cases (870) followed by Maharashtra (634). These two States together accounted for 37.3% of the total child rape cases reported in the country. Highlighting cases related to kidnapping and abduction, the Report mentions that a total of 3518 cases were reported during the year as compared to 3196 cases reported in the previous year accounting for an increase of 10.1%. Delhi reported the highest percentage of such cases among children up to 15 years. The analysis of data clearly reveals the increase of number of crimes against children in the country.

The aforesaid data reveals the predicament of missing children in many ways. Apart from the NCRB, there are some regional police websites like the Zonal Integrated Police Network (ZIPNET) and a few State police websites, which provide data on missing persons, including data on missing children. But the information provided therein remains largely incomplete. Since awareness about these databases – particularly, among police personnel – is low, it has not drawn adequate attention in the investigation and tracing of missing children.'

From a reading of these extracts, it transpires that thousands of cases are registered in various police stations regarding children and adults who go missing every year in India. The list of reasons for which such children are kidnapped is unending. Children and women specifically are the worst sufferers of such situations where they are either forced into begging or prostitution. It is in the context of seeking the proper investigation of such cases of missing children reported all over India that the following suggestions are mooted.

V. SUGGESTIONS IN THE EXISTING FRAMEWORK OF INDIAN LAWS

(a) Suggestions for tracing missing children and preventing future incidents in India

The suggestions given here are based on the 2011 report of the BBA, the 2007 report of the NHRC and the guidelines given by the Supreme Court in *Horilal* v. *Commissioner of Police, Delhi*, WP (Criminal) No. 610 of 1996, decided on 14 November, 2002, as well as a study of subsequent judgments of different High Courts in India on the subject of tracing missing children. Accordingly, the following suggestions can take the shape of guidelines in order to trace the missing children effectively in a lesser period of time. These suggestions are a compilation of the collective study of all the above reports on the subject with our various independent inputs. The guidelines are laid down in the following steps:

(i) Compulsory registration and investigation of all cases of missing children

The first and the foremost step with a view to starting the investigation and to moving a step closer to finding the missing child is the prompt and compulsory registration of the case with the police. The earlier the case gets reported/registered and the police start their investigation, the better the chances that the missing child is located in a short period of time. Police have to promptly and compulsorily register the case of missing children and initiate actions on all fronts to trace the missing child. A centralised system is to be established by which any one aggrieved by non-registration at the police station can, through this centralised system, forward their petition to senior police officers for appropriate intervention. An acknowledgement has to be provided to the aggrieved person. Once the case gets registered and the investigation starts soon after the crime is committed, it is possible that the missing child is found before being removed from the territorial limits of India or any state within the territory of India.

(ii) Immediate action to be taken to secure any evidence that might be of help

Immediate action is to be taken to secure evidence necessary to compare and conclusively establish the identity of the missing child through DNA/DMA analysis, in case only the mortal remains of the missing person were to be located. This would aid and assist in establishing the identity of the missing child as well as giving suitable clues to detect the identity of persons responsible for abduction if the missing child has been kidnapped or removed by force.

Subjecting the suspects to further narco-analysis may be of further help in eliciting finer details pertaining to the revelations already made and the activities that took place at the alleged time of disappearance so that the field verification of the revelations made is possible. Subjecting some key witnesses also to narco-analysis will help in checking and verifying their statements made earlier to the police.

(iii) Speeding up the investigation

A senior police officer in every state in India has to be entrusted with the investigation. Regular reviews at periodic intervals with respect to the progress should be taken by the police officers in the state. The officer should also get the details with regard to pending cases of children missing and in identifying dead bodies. Special squads if needed should be appointed to pursue further investigation. The state should issue strict instructions directing all police officers to treat matters of missing children as high priority cases.

Further, police investigation cells can be made in the police stations in a state to look immediately into the matters of missing children. The cells, however, should have an adequate number of police officials to work on a case immediately and the police officials included in the police investigation cell should be qualified to do the job successfully. Introduction of these special cells will speed up the investigation process considering the fact that the team of such officers will look only into the matter of missing children and with time and experience will get better in the field.

(iv) Setting up a police information network or a national database for quick information on missing children in India

It is very important that the present methods of collecting information about missing children be modified by way of a centralised network in India. It is necessary that the network is web-enabled, maintained and most importantly updated. A national tracking system that would encompass the grass roots in locating and tracing missing children should be introduced. There should be prompt reporting of not only missing children cases, but also return, rescue or recovery. All instances where children are rescued from places of exploitation including places of sexual exploitation and also exploitative labour should be updated in the national database. The database should be updated on a regular and systematic basis. This would help the investigating authorities to know the complete details of the children missing and those found, and keep themselves updated on the pending cases as well. The details of previous missing children and the places and the way they were found would help the authorities to track the culprit very soon in the future.

The Government of India should establish a centre for such missing children at the national level. The centre if established should be the repository of all the data on the missing children including the collection, analysis, interpretation and documentation of data. However, it is very important that the centre for missing children is adopted and implemented by the government of India without any delay.

Another step that might be taken is to have a separate website for all the state police authorities like the Delhi Police web-based Zipnet programme to upload all the details of the cases regarding missing children and to update it with the latest details on the case to help the family of the missing children to know more about the case.

(v) Improvement in the mechanism of publishing details of missing children and the role of media

Publication of look-out notices in local dailies, TV and cable networks including private TV channels/Doordarshan government programme, vernacular newspapers and other electronic media agencies needs to be devised. Improved arrangements are required to instantly communicate the disseminated details of missing children to important hospitals, mortuaries, all police stations, outposts, entry and exit points in every state to help them to correlate and give feedback of any information of relevance in tracing the missing child. Such details should also be made available to officials in charge of temples, churches, mosques, marriage registration offices as well as hospitals etc. automatically, with photographs of missing children for any useful feedback and intervention as required.

In view of the current alarming situation, the media can play an important role in increasing public awareness of missing children and the plight of the thousands of hapless families whose family members/children are listed as untraced. This could be achieved by taking the following steps:

(a) At the newsroom level, crime reporters and metro editors need to include the category of missing children as a regular beat and as part of their daily news grind. Regular follow-up news reports and look-out notices in the media would help a lot.

(b) These stories need to be followed up and tracked regularly just like other stories of murder, human trafficking, abduction and kidnapping.

(c) Newspapers can make a separate section in their classified sections on missing children. The notices and advertisements on missing children need to have a better display and be given more prominence and space in newspapers and TV bulletins. TV channels should have a repetitive telecast on missing children details.

The above suggested measures will help to a great extent to create awareness among the citizens of India and also to be careful and cautious and help prevention of any further increase in the number of missing children.

(vi) Speedy communication of information by the police personnel

One of the important aspects of a police investigation in such cases is communication of the crime to other states or places where the missing children are likely to be taken and further to communicate important messages during the continuation of the investigation. However, the communication between police personnel in India is not very prompt resulting in losing the chances of finding the missing children. Therefore, it is very important that the communication techniques between police personnel for transfer of important information are modified. Police personnel should be able to communicate and pass on information promptly. It is suggested that e-communications and Skype contact must be promoted for use by state police and police personnel must be educated/updated with using latest technology communication methods for tracing missing children. This would greatly facilitate faster communication by the police forces in India.

(vii) Collection of forensic evidence for establishing identity of unidentified dead bodies

No unidentified dead body should be permitted to be disposed of without ensuring collection of all possible evidence that will enable conclusive identity to be established by comparison of necessary forensic samples. A mandate must be issued to all police stations not to cremate the body of any missing/unclaimed child/person till a conclusive effort has been made to consolidate all evidence necessary which may lead to establishing the identity of the missing unclaimed child's remains.

Finger and palm prints, DNA comparison and skull superimposition techniques are being used now to conclusively establish the identity of a person. Since these techniques require some control samples for the purpose of comparison, immediately after a person goes missing, it is necessary to arrange for collection and preservation of control samples of the finger/palm print, DNA specimen, good photographs of the face, etc .of the missing person. Some of these can be collected from the already available personal effects or through samples taken from parents, siblings etc.

The photograph of an unidentified dead body should be taken in such a manner that it assists in identification of facial features, personal items, any personal identification marks, shoes, watches, jewellery, tattoo marks, finger prints/palm print, DNA finger print, etc. Dental records must be preserved to establish the identity.

(viii) Introduction of a child tracking system

Children who go missing are likely to be unwary victims of exploitation and trafficking. A child tracking system should be part of the national database to prevent trafficking and exploitation of the person missing. It is extremely important that both at state and central level a missing children database should be established which facilitates countrywide exchange of information for locating/tracing missing children. Compilation of data of missing children and the mode/methods utilised for their location and search will help to resolve future cases of missing children and aid in the compilation of statistics for future reference. Exchange of data state-wide will greatly help police authorities to resolve cases of missing children.

(ix) Public co-operation

Police help centres should be established in the jurisdiction of all the police stations in a state or union territory (UT) as well as in public places such as malls, public amusement places, bus stations, railway stations, etc so that the information on the missing children and unnatural and unidentified bodies may be disseminated to the public for possible clues or information exchange. These centres should be integrated with closed circuit television systems to be put at all public places covering the ports of entry/exit, malls, prominent public amusement places, eateries, etc to facilitate public-spirited persons to assist the police in tracing missing persons.

(b) Further suggestions to help in prevention of abduction, kidnapping and forcible removal of children in future

(i) Necessity of defining the term 'missing children'

Defining a 'missing child' is very important to help investigating agencies to deal with the problem. It is important to have a clear mandate on definitions of 'human trafficking' and 'missing children'. The reason for the need of a clear and specific definition lies in the fact that, because the term 'missing children' is not specifically defined in Indian penal laws, many cases are not registered by the police authorities in the state claiming that the matter is not of a 'missing child'. The special operating procedure developed by the Delhi Police has defined a missing child in the following words:

> 'A child (a person who is below 18 years of the age) whose whereabouts are not known to the parents, legal guardians or any other person who may be legally entrusted with knowing whereabouts/well being of the child whatever may be the circumstances/causes of disappearance. The child in need of care and protection will be considered missing until located and/or his/her safety/well-being is established.'

Once, the term 'missing persons' is defined exhaustively, it will be much easier for the family members of such a child to get the case registered and the investigation can be started at the earliest without any ambiguity or uncertainty.

(ii) Missing children squad or children's desk in police stations

Creation of a skilled investigation and rapid response squad on missing children is a necessity. One of the recommendations is that every police station across the respective states should have a special squad/missing persons desk to trace missing children. This squad/desk should have a registering officer who should be made responsible for registering complaints of missing children. The officer should maintain complete records of efforts made by them to trace missing children as well as by the special squad. The registering officer should also work as an enquiry officer, responsible for following up the entire procedure of tracing/tracking the missing child. The squad should also be regularly updated with the small details they have about the missing persons so that the families of the missing persons are well aware of the steps being taken by the authorities in finding their lost family members. The records should also be updated with the information of the missing persons who have been traced and returned back to their respective families at least in the past 6 months.

(iii) Involving Panchayati Raj Institutions (PRIs) (village bodies) etc

In order to make the investigative procedures concerning missing children more transparent and user-friendly, it would be preferable for the police investigating team to involve the community at large, such as representatives of Panchayati Raj Institutions (village level bodies), municipal committees, neighbourhood committees, resident welfare associations, in addition to existing helplines. This will enable the community to get fully involved along with the police in tracing missing children and also if these institutions at a lower level are involved, it is easy to pass on the information of the missing children to more and more people making the search of such children or adults easier and faster. The Director-General of Police (DGP) in every state and UT in India should seriously consider taking full advantage of these agencies in the task of not only investigating crimes relating to children but also tracking down missing children. The role of Panchayats and such bodies should be extended to:

- prompt reporting of missing children;
- prompt dissemination of information, if any, to the law enforcement agencies;
- rendering assistance to law enforcement agencies for tracing children;
- provide timely feedback to the law enforcement agencies about the return of the child.

This would not only help in finding missing children whose complaints have been registered but, because of the involvement of the agencies at a lower level, also help people in villages and the surrounding areas to report more cases of missing children, making them more aware in their daily lives and thus preventing the increase of crime at such a fast rate.

(iv) Involving non-government organisations (NGOs)/state legal services authorities and setting up of advisory boards

In places where vulnerable groups of children are found in large numbers, there is need for enforcement agencies to evolve some kind of a mechanism in partnership with non-governmental organisations and social workers, whereby apart from rendering counselling to them, awareness raising activities are also carried out. The involvement of the state legal services authority and its district level units can be extremely useful in this regard. This would not only instill confidence in the general public but also empower people and give them special protection so that they are in no way lured by external agencies/factors. This initiative could be taken by the missing children squad/cell in the districts. The DGPs need to ensure action on this initiative of public–private partnership.

Each state government in India should set up an advisory body including all government departments concerned as well as appropriate NGOs working in the field of missing children, trafficked children, child labour, etc. The body should be given statutory powers to ensure monitoring of the enforcement of child welfare legislative provisions.

(v) Establishing helplines

There is a need to establish a child helpline through NGOs and other agencies with adequate support from the government in all districts in India. The Department of Women and Child Development, Government of India, may take the initiative to set up such a national network. Such a helpline helps in immediate registration or providing the police with the information of missing children immediately, thereby improving the chances of finding the missing children or persons sooner.

(vi) Importance of registration of the cases of 'missing children' as a cognisable offence

It should be made mandatory for the police to promptly register without any delay all complaints of missing children as a First Information Report (FIR). At the moment the issue of missing children is not a cognisable offence and the very fact that a child is missing does not convey occurrence of a crime. However, some states like Andhra Pradesh, Tamil Nadu and New Delhi allow police to register FIRs and take up investigation. In order to facilitate proper enquiry/

investigation, it is advisable that a FIR is registered by the police with respect to the issue of missing children at the very inception without awaiting initial police preliminary inquiries. However, experience shows that in many cases a child may not have gone missing and the panic reaction of the parents or wards leads to such reporting. Therefore, all such issues may not warrant registration of an FIR immediately. Nevertheless, it is advisable to register a FIR if a missing child does not come back or is not traced within a reasonable time. State governments are advised to consider the issue of appropriate directions to law enforcement agencies to set a time-limit of 15 days from the date of reporting, that if a missing child is not traced back within that time, a presumption may be made of some *mala fides* and a FIR must be registered with respect to all such issues of missing children. Filing of a FIR greatly assists in finding missing children in a country like India, where the population is large and the criminal rate is very high. Registering a FIR makes it incumbent on the police authorities to look into the matter and they become responsible to the family of the missing child or person, thereby leading to good chances of finding the missing children or persons.

(vii) Mandatory intimation of missing children FIRs to state legal services authorities

It should be mandatory for police authorities in all states and UTs in India to forward both by e-mail and by post a copy of each FIR registered with regard to missing children to the respective state legal services authority or its district level chapters. In turn the legal services authority should provide all possible legal aid to parents and families of missing children and act as an interface between the parents of the missing children and the police authorities. This will help in keeping a vigil on any large scale kidnapping by organised gangs and provide a monitoring avenue whereby the police authorities can be asked to give regular feedback on the FIR so lodged.

(viii) Attention to transit points of trafficking

There is a need to keep special vigils at railway stations, bus stands, airports, seaports and such other places, which act as transit points for missing children, including children who run away or are made to run away. In this context, the government railway police, the Railway Protection Force, airport and seaport authorities need to be oriented about the issue of missing children. It is important that, as soon as the information about a missing child or person is received, authorities and police posts at all the nearest airports, railway stations, bus stands and seaports are informed about them and photographs/ details are displayed at such places.

(ix) Nodal officers

Nodal officers on missing children in every district should be appointed. The officer should be notified by the respective state governments and should be made accountable to take all steps to trace/give care and protection to the missing child. Adequate legal administrative and financial support should be provided by the state government. The family members of the missing child would have another option to get the complaint registered if it is refused by the police officers.

(x) Cross-border missing children

This is a grey area, which largely remains unaddressed. It has been reported that several foreign children who have been trafficked into India have been punished as illegal immigrants and are made to suffer. In this regard the National Human Rights Commission (NHRC) has already recommended that state governments undertake a review of all such cases and provide relief to such children, as all trafficked children, irrespective of their nationality, are children in need of care and attention. Moreover, there is a need of developing a protocol on this issue. It is learnt that United Nations Office on Drugs and Crime (UNODC) in its anti-human trafficking project can provide the required technical assistance. In this regard the Ministry of Women and Child Development can utilise the technical assistance of UNODC and, in close coordination with the Ministry of External Affairs (MEA), develop a protocol on this topic.

(xi) Interparental child abduction issues

Interparental child removal both within India and across international borders (both inbound and outbound) is a common phenomenon today. Parental child removal is neither defined in any law as an offence nor is it taken cognisance of by the police unless there is court intervention. India is not a signatory to the Hague Convention on Civil Aspects of International Child Abduction, 1980 and children forcibly brought to India or taken out of India by estranged parents do not fall within the ambit of any penal law. This grey area seriously needs legislation. Until that is done, the state/district legal services authorities and/or the mediation cells at the High Court/District Court levels must be associated or involved by police authorities and the courts to whom these matters get reported. Alternative dispute resolution and mediation in such cases can play a major role in the return of children to the place/country of their habitual and permanent residence. Return of children, their forcible removal and/or abduction by parents must be stopped forthwith.

(xii) Procedure after return of the child

The duty of the police authorities should not end with the child returning back home. Rather, whenever a missing child is traced or comes back on his or her own, the police or investigating officer should make sure that all relevant angles such as involvement of organised gangs, application of provisions of Bonded Labour Act and such other relevant Acts applicable in India are looked into as probable causes of the child going missing.

If the involvement of an organised gang is found, it is the responsibility of the police or investigating officer to refer the matter to the Crime Branch of the respective state police or the special cell constituted by the Central Bureau of Investigation (CBI) in this regard to prevent future recurrence.

(xiii) Comprehensive plan for the rehabilitation of the missing child

Another very important step that should be kept in mind once the missing child comes back to the family or is found by the police is their rehabilitation. So, to achieve this purpose it is important that the government of India or of the respective state takes steps for creation of a comprehensive plan for rehabilitation of the rescued children who need rehabilitation or any other assistance to come back to the mainstream of life.

Hence, the above-mentioned steps for protection and prevention of cases of missing children in future, and for tracing the already missing minor children all over the country, if followed diligently, can help solve the problem of kidnapping and abduction of innocent minor children. It is further stated that, if the guidelines are strictly looked into and followed by the concerned state departments, it can be an important step in saving lives of many children in the future.

VI. SUGGESTIONS IN THE ALTERNATIVE FRAMEWORK – THE COMMISSION FOR PROTECTION OF CHILD RIGHTS ACT, 2005

(a) Introduction

Besides the above steps that can be taken in the framework of existing statutory laws, another suggestion can be mooted within the framework of the Commission for Protection of Child Rights Act, 2005 (CPCRA). In this context, it is relevant to quote the Preamble of the CPCRA:

> *'An Act to provide for the constitution of a National Commission and State Commissions for Protection of Child Rights and Children's Courts for providing speedy trial of offences against children or of violation of child rights and for matters connected therewith or incidental thereto.*
>
> *WHEREAS India participated in the United Nations (UN) General Assembly Summit in 1990, which adopted a Declaration on Survival, Protection and Development of Children;*
>
> *AND WHEREAS India has also acceded to the Convention on the Rights of the Child (CRC) on the 11th December, 1992;*
>
> *AND WHEREAS CRC is an international treaty that makes it incumbent upon the signatory States to take all necessary steps to protect children's rights enumerated in the Convention;*
>
> *AND WHEREAS in order to ensure protection of rights of children one of the recent initiatives that the Government have taken for Children is the adoption of National Charter for Children, 2003;*
>
> *AND WHEREAS the UN General Assembly Special Session on Children held in May, 2002 adopted an Outcome Document titled "A World Fit for Children" containing the goals, objectives, strategies and activities to be undertaken by the member countries for the current decade;*
>
> *AND WHEREAS it is expedient to enact a law relating to children to give effect to the policies adopted by the Government in this regard, standards prescribed in the CRC, and all other relevant international instruments.'*

(b) Sections 13, 17, 24, 25 and 26 of the CPCRA

It may now be useful to quote sections 13, 17, 24, 25 and 26 of the CPCRA which are extracted for ready reference.

> ***'13. Functions of Commission.***
>
> *(1) The Commission shall perform all or any of the following functions, namely:—*

(a) *examine and review the safeguards provided by or under any law for the time being in force for the protection of child rights and recommend measures for their effective implementation;*

(b) *present to the Central Government, annually and at such other intervals, as the Commission may deem fit, reports upon the working of those safeguards;*

(c) *inquire into violation of child rights and recommend initiation of proceedings in such cases;*

(d) *examine all factors that inhibit the enjoyment of rights of children affected by terrorism, communal violence, riots, natural disaster, domestic violence, HIV/AIDS, trafficking, maltreatment, torture and exploitation, pornography and prostitution and recommend appropriate remedial measures;*

(e) *look into the matters relating to children in need of special care and protection including children in distress, marginalized and disadvantaged children, children in conflict with law, juveniles, children without family and children of prisoners and recommend appropriate remedial measures;*

(f) *study treaties and other international instruments and undertake periodical review of existing policies, programmes and other activities on child rights and make recommendations for their effective implementation in the best interest of children;*

(g) *undertake and promote research in the field of child rights;*

(h) *spread child rights literacy among various sections of the society and promote awareness of the safeguards available for protection of these rights through publications, the media, seminars and other available means;*

(i) *inspect or cause to be inspected any juvenile custodial home, or any other place of residence or institution meant for children, under the control of the Central Government or any State Government or any other authority, including any institution run by a social organisation; where children are detained or lodged for the purpose of treatment, reformation or protection and take up with these authorities for remedial action, if found necessary;*

(i) *inquire into complaints and take* suo motu *notice of matters relating to,–*

  i. *deprivation and violation of child rights;*

  ii. *non-implementation of laws providing for protection and development of children;*

  iii. *non-compliance of policy decisions, guidelines or instructions aimed at mitigating hardships to and ensuring welfare of the children and to provide relief to such children, or take up the issues arising out of such matters with appropriate authorities; and*

(j) *such other functions as it may consider necessary for the promotion of child rights and any other matter incidental to the above functions.*

(2) The Commission shall not inquire into any matter which is pending before a State Commission or any other Commission duly constituted under any law for the time being in force.'

'17. Constitution of State Commission for Protection of Child Rights.

(1) A State Government may constitute a body to be known as the (name of the State) Commission for Protection of Child Rights to exercise the powers conferred upon, and to perform the functions assigned to, a State Commission under this Chapter.

(2) he State Commission shall consist of the following Members, namely:—

(a) a Chairperson who is a person of eminence and has done outstanding work for promoting the welfare of children; and

(k) six Members, out of which at least two shall be women, from the following fields, to be appointed by the State Government from amongst persons of eminence, ability, integrity, standing and experience in,—

i. education;

ii. child health, care, welfare or child development;

iii. juvenile justice or care of neglected or marginalized children or children with disabilities;

iv. elimination of child labour or children in distress;

v. child psychology or sociology; and

vi. laws relating to children.

(3) The headquarters of the State Commission shall be at such place as the State Government may, by notification, specify.'

'24. Application of certain provisions relating to National Commission for Protection of Child Rights to State Commissions.

The provisions of sections 7, 8, 9, 10, sub-section (1) of section 13 and sections 14 and 15 shall apply to a State Commission and shall have effect, subject to the following modifications, namely:—

(l) references to "Commission" shall be construed as references to "State Commission";

(m) references to "Central Government" shall be construed as references to "State Government"; and

(n) references to "Member-Secretary" shall be construed as references to "Secretary".

25. Children's Courts.

For the purpose of providing speedy trial of offences against children or of violation of child rights, the State Government may, with the concurrence of the Chief Justice of the High Court, by notification, specify at least a court in the State or specify, for each district, a Court of Session to be a Children's Court to try the said offences:

Provided that nothing in this section shall apply if—

(a) a Court of Session is already specified as a special court; or

(b) a special court is already constituted,

for such offences under any other law for the time being in force.

26. Special Public Prosecutor.

For every Children's Court, the State Government shall, by notification, specify a Public Prosecutor or appoint an advocate who has been in practice as an advocate for not less than seven years, as a Special Public Prosecutor for the purpose of conducting cases in that Court.'

(c) Suggested measures under CPCRA

In the light of the above provisions of the CPCRA, it is incumbent on governments of all states and UTs of the country to take all necessary steps to protect children's rights enumerated in the Convention on the Rights of the Child (CRC). Sections 13 and 24 of the CPCRA provide ample powers both to the national commission and the state commissions for inter alia taking necessary steps and recommending appropriate remedial measures with regard to issues pertaining to missing children and all children in distress. These can be enforced in all states and UTs by setting up and/or constituting state commissions for protection of child rights under section 17 of the CPCRA in the respective territories of the individual governments. Hence, as a starting point, states and UTs should forthwith set up such state commissions so that the entire machinery can be galvanised under their regime.

It is suggested that any averment by State or UT governments against setting up state commissions for protection of child rights in their territories should not be entertained due to the sensitivity and magnitude of the problems relating to missing children. This is supported by the following contentions. A news report in the *English Tribune* dated 29 December, 2011, quoting the Bureau of Police Research and Development (BPRD) of the Union Home Ministry which organised a workshop to study the problem of disappearance of children in the northern States showing the concern in this matter. The news report quotes that over 200 of the 800 missing persons in Haryana in the last 6 months are minors. 72 of these 200 missing children are girls, which indicates the direct bearing on the safety of children. Likewise, a news report in *The Pioneer* dated 3 October, 2010 indicates that:

> *'Child protection continues to be the last priority of the city administration. Even after the recent study of the UT Health Department, which stated that child abuse is rampant in the city of Chandigarh, the Chandigarh Administration continues to overlook the need to implement the Integrated Child Protection Scheme (ICPS) here.'*

Hence, all states and UTs in India need to set up state commissions as a priority.

To complete the setting up of a fully operational system under the CPCRA, children's courts can be constituted in the said respective territories under section 25 of the CPCRA and special public prosecutors can be appointed in these territories under section 26 of the CPCRA. Thus, independent of other statutory enactments dealing with criminal laws or other penal provisions in general, CPCRA can be very effectively utilised for individually setting up a statutory system for enforcement of child rights specifically and particularly in the larger interest of children. This will create a special, exclusive and individual forum to redress breaches of children's rights and will provide effective, speedy and timely relief in the case of any individual incident of missing or distressed children.

The issues pertaining to missing children and children in distress can be exclusively looked into by the respective state commissions in their individual territories in view of the powers vested in them under sections 13 and 24 of the CPCRA. Clearly, if the state commission concerned *suo motu* or upon inquiry into complaints regarding missing children or children in distress comes to a conclusion that there is a violation of child rights, there is non-implementation of laws relating to children or there is non-compliance of decisions, guidelines or instructions pertaining to the welfare of children, such commission under section 15 of the CPCRA can approach the Supreme Court or High Court for issuance of directions, orders or writs as may be deemed necessary by the court, besides recommending that concerned governments grant interim relief as deemed necessary. Thus, any individual case of missing children or children in distress can be immediately remedied by the state commission by enforcing the above provisions of the CPCRA.

The composition of the state commission with its six members, out of which at least two should be women specialising in child health, care, welfare or child development, juvenile justice, child psychology, laws related to children and/or having knowledge of children in distress will give adequate opportunity to the state commission to receive complaints or act *suo moto* whenever there is any issue of kidnapping or removal of children and deprivation or violation of child rights. The commission is vastly empowered to examine all factors affecting children and relating to trafficking, torture, exploitation, pornography and prostitution and to recommend appropriate remedial measures. The commission has mandatory powers to forward cases to any magistrate and hear them as complaints. Independently, the commission upon inquiry can recommend initiation of proceedings for prosecution or such other action as deemed fit. Hence, all cases of trafficking of children particularly for exploitation, begging, prostitution and pornography can be monitored and future recurrence can be checked. All organised child mafias can therefore be attempted to be eliminated.

(d) Conclusion of suggested measures under CPCRA

A reading of the provisions, remedies and suggestions made above under the CPCRA indicates that a separate and independent machinery can be set into motion under the auspices of the CPCRA to specifically look into all issues related to child rights while the process of the criminal law moves in the mainstream.

The menace of missing children in large numbers can be curbed with a heavy hand only if the issues relating to children are segregated and dealt with under separate parameters under the watchful eye of child specialists, *i.e.* qualified members of the state commissions for protection of child rights. Only if qualified, trained and experienced persons sensitive to child rights are empowered to handle the problems of missing children can the process and machinery of the criminal law work in tandem.

Once offenders are apprehended, speedy trials of offences against children or of violation of child rights can be ensured in children's courts which can be set up under the CPCRA. This can prevent recurrence of organised children-related offences.

A vigilant state commission for protection of child rights both as a watch dog and as an investigator can serve a very significant role in the removal of problems of missing children. Hence, only if the issue of missing children is taken out of the general stream of treatment and handed over to child specialists to monitor it from the outside can the necessary attention, time and energy be devoted to this highly sensitive issue of missing children.

VII. DIRECTIONS ISSUED BY THE PUNJAB AND HARYANA HIGH COURT TO IMPLIMENT CHILD RIGHTS

As a watershed verdict pronouncing on child rights, Mr. Justice A.K. Sikri, as Chief Justice of Punjab and Haryana High Court, delivered a landmark judgment dated April 9, 2013 ruling on implementation of child rights under the provisions of the Commission for Protection of Child Rights Act, 2005, and the Juvenile Justice (Care and Protection of Children) Act, 2000. The National Commission for Protection of Child Rights (NCPCR) had moved the High Court seeking implementation of these child rights and the judgment is reported as *Court of its own Motion* v. *State of Punjab*, 2013 (2) ILR 533 (P&H). By a common verdict for a number of petitions heard together, the High Court laid down substantial directions in the petition of NCPCR under four broad headings for which relief had been claimed for meaningful implementation of child rights. To bring out these important directives, it would be best to quote from the judgment itself reported as ILR 2013 (2) P&H 533 by reproducing paras 22 to 29 as below:

> ***"First Relief – Constitution of State Commissions for protection of child rights.***
>
> *22. Insofar as appointments of six Members are concerned, it is clear that no procedure or guidelines have been stipulated in section 17 or section 18 of the CPCR Act. The petitioner, thus, suggests that a High-Powered Selection Committee should be constituted by the State Governments headed by retired Judge of the High Court as Chairperson along with suitable Members to make recommendations for appointment of the remaining six Members of the State Commissions. The process of selection should entail issuance of public advertisement for inviting applications, interviewing eligible candidates and recommending a penal of names of suitable persons. The Union Territory, Chandigarh is directed to speed up its actions for setting up State Commission. The States of Punjab and Haryana as well as U.T., Chandigarh shall also ensure that these State Commissions become fully functional by appointing Chairpersons and Members in the manner as highlighted above.*
>
> *23. In order to have transparency in the system and fair chance of consideration to all eligible persons, the selection should be after issuing public advertisement for inviting applications and after interview/discussion with the eligible candidates. It would be appropriate if the rules are framed containing the constitution of the Selection Committee for appointment of these Members and also stipulating*

the procedure for appointment. Till that is done, we direct that the Committee which is constituted for the appointment of Chairperson as per proviso to Section 18 of the CPCR Act shall make appointment of the six Members of the State Commission as well. In the alternative, the State Governments can constitute the Selection Committee on the lines contained in Rule 91 of the Juvenile Justice (Care and Protection of Children) Rules, 2007 (for short 'J.J. Rules').

Second Relief - Mandatory Registration of all Children Homes:

24. It is the submission of the petitioner that for the effective implementation of the provisions of section 34 of the J.J. Act, 2000, the registration of Children Homes should be made compulsory. The respondents concur with the same and the stand taken by them is that there is necessity of mandatory registration of these children homes and taking action against those Children Homes which are not registered. It is also stated that no Government grant or financial aid or any other benefit be given to such Children Homes which are not registered. It hardly needs to be emphasised that to check malpractices in various Children Homes, which have surfaced over a period of time, it becomes necessary to make the registration of such children homes not only mandatory but there has to be direct compliance of this provision. There is need to create awareness about this as well for which requisite steps should be taken by the respondents. In order to ensure that these Children Homes function properly, the State Commissions should undertake the job of overlooking the functioning of these bodies which is also the power given to it under section 13 of the CPCR Act.

Third Relief - Constitution of Selection Committee under rule 91 of J.J. Rules to make selection of Child Welfare Committee (Rule 20), Inspection Committee (Rule 63) and Advisory Boards (Rule 93) under the J.J. Act and Rules :

25. We find from the replies filed by the States of Punjab and Haryana as well as U.T., Chandigarh that Committees under the aforesaid provisions have already been constituted and working in these States/Union Territory. Apart from constitution of these Committees, the petitioner has given the following two suggestions:—

"vii. The Inspection Committee must ensure that all accounts of all privately run homes/institutions are regularly compulsorily audited by a firm of Chartered Accountants who should also ensure that proper account books are regularly maintained of all financial transactions and all payments are made or received through cheques/bank drafts with minimal cash payments. The regularly audited account statement must be sent to the inspection committee by all privately run homes/institutions. It is also suggested that SCPCR may maintain a panel of approved Chartered Accountants at various district levels through whom these audits of accounts should be got done for all privately run institutions/children homes.

vii. The Inspection Committee must ensure that in accordance with the provisions of Section 3 of the Right of Children to Free and Compulsory Education Act, 2009 (RTE Act), every child of the age of 6 to 14 years shall have a right to free and compulsory education in a neighbourhood school till completion of elementary education as also ensure that no form of child labour of employment of children in any vocation, trade, business or employment is permitted in any form whatsoever. Any children home or institution found violating this condition should be reported to the SCPCR by the inspection committee for prosecution and legal action."

The respondents have stated that they would consider these suggestions positively. We direct that such an exercise be done within a period of two months, on the feasibility of accepting these suggestions by passing necessary orders.

Fourth Relief - Constitution and notification of Children's Courts and appointment of Special Public Prosecutors under sections 25 and 26 of the CPCR Act.

26. The petitioner submits that for the purpose of conducting speedy trial of offences relating to violation of child rights, the provisions incorporated in section 25 of the CPCR Act require that State Government may by notification with the concurrence of the Chief Justice of the High Court, specify a Children's Court and notify Special Public Prosecutors for conducting cases in such a court. We find that States of Punjab and Haryana as well as U.T., Chandigarh have already designated specific Courts of Sessions to be the Children's Courts and also appointed Special Public Prosecutors for conducting cases in the Children's Courts. Sensitisation courses are organised as well from time to time by the Chandigarh Judicial Academy as well as by the Government at their level. Still, we would impress upon the Chandigarh Judicial Academy to evolve a module/ training programme for sensitizing all the stake-holders on child rights and also to deal with the cases in the Children's Courts.

27. We also issue a direction for creating Children's Courts with specialised infrastructure. Such a court has been established in District Court, Karkardooma in Delhi with child witness courtroom. We impress upon the High Court as well as the Governments to establish similar child witness courtrooms in all court complexes. The concerned Building Committees of the High Court would look into this aspect and take steps for establishing child witness courtrooms at the earliest. It would go a long way for proper deposition of children as witnesses and even in those cases which are against child offenders.

28. We would like to mention at this stage that recently, the Parliament has enacted the 'Protection of Children from Sexual Offences Act, 2012'. This is an Act to protect children from offences of sexual assault, sexual harassment and pornography. It becomes necessary to have effective implementation of this enactment as well. Under the Act, the National Commission and State Commissions have been made the designated authorities to monitor the implementation. Rules, 2012 have also been framed under this Act and Rule-6 prescribes for such monitoring with specific functions assigned to National Commission and State Commissions. Needless to mention, National Commission as well as State Commissions shall start discharging their functions under this Act in a meaningful manner. Similar duties assigned to National Commission as well as State Commissions under section 31 of the Right to Education Act shall also be diligently discharged.

29. These writ petitions are disposed of with the directions aforesaid.

Petition disposed of."

This land mark and authoritative verdict has far reaching significant dimensions, if accepted and actually executed by the administrative authorities in the true import of the spirit in which the verdict was rendered. Provisions for protection of children are often a neglected and ignored subject. However, this judgment is a wake up clarion call to which executive must yield and respond in the positive perspective. Beneficial provisions in child protection enactments will only find a momentous impact if the authorities responsible for their genuine realization follow the mandate given by the High Court.

VIII. CONCLUSION

In the backdrop of the above study, all missing children whose whereabouts are not known even after years of investigations and all the new cases registered every day in the police stations across the country can benefit and be traced if the above suggestions and recommendations are taken into account by the police or the investigating authorities while searching for the missing children. It may be suggested that not only should the police or the investigating authorities be responsible for finding the missing children whose cases have been reported in the police stations but the public bodies, NGOs/state legal services authorities should also be made a part of the support services. That would help and speed up the investigation process making it possible for missing children to come back home. If all authorities at all levels, *i.e.* village, district, state and centre, as well as public bodies, work together to find missing children, it will not be very difficult to find the missing children. Therefore, keeping in mind the above guidelines and suggestions it is possible to efficiently investigate and find the missing children besides preventing future instances of kidnapping of children. Considering that India is a large nation geographically with vast territories housing a multicultural society and a huge population of over 1.2 billion people, resolving critical issues like missing children is not an easy task. However, keeping in view that this vulnerable section of society is at a very high risk rate, every effort, step and endeavour should be made to adapt means and methods to protect the future of the nation's children. Therefore, it should be the endeavour of every official body of the system to contribute and do whatever is possible for the plight of missing children who must be helped. Resolving their problems should be the top priority in all walks of life.

Some Perspectives on Indian Family Law

The present India chapter analyses three areas of Indian family law: validity of marriages in the context of unmarried cohabitation under Hindu law; recent developments in international child abduction law; and the law of guardianship and inter-country adoption in India. The reason for focus on these select branches of law is because these areas are of immense interest to an international legal readership given the large size of the Indian population residing overseas.

I. HINDU LAW OF MARRIAGE

The principal law of marriage and divorce relating to Hindus is contained in the Hindu Marriage Act, 1955 (hereafter HMA, 1955), which came into force on 18 May, 1955. The HMA, 1955 also governs validity of marriages of those Indian spouses who are permanently resident overseas. It is an Act to amend and codify the law relating to marriage among Hindus. After outlining the main provisions of the HMA, 1955 they will be discussed in appropriate detail.

A. Main provisions of the HMA, 1955

Section 1 states the territorial application of the HMA, 1955. In terms of section 2, the Act is applicable only to Hindus. Section 5 of the HMA, 1955 stipulates the conditions for a valid Hindu marriage. Essential ceremonies for a Hindu marriage are laid down in section 7 of the Act. Registration of marriages is dealt with in section 8 of the Act. Sections 9 and 10 of the Act provide for restitution of conjugal rights and judicial separation.

Nullity of marriage and divorce are dealt with in detail in Chapter IV of the HMA, 1955. The grounds for divorce are detailed in section 13 of the Act. Divorce by mutual consent is recognised under section 13B of the Act.

The issue of jurisdiction and the procedure for obtaining divorce is provided in Chapter V of this Act. Provisions for maintenance *pendente lite* and permanent alimony are made in sections 24 and 25 of the Act, respectively. It is important to mention that section 29(2) of the Act recognises dissolution of marriage by custom, pleaded by parties to the marriage. The main provisions of the HMA, 1955 are discussed below.

B. Extent and jurisdiction of the HMA, 1955

Section 1 of the HMA, 1955 states that the Act extends to the whole of India, except the State of Jammu and Kashmir, and applies also to Hindus domiciled in the territories to which this Act extends who are outside the said territories. In effect, the Act has extra-territorial application, because a Hindu carries with him the personal law of marriage.

C. Application of the HMA, 1955

In terms of section 2 of the HMA, 1955, Hindu law applies to the following three categories:

(a) any person who is a Hindu, Jain, Sikh or Buddhist by religion;

(b) any person who is born of Hindu parents; and

(c) any other person domiciled in the territories to which this act extends who is not a Muslim, Christian, Parsi or Jew.

The Calcutta High Court in *Prem Singh* v. *Dulari Bai*, AIR 1973 Cal 425. While interpreting sections 1 and 2 of the HMA, 1955 held in para 5 of the judgment at p. 426:

> *'This section read with section 2(1)(a)(b) makes it equally clear that as regards the intra-territorial operation of the Act it applies to all Hindus, Buddhists, Jains or Sikhs irrespective of the question whether they are domiciled in India or not. The provisions of clause (c) of the same section contemplates extra-territorial operation in the sense that the persons domiciled in other territory to which this Act may extend, if governed by Hindu Law, even though, residing outside the territory, would come within the purview of this Act.'*

The court further held that the question of domicile assumes importance only when the marriage between the parties is prohibited by the domestic rule or law of the land to which one of the parties to the marriage, a foreigner, may belong.

D. Validity of marriages in the context of unmarried cohabitation under Hindu law

Before jumping to the main issue and the area of focus in this analysis, it would be pertinent to note the views of the Supreme Court on live in relationships which were stated by the Court in a recent judgment in the case of *S. Khushboo* v. *Kanniammal*, AIR 2010 SC 3196 which would give an effective background to demonstrate the view of the Court as follows:

> *"21. While it is true that the mainstream view in our society is that sexual contact should take place only between marital partners, there is no statutory offence that takes place when adults willingly engage in sexual relations outside the marital setting, with the exception of 'adultery' as defined under section 497 Indian Penal Code. At this juncture, we may refer to the decision given by this Court in* Lata Singh v. State of Uttar Pradesh, *2006 (3) RCR (Cri) 870: 2006 (3) RCR (Civil) 738: 2006 (2) Apex Criminal 670, wherein it was observed that a live -in relationship between two consenting adults of heterogenic sex does not amount to any offence (with the obvious exception of 'adultery'), even though it may be perceived as immoral. A major girl is free to marry anyone she likes or " live with anyone she likes". In that case, the petitioner was a woman who had married a man belonging to another caste and had begun cohabitation with him. The petitioner's brother had filed a criminal complaint accusing her husband of*

> *offences under sections 366 and 368 Indian Penal Code, thereby leading to the commencement of trial proceedings. This Court had entertained a writ petition and granted relief by quashing the criminal trial. Furthermore, the Court had noted that 'no offence was committed by any of the accused and the whole criminal case in question is an abuse of the process of the Court".*

A similar opinion was expressed in the case of *Indra Sarma* v. *V.K.V. Sarma*, AIR 2014 SC 309 by the Supreme Court of India in para no. 2 as follows:

> "2. *Live -in or marriage like relationship is neither a crime nor a sin though socially unacceptable in this country. The decision to marry or not to marry or to have a heterosexual relationship is intensely personal".*

Thus, the recognition of live in relationships by the Court give rise to several legal issues. However, the specific area of focus in this analysis is situations where a Hindu couple, in the country of their origin, have been cohabiting as husband and wife without performance of any religious ceremonies and without the registration of the marriage and, subsequently, the male Indian spouse has migrated and married abroad.

Cohabitation in this context would mean that the couple have initially been living under one roof, with family approval and public recognition. Some sort of token customary ceremony may also have been performed of which there exists no evidence at all. They are not ceremonies as envisaged in section 7 of the HMA, 1955.

This is a common phenomenon with a certain category of non-resident Indians residing overseas, especially in England, Canada and Australia. Quite often, the male migrant Hindu spouse gets married abroad with the prime agenda of securing overseas citizenship. Once this purpose has been achieved, the earlier Indian spouse and the children may very conveniently be dumped and deserted. In the event of any litigation during the process of acquiring overseas citizenship, foreign immigration and family lawyers are confronted with the problem of addressing the validity of the alleged initial marriage on the home soil. Problems also arise with regard to alimony payable to the previous deserted Indian spouse. Quite often the couple may have been living in a joint family before the husband migrated abroad. The bitter battle starts when the Indian spouse demands her share of the family property or from any agricultural land holdings or any other assets owned by the husband, as the case may be.

The core issue in such a situation is the legal status of the previous unmarried cohabitation in the country of origin of the male migrated spouse under the main Indian law of marriage, *i.e.*, the HMA, 1955. If this previous relationship is a valid marriage, then the male migrant Indian spouse is a bigamist. Bigamy is a criminal offence under the Indian Penal Code and invites very serious consequences. The marriage performed overseas, in such a situation, would then stand nullified under the HMA, 1955. The end result is that the prospects of acquiring overseas citizenship will be devastated.

The current debate on this situation has been triggered on account of a recent decision of the Supreme Court of India in *Surjit Kaur* v. *Gajra Singh*, AIR 1994 SC 135, which has substantially altered and rather reversed the tide of earlier judicial dicta. The Supreme Court of India held therein that, even if the parties hold themselves out before society as husband and wife and society treats them as such, without the proof of proper ceremonies of marriage they could not be considered as husband and wife. Long cohabitation creates no presumption of a valid marriage in such a situation. This decision contemplates the situation where the marriage has not been registered in terms of section 8 of the HMA, 1955. It is pertinent to mention that registration of marriages is not compulsory under the HMA, 1955.

On the other hand, there is ample earlier case law, contrary to this recent ruling, giving explicit legal recognition to a presumption of a valid marriage in such circumstances. The reverse proposition is discussed in detail in the subsequent portion of this chapter. However, it is pertinent to note a very recent judgment categorically opposite to the above mentioned case.

In the recent case of *Aysha* v. *Ozir Hassan*, Crl. R.C. No. 674 of 2007, decided on 17 June, 2013 by the High Court of Judicature at Madras has held a different opinion on ceremonies and customs related to the marriage as is stated below in the following words in para 16 of the judgment:

> *"16. After scrutinizing the trial Court judgment and on perusing the list of documents marked on the side of the petitioner, this Court is of the view that:—*
>
> *(i) A valid marriage does not necessarily mean that all the customary rights pertaining to the married couple are to be followed and subsequently solemnized...*
>
> ... *(v) Without legal encumbrance or third party interference or without affecting third party's rights, both the petitioner and the respondent lived together as spouses and begot two children. Therefore, illegitimate relationship does not arise in this case. Marriage solemnization is only a customary right and obligation, but not a mandatory one. Hence, this Court treats the petitioner and the respondent as spouses in normal life with a typical identity of their own.*
>
> *(vi) It is not disputed that the petitioner has been a spinster before she gave birth and that the respondent was a bachelor before developing sexual relationship with the petitioner. Both of them led their marital life under the same shelter and begot two children. Therefore, the petitioner's rank has been elevated as the 'wife' of the respondent and likewise the respondent's rank had been elevated as the 'husband' of the petitioner. Therefore, the children born to them are 'legitimate' children and the petitioner is the 'legitimate' wife of the respondent. This Court is of the view that if a women aged 18 or above has a sexual relationship with a man, aged 21 or above, and during the course of such relationship, if the woman becomes pregnant, she would henceforth be treated as the 'wife' and the man would be treated as the 'husband'. Even if the girl does not become pregnant after having such sexual relationship with a man but if there is strong documentary evidence to show the existence of such relationship then also the couple involved in such acts would be termed as "wife" and "husband".*

(vii) This Court is of the further view that even after such a sexual relationship, if both decide to separate due to difference of opinion, the 'husband' cannot marry without getting a decree of divorce from the Court of law against the 'wife'. He could not marry a second time without getting such a decree as it had been established that the sexual relationship had existed between them and consummation had taken place.

(viii) This Court is of the further view that if the bachelor has completed 21 years of age and the spinster 18 years of age respectively then they acquire the freedom of choice as guaranteed by the Indian Constitution. Consequently, any couple who choose to consummate their sexual cravings then that act becomes a total commitment with adherence to all consequences that may follow except on certain exceptional considerations. Therefore, the marriage formalities as per respective religious customs viz., *tying of thali, exchange of garlands, exchanging of finger rings, circling around the matrimonial fire pit or registering of marriage at a Government Registration Office is only to comply with each one's respective religious customs for the satisfaction of the society. However, if any couple, subject to their attaining the mandatory age of freedom, who indulge in sexual gratification, then that would be considered as valid marriage and they could be termed as "husband and wife", as a result of their choice of freedom. On the other hand, in some cases, both bachelors and spinsters, who adhering to all formalities of their respective religion and culture with marriage solemnized, find it that their conjugal rights for sexual consummation had not been fulfilled, then such a marriage is deemed to be a failure, void or lapse. So, in total, what is expected after adhering to norms and formalities is the sexual consummation by the couple which has occurred in the case on hand. Hence, the main legal aspect for valid marriage is consummation or sexual interaction such as in the instant case, the point is squarely and wholly applicable. Of course, this Court's further view is that if necessary, either party may approach the Family Court for declaration to the effect of marital status by supplementing documentary proof of evidence in order to prove the sexual relationship. After such a declaration from the concerned forum, the victim can establish herself in all the government records or any other relevant records where she can encrypt her name as wife to her counterpart. Legal rights applicable to the normal wedded couples will also be applicable to couples who have had sexual relationships which are established.*

(ix) In some cases, both the bachelor and spinster even after observing all the formalities of their religious customs and solemnization of marriage, are unable to have sexual relationship, as such consummation is deemed to be non-occurring, such a marriage would be referred to as an invalid marriage. What is expected after adhering to normal formalities is the consummation by the union (spouses) which has occurred in the present case.

(x) That the main legal aspect for valid marriage viz., consummation between both spouses has happened even before the formalities. Therefore, in the instant case, the point is elaborately explained. If the consummation has taken place between the spouses (bachelors and spinsters) then from

that time onwards both are declared husband and wife. This declaration will not be prejudicial to either party. This Court's further view is that this declaration would strengthen the Indian Culture and would protect the young womens welfare, character and status among the society. This pertinent view of this Court is in order to protect Womens Civil Rights and personal life. This Court further opines that it is an appropriate time to prevent the Indian Culture from deteriorating further when it comes to living honestly as spouses. It is an imperative need that the morals and ethics of Indian Culture is taken to the next level and maintained so as to never slander the life of an innocent woman. Finally and most importantly the Courts do give paramount importance to the customs and rights to every religion so long as it remains in tandem with civil rights that are controlled by the Courts. The instant case concludes with the main perceivable details as detailed above."

However, the above judgment caused spur in the minds of legal thinkers and it also raised serious questions and confusions. Thus, in the recent case of *Uday Gupta* v. *Aysha,* 2014 (3) RAJ 5, the above judgment was challenged considering it to be not legally tenable. The submission made by the learned counsel for the petitioner before the Apex Court is stated in para no. 3 of the judgment of the Supreme Court as under:

"3. Mr. M.R. Calla, learned senior counsel appearing for the petitioner has submitted that the observations made by the High Court that "a valid marriage does not necessarily mean that all the customary rights pertaining to the married couple are to be followed and subsequently solemnized" are not legally tenable. It has been pointed out by Mr. Calla, learned senior counsel that such observations demolish the very institution of marriage itself, and therefore, are liable to be set aside."

The Apex Court thus looked into the judgment challenged and stated that the judgment is not universally applicable. The Apex Court made the following observations in para no. 6, 7 and 8 of the judgment as quoted below to come to the conclusion reproduced here under:

"6. We are of the view that such observations had been made in the facts of that case. In fact, what the learned Judge wanted to say is that if a man and woman are **living** *together for a long time as husband and wife, though never married, there would be a presumption of marriage and their children could not be called to be illegitimate. Such a view stands fully fortified by a very large number of judgments.*

7. This Court in Madan Mohan Singh *v.* Rajni Kant, *2011 (1) RCR (Civil) 152: 2010 (6) RAJ 393: AIR 2010 SC 2933 held as under:—*

"The courts have consistently held that the law presumes in favour of marriage and against concubinage, when a man and woman have cohabited continuously for a number of years. However, such presumption can be rebutted by leading unimpeachable evidence. [Vide: Mohabbat Ali Khan *v.* Mohd. Ibrahim Khan, *AIR 1929 PC 135;* Gokalchand *v.* Parvin Kumar, *AIR 1952 SC 231;* S.P.S. Balasubramanyam *v.* Suruttayan, *(1994) 1*

SCC 460; Ranganath Parmeshwar Panditrao Mali *v.* Eknath Gajanan Kulkarni, *(1996) 7 SCC 681; and* Sobha Hymavathi Devi *v.* Setti Gangadhara Swamy, *2005 (1) RCR (Civil) 799: (2005) 2 SCC 244].”*

8. In Bharatha Matha *v.* R. Vijaya Ranganathan, *2010 (3) RCR (Civil) 252: 2010 (3) RAJ 515: AIR 2010 SC 2685, this Court dealt with the legitimacy of the children born out of such relationship observing:*

> *“Thus, it is evident that section 16 of the (Hindu Marriage) Act intends to bring about social reforms, conferment of social status of legitimacy on a group of children, otherwise treated as illegitimate, as its prime object.”*

In the instant case, the High Court made the aforesaid observations in the facts of that case as the alleged marriage took place in 1994 and two children were born in 1996 and 1999 respectively. Therefore, the observations made by the High Court in the said judgment are restricted to the facts of that case and do not lay down the law of universal application.”

Thus, it was concluded that if a man and woman are living together for a long time as husband and wife, though never married, there would be a presumption of marriage and their children could not be called to be illegitimate. The validity of such a purported marriage, as described above, will be governed by the provisions of the HMA, 1955.

E. Requirements of a valid Hindu marriage

The legal validity of such an alleged marriage has to be scrutinised in terms of sections 5 and 7 of the HMA, 1955. Section 5 provides as follows:

> ‘5: Conditions for a Hindu Marriage – A marriage may be solemnised between any two Hindus, if the following conditions are fulfilled, namely:
>
> (i) neither party has a spouse living at the time of the marriage;
>
> (ii) at the time of the marriage, neither party—
>
> (a) is incapable of giving a valid consent to it in consequence of unsoundness of mind; or
>
> (b) though capable of giving a valid consent, has been suffering from mental disorder of such a kind or to such an extent as to be unfit for marriage and the procreation of children: or
>
> (c) has been subject to recurrent attacks of insanity or epilepsy;
>
> (iii) the bridegroom has completed the age of twenty one years and the bride the age of eighteen years at the time of the marriage;
>
> (iv) the parties are not within the degrees of prohibited relationship unless the custom or usage governing each of them permits of a marriage between the two;
>
> (v) the parties are not sapindas of each other, unless the custom or usage governing each of them permits of a marriage between the two ...’

Section 7 deals with ceremonial aspects:

'7. Ceremonies for a Hindu Marriage.

(1) A Hindu marriage may be solemnized in accordance with the customary rites and ceremonies of either party thereto.

(2) Where such rites and ceremonies include the Saptapadi (that is, the taking of seven steps by the bridegroom and the bride jointly before the sacred fire), the marriage becomes complete and binding when the seventh step is taken.'

Where the requisite ceremonies of marriage as envisaged in section 7 of the HMA, 1955 are not performed, nor any custom is invoked by the couple rendering the performance of such ceremonies unnecessary, neither of the spouses in such a situation can claim the status of marriage in terms of section 7 of the HMA, 1955.

Some of the relevant case-law on sections 5 and 7 of the HMA, 1955 coupled with the issue of bigamy is discussed below.

F. Marriage registration under Hindu law not compulsory

Section 8 of the HMA, 1955 deals with registration of marriages. The Act does not make the registration of marriages compulsory. This is primarily because Hindu marriages and most marriages in India have been always performed in public with wide publicity. Section 8(2) of the HMA, 1955 provides that any State Government may make rules for compulsory registration of Hindu marriages. Furthermore, section 8(5) specifically lays down that failure to register a Hindu marriage shall in no way affect its validity. Even where compulsory registration of marriage is laid down under the rules, non registration does not affect the validity of the marriage. It merely entails a nominal fine. Unlike the entry of marriage pursuant to the English Marriage Act, 1949, mere registration under section 8 of the HMA, 1955 will not *ipso facto* make the marriage valid.

G. Proof of marriages solemnised outside England and Wales

In England, rule 10.14 of the Family Proceedings Rules, 1991 (subject to certain exceptions) stipulates requirements to prove the validity of a marriage celebrated outside England and Wales. Rule 10.14 provides that the validity of such a marriage under the law of the country where it was celebrated may, in any family proceedings in which the existence and the validity of the marriage is not disputed, be proved by the evidence of one of the parties to the marriage and the furnishing of a document purporting to be a marriage certificate or a similar document issued under the law in force in that country. Additionally, the evidence of a local expert in law is necessary to prove that such a certificate would be accepted in the country of origin as *prima facie* evidence that a valid marriage has taken place [*Rayden and Jackson's Law and Practice in Divorce and Family Matters*, Vol. 1 (Butterworths, London, 1997) at pp. 122 and 127].

H. Case-law analysis – validity of marriages

1. Case-law not supporting a presumption in favour of a valid marriage

Coming to the recent Supreme Court of India decision in the matter of *Surjit Kaur* v. *Garja Singh,* AIR 1994 SC 135, the operative part of which is found in para 13 at p. 137.

'*Prima facie*, the expression "whoever ... marries" must mean "whoever ... marries validly" or "whoever ... marries and whose marriage is a valid one". If the marriage is not a valid one, according to the law applicable to the parties, no question of its being void by reason of its taking place during the life of the husband or wife of the person marrying arises. If the marriage is not a valid marriage, it is no marriage in the eye of law. *The bare fact of a man and a woman living as husband and wife does not, at any rate, normally give them the status of husband and wife even though they may hold themselves out before society as husband and wife and the society treats them as husband and wife.*'

However, in the recent case of *D. Velusamy* v. *D. Patchaiammal*, AIR 2011 SC (Cri) 225, the Supreme Court of India held a completely different view and has recognized certain live-in relationships as 'relationship in the form of marriage' as common law marriage if they met the requisites as given below:

> *"32. Some countries in the world recognize common law marriages. A common law marriage, sometimes called de facto marriage, or informal marriage is recognized in some countries as a marriage though no legally recognized marriage ceremony is performed or civil marriage contract is entered into or the marriage registered in a civil registry (see details on Google).*
>
> *33. In our opinion a '***relationship** *in the nature of marriage' is akin to a common law marriage. Common law marriages require that although not being formally married:—*
>
> *(a) The couple must hold themselves out to society as being akin to spouses.*
>
> *(b) They must be of legal age to marry.*
>
> *(c) They must be otherwise qualified to enter into a legal marriage, including being unmarried.*
>
> *(d) They must have voluntarily cohabited and held themselves out to the world as being akin to spouses for a significant period of time.*
>
> *(see 'Common Law Marriage' in Wikipedia on Google)*
>
> *In our opinion a '* **relationship** *in the nature of marriage' under the 2005 Act must also fulfill the above requirements, and in addition the parties must have* **lived** *together in a 'shared household' as defined in section 2(s) of the Act. Merely spending weekends together or a one night stand would not make it a 'domestic* **relationship** *'.*
>
> *34. In our opinion not all* **live** *in* **relationships** *will amount to a* **relationship** *in the nature of marriage to get the benefit of the Act of 2005. To get such benefit the conditions mentioned by us above must be satisfied, and this has to be proved by evidence. If a man has a 'keep' whom he maintains financially and uses mainly for sexual purpose and/or as a servant it would not, in our opinion, be a* **relationship** *in the nature of marriage"*

In the case of *Surjit Kaur* (supra), it was held that the fact of a couple living together as husband and wife does not, at any rate, normally give them the status of husband and wife even though they may hold themselves out before society as husband and wife. Even if the society treats them as husband and wife, this position in law is now different and as has been established by a different legal position as is stated above in the case of *D. Velusamy* (supra).

2. ***Case Law for Marriage Ceremony to be essential to establish the fact of marriage.***

Saptapadi, being an essential ceremony, establishes the fact of marriage. Saptapadi is the taking of seven steps by the bridegroom and the bride jointly before the sacred fire. Without proof of such a ceremony, the first 'marriage', does not exist and a case for bigamy cannot arise. This was the mandate of law laid down by the Supreme Court of India in *Smt. Laxmi Devi* v. *Satya Narayan,* 1994 (30) HLR 449.

Where the parties are governed by the customary law of marriage and divorce, there has to be a specific averment in support of the same. In the instant case it was also held that, where the parties to the marriage had not proved that they were governed by any custom under which the essential ceremonies stipulated in section 7 of the HMA, 1955 were not required to be performed, the fact of marriage could not be established.

The High Court of Punjab and Haryana has held in the matter of *Ashok Kumar Chopra* v. *Krishna Kumari,* 1993 (27) HLR 111 (114):

> 'In view of the above mentioned authorities it is very well made out that in order to make out a prima facie case for the commission of bigamy it is necessary to allege form of marriage as well as essential ceremonies required for solemnisation of a valid marriage and then to lead some evidence in support thereof. Even the admission of second marriage by the petitioner is of no avail to the complainant. This inherent infirmity exists in the pleadings as well as in pre-charge evidence which cannot be cured at the stage of trial and under these circumstances continuance of proceedings will amount to abuse of process of Court.'

As stated above, a typical situation is that no religious rights or ceremonies may have been performed between the cohabiting couple during the currency of their stay in the country of origin. Also relevant to the status of such an alleged marriage is the decision of the Supreme Court of India in the case of *Santi Deb Berma* v. *Kanchan Prava Devi,* AIR 1991, SC 816. In this case the performance of 'saptapadi' was not proved, neither was the accused's marriage performed by any custom which dispensed with saptapadi. The accused and his alleged second wife were living as husband and wife, but there was no specific evidence regarding the performance of the essential rites, namely Saptapadi. The Supreme Court categorically held in paras 6 and 7 of the judgment (at p. 817) that, in the absence of any reliable and acceptable evidence, it was not sustainable to draw an inference as to the performance of ceremonies essential for a valid marriage. Accordingly, the accused was acquitted of the alleged offence of bigamy.

The Supreme Court of India held in *Lingari Obulamma* v. *Venkata Reddy,* AIR 1979 SC 848 that while assailing the second marriage where there was absolutely no evidence to prove Saptapadi or performance of prevailing customs in the community, which was neither mentioned in the complaint nor proved in the evidence, the conviction under section 494 of the Indian Penal Code for the offence of bigamy could not be sustained.

As early as 1966 the Supreme Court of India held in *Kanwal Ram* v. *Himachal Pradesh Administration*, AIR 1966 SC 614 (615) that, in a bigamy case, the essential ceremonies constituting an alleged second marriage must be proved. Admission of marriage by the accused is not sufficient for the purpose of proving marriage in an adultery or bigamy case. This ruling in *Kanwal Ram* has been recently reiterated in the above-mentioned case of *Smt. Laxmi*, 1994 (30) HLR 449.

Merely because the parties to the marriage have lived as husband and wife, the status of wife is not conferred as laid down by the Supreme Court of India in *B.S. Lokhande* v. *State of Maharashtra (AIR 1965 SC 1564)* It was further held that merely going through certain ceremonies with the intention that the parties be considered married will not constitute the ceremonies prescribed by law or approved by any established custom. This Supreme Court ruling has been very recently reiterated by the Supreme Court of India itself in the above-mentioned case of *Surjit Kaur*.

In *Brij Lal Bishnoi* v. *State*, 1996 (3) RCR 299 (302) the Delhi High Court held as follows:

> '11. I have already noticed above the law and it is that in a case like the one in hand the complainant has to provide strict proof of the marriage. The mere fact that they had been living together as husband and wife giving birth to their progeny would not do in a prosecution for matrimonial offences. And, as for section 50 of the Evidence Act, the fact that the man and woman spoke of each other as husband and wife, that others coming into their life in the passing or to endure also took them as husband and wife, proves nothing more than conduct, and conduct alone is no substitute of strict proof.'

The Supreme Court of India in the case of *P. Satyanarayana* v. *P. Mallaiah*, JT 1996 (8) SC 203 held that legal evidence is necessary to prove the fact of marriage on the basis of the tests laid down by this Court in *Bhaurao Shankar Lokhande* v. *State of Maharashtra*, AIR 1965 SC 1564; *Kanwal Ram* v. *Himachal Pradesh Administration*, AIR 1966 SC 614 (615) and *Priya Bala Ghosh* v. *Suresh Chandra Ghosh*, (1971) 1 SCC 864. The two earlier Supreme Court rulings, *i.e. Kanwal Ram* and *B.S. Lokhande*, reiterated by the Supreme Court in this ruling have already been elaborated upon above.

Furthermore, the Supreme Court of India has also held in the matter of *Valsamma Paul* v. *Cochin University*, AIR 1996 SC 1011 (1022) that: '[R]ecognition by family or community is not a pre-condition for married status'.

However, there are now cases to the contrary, as in the recent case of *Aysha* v. *Ozir Hassan* (supra) by the High Court of Judicature at Madras, which has held a different opinion on ceremonies and customs related to the marriage which is stated below in the following words in para 16 of the judgment:

> *"16. After scrutinizing the trial Court judgment and on perusing the list of documents marked on the side of the petitioner, this Court is of the view that:—*
>
> *(i) A valid marriage does not necessarily mean that all the customary rights pertaining to the married couple are to be followed and subsequently solemnized...*

The aforementioned case was challenged in the Supreme Court in the verdict rendered in *Uday Gupta* (supra), and the Apex Court made the following observations in para no. 6 of the judgment as quoted below to come to the conclusion reproduced here under:

> *"6. We are of the view that such observations had been made in the facts of that case. In fact, what the learned Judge wanted to say is that if a man and woman are* **living** *together for a long time as husband and wife, though never married, there would be a presumption of marriage and their children could not be called to be illegitimate. Such a view stands fully fortified by a very large number of judgments."*

3. *Case-law to the contrary: raising a presumption in favour of a valid marriage*

There is also ample case-law contrary to the above-mentioned proposition of law. Some of the decisions of the Supreme Court of India and various of the High Courts on the reverse proposition are discussed below.

In *S.P.S. Balasubramanyam* v. *Suruttayan* alias *Andali Padayachi,* AIR 1994 SC 133 (134) the Supreme Court of India further held:

> 'What has been settled by this court is that if a man and woman live together for long years as husband and wife then a presumption arises in law of legality of marriage existing between the two. But the presumption is rebuttable ... In the Hindu society no father would normally tolerate behaviour of his son having a concubine ...'

In *Chalakuttiyil Mutteri Karthiyayani Amma* v. *Padinhare Talasseri Veettil Narayanan Nair,* 1998 (1) HLR 393 (397) the Kerala High Court observed as follows:

> 'Unnikrishna Kurup, J. in the decision reported in *Kunji Pillai Amma* v. *Somanathan Pillai,* 1971 KLJ 105 held as follows:
>
> "The law appears to be clear that when the factum of marriage has been proved, the conditions required for a valid marriage would be presumed to have been fulfilled. The long course of conduct, the fact that the husband had openly acknowledged the 1st plaintiff as his wife and the 2nd plaintiff as his son, the marriage certificate and the various other circumstances afford ample proof that there was a valid subsisting marriage."'

In that case, the contention was that there was no legal evidence to show the presentation of cloth by the bridegroom to the bride as required by the provisions of the Nair Act. His Lordship relied on the decision of the Supreme Court in *Veerappa* v. *Michael,* AIR 1963 SC 23 and held that in so far as there is proof to show that the marriage had taken place, the law will presume that all the necessary ingredients have been performed.

In para 15 of this judgment at p. 398, the Court followed *Badri Prasad,* which is discussed in the subsequent portion of this chapter.

In *Subhash Popatlal Shah* v. *Smt. Lata Subhash Shah,* AIR 1994 Bom 43 (45) it was held by the High Court of Bombay as follows:

> 'However, at the hearing of these appeals, Mr. Abhyankar, learned advocate appearing on behalf of the appellant, very vehemently urged that as per section 7 of the Hindu Marriage Act, 1955, it had to be proved that a religious rite of completing saptapadi was performed and since there is no such evidence on record, a conclusion could not be drawn that the appellant and the respondent were legally wedded husband and wife. We are unable to persuade ourselves to agree with the submission of Mr. Abhyankar for the simple reason that it is only when the marriage rites and ceremonies include saptapadi that the marriage becomes complete and binding when the seventh step is taken. There is nothing on record that there was such custom or rites and ceremonies between the parties before us. Thus, saptapadi is not always a must to prove valid marriage between the parties ... Therefore, even if saptapadi was not one of the items of the marriage ceremony undertaken by the parties before us, we are of the opinion that the marriage between the appellant and the respondent cannot be held to be illegal and invalid. In fact, when some sort of marriage ceremony was undergone by and between the parties, there is always a presumption of validity of marriage unless the presumption is rebutted by quite cogent and satisfactory evidence.'

Subsequently, in para 8 of this judgment, the Bombay High Court reiterated quotes from *Ningu* and *Badri Prasad*, which have already been reproduced above.

In *S.P.S. Balasubramanyam* v. *Suruttayan* alias *Andali Padayachi*, AIR 1994 SC 133 (134) the Supreme Court of India has held that where a man and a woman were living under the same roof and cohabiting for a number of years, a presumption arises that they lived as husband and wife; and such presumption could not be destroyed by the circumstance and evidence proved in the instant case; and that the children were not illegitimate.

In *Smt. Nirmala* v. *Smt. Rukminibai*, AIR 1994 Kant 247 the Karnataka High Court expressly reiterated *Badri Prasad* and *S.P.S. Balasubramanyam*.

In *Ningu Vithu Bamane* v. *Sadashiv Ningu Bamane*, AIR 1987 Bom 27, it was held in para 20 of the judgment as follows:

> 'I am of the opinion that in a well-organised, orderly and civilised society like ours which is not of loose and uncertain morals, the institution of marriage occupies an important place and plays a very vital role in the process of development of human personality. We have definite views and strong convictions about marital relations. The law as to presumption in favour of marriage under sections 50 and 114, Evidence Act, is well crystallised. Thus when a man and woman, live together as husband and wife for sufficiently long time and were treated as husband and wife by friends, relatives and neighbours there is always a presumption in favour of their marriage. If children are born to such a couple, there is a further presumption in favour of their legitimacy. The presumption in favour of marriage does not get mitigated or weakened merely because there may not be positive evidence of any marriage having taken place. But if there is some evidence on record that the couple had gone through

some form of marriage, the presumption gets strengthened. Therefore, though marriage ceremony said to have taken place may not be valid, the marriage can be held to be valid by force of habit and repute and the onus of rebutting such a marriage would be on the person who denies the marriage. It may also be stated here that this presumption of law in favour of marriage and legitimacy is not to be repelled lightly by mere balance of probability. The evidence for that should be strong, satisfactory and conclusive. If the presumption is permitted to be rebutted lightly, the weaker and vulnerable sections of the society, *viz*, the women and the children could be the victims of the vagaries of uncertainties as to their positions and status in life. This would be very much detrimental in the development of their human personality. They would be the worst sufferers in the society.'

Section 114 of the Indian Evidence Act, 1872 reads as follows:

'114. The Court may presume the existence of any fact which it thinks likely to have happened, regard being had to the common course of natural events, human conduct and public and private business, in their relation to the facts of the particular case.'

In the case of *Madan Mohan Singh* v. *Rajni Kant*, AIR 2010 SC 2933, the Apex Court followed earlier precedents wherein living together satisfied the presumption under section 114 of the Evidence Act. In the following words of the Apex Court:

"20. In S.P.S. Balasubramanyam *v.* Suruttayan @ Andali Padayachi, *AIR 1992 SC 756, this Court held that if man and woman are living under the same roof and cohabiting for a number of years, there will be a presumption under section 114 of the Evidence Act, that they live as husband and wife and the children born to them will not be illegitimate.*

21. The courts have consistently held that the law presumes in favour of marriage and against concubinage, when a man and woman have cohabited continuously for a number of years. However, such presumption can be rebutted by leading unimpeachable evidence. [Vide: Mohabbat Ali Khan *v.* Mohd. Ibrahim Khan, *AIR 1929 PC 135;* Gokalchand *v.* Parvin Kumar, *AIR 1952 SC 231;* S.P.S. Balasubramanyam *v.* Suruttayan, *1992 (1) RCR (Cri) 524: 1992 (2) RRR 381: (1994) 1 SCC 460;* Ranganath Parmeshwar Panditrao Mali *v.* Eknath Gajanan Kulkarni, *(1996) 7 SCC 681; and* Sobha Hymavathi Devi *v.* Setti Gangadhara Swamy, *2005 (1) RCR (Civil) 799: (2005) 2 SCC 244]."*

The Court concluded that:

"**The live-in-relationship if continued for such a long time, cannot be termed in as "walk in and walk out" relationship and there is a presumption of marriage between them** which the appellants failed to rebut"

In *Badri Prasad* v. *Dy. Director of Consolidation*, AIR 1978 SC 1557, the relevant portion of the judgment reads as follows:

'A strong presumption arises in favour wedlock where the partners have lived together for a long spell as husband and wife. Although the presumption is rebuttable, a heavy burden lies on him who seeks to deprive the relationship of legal origin. Law leans in favour of legitimacy and frowns upon bastardy. In this view, the contention of Shri Garg for the petitioner, that long after the alleged marriage, evidence has not been produced to sustain its ceremonial process by examining the priest or other witnesses, deserves no consideration. If a man and woman who live as husband and wife in society are compelled to prove, half a century later, by eye witness evidence that they were validly married, few will succeed.'

In the case of *Chanmuniya* v. *Virendra Kumar Singh Kushwaha,* (2011) 1 SCC 14, the Supreme Court of India while dealing with the case where a man and a woman lived together for a long time giving rise to the issue whether the woman is entitled to get maintenance under section 125 of CrPC, reiterated several precedents that raised presumption in the favour of a valid marriage if a couple stayed together for a long time, in the following paras of the judgement quoted above:

"*14. Again in* Sastry Velaider Aronegary & his wife *v.* Sembecutty Viagalie, *(1881) 6 AC 364, it was held that where a man and woman are proved to have lived together as man and wife, the law will presume, unless the contrary is clearly proved, that they were living together in consequence of a valid marriage, and not in a state of concubinage.*

15. In India, the same principles have been followed in the case of A. Dinohamy *v.* W.L. Balahamy, *AIR 1927 PC 185, in which the Privy Council laid down the general proposition that where a man and woman are proved to have lived together as man and wife, the law will presume, unless, the contrary is clearly proved, that they were living together in consequence of a valid marriage, and not in a state of concubinage.*

16. In Mohabbat Ali Khan *v.* Muhammad Ibrahim Khan, *AIR 1929 PC 135, the Privy Council has laid down that the law presumes in favour of marriage and against concubinage when a man and woman have cohabited continuously for number of years.*

17. In the case of Gokal Chand *v.* Parvin Kumari, *AIR 1952 SC 231, this Court held that continuous co-habitation of man and woman as husband and wife may raise the presumption of marriage, but the presumption which may be drawn from long co-habitation is rebuttable and if there are circumstances which weaken and destroy that presumption, the Court cannot ignore them.*

18. Further, in the case of Badri Prasad *v.* Dy. Director of Consolidation, *(1978) 3 SCC 527, the Supreme Court held that a strong presumption arises in favour of wedlock where the partners have lived together for a long spell as husband and wife. Although the presumption is rebuttable, a heavy burden lies on him who seeks to deprive the relationship of legal origin.*

19. Again, in Tulsa *v.* Durghatiya, *2008 (1) RCR (Civil) 814: 2008 (1) RAJ 316: (2008) 4 SCC 520, this Court held that where the partners lived together for a long spell as husband and wife, a presumption would arise in favour of a valid wedlock".*

Thus the Apex Court finally expressed its views in favour of providing maintenance to the deserted woman thus, putting on the man the obligation of maintaining a woman out of a live-in relationship that usually arise in cases of marital union. The Court expressed its views in the following words:

> *"26. Thus, in those cases where a man, who lived with a woman for a long time and even though they may not have undergone legal necessities of a valid marriage, should be made liable to pay the woman maintenance if he deserts her. The man should not be allowed to benefit from the legal loopholes by enjoying the advantages of a de facto marriage without undertaking the duties and obligations. Any other interpretation would lead the woman to vagrancy and destitution, which the provision of maintenance in section 125 is meant to prevent."*

After analysing the law, it is clear that there is a conflict of law situation as far as presumption in favour of valid marriages is concerned, on the basis of cohabitation without cogent evidence of performance of ceremonies as envisaged in section 7 of the HMA, 1955. This is a situation which needs to be remedied by the Apex Court. In an appropriate case this issue should be referred to a Supreme Court Constitution bench for finality.

Dr. W.F. Menski, in one of his articles, has discussed the far-reaching implications of *Surjit Kaur*. He is of the opinion that this judgment particularly affects women who remarry after a divorce or after the death of their first husband. In such situations, it is customary not to have the full marriage rituals as done for a first marriage. Menski further states that in some instances it will be customary to have no marriage rituals at all. He further states that there are many cases in which a man and woman simply contract to marry, and whether or not it is done in writing is immaterial. However, it may be added by way of clarification that marriage is a sacramental union under Hindu law and the English concept of contract to marry is alien to the Indian system. Under the HMA, 1955, no form of writing is necessary to solemnise a marriage.

In *Surjit Kaur's* case gur (jaggery) was distributed to friends of the newly married couple. There was public recognition in addition to a document purporting to be registration of the customary marriage. Menski's interpretation of section 7 of the HMA, 1955 is that it is perfectly possible to enter a legally valid Hindu marriage without going through elaborate Sanskrit rituals. He opines that *Surjit Kaur's* case looks even more out of line, especially in comparison to *S.P.S. Balasubramanyam*, a judgment delivered by the Supreme Court of India at the same time as *Surjit Kaur*. *Balasubramanyam's* case relaxes the burden of proof and is exactly opposite to the law laid down in *Surjit Kaur*. Menski concludes: 'Bad decisions of this kind no doubt contribute to keeping women in subordination.' [*See number 89 (July-August 1995) Manushi, pp. 15-16*]

Here, at this point, it is pertinent to mention that in view of a number of cases with conflicting views, the Supreme Court of India in the case of *Chanmuniya* v. *Virendra Kumar Singh Kushwaha* (supra), summed up the whole of the conflict as depicted by various judgments above and framed three questions to be decided by a Larger Bench of the Apex Court. The questions mentioned in the judgment which are referred for consideration to a Larger Bench are as follows:

> *"45. We, therefore, request the Hon'ble Chief Justice to refer the following, amongst other, questions to be decided by a larger Bench. According to us, the questions are:*
>
> 1. *Whether the* ***living*** *together of a man and woman as husband and wife for a considerable period of time would raise the presumption of a valid marriage between them and whether such a presumption would entitle the woman to maintenance under section 125 Criminal Procedure Code?*
> 2. *Whether strict proof of marriage is essential for a claim of maintenance under section 125 Criminal Procedure Code having regard to the provisions of Domestic Violence Act, 2005?*
> 3. *Whether a marriage performed according to customary rites and ceremonies, without strictly fulfilling the requisites of section 7(1) of the Hindu Marriage Act, 1955, or any other personal law would entitle the woman to maintenance under section 125 Criminal Procedure Code?*
>
> *46. We are of the opinion that a broad and expansive interpretation should be given to the term 'wife' to include even those cases where a man and woman have been* **living** *together as husband and wife for a reasonably long period of time, and strict proof of marriage should not be a pre-condition for maintenance under section 125 of the Criminal Procedure Code, so as to fulfil the true spirit and essence of the beneficial provision of maintenance under section 125."*

I. Presumption of valid marriage – recent English law decision

As far as the position in English law is concerned, the Court of Appeal very recently held in *Chief Adjudication Officer* v. *Bath* that where there was an irregular marriage ceremony followed by a period of long cohabitation, it would be contrary to the general policy of the law to refuse to extend to the parties the benefit of a presumption of marriage, which would apply to them if there were no evidence of any ceremony at all.

The Court of Appeal so held in a reserved judgment when it dismissed the appeal of the Chief Adjudication Officer challenging the decision of a social security commissioner, who on 7 May, 1998, allowed the appeal of the claimant, Mrs. Kirpal Kaur Bath, for benefits due to her as a widow. Initially, the social security appeal tribunal dismissed her appeal on 12 August, 1994. The tribunal held that it was not established and it could not be presumed that there was a valid marriage, because there was no evidence of a valid ceremony in accordance with the English Marriage Act, 1949.

The claimant, aged 59, went through a Sikh marriage in 1956, when aged 16, with Zora Singh Bath, then aged 19, at the Sikh temple, the Central Gurdwara, 79 Sinclair Road, West Kensington, London, at a marriage ceremony administered by a Sikh priest in accordance with Sikh custom and religion.

They lived together as man and wife for 37 years until his death in January 1994. The temple moved to a new address some time between 1956 and 1983, at which latter date it was registered for marriages. There was some evidence that it was not a registered building for performing marriages in 1956 (*For details see the legal page of The Times, London, 28 October, 1999).*

The facts of the above-mentioned case are a typical situation common to British Asians of Indian origin who migrated from the state of Punjab in the early sixties and seventies. The English ruling above will be of immense help to spouses of immigrants, in the event of any litigation, who had migrated at that point of time. From England itself, there are numerous instances where this class of early migrants altogether denied existence of their marriages to their Indian spouses, in divorce proceedings. This is with the ultimate agenda of avoiding paying any maintenance or stalling the distribution of assets. It is easy for the husband to deny the existence of the marriage, as registration of marriages in India is not compulsory under section 8 of the HMA, 1955.

J. Recent developments- Case law analysis: Tests to determine whether a particular relationship is a relationship in the nature of marriage.

In the recent case of *Indra Sarma* v. *V.K.V. Sarma,* AIR 2014 SC 309, the Supreme Court had dealt with a question related to live in relationship and the Domestic Violence Act, 2005 before it. This issue was stated in different paras of the judgement in the following words:

> *"3. We are, in this case, concerned with the question whether a " live -in relationship " would amount to a " relationship in the nature of marriage" falling within the definition of "domestic relationship " under section 2(f) of the Protection of Women from Domestic Violence Act, 2005 (for short "the DV Act") and the disruption of such a relationship by failure to maintain a women involved in such a relationship amounts to "domestic violence" within the meaning of section 3 of the DV Act."*
>
> *12. We have to examine whether the non maintenance of the appellant in a broken live-in-relationship, which is stated to be a relationship not in the nature of a marriage, will amount to "domestic violence" within the definition of section 3 of the DV Act, enabling the appellant to seek one or more reliefs provided under section 12 of the DV Act.*
>
> *20. We are, in this case, concerned with a " live-in relationship " which, according to the aggrieved person, is a " relationship in the nature of marriage" and it is that relationship which has been disrupted in the sense that the respondent failed to maintain the aggrieved person, which, according to the appellant, amounts to "domestic violence". The respondent maintained the stand that the relationship between the appellant and the respondent was not a relationship in the nature of marriage but a live -in- relationship simplicitor and the alleged act, omission, commission or conduct of the respondent would not constitute "domestic violence" so as to claim any protection orders under section 18, 19 or 20 of the DV Act."*

In order to deal with these questions, the Apex Court deemed it fit to first make a distinction between ***marriage and marital relationship, and relationship in the nature of marriage*** in order to arrive at the status of the appellant. The Court explained about marriage and marital relationship in para 23 and 24 of the judgment in the following words:

"23. Marriage is often described as one of the basic civil rights of man/woman, which is voluntarily undertaken by the parties in public in a formal way, and once concluded, recognizes the parties as husband and wife. Three elements of common law marriage are (1) agreement to be married (2) living together as husband and wife, (3) holding out to the public that they are married. Sharing a common household and duty to live together form part of the 'Consortium Omnis Vitae" which obliges spouses to live together, afford each other reasonable marital privileges and rights and be honest and faithful to each other. One of the most important invariable consequences of marriage is the reciprocal support and the responsibility of maintenance of the common household, jointly and severally. Marriage as an institution has great legal significance and various obligations and duties flow out of marital relationship , as per law, in the matter of inheritance of property, successionship, etc. Marriage, therefore, involves legal requirements of formality, publicity, exclusivity and all the legal consequences flow out of that relationship .

24. Marriages in India take place either following the personal Law of the Religion to which a party is belonged or following the provisions of the Special Marriage Act, 1954. Marriage, as per the Common Law, constitutes a contract between a man and a woman, in which the parties undertake to live together and support each other. Marriage, as a concept, is also nationally and internationally recognized. O'Regan, J., in Dawood *v.* Minister of Home Affairs, *2000 (3) SA 936 (CC) noted as follows:*

"Marriage and the family are social institutions of vital importance. Entering into and sustaining a marriage is a matter of intense private significance to the parties to that marriage for they make a promise to one another to establish and maintain an intimate relationship for the rest of their lives which they acknowledge obliges them to support one another, to live together and to be faithful to one another. Such relationships are of profound significance to the individuals concerned. But such relationships have more than personal significance at least in part because human beings are social beings whose humanity is expressed through their relationships with others. Entering into marriage therefore is to enter into a relationship that has public significance as well.

The institutions of marriage and the family are important social institutions that provide for the security, support and companionship of members of our society and bear an important role in the rearing of children. The celebration of a marriage gives rise to moral and legal obligations, particularly the reciprocal duty of support placed upon spouses and their joint responsibility for supporting and raising children born of the marriage. These legal obligations perform an important social function. This importance is symbolically acknowledged in part by the fact that marriage is celebrated generally in a public ceremony, often before family and close friends....""

The Court further went on to explain the rights and obligations of marriage and marital relationship in the following words:

"30. Entering into a marriage, therefore, either through the Hindu Marriage Act, 1955 or the Special Marriage Act, 1954 or any other Personal Law, applicable

> *to the parties, is entering into a relationship of "public significance", since marriage being a social institution, many rights and liabilities flow out of that legal relationship. The concept of marriage as a "civil right" has been recognised by various courts all over the world, for example,* Skinner v. Oklahoma, *316 US 535 (1942);* Perez *v.* Lippold, *198 P.2d 17, 20.1 (1948);* Loving *v.* Virginia, *388 US 1 (1967).*
>
> *31. We have referred to, in extenso, about the concept of "marriage and marital relationship " to indicate that the law has distinguished between married and unmarried people, which cannot be said to be unfair when we look at the rights and obligations which flow out of the legally wedded marriage. A married couple has to discharge legally various rights and obligations, unlike the case of persons having live-in relationship or, marriage-like relationship or* de facto *relationship.*
>
> *32. Married couples who choose to marry are fully cognizant of the legal obligation which arises by the operation of law on solemnization of the marriage and the rights and duties they owe to their children and the family as a whole, unlike the case of persons entering into live-in relationship. This Court in* Pinakin Mahipatray Rawal *v.* State of Gujarat, *2013 (4) RCR (Cri) 271: 2013 (5) RAJ 243: (2013) 2 SCALE 198 held that marital relationship means the legally protected marital interest of one spouse to another which include marital obligation to another like companionship, living under the same roof, sexual relation and the exclusive enjoyment of them, to have children, their up-bringing, services in the home, support, affection, love, liking and so on."*

The Court then went on to distinguish relationship in the form of marriage and also provided with some illustrative category of cases. The Court mentioned these, in the following words as stated below:

> *"35. We have already dealt with what is "marriage", "marital relationship" and "marital obligations". Let us now examine the meaning and scope of the expression "relationship in the nature of marriage" which falls within the definition of section 2(f) of the DV Act. Our concern in this case is of the third enumerated category that is "relationship in the nature of marriage" which means a relationship which has some inherent or essential characteristics of a marriage though not a marriage legally recognized, and, hence, a comparison of both will have to be resorted, to determine whether the relationship in a given case constitutes the characteristics of a regular marriage.*
>
> *36. Distinction between the relationship in the nature of marriage and marital relationship has to be noted first. Relationship of marriage continues, notwithstanding the fact that there are differences of opinions, marital unrest etc., even if they are not sharing a shared household, being based on law. But live-in-relationship is purely an arrangement between the parties unlike, a legal marriage. Once a party to a live-in-relationship determines that he/she does not wish to live in such a relationship, that relationship comes to an end. Further, in a relationship in the nature of marriage, the party asserting the existence of the relationship, at any stage or at any point of time, must positively prove the existence of the identifying characteristics of that relationship, since the legislature has used the expression "in the nature of".*

37. Reference to certain situations, in which the relationship between an aggrieved person referred to in section 2(a) and the respondent referred to in section 2(q) of the DV Act, would or would not amount to a relationship in the nature of marriage, would be apposite. Following are some of the categories of cases which are only illustrative:

(a) Domestic relationship between an unmarried adult woman and an unmarried adult male: Relationship between an unmarried adult woman and an unmarried adult male who lived or, at any point of time lived together in a shared household, will fall under the definition of section 2(f) of the DV Act and in case, there is any domestic violence, the same will fall under section 3 of the DV Act and the aggrieved person can always seek reliefs provided under Chapter IV of the DV Act.

(b) Domestic relationship between an unmarried woman and a married adult male: Situations may arise when an unmarried adult women knowingly enters into a relationship with a married adult male. The question is whether such a relationship is a relationship "in the nature of marriage" so as to fall within the definition of section 2(f) of the DV Act.

(c) Domestic relationship between a married adult woman and an unmarried adult male: Situations may also arise where an adult married woman, knowingly enters into a relationship with an unmarried adult male, the question is whether such a relationship would fall within the expression relationship "in the nature of marriage".

(d) Domestic relationship between an unmarried woman unknowingly enters into a relationship with a married adult male: An unmarried woman unknowingly enters into a relationship with a married adult male, may, in a given situation, fall within the definition of section 2(f) of the DV Act and such a relationship may be a relationship in the "nature of marriage", so far as the aggrieved person is concerned.

(e) Domestic relationship between same sex partners (Gay and Lesbians): DV Act does not recognize such a relationship and that relationship cannot be termed as a relationship in the nature of marriage under the Act. Legislatures in some countries, like the Interpretation Act, 1984 (Western Australia), the Interpretation Act, 1999 (New Zealand), the Domestic Violence Act, 1998 (South Africa), the Domestic Violence, Crime and Victims Act, 2004 (U.K.), have recognized the relationship between the same sex couples and have brought these relationships into the definition of Domestic relationship.

38. Section 2(f) of the DV Act though uses the expression "two persons", the expression "aggrieved person" under section 2(a) takes in only "woman", hence, the Act does not recognize the relationship of same sex (gay or lesbian) and, hence, any act, omission, commission or conduct of any of the parties, would not lead to domestic violence, entitling any relief under the DV Act."

The case assumes importance in the light of certain tests that were provided by the Apex Court in the body of the judgment to determine whether a particular relationship would amount to relationship in the form of marriage. The Court expressed the need of such guidelines in para no. 40 and 54, while it provided for the test in para no. 55 in the following words:

> *"40. We have, therefore, come across various permutations and combinations, in such relationships, and to test whether a particular relationship would fall within the expression "relationship in the nature of marriage", certain guiding principles have to be evolved since the expression has not been defined in the Act.*
>
> *54. We have already stated, when we examine whether a relationship will fall within the expression "relationship in the nature of marriage" within the meaning of section 2(f) of the DV Act, we should have a close analysis of the entire relationship, in other words, all facets of the interpersonal relationship need to be taken into account. We cannot isolate individual factors, because there may be endless scope for differences in human attitudes and activities and a variety of combinations of circumstances which may fall for consideration. Invariably, it may be a question of fact and degree, whether a relationship between two unrelated persons of the opposite sex meets the tests judicially evolved.*
>
> *55. We may, on the basis of above discussion cull out some guidelines for testing under what circumstances, a live-in relationship will fall within the expression "relationship in the nature of marriage" under section 2(f) of the DV Act. The guidelines, of course, are not exhaustive, but will definitely give some insight to such relationships.*
>
> *(1) Duration of period of relationship*
>
> *Section 2(f) of the DV Act has used the expression "at any point of time", which means a reasonable period of time to maintain and continue a relationship which may vary from case to case, depending upon the fact situation.*
>
> *(2) Shared household*
>
> *The expression has been defined under section 2(s) of the DV Act and, hence, need no further elaboration.*
>
> *(3) Pooling of Resources and Financial Arrangements*
>
> *Supporting each other, or any one of them, financially, sharing bank accounts, acquiring immovable properties in joint names or in the name of the woman, long term investments in business, shares in separate and joint names, so as to have a long standing relationship, may be a guiding factor.*
>
> *(4) Domestic Arrangements*
>
> *Entrusting the responsibility, especially on the woman to run the home, do the household activities like cleaning, cooking, maintaining or upkeeping the house, etc. is an indication of a relationship in the nature of marriage.*
>
> *(5) Sexual Relationship*
>
> *Marriage like relationship refers to sexual relationship, not just for pleasure, but for emotional and intimate relationship, for procreation of children, so as to give emotional support, companionship and also material affection, caring etc.*
>
> *(6) Children*
>
> *Having children is a strong indication of a relationship in the nature of marriage. Parties, therefore, intend to have a long standing relationship. Sharing the responsibility for bringing up and supporting them is also a strong indication.*

(7) Socialization in Public

Holding out to the public and socializing with friends, relations and others, as if they are husband and wife is a strong circumstance to hold the relationship is in the nature of marriage.

(8) Intention and conduct of the parties

Common intention of parties as to what their relationship is to be and to involve, and as to their respective roles and responsibilities, primarily determines the nature of that relationship."

Based on various observations and precedents, the Apex Court adjudged the status of the appellant on the basis of the test devised by it, as expressed in the following words:

> *"56. Appellant, admittedly, entered into a live-in-relationship with the respondent knowing that he was married person, with wife and two children, hence, the generic proposition laid down by the Privy Council in* Andrahennedige Dinohamy *v.* Wiketunge Liyanapatabendage Balshamy, *AIR 1927 PC 185, that where a man and a woman are proved to have lived together as husband and wife, the law presumes that they are living together in consequence of a valid marriage will not apply and, hence, the relationship between the appellant and the respondent was not a relationship in the nature of a marriage, and the status of the appellant was that of a concubine. A concubine cannot maintain a relationship in the nature of marriage because such a relationship will not have exclusivity and will not be monogamous in character. Reference may also be made to the judgments of this Court in* Badri Prasad *v.* Director of Consolidation, *(1978) 3 SCC 527 and* Tulsa *v.* Durghatiya, *2008 (1) RCR (Civil) 814: (2008) 4 SCC 520. In* Gokal Chand *v.* Parvin Kumari, *AIR 1952 SC 231 this Court held that the continuous cohabitation of man and woman as husband and wife may raise the presumption of marriage, but the presumption which may be drawn from long cohabition is a rebuttable one and if there are circumstances which weaken and destroy that presumption, the Court cannot ignore them".*

The Hon'ble Supreme Court in the following case understanding the seriousness of the legal issues arising out of live in relationships expressed the need for proper legislation in the following words:

> *62. Parliament has to ponder over these issues, bring in proper legislation or make a proper amendment of the Act, so that women and the children, born out of such kinds of relationships be protected, though those types of relationship might not be a relationship in the nature of a marriage.*

K. Right to marry is not absolute

In a recent case of *Indra Sarma* v. *V.K.V. Sarma* (*supra*), the Supreme Court of India talked on Right to marry and right to raise in para 25, 26 and 27 of the judgement in the following words:

> *"25. South African Constitutional Court in various judgments recognized the above mentioned principle. In* Satchwell v. President of the Republic of South Africa, *2002 (6) SA 1 (CC);* Du Toit *v.* Minister of Welfare and Population Development *(Lesbian and Gay Equality Project as Amicus Curiae), 2003 (2)*

SA 198 (CC), the Constitutional Court of South Africa recognized the right "free to marry and to raise family". Section 15(3)(a)(i) of the Constitution of South Africa, in substance makes provision for the recognition of "marriages concluded under the tradition, or a system of religious, personal or family law." Section 9(3) of the Constitution of South Africa reads as follows:

"The State may not unfairly discriminate directly or indirectly against anyone on one or more grounds, including race, gender, sex, pregnancy, marital status, ethnic or social origin, colour, sexual orientation, age, disability, religion, conscience, belief, culture, language and birth."

26. Article 23 of the International Covenant on Civil and Political Rights, 1966 (ICCPR) provides that:

"1. The family is the natural and fundamental group unit of society and is entitled to protection by society and the State.

2. The right of men and women of marriageable age to marry and to found a family shall be recognized.

3. No marriage shall be entered into without the free and full consent of the intending spouses.

4. States Parties to the present Covenant shall take appropriate steps to ensure equality of rights and responsibilities of spouses as to marriage, during marriage and at its dissolution. In the case of dissolution, provision shall be made for the necessary protection of any children."

27. Article 16 of the Universal Declaration of Human Rights, 1948 provides that:

"1. Men and women of full age, without any limitation due to race, nationality or religion, have the right to marry and to found a family. They are entitled to equal rights as to marriage, during marriage and at it dissolution.

2. Marriage shall be entered into only with the free and full consent of the intending spouses.

3. The family is the natural and fundamental group unit of society and is entitled to protection by society and the State.""

In a first of its kind judgment on the right of a patient suffering from contagious venereal disease to marry, the Supreme Court of India has ruled that, so long as the person is not cured of the disease or impotency, his right to marry cannot be enforced through a court of law. The judgment is reported as *Mr. 'X'* v. *Hospital 'Z'*, AIR 1999 SC 495.

The Apex Court firmly held that if the man's marriage has been cancelled owing to his being an AIDS patient, his right to marry will remain a *suspended right*. Furthermore, he is not entitled to claim any compensation from the hospital which has disclosed his medical condition to the would-be bride's family.

The judgment came in the wake of a doctor's petition seeking compensation from the Apollo Hospital in Chennai. The hospital had detected that he was an HIV -positive patient. This fact was also disclosed to his would-be bride's family. The marriage was called off immediately. The doctor contended that the hospital had violated medical ethics by disclosing his medical condition to the bride's family. This led to his social ostracism.

The court dealt with yet another aspect of the matter in paras 40 and 41 of the judgment at p. 503:

> 'Therefore, if a person suffering from the dreadful disease "AIDS," knowingly marries a woman and thereby transmits infection to that woman, he would be guilty of offences indicated in sections 269 and 270 of the Indian Penal Code.
>
> 41. The above statutory provisions thus impose a duty upon the appellant not to marry as the marriage would have the effect of spreading the infection of his own disease, which obviously is dangerous to life, to the woman whom he marries apart from being an offence.'

Sections 269 and 270 of the Indian Penal Code read as follows:

> '*269 Negligent act likely to spread infection of disease dangerous to life.*— Whoever unlawfully or negligently does any act which is, and which he knows or has reason to believe to be, likely to spread the infection of any disease dangerous to life, shall be punished with imprisonment of either description for a term which may extend to six months, or with fine, or with both.
>
> *270 Malignant act likely to spread infection of disease dangerous to life.*—Whoever malignantly does any act which is, and which he knows or has reason to believe to be, likely to spread the infection of any disease dangerous to life, shall be punished with imprisonment of either description for a term which may extend to two years, or with fine, or with both.'

The issue in the above-mentioned case has gone a step further. A petition has been filed in the Supreme Court of India, seeking clarification of the above-mentioned judgment to facilitate marriage of an HIV-positive person after 'full, free and informed consent is taken for the marriage.' *(For details see: 'SC seeks opinion on AIDS patients' right to marry,' The Times of India, New Delhi, 8 February 2000)*

The same Supreme Court Bench comprising of Justice B.N. Kirpal and Justice S. Saghir Ahmad, which had handed down the earlier above mentioned judgment has issued notices to the Union of India and the Medical Council of India to ascertain their views. The second petition on this subject has been filed by Sahara, a centre for residential care and rehabilitation of HIV-positive persons under the AIDS care project.

L Children born out of Live-in Relationship

Legalizing live-in relationship gave rise to the issue of the status of children as to whether they would be legitimate or illegitimate. In answer to this question the Supreme Court of India in the case of *Bharatha Matha* v. *R. Vijaya Renganathan*, AIR 2010 SC 2685 held that children born out of live in relationship are not to be termed as illegitimate. It stated that Evidence Act provides for a presumption of the child being legitimate, until proved by strong preponderance of evidence to the contrary. In this context para 16 and 21 of the judgment is quoted below:

"16. Section 112 of the Evidence Act provides for a presumption of a child being legitimate and such a presumption can only be displaced by a strong preponderance of evidence and not merely by a balance of probabilities as the law has to live in favour of innocent child from being bastardised.

21. In S.P.S. Balasubramanyam *v.* Suruttayan @ Andali Padayachi, AIR 1992 SC 756, *this Court held that if man and woman are living under the same roof and cohabiting for a number of years,* **there will be a presumption under section 114 of the Evidence Act that they live as husband and wife and the children born to them will not be illegitimate**".

The Court further talking on the right to succession of property by a child born out of a live in relationship stated in the following words:

23. In Smt. P.E.K. Kalliani Amma *v.* K. Devi, AIR 1996 SC 1963, *this Court held that section 16 of the Act is not ultra vires of the Constitution of India. In view of the legal fiction contained in section 16, the illegitimate children, for all practical purposes, including succession to the properties of their parents, have to be treated as legitimate. They cannot, however, succeed to the properties of any other relation on the basis of this rule, which in its operation, is limited to the properties of the parents.*

25. In Jinia Keotin *v.* Kumar Sitaram Manjhi, *2003 (1) RCR (Civil) 469: (2003) 1 SCC 730, this Court held that while engrafting a rule of fiction in section 16 of the Act, the illegitimate children have become entitled to get share only in self-acquired properties of their parents. The Court held as under:—*

"4...........Under the ordinary law, a child for being treated as legitimate must be born in lawful wedlock. If the marriage itself is void on account of contravention of the statutory prescriptions, any child born of such marriage would have the effect, per se, or on being so declared or annulled, as the case may be, of bastardising the children born of the parties to such marriage. Polygamy, which was permissible and widely prevalent among the Hindus in the past and considered to have evil effects on society, came to be put an end to by the mandate of the Parliament in enacting the Hindu Marriage Act, 1955. The legitimate status of the children which depended very much upon the marriage between their parents being valid or void, thus turned on the act of parents over which the innocent child had no hold or control. But for no fault of it, the innocent baby had to suffer a permanent set back in life and in the eyes of society by being treated as illegitimate. A laudable and noble act of the legislature indeed in enacting section 16 to put an end to a great social evil. At the same time, section 16 of the Act, while engrafting a rule of fiction in ordaining the children, though illegitimate, to be treated as legitimate, notwithstanding that the marriage was void or voidable chose also to confine its application, so far as succession or inheritance by such children are concerned to the properties of the parents only.

5. So far as section 16 of the Act is concerned, though it was enacted to legitimise children, who would otherwise suffer by becoming illegitimate, at the same time it expressly provide in sub-section (3) by engrafting a provision with a non-obstante clause *stipulating specifically that nothing contained in sub-section (1) or sub-section (2) shall be construed as conferring upon any child of a marriage, which is null and void or which is annulled by a decree of nullity under section 12, 'any rights in or to the property of any person, other than the parents, in any case where, but for the passing of this Act, such child would have been incapable of possessing or acquiring any such rights by reason of this not being the legitimate child of his parents'. In the light of such an express mandate of the legislature itself there is no room for according upon such children who but for section 16 would have been branded as illegitimate any further rights than envisaged therein by resorting to any presumptive or inferential process of reasoning, having recourse to the mere object or purpose of enacting section 16 of the Act. Any attempt to do so would amount to doing not only violence to the provision specifically engrafted in sub-section (3) of section 16 of the Act but also would attempt to court relegislating on the subject under the guise of interpretation, against even the will expressed in the enactment itself. Consequently, we are unable to countenance the submissions on behalf of the appellants......."*

26. This view has been approved and followed by this Court in Neelamma *v.* Sarojamma, *(2006) 9 SCC 612.*

27. **Thus, it is evident that in such a fact-situation, a child born of void or voidable marriage is not entitled to claim inheritance in ancestral coparcenery property but is entitled only to claim share in self acquired properties, if any".**

Hence, children born out of a live in relationship would have full rights of maintenance, upkeep and their education besides share of self-acquired properties of their parents. As per the above judgment they will not be able to claim inheritance in ancestral property at par with legal heirs born from a valid and subsisting marriage between their parents as per their statutory personal laws. But, In the recent of *Revanasiddappa* v. *Mallikarjun*, (2011) 11 SCC 1, a matter came up before the Apex Court to examine whether the illegitimate children are entitled to a share in the coparcenary property or whether their share is limited only to the self-acquired property of their parents under section 16(3) of the Hindu Marriage Act, 1955. In the present appeal, the court has referred the said matter to a larger bench due to its view different from that of the earlier cases of *Jinia Keotin* v. *Kumar Sitaram Manjhi*, (2003) 1 SCC 730; *Neelamma* v. *Sarojamma*, (2006) 9 SCC 612; and *Bharatha Matha* v. *R. Vijaya Renganathan*, AIR 2010 SC 2685. All these cases held that where an illegitimate child is entitled to a share of his parents, such share must relate to the self-acquired properties and not the ancestral ones.

The Court is of the opinion that these cases represent a narrow view of section 16(3). Also, such entitlement of the illegitimate children in the coparcenary property as well, is in conformity with the article 37 of the Constitution of India and the same is stated below:

"35. In our view, in the case of joint family property such children will be entitled only to a share in their parents' property but they cannot claim it on their own right. Logically, on the partition of an ancestral property, the property falling in the share of the parents of such children is regarded as their self acquired **and** *absolute property. In view of the amendment, we see no reason why such children*

will have no share in such property since such children are equated under the amended law with legitimate offspring of valid marriage. The only limitation even after the amendment seems to be that during the life time of their parents such children cannot ask for partition but they can exercise this right only after the death of their parents.

36. We are constrained to differ from the interpretation of section 16(3) rendered by this Court in Jinia Keotin *(supra) and, thereafter, in* Neelamma *(supra) and* Bharatha Matha *(supra) in view of the constitutional values enshrined in the preamble of our Constitution which focuses on the concept of equality of status and opportunity and also on individual dignity. The Court has to remember that relationship between the parents may not be sanctioned by law but the birth of a child in such relationship has to be viewed independently of the relationship of the parents. A child born in such relationship is innocent and is entitled to all the rights which are given to other children born in valid marriage. This is the crux of the amendment in section 16(3). However, some limitation on the property rights of such children is still there in the sense their right is confined to the property of their parents. Such rights cannot be further restricted in view of the preexisting common law view discussed above. It is well known that this Court cannot interpret a socially beneficial legislation on the basis as if the words therein are cast in stone. Such legislation must be given a purposive interpretation to further and not to frustrate the eminently desirable social purpose of removing the stigma on such children. In doing so, the Court must have regard to the equity of the Statute and the principles voiced under Part IV of the Constitution, namely, the Directive Principles of State Policy. In our view this flows from the mandate of article 37 which provides that it is the duty of the State to apply the principles enshrined in Chapter IV in making laws. It is no longer in dispute that today State would include the higher judiciary in this country. Considering article 37 in the context of the duty of judiciary, Justice Mathew in* Kesavananda Bharati Sripadagalvaru *v.* State of Kerala, *(1973) 4 SCC 225 held:*

"I can see no incongruity in holding, when article 37 says in its latter part "it shall be the duty of the State to apply these principles in making laws", that judicial process is 'State action' and that the judiciary is bound to apply the Directive Principles in making its judgment."

Hence, the view that when an illegitimate child is entitled to a share of his parents' properties, such share must relate to the self-acquired properties and not the ancestral ones, is now to be adjudicated by a larger Bench of the Apex Court. However, till then the settled view prevails and children will have a right to whatever becomes the property of their parents whether self acquired or ancestral. This is the position of law now prevailing as of date.

II. CHILD ABDUCTION AND GUARDIANSHIP

A. Child abduction principles

International child abduction law in India stands substantially modified in terms of a recent Supreme Court judgment in the matter of *Dhanwanti Joshi* v. *Madhav Unde*, JT 1997 (8) SC 720. This judgment was handed down on

4 November, 1997. The said judgment deals with the provisions and case law analysis relating to the Hindu Minority and Guardianship Act, 1980 read with the Guardian and Wards Act, 1890. These two enactments principally govern the law relating to child custody under the Indian laws.

Under Indian law, *i.e.*, the Guardian and Wards Act 1890 and Hindu Minority and Guardianship Act, 1956, the prime consideration is the welfare of the child, though section 6(a) of the latter Act says that the custody of a minor who has not attained the age of five shall ordinarily be with the mother.

It has been held in para 31 at pp. 733-734 of the judgment, which is reproduced below for the purposes of ready reference:

> 'So far as non-Convention countries are concerned, or where the removal related to a period before adopting the Convention, the law is that the Court to which the child is removed will consider the question on merits bearing the welfare of the child as of paramount importance and consider the order of the foreign court as only a factor to be taken into consideration as stated in *McKee* v. *McKee,* 1951 AC 352, unless the Court thinks it fit to exercise summary jurisdiction in the interests of the child and its prompt return is for its welfare, as explained in *Re L,* [1974] 1 All ER 913 (CA). As recently as 1996–1997, it has been held in *P (A Minor) (Child Abduction: Non Convention Country), Re:,* (1996) 3 FCR 233 (CA) by Ward LJ 1996 (Current Law) (Year Book) (pp. 165-166) that in deciding whether to order the return of a child who has been abducted from his or her country of habitual residence – which was not a party to the Hague Convention 1980 – the Courts' overriding consideration must be the child's welfare. There is no need for the judge to attempt to apply the provisions of article 13 of the Convention by ordering the child's return unless a grave risk of harm was established.'

From the above mandate of law, it is clear that the Courts in India would not now exercise a summary jurisdiction to return children to the foreign country of habitual residence.

It has also been held, in para 21 of the above judgment, that orders relating to the custody of children are by their very nature not final, but are interlocutory in nature and subject to modification at any future time upon proof of change of circumstances requiring change of custody, but such change in custody must be proved to be in the paramount interests of the child. This was the position of law laid down by the Supreme Court of India in *Rosy Jacob* v. *Jacob A. Chakramakkal,* (1973) 1 SCC 840. The law laid down in *Rosy Jacob*'s case has been explicitly reiterated in the above mentioned 1997 ruling.

It has been further held in this judgment that the custody order of a foreign court is only one of the factors which will be taken into consideration by a court of law in India. The Court in India will form an independent judgment on the merits of the matter with regard to the welfare of the children. Lastly, superior financial capacity cannot be a sole ground for disturbing the children from their mother's custody.

The tenor of law laid down in the above-mentioned judgment of *Dhanwanti Joshi* has very recently been reiterated by the Supreme Court of India in *Sarita Sharma* v. *Sushil Sharma,* JT 2000 (2) SC 158. The brief facts of this case are mentioned below.

The parents of the children were living in the USA. The children were put in the custody of the father, while the mother was given visiting rights. In exercise of visiting rights on 7 May, 1997, the mother picked up the children from the father's residence. She was to leave the children next morning. The father got the information that the children were not brought back to the school. Eventually, the mother without obtaining any order from the American Court, flew to India with the children.

The father filed a habeas corpus writ petition in the Delhi High Court on 9 September, 1997. The wife's contention was that by virtue of the orders dated 5 February, 1996 and 2 April, 1997 made by the courts in America, both of them were appointed as possessory conservators. Hence, both the children were in her lawful custody.

The Delhi High Court held that in view of the interim orders made by the American Court, the wife had committed a wrong in not informing that Court and obtaining its permission to remove the children from the jurisdiction of that Court. The Delhi High Court took note of the fact that a competent court having territorial jurisdiction had granted a decree of divorce and had ordered that only the father should have the custody of the children. The Delhi High Court allowed the petition and directed the wife to restore the custody of the two children to the father. It was also declared that it was open to the husband to take the children to the USA without any hindrance. The wife appealed to the Supreme Court of India.

The Supreme Court, in para 4 of the judgment at p. 263, noticed from the record that there were serious differences between the two. The husband was an alcoholic and had indulged in violence against the wife. The conduct of the wife was also not very satisfactory.

In para 4 of the judgment itself, the court framed the following issues:

> 'The question is whether the custody became illegal as she had committed a breach of the order of the American Court directing her not to remove the children from the jurisdiction of that Court without its permission. After she came to India a decree of divorce and the order for the custody of the children have been passed. Therefore, it is also required to be considered whether the mother's custody became illegal thereafter.'

The Supreme Court of India held, in para 6 of the judgment at pp. 264 and 265, as follows:

> '6. Therefore, it will not be proper to be guided entirely by the fact that the appellant Sarita had removed the children from USA despite the order of the Court of that country. So also, in view of the facts and circumstances of the case, the decree passed by the American Court though a relevant factor, cannot override the consideration of welfare of the minor children.

We have already stated earlier that in USA respondent Sushil is staying along with his mother aged about 80 years. There is no one else in the family. The respondent appears to be in the habit of taking excessive alcohol. Though it is true that both the children have the American citizenship and there is a possibility that in USA they may be able to get better education, it is doubtful if the respondent will be in a position to take proper care of the children when they are so young. Out of them one is a female child. She is aged about 5 years. Ordinarily, a female child should be allowed to remain with the mother so that she can be properly looked after. It is also not desirable that two children are separated from each other. If a female child has to stay with the mother, it will be in the interest of both the children that they both stay with the mother. Here in India also proper care of the children is taken and they are at present studying in good schools. We have not found the appellant wanting in taking proper care of the children. Both the children have a desire to stay with the mother. At the same time it must be said that the son, who is elder than the daughter, has good feelings for his father also. Considering all the aspects relating to the welfare of the children, we are of the opinion that in spite of the order passed by the Court in USA it was not proper for the High Court to have allowed the Habeas Corpus writ petition and directed the appellant to hand over custody of the children to the respondent and permit him to take them away to USA. What would be in the interest of the children requires a full and thorough inquiry and, therefore, the High Court should have directed the respondent to initiate appropriate proceedings in which such an inquiry can be held.'

Furthermore, para 31 of the judgment in *Dhanwanti Joshi's* case, which has been already reproduced above was expressly reiterated by the Supreme Court of India in para 5 of the judgment in *Sarita Sharma's* case. *Sarita Sharma's* case is second in line of ruling of its kind handed down by the Supreme Court of India, altering the earlier dicta of child abduction law.

Before the above-mentioned 1997 and 1999 rulings were handed down by the Supreme Court of India, there was case-law to the contrary, allowing enforcement of foreign court custody orders on the principle of comity on a case-by-case basis. Such orders were normally enforced by initiating *habeas corpus* petitions under article 226 of the Constitution of India in the High Court of the region where the child was situated, or directly in the Supreme Court of India under article 32 of the Constitution of India.

It is pertinent to mention that article 137 of the Constitution of India provides for review of judgments or orders made by the Supreme Court of India. Article 141 of the Constitution of India mandates that the law declared by the Supreme Court of India shall be binding on all courts within the territory of India.

There is ample earlier case-law contrary to the law recently laid down in *Dhanwanti Joshi* and *Sarita Sharma*. One such Supreme Court of India ruling—

Surinder Kaur Sandhu v. *Harbax Singh Sandhu,* AIR 1984 SC 1224 has been noticed in para 5 at p. 262 in *Sarita Sharma*'s case. Para 10 of the judgment in

Sandhu's case has been reproduced in para 5 of *Sarita Sharma*'s case, which is reproduced hereunder for ready reference:

> 'We may add that the spouses had set up their matrimonial home in England where the wife was working as a clerk and the husband as a bus driver. The boy is a British citizen, having been born in England, and he holds a British passport. It cannot be controverted that, in these circumstances, the English Court had jurisdiction to decide the question of his custody. The modern theory of conflict of Laws recognises and, in any event, prefers the jurisdiction of the State which has the most intimate contact with the issues arising in the case. Jurisdiction is not attracted by the operation or creation of fortuitous circumstances such as the circumstance as to where the child, whose custody is in issue, is brought or for the time being lodged. To allow the assumption of jurisdiction by another State in such circumstances will only result in encouraging forum-shopping. Ordinarily, jurisdiction must follow upon functional lines. That is to say, for example, that in matters relating to matrimony and custody, the law of that place must govern which has the closest concern with the well-being of the spouses and the welfare of the offsprings of marriage. The spouses in this case had made England their home where this boy was born to them. The father cannot deprive the English Court of its jurisdiction to decide upon his custody by removing him to India, not in the normal movement of the matrimonial home but, by an act which was gravely detrimental to the peace of that home. The fact that the matrimonial home of the spouses was in England, establishes sufficient contacts or ties with that State in order to make it reasonable and just for the courts of that State to assume jurisdiction to enforce obligations which were incurred therein by the spouses. [See *International Shoe Company* v. *State of Washington,* 90 L Ed 95 (1945): 326 US 310], which was not a matrimonial case but which is regarded as the fountainhead of the subsequent developments of jurisdictional issues like the one involved in the instant case). It is our duty and function to protect the wife against the burden of litigating in an inconvenient forum which she and her husband had left voluntarily in order to make their living in England, where they gave birth to this unfortunate boy.'

The earlier mandate of law as laid down in *Sandhu*'s case elaborated above has not been followed by the Supreme Court of India in *Sarita Sharma*'s case.

In *Sarita Sharma*'s case, the Supreme Court has also noticed the earlier law laid down in *Elizabeth Dinshaw* v. *Arvand M. Dinshaw,* AIR 1987 SC 3. In this ruling the Apex Court had exercised summary jurisdiction regarding the return of the minor child. In *Dinshaw*'s case it was also stressed that the interest and the welfare of the minor child is the predominant criterion in child custody matters.

The earlier law laid down in *Sandhu* and *Dinshaw* stands substantially modified with the recent mandate of law in *Dhanwanti Joshi* and *Sarita Sharma.* However, in view of four recent judgements of the Apex Court in 2009, 2010 and 2014, the trend seems to be changing again. A brief description of these four recent decisions is summarized as hereunder:

In *Shilpa Aggarwal* v. *Aviral Mittal,* decided on 9 December, 2009, 2010 (1) SCC 591, a three and a half year old girl child, who was a British citizen born in USA to Indian parents was removed to India from USA by the mother in contravention of British Court orders. The mother was directed by the Supreme Court of India to return with the child to USA.

In *Dr. V. Ravi Chandaran* v. *Union of India,* decided on 17 November, 2009, (2010) 1 SCC 174, a seven year old boy, who was a US citizen and was born in USA to Indian Parents (who had become US citizens) was removed to India from USA by the mother contrary to US Court orders. The mother was directed by the Supreme Court of India to return to USA with the child failing which the father would be entitled to do so to take the child to USA.

In *Vikramvir Vohra* v. *Shalini Bhalla,* decided on 25 March, 2010, JT 2010 (3) SC 213, it was held by the Supreme Court of India that child custody orders are interlocutory in nature and can be altered for the welfare of the child. Consequently, the Supreme Court permitted the mother to take her minor son aged about ten years to Australia as per the wishes of the child to stay with the mother upholding the welfare of the child as a paramount consideration.

In *Arathi Bandi* v. *Bandi Jagadrakshaka Rao,* AIR 2014 SC 918, a decree of dissolution of marriage was obtained from a US Court. The custody of child was given to husband. The wife thereafter travelled to India along with child in defiance of the US Court order. The husband then came to India and filed a *Habeas Corpus* petition before the High Court seeking production of the child and permitting him to take custody of the minor in compliance with the order passed by the US Court. The High Court directed the wife to submit to the jurisdiction of the US Courts. An appeal by the wife was dismissed by Supreme Court which held that: *"(i) A parent doing wrong by removing children out of the country does not gain any advantage by his or her wrongdoing; and (ii) Contention that the American court, which passed the order/decree has no jurisdiction and being inconsistent in Indian Laws cannot be executed in India is not tenable"*

Hence, as of now, every case stands to be determined afresh based on the consideration of the best interest of the removed child to be determined by an Indian Court of competent jurisdiction, where the decision is taken to return the child or not to the country from where the child was removed.

B. Forum for custody proceedings

As far as the forum for securing the return of children is concerned, it is important to mention that India is not a signatory to the Hague Convention on the Civil Aspects of International Child Abduction, 1980. Under article 226 of the Constitution of India, a parent whose child has been abducted can petition the State High Court to issue a writ of habeas corpus against the abducting spouse for the return of the child. Alternatively, a habeas corpus petition seeking recovery of the abducted child can also be directly filed in the Supreme Court of India under article 32 of the Constitution of India.

C. Visiting rights cannot be denied

The Supreme Court of India, in a recent ruling reported as *N. Nirmala* v. *Nelson Jeyakumar*, JT 1999 (5) SC 223 held that deprivation of visiting rights is not justified. The question involved in this appeal concerned the custody of a minor daughter. The respondent-father was permitted to continue the custody as legal guardian. The learned single judge of the High Court confirmed the custody of the minor daughter with the father but gave visiting rights to the appellant-mother. Against the order passed by the learned single judge, the appellant- mother in search of an actual order of custody, appealed before a Division Bench of the High Court, which by the impugned judgment dismissed the appeal and deprived the mother of her visiting rights for which there was no cross-objection on the part of the respondent. The matter went on further appeal to the Supreme Court on this judgment being question by the mother.

The Apex Court held in para 3 at p. 223 of the judgment:

> 'In our opinion, such a further adverse order against the appellant was not justified. The interest of justice will be served if the order of the learned Single Judge continuing the custody of the minor child with the respondent and as confirmed by the Division Bench is maintained subject to the modification that visiting right which was denied to the appellant by the Division Bench be continued.'

D. Welfare of the minor child is the paramount consideration

In *Om Prakash Bharuka* v. *Shakuntala Modi*, AIR 1993 Gau 38 a custody dispute between the mother and father of the three minor children, custody had been granted to the mother. The wishes of the children were ascertained. They flatly refused to go and stay with their father. The court held, in para 17, at p. 42 of the judgment:

> '17. Merely because the father loves his children and is not shown to be otherwise undesirable cannot necessarily lead to the conclusion that the welfare of the children would be better promoted by granting their custody to him as against the wife who may also be equally affectionate towards her children and otherwise equally free from blemish, and, who, in addition because of her profession and financial resources, may be in a position to guarantee better health, education and maintenance for them. Thus therefore, the Court in case of a dispute between the father and mother is expected to strike a just and proper balance between the requirements of welfare of the minor children and the rights of their respective parents over them. In short, while giving custody of the children, the welfare of the children should be regarded as a paramount consideration.'

E. Foreign orders

The principles governing the validity of foreign court orders are laid down in section 13 of the CPC. This has already been discussed under the sub-heading, guidelines laid down by the Supreme Court of India on recognition of foreign matrimonial judgments.

It is reiterated, as elaborated above, that the Indian Courts would not exercise summary jurisdiction to return children to the country of habitual residence. The Courts in India would consider the question on its merits bearing in mind the welfare of the children as of paramount importance.

Section 14 of the CPC talks of a presumption as to foreign judgments. It provides that the court shall presume, upon the production of any document purporting to be a certified copy of a foreign judgment, that such judgment was pronounced by a court of competent jurisdiction, unless the contrary appears on the record; but such presumption may be displaced by proving want of jurisdiction.

F. No provision for mirror orders in India

In light of the prevailing child abduction law in India as elaborated above, it is not possible to obtain mirror orders – a concept known to the English legal system – as there exists no provision for the same in the Indian legal mechanisms. Since foreign court custody orders cannot now be mechanically enforced, it is suggested that in the event of any litigation in the foreign country of habitual residence, a Letter of Request be obtained by the foreign court in which litigation is pending, incorporating safeguards and conditions to ensure the return of the minor child to the country of normal residence.

This Letter of Request should be addressed by the foreign court to the Registrar General of the High Court within whose jurisdiction the estranged spouse is residing with the minor child. It should also be categorically mentioned that the passports of the parent and the child should be deposited with the Registrar General of the State High Court.

G. *Habeas corpus* can also be issued by a person who is not a citizen of India

It is well established that a writ of habeas corpus can be issued to secure the custody of a minor child. This can also be sought even by a person who is not a citizen of this country as recently held in *Miss Atya Shamim* v. *Deputy Commissioner/Collector, Delhi (Prescribed Authority under Citizenship Act)*, AIR 1999 J&K 140. The Jammu and Kashmir High Court in this ruling reiterated *Elizabeth Dinshaw's* case, AIR 1987 SC 3 where the Supreme Court of India had issued a writ at the instance of a person who was not a citizen of this country.

H. Child abduction and forced marriages

In a somewhat extreme and unusual set of circumstances, Mr. Justice Singer of the High Court of London ruled that parents who take their children abroad to marry them off against their wishes were guilty of child abduction. This judgment was handed down by the Family Division, Principal Registry on 18 May, 1999 and was reported as *Re KR (Abduction: Forcible Removal by Parents)*, [1999] 2 FLR 542.

The Judge, in the opening paragraph of the judgment, highlights the extent to which courts and other agencies concerned need to be alert to safeguard the individual integrity of children from attack, even from their own family. This case has also highlighted the risk which adolescents, particularly girls of a marriageable age, encounter when they seek to depart from the traditional norms of their religious, cultural or ethnic group.

The ruling pertains to a 17-year-old British Sikh girl who had been taken by her parents to a remote village in India to be married to one of the suitors they had chosen for her. The judge employed the services of the British Foreign Office, Interpol, British High Commission, New Delhi and the Indian police to help the girl return to Britain.

The girl had left her home in April 1998 to avoid being married. She went to live with her 19-year-old sister, who had also left home to escape being forced into a marriage against her wishes.

In June 1998, the girl was taken to India where she stayed with her aunt in Punjab. Her passport was confiscated by the family. She was kept under a close watch. She managed to smuggle a letter to her sister in England pleading for help.

Her sister contacted Reunite, a renowned London-based international charity organisation, whose purpose is to give impartial and expert advice and support to the parents of children abducted or believed to be at risk of abduction. With Reunite's assistance, legal proceedings were initiated to make the girl a ward of the court and remove her from her parents' control.

Reunite had to act quickly because once the abducted girl was 18, she could no longer be a ward of the court. The English court wanted to be sure as to what were the intentions of the girl before it took any judicial steps. Her parents insisted that she wanted to stay in India and even provided taped telephone conversations and fax communications from her as proof. The court insisted that officials from the British High Commission should interview the girl. It was discovered that the girl was being moved from place to place to evade them.

Eventually, the girl convinced her parents that she should be taken to the British High Commission at New Delhi. She told the officials that she wanted to return to London.

During the course of the proceedings, Mr. Justice Singer had drawn up an order which would have some extra-territorial effect, in the sense that it might encourage relevant authorities in India to give assistance. The judge rightly pointed out in the judgment that the order might be of assistance in comparable situations and it is reproduced hereunder:

> 'UPON hearing …
>
> AND UPON the application of all parties herein and by consent of all parties herein and upon reading … and upon hearing …
>
> AND WHEREAS KR is a Ward of this Honourable Court and is a British citizen; born in and domiciled in the United Kingdom; and currently travelling with a United Kingdom passport
>
> AND WHEREAS in consequence of the fact that this Court has ordered that KR remain a Ward of this Court while (until she attains the age of 18 years on [date]) she remains a minor, this Court is empowered and required to exercise its custodial jurisdiction over her and to ascertain her best interests and to facilitate and protect those best interests

> AND WHEREAS this Honourable Court is anxious to protect and secure her well-being and best interests and to ensure that she may freely express her wishes concerning her country and place of residence
>
> AND WHEREAS this Honourable Court is anxious to ensure that she is not induced or coerced into contracting any marriage or betrothal against her will
>
> AND WHEREAS this Honourable Court is satisfied that all interested parties are before the Court including the Official Solicitor appointed by the Court to represent the Ward
>
> AND WHEREAS this Honourable Court having heard limited oral evidence from [F and M] is of the view that serious grounds exist in the present circumstances to question whether this Honourable Court's Ward KR is able freely to express her views and wishes and in particular with regard to her country of residence
>
> IT IS ORDERED that every person in a position to do so shall co-operate in assisting and securing the immediate return to England of KR, a Ward of this Honourable Court
>
> AND NOW THEREFORE this Court invites all judicial and administrative bodies in the State of India to render assistance in establishing the whereabouts of the Ward of this Honourable Court and in arranging for her to be placed in contact with the British High Commission in New Delhi (Reference: [a named individual]) and to facilitate her travel to the British High Commission with a view to her immediate return to the United Kingdom.'

Indeed, the order was of assistance. The girl flew back to England on 5 March 1999. The court issued a protection order preventing her family from abducting her or trying forcibly to take her back to India.

The judge held at p. 10 in the concluding portion of the judgment:

> 'Sensitivity to these traditional and/or religious influences is however likely, in English courts, usually to give way to the integrity of the individual child or young person concerned. In the courts of this country the voice of the young person will be heard and, in so personal a context as opposition to an arranged or enforced marriage, will prevail. The courts will not permit what is at best the exploitation of an individual and may in the worst case amount to outright trafficking for financial consideration.'

I. The Hindu Minority and Guardianship Act, 1956 (hereafter HMGA, 1956)

It is important to advert to the provisions of the HMGA, 1956, which is an act to amend and codify certain parts of the law relating to minority and guardianship among Hindus. The provisions of the HMGA, 1956 are supplemental to the earlier Guardians and Wards Act, 1890. The HMGA, 1956, like the HMA, 1955, has extra-territorial application. It extends to the whole of India except the States of Jammu and Kashmir.

In terms of section 4(a) of the 1956 Act 'minor' means a person who has not completed the age of 18 years. A 'guardian' in section 4(b) is defined as the natural guardian or one appointed by will or a court of law.

Section 6 of the HMGA, 1956 defines the natural guardians of a Hindu minor, which recently came up for interpretation by the Supreme Court of India in the matter of *Githa Hariharan* v. *Reserve Bank of India*, (1999) 2 SCC 228. Two cases involving a similar point of law were decided by the Apex court. In this landmark judgement the Supreme Court has given the mother her due place in the HMGA, 1956 by ruling that both the mother and father would be treated as the natural guardians of their minor children.

In Writ Petition number 489 of 1995, the first petitioner and her husband, the second petitioner, jointly applied to the Reserve Bank of India, the first respondent, for the issue of Relief Bonds in the name of their son. They stated expressly that both of them agreed that the mother of the child, *i.e.* the first petitioner would act as the guardian of the minor for the purpose of investments made with the money held by their minor son. Accordingly, in the prescribed form of application, the first petitioner signed as the guardian of the minor. RBI replied to the petitioners advising them either to produce the application form signed by the father of the minor or a certificate of guardianship from a competent authority in favour of the mother. The bank contended that the mother was not the natural guardian of a minor in terms of section 6(a) of the HMGA, 1956. Ultimately, the petitioners filed a writ petition under article 32 of the Constitution of India seeking to strike down section 6(a) of the HMGA, 1956 and section 19(b) of the GWA, 1890 as a violation of articles 14 and 15 of the Constitution of India. The petitioners also sought to quash and set aside RBI's decision not to accept the deposit from them and to issue a mandamus directing the acceptance of the same after declaring the first petitioner as the natural guardian of the minor. Article 14 mandates that the State shall not deny to any person equality before the law or the equal protection of laws within the territory of India, while article 15 prohibits discrimination on grounds of religion, race, caste, sex or place of birth. Section 19 of the GWA, 1890 contemplates three contingencies in which the Court has no authority to appoint or declare a guardian of a minor at all. By virtue of section 19(b), no order declaring a guardian can be made during the lifetime of a minor's father, unless in the opinion of the court he is unfit to be the guardian of the minor.

Section 6 of the HMGA, 1956 is reproduced hereunder for ready reference:

> '6. The natural guardians of a Hindu minor, in respect of the minor's person as well as in respect of the minor's property (excluding his or her undivided interest in joint family property), are—
>
> (a) in the case of a boy or an unmarried girl – the father, and after him, the mother: Provided that the custody of a minor who has not completed the age of five years shall ordinarily be with the mother;
>
> (b) in the case of an illegitimate boy or an illegitimate unmarried girl – the mother, and after her, the father;
>
> (c) in the case of a married girl – the husband:

Provided that no person shall be entitled to act as the natural guardian of a minor under the provisions of this section—

(a) if he has ceased to be a Hindu, or

(b) if he has completely and finally renounced the world by becoming a hermit (vanaprastha) or an ascetic (yati or sanyasi).'

The judgment of the Chief Justice of India Dr. A.S. Anand assumes significance as he ruled, in para 7 of the judgment at p. 234:

> 'The expression "natural guardian" is defined in section 4(c) of the HMG Act as any of the guardians mentioned in section 6 (supra). The term "guardian" is defined in section 4(b) of the HMG Act as a person having the care of the person of a minor or of his property or of both, his person and property, and includes a natural guardian among others. Thus, it is seen that the definitions of "guardian" and "natural guardian" do not make any discrimination against mother and she being one of the guardians mentioned in section 6 would undoubtedly be a natural guardian as defined in section 4(c). The only provision to which exception is taken is found in section 6(a) which reads "the father, and *after* him, the mother". (emphasis ours) That phrase, on a cursory reading, does give an impression that the mother can be considered to be the natural guardian of the minor only after the lifetime of the father. In fact, that appears to be the basis of the stand taken by the Reserve Bank of India also. It is not in dispute and is otherwise well settled also that the welfare of the minor in the widest sense is the paramount consideration and even during the lifetime of the father, if necessary, he can be replaced by the mother or any other suitable person by an order of the court, where to do so would be in the interest of the welfare of the minor.'

Both the authors of the judgment, Justices Dr. Anand and Srinivasan, interpreting section 6(a) of the HMGA, 1956 in a manner to keep it in the ambit of constitutional validity held that the word 'after' need not necessarily mean 'after the lifetime.' It means 'in the absence of', the word 'absence' referring to the father's absence from the care of the minor's property or person for any reasons whatever.

The court held, in para 10 of the judgment at p. 235, that on the following grounds the father would be treated as absent and the mother being the recognised natural guardian, can act validly on behalf of a minor as the guardian:

(a) If the father is wholly indifferent to the matters of the minor even if he is living with the mother.

(b) If by virtue of mutual understanding between the father and the mother, the latter is put exclusively in charge of the minor.

(c) If the father is physically unable to take care of the minor either because of his staying away from the place where the mother and the minor are living or because of his physical or mental incapacity.

This progressive ruling also has a beneficial aspect for private international law. Paragraph 14 of the judgment at p. 238 recites:

'The message of international instruments – the Convention on the Elimination of All Forms of Discrimination Against Women, 1979 ("CEDAW") and the Beijing Declaration, which directs all State parties to take appropriate measures to prevent discrimination of all forms against women is quite clear. India is a signatory to CEDAW having accepted and ratified it in June 1993. The interpretation that we have placed on section 6(a) (supra) gives effect to the principles contained in these instruments. The domestic courts are under an obligation to give due regard to international conventions and norms for construing domestic laws when there is no inconsistency between them.'

Furthermore, Justice Banerjee, in para 35 of the judgment at pp. 242 to 243, has drawn a parallel between English law and Indian law on the subject. It will be noticed from the English rulings below that the welfare of the child is the common denominator in both the jurisdictions. In *Re McGrath*, (1893) 1 Ch 143: 62 LJ Ch 208 Lindley LJ observed:

'The dominant matter for the consideration of the court is the welfare of the child. But the welfare of a child is not to be measured by money only, nor by physical comfort only. The word 'welfare' must be taken in its widest sense. The moral and religious welfare of the child must be considered as well as its physical well-being. Nor can the ties of affection be disregarded.'

Lord Esher MR in *Re Gyngall*, (1893) 2 QB 232 stated:

'The court has to consider, therefore, the whole of the circumstances of the case, the position of the parent, the position of the child, the age of the child, the religion of the child, so far as it can be said to have any religion and the happiness of the child. Prima facie, it would not be for the welfare of the child to be taken away from its natural parent and given over to other people who have not that natural relation to it. Every wise man would say that, generally speaking, the best place for a child is with its parent. If a child is brought up, as one may say from its mother's lap in one form of religion, it would not, I should say be for its happiness and welfare that a stranger should take it away in order to alter its religious views. Again, it cannot be merely because the parent is poor and the person who seeks to have the possession of the child as against the parent is rich, that, without regard to any other consideration, to the natural rights and feelings of the parent, or the feelings and views that have been introduced into the heart and mind of the child, the child ought not to be taken away from its parent merely because its pecuniary position will be thereby bettered. No wise man would entertain such suggestions as these.'

Justice Banerjee has observed that English law has been consistent with the concept of welfare of the child. Likewise, Indian law also does not make any departure therefrom.

III. INTER-COUNTRY ADOPTION IN INDIA

At the outset it is important to emphasize that at present there exists no exclusive general law of adoption of children governing non-Hindus and foreigners. Adoption is permitted by statute among Hindus and by customs among some other communities. At present non-Hindu and foreigners can only be guardians under the Guardian and Wards Act, 1890. In India, in the last few years a new dimension has also emerged on account of tedious and complicated inter-country adoption laws and procedures. This gives rise to surrogacy arrangements, preferred especially by the Non-Resident Indians Community resident overseas.

In actual practice, earlier, foreign nationals and Persons of Indian Origin domiciled overseas wishing to adopt children from India had to also obtain guardianship orders from District Court or High Court, as the case may be, within whose territorial jurisdiction the child is residing. This was done with a view to adopt formally under the legal system of the country of their habitual residence. However, with the enactment of the new CARA Guidelines of 2011, now the Courts have the power to directly grant a child to be placed in adoption and grant adoption order if the adoptive parents want to adopt the child. There is no need now to take a guardianship order from the Court and then adopt the child in the foreign country through their foreign laws. This is indeed a big step to simplify the procedures and provide for adoption through Indian law.

The Ministry of Welfare pursuant to certain guidelines issued by the Supreme Court of India, in a public interest litigation petition reported as *Lakshmi Kanta Pandey* v. *Union of India,* AIR 1984 SC 469, framed guidelines governing inter-country adoption. This case was monitored by the Supreme Court from time to time until the year 1991. The Apex Court scrupulously reviewed the existing procedure and practices followed in inter-country adoptions. The objective was to prevent trafficking of children and to protect the welfare of adopted children.

After the implementation of the initial guidelines in 1989, it was felt necessary to revise them. Accordingly, a task force comprising a cross-section of representatives of adoption agencies under the chairmanship of former Chief Justice of India Mr. Justice P.N. Bhagwati was constituted on 12 August, 1992. The Chairman of the Task Force submitted its report on 28 August, 1993. The Indian Government accepted the recommendations of the above mentioned task force, and accordingly, circulated revised guidelines to regulate matters relating to adoption of Indian children (1994). These guidelines were published by the Government in the *Gazette of India* on 20 June, 1995. Subsequently, further new guidelines were enacted on 14 February, 2006. CARA earlier had two sets of guidelines: Guidelines of 2004 that governed in-country adoption and Guidelines of 2006 that governed inter-country adoption. Now, the latest enactment *i.e.* Guidelines Governing the Adoption of Children, 2011 replaces all earlier guidelines and consolidates as well as updates the earlier two guidelines that were enacted in all previous years.

A. Procedure to be followed in inter-country adoption

CARA Guidelines stipulate that every application from a foreigner wishing to adopt a child must be sponsored by a social or child welfare agency recognized or licensed by the Government of the country in which the foreigner is resident. Furthermore, the agency should be recognized by the Central Adoption Resource

Agency (hereafter CARA') set up under the aegis of the Indian Ministry of Welfare. CARA is the principal monitoring agency of the Indian Government handling all affairs connected with national and inter-country adoptions.

After receiving an application, the Authorised Foreign Adoption Agency conducts a Home Study Report of the prospective adoptive parents and if it finds the prima facie suitability of the prospective parents, it forwards the same to CARA for identification of Recognised Indian Placement Agency (RIPA). On recognition of the RIPA, process of referral of the child to the prospective parents and acceptance of the same is followed. Adoption Recommendation Committee (ARC) ensures that all the procedures are duly followed and issues a Recommendation Certificate. After the receipt of Recommendation Certificate, CARA constitutes a NOC (No Objection Certificate) Committee, which examines all the documents furnished and issues a No Objection Certificate and intimates about it to all the concerned authorities. RIPA then proceeds to the Court of the Guardian Judge in the concerned jurisdiction to obtain an order for Guardianship or Adoption.

No application by a foreigner to adopt a child should be entertained directly by any social or child welfare agency in India working in the areas of inter-country adoption or by any institution or Centre to which the children are sent by the Juvenile Court. The reasons behind this directive have been summed up by M.N. Das in his book *Guardians and Wards Act* (Eastern Law House, 14th Edn., 1995) at pages 80-81, which are reproduced here under for ready reference:

> *'Firstly, it will help to reduce, if not eliminate altogether, the possibility of profiteering and trafficking in children, because if a foreigner were allowed to contact directly agencies or individuals in India for the purpose of obtaining a child in adoption, he might, in his anxiety to secure a child for adoption, be induced or persuaded to pay any unconscionable or unreasonable amount which might be demanded by the agency or individual procuring the child. Secondly, it would be almost impossible for the court to satisfy itself that the foreigner who wishes to take the child in adoption would be suitable as a parent for the child and whether he would be able to provide a stable and secured family life to the child and would be able to handle trans-racial, trans-cultural and trans-national problems likely to arise from such adoption, because, where the application for adopting a child has not been sponsored by a social or child welfare agency in the country of the foreigner, there would be no proper and satisfactory home study report on which the court can rely. Thirdly, in such a case, where the application of a foreigner for taking a child in adoption is made directly without the intervention of social or child welfare agency, there would be no authority or agency in the country of the foreigner who could be made responsible for supervising the progress of the child and ensuring that the child is adopted at the earliest in accordance with law and grows up in an atmosphere of warmth and affection with moral and material security assured to it.'*

B. Home study report

The new Guidelines categorically and emphatically enumerate the contents of the Home Study Report and state that the Home Study Report shall be based on procedures as laid down at Schedule VI of the Guidelines. Since the Home Study Report is a crucial document, it is mandatory that it should include the following information:

(1) social status and family background;
(2) description of the home;
(3) standard of living as it appears in the home;
(4) current relationship between the husband and wife;
(5) current relationship between the parents and children (if there are any children);
(6) development of the already adopted children (if any);
(7) current relationship between the couple and the members of each other's family;
(8) employment status of the couple;
(9) health details such as clinical test, hearing condition, past illness etc (medical certificate etc.);
(10) economic status of the couple;
(11) accommodation for the child;
(12) schooling facilities;
(13) amenities in the home;
(14) reasons for wanting to adopt an Indian child;
(15) attitude of grandparent/s and relatives towards the adoption;
(16) anticipated plans for the adoptive child;
(17) legal status of the prospective adoptive parents.
(18) Capacity for Parenthood and Expectations of a Child;
(19) Attitude of Significant Others;

Mere receipt of the application as well as other original documents will not entitle the Indian placement agency to proceed with the case. The Indian placement agency can proceed only after obtaining a 'no objection certificate' from CARA.

The new CARA regulations further state that CARA should endeavour, as far as possible, to see that this no objection certificate should be issued within a reasonable period of time, say two weeks from the date of the receipt of the certified copies of the application and other relevant documents.

After the receipt of the original application and the original documents from the enlisted foreign agency by the CARA, it will then register the name of the prospective foreign parents in the appropriate register.

On receiving the application by CARA, the recognised Indian placement agency will then proceed to examine carefully the Home Study Report of the prospective foreign adoptive parents and start the exercise in matching the Home Study Report with the Child Study Report. When it arrives at the conclusion that a child can be placed with that particular family, then they will have to ensure that the concerned child is cleared by the Voluntary Coordinating Agency (hereafter VCA) for inter-country adoption. It is pertinent to mention that there exist separate VCAs in every State for that particular jurisdiction.

Thereafter, the recognised placement agency will send the Child Study Report, the photograph of the child and the medical report to the sponsoring foreign agency for the approval of the prospective adoptive parents. After obtaining the approval of the child by the prospective adoptive parents, the recognised placement agency concerned will apply to CARA to get a clearance for the child.

It is at this stage that CARA will have to ensure that the recognised placement agency has put in adequate efforts to find an Indian family for the said child.

C. Guardianship/adoption Order

The RIPA will then process the case with the local court having jurisdiction to decide adoption/guardianship issues for the guardianship/adoption of the child to the foreign prospective adoptive parents.

Once again, the scrutinising agency must, at this stage, inspect all the documents and advise the Competent Court that the inter-country adoption is in the best interest of the child. The Competent Courts are to dispose of the case within a maximum period of two months from the date of its filing, in accordance with the directions of the Supreme Court of India in *L.K Pandey* v. *Union of India (supra).*

On the basis of the guardianship/adoption Order, the recognised placement agency must apply to the regional passport office for an Indian passport for the child. Thereafter, the entry clearance/visa is to be obtained from the Embassy/High Commission of the country where the child is to live. After this rigorous drill has been carried out, the child leaves the country along with the prospective adoptive parents or with the escort, as the case may be, to go to the country of the prospective adoptive parents.

The Supreme Court of India in *Karnataka State Council for Child Welfare* v. *Society of Sisters of Charity St. Gerosa Convent,* AIR 1994 SC 658, held that the rationale behind finding Indian parents or parents of Indian origin is to ensure that the children should grow up in Indian surroundings so that they retain their culture and heritage. This is definitely an issue which has a bearing on the question of the welfare of the children. The welfare of the children is the main and prime consideration.

The Gujarat High Court, in a progressive judgment, upheld the validity of guardianship orders in favour of two Norwegian couples who were appointed as guardians of Hindu children. In this particular matter, reported as *Jayantilal* v. *Asha,* AIR 1989 Guj 152, the Court tersely held in para 12 of the judgment at p. 156 as follows:

> *'... if the biological parents have died rendering the child an orphan then the society owes a duty to the child that at least a semblance of comfort and care which the biological parents could have provided will be provided to the child, if some people from howsoever distant a corner of this planet, come forth to do so. In such a case a petty contention like the change of religion or culture of*

the child can hardly stand in the way of the court in sanctioning inter-country adoption. Unfounded and imaginary apprehensions also are of little consequence and once the court is assured that there is no possibility of the child being abused, which assurance can flow from the independent agencies which are ordained for the purpose, then nothing can and need prevent the court from sanctioning an inter-country adoption.'

Experience of counsel while dealing with the Ministry of Welfare suggests that the documentation should be compiled meticulously. This is in order to avoid bureaucratic delays. In addition to the Home Study Report, the following additional documents (*see* annex A of the Regulations) are required to be submitted by the foreign adoptive parents. Here, it will be noticed that the Indian requirements are quite similar to the stipulations prescribed in various appendices of RON 117 issued by the Home Office in Britain.

(1) recent photographs of the adoptive family;
(2) marriage certificate;
(3) declaration concerning health of adoptive parents;
(4) certificate of medical fitness duly certified by a medical doctor;
(5) declaration regarding financial status with supporting documents, including employer's certificate, wherever applicable;
(6) employment certificate, if applicable;
(7) income tax assessment order;
(8) bank references;
(9) particulars of properties owned;
(10) joint declaration stating willingness to be appointed guardian of the child;
(11) undertaking from the social or child welfare enlisted agency sponsoring the foreigner to the effect that the child would be legally adopted by the foreign adoptive parents, according to the law of the country, within a period not exceeding two years from the time of arrival of the child;
(12) undertaking to the effect that the child would be provided necessary education and upbringing according to status of the adoptive parents;
(13) undertaking from the recognised foreign social or child welfare agency that the report relating to the progress of the child along with his/her recent photograph would be sent quarterly during first two years and half yearly for the next three years in the prescribed proforma through the Indian Diplomatic post in the country of the adoptive parents;
(14) power of attorney conferred by the intending parents in favour of the social or the child welfare agency in India which will be required to process the case and such power of attorney should also authorise the lawyer in India to handle the case on behalf of the foreign adoptive parents, if they are not in a position to come to India;
(15) certificate from the foreign enlisted social or child welfare agency sponsoring the application to the effect that they are permitted to adopt a child according to the laws of their country;

(16) undertaking from the overseas social or child welfare agency to the effect that in case of disruption of the adoptive family, before the legal adoption has been effected, it will take care of child and find a suitable alternative placement for the child with prior approval of CARA;

(17) undertaking from the overseas social or child welfare enlisted agency that it will reimburse all expenses to the concerned Indian social or child welfare agency as fixed by the competent court towards maintenance of the child and the processing charge fees.

It is important to reiterate that all the above certificates/declarations/ documents in support of the application have to be notarised, as already explained in the preceding paragraphs.

It is pertinent to mention that even after the enactment of new CARA Guidelines of 2011, there are several loopholes in the system such as the applicability of the guidelines in cases where adoption takes place directly from biological parents, questions as to adoption of children by gay, lesbian, bisexuals and transgender sections of society is unidentified, cumbersome with stringent procedural hurdles. New cases arising out of new facts are within the domain of CARA and the sole authority of interpretation and relaxation of the Guidelines still lies with CARA, thus giving rise to no uniform rule. There is just one rule that the case uniformly sticks to and that is the 'best interest of the child' in adoption matters which is a universal principle.

In sum and substance it can be stated that a uniform but strict procedure must be evolved which can be easily followed and adhered to both in letter and spirit. No doubt procedural hurdles and legal formalities are necessary to prevent abuse of the process but separate and intricate adoption and immigration procedures often leave foreign adopting parents in confusion over differing interpretations. Therefore, if the adoption process and procedures are overhauled so that they conform to a uniform pattern, it may make the process more convenient, less cumbersome and easier to follow. All of this would be in the best interests of the child, which is undoubtedly the paramount consideration, and at the same time would allow both the letter and spirit of law to be adhered to. Considered and deliberated changes are thus urgently required in the field of inter-country adoption from India. Time has also come to enact legislation dealing with legal parentage issues of children born out of surrogacy arrangements as well.

D. Domestic law

The principal law relating to adoption in India by Hindus only is contained in the Hindu Adoptions and Maintenance Act, 1956 (hereafter the HAMA, 1956). Having elaborated the law and procedure relating to inter-country adoptions, brief reference is made to the domestic law governing adoptions by Hindus.

E. Requisites of a valid adoption

Section 6 stipulates four conditions for a valid adoption which are reproduced hereunder:

(1) the person adopting has the capacity, and also the right, to adopt;

(2) the person consenting to adoption has the capacity to do so;

(3) the person adopted is capable of being adopted; and

(4) the adoption is made in compliance with the other conditions mentioned in Chapter 2 of HAMA, 1956.

Section 6(iv) requires that the adoption should be made in compliance with other conditions mentioned in Chapter 2 of HAMA, 1956. In other words, in order that the adoption should be valid the provisions of section 7 to section 11 must be satisfied. Section 7 deals with capacity of a male Hindu to adopt; while section 8 talks of capacity of a female Hindu to adopt; section 9 qualifies persons capable of giving up children for adoption; section 10 categorises persons who may be adopted; section 11 enumerates other conditions for valid adoption. Thereafter, section 12 elaborates the effects of a valid adoption.

F. Effects of a valid adoption

Section 12 categorically deals with the legal effects of an adoption made in accordance with the provisions of HAMA, 1956. Here it can be pointed out that section 12 of HAMA, 1956 satisfies the requirements of clause (ix) of para 310 of H.C. 395 of the current British Immigration Rules governing adoption. This clause (ix) of para 310 in very harsh terms states that the adopted child 'has lost or broken his ties with his family of origin'.

Insofar as relating to the legal effects of a valid adoption, it is important to cite certain decisions of the Supreme Court of India. It was held by the Supreme Court of India in *Smt. Sitabai* v. *Ramchandra*, AIR 1970 SC 343, in para 6 at p. 348 as follows:

> 'The true effect and interpretation of sections 11 and 12 of Act No. 78 of 1956 therefore is that when either of the spouses adopts a child, all the ties of the child in the family of his or her birth become completely severed and these are all replaced by those created by the adoption in the adoptive family.'

Similarly, it was held by the Supreme Court in the matter of *Kartar Singh* v. *Surjan Singh*, AIR 1974 SC 216 that the wording in section 11(vi) 'with intent to transfer the child from the family of its birth to the family of its adoption' is merely indicative of the result of the actual giving and taking by the parents or guardians concerned referred to in the earlier part of the clause. Where an adoption ceremony is gone through and the giving and taking takes place, there cannot be any other intention. Much more recently, the Supreme Court of India, in the matter of *Chandan Bilasini* v. *Aftabuddin Khan*, 1996 (1) HLR 79 (SC) held in para 6 of the judgment at p. 81 as follows:

> 'Section 12 of the Hindu Adoptions and Maintenance Act clearly provides that an adopted child shall be deemed to be the child of his adoptive father or mother for all purposes with effect from the date of the adoption and from such date all ties of the child in the family of his or her birth shall be deemed to be severed and replaced by those created by the adoption in the adoptive family.'

Finally, section 15 of the 1956 Act underlines the irrevocability of the validly performed adoption.

G. Problems faced in inter-country adoption

At present non-Hindus and foreign nationals can only be guardians of children under the Guardianship and Wards Act, 1890. They cannot adopt children. The child is a loser by being deprived of the benefits that are available in course of a valid adoption. There have been disturbing press reports about greedy social activists *(See Sharma Vinod, 'Indian child losing out in adoption mart', Hindustan Times, New Delhi, 9 September, 1997)*. It has been pointed out that at the root of the problem is certain placement agencies' love for lucre and their propensity to extort money from childless foreigners. *Secondly*, it has been observed in this report that the paper work in practice is complex. The system is not working, on account of long delays at different levels of scrutiny. *Thirdly*, India has not ratified the Hague Convention on the Protection of Children and Co-operation in Respect of Inter-country Adoption (29 May, 1993). As pointed out by the *Bhagwati* Panel, the political and legal rights of the Indian child with foreign adoptive parents can be best assured through bilateral pacts under the Convention.

H. Conflict of laws

As counsel dealing with adoption applications at the British High Commission, New Delhi, we have encountered a conflict of laws situation. Quite often non-resident Indians, who have been residing abroad for several decades, adopt children within the family itself. The preference is for immediate blood relatives. This is a common South Asian phenomenon.

The unsuspecting adoptive parents duly comply with the above-mentioned requirements of HAMA, 1956 while taking the child in adoption. The adoption deed is flashed with pride and authority before the immigration authorities, and this is where the trouble begins. The UK immigration authorities completely disregard the Indian adoption deed. They are legally justified in doing so in terms of the Adoption (Designation of Overseas Adoptions) Order, 1973 (SI 1973/19).

In terms of the 2013 Order, if a child has been legally adopted from a country whose adoption orders are recognised as valid for UK law (a 'designated' country), then the parents may apply for the child to join them in the United Kingdom as their adopted child. However, this issue now stands resolved as India is a designated Country for the purposes of inter-country adoptions.

If the child has not been legally adopted from a 'designated' country or the adoption is from a country whose adoption orders are not recognised as valid in UK law (a 'non-designated' country), entry clearance will have to be obtained for the child to travel to the UK for adoption through the English Courts. India is now specified as a 'designated' country in terms of the 1973 Order and hence, the problem to this extent stands resolved.

Previously, the adoptive parents, were confronted with a refusal by the immigration authorities on the ground that the adoption deed was not valid under the above-mentioned 1973 Order although there had been due compliance of the provisions of HAMA, 1956. The only avenue then available to the parents was to challenge the refusal by way of appeal or lodge a fresh application.

However, this situation will not arise in fresh matters as India is a designated Country.

The real dilemma in such previous situations was to set back the clock to satisfy the requirements of British immigration law. How could a non-resident Indian adoptee couple obtained a guardianship order from a local court once a formal irrevocable adoption process has taken place. Certainly, a guardianship order was not on a better footing than a valid adoption under HAMA, 1956. This testing proposition, is now however put to rest as India is a designated Country for inter-country adoptions and there is no requirement of obtaining any Court declaration as well.

However, regardless of the above, there has been a growing demand for a general law of adoption enabling any person irrespective of his religion, race or caste to adopt a child. There is now a clear case for overhauling the existing adoption law in India.

IV. CONCLUSION

From the above analysis, it is clear that there is a conflict of law situation as far as the presumption in favour of valid marriages is concerned. On the basis of cohabitation without clear evidence of performance of ceremonies as envisaged in section 7 of the HMA, 1955 and the marriage not having been registered, the matter rests on a case to case basis. Therefore, this is a situation which needs to be decided by a Larger Bench of the Supreme Court of India. As far as foreign Court child custody orders are concerned, they cannot be mechanically enforced in the Indian courts. The Courts would come to an independent judgment, the prime consideration being the welfare of the minor children. The law of adoption also needs to be overhauled, to permit formal adoption by non-Hindus and foreigners rather than limiting them to mere custody orders.

Maintenance, Non-Resident Indians and the Law

EXISTING FAMILY LAW LEGISLATIONS PREVALENT IN INDIA

It may be relevant to give a background on the Indian position of family laws in the context of the existing and prevailing situation, keeping in mind that there is no uniform civil matrimonial legislation in India governing all religions, caste, communities, denominations and groups in India. There being no uniform civil or matrimonial code, all Indian citizens are governed by their respective codified personal statutory laws enacted or approved by Parliament.

A. THE INDIAN BACKGROUND

The Constitution of India enacted on the 26th day of November, 1949 resolved to constitute India as a Union of States and a Sovereign, Socialist, Secular, Democratic Republic. Today, a population of over one billion Indians live in twenty nine States and seven Union Territories within India besides about twenty five million Indians who reside in foreign jurisdictions and are called Non-Resident Indians. Within the territory of India spread over an area of 3.28 million sq. kms., the large Indian population comprised of multicultural societies professing and practicing different religions and speaking different local languages coexist in harmony in one of the largest democracies in the world.

The Indian Parliament at the helm of affairs legislates on central subjects in the Union and Concurrent lists and State legislatures enact laws pertaining to State subjects as per the State and Concurrent lists with regard to the subjects enumerated in the Constitution of India. Likewise, pertaining to the Judiciary, under article 214 of the Indian Constitution there shall be a High Court for each State and under article 124 there shall be a Supreme Court of India. Under article 141 of the Constitution, the law declared by the Supreme Court shall be binding on all Courts within the territory of India. However, the Supreme Court may not be bound by its own earlier views and can render new decisions.

Part III of the Constitution of India secures to its citizens "Fundamental Rights" which can be enforced directly in the respective High Courts of the States or directly in the Supreme Court of India by issue of prerogative writs under articles 226 and 32 respectively of the Constitution of India. Under the Constitutional scheme, amongst others, Freedom of Religion and the right to freely profess, practice and propagate religion is sacrosanct and is thus enforceable by a prerogative writ issued by any of the High Courts or the Supreme Court.

Simultaneously Part IV of the Indian Constitution lays down "Directive Principles of State Policy" which are not enforceable by any Court but are nevertheless fundamental in the governance of the country and it shall be the duty of the State to apply these principles while making laws. Under **article 44 of the Constitution** in this Part, the State shall endeavour to secure for the citizens a Uniform Civil Code throughout the territory of India. However, realistically speaking, till date a uniform civil code remains an aspiration which India has yet to achieve and enact. Hence, there is no uniform matrimonial or civil law statutorily enacted by Parliament in India and Indian Citizens are governed by separate codified personal laws. All matrimonial matters are adjudicated at the first level in Family Courts or a District Court (if there is no Family Court) exercising territorial and subject matter jurisdiction as per relevant statutes being the principal Courts of original jurisdiction in all matrimonial matters. Against the decisions rendered by these Courts, appeals are preferred to the concerned High Court exercising territorial jurisdiction within the specific States in which these Family Courts or District Courts are situated. Against the decisions rendered by the respective High Courts, final appeals can be instituted in the Supreme Court of India whose judgments are final and applicable on all Courts throughout the territory of India. However, the Supreme Court of India is not bound by its own decisions and can differ, vary, confirm or change its view in latter decisions.

B. PREVALENT STATUTORY FAMILY LAWS OF DIFFERENT COMMUNITIES

India is a land of diversities with several religions with Hindus dominating with the largest number. The oldest part of Indian Legal System is the personal laws governing the Hindus and the Muslims. The Hindu personal law has undergone changes by a continuous process of codification. The process of change in society has brought changes in law reflecting the changed social conditions and attempts the solution of social problems by new methods in the light of experience of legislations in other countries of the world. The Muslim personal law has been comparatively left untouched by legislations over a period of time.

The Indian Legal system is basically a common law system. The Indian Parliament has enacted the following family laws which are applicable to the religious communities defined in the respective enactments themselves. A brief description of each of these separate enactments is given as hereunder.

(a) The main marriage law legislation in India applicable to the majority population constituted of Hindus is known as **the Hindu Marriage Act, 1955 (HMA)**, which is an Act to amend and codify the law relating to marriage among Hindus. It applies to parties who are Hindus by religion. Ceremonial marriage is essential under this Act and registration is optional. It applies to any person who is a Hindu, Buddhist, Jaina or Sikh by religion and to any other person who is not a Muslim, Christian, Parsi or Jew by religion. The Act also applies to Hindus resident outside the territory of India. Nothing contained in this Act shall be deemed to affect any right recognized by custom or conferred by any special enactment. Likewise, in other personal law matters, Hindus are governed by the Hindu Succession Act, 1956, which is an Act to amend and codify the law relating to intestate succession among Hindus. The Hindu Minority and Guardianship Act, 1956 is an Act to amend and codify certain parts of the law relating to Minority and Guardianship among Hindus and the Hindu Adoptions and Maintenance Act, 1956 is an Act to amend and codify the law relating to adoptions and maintenance among Hindus.

It may be pertinent to point out that the **Indian Succession Act, 1925**, is an Act to consolidate the law applicable to intestate and testamentary succession in India unless parties opt and choose to be governed by their respective codified law otherwise applicable to them. In respect of issues relating to Guardianship, the **Guardian and Wards Act, 1890** would apply to non-Hindus. Interestingly, section 125 of the **Code of Criminal Procedure, 1973**, provides that irrespective of religion, any person belonging to any religion can approach a Magistrate for being provided maintenance. Therefore, apart from personal family law legislations, both Hindus and non-Hindus have an independent right of maintenance under the general law of the land, if he or she is otherwise entitled to maintenance under this Code.

(b) The Indian Parliament also enacted the **Special Marriage Act, 1954** (SMA), as an Act to provide a special form of marriage in certain cases, for the registration of such and certain other marriages and for divorces under this Act. This enactment of solemnizing marriage by registration is resorted to by Hindus, Non-Hindus and foreigners marrying in India who opt out of the ceremonial marriage under their respective personal laws. Registration is compulsory under this enactment. Divorce can also be obtained by non-Hindus under this Act. This legislation governs people of all religions and communities in India, irrespective of their personal faith. Likewise, under the **Foreign Marriage Act, 1969**, a person has only to be a citizen of India to have a marriage solemnized under this Act outside the territorial limits of India.

(c) The **Parsi Marriage and Divorce Act, 1936** as amended in 1988, is an Act to amend the law relating to marriage and divorce among the Parsis in India.

(d) The **Christian Marriage Act, 1872**, was enacted as an Act to consolidate and amend the law relating to the solemnization of the marriages of Christians in India and the **Divorce Act, 1869 as amended in 2001**, is an Act to amend the law relating to divorce and matrimonial causes relating to Christians in India.

(e) The **Muslim Personal Law (Shariat) Application Act, 1937, the Dissolution of Muslim Marriages Act, 1939, the Muslim Women (Protection of Rights on Divorce) Act, 1986 and the Muslim Women (Protection of Rights on Divorce) Rules, 1986**, applies to Muslims living in India.

For enforcement and adjudication of all matrimonial and other related disputes of any person in any of the different religious or non-religious communities under the respective legislations mentioned above, the designated judicial forum or court where such petition is to be lodged is prescribed in the respective enactments themselves. There is an organized system of uniform designated civil and criminal judicial courts within every State in India which works under the overall jurisdiction of the respective High Court in the State. It is in the hierarchy of these courts that all family and matrimonial causes are lodged and decided. In addition, the Indian Parliament has enacted **the Family Courts Act, 1984** to provide for the establishment of Family Courts with a view to promote conciliation in and to secure speedy settlement of disputes relating to marriage and family affairs. Despite the existence of an organized, well regulated and established hierarchy of judicial courts in India, there are still unrecognized parallel community and religious courts under Muslim religion in existence whose interference has been deprecated by the judicial courts since such unauthorized and unwarranted bodies work without the authority of law and are not parts of the Indian judicial system applicable to all.

Accordingly, maintenance *pendente lite* (maintenance during the pendency of the matrimonial litigation) and litigation expenses, permanent alimony and maintenance, maintenance of children as also settlement/division of matrimonial property/home as also rights of residence in the matrimonial home will be examined in this expert report in the light of all personal laws currently prevalent in India besides looking at the parallel provisions for these heads under the **Special Marriage Act, 1954 (SMA)** and other laws referred to above. It may be reiterated that the SMA, 1954 is applicable between any two persons who fulfil the conditions of solemnization of special marriages under the SMA, 1954, irrespective of religion, nationality, caste, creed or faith. It may be repeated that since there is no universal matrimonial civil law in India enacted by Parliament or uniform Civil Code applicable to all persons or citizens in India, and, hence there is no reference or discussion with regards to any uniform matrimonial civil law in India, as there is no such Code.

C. MAINTENANCE UNDER FAMILY LAWS IN INDIA

The wife is entitled to maintenance from the husband, as is invariably the case made out under section 24 or 25 of the Hindu Marriage Act, 1955, or section 37 of the Special Marriage Act, 1954. Section 125, Cr.P.C. gives the wife an additional claim for maintenance, irrespective of any matrimonial proceedings under the personal laws of the parties or the Special Marriage Act, 1954, as the case may be. The statutory provisions under various laws in India may be summarised as here under:

Position of maintenance under personal Laws and Special Marriage Act, 1954

1. Position of maintenance under Hindu Laws

In Hindu Law, there are two statutes, which provide for maintenance, *viz.*, the Hindu Marriage Act, 1955 (HMA) & the Hindu Adoptions & Maintenance Act, 1956 (HAMA)

1.1 Position of maintenance under the Hindu Marriage Act, 1955 (HMA)

Section 24 (HMA, 1955) of the Act provides for interim maintenance and states:

> *"Maintenance* **pendente lite** *and expenses of proceedings.- Where in any proceeding under this Act it appears to the court that either the wife or the husband, as the case may be, has no independent income sufficient for her or his support and the necessary expenses of the proceeding, it may, on the application of the wife or the husband, order the respondent to pay to the petitioner the expenses of the proceeding, and monthly during the proceeding such sum as, having regard to the petitioner's own income and the income of the respondent, it may seem to the court to be reasonable.*
>
> *Provided that the application for the payment of the expenses of the proceeding and such monthly sum during the proceeding, shall, as far as possible, be disposed of within sixty days from the date of service of the notice on the wife or the husband, as the case may be."*

Section 25 of the HMA, 1955 dealing with permanent alimony and maintenance, to be decided at the time of passing a decree or subsequently, reads as follows:

> *"Permanent alimony and maintenance.—(1) Any court exercising jurisdiction under this Act may, at the time of passing any decree or at any time subsequent thereto, on application made to it for the purpose by either the wife or the husband, as the case may be, order that the respondent shall pay to the applicant for her or his maintenance and support such gross sum or such monthly or periodical sum for a term not exceeding the life of the applicant as, having regard to the respondent's own income and other property, if any, the income and the property of the applicant, the conduct of the parties and other circumstances of the case, it may seem to the court to be just, and any such payment may be secured, if necessary, by a charge on the immovable property of the respondent.*
>
> **(2) If the court is satisfied that there is a change in the circumstances of either party at any time after it has made an order under sub-section (1), it may at the instance of either party, vary, modify or rescind any such order in such manner as the court may deem just.**
>
> *(3) If the court is satisfied that the party in whose favour an order has been made under this section has remarried, or if such party is the wife, that she has not remained chaste, or if such party is the husband, that he has had sexual intercourse with any women outside the wedlock, it may, at the instance of the other party, vary, modify or rescind any such order in such manner as the court may deem just."*

1.2 Position of maintenance under Hindu Adoptions and Maintenance Act

A Hindu wife has the advantage of an additional statute *viz.* **the Hindu Adoptions and Maintenance Act, 1956 (HAMA)**. Under section 18 of the HAMA, a Hindu wife is entitled to live separately from her husband without forfeiting her claim to maintenance, provided her separate living is justified which means that the husband:

(i) is guilty of desertion;

(ii) has treated her with cruelty;

(iii) is suffering from a virulent form of leprosy;

(iv) has any other wife living;

(v) keeps a concubine in the same house, or is living or habitually resides with a concubine elsewhere;

(vi) has ceased to be a Hindu by conversion to another religion; or

(vii) if there is any other cause justifying living separately.

The section provides two specific bars which would disentitle a wife from claiming maintenance under this Act, *viz.*, **(i) if she is unchaste or (ii) if she ceases to be a Hindu by conversion to another religion.**

2. Position of maintenance under the Special Marriage Act, 1954 (SMA)

This is a secular law applicable to all those persons who are married in India under this Act, irrespective of their caste, community, nationality or religion.

Section 36 and 37 of the Special Marriage Act, 1954 [SMA] also provides for maintenance *pendente lite* other than permanent alimony and maintenance for the wife, respectively. Unlike the **Hindu Marriage Act, 1955**, there is no provision in SMA, 1954 for maintenance for the husband. The said sections read as follows:

> *"Section 36. Alimony* **pendente lite.**—*Where in any proceeding under Chapter V or Chapter VI it appears to the district court that the wife has no independent income sufficient for her support and the necessary expenses of the proceeding, it may, on the application of the wife, order the husband to pay her the expenses of the proceeding, and weekly or monthly during the proceeding such sum as, having regard to the husband's income, it may seem to the court to be reasonable.*
>
> *Provided that the application for the payment of the expenses of the proceeding and such weekly or monthly sum during the proceeding under Chapter V or Chapter VI, shall, as far as possible, be disposed of within sixty days from the date of service of notice on the husband.*
>
> *Section 37. Permanent alimony and maintenance.—(1) Any court exercising jurisdiction under Chapter V or Chapter VI may, at the time of passing any decree or at any time subsequent to the decree, on application made to it for the purpose, order that the husband shall secure to the wife for her maintenance and support if necessary, by a charge on the husband's property such gross sum or such monthly or periodical payment of money for a term not exceeding her life, as, having regard to her own property, if any, her husband's property and ability, the conduct of the parties and other circumstances of the case, as it may seem to the court to be just.*
>
> *(2) If the district court is satisfied that there is a change in the circumstances of either party at any time after it has made an order under sub-section (1), it may, at the instance of either party, vary, modify or rescind any such order in such manner as it may seem to the court to be just.*

(3) If the district court is satisfied that the wife in whose favour an order has been made under this section has remarried or is not leading a chaste life, it may, at the instance of the husband, vary, modify or rescind any such order and in such manner as the court may deem just."

3. Position of maintenance under Parsi Law

The **Parsi Marriage and Divorce Act, 1936** provides for maintenance *pendente lite* and for permanent alimony and maintenance. It is significant to note that prior to Amendment Act 5 of 1988 only a wife was entitled to maintenance under the provisions of the Act. After the Amendment the provision has been brought at par with the Hindu Marriage Act, 1955 and now even a husband can seek maintenance. The relevant sections of this enactment provide for maintenance as follows:

"S. 39. Alimony **pendente lite.**—*Where in any suit under this Act, it appears to the Court that either the wife or the husband, as the case may be, has no independent income sufficient for her or his support and the necessary expenses of the suit, it may, on the application of the wife or the husband, order the defendant to pay to the plaintiff, the expenses of the suit, and such weekly or monthly sum, during suit, as having regard to the plaintiff's own income and the income of the defendant, it may seem to the court to be reasonable.*

Provided that the application for the payment of the expenses of the suit and such weekly or monthly sum during the suit, shall, as far as possible, be disposed of within sixty days from the date of service of notice on the wife or the husband, as the case may be.

S. 40. Permanent alimony and maintenance.—(1) Any Court exercising jurisdiction under this Act may, at the time of passing decree or at any time subsequent thereto, on an application made to it for the purpose by either the wife or the husband, order that the defendant shall pay to the plaintiff for her or his maintenance and support, such gross sum or such monthly or periodical sum, for a term not exceeding the life of the plaintiff as having regard to the defendant's own income and other property, if any, the income and other property of the plaintiff, the conduct of the parties and other circumstances of the case, it may seem to the court to be just, and any such payment may be secured, if necessary, by a charge on the movable or immovable property of the defendant.

(2) The Court, if it is satisfied that there is a change in the circumstances of either party at any time after it has made an order under sub-section (1), it may, at the instance of either party, vary, modify or rescind any such order in such manner as the court may deem just.

(3) The Court if it is satisfied that the party in whose favour an order has been made under this section has remarried or, if such party is the wife, that she has not remained chaste, or if such party is the husband, that he had sexual intercourse with any woman outside the wedlock, it may, at the instance of the other party, vary, modify or rescind any such order in such manner as the court may deem just.

Section 41. Payment of alimony to wife or to her trustee.—In all cases in which the Court shall make any decree or order for alimony it may direct the same to be paid either to the wife herself, or to any trustee on her behalf to be approved by the Court or to a guardian appointed by the Court and may impose any terms of restrictions which to the Court may seem expedient, and may from time to time, appoint a new trustee or guardian, if for any reason it shall appear to the Court expedient so to do."

4. Position of maintenance under Christian Law

Provisions for maintenance under the Christian Law are contained in the Indian Divorce Act, 1869 as amended in 2001. The relevant sections in this regard are:

"Section 36. Alimony **pendente lite.**—*In any suit under this Act, whether it be instituted by a husband or a wife, and whether or not she has obtained an order of protection, the wife may present a petition for expenses of the proceedings and alimony pending the suit.*

Such petition shall be served on the husband, and the court, on being satisfied of the truth of the statements therein contained, may make such order on the husband for payment to the wife of expenses of the proceedings and alimony pending the suit as it may deem just.

Provided that the petition for the expenses of the proceedings and alimony pending the suit shall, as far as possible, be disposed of within sixty days of service of such petition on the husband.

Section 37. Power to order permanent alimony.—Where a decree of dissolution of the marriage or a decree of judicial separation is obtained by the wife, the District Court may order that the husband shall, to the satisfaction of the Court, secure to the wife such gross sum of money, or such annual sum of money for any term not exceeding her own life, as having regard to her fortune (if any), to the ability of the husband, and to the conduct of the parties, it thinks reasonable, and for that purpose may cause a proper instrument to be executed by all necessary parties.

Power to order monthly or weekly payments.-In every such case the Court may make an order on the husband for payment to the wife of such monthly or weekly sums for her maintenance and support as the court may think reasonable.

Provided that if the husband afterwards from any cause becomes unable to make such payments, it shall be lawful for the court to discharge or modify the order, or temporarily to suspend the same as to the whole or any part of the money so ordered to be paid, and again to revive the same order wholly or in part, as to the court seems fit.

Section 38. Court may direct payment of alimony to wife or to her trustees.—In all cases in which the court makes any decree or order for alimony it may direct the same to be paid either to the wife herself or to any trustee on her behalf to be approved by the court and may impose any terms or restrictions, which to the court seem expedient and may from time to time appoint a new trustee if it appears to the court expedient so to do."

5. Position of maintenance under Muslim Law

The personal law statutes governing a Muslim woman's right to maintenance are the **Dissolution of Muslim Marriages Act, 1939** and the **Muslim Women (Protection of Rights on Divorce) Act, 1986**. The former Act provides for grounds under which a women married under the Muslim law can seek dissolution of the marriage. One of the grounds provided is that 'the husband has neglected or has failed to provide for her maintenance for a period of two years', as under section 2(ii) of the **Dissolution of Muslim Marriages Act, 1939**. The latter Act, as its very title indicates, makes provision for protection of rights of Muslim women who have been divorced by, or have obtained divorce from, their husbands, which includes right of maintenance as well. Section 2(ii) of the **Dissolution of Muslim Marriages Act, 1939** is quoted as hereunder for purposes of ready reference:

"**2.** *Grounds for decree for dissolution of marriage.*

A woman married under Muslim law shall be entitled to obtain a decree for the dissolution of her marriage on any one or more of the following grounds, name:—

i. xxxxx

ii. that the husband has neglected or has failed to provide for her maintenance for a period of two years."

The Muslim Women (Protection of Rights on Divorce) Act, 1986, which is an Act to protect the rights of Muslim women who have been divorced by, or have obtained divorce from their husbands provides for making of an order for payment of maintenance under sections 3 and 4 of this Act by making an application to a Magistrate in the area where the divorced woman unable to maintain herself resides. This is apart from the right of the Muslim Woman to claim *Mahr* under section 3 of this Act which provides for *Mahr or other properties of Muslim woman to be given to her at the time of divorce* by her former husband and which can also be enforced by making an application to a Magistrate. In this regard sections 3 and 4 of **the Muslim Women (Protection of Rights on Divorce) Act, 1986** is as follows:

3. Mahr or other properties of Muslim woman to be given to her at the time of divorce.—

(1) Notwithstanding anything contained in any other law for the time being in force, a divorced woman shall be entitled to—

(a) a reasonable and fair provision and maintenance to be made and paid to her within the iddat period by her former husband;

(b) where she herself maintains the children born to her before or after her divorce, a reasonable and fair provision and maintenance to be made and paid by her former husband for a period of two years from the respective dates of birth of such children;

(c) an amount equal to the sum of mahr or dower agreed to be paid to her at the time of her marriage or at any time thereafter according to Muslim law; and

(d) all the properties given to her before or at the time of marriage or after the marriage by her relatives or friends or the husband or any relatives of the husband or his friends.

(2) where a reasonable and fair provision and maintenance or the amount of mahr or dower due has not been made or paid or the properties referred to in clause (d) of sub-section (1) have not been delivered to a divorced woman on her divorce, she or any one duly authorised by her may, on her behalf, make an application to a Magistrate for an order for payment of such provision and maintenance, mahr or dower or the delivery of properties, as the case may be.

(3) Where an application has been made under sub-section (2) by a divorced woman, the Magistrate may, if he is satisfied that—

(a) her husband having sufficient means, has failed or neglected to make or pay her within the iddat period a reasonable and fair provision and maintenance for her and the children; or

(b) the amount equal to the sum of mahr or dower has not been paid or that the properties referred to in clause (d) of sub-section (1) have not been delivered to her,

make an order, within one month of the date of the filing of the application, directing her former husband to pay such reasonable and fair provision and maintenance to the divorced woman as he may determine as fit and proper having regard to the needs of the divorced woman, the standard of life enjoyed by her during her marriage and the means of her former husband or, as the case may be, for the payment of such mahr or dower or the delivery of such properties referred to in clause (d) of sub-section (1) to the divorced woman:

Provided that if the Magistrate finds it impracticable to dispose of the application within the said period, he may, for reasons to be recorded by him, dispose of the application after the said period.

(4) If any person against whom an order has been made under sub-section (3) fails without sufficient cause to comply with the order, the Magistrate may issue a warrant for levying the amount of maintenance or mahr or dower due in the manner provided for levying fines under the Code of Criminal Procedure, 1973 (2 of 1974) and may sentence such person, for the whole or part of any amount remaining unpaid after the execution of the warrant, to imprisonment for a term which may extend to one year or until payment if sooner made, subject to such person being heard in defence and the said sentence being imposed according to the provisions of the said Code.

4. Order for payment of maintenance.—

(1) Notwithstanding anything contained in the foregoing provisions of this Act or in any other law for the time being in force, where the

Magistrate is satisfied that a divorced woman has not re-married and is not able to maintain herself after the iddat period, he may make an order directing such of her relatives as would be entitled to inherit her property on her death according to Muslim law to pay such reasonable and fair maintenance to her as he may determine fit and proper, having regard to the needs of the divorced woman, the standard of life enjoyed by her during her marriage and the means of such relatives and such maintenance shall be payable by such relatives in the proportions in which they would inherit her property and at such periods as he may specify in his order:

Provided that where such divorced woman has children, the Magistrate shall order only such children to pay maintenance to her, and in the event of any such children being unable to pay such maintenance, the Magistrate shall order the parents of such divorced woman to pay maintenance to her:

Provided further that if any of the parents is unable to pay his or her share of the maintenance ordered by the Magistrate on the ground of his or her not having the means to pay the same, the Magistrate may, on proof of such inability being furnished to him, order that the share of such relatives in the maintenance ordered by him be paid by such of the other relatives as may appear to the Magistrate to have the means of paying the same in such proportions as the Magistrate may think fit to order.

(2) Where a divorced woman is unable to maintain herself and she has no relative as mentioned in sub-section (1) or such relatives or any one of them have not enough means to pay the maintenance ordered by the Magistrate or the other relatives have not the means to pay the shares of those relatives whose shares have been ordered by the Magistrate to be paid by such other relatives under the second proviso to sub-section (1), the Magistrate may, by order direct the State Wakf Board established under section 9 of the Wakf Act, 1954 (29 of 1954), or under any other law for the time being in force in a State, functioning in the area in which the woman resides, to pay such maintenance as determined by him under sub-section (1) or, as the case may be, to pay the shares of such of the relatives who are unable to pay, at such periods as he may specify in his order."

D. DIVORCED WIFE'S RIGHT TO RESIDENTIAL ACCOMMODATION

The Bombay High Court in two rulings reported as ***Ajit Bhagwandas Udeshi* v. *Kumud Ajit Udeshi*, AIR 2003 Bom 120** *and* ***Sunita Shankar Salvi v. Shankar Laxman Salvi***, reported as **AIR 2003 Bom 431** held that the divorced wife cannot be left without a roof over her head. In the case of ***Udeshi (2003)***, the tenancy of the flat was for the benefit of the family and the wife occupied the same as member of the family. While, the case of ***Salvi (2003)***, is important from the point of view, that irrespective of the financial contribution or joint ownership on record, the Courts in India are concerned about providing residential accommodation to a divorced wife, who has no resources of her own.

In the judgment of ***Komalam* Amma v. *Kumara Pillai Raghavan Pillai*, AIR 2009 SC 636**, the Hon'ble Supreme Court of India endorsed the right of a woman to a residence as included in the general term *'**maintenance**.'*

The Apex Court elaborated on the concept of maintenance in **AIR 2009 SC 636** para 9 at page 637 of the judgment as follows:

> ***"9. Maintenance, as we see it, necessarily must encompass a provision for residence. Maintenance is given so that the lady can live in the manner, more or less, to which she was accustomed. The concept of maintenance must, therefore, include provision for food and clothing and the like and take into account the basic need of a roof over the head. Provision for residence may be made either by giving a lump sum in money, or property in lieu thereof. It may also be made by providing, for the course of the lady`s life, a residence and money for other necessary expenditure. Where provision is made in this manner, by giving a life interest in property for the purposes of residence, that provision is made in lieu of a pre-existing right to maintenance and the Hindu lady acquires far more than the vestige of title which is deemed sufficient to attract section 14(1)."***

Basically, the law in the Indian jurisdiction in so far relating to the concept of maintenance for the wife under the provisions of the HMA, 1955 and the HAMA, 1956 includes the amount of maintenance given to her to generally sustain the same lifestyle to which she was accustomed. As it will be noticed, this view also stands reiterated in the above mentioned ruling of the Supreme Court of India.

Furthermore, the judgment above in **AIR 2009 SC 636** para 12 at page 638 of the said judgment has reiterated the position of law as enunciated by the Supreme Court of India in one of its earlier judgments of the year 2005. This particular judgment of the year 2005 very succinctly elaborates on the concept of maintenance as statutorily provided under the provisions of the HAMA, 1956. ***AIR 2009 SC 636*** para 12 at page 638 in this regard reiterates as follows:

"12. In ***B.P. Achala Anand* v. *S. Appi Reddy*, (2005) 2 SCALE 105**, it was observed as follows:

> ***"Having said so generally, we may now deal with the right of a wife to reside in the matrimonial home under personal laws. In the factual context of the present case, we are confining ourselves to dealing with the personal law as applicable to Hindus as the parties are so. A Hindu wife is entitled to be maintained by her husband. She is entitled to remain under his roof and protection. She is also entitled to separate residence if by reason of the husband's conduct or by his refusal to maintain her in his own place of residence or for other just cause she is compelled to live apart from him. Right to residence is a part and parcel of wife's right to maintenance. The right to maintenance cannot be defeated by the husband executing a will to defeat such a right (See:*** **MULLA, Principles of Hindu Law, Vol. I, 18th Edn., 2001, paras 554 and 555).** ***The right has come to be statutorily recognized with the enactment of the Hindu Adoption and Maintenance Act, 1956. Section 18 of the Act provides for***

> ***maintenance of wife. Maintenance has been so defined in clause (b) of section 3 of the Hindu Adoption and Maintenance Act, 1956 as to include therein provision for residence amongst other things. For the purpose of maintenance the term 'wife' includes a divorced wife."***

Hence, it is clear from the above mentioned caselaw analysis that the right of wife to get maintenance from her husband also encompasses a right of residence either in the matrimonial home or a separate residence.

Furthermore, the estranged wife alongwith her maintenance claim can also stake a claim for her right to separate residence from her husband in light of the settled position of law.

That out of abundant caution, it is equally important to refer to the provisions of **the Protection of Women from Domestic Violence Act, 2005** (**Domestic Violence Act, 2005 or DVA, 2005**), which is a very women rights favorable legislation in actual implementation, and is certainly not advantageous where the alleged erring spouse is a husband.

E. DISPOSAL OF PROPERTY UNDER THE PROVISIONS OF THE HINDU MARRIAGE ACT, 1955 AND PROTECTION OF WOMEN FROM DOMESTIC VIOLENCE ACT, 2005.

There is no talk of division of assets in Indian divorce laws. Financial settlements are limited to paying maintenance. On this aspect of the matter, both the HMA, 1955 and the Special Marriage Act, 1954 (SMA) are gender-neutral, allowing the spouse with the smaller income to seek maintenance.

However, there are some provisions under the Indian laws which talk about the division of properties between the parties on divorce.

Section 27 of HMA, 1955 empowers the Court to adjudicate upon the division and distribution of the property of the divorced couple at the time of the passing of the divorce decree, and is reproduced below for ease of reference:

> '27. *Disposal of property*
>
> **In any proceeding under this Act, the court may make such provisions in the decree as it deems just and proper with respect to any property presented, at or about the time of marriage, which may belong jointly to both the husband and the wife.**'

The Delhi High Court held in *Subhash Lata* **v.** *V.N. Khanna,* AIR 1992 Del 14 that section 27 of the Act concerns only property presented at or about the time of marriage, which are alleged to belong jointly to both the spouses. It is a pre-condition for getting relief that such property must belong jointly to both the spouses.

However, many High Courts have differently interpreted section 27 of the HMA, 1955 and have elaborated the scope of the application of the section. Some of the judgments interpreting section 27, HMA, 1955 are referred as hereunder.

The Punjab and Haryana High Court held in the case of *Inderjit Singh* v. *Manjit Kaur,* 1987 (2) HLR 496, that no order under section 27 can be passed with respect to the property which exclusively belongs to the wife.

A Division Bench of the Allahabad High Court in the case of *Hemant Kumar Agrahari* v. *Lakshmi Devi,* AIR 2004 All 126 (DB), held that section 27 of the Hindu

Marriage Act, 1955 does not confine or restrict the jurisdiction of matrimonial Courts to deal only with the joint property of the parties, which is presented at or about the time of marriage but also permits disposal of exclusive property of the parties provided they were presented at or about the time of marriage.

Hence, the Court has the right to deal with the property of the parties acquired jointly at or about the time of the marriage and also with the exclusive property of the parties presented at or about the time of the marriage with a clear exception to the '**istridhan**' (woman's property given to her at time of marriage) of a woman. A court has no right to pass orders regarding the '**istridhan**' of the woman as stated above.

Furthermore, sections 17 and 19 of the Domestic Violence Act, 2005, (hereafter DVA, 2005) provide for the right of a woman to reside in her matrimonial home when in a domestic relationship and empowers the Courts to provide for a residential accommodation for the aggrieved spouse in cases where the domestic violence is proved. Sections 17 and 19 of the DVA, 2005 read as follows:

> ***"SECTION 17 OF DOMESTIC VIOLENCE ACT, 2005:***
>
> *SECTION 17: Right to reside in a shared household:*
>
> *(1) Notwithstanding anything contained in any other law for the time being in force, every woman in a domestic relationship shall have the right to reside in the shared household, whether or not she has any right, title or beneficial interest in the same.*
>
> *(2) The aggrieved person shall not be evicted or excluded from the shared household or any part of it by the respondent save in accordance with the procedure established by law."*
>
> ***"SECTION 19 OF DOMESTIC VIOLENCE ACT, 2005:***
>
> *SECTION 19: Residence orders.—*
>
> *(1) While disposing of an application under sub-section (1) of section 12, the Magistrate may, on being satisfied that domestic violence has taken place, pass a residence order—*
>
> *(a) restraining the respondent from dispossessing or in any other manner disturbing the possession of the aggrieved person from the shared household, whether or not the respondent has a legal or equitable interest in the shared household;*
>
> *(b) directing the respondent to remove himself from the shared household;*
>
> *(c) restraining the respondent or any of his relatives from entering any portion of the shared household in which the aggrieved person resides;*
>
> *(d) restraining the respondent from alienating or disposing off the shared household or encumbering the same;*
>
> *(e) restraining the respondent from renouncing his rights in the shared household except with the leave of the Magistrate; or*
>
> *(f) directing the respondent to secure same level of alternate accommodation for the aggrieved person as enjoyed by her in the shared household or to pay rent for the same, if the circumstances so require:*

Provided that no order under clause (b) shall be passed against any person who is a woman."

The Hon'ble Supreme Court of India in the case of *Vimlaben Ajitbhai Patel* **v.** *Vatslaben Ashokbhai Patel* with *Ajitbhai Revandas Patel* **v.** *State of Gujarat*, (2008) 4 SCC 649, has held that the statutory right of a woman to reside in her matrimonial home arises only in cases where the matrimonial home is the property of the husband. This judgment reported as (2008) 4 SCC 649 Para 21 at page 660 of the said judgment carves out the obligations of a husband towards his wife in the following categoric terms:

"21. Maintenance of a married wife, during subsistence of marriage, is on the husband. It is a personal obligation. The obligation to maintain a daughter-in-law arises only when the husband has died. Such an obligation can also be met from the properties of which the husband is a co-sharer and not otherwise. For invoking the said provision, the husband must have a share in the property. The property in the name of the mother-in-law can neither be a subject matter of attachment nor during the life time of the husband, his personal liability to maintain his wife can be directed to be enforced against such property."

Clearly, the import of the above mentioned judgment rendered by the Hon'ble Supreme Court of India, lays down that the issue of maintenance of a wife is the personal obligation of the **husband** and the liability is solely fastened on him till the time he is alive.

Further, in (2008) 4 SCC 649 paras 27 and 28 of the said judgment the Supreme Court has interpreted the provisions of the DVA, 2005 dealing with the wife's right to reside in her matrimonial home and paras 27 and 28 at page 662 read as under:

"27. The Domestic Violence Act provides for a higher right in favour of a wife. She not only acquires a right to be maintained but also thereunder acquires a right of residence. The right of residence is a higher right. The said right as per the legislation extends to joint properties in which the husband has a share.

28. Interpreting the provisions of the Domestic Violence Act this Court in **S.R. Batra** *v.* **Taruna Batra**, *(2007) 3 SCC 169 held that even a wife could not claim a right of residence in the property belonging to her mother-in-law, stating :*

> *"17. There is no such law in India like the British Matrimonial Homes Act, 1967, and in any case, the rights which may be available under any law can only be as against the husband and not against the father-in- law or mother-in-law....*
>
> *Hence, the DVA, 2005 gives a right to the aggrieved spouse to reside in the matrimonial home. Where the aggrieved wife qualifies for maintenance from her husband, she also has a right to only reside in the properties belonging to her husband and not the mother-in-law.""*

In another Bombay High Court judgment in the case of, *Abhijit Bhikaseth Auti* v. *State of Maharashtra*, AIR 2009 (NOC) 808 (Bom), the provisions under sections 17 and 19 of the DVA, 2005 have been elaborated. The case was filed by the wife against the husband on the ground of domestic violence committed by him. AIR 2009 (NOC) 808 (Bom) **p**aras 12 and 13 of the said judgment explains the extent of the applicability of the provisions of sections 17 and 19 of the Act in the following terms:

"12. Section 17 reads thus:

> ***17. Right to reside as in a shared household.—(1) Notwithstanding anything contained household: in any other law for the time being in force, every woman in a domestic relationship shall have the right to reside in the shared household, whether or not she has any right, title or beneficial interest in the same.***
>
> ***(2) The aggrieved person shall not be evicted or excluded from the shared household or any part of it by the respondent save in accordance with the procedure established by law.***

13. Sub-section (1) of section 17 starts with a **non-obstante clause** ***which has over-riding effect over other statutes. The sub-section provides that every women in a domestic relationship shall have right to reside in a shared household whether or not she has any right, title or beneficial interest in the same. This is indeed a provision which enlarges the scope of the concept of matrimonial home under the existing laws dealing with matrimonial relationship. This is in the context of the definition of domestic relationship under clause (f) of section 2 which means relationship between two persons who live or have, at any point of time lived together in a shared household, when they are related by consanguinity, marriage, or through a relationship in the nature of a marriage. The definition of shared household under section 2(s) of the said Act is very wide. It even includes a household which may belong to the joint family of which the respondent is a member. Section 19 which gives power to the Magistrate to pass residence orders providing for grant of various orders in relation to a shared household for protecting the rights of the aggrieved person to occupy a shared household. The learned Magistrate in a given case can even direct the respondent to remove himself from a shared household."***

Hence, under the Indian laws the division of property in cases where marriage ends up in a divorce has been specifically dealt only under the provisions mentioned in the above mentioned legislation *i.e.*, the provisions of the DVA, 2005. That whether or not a foreign national can be charged under the provisions of the DVA, 2005 is a debatable point. In the Indian context, it is a very powerful tool to nail down the husband, especially in matters of alimony, maintenance and right of residence.

Thus, on the basis of the above discussion, the position regarding the property of the parties to the marriage is very clear and unambiguous. The Court may or may not deal with the property of the parties acquired after the marriage. In the facts and circumstances of a case, if the wife feels that some specific property was bought by the parties after the marriage, she can very much claim the share in the property under section 27 of the HMA, 1955 as well.

In terms of the provisions of the DVA, 2005, it is important to note, that another efficacious alternative remedy is available for Hindu wives in cases where they are ill treated and not kept properly by the Husband. The DVA, 2005 not only provides for a right to maintenance that might be granted to a wife but also a right to residence that has to be provided to the wife by the husband in such like cases, depending on the facts and circumstances of each case. Hence, claiming a right to maintenance alongwith the right to residence is yet another remedy available under DVA, 2005, with the wife.

F. WHETHER THE INDIAN COURTS ARE IN A POSITION TO DETERMINE AN APPLICATION FOR MAINTENANCE WHILE THE HUSBAND IS NOT RESIDENT WITHIN THE INDIAN JURISDICTION

The concept of '**maintenance**' in India is statutorily defined under section 125 of the Code of Criminal Procedure, 1973 (section 125), sections 24 and 25 of the HMA, 1955 and section 18 of the HAMA, 1956. Under Indian law, the term 'maintenance' is a measure of social justice and an outcome of the natural duty of a man to maintain his wife, children and parents, when they are unable to maintain themselves. The object of maintenance is to ameliorate the economic condition of women and children, as it lowers down in the society after the divorce proceedings are started in a Court of law as a result of which the husband refuses to maintain the wife and the child anymore.

The remedy available to the Hindu wife under sections 24 and 25 of the HMA, 1955 and section 18 of the HAMA, 1956 are civil in nature.

However, it is very important to mention that proceedings initiated under section 125 of the Indian CrPC, 1973, however, are criminal proceedings and, unlike the personal laws, are of a summary nature and apply to everyone regardless of caste, creed or religion. The object of such proceedings however, is not to punish a person for his past neglect. The said provision has been enacted to compel those who can provide support to give support to those who are unable to support themselves. Maintenance can be claimed either at the interim stage, *i.e.,* during the pendency of proceedings, or the final stages of proceedings under the relevant provisions both of the HMA, 1955 and/or the CrPC, 1973.

But, at the same time it is very important to mention that contested divorce proceedings under the provisions of the HMA, 1955, as also claims for maintenance can be protracted time consuming cumbersome proceedings and sometimes leading to inordinate delay as well.

With regard to the determination of an application for maintenance by the Courts in India when the husband is not residing with the Indian jurisdiction it is stated that even though the husband in such cases is not ordinarily resident in India, maintenance will still be granted to the wife and the children, by the Courts in India adjudicating upon maintenance applications under the above mentioned provisions of law. The reasons for the same are that in divorce proceedings, the spouse who is not able to earn his/her livelihood, is bound to get maintenance from the other spouse during and after the divorce proceedings subject to fulfillment of all other requirements of law.

There is a specific direct ruling, clearly and categorically addressing the issue as stated above. The legal position in this regard was dealt by the Delhi High Court in the year 2004. In a lucid and an erudite judgment of *Anubha* v. *Vikas Aggarwal,* Regular First Appeal 38/2002, decided on 17 November, 2004, the Hon'ble Delhi High Court handed down an authoritative pronouncement taking into account a humanitarian approach especially on the rights of deserted/abandoned Non Resident Indian spouses (commonly referred to as NRI's). This particular judgment is also posted on the Delhi High Court website and the most relevant portions of this judgment crucial to the facts and circumstances of the case in hand read as follows:

> ***"This is one of those classic cases where Indian citizens who go abroad and marry Indian women and thereafter maltreat such women and inflict cruelty and dump them in alien and hostile environment without even bothering to give adequate maintenance. Such persons take advantage of the fact that they are outside the jurisdiction of the Courts of India and most of the time battered married women do not have resources to fight back and bring the culprits to face the consequences of their wrong doings. To deal with such kind of cases and to counter the mischief of such people who exploit the women of this country, and who feel that the strong arms of law cannot reach them, stern action should be taken at every level against them and they should be made to pay such amount of maintenance as would be necessary to restore some dignity and comforts to such women to lead a normal life again. Therefore, in this regard, the duty is cast on the State that such persons who marry Indian women and then dump them in foreign countries by resorting to the laws of those countries for taking divorce, which may not be valid in India, and without giving any maintenance and without discharging their liabilities, to be served with the notices and the orders passed by the court through the embassies and High Commissions of India in those countries so as to bring them under the jurisdiction of the Courts to enforce the liabilities fastened on them under India law and to make them comply with the orders passed by the Courts in India. Indian citizens residing outside as NRIs either on account of having a residency permit or on account of having work permit should not be allowed to violate the rule of law of this country. So long they are citizens of India, they are not immune from the laws of this country and must be made to comply with the orders passed by the Courts in India."***

Similarly, in a Delhi High Court decision in the case of *Radhika* v. *Vineet Rungta,* AIR 2004 Del 323, an application for maintenance was filed by a wife who was residing in India before the Indian Courts, against her husband who was working and residing in the United States of America. In this case as well, the maintenance was granted to wife by the Delhi High Court even though the husband was not ordinarily resident in India at the time of the judgment was handed down by the Delhi High Court in this particular case.

G. THE LIKELY VIEW OF THE INDIAN COURTS OF THE HUSBAND'S INCOME BEING PAID TO HIM IN A FOREIGN OR OVERSEAS JURISDICTION

This particular issue specifically deals with the consequential impact of the salary income or other income of the husband in the foreign or overseas jurisdiction on the amount of maintenance that might be or other income potentially awarded to the wife presently residing in India. In India, the quantum of maintenance provided to one of the parties in a divorce proceeding is the discretion of the Court in awarding the amount of maintenance depending on the facts and circumstances of each case. The test employed by the courts in the Indian jurisdiction is the means test, as to what amount of money the estranged wife would need to sustain herself and her children.

However, in so far relating to the quantum of maintenance, section 23 of the HAMA, 1956, categorically lays down the conditions that will be taken into account by the Court in awarding maintenance to the aggrieved spouse.

Section 23 of the HAMA, 1956 provides that it shall be at the discretion of the Court to determine the amount of maintenance, if any, payable; and in doing so the court shall be guided by the considerations set out in section 23(2) or (3) of the HAMA, 1956, which are set out below.

> '23. *Amount of maintenance*
>
> ***(1) It shall be in the discretion of the Court to determine whether any, and if so what, maintenance shall be awarded under the provisions of this Act, and in doing so, the Court shall have due regard to the considerations set out in sub-section (2), or sub-section (3), as the case may be, so far as they are applicable.***
>
> ***(2) In determining the amount of maintenance, if any, to be awarded to a wife, children or aged or infirm parents under this Act, the following factors shall be taken into account—***
>
> ***(a) the position and status of the parties;***
>
> ***(b) the reasonable wants of the claimant;***
>
> ***(c) if the claimant is living separately, whether the claimant is justified in doing so;***
>
> ***(d) the value of the claimant's property and any income derived from such property, or from the claimant's own earnings or from any other source;***
>
> ***(e) the number of persons entitled to maintenance under this Act.***
>
> ***(3) In determining the amount of maintenance, if any, to be awarded to a dependant under this Act, regard shall be had to—***
>
> ***(a) the net value of the estate of the deceased after providing for the payment of his debts;***
>
> ***(b) the provision, if any, made under a will of the deceased in respect of the dependant;***
>
> ***(c) the degree of relationship between the two;***

(d) the reasonable wants of the dependant;

(e) the past relations between the dependant and the deceased;

(f) the value of the property of the dependant and any income derived from such property, or from his or her earnings or from any other source;

(g) the number of dependants entitled to maintenance under this Act.' Section 25 of the HAMA, 1956 also provides that the amount of maintenance may be altered on change of circumstances."

The Delhi High Court in the above mentioned case of *Radhika* v. *Vineet Rungta*, AIR 2004 Del 323, lamented at the practice of the parties to the litigation not disclosing their actual income. In a terse ruling, Justice Vikramjit Sen held in AIR 2004 Del 323 para 3 at pages 323 and 324 of the judgment as follows:

> *"3. Cases where the parties disclose their actual income are extremely rare. Experience, therefore, dictates that where a decision has to be taken pertaining to the claim for maintenance, and the quantum to be granted, the safer and surer method to be employed for coming to a realistic conclusion is to look at the status of the parties, since whilst incomes can be concealed, the status is palpably evident to all concerned. If any opulent lifestyle is enjoyed by warring spouses he should not be heard to complaint or plead that he has only a meagre income. If this approach had been followed, it would have been evident that the warring spouses enjoy an affluent lifestyle. It has already been noted that the learned trial Court has not discussed the Husband's income. While granting maintenance it is incumbent on the Court to make such monetary arrangements as would be conducive to the spouses continuing a lifestyle to which they were accustomed before the matrimonial discord. In the application under section 24 of the Hindu Marriage Act, 1955, it has been categorically pleaded that the Husband is getting a salary of US$ 72,000 per annum which is equivalent to Rs. 30,24,000 per annum along with the perquisites. A mention is made of the receipt of interest of approximately US$ 1,000 per month as also accounts in various banks. It is pleaded that the Husband is a joint owner of properties valued at over Rs. 2,00,00,000. The wife has pleaded that since 5-10-1998 she has been living at the mercy of her parents; that she has no movable or immovable properties or other assets in her name except a nominal amount of interest from deposits. It has been categorically stated that the Wife has no income to support herself and to meet her necessary expenses."*

AIR 2004 Del 323, para 8 at page 324 of the above mentioned judgment after making an assessment of the overseas income of the husband resident abroad, awarded the maintenance to the wife resident in India. AIR 2004 Del 323 Para 8 at page 324 of the said judgment concluded as follows:

> *"8. Discounting all other incomes, I find that the Husband should be held to have an income of at least US $ 50,000 annually. Considering the lifestyle to which the spouses would be accustomed, and the above minimum assessment of the disposable income of the Petitioner, I am*

> *of the considered view that the learned Trial Court should have granted Rs. 15,000 per month towards maintenance* **pendente lite.** *It is ordered accordingly. By adopting this approach an effort has been made to balance the income and the earnings of the Husband against the income of the Wife, and ensuring that the normal lifestyle and status can be preserved in some measure."*

Here, it will be noticed that the Court assessed the annual income of the husband to be at least 50,000 USD, but awarded the wife a sum of Rs. 15,000 per month towards maintenance *pendente lite* which after conversion at present exchange rates works out to 300 USD per month only.

Furthermore, the Hon'ble Supreme Court of India in the case of *Vinny Parmar* v. *Paramvir Parmar,* AIR 2011 SC 2748, dealt with the question of the reasonable amount of maintenance that the appellant wife was entitled to be payable by the husband in a case of divorce on the grounds of cruelty. The trial Court and the High Court in the present case did not take note of the actual income of the husband and the amount of maintenance granted to the appellant wife in the present case was considered to be low as per the lifestyle of the husband. The Supreme Court in this very recent judgment has elaborated upon the broad principles to be kept in mind by the Courts while dealing with the question of award of maintenance and permanent alimony.

In AIR 2011 SC 2748 paras 10 to 12 of the judgment at page 2750 elaborate the legal position in this regard in the following terms:

> *"10. In* **Shri Bhagwan Dutt** *v.* **Smt. Kamla Devi,** *(1975) 2 SCC 386, though this Court has considered the amount of maintenance payable to wife under section 488 of the Code of Criminal Procedure, 1898, the principle laid down is applicable to the case on hand. In para 19, this Court held "The object of these provisions being to prevent vagrancy and destitution, the Magistrate has to find out as to what is required by the wife to maintain a standard of living which is neither luxurious nor penurious, but is modestly consistent with the status of the family. The needs and requirements of the wife for such moderate living can be fairly determined, only if her separate income, also, is taken into account together with the earnings of the husband and his commitments.*
>
> *11. In* **Chaturbhuj** *v.* **Sita Bai,** *(2008) 2 SCC 316, which also relates to maintenance claim by deserted wife under section 125 of the Code of Criminal Procedure, 1973. The following statement in para 8 is relevant which reads as under:*
>
> > *"Where the personal income of the wife is insufficient she can claim maintenance under section 125, CrPC. The test is whether the wife is in a position to maintain herself in the way she was used to in the place of her husband. In* **Bhagwan Dutt** *v.* **Kamla Devi** *it was observed that the wife should be in a position to maintain a standard of living which is neither luxurious nor penurious but what is consistent with status of a family. The expression unable to maintain herself does not mean that the wife must be absolutely destitute before she can apply for maintenance under section 125, CrPC."*

> ***12. As per section 25, while considering the claim for permanent alimony and maintenance of either spouse, the respondent's own income and other property, and the income and other property of the applicant are all relevant material in addition to the conduct of the parties and other circumstances of the case. It is further seen that the court considering such claim has to consider all the above relevant materials and determine the amount which is to be just for living standard. No fixed formula can be laid for fixing the amount of maintenance. It has to be in the nature of things which depend on various facts and circumstances of each case. The court has to consider the status of the parties, their respective needs, the capacity of the husband to pay, having regard to reasonable expenses for his own maintenance and others whom he is obliged to maintain under the law and statute. The courts also have to take note of the fact that the amount of maintenance fixed for the wife should be such as she can live in reasonable comfort considering her status and mode of life she was used to live when she lived with her husband. At the same time, the amount so fixed cannot be excessive or affect the living condition of the other party. These are all the broad principles courts have to keep in mind while determining maintenance or permanent alimony."***

The Apex Court in the judgment above has in categorical terms laid down the factors and circumstances to be borne in mind by the Hon'ble Courts while adjudicating upon the issue of grant of maintenance to the aggrieved spouse in divorce cases.

Further, the Hon'ble Apex Court in the penultimate paragraph of the judgment while allowing the appeal of the appellant wife had enhanced the maintenance earlier granted to the wife by the trial court and the High Court. This was on the basis of detailed reasons advanced by the Hon'ble Apex Court in AIR 2011 SC 2748 para 15 at page 2751 of the judgment as follows:

> ***"15. In the light of the details furnished by both the parties, we are of the view that the amount of Rs. 1,40,000 determined as net monthly income of the respondent-husband is not acceptable. Equally, direction for payment of maintenance at the rate of Rs. 20,000 per month to the appellant-wife is also inadequate. It is relevant to point out that the status of the appellant before her marriage is also one of the relevant factors for determining the amount of maintenance. It is not in dispute that before her marriage with the respondent, she was working as an Air Hostess in Cathay Pacific Airlines and after marriage she resigned from the said post. Considering the conditions prescribed in section 25 of the Act relating to claim of permanent alimony/maintenance and the fact that the appellant is not permanently employed as on date and residing with her sister at Mumbai, taking note of the respondent's income from salary as Sr. Commander in Air India, other properties standing in his name, age being 42 years, future employment prospects and also considering the fact that the respondent re-married, having a child and also to look after his parents, we feel that the ends of justice would be met by fixing maintenance at the rate of Rs. 40,000 per month instead of Rs. 20,000 per month as fixed***

by the Family Court and affirmed by the High Court. The same shall be payable from the date of her application and continue to pay in terms of section 25 of the Act. The respondent is granted one year time from 1-8-2011 to pay all the arrears payable in six equal instalments. It is made clear that if there is any change in the circumstance of either party, they are free to approach the Court concerned to modify or rescind. As suggested and fixed by the High Court, in the alternative, we fix the amount of permanent alimony/maintenance at Rs. 40 lakhs in lump sum to be paid by the respondent within a period of six months from 01.08.2011 which will forfeit all her claims. The respondent is free to opt any one mode to comply with the same. If the respondent opts the first method, the same is subject to the conditions prescribed in sub-section (3) of section 25 of the Act. The appeals are allowed to the extent mentioned hereinabove. No order as to costs."

It will be noticed from the above-mentioned judgment that the Hon'ble Apex Court *firstly,* doubled the monthly maintenance to be provided to the aggrieved wife. In the alternative, the Court also provided the one time option to the husband to pay consolidated lump sum payment towards permanent alimony/maintenance. It is important to mention that the amount of permanent alimony/maintenance in the facts and circumstances of the case was doubled from 20 lakhs to 40 lakhs. This, after conversion at that time, had worked out to 24,494.6 British Pounds to 48,989.3 British Pounds (approximately as per the current exchange rate at that time on a prominent currency converter website *i.e.,* www.oanda.com – Current Rates of Exchange now may vary). The Supreme Court in the present case has reiterated the earlier law of the means test as also taking into account the factors to be taken into consideration while deciding the quantum of maintenance and permanent alimony by the Courts.

In another case of *Mr. Rajat Taneja* v. *Ms. Harmeeta Singh,* (2008) 149 PLR 18, the Hon'ble Delhi High Court specifically dealt with the question of quantum of maintenance to be paid to an aggrieved wife in divorce proceedings who is staying in India while the husband is residing outside India. The observations of the Delhi High Court in this regard have been elaborated very clearly in (2008) 149 PLR 18 paras 38 and 39 at pages 21 and 22 of the judgment held as under:

"38. As held by the Supreme Court in the decision reported as **United India Insurance** *v.* **Patricia Jean Mahajan,** *AIR 2002 SC 2607: (2002) 6 SCC 281, when compensation has to be paid in India to the claimants of a deceased working abroad, standard of living in India, cost of living in India and other related factors have to be considered and in light of the said facts considering income of the husband in a foreign country further taking note of the fact as to what is the cost of living in the said foreign country, loss of dependence has to be worked out.*

39. Similar principles would apply to grant of monthly maintenance to a wife stationed in India but husband being abroad and earning in foreign currency."

Hence, according to the Delhi High Court in cases where the wife is resident in India and has to be paid maintenance by the husband working outside India, the cost of living and the expenditure in both the countries where the parties are residing has to be kept in mind while calculating the quantum of maintenance to be paid to the wife.

Therefore, from the position of law as elaborated above, the relevant considerations laid down in the HAMA, 1956, HMA, 1955 and/or the CrPC, 1973 depending on the recourse sought by the aggrieved wife, will have to be taken into consideration by the Hon'ble Court while arriving at a decision on the quantum of maintenance to be provided to the wife. Hence, alongwith the salary of the husband, the Hon'ble Court will also take into consideration other relevant factors before granting the maintenance, *i.e.,* the status of the parties, the number of claimants, other properties of the husband and any income from such properties, cost of living in both the countries etc. Hence, it can be asserted that the quantum of maintenance to be paid to the aggrieved wife cannot be decided on the basis of the salary of the husband alone.

Therefore, to sum up it can be stated that if the aggrieved wife has no means of livelihood to maintain herself, she can claim any of the financial remedies as discussed and analysed above. The relevant provisions in this regard that could potentially be invoked free of personal laws, are under section 125 of the CrPC, 1973, as it is a religion neutral provision.

H. MAINTENANCE UNDER SECTION 125 OF THE CRIMINAL PROCEDURE CODE, 1973

Apart from the personal laws, the Code of Criminal Procedure, 1973 (Cr.PC) also provides for maintenance of wives, under Chapter IX containing sections 125 to 128.

Unlike the personal laws which are applicable only to persons belonging to particular religions, the provisions of the Code of Criminal Procedure, 1973 are applicable to all persons irrespective of religion. Relief under this Code is speedy and is available irrespective of whether or not any matrimonial proceedings are pending. Maintenance under Cr.P.C is also available separately even if matrimonial proceedings are separately pending under separate provisions of law, though the quantum may get reduced if separate maintenance under any other statutory provision of a matrimonial law has already been awarded and is being paid. The bare provision [relevant extract] of section 125, Cr.P.C is quoted as hereunder:

> ***"Section 125. Order for maintenance of wives, children and parents.—(1) if any person having sufficient means neglects or refuses to maintain—***
>
> ***(a) his wife, unable to maintain herself, or***
>
> *(b) .....*
>
> *(c) ......*
>
> *(d) .....*
>
> ***a magistrate of the first class may, upon proof of such neglect or refusal, order such person to make a monthly allowance for the maintenance of***

his wife... at such monthly rate, as such magistrate thinks fit, and to pay the same to such person as the magistrate may from time to time direct

.....

Provided .... that the Magistrate may, during the pendency of the proceeding regarding monthly allowance for the maintenance under this sub-section, order such person to make a monthly allowance for the interim maintenance of his wife., and the expenses of such proceeding which the Magistrate considers reasonable, and to pay the same to such person as the Magistrate may from time to time direct

Explanation: For the purpose of this chapter....

(a) ....

(b) "Wife" includes a woman who has been divorced or has obtained a divorce, from her husband and has not remarried.

(2) Any such allowance for the maintenance or interim maintenance and expenses for proceeding shall be payable from the date of the order or, if so ordered, from the date of the application for maintenance or interim maintenance and expenses of proceeding , as the case may be.

(3) If any person so ordered fails without sufficient cause to comply with the order, any such Magistrate may, for every breach of the order, issue a warrant for levying the amount due in the manner provided for levying fines, and may sentence such person, for the whole or any part of each month's allowance for the maintenance or the interim maintenance and expenses of proceeding, as the case may be, remaining unpaid after the execution of the warrant, to imprisonment for a term which may extend to one month or until payment if sooner made:

Provided that no warrant shall be issued for the recovery of any amount due under this section unless application be made to the court to levy such amount within a period of one year from the date on which it became due:

Provided further that if such person offers to maintain his wife on condition of her living with him, and she refuses to live with him, such Magistrate may consider any grounds of refusal stated by her, and may make an order under this section notwithstanding such offer, if he is satisfied that there is just ground for so doing.

Explanation.—If a husband has contracted marriage with another woman or keeps a mistress, it shall be considered to be just ground for his wife's refusal to live with him.

(4) No wife shall be entitled to receive an allowance for the maintenance or the interim maintenance and expenses of proceeding, as the case may be, from her husband under this section if she is living in adultery, or if, without any sufficient reason, she refuses to live with her husband, or if they are living separately by mutual consent.

(5) On proof that any wife in whose favor an order has been made under this section is living in adultery, or that without sufficient reason she refuses to live with her husband, or that they are living separately by mutual consent, the Magistrate shall cancel the order."

The salient features of section 125, Cr.P.C may be summarised as hereunder:

(i) A wife includes a divorced wife.

(ii) Only lawful wife is entitled to maintenance under this section.

(iii) A wife may seek maintenance even without any matrimonial litigation.

(iv) She may stay separate if there are sufficient grounds justifying that and yet get maintenance.

(v) There must be neglect or refusal on part of husband to maintain her.

(vi) Wife must be unable to maintain herself.

(vii) The court can grant interim maintenance also.

(viii) The amount may be varied or cancelled if there is change in circumstances.

(ix) In certain situations a wife may be debarred from claiming maintenance.

(x) Her right terminates on remarriage.

(xi) The proceedings are summary and expeditious."

I. SOME RECENT DECISIONS OF INDIAN COURTS ON ALIMONY

A compilation of some recent decisions are given hereunder in cases where parties have either settled or have been directed to pay lumpsum alimony or an agreed negotiated amount towards parting by a decree of divorce or consensual termination. These recent decisions are given case wise as hereunder:

(a) In *Sarla Singh* v. *Kr. Ajay Partap Singh*, 2011 (2) Marri LJ 372, the High Court of Punjab and Haryana held as follows:

"It is settled law, that in estimating the amount of permanent alimony or permanent maintenance, the Court, while dealing with the fact of income, is not to focus its attention only on the disposable income of a spouse in the year of proceedings but would also normally have regard to the earnings in the previous years and probable earnings in the future. The Court is also to look into the position and the status of parties and in absence of any reliable data on the point of income, the Court is to take into consideration overall financial position of the spouses and their necessities having regards not merely to their income but their properties, debts and liabilities.

It is well settled that the wife besides maintenance is now also entitled to right of residence with the equal status as that of husband. Even a flat of two rooms is worth more than Rs.80 lacs (Rupees eighty lac

only). However, the right of residence along with right to maintenance is assessed at Rs. 1,00,000,00 (Rupees one crore only), if paid in lump sum.

For the reasons stated, this appeal is allowed, the permanent alimony payable is enhanced to Rs. 40,000 (Rupees forty thousand only) per month with right of residence or in the alternative a sum of Rs. 1,00,000,00 (Rupees one crore only) as one time alimony which would not represent even 1/10th of the property owned by the respondent."

Hence, in the above decision, the High Court was pleased to hold that the wife besides maintenance is also entitled to a right of residence with status equal to that of the husband which in the facts of the case was quantified to Indian rupees one hundred thousand, if paid in lumpsum as one time alimony to be paid by the husband.

(b) In *Vinny Parmvir Parmar* v. *Parmvir Parmar,* AIR 2011 SC 2748, the Supreme Court of India was pleased to hold as follow in a case to determine as to what would be the reasonable amount the wife is entitled by way of maintenance from the husband under section 25, HMA, 1955. The Court held

"12. As per section 25, while considering the claim for permanent alimony and maintenance of either spouse, the respondent's own income and other property, and the income and other property of the applicant are all relevant material in addition to the conduct of the parties and other circumstances of the case. It is further seen that the court considering such claim has to consider all the above relevant materials and determine the amount which is to be just for living standard. No fixed formula can be laid for fixing the amount of maintenance. It has to be in the nature of things which depend on various facts and circumstances of each case. The court has to consider the status of the parties, their respective needs, the capacity of the husband to pay, having regard to reasonable expenses for his own maintenance and others whom he is obliged to maintain under the law and statute. The courts also have to take note of the fact that the amount of maintenance fixed for the wife should be such as she can live in reasonable comfort considering her status and mode of life she was used to live when she lived with her husband. At the same time, the amount so fixed cannot be excessive or affect the living condition of the other party. These are all the broad principles courts have to keep in mind while determining maintenance or permanent alimony.

"15. ...It is not in dispute that before her marriage with the respondent, she was working as an Air Hostess in Cathay Pacific Airlines and after marriage she resigned from the said post. Considering the conditions prescribed in section 25 of the Act relating to claim of permanent alimony/ maintenance and the fact that the appellant is not permanently employed as on date and residing with her sister at Mumbai, taking note of the respondent's income from salary as Sr. Commander in Air India, other properties standing in his name, age being 42 years, future employment prospects and also considering the fact that the respondent re-married,

having a child and also to look after his parents, we feel that the ends of justice would be met by fixing maintenance at the rate of Rs. 40,000 per month instead of Rs. 20,000 per month as fixed by the Family Court and affirmed by the High Court. The same shall be payable from the date of her application and continue to pay in terms of section 25 of the Act. The respondent is granted one year time from 01.08.2011 to pay all the arrears payable in six equal instalments. It is made clear that if there is any change in the circumstance of either party, they are free to approach the Court concerned to modify or rescind. As suggested and fixed by the High Court, in the alternative, we fix the amount of permanent alimony/ maintenance at Rs. 40 lakhs in lump sum to be paid by the respondent within a period of six months from 1-8-2011 which will forfeit all her claims. The respondent is free to opt any one mode to comply with the same. If the respondent opts the first method, the same is subject to the conditions prescribed in sub-section (3) of section 25 of the Act. The appeals are allowed to the extent mentioned hereinabove. No order as to costs."

In the aforesaid case, the Supreme Court while holding that no fix formula can be laid down for fixing the amount of permanent alimony, fixed the amount of permanent maintenance quantified at Indian rupees 400,000 (Rs.40 lacs) to be paid in lumpsum which would forfeit all the claims of the respondent wife as a one time payment or be paid Indian rupees 40,000 per month during her life time.

(c) In *Vishwanath* v. *Sau Sarla Vishwanath Agrawal*, (2012) 7 SCC 288, while deciding permanent alimony, it was held:

"41. Presently, we shall deal with the aspect pertaining to the grant of permanent alimony. The court of first instance has rejected the application filed by the respondent-wife as no decree for divorce was granted and there was no severance of marital status. We refrain from commenting on the said view as we have opined that the husband is entitled to a decree for divorce. Permanent alimony is to be granted taking into consideration the social status, the conduct of the parties, the way of living of the spouse and such other ancillary aspects. During the course of hearing of the matter, we have heard the learned counsel for the parties on this aspect. After taking instructions from the respective parties, they have addressed us. The learned senior counsel for the appellant has submitted that till 21-2-2012, an amount of Rs. 17,60,000 has been paid towards maintenance to the wife as directed by the courts below and hence, that should be deducted from the amount to be fixed. He has further submitted that the permanent alimony should be fixed at Rs. 25 lacs. The learned counsel for the respondent, while insisting for affirmance of the decisions of the High Court as well as by the courts below, has submitted that the amount that has already been paid should not be taken into consideration as the same has been paid within a span of number of years and the deduction would affect the future sustenance. He has emphasised on the income of the husband, the progress in the business, the inflation in the

cost of living and the way of life the respondent is expected to lead. He has also canvassed that the age factor and the medical aid and assistance that are likely to be needed should be considered and the permanent alimony should be fixed at Rs. 75 lacs.

42. In our considered opinion, the amount that has already been paid to the respondent-wife towards alimony is to be ignored as the same had been paid by virtue of the interim orders passed by the courts. It is not expected that the respondent-wife has sustained herself without spending the said money. Keeping in view the totality of the circumstances and the social strata from which the parties come from and regard being had to the business prospects of the appellant, permanent alimony of Rs. 50 lacs (rupees fifty lacs only) should be fixed and, accordingly, we so do. The said amount of Rs. 50 lacs (rupees fifty lacs only) shall be deposited by way of bank draft before the trial court within a period of four months and the same shall be handed over to the respondent-wife on proper identification."

In the aforesaid decision rendered by the Supreme Court of India, the Court keeping in mind, inflation and the cost of living besides the life the respondent wife was expected to lead as also ignoring earlier amounts paid, held that keeping in view the social strata of the parties, a permanent alimony of Indian rupees 500,000 (Rs.50 lacs) be paid as a lumpsum settlement to the wife for settlement in divorce.

(d) In *U. Sree* v. *U. Srinivas,* AIR 2013 SC 415, the Apex Court holding that no arithmetic formula was possible to be devised in calculating permanent maintenance, was pleased to hold as follows:

"33. We have reproduced the **aforesaid orders** *to highlight that the husband had agreed to buy a flat at* **Hyderabad.** *However, when the matter was listed thereafter, there was* **disagreement** *with regard to the locality of the flat arranged by the husband and, therefore, the matter was heard on merits. We have already opined that the husband has made out a case for divorce by proving mental cruelty. As a decree is passed, the wife is entitled to permanent alimony for her sustenance. Be it stated, while granting permanent alimony , no arithmetic formula can be adopted as there cannot be mathematical exactitude. It shall depend upon the status of the parties, their respective social needs, the financial capacity of the husband and other obligations. In* **Vinny Parmvir Parmar** *v.* **Parmvir Parmar,** *2011 (3) RCR (Civil) 900: 2011 (4) RAJ 357: (2011) 13 SCC 112, while dealing with the concept of permanent alimony , this Court has observed that while granting permanent alimony, the Court is required to take note of the fact that the amount of maintenance fixed for the wife should be such as she can live in reasonable comfort considering her status and the mode of life she was used to when she lived with her husband. At the same time, the amount so fixed cannot be excessive or affect the living condition of the other party.*

34. Keeping in mind the aforesaid broad principles, we may proceed to address the issue. The respondent himself has asserted that he has earned

name and fame in the world of music and has been performing concerts in various parts of India and abroad. He had agreed to buy a flat in Hyderabad though it did not materialise because of the demand of the wife to have a flat in a different locality where the price of the flat is extremely high. Be that as it may, it is the duty of the Court to see that the wife lives with dignity and comfort and not in penury. The living need not be luxurious but simultaneously she should not be left to live in discomfort. The Court has to act with pragmatic sensibility to such an issue so that the wife does not meet any kind of man-made misfortune. Regard being had to the status of the husband, the social strata to which the parties belong and further taking note of the orders of this Court on earlier occasions, we think it appropriate to fix the permanent alimony at Rs. 50 lacs which shall be deposited before the learned Family Judge within a period of four months out of which ? 20 lacs shall be kept in a fixed deposit in the name of the son in a nationalized bank which would be utilised for his benefit. The deposit shall be made in such a manner so that the respondent wife would be in a position to draw maximum quarterly interest. We may want to clarify that any amount deposited earlier shall stand excluded."

In the aforesaid decision, it was held that the wife was entitled to a status depending on the financial capability of the husband. Further, it was held that no arithmetic formula can be adopted as there cannot be a mathematical exactitude. The Court was pleased to award a sum of Indian Rupees 500,000 (Rs. 50 lacs) as permanent alimony, out of which Indian Rupees 200,000 (Rs.20 lacs) was to be kept in the name of the son in a fixed deposit to be utilised for his benefit.

(e) In *Biswajit Dash* v. *Milan Dash*, 2014 (134) AIC 333, interpreting section 25 of the Hindu Marriage Act, 1955 dealing with permanent alimony, it was held by the Orissa High Court as follows:

"A perusal of the above provision makes it clear that any Court exercising jurisdiction under the Hindu Marriage Act, 1955, before granting permanent alimony under section 25 of the Act, is required to consider the following:

(a) that the order granting permanent alimony is made at the time of passing any decree under the Act, 1955 or at any time subsequent thereto,

(b) the income and other property of the applicant,

(c) the respondent's own income and other property,

(d) the conduct of the parties, and

(e) other circumstances of the case.

12. The apex Ccurt in **Vinny Parmvir Parmar** *v.* **Parmvir Parmar, AIR 2011 SC 2748** *held as follows:—*

"It is further seen that the court considering such claim has to consider all the above relevant materials and determine the amount which is to be just for living standard. No fixed formula can be laid for fixing

the amount of maintenance. It has to be in the nature of things which depend on various facts and circumstances of each case. The court has to consider the status of the parties, their respective needs, the capacity of the husband to pay, having regard to reasonable expenses for his own maintenance and others whom he is obliged to maintain under the law and statute. The courts also have to take note of the fact that the amount of maintenance fixed for the wife should be such as she can live in reasonable comfort as she was used to live when she lived with her husband. At the same time, the amount so fixed cannot be excessive or affect the living condition of the other party. These are all the broad principles courts have to keep in mind while determining maintenance or permanent alimony.

13. In **Vishwanath Sitaram Agrawal** *v.* **Sau. Sarla Vishwanath Agrawal,** *2012 (117) AIC 111 (SC): AIR 2012 SC 2586 the Apex Court while granting permanent alimony has observed that the amount that has already been paid to the respondent-wife towards alimony is to be ignored as the same had been paid by virtue of the interim orders passed by the courts. It is not expected that the respondent-wife has sustained herself without spending the said money."*

14. In **U. Sree** *v.* **U. Srinivas,** *AIR 2013 SC 415, the apex Court while dealing with section 25 of the Act has observed as follows:—*

".. while granting permanent alimony, no arithmetic formula can be adopted as there can not be mathematical exactitude. It shall depend upon the status of the parties their respective social needs, the financial capacity of the husband and other obligations."

In the said judgment the apex Court has also observed that ".. it is the duty of the court to see that the wife lives with dignity and comfort and not in penury. The living need not be luxurious but simultaneously she should not be left to live in discomfort. The court has to act with pragmatic sensibility to such an issue so that the wife does not meet any kind of man made misfortune"

Hence, summarising the position of law as elucidated by the Supreme Court, the High Court laid down general principles for grant of permanent alimony to the wife.

(f) In another unique financial settlement between parties for agreeing to a divorce by mutual consent, which was decided by the 8th Court of the Additional District Judge, Alipore, Calcutta (India) in Matrimonial Suit No. 104 of 2013, in *Aritra Sarkar* v. *Alison Gansell Sarkar*, decided on 18 December, 2013, the parties negotiated and settled terms for grant of a divorce by mutual consent under section 13(B) of the Hindu Marriage Act, 1955. The parties mutually settled that the husband would pay to the wife a sum of 2 million USD (2,000, 000 US dollars) as a one time payment of permanent alimony as stated in Schedule B Part I, besides giving to the wife all the 50 items of jewellery and ornaments mentioned in Schedule B Part II besides also giving the Ganesh Pyne Painting mentioned in Schedule B Part III of the Deed of Settlement. This agreement between the parties was arrived at by mutual negotiation and settlement after parties had amicably decided to divorce by mutual consent. The transfer of the permanent alimony was done in US dollars to enable the wife to have the alimony given to her in USA alongwith all other jewellery items and the painting.

J. MAINTENANCE OF CHILDREN UNDER FAMILY LAWS IN INDIA

Maintenance under Personal Laws and Special Marriage Act, 1954

The obligation of parents to maintain minor children arises both out of blood relationships as well as moral duty, which is reinforced by statutory provisions. Almost every society recognises the duty of a parent to maintain his minor child so long as he is a minor or unable to maintain himself. The degree and extent of such obligation varies from society to society and from time to time.

Minor children in India are entitled to be maintained under two sets of laws, *viz.*, (i) their personal law; and (ii) the secular law, which is the Code of Criminal Procedure, 1973. It may be added here that under **section 38 of the Special Marriage Act, 1954,** in any proceeding under the act the Court can pass both interim and final orders for the custody, maintenance and education of minor children consistently with the wishes wherever possible and may make further orders if so required.

Hindu Law for maintenance of children

There are two personal law statutes amongst the Hindus where under children are entitled to claim maintenance. These are the Hindu Marriage Act, 1955 and the Hindu Adoptions and Maintenance Act, 1956.

The Hindu Marriage Act, 1955 is primarily a statute governing matrimonial relations and providing reliefs to parties but children being an integral component of matrimony, the Act makes provisions to safeguard the interest of the minor children of marriage. Section 26 of the Act says:

> ***"Section 26. Custody of Children.—In any proceeding lunder this Act, the court may, from time to time pass such interim orders and make such provisions... as it may deem just and proper with respect to the custody, maintenance and education of minor children..."***

Apart from section 26, the court may grant maintenance for minor children also on an application by the wife under sections 24 and 25 of the Act.

A relevant extract of section 20 Hindu Adoptions and Maintenance Act, 1956 providing for maintenance of children is as reproduced hereunder for ready reference.

> ***"S.20. Maintenance of Children and aged parents.—(1) ...a Hindu is bound, during his or her lifetime, to maintain his or her legitimate or illegitimate children...***
>
> ***(2) A legitimate or illegitimate child may claim maintenance from his or her father or mother so long as the child is minor.***
>
> ***(3) The obligation of a person to maintain his or her daughter who is unmarried extends in so far as... the unmarried daughter... is unable to maintain... herself out of... her own earnings or other property."***

"Maintenance", under section 3(b) of the Act includes:

(i) in all cases, provision for food, clothing, residence, education and medical attendance and treatment;

(ii) in the case of unmarried daughter, also the reasonable expenses of an incident to her marriage."

A reading of the above enactments leads to the following conclusions:

(a) The children are to be maintained by both the mother and the father.

(b) Children, legitimate or illegitimate, have a right to maintenance.

(c) Children have a right of maintenance until they attain the age of 18 years.

(d) However, an unmarried daughter is entitled to maintenance beyond the age of 18 years, if she is not in a position to maintain herself

(e) The responsibility of maintaining minor children does not depend on the parents possessing any property or assets and it is an absolute personal right of the minor children.

(f) The scope for maintenance is much larger under the Hindu Adoptions and Maintenance Act as it does not require any pending or existing litigation between the parents.

(g) Under the Hindu Marriage Act, 1955, right of maintenance is an ancillary relief in a pending proceeding between parents for some matrimonial relief.

(h) There is no scope for maintenance of an unmarried adult daughter under the Hindu Marriage Act, 1955 since it provides maintenance only for minor children.

Other Personal Laws for maintenance of children

Section 49 of the Parsi Marriage and Divorce Act, 1936 provides maintenance for children as also sections 41-44 of the Indian Divorce Act, 1869, deals with provisions for custody, maintenance and education of minor Christian children. Similarly, under section 38 of the Special Marriage Act, 1954, issues of maintenance, custody and education of children regardless of their religion are dealt with. Like the Hindu Marriage Act, 1955, these provisions provide for maintenance when there is a pending matrimonial litigation between their parents. However, Hindu Adoptions and Maintenance Act, 1956, does not require any pending litigation between parents, as a requirement for a claim for maintenance by the children against the parents.

Muslim Law for maintenance of children

Muslim law has different provisions for maintenance of sons and daughters. Sons are entitled to maintenance until the age of 15 and daughters are entitled to maintenance till they are married. The children have a right of maintenance irrespective of the fact that they are in the custody of their mother. However, the children who are in a position of being maintained out of property with them, would not be entitled to maintenance from their father.

Provision for maintenance of children under the Code of Criminal Procedure, 1973

Under sections 125 to 128 of the Criminal Procedure Code, other than wives and parents, children have a right of maintenance regardless of their religion. The relevant extract of section 125 of the Criminal Procedure Code reads in the following terms:

> ***"Section 125.Order for maintenance of wives, children, and parents.—(1) If any person having sufficient means neglects or refuses to maintain—***
>
> ***(a) ....***
>
> ***(b) his legitimate or illegitimate minor child, whether married or not, unable to maintain itself , or***
>
> ***(c) his legitimate or illegitimate child (not being a married daughter) who has attained majority, where such child is, by reason of any physical or mental abnormality or injury unable to maintain itself, or***
>
> ***(d) ....***
>
> ***A Magistrate of the first class may, upon proof of such neglect or refusal, order such person to make a monthly allowance for the maintenance.... of such child.... at such monthly rate as such Magistrate thinks fit..."***

It may be added here that the provisions of section 125 of the Criminal Procedure Code, can be invoked irrespective of any existing proceedings between the parents and the children. Further, claim for maintenance under this provision is not dependant on the award of any maintenance under the provisions of any proceedings or amount awarded under the Hindu Marriage Act, 1955 or the Hindu Adoption and Maintenance Act or any other Personal law applicable to the parties.

CONCLUSIONS ON THE ISSUE OF MAINTENANCE OF CHILDREN

(i) The rights of maintenance for children in pending proceedings are available by way of ancillary relief under all Personal laws of parties as also under the Special Marriage Act, 1954.

(ii) Under the Hindu Adoptions and Maintenance Act, 1956, maintenance of minor children does not depend on any previous proceedings or any existing or pending litigation between the parents.

(iii) Maintenance under section 125 of the Criminal Procedure Code, for children does not depend on any maintenance awarded under any Personal laws and is an independent provision regardless of the pendency of any pending proceedings between the parents under their Personal laws.

(iv) The responsibility to maintain children is absolute irrespective of the financial status of the parents and is confined to minor children only, under personal laws of the parties.

K. DISPOSAL OF MATRIMONIAL PROPERTY AND CLAIM FOR RIGHTS OF RESIDENCE

Section 27 of the Hindu Marriage Act, 1955 provides that in any proceedings under the Act, the Court may make such provisions as it deems fit with respect to any property presented at or about the time of marriage, which may belong jointly to both the husband and the wife. The Supreme Court in *B.R. Kadam* v. *S.B. Kadam,* AIR 1997 SC 3562, interpreted the expression "at or about the time of marriage" to mean and include even the property given before or after marriage so long as it is related to the marriage. The right of residence of an estranged wife is part of a maintenance rights as there is no separate provision in the Hindu Marriage Act, 1955 for rights of residence. As held by the Supreme Court in *Komalam Amma* v. *Kumara Pillai,* AIR 2009 SC 636, maintenance includes right to matrimonial assets. Under the HMA, 1955, the estranged wife cannot be denied the right of residence in the matrimonial home.

It may also be added that under section 3(b) of the Hindu Adoptions and Maintenance Act, 1956, read with section 18, a Hindu wife is entitled to live separately from her husband, without forfeiting her claim to maintenance, if her husband is guilty of any matrimonial wrong. Section 3(b) defines maintenance by including provisions for residence. Thus, the right of maintenance and separate residence under section 18 is a substantive right, and not dependent on any existing proceedings, unlike the Hindu Marriage Act, 1955.

Under section 37 of the Special Marriage Act, 1954, permanent alimony and maintenance is available to the wife at the time of passing any decree or subsequent thereto. This would include a charge on the husband's property for such gross sum or monthly or periodical payment, as the court may deem fit to award. Therefore, under the SMA, 1954, the right of residence in the matrimonial home would be a part of her right to maintenance to be adjudicated under section 37 of the Act.

Under sections 17 and 19 of the Protection of Women from Domestic Violence Act, 2005, every woman in a domestic violence shall have the right to reside in a shared household, whether or not she has any right, title or beneficial interest in the same. Residence Orders can be obtained by the wife against the husband under section 19 of the said Act. In *S.R. Batra* v. *Tarun Batra,* AIR 2007 SC 118, it was held that the estranged wife cannot claim any rights under this Act against the father-in-law, mother-in-law and other relatives. It was further held that shared household accommodation, owned by the mother-in-law, does not become a shared household of the husband and wife for the purposes of the Act. Hence, it was held that a claim for a right to alternative accommodation can be made against the husband only in respect of a house owned or taken on rent by the husband or a house that belongs to the joint family of which the husband is a member.

In a unique unreported case decided by the Supreme Court of India on 15 July 2013 in the matter of *Pamela Sharda* v. *Rama Sharda,* a petition for Special Leave to Appeal (Civil) No. 11714 of 2012, preferred against a Judgment of the High Court of Delhi, the Apex Court was pleased to uphold a settlement arrived at between the parties at the Supreme Court Mediation Centre. It may be mentioned that this Centre assists parties for resolution of disputes through process of mediation. Clauses 2, 5, 7 and 9 of the Settlement between parties read as follows:

"2. That the First Party shall pay a sum of Rs. 45,00,000 (Rupees Forty Five Lakhs only) to the Third Party in full and final settlement of her claims towards Istridhan, maintenance pendente lite, *alimony temporary and permanent and pursuant to the receipt of Rs. 45,00,000 (Rupees Forty Five Lakhs only) the Third Party shall have no claim whatsoever against the First Party. The Third Party shall also make no claim in future qua the rights of residence as envisaged under section 19 of the Domestic Violence Act, Hindu Adoption and Maintenance Act, 1956 and Hindu Marriage Act, 1955 or under any other statutory enactment and all her statutory rights, claims* qua *the First Party shall stand extinguished upon the payment of Rs. 45,00,000 (Rupees Forty Five Lakhs only).*

5. That it has been agreed between the First Party and the Third Party that the amount received by the Third Party from the First Party shall not be considered as an amount towards dissolution of marriage as permanent alimony. Further the First Party had assured the Third Party that he shall not file any proceedings for obtaining divorce on any ground and in lieu of that assurance the Third Party has undertaken that she will not claim any maintenance past, present or future or permanent alimony or expenses of the proceedings, costs, etc., from the First Party in any form whatsoever or under any statutory enactment.

7. That pursuant to the receipt of Rs. 45,00,000 (Rupees Forty Five Lakhs only) from the First Party the Third Party shall cease to have any right to reside with the First Party nor shall claim any right of residence from the First Party nor claim any restitution of conjugal rights or any form of matrimonial relationship with the First Party before any Court, Tribunal or Forum. The Third Party shall have no right to stay with the First and the Second Parties and shall not cause any disturbance in the normal day to day life of the First and the Second Parties and in the event the Third Party tries to invade the privacy of the First and the Second Party, then in that event, the First and the Second Party shall be entitled to seek injunction against the third party. However, it is agreed that for the three months i.e. *August, September and October, 2013 the first party shall pay maintenance of Rs. 15,000 per month to the third party and thereafter all the rights of the third party to claim any maintenance, permanent alimony, istridhan shall stand extinguished in law, against the first party.*

9. That pursuant to the receipt of the amount of Rs. 45,00,000 (Rupees Forty Five Lakhs only) the Third Party shall have no right, title or interest in the said property or any other property belonging to the First and the Second Parties and further undertakes that she shall not file any claim, case or action against the First and the Second Parties nor shall stake any claim qua *the movable and immovable properties of the First and the Second Parties and even upon the demise of the first and second party, the third party shall not claim any right, title or interest over the said property or over any movable or immovable properties of the first and the second party, including the said property."*

In this inimitable decision rendered on 15 July, 2013, the Supreme Court, accepting the tripartite settlement deed executed between the wife, husband and his mother through mediation, permitted parties to part ways upon a onetime payment of Indian Rupees 450,000 (Rs.45 lacs) to the wife with the condition that both would not seek divorce on any ground. The couple married for 30 years agreed to withdraw all their pending litigations and the wife agreed not to cause any disturbance or invade the privacy of her husband and his 83 year old mother living in their household property. The sum of Indian Rupees 450,000 (Rs. 45 lacs) paid in full and final settlement to the wife was towards all her financial claims. Both parties living separately since 2009, agreed that they shall have nothing to do with each other's lives and will not undergo any divorce proceedings. The wife would also not claim restitution of conjugal rights or rights of residence in the household. However, in the event of remarriage of the husband, the agreement shall stand terminated and the wife would be entitled to revive her claim of maintenance or alimony for the present and future, since the sum of Indian Rupees 450,000 (Rs.45 lacs) shall not be considered as an amount towards dissolution of marriage and payment of permanent alimony. The Apex Court by its Judgment of 15 July, 2013 accepting the *Settlement Deed* and the *Undertakings* of the parties, disposed off the matter and permitted parties to file the same before all Courts where litigations were pending with liberty to invoke the provisions of the Contempt of Courts Act, 1971 upon breach if any. Hence, prior to divorce or at the time of settlement of permanent alimony upon divorce, the wife can claim her right of residence in a property owned by the husband or demand an equivalent share to compensate her for her right to residence so that the wife and her children can have suitable living accommodation as per the standards they were living in when the parties were married and were enjoying residential facilities jointly.

L. CONCLUSION: NEED BASED ASSESSMENT, NO ARITHMETIC FORMULA

Hence, all personal laws provide for maintenance of women and children. The Special Marriage Act, 1954, as a secular law, also provides for maintenance, alimony and support for both women and children. The provisions of the Criminal Procedure Code can be invoked irrespective of religion by both women and children regardless of the pendency of any matrimonial litigation between the parties. The Protection of Women from Domestic Violence Act provides rights to reside in a shared household. The quantum of maintenance under all laws is a **need based means requirement** depending upon the status of parties and maintenance can be claimed simultaneously under personal laws and the Cr.P.C, though the quantum may be reduced in such parallel claims.

A Hindu wife has an added advantage of invoking a right to claim maintenance under the Hindu Adoptions and Maintenance Act, 1956 for which there is no requirement of any matrimonial litigation and can be availed of irrespective of maintenance under other laws. However, the quantum of maintenance may be reduced if parallel claims are made under different laws.

Permanent Alimony, right of residence and maintenance is determined by Indian Courts depending upon the income and properties of both parties, status of parties, their respective needs, standards or amenities the wife is entitled to as per facilities enjoyed by the husband when she lived with the husband, and their respective lifestyles as also the conduct of both parties. The Courts will consider not only the present income of the earning spouse, but would also look at previous and probable future earnings. Overall financial position, properties owned, debts, liabilities, future earnings, pensions, rents, and other accruals will also fall in the zone of consideration. Thus, no fixed or arithmetical formula in general can be laid down for calculating maintenance which would vary in the individual facts and circumstances of each case. Right of residence is a component of the wife's right to maintenance. Besides, the wife would also have right of residence in the matrimonial home under the Protection of Women from Domestic Violence Act, 2005.

Based on the precedents of various Courts, the factors and remedies which would possibly merit consideration in an application for maintenance and alimony as also right of residence by the wife as also her children by a Court can now be broadly identified. In determining an application for maintenance, residence or permanent alimony by the wife and the adult children, a Court is likely to ascertain a monthly or lumpsum amount on a **need based formula** of **means test,** to be evaluated after assessing the following factors which are listed as hereunder for ready reference:

a. On termination of marriage, a spouse can claim permanent maintenance and alimony including a right of residence as part of maintenance. This claim can be made by a spouse under section 25 of the Hindu Marriage Act, 1955 (for Hindus), section 37 of the Special Marriage Act, 1954 (for all persons), section 40 of the Parsi Marriage and Divorce Act, 1936 (for Parsis), or section 37 of the Indian Divorce Act, 1869 as amended in 2001 (for Christians) and sections 3 and 4 of the Muslim Women (Protection of Rights on Divorce) Act, 1986 (for Muslims), depending on the applicability of the relevant law to the parties based on their religion or application of Special Marriage Act, 1954, if parties do not invoke application of personal laws. Besides, independent of these provisions, there are also remedies available under section 125 of the Criminal Procedure Code as also under sections 17 and 18 of the Protection of Women from Domestic Violence Act, 2005.

b. It may be stated that under all statutory provisions of different religious communities (except Muslims) as also under the provisions of the Special Marriage Act, 1954, the factors and considerations weighing with a Court in making an order for financial relief in the nature of permanent alimony and maintenance are by and large uniform and consistent as they follow a need based requirement. In Indian Jurisprudence and interpretation of matrimonial laws in giving financial relief, the practice of making individual or distinct capital orders by way of property adjustment or sharing of pensions has not been noticed in precedents. Instead, the Courts estimate the value of all the assets of spouses to proportionately determine on a need based means test, the lumpsum amount of maintenance to be awarded to the non-earning spouse. In most matters, when the claim for permanent maintenance and alimony is made by the wife, Courts consolidate the value of all the assets of the husband by including his income, properties, other assets, future earnings etc to assess the net worth. **The practice of making pension sharing orders separately is not adopted in the Indian jurisdiction.** In so far property adjustment is concerned, it is made a part of lumpsum maintenance, unless parties chose to separately make a property arrangement. However, there is no such statutory requirement and any such arrangement is purely on volition of parties. Accordingly, maintenance and alimony club under it all ingredients of assets to form one composite figure from which the Court decides lumpsum maintenance on a need based requirement which may be paid in one or separate instalments. Once a consolidated figure of the total income and assets of the earning spouse is arrived at, the Court awards a proportionate amount as lumpsum alimony after determining the need based requirement on the means test basis for granting this lumpsum amount without any separate or segregated arrangements.

c. It may be stated that once Courts arrive at a consolidated figure of lumpsum maintenance or alimony, **the Court itself lays down a lumpsum package or a monthly ongoing payment plan after fixing the lumpsum amount**. It may be the option of the wife *i.e.*, the receiving spouse invariably to make her choice upon a request to the Court depending on the need based requirements varying from the facts and circumstances in an individual case. There is no statutory rule or mandate in any enactment for any lumpsum or monthly payment process and it is the discretion of the Court adjudicating any such matter to take an appropriate decision upon the request of parties or keeping in mind the need based requirement in a specific case. There is no hard and fast rule to make an ongoing monthly payment or lumpsum payment once the consolidated figure of permanent alimony is settled. The payment will subsist only to the extent of the amount payable as agreed and settled and the husband's estate cannot be burdened beyond the settled amount after his death. A decree for maintenance does not get extinguished with the death of the husband and the decree of maintenance would have to be satisfied first and thereafter the legal heirs would succeed to his property from the amount remaining after such satisfaction of a matrimonial decree. Hence, any ongoing monthly payment would subsist after the death of the husband till the lumpsum decretal amount is settled but would not go beyond it. **In so far remarriage is concerned, most Courts invariably hold upon awarding a lumpsum or monthly amount that no maintenance shall be payable on remarriage of a spouse**. The logic clearly is that maintenance is a need based requirement and upon remarriage the need based requirement ceases. Furthermore, even on the death of the wife, the maintenance for the wife would be not payable in the case of a monthly payment plan to the extent to which it remains unpaid till death of the wife. However, if paid in lumpsum, no refunds are possible on the death or the remarriage of the wife as lumpsum payments cannot be refunded.

d. It may be stated that there are no statutory criteria or principles laid down in any of the enactments to guide the award of maintenance which are purely discretionary in every matter depending on the facts and circumstances of each case. **The underlining basic principle for all these factors is a need based means test or requirement of the spouse claiming maintenance and alimony**. A number of factors and considerations can be possibly termed as guiding sub-principles to understand and appreciate the import of the basic need based test principle as everything revolves around this basic primary test. The general principles and grounds on which the claims for maintenance and permanent alimony are awarded by Courts generally have been identified on the basis of the large number of precedents cited and relied upon over a period of time.

e. There is no statutory law in matrimonial jurisprudence for any separate maintenance or other benefits to be paid to adult children. Hence, any award of ongoing financial support to adult children for higher education on a need basis, would require special facts and circumstances to be pleaded before a Court to merit any attention. Thereafter, it is in the total discretion that, in the special situation of a given case, that a Court may award maintenance and financial support to adult children for higher education or other specified purposes. This would require special pleadings, specific evidence and documentary proof to enable the Court to be satisfied of any such special need. However, there is no specific bar to disentitle adult children from receiving any such benefits and it is purely the discretion of the Court to see and award any such benefit of financial aid for higher education to be given to adult children. This may require the Court to give reasons and justification in doing so. However, it may be added that nothing prevents the parties from consenting to giving on their own benefits to adult children for higher education or other need based emergent situations like medical treatment or special facilities, in case of adult children having special needs due to disabilities or medical conditions.

f. Gross income of the husband for a period of 3-5 years before filing of the divorce petition as well as the application for permanent alimony and maintenance. Earnings of previous year may also be examined by the Court, for a better assessment. The income of the husband will be examined in a foreign currency, if he is earning abroad and if the wife is also abroad.

g. Future earnings prospects of the husband from salary and other benefits. Rents, accruals, profits, annuities, pension or any other income from any other capital moveable and immoveable assets will fall in the zone of consideration to assess the net value of the wealth of the husband. Income, assets, properties and all financial gains of the wife may be kept in mind by the Court to make a need based assessment of maintenance for her.

h. If the husband has properties abroad and a pension also in a foreign country, which are substantial assets, a Court in India in every likelihood would take into consideration these assets in deciding the permanent alimony of the wife as the wife would certainly make a claim on these foreign based assets considering that she is resident overseas and would need funds in the foreign currency. The foreign based Pension or other assets of the husband would certainly be relied upon by the wife and therefore be considered by an Indian Court as an asset of the husband to determine permanent alimony to be paid to the wife.

i. It may be the claim of the wife that the property located abroad of the husband was their former, "***matrimonial home***" which however, may be disputed by the husband who claims that the "***matrimonial home***" of the parties is in India where the parties may have lived together as husband and wife. Be that as it may, the wife has a right of residence after divorce, irrespective of where the parties last resided or had the locus of their "***matrimonial home***". Therefore, the wife would have to be either given a right of residence in a foreign country in a property owned by the husband commensurate to the status the parties had when they were living as a family and if that is not possible, the wife would have to be compensated monetarily to live in the foreign country with the children (if they are still living with the mother in the foreign country) in accordance with the standards the wife and children enjoyed when they lived as a family.

j. Previous employment of the wife, her current position of non employment and any other possible source of income of the wife may also be looked into by the Court in making an assessment of her dependency on the husband.

k. Since the wife has a right of residence in a property owned by the husband, the wife would be entitled to a proportionate share in case she is not provided with suitable accommodation in the foreign country. If no residence is made available by the husband, he will have to compensate the wife with a monetary compensation so that the wife would have comfortable accommodation which the husband enjoys.

l. The permanent alimony will be determined in accordance with expenses commensurate to the standards of living the wife would have been entitled to had she been living with the husband keeping in mind the status of the parties, their respective social and family needs as also other obligations.

m. The permanent alimony would be assessed in accordance with standards as per which the wife can live in reasonable comfort and the mode of life she was used to when she lived with her husband.

n. The conduct of both parties *i.e.* husband and wife will be relevant for determining permanent alimony though for interim maintenance, conduct of parties is not to be kept in mind by the Court at the initial stages of proceedings for grant of interim maintenance.

o. If the parties have any children, their maintenance and education expenses as also any other upbringing costs may have to be borne in mind in calculating the monthly or lumpsum payment of alimony for the wife and children. The Court may segregate the amounts or determine a lumpsum. However, since statutory provisions only provide for maintenance and education of minor children, the grant of any financial benefit or support to adult children may be totally discretionary. If the adult children can establish independently need for financial support for higher education, they may be required to make out a special case for claiming dependency on their father and it would be totally discretionary for the Court in India to award any financial benefit to them in any special situation. There is no mandatory and statutory obligation for maintenance of adult children. However, parties may voluntarily opt to provide for their maintenance in the facts and circumstances of the given case.

p. If the wife resides in a foreign jurisdiction and all her expenses, living costs, funds (if any) for adult children and other maintenance claims would be in a foreign currency, as also keeping in mind that the husband has assets, income, property and other wealth in that foreign jurisdiction, the Court in India is likely to award a lumpsum monthly or total amount in the currency of that foreign jurisdiction and not in Indian Rupees.

q. Rising costs due to inflation, escalating living costs, future expenses of adult children towards higher education and medical expenses of the wife will also be kept in mind by an Indian Court for assessing permanent alimony.

r. As per Indian law there is no mathematical or set formula of determining percentage of an amount towards permanent alimony, maintenance and right of residence to be assessed from the collective earnings of the husband. The Court would make its own **need based assessment** by a **means test** and then arrive at a figure by which assessed lumpsum permanent alimony can be paid either on monthly basis or a onetime single payment.

s. In Criminal Appeal No. 1331 of 2014 *Bhuwan Mohan Singh* v. *Meena*, 2014 STPL (Web) 467 SC decided on 15 July, 2014, the Supreme Court held:

11. The Family Courts have been established for adopting and facilitating the conciliation procedure and to deal with family disputes in a speedy and expeditious manner.

12. A three-Judge Bench in *K.A. Abdul Jalee*l v. *T.A. Shahida*, (2003) 4 SCC 166, while highlighting on the purpose of bringing in the Family Courts Act by the legislature, opined thus:—

> "The Family Courts Act was enacted to provide for the establishment of Family Courts with a view to promote conciliation in, and secure speedy settlement of, disputes relating to marriage and family affairs and for matters connected therewith."

13. The purpose of highlighting this aspect is that in the case at hand the proceeding before the Family Court was conducted without being alive to the objects and reasons of the Act and the spirit of the provisions under section 125 of the Code. It is unfortunate that the case continued for nine

> years before the Family Court. It has come to the notice of the Court that on certain occasions the Family Courts have been granting adjournments in a routine manner as a consequence of which both the parties suffer or, on certain occasions, the wife becomes the worst victim. When such a situation occurs, the purpose of the law gets totally atrophied. The Family Judge is expected to be sensitive to the issues, for he is dealing with extremely delicate and sensitive issues pertaining to the marriage and issues ancillary thereto. When we say this, we do not mean that the Family Courts should show undue haste or impatience, but there is a distinction between impatience and to be wisely anxious and conscious about dealing with a situation. A Family Court Judge should remember that the procrastination is the greatest assassin of the *lis* before it. It not only gives rise to more family problems but also gradually builds unthinkable and Everestine bitterness. It leads to the cold refrigeration of the hidden feelings, if still left. The delineation of the *lis* by the Family Judge must reveal the awareness and balance. Dilatory tactics by any of the parties has to be sternly dealt with, for the Family Court Judge has to be alive to the fact that the *lis* before him pertains to emotional fragmentation and delay can feed it to grow. We hope and trust that the Family Court Judges shall remain alert to this and decide the matters as expeditiously as possible keeping in view the objects and reasons of the Act and the scheme of various provisions pertaining to grant of maintenance, divorce, custody of child, property disputes, etc.

Hence, the law of maintenance in India is a need based requirement assessed and evaluated by a Court in independent or ancillary proceedings depending on the facts and circumstances of a case. No rigid or mathematical formula determines a set precedent. However, the Supreme Court has clearly held that time is the essence of the matter in such claims to maintenance and Family Courts have been directed to decide all such claims expeditiously in the interest of parties.

Family Settlements – Governing Legal Principles, Statutory Requirements and Caselaw Analysis

BRIEF BACKGROUND TO NATURE AND REQUIREMENTS OF FAMILY SETTLEMENTS EXECUTED IN FAMILY RUN COMPANIES IN INDIA AND IN THE EVENT OF FAMILY DISPUTES IN THE INDIAN JURISDICTION

It is necessary to advert to the nature and background of family arrangements with well known corporate families of India. Reported ample evidence abounds of family arrangements executed even by family members of well known listed companies, which have a strong domestic and an international presence as well.

In this chapter, there is an analytical compilation under different brief headings a list of handful of key judgments on the subject decided by the Supreme Court of India and various High Courts of the country right from 1965 to 2010. This is with a limited perspective to demonstrate on the basis of settled caselaw on different aspects, components, governing principles and legal requirements of family arrangements in the Indian jurisdiction.

In particular, reference is also drawn to the exhaustive judgment in the case of ***Reliance Natural Resources Ltd.* v. *Reliance Industries Ltd.*, (2010) 7 SCC 1**. The said judgment handed down by the Supreme Court of India has direct substantial relevance, in so far specifically relating to the issue of family settlements. This judgment categorically emphasises and distinguishes on the non-binding nature of family settlements on corporate entities. Clearly, this judgment is important for powerful family run stakeholders, who own, operate and manage family run companies.

A summary of the fundamental benchmark principles governing family settlements on the basis of caselaw analysis is discussed below:

PRINCIPLES AND CONDITIONS GOVERNING VALIDITY AND EXECUTION OF FAMILY/SETTLEMENT ARRANGEMENTS ELUCIDATED AND SUMMARISED ON BASIS OF CASE LAW ANALYSIS OF JUDGMENTS OF THE SUPREME COURT OF INDIA AND VARIOUS HIGH COURTS COUNTRY WIDE.

(1) SIX BASIC PRINCIPLES GOVERNING FAMILY SETTLEMENTS LAID DOWN BY THE SUPREME COURT OF INDIA IN 1976 IN THE CASE OF KALE

The Supreme Court of India in ***Kale* v. *Deputy Director of Consolidation*, AIR 1976 SC 807** very lucidly enunciated principles and propositions governing family settlements. It was held in para 10 of the judgment as follows:

"10. *In other words to put the binding effect and the essentials of a family settlement in a concretised form, the matter may be reduced into the form of the following propositions:*

(1) *The family settlement must be a bona fide one so as to resolve family disputes and rival claims by a fair and equitable division or allotment of properties between the various members of the family.*

(2) *The said settlement must be voluntary and should not be induced by fraud, coercion or undue influence.*

(3) *The family arrangements may be even oral in which case no registration is necessary;*

(4) *It is well settled that registration would be necessary only if the terms of the family arrangement are reduced into writing. Here also, a distinction should be made between a document containing the terms and recitals of a family arrangement made under the document and a mere memorandum prepared after the family arrangement had already been made either for the purpose of the record or for information of the Court for making necessary mutation. In such a case the memorandum itself does not create or extinguish any rights in immovable properties and therefore does not fall within the mischief of section 17(2) (sic) section 17(1)(b) of the Registration Act and is, therefore, not compulsorily registrable;*

(5) *The members who may be parties to the family arrangement must have some antecedent title, claim or interest even a possible claim in the property which is acknowledged by the parties to the settlement. Even if one of the parties to the settlement has no title but under the arrangement the other party relinquishes all its claims or titles in favour of such a person and acknowledges him to be the sole owner, then the antecedent title must be assumed and the family arrangement will be upheld and the Courts will find no difficulty in giving assent to the same;*

(6) *Even if* bona fide *disputes, present or possible, which may not involve legal claims are settled by a bona fide family arrangement which is fair and equitable the family arrangement is final and binding on the parties to the settlement*

It will be noticed that the above mentioned principles have been summed up very succinctly, and are a clear cut judicial guideline on the subject.

The other important requirements, basis, legal requirements and principles governing family settlements are tabulated hereunder as follows:

(2) BASIC PURPOSE BEHIND EXECUTION OF FAMILY ARRANGEMENTS

The Supreme Court of India in ***Maturi Pullaiah* v. *Maturi Narasimham*, AIR 1966 SC 1836** held in para 17 of the judgment as follows:

> *"17. Briefly stated, though conflict of legal claims in present or in future is generally a condition for the validity of a family arrangement, it is not necessarily so. Even bona fide disputes, present or possible which may not involve legal claims will suffice. Members of a joint Hindu family may, to maintain peace or to bring about harmony in the family, enter into such a family arrangement. If such an arrangement is entered into bona fide and the terms thereof are fair in the circumstances of a particular case, Courts will more readily give assent to such an arrangement than to avoid it."*

Thus, in order for the Deed of Family Arrangement to be valid, the parties to the same will have to demonstrate that it was executed for bona fide purposes.

(3) CIRCUMSTANCES IN WHICH A FAMILY ARRANGEMENT CAN BE ENFORCED IN A COURT OF LAW

The Supreme Court of India in ***Potti Lakshmi Perumallu* v. *Potti Krishnavenamma*, AIR 1965 SC 825** held that no doubt, a family arrangement which is for the benefit of the family generally can be enforced in a court of law. But before the Court would do so, it must be shown that there was an occasion for effecting a family arrangement and that it was accordingly acted upon.

(4) IT IS NOT NECESSARY THAT PARTIES TO A FAMILY ARRANGEMENT SHOULD ALL BELONG TO ONE FAMILY

Para 10 of the judgment in ***Krishna Beharilal (dead) by his legal representatives* v. *Gulabchand*, AIR 1971 SC 1041,** the Supreme Court of India held as follows:

> *"...To consider a settlement as a family arrangement, it is not necessary that the parties to the compromise should all belong to one family. As observed by this Court in* Ram Charan Das *v.* Girjia Nandini Devi, *(1965) 3 SCR 841 (850 and 851): AIR 1966 SC 323 (328 and 329) the word "family" in the context of the family arrangement is not to be understood in a narrow sense of being a group of persons who are recognised in law as having a right of succession or having a claim to a share in the property in dispute. If the dispute which is settled is one between near relations then the settlement of such a dispute can be considered as a family arrangement – see* Ramcharan Das's *case, (1965) 3 SCR 841: AIR 1966 SC 323 (*supra*).*
>
> *9. The Courts lean strongly in favour of the family arrangements to bring about harmony in a family and do justice to its various members and avoid in*

anticipation future disputes which might ruin them all – see Sahu Madho Das *v.* Pandit Mukand."

(5) CIRCUMSTANCES IN WHICH REGISTRATION OF THE FAMILY ARRANGEMENT IS REQUIRED

The Supreme Court of India in ***Tek Bahadur Bhujil* v. Debi *Singh Bhujil*, AIR 1966 SC 292** elaborated the circumstances in which registration of family arrangements is required.

Para 12 of the above mentioned judgment in this regard reads as follows:

> *"12. Family arrangement as such can be arrived at orally. Its terms may be recorded in writing as a memorandum of what had been agreed upon between the parties. The memorandum need not be prepared for the purpose of being used as a document on which future title of the parties be founded. It is usually prepared as a record of what had been agreed upon so that there be no hazy notions about it in future. It is only when the parties reduce the family arrangement in writing with the purpose of using that writing as proof of what they had arranged and where the arrangement is brought about the document as such, that the document would require registration as it is then that it would be a document of title declaring for future what rights in what properties the parties possess.....*
>
> *....The document, to our mind, is nothing but a memorandum of what had taken place and, therefore, is not a document which would require compulsory registration under section 17 of the Registration Act."*

(6) COURTS GIVE ASSENT TO *BONA FIDE* FAMILY ARRANGEMENTS

There are several reported cases to the effect that Courts in India "give assent to *bona fide* family arrangements". The Supreme Court of India reiterated and expounded this concept in ***S. Shanmugam Pillai* v. K. Shanmugam Pillai, AIR 1972 SC 2069.**

Para 24 of the above mentioned judgment in this regard reiterates as follows:

> *"24. Now turning to the plea of family arrangement, as observed by this Court in* Sahu Madho Das *v.* Pandit Mukand Ram, *(1955) 2 SCR 22: AIR 1955 SC 481 the courts lean strongly in favour of family arrangements that bring about harmony in a family and do justice to its various members and avoid, in anticipation, future disputes which might ruin them all. As observed in that case the family arrangement can as a matter of law be inferred from a long course of dealings between the parties.*
>
> *25. In* Maturi Pullaiah *v.* Maturi Narasimham, *AIR 1966 SC 1836 this Court held that although conflict of legal claims in praesent or in future is generally a condition for the validity of family arrangements, it is not necessarily so. Even bona fide disputes, present or possible which, may not involve legal claims will suffice. Members of a joint Hindu family may, to maintain peace or to bring about harmony in the family, enter into such a family arrangement. If such an arrangement is entered into bona fide and the terms thereof are fair in the circumstances of a particular case, Courts will more readily give assent to such an arrangement than to avoid it."*

Prima facie, in a given situation if there are a cumulative set of inherent contradictions with regard to the clauses contained in a particular Deed of Family Arrangement, it is highly unlikely that the court of competent jurisdiction will grant its assent or endorsement to effectuate such an arrangement.

(7) CONDITIONS PRECEDENT TO TEST A FAMILY ARRANGEMENT

In ***Shambhu Prasad Singh* v. *Mst. Phool Kumari,* (1971) 2 SCC 28** the Apex Court elaborated upon the tests of a family arrangement in the given facts and circumstances of the said case.

The Supreme Court held in para 17 of the judgment that the parties to Exhibit in the said case arrived at a settlement in view of claims and cross-claims by some against the others. Taken as a whole and in the light of the recitals and statements in the operative part of the document indicating conflict amongst the members of the family, the document represented an arrangement *bona fide* entered into, for settling existing or at any rate apprehended disputes and therefore, satisfied the tests of a family arrangement.

Para 11 of the above mentioned judgement categorically held as follows:

> *"11. The arrangement under challenge has to be considered as a whole for ascertaining whether it was made to allay disputes, existing or apprehended, in the interest of harmony in the family or the preservation of property. It is not necessary that there must exist a dispute, actual or possible in the future, in respect of each and every item of property and amongst all members arrayed one against the other. It would be sufficient if it is shown that there were actual or possible claim and counter claims by parties in settlement whereof the arrangement as a whole had been arrived at, thereby acknowledging title in one to whom a particular property falls on the assumption (not actual existence in law) that he had an another title therein."*

(8) MERE MIXING OF SELF ACQUIRED PROPERTY WITH JOINT FAMILY PROPERTY CANNOT ORDINARILY BE REGARDED AS AN ADMISSION OF A LEGAL OBLIGATION

In so far relating to the voluntary addition of the self acquired property of a member of the joint Hindu family with the common family property, the Supreme Court of India in ***K.V. Narayanan* v. *K.V. Ranganadhan,* AIR 1976 SC 1715** gave important clarification regarding the character and status of self acquired property in such a situation.

Para 13 of the above mentioned judgment was in the following specific terms as follows:

> *"...It is true that property separate or self acquired of a member of a joint Hindu Family may be impressed with the character of a joint family property if it is voluntarily thrown by the owner into the common stock with intention of abandoning his separate claim therein but the question whether a coparcener has done so or not is entirely a question of fact to be decided in the light of all the circumstances of the case. It must be established that there was a clear intention on the part of the coparcener to waive his separate rights, such an intention cannot be inferred merely from the physical mixing of the property with his joint*

family or from the fact that other members of the family are allowed to use the property jointly with himself or that the income of the separate property is utilised out of generosity or kindness to support or from the failure to maintain separate accounts for an act of generosity or kindness cannot ordinarily be regarded as an admission of a legal obligation...."

In terms of the above mentioned judgment of the Supreme Court of India, under Hindu Law self acquired property will not lose its character, simply by blending the property with the joint family property.

(9) ANTICIPATED DISPUTE MUST BE REAL AND NOT IMAGINARY

The Kerala High Court in ***Mythili Nalini* v. *Kowmari*, AIR 1991 Ker 266,** after reiterating the earlier settled position of law made an important clarification to the effect that the anticipated dispute must be real and not imaginary.

Para 14 of the above mentioned judgment of the Kerala High Court held as follows;

"In Shamhu Prasad Singh *v.* Mst. Phool Kumari, *AIR 1971 SC 1337, also the Supreme Court had occasion to consider the effect of a family settlement. In the course of the judgment, the Supreme Court observed as follows (at page SC 1343; AIR 1971:*

"The arrangement under challenge has to be considered as a whole for ascertaining whether it was made to allay disputes, existing or apprehended, in the interest of harmony in the family or the preservation of property. It is not necessary that there must exist a dispute, actval or possible in the future, in respect of each and every item of property and amongst all members arrayed one against the other. It would be sufficient if it is shown that there were actual or possible claims and counter-claims by parties in settlement whereof the arrangement as a whole had been arrived at, thereby acknowledging title in one to whom a particular property falls on the assumption (not actual existence in law) that he had an enterior title therein".

In Kisto Chandra Mandal *v.* Lt. Anila Bala Dasi, *AIR 1968 Pat 487, the Patna High Court considered the scope of family settlement. The Court observed (at page Pat 492; AIR 1968):*

"14A. It is also now well settled that the court will lean towards upholding the family settlement as it is intended to bring about family peace and to avoid future disputes which may ruin the family. But while determining whether a particular transaction is a family settlement or not, it is necessary to bear in mind whether the settlement entered into by the parties concerned is bona fide settlement of conflicting claims of the parties. It is not for the court to determine whether at the time of the settlement the parties have antecedent title or not. It is sufficient that the parties asserted some kind of antecedent title or semblance of title.

In AIR 1968 Pat 493.

The basis of all compromises and family settlement is the existence of doubtful claims or semblance of claim of the parties concerned in respect of the properties in dispute. The motive for settlement is to settle the existing disputes or anticipated disputes, which are likely to arise in future and to secure peace to the family so that the properties in dispute and the family concerned may not be ruined. The anticipated dispute must be real and not imaginary. The end is secured by settlement amongst the parties by resolving the conflicting claims by the process of giving and taking, which is the consideration of the compromise or family settlement. In all compromises, there is some kind of consideration. If there is none, no compromise would be valid."

(10) THE MEANING OF WORD CONSIDERATION IN THE CONTEXT OF FAMILY ARRANGEMENTS WITH SPECIAL REFERENCE TO SECTION 10 OF THE INDIAN CONTRACT ACT, 1872

The Supreme Court of India in ***Ram Charan Das* v. *Girja Nandini Devi*, AIR 1966 SC 323** elaborated on the concept of consideration in the context of family settlements in para 10 of the judgment as follows:

> *"The consideration for such a settlement, if one may put it that way, is the expectation that such a settlement will result in establishing or ensuring amity and goodwill amongst persons bearing relationship with one another. That consideration having passed by each of the disputants the settlement consisting of recognition of the right asserted by each other cannot be permitted to be impeached thereafter."*

Para 11 of the above mentioned judgment further held as follows:

> *"...Here the transaction in question is a family settlement entered into by the parties bona fide for the purpose of putting an end to the dispute among family members. Could it be said that this amounts to a transfer of or creation of an interest in property? For, unless it does, the action of Kadma Kuar would not fall within the purview of the aforesaid clause of section 37. In* Mst. Hiran Bibi *v.* Mst. Sohan Bibi, *AIR 1914 PC 44, approving the earlier decision in* Khunni Lal *v.* Govind Krishna Narain, *ILR 33 All 356 (PC), the Privy Council held that a compromise by way of family settlement is in no sense an alienation by a limited owner of family property. This case, therefore, would support the conclusion that the transaction does not amount to a transfer. Mr. Sinha, however, contends that the transaction amounts to creation of an interest by the ward in property which was under the superintendence of the Court of Wards and in support of his contention relies on* Maan Singh *v.* Nowlakhbati, *53 Ind App: AIR 1926 PC 2. In the first place once it is held that the transaction being a family settlement is not an alienation, it cannot amount to the creation of an interest. For, as the Privy Council pointed out in* Mst. Hiran Bibi's *case, AIR 1914 PC 44 in a family settlement each party takes a share in the property by virtue of the independent title which is admitted to that extent by the other parties. It is not necessary, as would appear from the decision in* Rangasami Gounden *v.* Nachiappa Gounden, *46 Ind App 72: AIR 1918 PC 196, that every party taking benefit under a family settlement must necessarily be shown to have, under the law, a claim to a share in the property. All that is necessary is that the parties must be related to one another in some way and have a possible claim to the property or a claim or even a semblance of a claim on some other ground as, say, affection."*

It is equally important to touch upon the issue of public policy considerations, which briefly find mention as hereunder:

(11) PUBLIC POLICY CONSIDERATIONS

The concept of public policy is not defined under the provisions of the India Contract Act 1872. The Supreme Court of India in ***Central Inland Water Transport Corporation Limited* v. *Brojo Nath Ganguly*, AIR 1986 SC 1571 (1)** clarified that the concept of public policy as envisaged in section 23 of that Act is not defined expressly in the said central legislation.

Para 93 of the above mentioned judgment appropriately clarified as follows:

> **"93.** *The Contract Act does not define the expression "public policy" or "opposed to public policy". From the very nature of things, the expressions "public policy," "opposed to public policy" or "contrary to public policy," are incapable of precise definition. Public policy, however, is not the policy of a particular government. It connotes some matter which concerns the public good and the public interest. The concept of what is for the public good or in the public interest or what would be injurious or harmful to the public good or the public interest has varied from time to time. As new concepts take the place of old transactions which were once considered against public policy are now being upheld by the courts and similarly where there has been a well-recognized head of public policy, the courts have not shirked from extending it to new transactions and changed circumstances and have at times not even flinched from inventing a new head of public policy...."*

Clearly, the provisions of the Deed of Family Arrangement should not be contrary to statute law and be not violative in any manner of the concept of public policy.

(12) DEED OF FAMILY ARRANGEMENT NOT BINDING ON COMPANIES OWNED BY PARTIES TO THE FAMILY ARRANGEMENT

The Supreme Court of India in the matter of ***Reliance Natural Resources Limited* v. *Reliance Industries Limited*, (2010) 7 SCC 1** had the occasion to examine as to whether a Memorandum of Family Understanding was binding on one of the companies run by the Reliance Group of Industries, which is a very well known powerful business conglomerate in India, with substantial diverse business interests both in India and abroad.

The Apex Court held that a Memorandum of Family Understanding was not binding on one of the companies run by the Reliance Group of Industries. The relevant extracts of this judgment are quoted and reproduced hereunder. The exact citation of this case is as follows:

RELIANCE NATURAL RESOURCES LIMITED APPELLANT

VERSUS

RELIANCE INDUSTRIES LIMITED RESPONDENT

WITH

CIVIL APPEAL NUMBER 4274 OF 2010

RELIANCE NATURAL RESOURCES LIMITED APPELLANT

VERSUS

RELIANCE INDUSTRIES LIMITED RESPONDENT

WITH

CIVIL APPEAL NUMBER 4275-76 OF 2010

RELIANCE INDUSTRIES LIMITED APPELLANT

VERSUS

RELIANCE NATURAL RESOURCES LIMITED RESPONDENT

WITH

CIVIL APPEAL NO.4277 OF 2010

UNION OF INDIA APPELLANT

VERSUS

RELIANCE INDUSTRIES LIMITED RESPONDENTS

The said memorandum of Family understanding executed by the Ambani family in this particular case appears at pages 54 and 55 of the electronic version of the above mentioned judgment and same is reproduced hereunder:

"(B) Memorandum of Understanding (MoU)

(i) In order to understand the position of RNRL and RIL as well as "suitable arrangement" under the "Scheme", it is but proper to refer the contents of MoU (placed before the Division Bench of the High Court) which are as under:

"STRICTLY CONFIDENTIAL MEMORANDUM OF UNDERSTANDING

This Memorandum of Understanding (this "MoU") is made at Mumbai this___ day of June, 2005 amongst Kokilaben D. Ambani ("Kokilaben"), Mukesh D. Ambani (Mukesh") and Anil D. Ambani ("Anil") (each of Kokilaben, Mukesh and Anil hereinafter referred to individually as a "Party" and collectively as the "Parties.")

WHEREAS

A. After the demise of Shri Dhirubhai H Ambani (late Dhirubhai) on July 6, 2002, Kokilaben is the head of the Ambani family and has complete moral authority over the family. Her four children, Mukesh, Anil, Dipti and Nina have, by Deed of Release dated October 17, 2002, released their entire interest in the estate of late Dhirubhai in her favour.

B. Mukesh and Anil have been managing the various businesses of the family comprised in the Reliance Group (the "Businesses"). Differences have arisen between them in this behalf, and having regard to recent events and with the intervention of Kokilaben, the Parties have now agreed that the best way forward would be to have a segregation of the ownership and Businesses into two groups, with one group owned, managed and controlled by Mukesh and the other owned, managed and controlled by Anil. Most of the key principles relating to the segregation of certain family assets including controlling interest in the Businesses and companies have been agreed to between the Parties."

The discussion on the validity of the said memorandum of Family Understanding is primarily contained at pages 54 to 66 of the above mentioned judgment and with regard to other issues as well in the context of the litigation that had reached the portals of the Supreme Court of India.

One of the key questions posed in the said judgment was as to whether the above mentioned MOU can be binding on the company. The discussion in this regard is at pages 239 to 247 of the electronic version of the above mentioned judgment.

"140. Can the MoU be binding on the company?:

It is absolutely clear that the MoU was executed in the private domain, with the help and aid of a lawyer and then marked confidential. Further, the individuals, from all indications have only executed it in their individual capacity and it was not purported to be in exercise of their positions in RIL or any other company of the Reliance Group. It is also very clear that the MoU itself recognizes that the reorganization that the promoters sought would have to be routed through the Board. The promoters also had the right to apply for a Scheme of Rearrangement under Section 391 of the Companies Act, 1956, in which case the mode of shareholder approvals and the classes formed would have been entirely different. As Shri. Rohinton Nariman points out, the MoU is an agreement between three promoters, and the Scheme is between two million shareholders, all of the same equity class and hence the MoU cannot now be imported into the Scheme. Otherwise the promoters who under the Scheme were the same as anyone else would now become special, thereby negating the very concept of class of members with similar interests voting on a proposal for reorganisation.

141. The minutes of the meetings of the Board of RIL dealing with various issues concerning the reorganization do not reveal anywhere whether the Board as a collective body ever took note of and approved the MoU. This is not a mere technicality. There is a certain legal sanctity associated with it, in the first place, in the form of presumptions that flow from Sections 193, 194 and 195 of the Companies Act, 1956 that they are an accurate record of the proceedings. The collective decision making, at a conjoint sitting allows for exchange of ideas. The idea of the Board working as a collective is also about the process of sharing of views and arriving at collective decisions to protect and enhance the interests of all the shareholders. And in the very first meeting, albeit on the same day that the MoU was announced, the various Directors of RIL after thanking KDA, quite effectively severed any umbilical cord that the eventual Scheme might have had with the MoU, when they asserted that any reorganization can only be premised on protection of the value of all the shareholders. There is not even a whisper of protection of a broader class of shareholders in the MoU. This is not some mere technicality; but a fundamental philosophical and attitudinal approach with regard to arrival at the decision to reorganize the businesses. The duty to protect the interests of the shareholders is cast upon the Board, and the Board has to act in a fiduciary capacity vis-à-vis the shareholders. This duty has been a part of broader understanding of company law from the days of Settlement Companies that were the precursors of joint stock companies. What RNRL is demanding, by implications that follow the insertion of the gas supply section of the MoU in Clause 19 of the Scheme, is that the Board of RIL only acted at the behest of the promoters and were mere rubber stamps of the decisions of the promoters. Acceptance of such demands would destroy the fabric of company law itself and the foundations of trust, faith and honest dealing with the shareholders. The actions of the Board of RIL clearly indicate that it did not conceive its role in that manner.

142. It is quite obvious, from the MoU itself, that the promoters family had a number of personal issues to settle, amongst which the issue relating to businesses and ownership over them was but one. It is also equally obvious that what has been revealed is but a portion of the total document. See part 1.103-1.104 of Palmer's Company Law, *page 1011, 25th Edn., Vol.1. document were to be filed as a proposal for arrangement, it would have to be thrown out at the very inception. The differences in details of the proposals for demerger as contained in the MoU, when contrasted with that of the Scheme, are staggering. Where no reasons for reorganization are adduced in the MoU, apart from a statement that having settled all the other family and other business related issues the best way forward would be a reorganization, it is the Scheme as framed and approved by the Board which provides the justification. The Scheme specifies that each of the businesses carry different sets of risks and prospects, and that they could attract different sets of investors, that a focused management is needed to enhance the prospects of each business, etc. Finally, it is the Board which recommended the Scheme to the shareholders saying that it would benefit them.*

143. The fact that the Board asked that an analysis of the pros and cons of such a reorganization be undertaken by the CG Committee of Independent Directors, along with the command that they propose a scheme of reorganization if any, with the help of professionals to study the various businesses and the implications with respect to statutory and legal issues, is prima facie evidence of independence and application of the mind.

Further, from the record it can be gleaned that the CG Committee with the help of professionals framed an outline of a Scheme, executed by representatives of both the MDA and the ADA Group and on that count too, it would have to be held that the Scheme was something more and fundamentally different from the MoU.

144. Clinchingly, with respect to the most contentious aspect - governmental approvals - which RNRL claims were not necessary, the minutes reveal that the Board actually commanded that it be made sure that any gas supply agreements, including terms of price, tenure etc., be subject to such approvals. Moreover, if MoU is considered, it actually runs counter to the entire claim of RNRL that it formed the basis of the Scheme regarding gas supply also in as much as the Board approved a Scheme in which the only provision with respect to gas supply was for a plan to set some uncrystallised "suitable arrangements" in place. If the Board had agreed to the commercial terms of agreement, as contained in the gas supply section of the MoU, then it would have been mandatory upon them to reveal the same to the shareholders of RIL, because of the sheer scale of monetary value of the gas supply contracts. RNRL itself claims that the potential monetary value of such gas supply arrangements could run into many thousands of crores of rupees, and we fail to see how prospective agreements involving such huge value, in which commercial terms are claimed to have been settled, cannot be revealed to the shareholders in the context of a scheme of arrangement. No rationale or justification can support such a proposition.

145. The Companies (Amendment) Act, 1965, based on the recommendations of Daphtary-Sastri Committee specifically provided that the applicants for a scheme shall "disclose by affidavit all material facts". [See: section 391(2) of the Companies Act, 1956]. In as much as the terms and conditions of gas supply, as specified in the MoU, were not specifically informed to all the shareholders and stakeholders, including in this case the GoI (as a party to the PSC), we simply fail to see how the MoU can be read into the Scheme itself. It doesn't matter whether one calls MoU the guiding light or a tool for interpretation or a foundation – the sheer fact that the terms of gas supply contained in the MoU were withheld from the shareholders implies that it cannot now be imported into the Scheme.

The argument that contracts are entered into all the time, and are treated as day to day affairs for the management and the Board, fails at the point of division of a company. Where, in regular times a shareholder or a stakeholder can demand and obtain information and have time to try and monitor such contracts and the actions of the management, the act of hiving off an undertaking is a much more crucial point, when the shareholders have to be even more careful about the transfer of value. The whole purpose of section 293 which prohibits the Board from hiving off an undertaking without shareholders approvals, is to prevent such transfers being effectuated on a permanent basis without the knowledge of the shareholders. The very essence of the requirement that all material facts be disclosed would have been decimated.

Consequently, we hold that the Scheme as propounded by the Board, placed before and approved by shareholders and stakeholders and sanctioned by the court is completely different from the MoU. The MoU may have been the starting point. The end point is significantly, substantially and materially different from it and it cannot now be brought back in the guise of interpretation."

The operative part of the conclusions in this complex litigation appearing at pages 263 to 265 of the electronic version of the said judgment is reproduced below.

CONCLUSIONS:

"163. In the result, we hold that:

(i) both the learned Single Judge and the Division Bench committed a serious error in exercising jurisdiction in the manner they did under section 392 of the Companies Act, 1956, for such interference has resulted in the provisions of a document (MoU) which was not before the shareholders supersede the Scheme of Arrangement. Such a document could not have been read into and incorporated in the Scheme propounded by the Board, approved by the shareholders and sanctioned by the Company Court;

(ii) *the courts below having rightly directed the parties to negotiate, and further having rightly refused to grant the prayers in the Company Application, however, fell into error directing the MoU to be binding and the basis for further negotiations between the parties. MoU is a private pact between the members of Ambani family which is not binding on RIL;*

(iii) *the EGOM decisions, regarding the utilization of the natural gas and the price formula/basis etc. do not suffer from any legal or constitutional infirmities. They shall apply to all supplies of natural gas under the PSC. The parties are bound by the governmental policy and approvals regarding price, quantity and tenure for supply of gas;*

(iv) *under the PSC in issue the Contractor (RIL) does not become the owner of natural gas, and there is nothing like specified physical quantities of natural gas to be shared by the GoI and the Contractor;*

(v) *we, accordingly, direct the parties to renegotiate as to the suitable arrangements for supply of gas de-hors the MoU. Such renegotiations shall be within the framework of governmental policy and approvals regarding price, quantity and tenure for supply of gas. The renegotiations shall commence within eight weeks from today at the initiative of RIL and shall be completed within a period of six weeks from the day of commencement of negotiations. Accordingly, the judgments of the learned Single Judge and the Division Bench of the Bombay High Court are set aside and we dispose of* all the appeals without any order as to costs. Intervention Applications do not require any adjudication.

They are also accordingly disposed of.

164. Before we part with the case, we consider it appropriate to observe and remind the GoI that it is high time it frames a comprehensive policy/suitable legislation with regard to energy security of India and supply of natural gas under production sharing contracts."

It will be noticed from the judgment in the Reliance case that there was a big dispute within the family *i.e.* the two Ambani brothers and the Apex Court categorically kept the family arrangement outside the purview of the corporate domain by firmly ruling that the deed of family arrangement was not binding on the family run companies of the Ambani brothers.

CONCLUSION:

That after a reading of the caselaw analysis, in sum and substance, the key legal issues and principles governing family settlements can be summarised as follows:

- One of the key requirements for a family arrangement is the existence of a dispute or a possible dispute, as also held in light of the settled position of law as described above. Indeed, it is generally the case that family settlements and agreements in the Indian jurisdiction are the outcome of protracted litigation, normally engineered and encouraged by court intervention.

- The above mentioned Kerala High Court judgment in ***Mythili Nalini (1991)*** goes to state that even the anticipated dispute must be existing or apprehended "but instances also abound in actual practice," whereby family members harmoniously and amicably execute family arrangements with regard to movable and immovable properties, especially when the kith and kin and siblings are residing abroad.
- That in light of the recent judgment of the Supreme Court of India in the case of reported as ***Reliance Natural Resources Limited,* (2010) 7 SCC 1,** it has been categorically held that the family memorandum of understanding is not binding on the company, as a separate corporate entity.
- That as per the settled position of law as already elaborated above, a family settlement must be a bona fide one so as **to resolve family dispute and rival claims by a fair and equitable division or allotment of properties** between the various members of the family. Of course, the bona fides and fairness of a family arrangement has to be judged by the circumstances prevailing at the time when such settlement was made. However, by way of instance if in any given situation, the Deed of Family Arrangement which singularly divests a major portion of the assets in question in favour of a particular family member only, which in actual practice of course would be highly unusual as per prevailing social and cultural norms and practices followed by business families of repute and eminence in India. Further, it is not a happy situation which any court would be prepared to accept as a "fair and equitable," arrangement. Another hypothetical situation could be of the said Deed of Family Arrangement so executed which attempts to divert and vest the immovable and moveable assets into the hands of a particular family member only. This again of course would not be logically acceptable as per prevailing trends and norms followed by eminent business families of high standing and repute in India, especially when it comes to future family succession and for providing a blue print for prospective successful running of the family owned and run companies, and managing the overall business interests of the family. Such a converse proposition would not be acceptable. This is because in family run businesses in India especially those running business empires, there is a strong marked emphasis on family business succession and the next generation taking over the reins of ongoing companies and business enterprises run by the immediate family as also the extended family. It might well be the case that the rights of the future daughters in law of the family have been completely ignored in the Deed of Family Arrangement so much so, there is no provision at all even for their day to day sustenance. Culturally, in modern metropolitan India no daughter in law would even remotely tolerate leave alone accept such one sided clauses by the head of the family, as in the present case.
- Statutory requirements are also enforced by court orders. The Supreme Court of India in ***Renusagar Power Company Ltd.* v. *General Electric***

Company, **AIR 1994 SC 860** held that it is the fundamental principle of law that orders of courts must be complied with for any action which involves disregard for such orders would adversely affect the administration of justice and would be destructive of the rule of law and would be contrary to public policy. That by way of yet another instance, if there is a failure in terms of the provisions of the family arrangement to comply with statutory land law requirements, it would then also be contrary to public policy, also in terms of the above mentioned judgment of the Supreme Court of India. Section 10 of the Indian Contract Act, 1872 defines as to what agreements are contracts. That as laid down by the Supreme Court of India in the case of **Ram Charan Das, AIR 1996 SC 323,** the consideration for a settlement is the expectation that such a settlement will result in establishing or ensuring amity and goodwill amongst persons bearing relationship with one another.

- Generally, family arrangements need not be registered barring certain situations, but the same is imperative, If the document itself creates an interest in an immovable property. The fact that it contemplates the execution of another document will not exempt the Deed of Family Arrangement from registration under section 17(2)(v) of the Indian Registration Act, 1908. From experience, it is strongly advised that any sort of family arrangement be registered in terms of the provisions of the Indian Registration Act, 1908 which is in fact so crucial and important in consolidating the family empire, and more than that leaving little scope for challenge in the event of any unforseen litigation at a later point of time. A copy of the said registered document would have to be ordinarily been deposited with the local administrative registering authority, depending on the requirement of the local rules, and certainly it is more than credible proof of the fact of actual registration of the document itself, so executed between the necessary parties. The same can be always readily inspected in the said Government office on the payment of prescribed nominal statutory fees. Generally, in most of the states in India there is official prescribed procedure for inspection of duly registered public documents, on the deposit of nominal statutory fees in the Government treasury. In such a situation, chances of vested interests are substantially dampened to deny the existence of any such family arrangement, subject to the compliance of other requirements of law.
- There is no statutory bar under Indian law with regard to the extra-territorial application of family arrangements especially with regard to the allocation and division any immovable or movable assets or business interests outside the territories of India. This would be of course subject to the law of the foreign land where the said assets are situated.
- Certainly, a duly contested and properly represented court order/ judgment by counsel duly authorised by the respective parties of a court of competent jurisdiction whether in India or abroad, and especially, if it is a foreign court order/judgment the same should meet strict compliance

of sections 13 and 44 of the Indian Civil Code of Procedure, 1908, and such a judicial verdict will certainly over ride the provisions of the Deed of Family Arrangement.

- That in the event of any litigation, especially when assets are situated abroad, family settlements may be allegedly executed pursuant to the commencement of the litigation, with a view to attempt to defeat the purpose of the litigation, thus missing out the vital clauses especially with regard to the applicability or exclusion of foreign law, choice of law or conflict of law, strongly suggesting that the Deed of Family Arrangement has been drafted in hot haste.
- Given the diversity of cultures and the size of our country it is pertinent to mention that family arrangements are not confined only to particular communities in India but are equally applicable to various other communities including Christians, Parsis, Muslims and people from other religions as well.

NRIs Property Related Problems – The Punjab Model

INTRODUCTION – THE GIST OF THE IDENTIFIABLE PROBLEMS

- A foreign based second or third generation descendant of a Non resident Indian (NRI) seeks transfer of title of family property inherited by him in rural or urban India. An ageing NRI battles in Court to recover possession of urban property in metropolitan India wrested away by unscrupulous elements. Enthusiastic NRI owner sitting abroad desperately seeks remedies to locate share in rural agricultural property to claim ownership on the basis of inheritance. NRI families battle over division of land and property in exclusive control with custodians in India. Horrified NRI shockingly discovers divested share of family property on arriving in India which was done on the basis of fraudulent documentation. Frantic NRI family members try to implement family settlement thwarted by local relatives occupying property locally. These real life instances are now common to NRIs and Persons of Indian Origin (PIO).
- During the last over 50 years, large number of Indians have migrated and permanently settled in foreign countries leaving behind their homes, ancestors and landed properties. Now, when the NRIs wish to recover their properties, they find them in forceful or illegal occupation of their trusted childhood guardians or overstaying tenants who have designs to grab the property. Agreements are dishonoured, trust is violated and faith is destroyed. Commercial real estate property of NRIs is grabbed with impunity. The NRI has neither the patience nor the time to fight a protracted legal battle in an Indian law Court which may last a life time, if fought, waged and litigated till the Apex Court. Legal processes are cumbersome, tedious, technical and move at a snail's pace. The bottom line is that the NRIs are at a great disadvantage leaving them disillusioned and disappointed. No existing legislation comes to their rescue or aid.
- Gullible, excited and patriotic NRIs with a fervour happily invests huge sums of Pounds, Sterling, Dollars or Euros in real estate, flats, or immovable property in India. When it comes to taking actual physical possession of their prized immovable asset in their homeland, the vulnerable NRI discovers to his horror that either the land or the flat does not exist or that he has been cheated into buying property which does not have any

trace. Unscrupulous, unethical and unprofessional brokers, builders or real estate agents who had made these deals with the NRIs and promised the moon have either disappeared, are untraceable or flatly deny having made any commitment. The dumbfounded NRI is too stunned to react. With little time at his hand on his Indian visit or sitting in a foreign land, he does not know what to do. Who will help him. Should he go to the police or the administrative authorities or to a Court of law for a judicial remedy. Where should he seek advice and how does he pursue the case. The questions are myriad but the solutions and answers lie submerged in a complicated web of long winded procedures which on initiation will proceed endlessly at a snail's pace. The frustrated, dejected and defeated NRI gives up not knowing what to do.

- The above summarization is in brief a nutshell of the NRIs ailing property problems for which he seeks a consolidated, composite, timely and effective remedy. The NRI wants to reconnect with his homeland but is disillusioned, disenchanted and disheartened. It is in this backdrop that this chapter looks at these peculiar problems with a focus on the State of Punjab which contributes highly to the migratory numbers to countries all over the world.
- Broadly, property related problems can be divided under four heads as follows:
  - **(A)** Issues relating to landlord-tenant relationships in Punjab and Chandigarh.
  - **(B)** Issues relating to succession, Wills and inheritance - India, NRIs & Wills.
  - **(C)** Problems arising out of revenue records and agricultural land disputes - the position prevailing in the State of Punjab.
  - **(D)** Propositions arising out of property investment related issues in India.
- It is in the above perspective, that this Chapter looks at the above issues and how they are handled and attempted to be resolved in the framework of the existing laws which prevail in the State of Punjab and the Union Territory of Chandigarh in the matters of tenancy and agricultural property related issues which are governed by State legislations.
- In so far, problems related to succession, Wills and inheritance, as also propositions arising out of property investment related issues, the same are governed by Central legislations (except where there are separate State laws), the problems and solutions are by and large common throughout the territory of India. Hence, wherever there is a Central legislation enacted by Indian Parliament, the Indian law will have universal application throughout the territory of India. To that extent, the issues and laws arising for succession and property investment related issues may be common for the entire Indian jurisdiction and applicable in all States of India.

(A) Issues relating to landlord-tenant relationships in Punjab and Chandigarh

In 2001, the Government of Punjab upon receiving representations from various NRI individuals, and through their associations highlighting the plight of Indian residents returning to India after long years abroad decided to amend the existing East Punjab Urban Rent Restriction Act, 1949, to provide NRIs a right to recover immediate possession of their properties. It was represented that the NRIs having spent long years of their life abroad did not find conditions congenial in their own country on their return either to settle down or to take up any business. On account of rigid legal provisions of existing rent laws, the NRIs were unable to recover possession of their own residential/non-residential buildings from the tenants. Accordingly, the Government of Punjab having considered the situation had decided that the existing rent legislation viz. East Punjab Urban Rent Restriction Act, 1949, should be amended to provide relief to NRIs to enable them to recover possession of a residential or scheduled building and/or one non residential building for their own use. By a notification dated 9 October, 2009, the Central Government has extended to the Union Territory of Chandigarh the benefit of the said amendment and hence as of now, NRI landlords are entitled to the benefit of immediate recovery of immediate possession of their properties in accordance with this Law as per details below.

In Civil Writ Petition No. 15378 of 2011 *Asha Chawla* v. *Union of India*, decided on August 23, 2011, by the High Court of Punjab and Haryana, the challenge to the East Punjab Urban Rent Restriction (Amendment) Act, 2001 and notification dated October 9, 2009 issued by the Central Government under section 87 of the Punjab Reorganisation Act, 1966 extending the aforesaid amendment Act to the Union Territory, Chandigarh, as unconstitutional, was dismissed by a Division Bench of the High Court. It was held by the High Court in para 9 its judgment as follows:

> *"9. The classification of Non-resident Indians, as a separate class of landlords, cannot be held to be violative of article 14 of the Constitution. Right to seek eviction on the ground of* bona fide *need is available to all landlords. Only difference in the case of NRIs and certain other specified landlords is that right to contest eviction proceedings is governed by special procedure of requirement of obtaining leave to defend by making out a case under section 18A of the Act. The classification is not shown to be irrational. The same is intelligible and has rational relationship with the object sought to be achieved* i.e. *providing speedy remedy to non-residents in* bona fide *need of premises let out to tenants."*

Upholding the validity of the beneficial provision for fast track eviction of properties owned by NRIs, the High Court repelled the challenge to the said law.

Summary eviction of tenants from properties of NRIs in Punjab and Chandigarh

- The East Punjab Urban Rent Restriction Act, 1949 (EPURRA), which extends to all urban areas in Punjab as also the Union Territory of

Chandigarh, is an Act to restrict the increase of rents of certain premises and to provide for eviction of tenants therefrom. Other than prescribing a normal process for eviction of tenants, it also provides a summary procedure for recovering immediate possession of residential or scheduled buildings to certain specified landlords. By an amendment in 2001, the Act also created a special class of NRI landlords reposing in them a special right to recover immediate possession from tenants occupying their premises by a special summary procedure.

- Now under section 13B of the EPURRA, once in a lifetime, possession can be given to a NRI landlord to get one building vacated in a summary manner. A NRI landlord is accordingly required to prove that he is an NRI, he has returned to India permanently or temporarily, the requirement of the accommodation by him or his dependent is genuine and that he is the owner of the property for the last five years before the institution of the ejectment proceedings.
- By a 2005 landmark judgment titled *Baldev Singh Bajwa* v. *Monish Saini*, AIR 2006 SC 59, the Supreme Court has given far reaching positive dimensions both to the definition of an NRI landlord and to the concept of 'his return' to India in the context of the NRIs right to recover possession of his property under the summary procedure under section 13B of the EPURRA. It does not distinguish between a Non-Resident Indian, Person of Indian Origin or an Overseas Citizen of India.
- To be an NRI, it is sufficient that a Person of Indian Origin establishes that he has permanently or temporarily settled outside India for his business or on account of his employment or for any other purpose which would indicate his intention to stay outside India for an uncertain period.
- A person to be an NRI should be of Indian origin. Since "Indian Origin" is not defined in the EPURRA, any person whose parents, grandparents or great grand parents were born in India and permanently resided in India would be an NRI. It is not necessary that the NRI should be a citizen of India. It is immaterial that the NRI holds a foreign passport or has shifted to a foreign country.
- Return to India cannot be read as return to India permanently with an intention to settle in India permanently. There is no requirement that the NRI has to permanently settle in India on his return or he has returned to India with an intention to permanently settle in India. Hence, "return to India" may not be of permanent nature as the premises may be required for the use of any dependent ordinarily living with the NRI. All that is required under section 13B is that a NRI should return to India to claim the premises.

NRI's can now get their multiple properties vacated from tenants under the Punjab Rent Act, 1995 (as Amended by the Punjab Rent (Amendment) Act, 2013 on April 10, 2013.

- The Punjab Rent Act, 1995, (PRA) which received the assent of the President of India on March 26, 1998 and which was notified upon publication in the Punjab Government Gazette on December 10, 2012, extends to all urban areas of Punjab. It is an Act to provide for the regulation of rents, repairs and maintenance, as also for eviction relating to premises in all urban areas of Punjab. The EPURRA has been repealed by section 75 of the PRA but pending proceedings under EPURRA are saved.

- Section 24 of the PRA as amended by the **Punjab Rent (Amendment) Act, 2013,** allows an NRI landlord to apply to the Rent Authority for recovery of immediate possession of his residential or/and non-residential premises.
- Section 24(3) of the **Punjab Rent (Amendment) Act, 2013,** is as under:

Right to recover immediate possession of premises to accrue to NRIs:

"24(3) Where an owner is a non-resident Indian and returns to India for permanent residence, he or she may apply to the Rent Authority for recovery of immediate possession of residential or/and non-residential premises let out by him or her on or prior to the commencement of this Act, which are required by him for his or her own use, or for the use of any one ordinarily living with and dependent on him or her."

Explanation: "non-resident Indian" means a person of Indian origin, who is either permanently or temporarily settled outside India, in either case—

(i) for or on taking up employment outside India ; or

(ii) for carrying on a business or vocation outside India; or

(iii) for any other purpose, in such circumstances, as would indicate his intention to stay outside India for an uncertain period."

Previously, under the original provision of section 24(2) PRA, the right to seek recovery of immediate possession was available, ***"in respect of anyone residential and one non-residential premises each chosen by him."*** However, under the amended provisions of section 24(3) of the **Punjab Rent (Amendment) Act, 2013,** this restriction does not exist, thereby allowing NRIs to get their multiple residential/non-residential properties vacated from tenants.

Judgments under section 13B, EPURRA for NRI Landlords

The right of summary eviction of an NRI landlord, under section 13B, EPURRA in the State of Punjab and U.T, Chandigarh, is a very expeditious and effective remedy to an NRI landlord for a fast track eviction process of urban residential and commercial properties since 2001. However, upon such litigation coming up before Rent Controllers in the State of Punjab, the provisions of section 13B, EPURRA have been interpreted by the High Court of Punjab and Haryana upon revision petitions being filed by aggrieved tenants or NRI landlords to impugn unfavourable decisions of Rent Controllers from time to time in individual cases. In this process, a number of decided cases have emerged to develop a jurisprudence of NRI landlord-tenancy law and a summary of judgments of the High Court of Punjab and Haryana following the landmark judgment of the Apex Court in *Baldev Singh Bajwa* v. *Monish Saini*, AIR 2006 SC 59, in interpreting section 13B, EPURRA and settling the law, are tabulated as hereunder:

Person Settled Abroad Temporarily and Does Not Need To Return

In interpreting the phrase NRI *"returns to India"* in section 13B, EPURRA, it has been held in *Baldev Singh Bajwa* v. *Monish Saini*, AIR 2006 SC 59, the Apex Court has been authoritatively pleased to hold in paras 25 and 26 as below:

> *"25. When we read section 13B along with the definition of the NRI it is apparent that the person who is permanently residing outside India can also claim possession under section 13B of the Act. All that is required under section 13B is that a NRI should return to India and claim the premises for his/her use or for the use of any dependent ordinarily living with him. There is no requirement that he has permanently settled in India on his return or he has returned to India with an intention to permanently settle in India. A NRI may require the accommodation for expansion of his business which he is carrying on in other country or requires the accommodation for his temporary stay. Under section 13B, a NRI can also claim ejectment of the tenant from the premises for the purposes of any other person who is dependent on him and is ordinarily living with him, which makes it clear that although a NRI resides permanently in other country, he could get the accommodation vacated for the need of his dependant who ordinarily lives with him and he intends to come to India, choosing it to be his permanent abode. We do not find any substance in the submissions made by the learned counsel that the words "return to India" under section 13B of the Act denote return to India permanently.*
>
> *26. On the interpretation given by us and on a plain reading of the provisions, once in a lifetime possession is given to a NRI to get one building vacated in a summary manner. A Non-resident Indian landlord is required to prove that:—(i) he is a NRI; (ii) that he has returned to India permanently or for the temporary period; (iii) requirement of the accommodation by him or his dependent is genuine; and (iv) he is the owner of the property for the last five years before the institution of the proceedings for ejectment before the Controller. The tenant's affidavit asking for leave to contest the NRI landlord's application should confine to the grounds which NRI landlord is required to prove, to get ejectment under section 13B of the Act. The Controller's power to give leave to contest the application filed under section 13B circumscribe to the grounds and inquiry to the aspects specified in the section 13B. The tenant would be entitled for leave to contest only if he makes a strong case to challenge those grounds. Inquiry would be confined to section 13B and no other aspect shall be considered by the Controller."*

Hence, the phrase "return to India" for an NRI under the EPURRA cannot be read as "return to India" permanently with an intention to settle in India forever. Further, it has been held by the Apex Court that to avail the benefit under section 13B, EPURRA, an NRI landlord is required to prove (i) that he is a NRI; (ii) that he has returned to India permanently or for a temporary period; (iii) the NRI has a requirement of the accommodation by him or his dependent which is genuine; and (iv) the NRI is the owner or co-owner of the property for the last five years before the institution of the proceedings for ejectment before the Controller.

Following the above dictum of law, the High Court of Punjab and Haryana has rendered the following decisions and a brief summary of each of these cases are given below for purposes of ready reference.

(a) *Mangwinder Chahal* v. *Ramesh Kumar Sudera,* 2013 (3) PLR 241, holding that a person who is residing outside India whether permanently or temporary qualifies for the definition as NRI and there is no bar for a person who is permanently residing outside India to seek for ejectment of his property.

(b) *Rakesh Rishi* v. *Bakshish Kaur,* 2013 (4) PLR 401, deciding that to be an NRI, it is sufficient that a person of Indian origin establishes that he has permanently or temporarily settled outside India for his business or on account of his employment, or for any other purpose which would indicate his intention to stay outside India for an uncertain period, as also that it is not necessary that the person should be a citizen of India or that because he holds a foreign passport, such NRI landlord would not be an NRI for the purposes of EPURRA.

(c) *Sheela Rani* v. *Minder Kaur,* 2013 (3) RCR (Civil) 744, holding that an NRI landlord has a right to seek eviction after a period of five years from the date of becoming owner of such building, irrespective of the fact that the building has been let out by him or her. Accordingly, it was held that a NRI landlord had to basically prove that he was an NRI, had returned to India permanently or temporarily, the requirement of the premises was genuine and bonafide, as also that the NRI was the owner of the premises for the last five years.

(d) *Renu Tiwari* v. *Balbir Dub,* 2010 (1) RLR 182, interpreting the meaning of the expression non-resident Indian, held that it contemplates a person who is either permanently or temporarily settled outside India for taking up employment outside India or for carrying on a business or vocation outside India or for any other purpose to stay outside India for an uncertain period.

(e) *Jasbir Kaur Sandhu* v. *Bihari Lal,* 2006 (2) RCR (Rent) 261, holding that under section 13B, EPURRA, a NRI landlord can also claim ejectment of the tenant from the premises for the purposes of any other person who is dependent on him and is ordinarily living with him.

(f) *Deepak Kumar* v. *Charanjit Rai,* 2014 (2) RCR (Rent) 108, holding that as per provisions of section 13B, EPURRA, a rent petition for eviction of tenant for the bona fide need of NRI landlord can be filed by the owner of the suit property and it is not necessary that the person who inducted the tenant can only file the petition.

(g) *Gurdial Singh* v. *Rajinder Kumar,* 2014 (2) RCR (Rent) 105, deciding that for eviction of tenants for bona fide need of NRI landlord, a co-owner of the tenanted premises can maintain an eviction petition. It is not necessary that a NRI landlord should first return to India and then only he can apply for eviction of the tenant under section 13B, EPURRA.

(h) *Lakhwinder Kumar* v. *Pavitter Kaur,* 2010 (2) RLR (Rent) 74, settling the proposition that it is not necessary for an NRI landlord to return permanently to India and it would suffice if the NRI landlord requires the demised premises for his occasional visits to India, the petition under section 13B, East Punjab Urban Rent Restriction Act, 1949 would be maintainable.

(i) *Narinder Kumar* v. *Chandroop Singh,* 2013 (3) RCR (Civil) 703, deciding that if an NRI landlord wanted to return to India to commence the business of a restaurant alongwith his dependent son, the need was *bona fide* and the son of the NRI landlord could file an eviction petition under section 13B, EPURRA as a power of attorney holder on behalf of his NRI father landlord.

(j) *Surinder Kumar* v. *Shukntala Devi,* 2006 (2) RCR (Rent) 373, deciding that it is not necessary to hold an Indian passport to be an NRI as also the contention that an NRI landlord being aged, would not return to India, since there is no requirement that the NRI should first return to India and then apply for eviction of the tenant under section 13B, EPURRA.

NRI landlord can select the premises for eviction

In the precedents quoted below, the High Court of Punjab and Haryana has been pleased to hold that it is upto the NRI landlord to choose and select the tenanted premises of which he desires eviction from the tenant under section 13B, EPURRA. A gist of judgments in this regard are set down as hereunder:

(a) *Ranjit Kaur* v. *Surinder Singh,* 2010 (2) ALR 330, holding that if an NRI landlord owns more than one premises, it is open to him to decide to relate the special provisions of section 13B, EPURRA to one particular premises and which will not extend to more than one premises.

(b) *Assa Singh* v. *Charanjiv Singh,* 2004 (2) RCR (Rent) 660, deciding that a NRI landlord who was a green card holder in USA had an intention to live outside India for an uncertain period, was entitled as co-owner to seek eviction of the tenant, as also that the ownership or possession of other suitable accommodation in the same area is no bar on a NRI landlord to get one building of his choice vacated under section 13B, EPURRA.

(c) *Lakhwinder Kumar* v. *Pavitter Kaur,* 2010 (2) RLR (Rent) 74, holding that if one building is occupied by different tenants, an NRI landlord can seek eviction of all the tenants, as also if the NRI landlord needs only a part of the building, he can restrict his requirement qua that part only under section 13B, EPURRA.

(d) *PSEB* v. *Kanwar Varinder Singh,* 2006 (1) RCR (Rent) 527,deciding that a heavy burden lies on a tenant to prove that the requirement of the NRI landlord is not genuine. If the application by the tenant seeking leave to defend is bereft of detailed particulars, much less of any documentary evidence to support the plea that the requirement of the landlord is not genuine and *bona fide*, the claim of the tenant deserves rejection and dismissal.

(e) *Kaki Nanda* v. *Nand Lal,* 2006 (2) RCR (Rent) 410, concluding that leave to contest granted to a tenant by the Rent Controller on the assumption that Courts should be liberal to grant permission to defend cannot be accepted and that leave to defend should only be granted to a tenant under section 13B, EPURRA only if he makes out a strong case on merits to challenge the averments of the NRI landlord made out in his petition for eviction.

(f) *Baljit Singh* v. *Raghubir Singh,* ALR 2010 (1) 418, holding that in summary proceedings under section 13B, EPURRA, it is not for the tenant to decide the size and portion of the tenanted property which would fulfill the requirement of the NRI landlord. Hence, it was decided that the argument of the tenant that he is the only tenant from whom the landlord is seeking possession, is not tenable as the demised premises is the only area which is on rent.

(g) *Narinder Singh* v. *Kirpa Singh,* 2006 (2) RCR (Rent) 218, deciding that the tenant would be entitled to leave to contest only if he makes out a strong case and that the tenant's affidavit should confine to grounds which NRI landlord is required to prove to get ejectment under section 13B, EPURRA.

Rent petition for eviction by co-owner of NRI maintainable

In petitions under section 13B, EPURRA for claiming possession of tenanted property, the NRI landlord may be a co-owner of a property which is jointly owned by him with other co-owners. In these circumstances, it has been consistently held that any such petition by a co-owner as an NRI landlord, even through a general power of attorney holder would entitle him to succeed as an NRI landlord to claim possession of his tenanted property under section 13B, EPURRA. In this regard, the following judgments are given hereunder in support of this proposition.

(a) *Satnam Channan* v. *Darshan Singh,* 2006 (2) RCJ 281, holding that where an NRI landlord was joint owner of the tenanted property with others, he could prefer a petition under section 13B, EPURRA through his son as an attorney holding his general power of attorney. The NRI landlord did not appear in court and his son was held competent to depose on his behalf as his attorney in respect of all matters, except which are required to be done personally by the principal.

(b) *Smt. Bachan Kaur* v. *Kabal Singh,* 2011 (1) RCR (Rent) 368, deciding that a co-owner who is not an NRI, can maintain a petition under section 13B, EPURRA for ejectment for benefit of all co-owners on behalf of an NRI landlord who is one of the co-owners. It was held that it is not necessary that all the other co-owners should be NRIs to maintain a petition for eviction of a tenanted property jointly owned by all the co-owners. It was also decided that a NRI co-owner can seek eviction of the tenant in such a building even though the tenant was not inducted by such NRI as it is not necessary that all co-owners should be NRIs.

(c) *Karnail Singh* v. *Surinder Singh,* 2006 (1) RCR (Rent) 214, concluding that an NRI landlord as co-owner of the premises is entitled to seek ejectment of a tenant and that it is not necessary for him to obtain express authority or consent of other co-owners. If one co-owner files an eviction petition as an agent of other co-owners, the consent of other co-owners is assumed as taken unless it is shown that the other co-owners were not agreeable to eject the tenant and the ejectment petition under section 13B, EPURRA was filed in spite of their disagreement.

(d) *Kewal Krishan* v. *Mohan Singh,* 2006 (2) RCJ 261, deciding that an NRI landlord who jointly owned property with other co-owners is entitled to evict the tenant under the summary procedure prescribed under section 13B, EPURRA unless it is shown that the other co-owners are objecting to the eviction of tenant by the NRI landlord. Even if a preliminary decree for partition of the joint property is passed, the property retains the joint character, till such time a final decree is passed by a court of competent jurisdiction in the suit for partition.

(e) *Dharampal Sood* v. *Sarwan Singh,* 2006 (2) RCJ 22, concluding that an NRI landlord as co-owner of a property is entitled to seek eviction of a joint property under section 13B, EPURRA, till such time the property is actually partitioned by metes and bounds as the NRI landlord owns every part and bit of the joint property alongwith others.

(f) *Ravinder Pal* v. *Gurbachan Singh,* 2006 (2) RCR (Rent) 211, holding that an NRI landlord who is co-owner of the tenanted premises is entitled to file a petition under section 13B, EPURRA and consent of other co-owners is presumed unless and until it is shown that other co-owners were not agreeable to eject the tenants or that the ejectment application has been filed without their consent.

Tenant has no *locus standi* to challenge the Will or title in favour of landlord as the owner of the tenanted property

In the precedents cited below, it has been settled by the High Courts of Delhi, Karnataka, Andhra Pradesh and the Punjab and Haryana High Court that a tenant cannot question the ownership and title vested in the landlord in an eviction petition before the Court under an enactment for eviction of tenants. Judgments, to this effect are tabulated as hereunder for ready reference;

(a) *Plasti Chemicals Co.* v. *Ashit Chadha,* 2004 (2) RCR (Rent) 667, holding that a landlord claiming ownership on the basis of registered Will has sufficient proof of ownership so far as the Delhi Rent Control Act, 1958 is concerned. The testament in favour of the landlord can only be questioned by the legal representatives of the earlier owner and the tenant has no *locus standi* to question the same.

(b) *Munni Devi* v. *Manmohan Verma,* 2007 (1) RCR (Rent) 223, deciding that it is not the domain of a tenant to challenge a Will if the landlord has inherited the premises from his father on the basis of a Will to this effect. The proceedings under the Delhi Rent Control Act, 1958 cannot be converted and utilised by a tenant to prevent eviction merely on the ground that he seeks to cast a doubt on the title of the property which has been inherited when there is really no one else claiming a right to such tenanted property.

(c) *Krishna Chopra* v. *Raksha,* 2000 (1) Rent LR 317, concluding that if a landlady has inherited a premises by virtue of a Will in her favour given by her father, the tenant cannot dispute the contents of the Will simply because there were other legal heirs also. The Will may be challenged by other heirs also. The Will may be challenged by other heirs or successors and tenant cannot question the Will in proceedings under the Delhi Rent Control Act, 1958.

(d) *Inderjit Kaur* v. *Baijnath,* 2003 (2) Rent LR 250, deciding that in a case where that wife of the tenant purchased a share of the land from another co-owner, it will not necessarily make her a landlady within meaning of section 2(c) of the EPURRA. The status of the tenant cannot merge with the status of the landlord and tenant is not entitled to deny the title of the landlord, even though his wife became co-owner as there is no axiomatic merger of the status of a tenant.

(e) *Babulal* v. *K. Sharadamma,* 2003 (2) RCR (Rent) 447, holding that in a petition for eviction under the Karnataka Rent Act, 2001, where the landlord claimed ownership under a Will, the tenant cannot raise a dispute with regard to the correctness or validity of a Will, even if it was a jointly owned property.

(f) *Jalal & Sons* v. *Sita Bai,* 2001 (2) Rent LR 85, deciding that if a landlord bequeathed property to a near relative by way of a Will, the tenant has no concern as to who could succeed and any denial of the title of the donnee under a gift deed or a legatee under a Will cannot be considered in law as *bona fide* denial of title.

(g) *Sham Lal Khera* v. *Sudershan Kumar,* 2011 (2) RCR (Rent) 400, holding that if an NRI landlord became owner of a ancestral property on the basis of a Will executed by his mother in his favour, it will not make any difference if the Will is challenged by another, legal heir and even discarded, since landlord being co-owner alongwith other legal heirs can maintain the petition for eviction under section 13B, EPURRA. Such a NRI landlord cannot be debarred from filing a eviction petition.

From a collective reading of the above precedents under different rent laws of different jurisdictions, it can be concluded that in any petition preferred by an NRI landlord under section 13B, EPURRA, the tenant may have little chances to succeed by disputing the inherited title of an NRI landlord co-owning any property.

In the latest erudite verdict of the Apex Court rendered by Justice T.S. Thakur in *Kamaljit Singh* v. *Sarabjit Singh,* JT 2014 (10) SC 134, it has been held that section 13B, EPURRA is a Code by itself providing a speedy remedy for a special category of cases of NRI landlords. Very lucidly, invoking the principles of estoppel, it has been aptly held by the Apex Court that the NRI landlord was not obliged to prove his title to the tenanted property, no matter the tenant clearly admits to the existence of a jural relationship of landlord and tenant. Reversing both judgments of the Trial Court and the High Court, it has been held that the tenant cannot question the title of the landlord in eviction proceedings.

Dismissal of ejectment petition does not debar fresh petition

In *Surinder Kaur* v. *Ramkishan,* 2012 (2) RCR (Rent) 181, it has been held that mere dismissal of an ejectment petition under section 13, EPURRA on normal grounds available for eviction of tenants, does not debar the landlord from subsequently filing an ejectment petition under section 13B, EPURRA as an NRI landlord and therefore, leave to contest the ejectment petition under section 13B, EPURRA could not have been granted to the tenant on the ground that an earlier ejectment petition filed by landlord under section 13, EPURRA stood dismissed.

In conclusion here it may be stated that the provisions of section 13-B EPURRA, had been enacted by the Government of Punjab on account of the rigid legal provisions of existing rent laws on account of which NRIs were unable to recover possession of their own residential and commercial buildings from tenants. The said legislation is a very effective law operating in the State of Punjab and in U.T Chandigarh. It is hoped that other States in India would also enact similar legislations to apply in their jurisdictions for the benefit of the NRI community.

(B) Issues relating to succession, Wills and inheritance – INDIA, NRIs and Wills

- As far as succession, inheritance and Wills are concerned, the Hindu Succession Act, 1956 and the Indian Succession Act, 1925 being Central legislations are applicable throughout the territory of India. Hence, in so far these issues are concerned, they apply uniformly throughout the territory of India to all States and Union Territories. The Indian Succession Act, 1925 is an Act to consolidate the law applicable to testamentary succession for Hindus and the Hindu Succession Act, 1956 is an Act to amend and codify the law relating to intestate succession among Hindus. Hence, in respect of the matter of Wills *i.e.*, testamentary succession, all NRIs with movable and immovable property in India shall be governed by the Indian Succession Act, 1925.
- The global Indian diaspora has some problems on the home soil which needs intercontinental solutions. In this perspective, the disposition of property of an NRI living in a foreign domicile, when such property is located partly in India and partly situated abroad, often poses awkward questions. Must an NRI make a Will or leave his property to natural succession. Should the NRI make a joint, composite or common Will of his assets and properties in India and abroad. If so, should such a Will be registered and where. Should a person be appointed to execute the Will in different jurisdictions. Would it be better if there are different Wills for separate properties in India and abroad. Should such different Wills be registered individually in separate jurisdictions. How should inheritance rights of beneficiaries of NRIs be safeguarded in India and abroad. Which law Indian or foreign would apply to assets and properties of NRIs in different countries.
- Two distinct Indian legislations exist. The Hindu Succession Act, 1956 (HSA) contains the codified law relating to intestate succession among Hindus *i.e.*, when there is no Will. The Indian Succession Act, 1925 (ISA) consolidates the law applicable to persons other than Hindus for intestate

succession and testamentary succession for all persons in India including Hindus. Hence, all NRIs (whether Hindus or non-Hindus) can make Wills governed by the provisions of the Indian Succession Act, 1925. To begin with, for an NRI, it is advisable to execute a written Will, get it witnessed and registered to avoid any intricate problems of succession and inheritance. With the abundance of problems of NRI properties in India, natural succession in the absence of a Will may pose problems from third party claimants. An NRI ought to Will his property by choice to his natural heirs or others and thus eliminate speculation or bogus claims from claimants and pawe a smooth succession. Thus, what ought to follow naturally must be better confirmed by a Will also.

- The HSA/ISA unlike the Hindu Marriage Act, 1955 does not have extra territorial application. In the wisdom of the Legislature, there are well defined principles of international law, which regulate succession to the movable and immovable properties of a Hindu NRI domiciled outside the territory of India. Thus, on the basis of international comity, the following three principles can be deduced regarding the application of HSA/ISA:-
- *Firstly*, for a Hindu domiciled outside India, succession to his immovable property in India is governed by HSA/ISA whereas succession to his movable property shall be governed by the law of the country of his foreign domicile.
- *Secondly*, where a Hindu is domiciled in India, succession to his immovable property outside India shall be governed by the law of the country where the property is situated. Movables outside India will be governed by HSA/ISA or by the local law of the foreign country in which the movable property is situated.
- *Thirdly*, in respect of a Hindu domiciled outside India, succession to his movable and immovable property outside India shall not be governed by HSA/ISA but by the law of the foreign domicile of the Hindu.
- In the event of there being no Will, natural succession among the category of heirs as per the order of succession will flow as per the HSA. Then, speculation, outsider claims, disputes among heirs and third party rights are rife. Hence, it is in the best interest of an NRI to pen a Will and put down his wishes and leave nothing to doubt.
- In the light of non-application of HSA/ISA outside India, it is strongly recommended that NRIs of Hindu origin having immovable assets in different countries should execute a joint composite Will pertaining to all their immovable properties located in different jurisdictions. For NRIs, execution of separate Wills for separate immovable properties in different countries is not advisable. Establishing genuineness of a composite Will is easier than proving multiple Wills. It is also recommended that the NRI must register the Will separately in every jurisdiction even though it is optional in India to do so. It may be mentioned that the registration in a particular country may hold good in respect of properties of the NRIs in that jurisdiction. Accordingly, separate rules of registration of different

countries ought to be complied with as per rules of the foreign domicile of the NRI.

- It is also advisable that the NRI should specifically appoint an executor to execute the Will in the particular jurisdiction where the property is situated. This assists the beneficiaries and simplifies the division of assets as per the Will. A written Will of an NRI duly witnessed and registered in respect of Indian properties identifies the claimants and legal heirs. Its multiple registration assures the seal of finality. The message for the NRI therefore is, to act well in advance and simplify the task of the beneficiaries who are to inherit their properties.

Thereafter, the law of the jurisdiction, where the property is situated will govern the process of succession on the basis of rights established under the Will. The global Indian must take advantage of this well codified position of Indian succession law. This is to ensure that there is no uncertainty and ambiguity.

(C) Problems arising out of revenue records and agricultural land disputes – the position prevailing in the State of Punjab

The love of land and the need to reconnect with his homeland are an ingrained part and parcel of every NRI originating from Punjab. The landed agricultural properties left by forefathers, ancestors and well wishers always creates the innate desire in the Punjabi NRI to visit his homeland and stake his ownership claim to his land he loves. Sometimes, the landed property in the hands of relatives, tenants, family members or employees is difficult to recover, creating a plethora of unforeseen problems which can take a long time to resolve in the Revenue Courts.

At times, title disputes are difficult to resolve and lack of documents to establish ownership can be difficult to obtain. This creates a very unpleasant and disturbing situation for the NRI. It is in this perspective that the State of Punjab has made some special endeavours to expedite the process of settling such disputes by simplified procedures and fast track resolution of such cases in this regard, the following summarized points are enumerated as under:—

- Superseding its earlier orders under which existing Courts of Tehsildars and Naib-Tehsildars were designated as Fast-Track Courts for NRI's, the Department of Revenue and Rehabilitation in a directive issued on December 28, 2005 declared that four Fast-Track Courts would be set-up at Jalandhar, Hoshiarpur, Moga and Nawanshahr to which neighbouring districts would be attached.
- The District Revenue Officer heads a Fast-Track Court and has the powers to decide on the correction of "Khasra girdwari", partition, contested and un-contested mutations, registered and un-registered Wills, "lambardari", demarcation, rent suit, and ejection under the Punjab Land Revenue Act. They also hear "chowkidari" cases. The Additional Deputy Commissioner or the Divisional Commissioner decide appeals against the orders of the Fast-Track Courts.

- The Government of Punjab by Notification dated 16 November, 2006, has also appointed District Revenue Officers at four district headquarters to decide Suits under the Punjab Tenancy Act, 1887, for Non-Resident Indians by conferring powers of Assistant Collector Ist Grade upon them.

Punjab Amends Acts: Under the New Punjab Security of Land Tenures (Amendment) Act, 2013, AND the Pepsu Tenancy and Agricultural Lands (Amendment) Act, 2013, now NRI's can get their ancestral agricultural property and property purchased by NRIs within five years vacated from tenants.

- On October 29, 2013, Punjab Vidhan Sabha unanimously passed the Punjab Security of Land Tenures (Amendment) Bill, 2013 and The Pepsu Tenancy and Agricultural Lands (Amendment) Bill, 2013, with which the Non-Resident Indians (NRIs) have got the right to get their property vacated from tenants in Punjab. Earlier, the Punjab Government had in 2008 enacted a law empowering the NRIs and Armed Forces personnel to get their single property vacated from tenants.
- Earlier also the Punjab government had given NRIs the liberty to get vacated a single property and now with these amendments, the NRIs can get their ancestral property and property owned by them for at least 5 years vacated from tenants.
- Under the new amendments, agricultural properties which have been given by NRIs on lease or rent, will now be able to get it back without providing alternate arrangements for stay and other stringent conditions. A single ownership proof and summary proceedings for eviction would provide an expeditious remedy to NRIs.
- Section 9B of the Punjab Security of Land Tenures (Amendment) Act, 2013 now reads in the following terms:

  "9B: One Time Concession – The concession given under sections 9 and 9A to the land owner, who is a Non-Resident Indian, shall be available only in respect of his ancestral property and the property, which has been purchased by him atleast five years before from the date he files the ejectment application."

- Section 7B of the Pepsu Tenancy and Agricultural Lands (Amendment) Act, 2013, now reads in the following terms:

  "7B: One Time Concession – The concession given under sections 7 and 7A to the land owner, who is a Non-Resident Indian, shall be available only in respect of his ancestral property and the property, which has been purchased by him atleast five years before from the date he files the ejectment application."

(D) Propositions arising out of property investment related issues in India

Investing in real estate, urban property, flats or apartments with builders, colonizers, estate agents and building companies can sometimes be a nightmare for NRIs. Colourful brochures, fancy promises, pictures of properties and attractive installment plans are used as inducement measures to extract huge sums of money from innocent NRIs who walk into such traps. At times, flats, houses, or apartments are not constructed as per the schedule and escalated costs are demanded failing which money already paid is forfeited. There are also times when the same property is sold to multiple owners and the unfortunate NRI has to face insurmountable problems. It is in this context that the following safeguards and remedies can be advocated which are applicable uniformly throughout the territory of India in all States & Union Territories.

- Before any investment in any property, flat or apartment is made in India, unless and until a physical verification is done through a reliable source or agency to conclusively establish the title or ownership of the builder, colonizer, company or estate agent, no money should be invested blindly without checking.
- Every step should be taken by an NRI to ask, confirm and verify whether the person, builder, colonizer or company possesses a valid license, permission or sanction as per local laws to build a colony, set of apartments or the prescribed number of flats which are advertised or propagated at the time of sale.
- If possible, through the assistance of local agencies or contacts, the title of the owner who is selling the property should be verified from the local land records to establish the ownership of the vendor. This will rule out the issues relating to ownership being disputed at a later stage.
- It should be an absolute certainty that proper documents must be executed at the time of paying any initial deposit and no payment should be made unless and until proper contracts or agreements are executed and signed by the builder, estate agent, colonizer or company selling any property.
- It must be clarified in writing that in case the property is not handed over in the stipulated time, there shall be no escalation clause in terms of building costs. Similarly, adequate caution and care should be taken not to sign any agreement or document by which consent is given to agree to escalated building costs .Agreements or documents should be signed only after consultation with solicitors and no blank documents should be signed at all.
- In case there is any failure to hand over property in a stipulated period of time or there is any breach of promise, an NRI should not wait indefinitely. Every effort should be made to put the grievance or complaint in writing to the concerned colonizer, builder, estate agent or property developer which can serve as written proof and evidence for initiating any legal proceeding later.
- The Consumer Protection Act, 1986, an Act for better protection of the interests of consumers and for the purpose to make provisions for establishment of Consumer Courts for settlement of consumer disputes is a very effective remedy in India against errant builder, colonizers and property developers. Consumer Courts exist in every district in India and complaints can be made in simple language with a very small amount of fee payable as court-fee. The complaints can be followed up in person

and the procedure of hearing is simple. Trial is expeditious and quick. It serves as a very effective remedy. Hence, it is strongly advised that in case of any deficiency in service or restrictive trade practice suffered by an NRI at the hands of any such errant builder, colonizer or estate agent, the provisions of the Consumer Protection Act, 1986 applicable throughout India should be invoked at the earliest possible. This is a easy, friendly and quick method for getting relief.

CONCLUSION:

As a common conclusion to all the above problems, some general suggestions can be mooted which can be a panacea to the NRI for the ills which ail him for his property problems. Though, no solution is universal but for the betterment of the properties of the NRI, these possible remedies can improve and make the situation better. These suggestions can be summarized in the following headings:

- At the outset it may be most useful for States and Union Territories all over India to constitute nodal cells for NRI affairs at State headquarters. These NRI cells with memberships of administration, police and legal authorities can be nodal bodies for entertaining NRI complaints online and in person from NRIs. They can forward these complaints to the respective departments to which they pertain to and advise NRIs what remedy to adopt for resolving the problem. If the issue can be resolved by seeking a response from the Government machinery internally, the matter can be concluded or the NRI can be guided to approach the appropriate Court for relief.
- The Constitution of the NRI nodal cell by the Chandigarh administration on August 12, 2009 which is headed by a retired High Court Judge and various officials including one of the authors as member is a role model for other States and Union Territories to adopt. This experiment is definitely worth emulating by other States in India.

  It is strongly advocated that in matters of landlord-tenant relationship, all States and Union Territories in India should enact local legislations on the lines of the special provisions for the Right to recover immediate possession of residential and non-residential buildings of NRIs. The Union Territory of Chandigarh by a notification dated 9 October, 2009 has made applicable the provisions of section 13(B) of the East Punjab Rent Restriction Act to the Union territory of Chandigarh whereby NRI landlords in Chandigarh can now recover immediate possession of their property. Wherever such a law does not exist in India, States and Union Territories should endeavour to make changes in local laws to incorporate such fast track changes in rent laws for NRIs.
- Further, it may be suggested that individual States and Union Territories should endeavour to create Fast Track NRI Courts in matters of agricultural properties, revenue affairs and land revenue disputes besides maintenance of revenue records. The changes in the State of Punjab in this regard are a helpful model to adapt.

- It may also be suggested that appropriate legislative changes may be brought about in matters of properties of NRIs involving cases where NRI properties have been retained, forcibly occupied or grabbed by unscrupulous or unethical persons. It may be in order if the Central Government seriously considers enacting a Central legislation applicable throughout the territory of India to take cognizance of such issues of NRI properties and bring them under purview of such Legislation. Such an enactment can create special Courts for speedy trials of property disputes of NRIs.
- In so far issues concerning obtaining copies of land revenue records, title deeds, title documents, ownership records, transfer of ownership papers etc. are concerned, the Government of India should endeavour having a module of public private partnership to whom the limited function of preparation and handing over copies can be out sourced after the data is computerised by the Government. By commercial bidding, an agency can be identified either at Central or State level to handle this limited function of preparing copies of records on the basis of a regularly updated website to be prepared on the instructions of the respective State Governments and Union Territories within India. This out sourced agency can fix rates at which copies of all individual ownership records can be supplied on payment of requisite charges either online or in person to the concerned NRI on a written request supported by his identity and his connection with the property. The local administration in every State can monitor the function of such agency & restrict its function only to disseminate limited information to concerned NRI.

It may be pointed out that the State of Punjab has made endeavours and taken steps for providing better, expeditious and more effective remedies to aid and assist the dispensation of relief to NRIs as also to provide a platform for giving them the right to information and the right to avail services. In this regard, the State of Punjab has taken the following steps in this regard as hereunder:

- The Registrar General of the Punjab and Haryana High Court, Chandigarh, by a communication dated November 21, 2013 has stated that the High Court has decided to establish one NRI Court at Magisterial level and one at Appellate level to function initially at Jalandhar only.
- Constituted an NRI Commission under the Punjab State Commission for NRIs Act, 2011.
- Constituted a Punjab Right to Service Commission under the Punjab Right to Service Act, 2011.
- Constituted a State Information Commission, Punjab under the Right to Information Act, 2005.
- A brief description of all the aforementioned above three fully functional Commissions operating in the city of Chandigarh is set down as hereunder:

Punjab State Commission for NRIs Act, 2011

The enacted law labelled as ***"The Punjab State Commission for NRIs Act, 2011"*** is stated to be ***"An Act to provide for the constitution of the Commission for NRIs in the State of Punjab with a view to protecting and safeguarding the interests of the NRIs in the State of Punjab, and to recommend remedial measures to State Government."*** It defines a ***"Complaint"*** by stating that it ***"means all petitions/communications received in State Commission for NRIs from an NRI or any other person on his behalf, in person, by post, by telegram, by fax or by any other means whatsoever, alleging, disputes or violations or abetment thereof or negligence in the prevention of such dispute or violation, by a public servant or a private person or the material on the basis of which the Punjab State Commission for NRIs takes suomotu cognizance."*** The powers and the functions of the Punjab State Commission for NRIs stipulated in sections 12 and 14 are reproduced as follows:

> ***"12. Powers and Functions o, the Commission***
>
> *(1) The Commission shall, while investigating any matter under this Act, have all the powers of a Civil court trying a suit and, in particular, in respect of the following matters namely:—*
>
> *(a) summoning and enforcing the attendance of any person and examining him on oath;*
>
> *(b) requiring the discovery and production of any documents;*
>
> *(c) receiving evidence on affidavits;*
>
> *(d) requisitioning any public record or copy thereof from any court or office;*
>
> *(e) issuing commissions for the examination of witnesses and documents; and*
>
> *(f) any other matter which may be prescribed.*
>
> *(2) The Commission shall function by holding "sittings" and "meetings" at any place within the State of Punjab.*
>
> *(3) The Members of the Commission including the Chairperson shall function in accordance with Rules framed by State Government.*
>
> ***14. Power of the Commission to utilize the services of certain officers and investigating agencies for conducting investigating***
>
> *The Commission may conduct enquiry or investigation into the matters falling within its authority:*
>
> *(a) either directly; or*
>
> *(b) through an Investigating team constituted by the Commission; or*
>
> *(c) through the Deputy Commissioner of the district concerned; or*
>
> *(d). through the Government."*

The Punjab State Commission for NRIs constituted by the Government of Punjab is the first NRI commission in the Country which is fully functional for the past two years and is receiving complaints in person, by post and by email as well. The two Member Commission headed by Mr. Justice Arvind Kumar, Former Judge Punjab and Haryana High Court, Chandigarh has its office premises in the Punjab Mini Secretariat on the ground floor in Room no. 6 at Sector 9, Chandigarh and is working very successfully under his able guidance. It receives large number of complaints in its office which are taken up by the NRI Commission which holds daily sittings. Enquiries or investigations are conducted by NRI Commission through its directions to Government agencies and follow up reports are obtained to ensure compliance. This is a very effective means of redressal of complaints and the opportunity to parties to appear in person or through counsel has resulted in settlement of grievances of large number of NRIs and other persons. The NRI Commission has been able to resolve a large number of matrimonial, property, immigration and other related NRIs disputes in a short span of time with their regular sittings and meetings. In its first Annual Report covering the period from 29 November 2011 to 31 March 2013, it is reported that the NRI Commission received 443 complaints in the very first year and that the Commission successfully resolved 225 complaints whilst 218 cases are still pending resolution.

The NRI Commission can be reached at nricommpb@gmail.com

The Official Address of the Punjab State Commission for NRIs is:

Punjab Civil Secretariat-2, Block 'A', Room No. 6, Sector 9, Chandigarh

The Punjab Right to Service Act, 2011 and Punjab Right to Service Commission

Punjab is the first State which has not only brought Punjab Right to Service Act, 2011 but also constituted a statutory Commission, called the Punjab Right to Service Commission as the highest forum of appeal under the Punjab Right to Service Act, 2011 as also to take measures to get the provisions of this Act implemented at the grass soot level through regular monitoring and supervision. The Commission is also vested with the duty to suggest changes in systems and procedures to make service delivery faster and more efficient. The Act seeks to achieve its objectives by authorizing the Government of Punjab for the performance of the following functions and duties:

(a) Notify services that are to be covered under the Act;

(b) Provide timelines for each service covered by the notification;

(c) Designate officers who are responsible for delivery of each service in the given timeline;

(d) Provide for two levels of appeal to the citizen in case the service is not provided in the given time, or is deficient in any manner;

(e) Empower the second appellate authority to impose penalty on the defaulting officer if the service has been refused or delayed without sufficient reason;

(f) Provide for compensation to the aggrieved citizen out of the amount recovered as penalty; and

(g) Constitute a commission to oversee and supervise the implementation of the Act and to act as the highest forum of revision or appeal under the Act.

Originally **67 services** were notified under section 3 of the said Act and as of now **149 services** have been brought under the ambit of this Act. The Commission started receiving regular information on receipt and disposal of services from August 2011. **Up to November 30, 2013 as many as 1,54,59,703 applicants** have availed the services under the provisions of this Act. **738 appeals** have been filed before the 1st Appellate Authorities and **10 appeals** before the 2nd Appellate Authorities. **14 Revision Petitions** have been filed with the Commission under the Punjab Right to Service Act, 2011.

On its part, the Commission has also taken up, on priority, the task of disseminating awareness about salient features of this Act to the public. For this purpose, apart from distributing literature, Members of the Commission have visited various districts in the field and have held discussions with different target groups.

The Commission stands committed to make recommendations to the Government of Punjab to further streamline and strengthen the public service delivery mechanism by expanding the canvas of services under the purview of this Act and by developing the infrastructure capable of meeting the requisite provisions. The Punjab Right to Service Commission constituted on October 20, 2011 is headed by Sh. S.C. Aggarwal, Chief Commissioner, who is assisted by 4 Commissioners and a Secretary to The Commission. The full time Commission functions at the following address:

Office of Punjab Right to Service Commission:

Office Address	*Mahatma Gandhi State Institute of Public Administration, VIP Suites, Institutional Area, Sector 26, Chandigarh – 160 019*
Telephone	*0172-2790181, Fax - 0172-2792182*
E-mail	*rtspunjab@punjab.gov.in, rtspunjab@gmail.com*

The Working of the State Information Commission, Punjab under the Right to Information Act, 2005

In 2005, The Government of Punjab was amongst the first States to set up the State Information Commission, *Punjab (SICP)* which reportedly has the highest disposal rate of complaint appeals in the country. Punjab State thus leads the nation in deciding matters of Right to Information under the RTI Act. The Right to Information Act, 2005 (RTI ACT, 2005) was enacted to provide for setting up a practical regime of Right to secure access to information under the control of public authorities to promote transparency and accountability. Section 15 of this Act requires every State Government to Constitute a State Information Commission and the State of Punjab set up its Commission in 2005 itself.

The RTI Act, 2005 lays down the procedure for access to information from Public Authorities and provides for an enforcement mechanism, in case of any alleged denial of the right. Each public authority is legally bound to appoint Public Information Officer/s [PIO], which are the single point of contact for any individual desirous of obtaining information from the concerned State department/Government organization. The concerned citizen has to submit a request to the PIO of the concerned department, specifying the information he wants and each application must be accompanied by a fee of Rs. 10 only. The PIO is legally bound to respond to a request for information within 30 days, either allowing access to the requested documents or in case information is to be denied on any of the grounds listed in section 8 of the Act, convey this in writing with supporting reasons. The aggrieved citizen has a right to file Appeal to the Departmental Appellate Authority and thereafter a second Appeal to the State Information Commission concerned. In this regard, The Central Government and State Governments have constituted Information Commissions to hear Appeals/Complaints against their respective public authorities in their respective territorial jurisdictions.

State Information Commission Punjab (SICP)

The Punjab Government had in 2005 set up Punjab State Information Commission to hear cases against the decisions of the PIO's/First Appellate Authorities of the State government departments/Public Authorities. The details may be seen at the website of the Commission ***www.infocommpunjab.com.*** Now very ably headed by Mr. S.S. Channy, IAS (Retd.) its office address at State Information commission, Punjab (SICP) SCO No. 84-85, Sector 17-C, Chandigarh.

The SICP was constituted under the able Chairmanship of **The Chief Information Commissioner Sh. R.I. Singh, IAS, (Retd.)** along with nine other State Information Commissioners. Punjab State Information Commission is to ensure citizens in the state of Punjab their Right to Information from public authorities; thereby fulfilling the mandate assigned in the Right to Information Act, 2005. Punjab State Information Commission exercises powers for implementation under **sections 18, 19, 20 and 25 of the RTI Act**. At the same time State Information Commission Punjab is itself a Public authority as defined in section 2(h) of RTI Act 2005. Since its inception, the State Information Commission, Punjab has heard Appeals from 2005 to 2013. Starting **from 20 appeals in 2005**, this Commission has disposed of a record of **5413 appeals in 2012** which is highest in the country. Undoubtedly, The SICP in the State of Punjab is the leader in the matters of disposal of appeals made to it which ensure expeditious decisions on people's Right to Information. SICP has the unique distinction of rendering exemplary services in State of Punjab.

Means to an end

By no means, the above suggestions, steps taken, Commissions constituted and the efforts made in making them practically workable are exhaustive or conclusive. They are the beginning of a new thought process initiated by the Government of Punjab in the very useful deliberation on property problems of NRIs/PIOs. Punjab is the first State in the country which has taken above steps as a pioneer to find effective ways and means to solve such problems by redressal of grievances of NRIs. Similar enactments are required in other States as well and forums need to be created at the Centre and other States also for providing such services in other jurisdictions. However, to generate more thoughts, have more suggestions and consider other view points, these limited views have been put forth for a fruitful, interactive and participative dialogue for the consideration of the welfare of the NRI brethren. It is a beginning without an end and a start of a new era for the NRI.

CHILD LAWS

CHILD LAWS

- Children in Distress – Remedies in Indian Law
- Norway, Leave the Indian Children Alone
- POCSO – A Child Law in Oblivion
- A New Child Law in the Making – A Positive Step
- Juveniles and Children in Conflict – A New Law

Children in Distress – Remedies in Indian Law

Today's children constitute tomorrow's future. Sad, but true, we are not protecting our children. Our future is in jeopardy. Abuse of child inmates of protection homes have recently shocked the conscience of the nation. Physical, mental and sexual harassment was rampant in these private institutions. Offences of molestation, rape, wrongful confinement, criminal intimidation and immoral trafficking have been reportedly registered against these protection houses where the care givers turned into predators. A plethora of laws exist to protect child rights. The Indian Protection of Children from Sexual Offences Act, 2012 has also become a deterrent law. However, enacting laws is not the solution. Sensitization of child rights, appointing Ombudsmen to protect children and above all providing special care to their privileges is the clarion call of the day. Lethargy, indifference, tardiness and insensitivity to protection of children must end. Callous treatment of children should be penalised by social ostracization of child offenders as law alone is not the remedy

A WHOLESOME LAW – CPCRA

India participated in the United Nations (UN) General Assembly Summit in 1990, which adopted a Declaration on Survival, Protection and Development of Children and acceded to the Convention on the Rights of the Child (CRC) on the 11th December, 1992. CRC is an international treaty that makes it incumbent upon the signatory States to take all necessary steps to protect children's rights enumerated in the Convention. In order to ensure protection of rights of children, one of the recent initiatives that the Government has taken for Children is, the adoption of National Charter for Children, 2003. The UN General Assembly Special Session on Children held in May, 2002 adopted an Outcome Document titled "A World Fit for Children" containing the goals, objectives, strategies and activities to be undertaken by the member countries for the current decade. Hence, in the wisdom of the Indian Parliament, it was thought expedient to enact a law relating to children to give effect to the policies adopted by the Government in this regard, standards prescribed in the CRC, and all other relevant international instruments. Hence, after the UN Convention on the Rights of the Child was signed by India, the Commission for Protection of Child Rights Act, 2005 (CPCRA) was enacted by Parliament to provide teeth and implement the UN Convention. CPCRA is an Act to provide for the constitution of a National Commission and State Commissions for Protection of Child Rights and Children's Courts for providing speedy trial of offences against children or of violation of child rights and for matters connected therewith or incidental thereto.

Suggested Measures under CPCRA:

- In the light of the above provisions of the CPCRA, it is incumbent on the Governments of all the States and the Union Territories (UT's) in India to take all necessary steps to protect children's rights enumerated in the Convention on the Rights of the Child (CRC). Sections 13 and 24 of the CPCRA provides ample powers both to the National Commission and the State Commissions for inter alia taking necessary steps and recommending appropriate remedial measures with regard to issues pertaining to all children in distress. These can be enforced in all the States and the UT's throughout India by setting up and/or constituting State Commissions for Protection of Child Rights under section 17 of the CPCRA in the respective territories of the individual Governments. Hence, as a starting point, the States and the UT's in India should forthwith set up the said State Commissions so that the entire machinery can be galvanized under its regime.
- It is suggested that any averment or contention by either of the State or UT Governments of not to set up State Commissions for Protection of Child Rights in their territories should not be entertained and accepted due to the sensitivity and magnitude of the problems relating to children in difficulty. This is supported by the following contentions. Hence, all the States and the UT's in India need to set up the said State Commissions on priority.
- To complete the setting up of a fully operational system under the CPCRA, Children's Courts can be constituted in the said respective territories in India under section 25 of the CPCRA and Special Public Prosecutors can be appointed in these territories under section 26 of the CPCRA. Thus, independent of the other statutory enactments dealing with criminal laws or other penal provisions in general, CPCRA can be very effectively utilized for individually setting up a statutory system for enforcement of child rights specifically and particularly in the larger interest of children only. This will create a special, exclusive and individual forum for in camera proceedings for redressal of Children's Rights and will provide effective, speedy and timely relief in the case of any individual incident of missing/distressed children.
- The issues pertaining to missing children and/or children in distress can be exclusively looked into by the respective State Commissions in their individual territories within India in view of the powers vested in them under sections 13 and 24 of the CPCRA. Clearly, if the State Commission concerned *suo moto* or upon inquiry into complaints regarding missing children or children in distress comes to a conclusion that there is a violation of Child Rights, there is non implementation of laws relating to

children or there is non-compliance of decisions/guidelines/instructions pertaining to welfare of children, such Commission under section 15 of the CPCRA, can approach the Supreme Court/High Court concerned for issuance of directions, Orders or Writs as may be deemed necessary by the Court, besides recommending concerned Governments for grant of interim relief as deemed necessary. Thus, any individual case of missing children/ children in distress can be immediately remedied by the concerned State Commission in India by enforcing the above provisions of the CPCRA.

- The composition of the State Commission with its six members, out of which at least two should be women specializing in child health, care, welfare or child development, Juvenile Justice, child psychology, laws related to children and/or having knowledge of children in distress will give adequate opportunity to the State Commission to receive complaints or act *suo moto* whenever there is any issue of kidnapping or removal of children and deprivation/violation of child rights. The Commission is vastly empowered to examine all factors affecting children and relating to trafficking, torture, exploitation, pornography and prostitution and recommend appropriate remedial measures. The Commission has mandatory powers to forward cases to any Magistrate and hear them as complaints. Independently, the Commission upon inquiry can recommend initiation of proceedings for prosecution or such other action as deemed fit. Hence, all cases of trafficking of children particularly for exploitation, begging, prostitution and pornography can be monitored and future recurrence can be checked. All organized Child Mafias can therefore be attempted to be eliminated.
- That as an overall additional suggestion for effective preventive measures for the future, every State and Union Territory in India must forthwith set up the statutory District Child Welfare Committees, besides State and District Inspection Committees, as required under sections 29 and 35 of the Juvenile Justice (Care and Protection of Children) Act, 2000. Under Rule 91 of The Juvenile Justice (Care and Protection of Children) Rules, 2007, every State and Union Territory in India must constitute a Selection Committee, to be headed by a Retired Judge of the High Court as its Chairperson to make selections of District Child Welfare Committees, besides making selections of State and District Inspection Committees. Also, as prescribed under section 62 of the Juvenile Justice (Care and Protection of Children) Act, 2000, every State and Union Territory in India must constitute a State Advisory Board by appointing independent professionals, in terms of section 62 of the above Act, on the matters relating to the establishment and maintenance of homes, mobilization of resources, provision of facilities for education, training and rehabilitation of children in need of care and protection. Nominating these committees with ex-officio government officials as full time members who have no inclination, time, energy or interest in child related matters is fatal.

Conclusion of suggested measures under CPCRA:

A conjoint reading of the provisions, remedies and suggestions made above under the CPCRA indicates that an altogether separate and independent machinery can be set into motion under the auspices of the CPCRA to specifically look into all issues related to Child Rights while the process of Criminal Law moves in the mainstream.

The menace of child abuse can be curbed with a heavy hand only if the issues relating to children are segregated and dealt with under separate parameters under the watchful eye of Child specialists *i.e.,* qualified members of the State Commissions for Protection of Child Rights, besides Child Welfare or Inspection Committees and Boards. Only if qualified, trained and experienced persons sensitive to Child Rights are empowered to handle the problems of children, can the process and machinery of Criminal Law work in tandem.

Once Child offenders are apprehended, speedy trials of offences against children or of violation of Child Rights can be ensured in Children's Courts which can be set up under the CPCRA. This can prevent recurrence of organized children related offences.

A vigilant State Commission for Protection of Child Rights both as a watch dog and as an investigator can serve a very significant role in the removal of problems of children in difficulty. Hence, only if the issue of children in trouble is taken out from the general stream of treatment and handed over to Child Specialists to start with and monitor/overlook it from the outside, can the necessary attention, time and energy be devoted to this highly sensitive issue of problems of children.

CONCLUDING THOUGHTS

Children go missing, are abused or are maltreated in silence. It may be suggested that not only the police or the investigating authorities should be solely responsible for identifying the children in distress, whose cases have been reported in the police stations, rather even the public bodies, NGO's, State Legal Services Authorities within their territories in India should be made a part of the support services as that would help and speed up the investigation process making it possible for the children in distress to be helped. If all the authorities at all levels *i.e.,* Village, District, State and Centre in their respective jurisdictions, including the public bodies work together to identify the children in distress, it will not be very difficult to solve their problems. Therefore, keeping in mind the above guidelines and suggestions it is stated that it is very much possible to efficiently investigate and locate children in difficulty besides preventing future instances of abuse and kidnapping of children. Considering that India is a large nation geographically spread over an area of 3.28 million square kilometres, with vast territories housing a multi-cultural society and a huge population of over 1.2 billion people spread over 29 States and 7 Union Territories, resolving critical issues of children in distress is not an easy task. However, keeping in view that this vulnerable section of society is at a very high risk rate, every effort, step and endeavour should be made to adapt means and methods to protect the future of the nation constituted of its precious children. Therefore, it should be the endeavour of every official body of the system in India to contribute and do whatever best is possible to be done for the plight of the children in distress who must be helped. Resolving their problems should be the top most priority in all walks of life. We have to work seriously to save our children and if we do not, no one else will do it.

COMPARATIVE LOOK OF ALL THE FOUR INDIAN ENACTMENTS ON THE RIGHTS OF THE CHILD

NAME OF INDIAN **ENACTMENT**	JUVENILE JUSTICE (CARE AND PROTECTION OF CHILDREN) ACT, 2000	COMMISSION FOR PROTECTION OF CHILD RIGHTS ACT, 2005	THE RIGHT OF CHILDREN TO FREE AND COMPULSORY EDUCATION, 2009	CHILD LABOUR (PROHIBITION AND REGULATION) ACT, 1986
Main Objective	To provide for the care, protection, treatment, development and rehabilitation of neglected or delinquent juveniles.	Provide for National & State Commissions, Courts for providing speedy trial of offences against children or of violation of child rights & for incidental/ connected matters.	To provide for free and compulsory education to all children of age 6 to 14 years.	Prohibiting the engagement of children in certain employments and to regulate the conditions of work for children in certain other employments.
Definition of Child under the Enactment	Child in need of care and protection is defined with 9 different points	Child Rights defined as per UN Convention on the Rights of the Child.	Child means a male or female child of the age six to fourteen years	Child means a person who has not completed his fourteenth year of age.
Important and relevant sections under the Enactment	Definition of child section 2(d), Juvenile Justice Board section 4-6, Important provisions for protection of juveniles section 15 & 16, Child Welfare Committee section 29-31, Benefits for children section 40-45	Definition of Child Rights section 2(b) National Commission formed under the Act section 3, with functions under section 13 &14, State Commission section 24, Children's Court section 25 and 26.	Definition of child section 2(c), (d),(e) Rights of child to free education section 3, 4 and 5 Protection of rights of child – Commission formed under CPCRA section 31-34	Definition of child section 2(ii) prohibition of employment of child section 3 Child Labour Technical Advisory Committee section 5 Benefits for children under the Act section 7, 8 and 13
Authority constituted under the Enactment	Juvenile Justice Board and Child Welfare Committee	National and State Commissions for Protection of Child Rights and Children's Court for speedy trial of offences against children.	Under section 31, National and State Commissions for Protection of Child Rights as constituted under section 3 & 17 of the CPCRA/ Advisory Councils sections 33, 34	Child Labour Technical Advisory Committee

Role of the authority constituted under the Enactment	JJ Board: deals with all the proceedings relating to the juvenile under law Child Welfare Committee: looks after the children in need of care and protection	National and State Commissions: Have the duty of protection of all kinds of rights of children as elaborated in section 13. Children's Court: speedy trial of offences against violation of child rights.	National and State Commissions: in addition to the functions under the CPCRA, also look after the rights of education of children and inquire into the complaints of violation of the same	Child Labour Technical Advisory Committee: to look into the complaints of violations under the Act *i.e.,* where children are engaged in employments in violation of the provisions under the Act
Benefits available to the children	Provides for the rehabilitation and social reintegration of the children or juveniles who are guilty under the law.	All kinds of rights of children on whole are protected under the Act due to diverse functions and powers under section 13 of the Act.	Protection of right of education of children of age 6 to 14 years.	Protection of children from being employed in places with high risks to the life of the children and providing better work environment for the children
Drawbacks of the Enactment	The Act specifically deals with the protection of juveniles who have committed crimes and the ways the Courts should deal with them. No effective machinery is provided for protection of rights of children who are being exploited.	None apparently, though, if qualified people as stipulated under section 3 and 17 are not appointed to the National/State Commissions, no meaningful purpose will be served in creating these specialist bodies with statutory powers created under the UN Convention of the Rights of the Child.	The major focus of the Act is on the right to provide free and compulsory education to children.	The Act only focuses on the prohibition of employment of children in certain work places which are harmful for the children.

After perusing the comparative study of the above enactments, it can be stated that it is best that a State Commission be formed under the Commission for Protection of Child Rights Act, 2005 (CPCRA) in every State, to look into the matters of protection of violation of Child Rights not visualized in other Acts. The State Commissions formed under the Act in India for protection of violation of Child rights have a vast scope to deal with the problems in hand. The Act talks about the protection of "child rights," in terms of the definition given in the UN Convention on the Rights of the Child and the functions/powers of the Commission are very broad giving ample authority to it in all areas of Child rights. Commissions formed under this Act in every State and at National level will not only help solve the problem of the children but will also look at other areas and give directions to State level bodies for effective implementation. Hence, as per the provisions of the four Indian enactments and the points raised above, it is best that the Commissions under the CPCRA are formed to deal with all the problems of child rights and they can further utilize powers of State level Boards, authorities, Committees for seeking effective implementation of all the four Acts.

Norway, Leave the Indian Children Alone

Shocking but true, Barnevarne, a child care service of Norway had taken custody of Indian children, Abhigyan and Aishwarya from their natural parents Anurup and Sagarika Bhattacharya in May, 2011 when they were two and a half years and six months old respectively and lodged them in separate foster homes. They charged the mother Sagarika with "negligence and unable to bring up" the children. A Norwegian Court had ruled that the two children would stay in two different foster homes until the age of 18 and their natural parents would be allowed to meet them only once a year for one hour. Shockingly, the Court had added that only if the couple separated, the custody of the children could be given to the natural father who is employed as a Geoscientist in Norway since 2007. After an international media outcry and a personal meeting of grandparents Monotosh and Shikha Chakravarty with the then President Pratibha Patil to seek her intervention in getting their two grandchildren back from foster care in Norway, a headway was reported, as Norway agreed to hand over the children to their uncle in India. Earlier letters sent to the Norwegian Government by the Ministry of External Affairs reportedly on December 28, 2011 and January 5, 2011, had not elicited any response. With the visas of Bhattacharyas to stay in Norway expiring in March, they had dreaded leaving the country without their loved ones. The happening, sorrowfully true was appalling. However, the entire episode ended happily and the children were returned back to India by the Norwegian authorities.

Should India have agreed and permitted its citizens in Norway to decide matters relating to personal laws. Ironically, as we celebrate our 65th Republic Day as a Sovereign, Socialist, Secular, Democratic Republic, our citizens abroad are still governed by foreign family laws. While a false sense of euphoria dawns on the horizon as Norway agrees to hand over the Indian children to their uncle subject to a Norwegian District Court accepting the arrangement, larger issues prevail raising disturbing questions. In upholding the applicability of Norwegian laws, Indian sovereignty cannot be subjugated to abdicate the majesty of Indian family laws. The precedent is therefore clearly wrong and this may not be a healthy trend for 30 million NRIs who live in 180 countries abroad. On 26 November, 1949, we gave to ourselves The Constitution of India and the power to the State to legislate on any subject. This power is reserved within ourselves and we cannot surrender it to any foreign jurisdiction. In other matters of local civil and criminal laws, Indians may have to follow the law of the foreign domicile, but in matters of personal laws in our homes, the exception of applicability of our family laws must prevail. The sanctity of personal family laws of Indian communities is overriding.

Norway, Denmark, Sweden and Finland have stringent State welfare policies for its nationals which empower them to place children in foster homes to live with strangers. Norwegian Child Protection Services however, ought not to have exercised such rights with respect to Indian children whose religious, ethnic, cultural and linguistic milieu was different and distinct. In any case, custody of children of Indian nationals in Norway ought not to have been taken away from their natural guardians *i.e.*, their parents, unless and until the action was warranted under Indian law applicable to the parties. In this respect, the lack of Consular assistance and non-availability of legal help to the Bhattacharya's in Norway may have contributed in this abrupt Nordic State action snatching their children away from them. The case thus did require close examination.

The moot proposition on which the Norwegian action is questionable, rests on the fundamental plank that Indian nationals are governed by the personal law applicable to the parties. In respect of Hindus, i.e., any person who is Hindu, Buddhist, Jain or Sikh by religion, The Hindu Minority and Guardianship Act, 1956 (HMGA) has extra territorial application. It also applies to Hindus domiciled in the territories to which HMGA extends who are outside the territory of India. Thus, the Bengali Bhattacharyas carry with them their personal law in their pockets when they live in Norway. Under HMGA, the natural Guardian of a Hindu minor is his father and after him the mother. The custody of a minor child under the age of 5 years shall ordinarily be with the mother. Alternatively, the welfare of the minor is the paramount consideration in the appointment or declaration of any person as a Guardian by a court of competent jurisdiction in India.

The process of appointment of Guardians in respect of minor children in India is governed by the Guardians and Wards Act, 1890 (GWA). Surprisingly, since the HMGA does not have any independent statutory provisions for appointment of Guardians of minors, all parties, whether Hindus or non-Hindus, have to invoke the provisions of the GWA for appointment of a Guardian with respect to a minor child in India. Needless to add, this process is adjudicated by a notified Guardian Judge as the Court of competent jurisdiction in the place where the minor ordinarily resides. There is an explicit provision in the GWA that if the natural father is living, no one else can be declared or appointed to be the Guardian of the minor, unless the Court is of the opinion that the father is "unfit" to be a guardian. This process, would of course, be tested on the fundamental principle resting on what appears to be in the circumstances better for the welfare and in the best interests of the minor. In considering what will be for the welfare of the minor, the Court shall have regard to the age, sex, and religion of the minor besides other factors.

The reported face saving resolution of Dr. Arunabhas Bhattacharya, the 27 year old bachelor brother of Anurup in Kolkata being given custody, subject to a Norwegian Court accepting the arrangement, seems to be an abject surrender to Norwegian laws without considering the applicability of Indian personal laws. Why was the applicability of the HMGA not raised and would the competent Court to decide the custody issue be not as per the HMGA. Hindu family law and not Norwegian laws ought to apply. Nobody probably raised the issue. Thus, these issues remain unanswered. The determination of the custody matter of Indian children of Hindu religion under custody laws of Norway is clearly a wrong application. Subjecting Indian citizens governed by their personal laws to the Norwegian jurisdiction in family law matters is an incorrect precedent contrary to settled Indian law. This fallacious practice will only mar future cases falling for similar determination and put applicability of Indian laws in jeopardy. This disturbing trend must be stalled.

In the backdrop of the above social milieu, the Norwegian action does not seem sustainable. Applying Nordic law to Indian nationals domiciled in Norway who are Hindus by religion does not meet the interpretation of the personal law applicable to the Indian parents. Further, applying European yardsticks of culture, habits and social mores to Bhattacharyas who profess Hindu religion and cultural practices, is not the correct application of the best interests principle for determining the welfare of children. An overzealous Norwegian social set up cannot change the personal law of the parties or usurp the interpretation of principles of upbringing of Indian children and thrust them upon foreign citizens domiciled temporarily in their territory. Furthermore, the yardsticks to be adopted in such a determination is by adjudication before the competent courts under the HMGA read with the GWA. Any Norwegian Court cannot close the rights of Indian parents till their children attain the age of majority. Rights of children cannot be flouted with such impunity. Another disturbing factor seems to be in separating the children and traumatizing them by not letting them grow as siblings is alarming. The brother and sister have a right to grow up in a family together as they were born. This natural order cannot be changed.

The United Nations Convention of the Rights of the Child has been brutally offended in the conduct of the Indian Children being confiscated and put in foster care. The concern is larger. The Right to Family Life guaranteed by the European Convention of Human Rights too has been violated. The dilemma is international and Nordic viewpoint needs to be tested. Forcibly removing children and putting them in foster homes and adoption to foreign parents whilst their natural parents are living, is not in the best interest or the welfare of the child. It would be best if Norway left Indian children alone. In its wisdom, the Indian jurisdiction must intervene and step forward to put its view point before it is too late. It will be a sad story with an unhappy ending if India does not intervene. It is time India expressed its sovereignty in the matter of Indian family laws to Indian citizens in foreign jurisdictions in affairs of personal laws. The future fate of similar matters must not be sealed with an incorrect precedent. Sovereignty of Indian law must prevail.

POCSO – A Child Law in Oblivion*

> ***"There is no trust more sacred than the one the world holds with children. There is no duty more important than ensuring that their rights are respected, that their welfare is protected, that their lives are free from fear and that they can grow up in peace – KOFI ANNAN"***

THE PROBLEM

With the repeated string of rape of children being reported across the nation and a public outcry raging on the streets like molten lava flowing uncontrolled from a bursting volcano, the victimised and abused child suffers in silence. Traumatised, dejected and horrified family members of unfortunate victims find themselves helpless, confused and unable to cope up with the heinous crime. Even though on 22 May, 2012, the Parliament passed the Protection of Children against Sexual Offences Act, 2012 (POCSO) and which came into force on 14 November, 2012, this special law to protect children from offences of sexual assault, sexual harassment and pornography, remains an unimplemented law, unknown to most and beyond knowledge or information of those who need to apply it. Sadly, the result is that POCSO, an Act, which is a necessity in India where 40 percent of the population is below the age of 18 and where over 53 percent of children reportedly surveyed in 2007 stated that they had experienced one or more forms of sexual abuse, is not complied with despite being on the statute book. Rhetoric demands stiff penalties, expeditious new laws and fast track courts little realising that POCSO, as a wholesome law already says it all.

---

* *Hon'ble Mr. Justice J.S. Verma breathed his last on 22 April, 2013. This article is a humble tribute devoted to the memory of Late Justice J.S. Verma, who as Chairman of The Committee on Amendments to Criminal Law furnished an exemplary time bound report to provide for quick trial and enhanced punishment for criminals committing sexual assault of extreme nature. Chapter 7 of the Report of Justice Verma Commission was devoted to child sexual abuse and reportedly "the first - person stories of young girls and a boy traumatised by years of sexual exploitation were so gut- wrenching that Justice Verma and his two colleagues broke down and wept." Today, Justice Verma Committee's salutary report is chronicled as a landmark exposition of human rights and he will be fondly remembered for his great work. May his soul rest in peace.*

POCSO AND ITS CONTENT

Until recently, various provisions of the Indian Penal Code (IPC) were used to deal with sexual offences against children as the law did not make a distinction between an adult and a child. POCSO deals with sexual offences against persons below age of 18 years. A child has been defined as a person below the age of 18 years. POCSO defines "Penetrative sexual assault," "sexual assault" and "sexual harassment" making the offence aggravated if it is committed by a police officer, public servant, staff member of jail, remand, protection or observation home, staff of a hospital or an educational institution or by a member of the armed or security forces. POCSO provides for relief and rehabilitation as soon as the complaint is made to the Special Juvenile Police Unit or the local police who are required to make immediate arrangements for care and protection. The intent to commit an offence defined under POCSO is also punishable besides abetment or aiding the sexual abuse of a child. Special emphasis has been provided for trial in special children's courts with speedy disposal and special procedures to avoid child not seeing accused at time of testifying.

AWARENESS OF POCSO

Despite POCSO laying down that the Central and State Governments shall take measures to give wide publicity through media including television, radio and print media and imparting periodic training to all stake holders on the matters relating to implementation of provisions of POCSO, the Act is relatively unknown. Shockingly, in the present most recent unfortunate rape case, the Delhi Police included the provisions of POCSO to the FIR reportedly after two days of the filing of the FIR on 15 April, 2013. In the infamous APNA GHAR Rohtak shelter home case of May 2012, despite rampant allegations of child sexual abuse of over 100 inmates, reportedly, the provisions of POCSO are still not stated to have been invoked against the accused. Most child sex abuse cases are not booked under POCSO. Child sex offenders get away despite a stringent law. The Act is unknown. Indoctrination, training, familiarisation and actual application by police officers and other stake holders still remains a far cry. POCSO remains an Act of law in oblivion.

A STEP FORWARD

The passing of the salutary law is more than significant for a variety of reasons. It defines exclusively the crime of sexual offences against children and fulfils the mandatory obligations of India as a signatory to the United Nations Convention on the Rights of The Child, acceded to on December 11, 1992. For monitoring and implementation of the provisions of POCSO, the Act enjoins that the National Commission and State Commissions for Protection of Child Rights constituted under the Commissions for Protection of Child Rights Act, 2005 shall ensure the effective carrying out of the provisions of POCSO. The Supreme Court in hard hitting directions on 7 February and 16 December, 2013 reported as *Re: Exploitation of Children in Orphanages in the State of Tamil Nadu* v. *Union of India,* (2014) 2 SCC 180 and (2014) 2 SCC 193, has directed that all States are to ensure that the regulatory and monitoring bodies are constituted and made functional. However, till date, the fully functional Commissions are non-existent or effectively non-functional.

A LANDMARK JUDGMENT

Upon the National Commission for Protection of Child Rights (NCPCR) petitioning the Punjab and Haryana High Court, in a path breaking judgment rendered on 9 April, 2013, reported as *NCPCR* v. *State of Haryana* 2013 (3) RCR (Cri) 298, it has been directed that the States of Punjab and Haryana as well as Union Territory of Chandigarh shall ensure, that, State Commissions for Protection of Child Rights headed by a Chair person who should be a person who has been a Judge of the High Court, shall become fully functional by appointing Chairpersons and six members appointed through a transparent selection process. The High Court has further directed mandatory registration of all children homes, constitution and notification of children's courts and appointment of special public prosecutors besides constituting a proper selection committee to make further selections of various committees to be set up for child welfare. Hence, the entire machinery of monitoring child rights has been galvanised. A further direction has been issued that the National Commissions and State Commissions shall start discharging their functions under POCSO for implementing its provisions and modules/training programmes for sensitizing all stake holders on child rights and for dealing with cases in Children's Court be also initiated in the Chandigarh Judicial Academy. It is now for the State Governments to implement this beneficial mandate and create an effective machinery to check heinous crimes of gross sexual abuse against children by enlightening all concerned about it. It is the duty of the State to now perform its obligations for the welfare of society.

THE NET EFFECT

The report of Justice Verma *Committee on Amendments to Criminal Law* in one of its conclusion on child sexual abuse holds *"there is an urgent need to audit the performance of all institutions of governance and law and order. It is indeed necessary that we must now have external social audit for the sake of transparency. We also wish to make it clear that every case of a missing child must be registered as FIR"*. The Committee further make suggestions of constituting "an oversight mechanism" through the High Court, special training needs programmes, sensitizing officials on sexual abuse of children and strict implementation of provisions of various enactments of child laws. Summing up, we need to consolidate our efforts and focus our energies on existing laws and not look to amending more laws and making still further newer laws, alien to our culture, society, habits, life styles and harsh realities of the common man. In so far child sex abuse is concerned, POCSO is a wholesome law. The Government must create the machinery to implement it and educate its officers besides all stake holders on what it contains. The remedy to handle the public outcry is by implementing POCSO. All child offenders must be charged, tried and punished in accordance with POCSO expeditiously. Speedy, stringent and relentless pursuit of POCSO is the remedy and a possible cure. The State must not waste its time in exploring alternatives when the answers exists in a law made by Parliament for these special offences against children, the most vulnerable section of society. Today's children are tomorrow's future. Let us protect them. The laudable endeavours of Late Justice Verma must find implementation.

CHILD FRIENDLY PROCEDURES ARE INCORPORATED IN POCSO

Recording the statement of the child at the residence of the child or at the place of his choice, preferably by a woman police officer not below the rank of sub-inspector. Evidence has to be recorded within 30 days.

- No child to be detained in the police station in the night for any reason.
- Police officer to not be in uniform while recording the statement of the child.
- The statement of the child to be recorded as spoken by the child.
- Assistance of an interpreter or translator or an expert as per the need of the child.
- Child not to see accused at the time of testifying. The evidence of the child shall be recorded within a period of 30 days of the cognizance of the offence.
- Assistance of special educator or any person familiar with the manner of communication of the child in case child is disabled.
- Medical examination of the child to be conducted in the presence of the parent of the child or any other person in whom the child has trust or confidence.
- In case the victim is a girl child, the medical examination shall be conducted by a female doctor.
- Child not to be called repeatedly to testify and frequent breaks to be given to the child during the trial.
- No aggressive questioning or character assassination of the child.
- Trial to be held in the special court *in camera.*

A New Child Law in the Making – A Positive Step

Repeal of the Juvenile Justice (Care and Protection of Children) Act, 2000 and re-enactment of The Juvenile Justice (Care and Protection of Children) Bill, 2014.

The Juvenile Justice (Care and Protection of Children) Act, 2000, relating to juveniles/ children in conflict with law besides dealing with children in need of care and protection have been amended earlier twice in 2006 and 2011. The further demands for amendments to the Juvenile Justice (Care and Protection of Children) Act, 2000 (56 of 2000) (JJ Act) have been in the reckoning again in 2012. After the unfortunate Delhi Gang-rape case, the juvenile who was the prime accused was given the maximum three year tenure imprisonment in a correctional home under the JJ Act. A public outcry agitated a more stringent punishment for this principal offender. Moreover, violence witnessed against juveniles themselves, is also emerging as an alarming issue required to be redressed on priority by strengthening of existing provisions in a new enactment through introduction of new clauses in the fresh Act.

The Apex Court in a public interest litigation decided on March 28, 2014, in *Dr. Subramanian Swamy* v. *Raju*, JT 2014 (4) SC 328, refused to read down the provisions of Juvenile Justice Act, 2000, in order to account for the mental and intellectual competence of a juvenile offender and refused to interfere with the age of a juvenile accused, in cases where juveniles were found guilty of heinous crimes. It was held by the Court that the provisions of the Act are in compliance with the Constitutional directives and international conventions. The Court further directed that the classification of juveniles as a special class stood the test of article 14 of the Constitution of India, and that it should restrict itself to the legitimacy and not the certainty of the law.

The Government of India is now contemplating amendments to the Act by repealing the existing JJ Act, 2000 and re-enacting a new JJ Act, 2014 for which a review committee has been constituted under the Ministry of Women and Child Development (WCD), Government of India.

The WCD Ministry has posted on its website a proposed draft of the the Juvenile Justice (Care and Protection of Children) Bill, 2014 suggesting broad amendments and enacting fresh better provisions for the welfare of the children in the following areas needing urgent legislative action:

(a) Increase in reported incidents of abuse of children in institutions, families and communities;

(b) Inadequate facilities, quality of care and rehabilitation measures in private and Government run children Homes;

(c) Delays in various processes under the JJ Act, such as decisions by Child Welfare Committees (CWCs) and Juvenile Justice Boards (JJBs) leading to high pendency of cases relating to juveniles;

(d) Delay in inter country adoption process under Central Adoption Resource Agency (CARA);

(e) Inadequate provisions to deal with offences against children;

(f) Provisions related to juveniles in conflict with law, in the age group of 16 to 18 years etc.

(g) The Draft JJ Act incorporates the principles of the Hague Convention on Protection of Children and Cooperation in Respect of Inter-Country Adoption (1993) which was absent in the original JJ Act, 2000.

The proposed JJ Bill, 2014 seeks to make the following provisions of law:

The JJ Bill, 2014 seeks to enact a law to consolidate and amend the law relating to children in need of care and protection by catering to their developmental needs through proper care, protection and treatment, and by adopting a child friendly approach in the adjudication and disposal of matters in the best interest of children and for their ultimate rehabilitation through processes provided, and institutions established, under the proposed new enactment.

The new JJ Bill, 2014 provides for application of the proposed Act in the following cases and matters:

(i) cases involving detention, prosecution or penalty of imprisonment;

(ii) matters or processes relating to apprehension, production before court, disposal orders and restoration, and

(iii) procedures and decisions related to adoption of children and rehabilitation and reintegration of children, in conflict with law or, as the case may be, in need of care and protection, under such other law.

It also defines an "abandoned child" as well as "aftercare", unlike the present enactment. According to the draft, an "abandoned child" means a child deserted by his biological or adoptive parents or guardians, who has been declared as abandoned by the Committee after due inquiry. Further, "aftercare" means provision of support, financial or otherwise, to young adults, who have completed the age of eighteen years but have not completed the age of twenty-one years, and have left institutional care, to help them to join mainstream society.

The draft bill also provides for a definition for "best interest of Child", "Central Adoption Resource Authority", "Chief Medical Officer", "child friendly", "child legally free for adoption", "open shelter", "Child Welfare Officer", "corporal punishment" and many others required for effective implementation of the proposed Act.

The word 'juvenile' is replaced with the word 'child' and the expression 'juvenile in conflict with the law' has been changed to 'child in conflict with law'. The responsibility affixed on the 'child' differs to the extent that while the JJ Act, 2000 defines juveniles in conflict with law as the 'accused', the Draft Bill, 2014 identifies a 'child in conflict with law' to be a child who is found by the Juvenile Justice Board to have actually committed an offence

Chapter II is the most noteworthy characteristic of the proposed Bill which provides for "Fundamental Principles for Care, Protection, Rehabilitation and Justice for Children". It incorporates internationally accepted principles of presumption of innocence, dignity and worth, participation, best interest, family responsibility, safety (no harm, no abuse, no neglect, no exploitation and no maltreatment), positive measures, non-stigmatizing semantics, non-waiver of rights, equality and non-discrimination, privacy and confidentiality, repatriation and restoration, fresh start, diversion and natural justice. Institutionalization as a measure of last resort is suggested if no other family based care option is possible or available.

The functions and responsibilities of the Juvenile Justice Board have also been defined clearly, keeping in mind the best interest of the child. Draft section 10 defines the role of the custodian of child in conflict with law and draft section 11 provides the conditions for bail of a child alleged to be in conflict of law.

Draft section 14 provides for inquiry by the JJ Board into commission of specific offences by a child who has completed 16 years of age. The inquiry, for offences alleged to have been committed under sections 302, 326A, 376, 376A or section 376D of the Indian Penal Code is provided to be committed within a month of the appearance of the child before the JJ Board.

With regard to the said specific offences, draft section 19 bars capital punishment or life imprisonment without the possibility of release, for any such offence, either under the provisions of this Act or under the provisions of Indian Penal Code.

Under section 17 of the draft Bill there is a provision for children in conflict with law who have attained 16 years of age who have committed an offence to be lodged in a Special Home, if the Board is satisfied that the offence is of serious nature or that the child's conduct and behaviour has been such that it would not be in the child's interest, or in the interest of other children housed in a special home, to send such child to the special home; or if the child is a habitual offender, or if the person is above eighteen years of age at the time of final orders; the JJ Board may order such child or person to be kept in a place of safety and in such manner as it thinks fit and the period of detention so ordered shall not exceed in any case the maximum period provided for under this Act.

Section 24 of the draft Bill includes provision with respect to a run-away child in conflict with law and section 28 of the draft Bill provides for the functions and responsibilities of the Child Welfare Committee.

Draft section 30 of the JJ Bill, 2014 provides for mandatory reporting in case of a child found separated and non-compliance is declared as an offence under section 32 of the draft Bill with an imprisonment up to 6 months, or fine of Rs. 10,000 or both.

Section 30 of the draft Bill provides for the provisions for surrender of a child and clearly defines, providing for a surrender deed before the Committee. An entire draft section 35 with regard to orders that can be passed regarding a child in need of care and protection has been added. This section provides for declaration of the child as being in need of care and protection and makes provision for restoration, placement, sponsorship, foster-care and draft section 37 of the Bill provides for a declaration of child as legally free for adoption. However, under section 36 of the draft Bill the committee is not empowered to pass adoption orders or resolve custodial matters in a marital dispute.

Under section 41 of the draft Bill, a penalty for non-registration of institutions housing children is provided and a penalty for non-registration is provided by imposition of punishment of imprisonment for 1 year or a fine of 1 lakh rupees or both.

Under section 42 of the draft Bill, the State Government is empowered to establish and maintain by itself or through voluntary or non-governmental organizations, as many "Open Shelters" as required.

Unlike the current JJ Act, 2000, section 42 of the draft Bill provides for a detailed procedure to place the child under foster care, and empowers the State Government to make rules for defining procedure, criteria and manner for providing foster care services. Draft section 45 of the Bill provides for the provision for after care of young adults leaving institutional care, along with rehabilitation and re-integration services in institutions registered under the Act.

Chapter VIII of the draft Bill deals with Adoption. Section 58 of the draft Bill lays down special emphasis on inter-country adoptions. It states that all applications for adoption by prospective adoptive parents shall be filed before a Principal Magistrate of the concerned jurisdiction where the specialised and registered adoption agency is located. However, the proposed provision for adoption orders to be passed by the Principal Magistrate on the first date of hearing itself or within a period of two weeks, failing which it will be construed by the higher authority of the Principal Magistrate, "as dereliction of duty" does not seem to be practical, realistic and possible for actual implementation. Judicial proceedings have to be regulated by the Code of Civil Procedure and hence, no short circuit fast track procedure by passing rules of evidence etc., can be proposed in contravention of law.

Sections 67-69 of the draft Bill gives a detailed insight into the functioning of the Central Adoption Resource Authority (CARA) which has been made a statutory body vested with functions of in-country and inter-country adoptions besides issuing guidelines on adoption as also carrying out the functions under the Hague Convention on protection of children.

Defining other offences against children in Chapter IX of the draft Bill, section 74 prohibits the media from disclosing the identity of children or propagating any such information which would lead to the same. All reports relating to the child are also provided to be treated as confidential under section 100 of the draft Bill. Sections 75 and 76 of the draft Bill relates to punishment for cruelty to child as also punishment for employment of child for begging. Corporal punishment and ragging is also made punishable under sections 82 and 83 of the draft Bill. Sections 80 and 81 of the draft Bill provide for punitive measures for adoption without following the proper procedure, as well as sale or procurement of children for any purpose.

Hence, the draft Bill provides a comprehensive mechanism to deal with children in conflict with law as well as children who are in need of care and protection. The issue of inter country adoption and the role of CARA has been simplified and made very comprehensive. The JJ Act, 2000 had been amended twice, in 2006 and 2011, but the amendments have never been these transparent or non-cumbersome. The Draft Bill, 2014 is an excellent comprehensive draft which is the need of the day. Rights of children of all categories need urgent attention, simplification and expeditious disposal. Any delay or insensitive handling of the rights of children must be remedied. The draft Bill is a positive step in that direction. The framers of the draft Bill have done well. The Ministry has invited comments over the draft till July 3, 2014. It is hoped that positive suggestions will come from all concerned to help in making the proposed enactment a better law for the welfare of children and juveniles.

Juveniles and Children in Conflict – A New Law

A BACKDROP

The Juvenile Justice (Care and Protection of Children) Act, 2000 (JJ Act), relating to juveniles and children in conflict with law, besides dealing with children in need of care and protection, has been amended earlier twice in 2006 and 2011. The further demands for amendments to the JJ Act have been in the reckoning again. After the unfortunate Delhi Gang-rape case in 2012, the juvenile, who was the prime accused, was given the maximum three year tenure imprisonment in a correctional home under the JJ Act. A public outcry agitated a more stringent punishment for this principal offender. Moreover, violence witnessed against juveniles themselves, is also emerging as an alarming issue which is required to be redressed on priority by strengthening of existing provisions in a new enactment. Cumbersome, protracted and technical inter-country adoption procedures in the existing JJ Act need urgent legislative resolution for over 12 million orphan children needing homes. Personal laws provide adoptions to its respective communities. Other persons can become only guardians under an archaic 125 year old Guardians and Wards Act, 1890. A secular gender free adoption law for all persons, irrespective of marital status and gender, answering the recent Supreme Court mandates is a clarion call to be heard and implemented. Now is the time to do it.

In *Stephanie Joan Becker*, (2013) 12 SCC 786, a single 53 year old lady was permitted to adopt a female orphan child aged 10 years by relaxing the rigor of the guidelines of CARA on the totality of the facts of the case that the proposed adoption would be beneficial to the child as the experts were of the view that the adoption process would end in successful blending of the child in the US. Likewise, in *Shabnam Hashmi* v. *Union of India*, (2014) 4 SCC 1, the Apex Court upholding the recognition of the right to adopt and to be adopted as a fundamental right has held that every person, including Muslims, irrespective of the religion they profess is entitled to adopt a child. The latest verdict of the Supreme Court in *National Legal Services Authority* v. *Union of India*, (2014) 5 SCALE 1 recognising transgender as the third gender have held *"that discrimination on the basis of sexual orientation or gender identity includes any discrimination, exclusion, restriction or preference, which has the effect of nullifying or transposing equality by the law or the equal protection of laws guaranteed under our Constitution.*" The Judgment in *Jan Balaz* v. *Anand Municipality,* AIR 2010 Guj 21, is under challenge in the Supreme Court by way of SLP (Civil) No. 31639 of 2009; *Union of India* v. *Jan Balaz,* where the twin German children born through surrogacy were granted an exit permit on Supreme Court directions to CARA to permit their adoption by German parents. Yeoman judicial innovation must be legislatively recognised. Rightly so, the Government of India is now contemplating amendments to the JJ Act by repealing the existing JJ Act, 2000 and re-enacting a new JJ Act, 2014 for which a review committee has been constituted under the Ministry of Women and Child Development (WCD), Government of India. The call for suggestions and comments in public domain to the draft Juvenile Justice (Care and Protection of Children) Bill, 2014, having sadly gone un-noticed, a brief overview for generating a thought perception is a must. A major change in child jurisprudence is evolving . All citizens must know of it. An umbrella child law legislation for current needs today must unravel with public participation on meaningful suggestions for Parliamentarians.

The Apex Court in a public interest litigation decided on March 28, 2014, in *Dr. Subramanian Swamy* v. *Raju,* JT 2014 (4) SC 328, refused to read down the provisions of Juvenile Justice Act, 2000, in order to account for the mental and intellectual competence of a juvenile offender and refused to interfere with the age of a juvenile accused, in cases where juveniles were found guilty of heinous crimes. It was held by the Court that the provisions of the Act are in compliance with the Constitutional directives and international conventions. The Court further directed that the classification of juveniles as a special class stood the test of article 14 of the Constitution of India, and that it should restrict itself to the legitimacy and not the certainty of the law. The baton has been passed on to the Parliament to finish the relay race in time by enacting a new law.

THE NEW BILL

The JJ Bill, 2014 seeks to enact a law to consolidate and amend the law relating to children in need of care and protection by catering to their developmental needs through proper care, protection and treatment, and by adopting a child friendly approach in the adjudication and disposal of matters in the best interest of children and for their ultimate rehabilitation through processes provided, and institutions established, under the proposed new enactment.

The WCD Ministry has posted on its website a proposed draft of The Juvenile Justice (Care and Protection of Children) Bill, 2014 suggesting broad amendments and enacting fresh better provisions for the welfare of the children in the following areas needing urgent legislative action:

(a) Increase in reported incidents of abuse of children in institutions, families and communities;

(b) Inadequate facilities, quality of care and rehabilitation measures in private and Government run children Homes;

(c) Delays in various processes under the JJ Act, such as decisions by Child Welfare Committees (CWCs) and Juvenile Justice Boards (JJBs) leading to high pendency of cases relating to juveniles;

(d) Delay in inter country adoption process under Central Adoption Resource Agency (CARA);

(e) Inadequate provisions to deal with offences against children;

(f) Provisions related to juveniles in conflict with law, in the age group of 16 to 18 years etc.

(g) The Draft JJ Act incorporates the principles of the Hague Convention on Protection of Children and Cooperation in Respect of Inter-Country Adoption (1993) which was absent in the original JJ Act, 2000.

The new JJ Bill, 2014 provides for application of the proposed Act in the following cases and matters:

(i) cases involving detention, prosecution or penalty of imprisonment;

(ii) matters or processes relating to apprehension, production before court, disposal orders and restoration, and

(iii) procedures and decisions related to adoption of children and rehabilitation and reintegration of children, in conflict with law or, as the case may be, in need of care and protection, under such other law.

A FLEETING GLIMPSE

The word 'juvenile' is replaced with the word 'child' and the expression 'juvenile in conflict with the law' has been changed to 'child in conflict with law'. The responsibility affixed on the 'child' differs to the extent, that while the JJ Act, 2000 defines juveniles in conflict with law as the 'accused', the Draft Bill, 2014 identifies a 'child in conflict with law' to be a child who is found by the Juvenile Justice Board to have actually committed an offence. It also defines an "abandoned child" as well as "aftercare", unlike the present enactment. According to the draft, an "abandoned child" means a child deserted by his biological or adoptive parents or guardians, who has been declared as abandoned by the Committee after due inquiry. Further, "aftercare" means provision of support, financial or otherwise, to young adults, who have completed the age of eighteen years but have not completed the age of twenty-one years, and have left institutional care, to help them to join mainstream society. Chapter II is the most noteworthy characteristic of the proposed Bill which provides for "Fundamental Principles for Care, Protection, Rehabilitation and Justice for Children". It incorporates internationally accepted principles of presumption of innocence, dignity and worth, participation, best interest, family responsibility, safety (no harm, no abuse, no neglect, no exploitation and no maltreatment), positive measures, non-stigmatizing semantics, non-waiver of rights, equality and non-discrimination, privacy and confidentiality, repatriation and restoration, fresh start, diversion and natural justice. Institutionalization as a measure of last resort is suggested if no other family based care option is possible or available.

NEW ADDITIONS

A new procedure for handling children in conflict with law and orders to be passed is proposed. A revamped Child Welfare Committee is identified, empowered and given statutory functions for orders to be passed for children in need of care and protection beside rehabilitation and social integration. Mandatory registration of child care institutions is provided with strict penalty for non-registration. Observation, shelter and special homes may be established by State Governments.

CARA has been made a statutory body vested with functions of in-country and inter-country adoptions besides issuing guidelines on adoption as also carrying out the functions under the Hague Convention on protection of children. Section 58 of the draft Bill lays down special emphasis on inter-country adoptions. It states that all applications for adoption by prospective adoptive parents shall be filed before a Principal Magistrate of the concerned jurisdiction where the specialised and registered adoption agency is located. However, the proposed provision for adoption orders to be passed by the Principal Magistrate on the first date of hearing itself or within a period of two weeks, failing which it will be construed by the higher authority of the Principal Magistrate, "as dereliction of duty" does not seem to be practical, realistic and possible for actual implementation. Judicial proceedings have to be regulated by the Code of Civil Procedure and hence, no short circuit fast track procedure by-passing rules of evidence can be proposed in contravention of law. Like wise, transgenders need adoption rights as much as parents having children born through surrogacy , till suitable independent laws vest appropriate rights. The JJ Bill must encompass these issues, which are as of now missing in the Bill.

The proposed Bill prohibits the media from disclosing the identity of children or propagating any such information which would lead to the same. All reports relating to the child are also provided to be treated as confidential. The draft Bill provides punishment for cruelty to a child, as also prescribes punishment for employment of child for begging. Corporal punishment and ragging is also made punishable under the draft Bill besides providing for punitive measures for adoption without following the proper procedure, as well as sale or procurement of children for any purpose.

The draft Bill provides a comprehensive mechanism to deal with children in conflict with law as well as children who are in need of care and protection. Private unregistered child care homes abusing, exploiting and selling children will be in the net. The issue of inter country adoption and the role of CARA has been simplified and made very comprehensive. The JJ Act, 2000 had been amended twice, in 2006 and 2011, but the amendments have never been these transparent or non cumbersome. The Draft Bill, 2014 is an excellent comprehensive draft which is the need of the day. Rights of children of all categories need urgent attention, simplification and expeditious disposal. Any delay or insensitive handling of the rights of children must be remedied. The draft Bill is a positive step in that direction. The framers of the draft Bill have done well. However, only if enacted, a stringent implementation can provide a meaningful disposition to make it a true letter of law. As of now, the dire need for legislative intervention is required. Any delay or insensitive handling of rights of children must be remedied. The draft Bill is a positive step in that direction. Its framers have done well. Children deserve it.

HUMAN SMUGGLING

HUMAN SMUGGLING

- Curbing Flights of Fancy – A Law to Curb Illegal Immigration from Punjab
- Emigration Act, 1983 – A Need for Dire Change
- Human Rights, Illegal Immigrants and the Law
- Roots of Human Smuggling – The Malady and the Cure
- A False Euphoria – Lessons not Learnt from Iraq

Curbing Flights of Fancy – A Law to Curb Illegal Immigration from Punjab

THE PROBLEM

With the merchants of death running thriving rackets of human smuggling in Punjab at the cost of gullible youth trapped everyday with dollar dreams, the waiting worsens the plight of duped innocent citizens and this organized crime perpetuates horror and misery flourishing with daring impunity. Smuggled migrants are vulnerable to exploitation and their lives are often put at risk. They have suffocated in containers, perished in deserts, drowned at sea or herded as forced labour in slave camps. Smugglers of migrants conduct their activities brazenly without fear or favour with no regard for human life. Survivors tell harrowing tales of their ordeal, forced to sit in human waste, deprived of food and water, while others around them die and their bodies are dumped at sea or on road sides. The smuggling of migrants generates high net worth profits at the hands of criminals who fuel corruption and organized crime. The smuggling of migrants is a deadly business that must be combated as a matter of grave urgency and happily Punjab is the first State ready to combat it.

THE PROPOSED SOLUTION IN THE NEW LAW

The Punjab Prevention of Human Smuggling Act, 2012, now known as the Punjab Travel Professional Regulation Act, 2012, is described as a law to provide for the regulation of the profession of travel agents with a view to check and curb their illegal, fraudulent activities, and malpractices of the persons involved in organized human smuggling in the State of Punjab and for the matters connected therewith or incidental thereto. This new law has nine noteworthy features.

- √ **It defines human smuggling and travel agent. It applies to travel agents, coaching institutes of IELTS, ticketing agents and general sales agents of airlines.**
- √ **Provides for a licensing regime for travel agents. Debars persons from operating without a license under the Act. Requires licence number to printed in any advertisement or permission to be sought if unlicenced.**

- √ **Gives power of search, seizure and arrest to Magistrates and Police Officials.**
- √ **Prescribes power of investigation by DSP to be completed within two months and to be verified by S.P./SSP to be Nodal Officer for all investigations under the Act. Prior verification of complaint to be done by Deputy Commissioner from Additional Deputy Commission and Sub Division Magistrate concerned.**
- √ **In addition to imposing penalties, provides award of reasonable compensation to be paid to aggrieved person by travel agent.**
- √ **Identifies defined variable punishment for offences under the Act which may be extended upto 7 years.**
- √ **Authorises Courts to decide whether any illegally acquired property is liable to be confiscated.**
- √ **Provides for liability of Director, Manager, Secretary of Companies responsible for conduct of business when negligence can be attributed.**
- √ **Cheating shall have the same meaning as under the Indian Penal Code.**

"**Travel Agent**" is defined as a person in a profession that involves arranging, managing or conducting affairs related to sending people abroad. It includes consultancy for permanent emigration, obtaining education, work, travel for tourism, cultural entertainment or musical shows, medical treatment, spreading or preaching religion, participating in sport tournaments, issuing advertisements for travel, holding seminars and lectures to promote emigration, arranging matrimonial alliances for purposes of emigration, and arranging overseas travel for any purpose whatsoever. Dishonest misrepresentation with intention to have wrongful gain for inducing, deception, cheating or allurement for above activities is punishable under the Bill. If any travel agent wants to advertise or hold seminars, he will have to notify the competent authority in writing giving complete details of advertisement of seminars. It does not include recruitment agents carrying on the business of recruitment who are governed and registered under the provision of the Emigration Act, 1983

THE GRAVE END

Naive youth fell prey to agents and landed up working as slave labour in ammunition dumps or fields in Iraq or end up condemned to live as illegal immigrants abroad in pitiable conditions with no hope of return if they manage to survive hazardous channels of death. Smuggling of migrants is a highly profitable business with a low risk of detection. For criminals, it is increasingly attractive to deal in human merchandise and this business of death is becoming more and more organized, in which professional international networks wantonly flourish transcending global borders and regions. India, as a nation, therefore, has a dire need to check this global menace. However, sadly, the Emigration Act, 1983, which is an Act to consolidate and amend the law relating to Emigration of citizens of India, neither defines human smuggling nor even looks at the problems connected with this deathly trade. Thus, the need for Parliament to legislate a Indian Human Smuggling law is a crying need. Piecemeal state legislations with limited ambit of application will restrict scope only to State territorial borders. A Central law is therefore, the composite solution. Initiatives of Parliament must set this ball rolling. Till then, any State legislation on the subject would be a welcome take off point and the Government of Punjab deserves kudos for this innovative pioneer excellent effort.

CENTRAL LAW IN EXISTENCE

The Emigration Act, 1983 provides for checks, controls, balances by enacting a licensing regime for "recruiting agents," for "emigration" purposes which find definition in the following words in the said Act.

- "Recruiting Agent" means a person engaged in India in the business of recruitment for an employer and representing such employer with respect to any matter in relation to such recruitment including dealings with persons so recruited or desiring to be so recruited.
- "Emigrate and Emigration" means the departure out of India of any person with a view to taking up any employment (whether or not under an agreement or other arrangements to take up such employment and whether with or without the assistance of a recruiting agent or a employer) in any country or place outside India.

The Emigration Act, 1983, creates a "Protector of Emigrants" for providing emigration clearance to ensure that conditions of employment of Indian citizens are not discriminatory, exploitative, unlawful, against public policy, violative of norms of human dignity & decency, besides, do not prescribe sub-standard working or living conditions. The ambit of the Act extends to Indian citizens only and exempts control of recruiting in India for service of foreign States. Clearly, the regulatory provisions of the Central Act, provides beneficial legislation to reign in Indian recruiting agents operating in India.

NEW PUNJAB LAW IN CONTRAST

In contrast, the Punjab Travel Professionals Regulation Act, 2012, enacted to provide a licensing regime for travel agents with penal provisions, has similar regulatory functions to check human smuggling. The words "travel agent" and "human smuggling" in the Punjab Act, find definition in the following words:

"**Travel Agent**" means a person doing the profession which involves arranging, managing or conducting affairs relating to sending persons abroad or which arise out of the affairs of persons sent to a foreign country, and shall include a range of activities covering diverse practices .

"**Human Smuggling**" shall mean and include illegally exporting, sending or transporting persons out of India by receiving money from them or their parents, relatives or any other persons interested in their welfare, by inducing, alluring or deceiving or cheating.

It is further stated in the Punjab Act, that "cheating" shall have the same meaning as assigned to it in sections 415 and 416 of the Indian Penal Code, 1860. Therefore, the Punjab Travel Professionals Regulation Act, 2012, looks at the menace of human smuggling by defining it as an offence and creates a process for its regulatory enforcement by compulsory registration and imposition of punishment upon violations through a legal process prescribed in the Punjab Act.

CONCLUSION

Hence, placing both the Acts *i.e.*, the Emigration Act, 1983 and the Punjab Travel Professionals Regulation Act, 2012, side by side clearly shows that they enshrine regulatory mechanisms for recruiting agents and travel agents separately. Viewed objectively, both carry complimentary purposes in their own spheres. They are neither inconsistent nor repugnant to each other. In fact, the two laws compliment each other as they provide similar objectives, aims and functions for recruiting and travel agents respectively. Punjab has enacted a law which no other State in the country has made. In fact, human smuggling is a silent issue in the Emigration Act. Thus, even though the subjects of both enactments relating to criminal law, criminal procedure, actionable claims, employment related issues etc., are in the Concurrent list and only Emigration is in the Union list of the 7th Schedule of the Indian Constitution, the State of Punjab is within its rights to enact a Human Smuggling Law for Punjab. Under article 246(1), the prerogative of the Parliament to legislate extends exclusively to the subject of Emigration prescribed in the Union list, whereas, for the aforesaid remaining subjects, article 246(2) of the Constitution, empowers the Punjab State to legislate on the remaining matters which are in the Concurrent list of the Constitution. There is thus, no legislative overreach and the Punjab law is enacted validly. Punjab supplements but does not supplant any existing Central law. The authority of law vested in the State must be exercised to enforce this law. Punjab will proceed with its own initiative and lead the nation in its yeoman spirit.

PUNJAB PREVENTION OF HUMAN SMUGGLING ACT, 2012, NOW KNOWN AS THE PUNJAB TRAVEL PROFESSIONAL REGULATION ACT, 2012

➢ *The Punjab Prevention of Human Smuggling Act, 2012, now known as The Punjab Travel Professional Regulation Act, 2012, passed by the Punjab Vidhan Sabha on 21 December, 2012 and implemented upon Notification in the Punjab Government Gazette on 20 August, 2013, is as an Act to provide for the regulation of the profession of travel agents with a view to check and curb their illegal, fraudulent activities, and malpractices of the persons involved in organized human smuggling in the State of Punjab and for the matters connected therewith or incidental thereto. This law has nine noteworthy features.*

√ **It defines human smuggling and travel agent.**

√ **Provides for a licensing regime for travel agents. Debars persons from operating without a license under the Act. Applies to travel agents, coaching institutes of IELTS, ticketing agents and general sales agents of airlines.**

√ **Gives power of search, seizure and arrest to Magistrates and Police Officials.**

- √ **Prescribes power of investigation by DSP to be completed within two months and to be verified by S.P. SSP to be Nodal Officer for all investigations under the Act.**
- √ **In addition to imposing penalties, provides award of reasonable compensation to be paid to aggrieved person by travel agent.**
- √ **Identifies defined variable punishment for offences under the Act.**
- √ **Authorises Courts to decide whether any illegally acquired property is liable to be confiscated.**
- √ **Provides for liability of Director, Manager, Secretary of Companies responsible for conduct of business when negligence can be attributed.**
- √ **Cheating shall have the same meaning as under the Indian Penal Code.**
- ➢ ***Travel agent is defined as a person in a profession that involves arranging, managing or conducting affairs related to sending people abroad.***
- √ It includes consultancy for permanent emigration, obtaining education, work, travel for tourism, cultural entertainment or musical shows, medical treatment, spreading or preaching religion, participating in sport tournaments, issuing advertisements for travel, holding seminars and lectures to promote emigration, arranging matrimonial alliances for purposes of emigration, and arranging overseas travel for any purpose whatsoever except for business of recruitment governed by registration under provision of the Emigration Act, 1983
- √ Dishonest misrepresentation with intention to have wrongful gain for inducing, deception, cheating or allurement for above activities and cheating by personation is punishable under the Act as having same meaning as IPC. If any travel agent wants to advertise or hold seminars, he will have to notify competent authority in writing with complete details of advertisement of seminars.
- ➢ ***The words "travel agent" and "human smuggling" in the Punjab Act, find definition in the following words:***
- √ "Travel Agent" means a person doing the profession which involves arranging, managing or conducting affairs relating to sending persons abroad or which arise out of the affairs of persons sent to a foreign country, and shall include a range of activities covering diverse practices.
- √ "Human Smuggling" shall mean and include illegally exporting, sending or transporting persons out of India by receiving money from them or their parents, relatives or any other persons interested in their welfare, by inducing, alluring or deceiving or cheating.

HIGHLIGHTS OF THE EMIGRATION ACT, 1983

- ➢ **The Emigration Act, 1983 provides for checks, controls, balances by enacting a licensing regime for "recruiting agents," for "emigration" purposes which find definition in the following words in the said Act.**

- √ **"Recruiting Agent" means a person engaged in India in the business of recruitment for an employer and representing such employer with respect to any matter in relation to such recruitment including dealings with persons so recruited or desiring to be so recruited. Recruiting agents doing business of recruitment have to obtain compulsory registration under the Emigration Act, 1983.**
- √ **"Emigrate and Emigration" means the departure out of India of any person with a view to taking up any employment (whether or not under an agreement or other arrangements to take up such employment and whether with or without the assistance of a recruiting agent or a employer) in any country or place outside India.**

CURBING FLIGHTS OF FANCY NEW PUNJAB PREVENTION OF HUMAN SMUGGLING RULES, 2013

Travel agencies, ticketing agents and immigration consultants will now be regulated under a licencing regime created under the Punjab Prevention of Human Smuggling Rules, 2013. It has been made mandatory that all persons falling under the definition of "travel agent" must register their business with District Magistrates all over Punjab notified on 3 September, 2013, as competent authorities for granting licences before 30 November, 2013. The Punjab Prevention of Human Smuggling Act, 2012, a first of its kind, was enacted on 21 December, 2012 to check and curb malpractices of organised illegal immigration and related fraudulent activities resulting in repeated tragic loss of human life and property.

EXISTING CENTRAL LEGISLATION

The Emigration Act, 1983, a law made by Parliament, consolidated and amended the law relating to Emigration of citizens of India. It applies only to *"recruitment"* and *"recruiting agents"* for whom the registering authority is the *Protector General of Emigrants (PGE)*. Under section 10 of the Emigration Act, 1983, no person can function as a *recruiting agent* to commence or carry on the business of recruitment unless registered with the PGE. Further, under section 15 of the Emigration Act, 1983, all *recruiting agents* carrying on the business of recruitment are required to be obtain a *permit* from the *Protector General of Emigrants*. Hence, this Act applies only to *recruitment* and *recruiting agents.*

A DIFFERENT CENTRAL LAW

The Emigration Act, 1983 (EA) is a law to consolidate and amend the law relating to emigration of citizens of India. All the recruiting agents or employers working in any place are duty bound to follow the provisions laid down under the EA, before carrying on or conducting the business of sending people outside India on the pretext of jobs or employment outside India. The recruiting agents or employers not working as per the EA are unlicensed and unauthorised. A Protector of Emigrants is appointed in every State and a Protector General of Emigrants functions at New Delhi under the EA. Both the Protector of Emigrants and the Protector General of Emigrants work under the authority of the Ministry of Overseas Indian Affairs (MOIA). The recruiting agents or employers in a

State before commencement and carrying on business of recruitment or overseas employment needs to get a valid registration certificate and a permit which is issued by the Protector of Emigrants in their respective States. Without getting any such registration certificate or a valid permit, the recruiting agent or employer cannot legally conduct the business or send any person abroad. As per the website of The MOIA, www.poeonline.gov.in, where a list of registered recruiting agents registered under the EA is maintained, there are only 47 recruiting agents currently registered in the State of Punjab under the EA. Sadly, lack of a strict law neither made nor enforced by the Government of India keeps the noose away.

UNDEFINED AGENTS

The words *"travel agent"* and *"human smuggling"* are not defined under the EA or under any other law made by Parliament. There are thousands of consultants in the State of Punjab who function under the banner or name of various kinds of agents and indulge in the unethical rackets of sending persons abroad by different means and practices. Such agents deny that they conduct the business of *recruitment* or *recruiting agents* and hence claim that the provisions of the EA do not apply to them. Those working under the law are outwitted Therefore, the illegal business of human smuggling is unchecked in Punjab and thousands of gullible youth are misled daily by unscrupulous agents who cheat them with impunity. All such unlicensed and unauthorized agents are not governed by any law and there is no check or control on them by virtue of the EA whose dragnet is evaded by them. Since such agents or consultants claim that they do not do the business of recruitment or are recruiting agents. Hence, they do not get registered under the EA or take any permit under the EA.

NEW INITIATIVE

The Government of Punjab is the first State in the country which has enacted the Punjab Prevention of Human Smuggling Act, 2012, now known as the Punjab Travel Professional Regulation Act, 2012, to provide for the regulation of the profession of travel agents with a view to check and curb their illegal and fraudulent activities, and malpractices involved in the organized human smuggling in the State of Punjab. This law has nine noteworthy features not covered by any existing Indian law.

- √ **It defines human smuggling and travel agent.**
- √ **Provides for a licensing regime for travel agents. Debars persons from operating without a license under the Act. Licence number to be printed in advertisement by a travel agent.**
- √ **Gives power of search, seizure and arrest to Magistrates and Police Officials.**
- √ **Prescribes power of investigation by DSP to be completed within two months and to be verified by S.P./SSP to be Nodal Officer for all investigations under the Act. Complaint in the first instance may be verified by the Deputy Commissioner or Additional Deputy Commissioner or Sub Division Magistrate concerned.**

- √ **In addition to imposing penalties, provides award of reasonable compensation to be paid to aggrieved person by travel agent.**
- √ **Identifies defined variable punishment for offences under the Act which may be extended upto 7 years.**
- √ **Authorises Courts to decide whether any illegally acquired property is liable to be confiscated.**
- √ **Provides for liability of Director, Manager, Secretary of Companies responsible for conduct of business when negligence can be attributed.**
- √ **Cheating shall have the same meaning as under the Indian Penal Code.**

Travel agent is defined as a person in a profession that involves arranging, managing or conducting affairs related to sending people abroad. It includes consultancy for permit emigration, obtaining education, work, travel for tourism, cultural entertainment or musical shows, medical treatment, spreading or preaching religion, participating in sport tournaments, issuing advertisements for travel, holding seminars and lectures to promote emigration, arranging matrimonial alliances for purposes of emigration, and arranging overseas travel for any purpose whatsoever. Dishonest misrepresentation with intention to have wrongful gain for inducing, deception, cheating or allurement for above activities is punishable under the Act. If any travel agent wants to advertise or hold seminars, he will have to notify the competent authority in writing giving complete details of advertisement of seminars.

JUSTIFICATION FOR NEW RULES

The licensing regime of travel agents is a positive step of the Government of Punjab in registering travel agents who otherwise have no law to check and control them. All such consultants, travel agents and other such persons or institutions carrying on business of sending persons abroad evade the definition of recruitment and recruitment agent under the EA and hence do not take any registration or permit under the EA. Hence all such travel agents and consultants cannot be registered with the Protector General of Emigrants under the EA. Therefore, the Punjab Prevention of Human Smuggling Act, 2012, now known as the Punjab Travel Professional Regulation Act, 2012, is a positive, healthy, productive and citizen oriented legislation meant for protecting the rights of the susceptible citizens of Punjab whose rights and valuable assets are protected by this well meaning law. A dire need has been fulfilled to create a separate machinery and mechanism for registering the travel agents and consultants under the Punjab Prevention of Human Smuggling Act, 2012, now known as the Punjab Travel Professional Regulation Act, 2012. There is no duplication or overlapping of powers with the EA and no conflict arises between the two laws which can have separate mechanisms for implementation. However, the Punjab law, a welcome move, will have jurisdictional constraints. The Parliament in its wisdom could consider enacting a Central law whose umbrella will protect and shield the entire nation from the unscrupulous activities of human smugglers. Trading in human lives for commercial gains must be obliterated.

HIGHLIGHTS – PUNJAB PREVENTION OF HUMAN SMUGGLING RULES, 2013

- *Punjab Prevention of Human Smuggling Rules, 2013 for regulating the trade of travel agencies or consultancies and ticketing agents were notified on August 20, 2013 and provide for a licensing regime through notified competent authorities.*
- *By notification dated September 3, 2013, District Magistrates/Additional District Magistrates of each district have been designated as the "Competent Authority" for issuing a licence to undertake the profession of a travel agent.*
- *Applications for licences to be accompanied by fee of Rupees one lac for agents in existence for more than five years, Rs. 25,000 for less than five years and Rs. 25,000 for ticketing agents. Records in electronic form and soft copies to be kept by agents.*
- *Residence certificates, proof of age, identity, passport, PAN card, Income Tax Returns, bank statements, satisfaction of credibility and no criminal record to accompany applications. For NRI agents, social security number, permission of foreign country of operations and RBI sanction additionally to be furnished.*
- *Applicants must not be insolvent or bankrupt, should have no involvement in crimes as per police records, should not hold office of profit, should not be barred by Agents Associations, must have adequate space or accommodation and must maintain records and fee charged by them to be furnished to State Government.*
- *Licences to be issued for five years, renewable upon furnishing Income Tax Return and Statement of Bank Accounts. Refusal to grant or renew license appealable to Government. All activities of agents to be monitored under the new rules.*
- *All illegally acquired property to be confiscated upon trial of offences under the law*

Emigration Act, 1983 – A Need for Dire Change

TRADE OF HUMAN BEINGS

Today, manpower export, legally called human smuggling or in local parlance called *kabootarbazi* is the most profitable trade which requires no technical skill, no educational or professional qualification, no financial investment and least but not the last has no fear of any law, checking, punishment or criminal action. *Smuggling of Migrants from India to Europe and in particular to UK: A Study on Punjab and Haryana,* a report released by the United Nations Office on Drugs and Crime (UNODC) in March 2010, based on extensive research revealed that over 20,000 youths from Punjab attempt irregular migration every year and that sub agents who sponsor this activity had proliferated in rural areas in Punjab, Haryana, Himachal Pradesh and Jammu Kashmir. Sadly, despite concrete remedial suggestions for curbing this human trade merchandise having been suggested in the UNODC report, nothing at all seems to have been done by any State or Central Government. The result is inevitable, gullible, innocent and foreign crazy youth board flights to fantasy land fuelled by dreams weaved by unscrupulous and unethical agents, which often lead them to misery, slavery and sometimes even death whilst law sleeps in its slumber.

LAW ON THE SUBJECT

The Emigration Act, 1983 (EA) was the culmination of the Supreme Court Orders in *Kanga* v. *Union of India,* WP2632/1978, decided on March 20, 1997, handed down in 1979 by the Apex Court and which resulted in the amendment of the Emigration Act, 1922. Today, under the EA, a notified Protector of Emigrants (POE) in a State, overseen by a Protector General of Emigrants (PGOE) at the Centre, is statutorily bound under the EA to ensure that no person functions as a recruiting agent without a registration certificate and that no employer shall conduct recruitments for foreign employment without a valid permit to be issued by the POE. The POE in turn under the EA must must protect and aid all intending emigrants with advice and support. Every recruiting agent has a mandate under the EA to maintain registers, records, besides file returns and the PGOE/POE exercising powers of the Civil Court can check, monitor, requisition and enforce compliance which is punishable on contravention with powers of suspension or cancellation of permits on violation. Factually, how much of this is observed or followed, does not need any guesses or answers.

OUTDATED LAW

The EA supported by Emigration Rules, 1983 providing the complete procedural machinery remains a paper law since the violation of the EA, flouted with impunity, has neither any redressal nor any remedy. Catchy advertisements in English and vernacular newspapers, gaudy display signboards and a potent pitch of illegal immigration abroad are galore promising treasures at the end of the rainbow in foreign countries. There is no regulation, rule, policy or law to check unethical and misleading advertisements. The innocent victims are not even aware of the compulsory registration and licensing permit scheme prescribed by the EA which they ought to check before they dole out exorbitant sums generated by selling, mortgaging or pawning land, jewellery or valuable assets. Once, shipped out illegally to Gulf or European destinations, the terrorized and duped youth lose their passports, their dignity and self respect and sometimes their lives, if not living a life of misery, shame and destitution abroad having no face or identity to return back home.

This unlawful human smuggling business is propelled by a large number of illegal immigration/emigration companies openly advertising their wares without any registration certificate or a permit/license required under the EA. These attractive advertisements carry no detail of registration or work permit numbers of the advertisers. Most such unethical individuals or firms operate under the guise of a consultancy company which needs no registration. No law monitors their misleading advertisements or checks their websites. Huge amounts of money transacted in cash change hands for illegally sending youths abroad under promised work permits without any covering safeguards prescribed under the EA. The performance of statutory duties of the POE under the EA are non existent. Nobody checks this flourishing business but everybody reads horror stories of innocent victims who are duped and defrauded. The existing EA law has teeth but no poison in its fangs. Thus, under the EA, there are no checks, inspections, penalties, suspensions or cancellations ever reported. The EA remains a dead letter law without implementation

LAW IN THE MAKING

The Government of Punjab in its far fetched wisdom passed the Punjab Prevention of Human Smuggling Act, 2012, now known as the Punjab Travel Professional Regulation Act, 2012, in the sitting of the Punjab Vidhan Sabha held on December 21, 2012, in an attempt to be the first State to define Human Smuggling and check all appurtenant malpractices associated as ancillary evils. This new law has met with suggestions from Central Government Ministries and reportedly, the amended Act was passed by the Punjab legislature in the subsequent sessions. Till then, *status quo* continues and victims of this tragic trade meet their fatal fates because of the lack of a similar law for the rest of the country.

The enactment of the Punjab law alone will not serve the purpose, if achieved in the first place, as all human smuggling traders will shift their operations out of Punjab to escape the wrath of this law in the making. A Central law to be enacted by Parliament is thus, the crying need of the day. The existing EA neither defines nor punishes human smuggling or illegal immigration. None of the evils of this unethical trade which has proliferated in society as a deadly virus has no befitting legal antidote under any existing law. Thus, the Government of India may seriously have to consider enacting an All India legislation or drastically amending the EA to take cognizance of malpractices which ails society daily in this unethical trade of human beings. This cancer spreading into lives of youth unless checked, will do irreparable damage. Law must not wait any longer.

PARALLEL CHANGES

To wean the youth from boarding unchartered illegal flights abroad, vocational training leading to self employment or creating means of livelihood are an absolute necessity if they are to be tied down by an anchor back home. At the same time, it should be a prime Government duty to generate official manpower overseas placement bureaus which legitimately permit overseas employment under legal and channelized safeguards. Simultaneously, educating youth with the pitfalls of human smuggling and immigrating the right way is an absolute necessity. Social thinking must be changed to educate all citizens to adapt to legal methods for emigration. All foreign embassies now arm themselves on their websites with educative and informative material routing applications through Visa Facilitation Services (VFS). Education curriculums in schools, colleges and universities must expose youth to these as a necessary learning part in their educative process. The media too must carry these messages. NGOs and socially spirited individuals must translate these empowered methods in vernacular languages appropriately. This combined and composite plan should be a prime agenda in the interest of the nation and society at large. No waiting is prescribed or recommended. Parliament too, must rise to the call and act for enacting a beneficial law to cap human smuggling.

EMIGRATION ACT – NEED FOR DIRE CHANGE

THE PROBLEM IN SUMMARY

- WTO Study says that India is seventh largest country in the world with a population of over1.1 billion people which accounts for 16.7% of the world population.
- About 30 million persons of Indian origin live in 130 countries abroad. 400,000 Indians immigrate every year to foreign destinations.
- Interpol study "Marco Polo" reports that India is one of the countries accounting for the largest number of illegal immigrants coming to Western Europe and UNODC has commissioned a special study on this issue.
- The UNODC report on "Smuggling of migrants from India to Europe and in particular to UK: A study on Punjab and Haryana 2009]" released in Chandigarh on 11 March, 2010, quotes that over one lakh illegal immigrants from India are behind bars in foreign jurisdictions and over 20,000 youths from Punjab alone attempt irregular immigration every year.

⇨ A multi-million dollar illegal immigration racket where 20,000 to 30,000 USD is charged by unscrupulous agents to send gullible Indians abroad flourishes in India, unabated and unchecked. Three examples are cited:

  ▫ In 1996, 289 South Asians including 170 Indians from Punjab found a watery grave in the Ionian Sea in their voyage of illegal immigration to Europe.

  ▫ UNODC quoted Indian-American Centre for Political Awareness in U.S.A. informs that 73 men from Punjab duped by employment agents in Punjab landed in Tehran after a 1500 mile journey on foot. They were frost-bitten and their toes had to be amputated.

  ▫ On June 24, 2007, Indian Police apprehended an agent with 300 fake travel documents including 25 forged passports, 114 fake visas of Schengen countries and duplicate passports with fake identities.

⇨ UNODC committed to combating global human trafficking estimates that about 2 million migrants cross international borders without authorization every year. The reasons for this in India are high population growth, increasing unemployment rate, quest for a better economic life and for improvement in status besides seeking professional growth in life.

⇨ U.K. Visas in India deals with over 500,000 applications every year and over 300,000 visas are issued every year. 80% illegal immigration from India takes place from Punjab. Over 500,000 illegal immigrants from India live in U.K. alone & thousands from Punjab attempt to sneak into U.K. every year.

⇨ The problem is not in Punjab alone. About 400,000 illegal workers from Andhra Pradesh without passports, travel documents or visas live in labor camps in UAE desperate to be jailed to enable their official return to India.

SOLUTION PROPOSED

The urge for illegal migration cannot be curbed. The need for managed migration needs to be channelized and the necessity for sustainable solutions requires to be explored. Legalized, managed, integrated and organized migration must be opted for. The only way of migration by legal means must be publicized.

SUGGESTIONS:

The suggested solutions possible are:

√ a comprehensive approach on migration setting out legal migration opportunities on selective and managed migration

√ migration profiling

√ regularization of over stay (and not amnesty) besides short term visas

√ comprehensive policy determination by categorization of classes of visas

- √ A two – fold approach can be seen in the Indian context in the perspective of India where managed migration is currently in experimental stages. Two set of ideologies can be drawn:
- √ Practicing promotion of managed migration
- √ Regulation of illegal migration.
- √ Both follow an educative thought oriented process.
- √ An active Government participation is a must for effective resolution of managed/illegal migration at operational levels in both these schools of thought.

Human Rights, Illegal Immigrants and the Law

This article highlights the return of illegal Indian immigrants who are languishing in jails abroad and have no means, resources or travel documents to return to India. In terms of the law laid down by the Apex Court in ***Satwant Singh Sawhney* v. *A.P.O., New Delhi,* AIR 1967 SC 1836**, holding that deprivation of passports amounts to infringement of right to personal liberty under article 21 of the Constitution and that right to travel abroad includes the right to return to India, all such Indian citizens detained abroad are entitled to emergency travel documents under section 4(2) of the Passports Act, 1967 read with rules 3 & 4 of the Passport Rules, 1980.

As per a report of The United Nations Office on Drugs and Crime (UNODC) on "Smuggling of Migrants from India to Europe and in particular to UK: A Study on Punjab and Haryana, 2009" which was released in Chandigarh on March 11, 2010, it is quoted that over one lac illegal immigrants from India have been caught by foreign police authorities and are behind bars in foreign jurisdictions. The report quotes that according to statistics sourced from the Ministry of External Affairs, over one lac residents of six districts of Punjab *i.e.*, Jalandhar, Nawanshahar, Gurdaspur, Amritsar, Hoshiarpur and Kapurthala, faced deportation from different countries for not travelling on valid travel documents during the last five years. The report also states that every year more than 20,000 youths from Punjab attempt irregular migration which is now spreading to the neighbouring States of Haryana etc.

A joint reading of various provisions of the Passports Act, 1967, amply clarifies that emergency certificates authorising an Indian citizen to enter India can be issued in exceptional and urgent cases for a period not exceeding 12 months. These provisions also provide that after doing so, the applications of such cases can be transferred to the concerned Indian Passport Authority having jurisdiction in the territory where such person who has been issued emergency certificates ordinarily resides. Before doing so, the antecedents, parental family, permanent residence and all other details of parentage of such Indian citizens from the respective States in India can be established.

The Protection of Human Rights Act, 1993 defines "human rights" in section 2(d) as follows;

"(d) human rights means the rights relating to life, liberty, equality and dignity of the individual guaranteed by the constitution or embodied in the International Covenants and enforceable by Courts in India."

Likewise, International Covenants in section 2(f) is defined as follows;

"(f) International Covenants means the International Covenant on Civil and Political Rights and the International Covenant on Economic, Social and Cultural Rights adopted by the General Assembly of the United Nations on the 16th December, 1966."

Article 6(1) of the International Covenant on Civil and Political Rights, 1966 is quoted hereunder for ready reference;

"Article 6(1) – Every human being has the inherent right to life. This right shall be protected by law. No one shall be arbitrarily deprived of his life."

It may also be relevant to quote articles 3 and 5 of the Universal Declaration of Human Rights, 1948, which provide for the Protection of Life and Human Rights of Human beings in the following words;

"Article 3 – Every one has the right to life, liberty and security of person."

"Article 5 – No one shall be subjected to torture or to cruel, inhuman or degrading treatment or punishment."

As per the UNODC report, more than one lac persons from India are reportedly detained in jails abroad of foreign jurisdictions after having travelled abroad illegally. Such Indian citizens are unfortunate victims of unscrupulous travel agents who have duped and defrauded them to travel by illegal means. These Indian citizens having been arrested and detained in foreign jurisdictions on being detected and caught have no resources, documents, financial or legal aid. They have no means of contact with their well wishers and families in India. In such a situation, they have lost their self respect, dignity and liberty and they are in no situation to secure their personal liberty by any legal or administrative means. The respective Consular offices of the Indian Embassies/ High Commissions abroad can come to the aid and rescue of such illegal Indian immigrants to aid and assist in their return home. The International Covenants quoted above clearly establish that such Indian citizens have a right to secure their liberty, respect and dignity. Article 21 of the Constitution also secures such right to life and personal liberty to them.

These gullible, innocent and unfortunate victims of human smuggling have been left to the mercy of fate. No tangible steps have been taken by the Government of India to secure their release and help them to return to India despite the matter having been publicized in the media over two years ago. There is no future hope of their release. International instruments, covenants and Indian legislation besides basic human rights warrants their release and return to India. The provisions of the Passports Act and Rules made thereunder clearly establish that all such Indian detenues abroad can be permitted to return on emergency travel documents upon verification of their antecedents by the respective State Governments.

An exercise has been conducted to review lists of black listed non-resident Indians who could not return to India on account of alleged offences said to have been committed by them. Such an exercise is also possible in the case of illegal immigrants detained abroad who wish to return to India being Indian citizens. Government of India can seek information regarding such detained Indian nationals from the respective Embassies/High Commissions in India where such persons have immigrated illegally. Upon such list being obtained from the foreign embassies/High Commissions in India, the States Governments can be asked to verify the antecedents and particulars of such Indian citizens. Thereafter, the Consular section of the Indian Embassies/High Commissions abroad in such foreign jurisdictions can grant them emergency travel documents to enable their return to India. These emergency certificates can be issued under the provisions of the Passport Act. In this way, the entire exercise can be conducted in the larger interest of Protection of human life and personal liberty guaranteed under articles 14, 19 and 21 of the Constitution, besides the International instruments quoted above.

If the above exercise is conducted, it will be a very big deterrent to future illegal immigrants who are proposing to travel abroad unlawfully. Moreover, even unethical and unscrupulous agents will be deterred by this process. State of Punjab has taken a task of enacting the Punjab Prevention of Human Smuggling Bill, in an attempt to end this menace. It is reported that this legislation is pending approval of the Government of India. In this backdrop, it can be mulled that even Government of India may seriously consider enacting an All India Legislation for the entire territory of India to make humans smuggling and human trafficking a punishable offence. The existing Emigration Act, 1983 neither defines nor punishes Human Smuggling or Human Trafficking and it is the need of the day that some possible law may be enacted to deal with this human problem in an attempt to stop the illegal trafficking of human beings. Traffickers of human merchandise cannot be allowed to trade in human beings. This menace must stop in the interest of human rights, civil liberties and fundamental rights.

Roots of Human Smuggling – The Malady and the Cure

The Social Problem

It is estimated that there were more than 10,000 Indian workers in the strife torn nation of Iraq in June 2014. Over 40 of these unfortunate young men from Punjab and Himachal Pradesh were reportedly trapped after being abducted as hostages, besides 201 other Punjabis and 112 youths from Haryana were stranded in a war zone in Iraq. Likewise, 700 of these migrants from Telangana were also in dire straits. 46 were nurses from Kerala and Tamil Nadu, who were stuck, but safe. Though, serious efforts were underway to secure their safety and return, a serious introspection was required to deliberate on the moot question as to why, how and when such gullible Indian citizens are trapped by unscrupulous agents with Dollar dreams of lucrative jobs in exchange for hefty fees. An ineffective Emigration Act, 1983 (EA) does little to remedy this situation. Sad, but true, palatial multicolour bungalows with water tanks shaped as footballs or mini aircrafts dot the skyline in the rural landscape of Punjab, propelling unguided youth to fall prey to hefty earnings on foreign shores for magically owning similar homes. Tall promises of unethical travel agents assuring astronomical earnings overseas to build similar castles in the air, vanish and evaporate in actual reality when innocent young denizens land up as bonded labour in captivity in Gulf countries or are made to work for a pittance, huddled like cattle with no documents. Most of these unfortunate victims reached Iraq from Dubai via Qatar and Kuwait through devious Indian travel agents, who work in connivance with illegal employment syndicates operating from Gulf Countries for luring these hapless youngsters. On one occasion, hundreds of Punjabi youths were clearing ammunition, bombs and mines from uncultivated Iraqi fields.

Central Law in Existence

The EA, which is an Act to consolidate and amend the law relating to Emigration of citizens of India applies only to *"recruitment"* and *"recruiting agents"*. Registration and obtaining permits are essential under the EA from a State *Protector of Emigrants* working under a *Protector General of Emigrants* (PGE) under the Ministry of Overseas Indian Affairs. Without getting any such registration certificate or a valid permit, no recruiting agent or employer can legally conduct this business or send any person abroad. On actual ground, reality is a far cry. Punjab has only 47 recruiting agents, and Andhra Pradesh has 46 such agents registered under the EA. Ironically, neither the word *"travel agent"*, nor the phrase *"human smuggling"* are defined or identified in the EA, which neither recognises this proliferating business of human trading nor seeks to check or punish it. All such nefarious traders escape the noose claiming that they do not need any registration or work permit under the EA as they do not conduct the business of recruitment and are thus not "recruiting agents". Law, thus, looks the other way. The illegal business of human smuggling is unchecked. Youth are cheated daily with impunity. A travel agent needs no educational qualification, no experience, no office or business premises and no registration or regulation under any law. Human lives are at stake. Regardless, the statute books silently watch the vacuum in law.

Punjab Leads the Way

The Government of Punjab is the first State in the country which has enacted the Punjab Prevention of Human Smuggling Act, 2012, now known as the Punjab Travel Professional Regulation Act, 2012, with supporting rules of 2013, to provide for the regulation of the profession of travel agents with a view to check and curb their illegal and fraudulent activities, as also to penalise malpractices involved in the organised human smuggling rackets flourishing in the State of Punjab. No other State has made any similar or other enactment, even though the problem afflicts all like a plague. This state law has 9 noteworthy features:

- √ **It defines human smuggling and travel agent. It applies to travel agents, coaching institutes of IELTS, ticketing agents and general sales agents of airlines.**
- √ **Provides for a licensing regime for travel agents. Debars persons from operating without a license under the Act. Requires licence number to printed in any advertisement or permission to be sought if unlicenced.**
- √ **Gives power of search, seizure and arrest to Magistrates and Police Officials.**
- √ **Prescribes power of investigation by DSP to be completed within two months and to be verified by S.P./SSP to be Nodal Officer for all investigations under the Act. Prior verification of complaint to be done by Deputy Commissioner from Additional Deputy Commission and Sub Division Magistrate concerned.**
- √ **In addition to imposing penalties, provides award of reasonable compensation to be paid to aggrieved person by travel agent.**
- √ **Identifies defined variable punishment for offences under the Act which may be extended upto 7 years.**
- √ **Authorises Courts to decide whether any illegally acquired property is liable to be confiscated.**
- √ **Provides for liability of Director, Manager, Secretary of Companies responsible for conduct of business when negligence can be attributed.**

√ **Cheating shall have the same meaning as under the Indian Penal Code.**

"**Travel Agent**" is defined as a person in a profession that involves arranging, managing or conducting affairs related to sending people abroad. It includes consultancy for permanent emigration, obtaining education, work, travel for tourism, cultural entertainment or musical shows, medical treatment, spreading or preaching religion, participating in sport tournaments, issuing advertisements for travel, holding seminars and lectures to promote emigration, arranging matrimonial alliances for purposes of emigration, and arranging overseas travel for any purpose whatsoever. Dishonest misrepresentation with intention to have wrongful gain for inducing, deception, cheating or allurement for above activities is punishable under the Act. If any travel agent wants to advertise or hold seminars, he will have to notify the competent authority in writing giving complete details of advertisement of seminars. It does not include recruitment agents carrying on the business of recruitment who are governed and registered under the provision of the Emigration Act, 1983

No Over-reach

Placing both the Acts, i.e., the Emigration Act, 1983 and the Punjab Prevention of Human Smuggling Act, 2012, now known as the Punjab Travel Professional Regulation Act, 2012, side by side clearly shows that they enshrine regulatory mechanisms for recruiting agents and travel agents separately. Viewed objectively, both carry regulatory functions in their own spheres. They are neither inconsistent nor repugnant to each other. In fact, the two laws complement each other as they provide similar objectives, aims and functions for recruiting and travel agents in separate compartments respectively as independent legislations. Since, in 1983, when the EA was enacted, human smuggling was never contemplated or visualized, the EA does not cover this subject, Punjab has enacted a law which no other State in the country has made. In fact, human smuggling is a silent issue in the Emigration Act. Even though the subjects of enactments relating to laws regarding professions, welfare of labour, education, employment related issues etc., are in the Concurrent list and only Emigration is in the Union list of the 7th Schedule of the Indian Constitution, the State of Punjab is within its rights to enact a Human Smuggling Law for Punjab under powers enjoyed under the Concurrent List. Even if such activity is termed as trade, the State Government, under the State List, is empowered to legislate on Human Smuggling. Under article 246(1), the prerogative of the Parliament to legislate extends exclusively on the subject of Emigration only as prescribed in the Union list. Whereas, for the aforesaid remaining subjects, article 246(2) of the Constitution, empowers the Punjab State or any other State Government to legislate on the remaining matters which are in the Concurrent list of the Constitution. There is thus, no legislative overreach and the Punjab law is enacted validly. Punjab supplements but does not supplant any existing Central law. The authority of law vested in the State must be exercised to enforce this law. Punjab will proceed with its own initiative and lead the nation in its yeoman spirit. All others may choose to follow suit for resolving the human problem.

THE GRAVE END

Naive youth fall prey to agents and land up working as slave labour in ammunition dumps or fields in Iraq or end up condemned to live as illegal immigrants abroad in pitiable conditions with no hope of return if they manage to survive hazardous channels of death. Smuggling of migrants is a highly profitable business with a low risk of detection. For criminals, it is increasingly attractive to deal in human merchandise and this business of death is becoming more and more organized, in which professional international networks wantonly flourish transcending global borders and regions. India, as a nation, therefore, has a dire need to check this global menace which is now a deathly trade. Thus, the need for Parliament to legislate an Indian Human Smuggling law is a crying need. Piecemeal State legislations with limited ambit of application will restrict scope only to State territorial borders. A Central law is therefore, the composite solution. Initiatives of Parliament must set this ball rolling. Till then, any State legislation on the subject would be a welcome take off point and the Government of Punjab deserves kudos for this innovative pioneer and excellent effort.

A False Euphoria – Lessons Not Learnt from Iraq

CURRENT DIMENSIONS

A horror story with shades of the Kandahar hijack incident and hostage exchange for release of terrorists has been circumvented. A *potpourri* of diplomatic parleys, Union Government intervention and active association of Malayalee businessman, pitched in with divine invocation, worked in tandem. This ordeal over, 46 Indian nurses released from captivity by Islamic State of Iraq and Syria (ISIS) militants, will be flown back to India in a special Air India flight along with 70 other Indians who wish to flee Iraq. The tale has not ended. The saga has just begun. The fate of 40 other Indian denizens mostly hailing from the north, reportedly in captivity of the Jihadi militant groups, still remains sealed on the first Friday of Ramzan. About ten thousand Indian workers struggle for existence in strife torn Iraq. How, when, where and through whom will they come back. How will India ensure their safety and security. Nobody knows. More channels and bridges in gulf nations will continue negotiations for hopeful release of those held captive. Till then we wait and we fervently pray. For some, propelled by poverty and despair, it is a point of no return.

THE PROBLEM

The sad chronicle is not of Punjab alone. Andhra, Tamil Nadu, Kerala and Karnataka pitch in their fair share. Reportedly, more than four lac nurses from Kerala work abroad and about one thousand are still said to be in Iraq. Exploitation is writ large. Thousands form Punjab add on. The diaspora of 30 million NRIs in 180 nations is swelling. Some have prospered. Others are devastated. Economic necessity, exploitation by unscrupulous agents and foreign demands glitter the path to the patch of grass which is not green on the other side. A 2012 Irregular Migration CARIM India study supplementing a 2009 report of UNODC reveal a flourishing immigration carrier – agent racket fleecing between rupees two to ten lacs for paving passages to hell with forged travel documents, fictitious employment promises and miserable living conditions. Day in and day out, more and more gullible Indian youth fall prey. Coercive exploitation, perpetuated misery and human rights abuses are rampant. No law checks them, nobody regulates this human smuggling trade and blissfully the merchants of death carry on their trade fearing none and defying all.

STUDY ON THE SUBJECT

The 2012 CARIM-India outlines *"the modus operandi of agents include jacket substitution, photo substitution in Indian and foreign passports, re-stitching and tampering of passports, use of forged and stolen visas, use of forged residence permits, employment visas and fabricated seals or stamps, exchange of boarding cards at security areas in airports, tutoring to claim asylum and encouraging over stay on tourist visas"* as commonly used methods for illegal immigration. Agents involved in this deathly trade of irregular migration are reported to work in collaboration with links of international chains emanating from the country of origin to transit to destination points with fee being shared at different levels. Sub-agents at the lowest hierarchy at village levels scout for semi-literate and unemployed youth for national level primary agents who liase with an international chain. The report reveals *"Punjabi fascination for alien shores translates into a fanatical mania bordering on suicidal desperation, tragic tales of illegal immigration, of unrequited ambition, of dreams turning sour, of precious lives lost, are written and re-written. Even today, an average Punjabi youth would go to any lengths, bear any costs and adopt any means – legal or illegal – to cross the seven seas to start a new life in a new country. The faster the law catches up , the more ingenuous he becomes. With each dawn, his mind devises newer means to immigrate. Immigration is a natural way of growth, both for the individual and the nations. Illegal immigrants are ready to brave anything, hide as stowaways in tankers or trucks, trek for several days at a stretch, bear frostbites lose limbs, starve, risk detention and serving jail terms, be exiled to live in Gurudwaras or be caught and shot by mercenaries."* The list goes on. The horror story is endless.

PAST EXPERIENCES

The Malta boat tragedy in 1996 saw 170 Indians, of which 88 were Punjabi youth drowning in the Ionian sea in their unsuccessful venture to immigrate illegally to Greece. Even their bodies were not recovered. In 2011, about 100 Punjabi youth, sold to American agents were held in captivity. Under the watchful eyes of AK 47 toting guards, they were forced to clear explosives from agricultural fields in which remnants of the 2003 Gulf war *i.e.*, bombs, rockets, shells, missiles, cartridges and other ammunition were scattered. With bare hands, these youth were made to run after tractors which unearthed these deadly explosive materials and thereafter physically pick them up to clear the fields for plantation. With a herculean effort and upon High Court intervention, their lives were spared and they reached back home. They were trained as para legal brand ambassadors to educate others not to follow the beaten path leading to despair. Regardless, history repeats itself. The trade flourishes with impunity. Tragic memories are short lived. All those who returned, venture again at risk of their lives. Nobody stops them. Agents send them through the tunnels of death with impunity, fearing no law or authority to check them.

AN INEFFECTIVE LAW

Whilst, precious human lives are traded like commercial merchandise by human smugglers, law looks the other way. The Emigration Act, 1983, (EA) which is an Act to consolidate and amend the law relating to emigration of citizens of India applies only to *"recruitment"* and *"recruiting agents"* for whom the registering authority is the *"Protector of Emigrants"* (POE) who also issues permits for this business. The Ministry of Overseas Indian Affairs website www.poeonline.gov.in indicates 47 recruiting agents registered in Punjab under this Act. Whilst advertisements of agents, consultants and employers in every vernacular newspaper are galore of every possible job, employment, contract or work position, every such individual claims to be a *"consultant"* and not a *"recruiting agent"* doing recruitment. Thus, all such *pseudo* agents claim immunity from registration or taking permits under the EA. A flaccid checking mechanism under the EA lets them get away. The Union Government does not look at human smuggling as an offence under this law. Hence, the long arm of law neither looks, nor thinks of catching up with these human sharks.

A NEW STATE LAW

The Government of Punjab is the first State in the country which has enacted The Punjab Travel Professionals Regulation Act, 2012, as amended in 2014 (previously known as The Punjab Prevention of Human Smuggling Act, 2012), with supporting rules of 2013, to provide for the regulation of the profession of travel agents with a view to check and curb their illegal and fraudulent activities, as also to penalise malpractices involved in the organised human smuggling rackets flourishing in the State of Punjab. No other State has made any similar or other enactment, even though the problem afflicts all like a plague. This State law has 12 note-worthy features:

- √ **It defines human smuggling and travel agent including all ticketing agents. It applies to travel agents, coaching institutes of IELTS, ticketing agents and general sales agents of airlines.**
- √ **Provides for a licensing regime for travel agents. Debars persons from operating without a license under the Act. Requires licence number to printed in any advertisement or permission to be sought if unlicenced.**
- √ **Provides licence numbers to be quoted in all advertisements of agents.**
- √ **Gives power of search, seizure and arrest to Magistrates and Police Officials.**
- √ **Complaints to be first verified by Deputy Commissioner or his nominee.**
- √ **Prescribes power of investigation by DSP to be completed within two months and to be verified by S.P. SSP to be Nodal Officer for all investigations under the Act.**
- √ **In addition to imposing penalties, provides award of reasonable compensation to be paid to aggrieved person by travel agent.**
- √ **Identifies defined punishment for offences under the Act which may be extended upto 7 years.**
- √ **Authorises Courts to decide whether any illegally acquired property is liable to be confiscated.**

√ **Provides for liability of Director, Manager, Secretary of Companies responsible for conduct of business when negligence can be attributed.**

√ **Cheating shall have the same meaning as under the Indian Penal Code.**

√ **Punishment depending on the crime or offence committed.**

CHINKS IN THE ARMOUR

Sadly, even though this benevolent legislation provides succour to the much needed cancerous ailment of regulating the profession of travel agents and consultants as a lawful solution, the implementation of this new law remains a far cry. It is agitated that the State Government is not competent to make this law and only Parliament can enact a law on this subject. Hence, either way, the agents and consultants wish to escape the net be it the EA or the Punjab Travel Professionals Regulation Act, 2012. Hence, while the law remains in limbo, the racket flourishes with no ethics.

A POSSIBLE SOLUTION

Where then does the solution lie. The remedy, whether in Andhra Pradesh, Tamil Nadu, Punjab or Kerala, is the same. The youth and their families need to be educated about the pitfalls of illegal migration. Also, meaningful sources of self employment or vocational avenues at home need to be identified and publicised. It is time the Parliament seriously contemplate enacting a composite law defining human smuggling. The long arm of the law must reach out to capture those who indulge in this business of human trading. Meanwhile, be it a consultant, an agent or a immigration professional, all must register, take permits and be bound by regulatory ethical practices. All those who indulge in clean practices in this business must realise that those who register will have credibility against those who do not and ultimately all illegal, unethical and unregistered agents will phase out. People will realise that only those who are registered and permitted can deal with them. It is thus for the consultants and agents to themselves realise the benefits of the State law. However, it is time that Parliament too delve in this subject to realise that the euphoria is short lived. The long term solution is legislation to rein and herd in all concerned. Changing times show an emergence of a new professional activity. Law requires that they be regulated. The 1983 EA has out lived its utility. It must be replaced with a new law. More human lives cannot be put to stake. We must learn from Iraq. Otherwise, the bubble will burst again and a crisis will proliferate again.

MARRIAGE & DIVORCE

MARRIAGE & DIVORCE

- A Secular Marriage Registration Law
- Domicile, Marriage and Divorce
- Hindu Marriages in Jammu and Kashmir
- Limping Marriages – Remedies and Solutions for Punjab
- NRI Marriage Law in a Limbo
- Religious Conversion in NRI Marriages
- Secular Indian Marriages Settlement
- Settlement Sans Divorce-Post Nuptial Agreements
- Trial of NRI Matrimonial Criminal Offences

A Secular Marriage Registration Law

A SECULAR LAW

On 13 August, 2012, The Rajya Sabha passed a Bill to make Registration of Marriages of all persons who are citizens of India belonging to various religious denominations mandatory thereby necessitating Registration of Marriages, irrespective of the religion of the parties. The Registration of Births and Deaths (Amendment) Bill, 2012, passed by a voice vote, adds marriages to the existing law and substitutes the words "Births, Marriages and Deaths" for the words "Births and Deaths" in the Registration of Births and Deaths Act, 1969. The proposed Law has been enacted to provide evidentiary value in matters of matrimonial status of parties, proof of age, and for establishing custody rights of children as also for conferring rights on children born out of marriages. The law also proposes to help women in maintenance cases as also to prevent unnecessary harassment meted out to women. It will now be tabled before the Lok Sabha and upon being passed will require Presidential assent to become a law.

BACKGROUND

The new marriage law is the outcome of the directions of the Supreme Court on 14 February, 2006 in *Seema* v. *Ashwani Kumar*, AIR 2006 SC 1158 and the 205th Report of the 18th Law Commission of India which had recommended a mandatory Parliamentary legislation on compulsory Registration of Marriages to bring country wide uniformity of marriages of all religious faiths. Further, the Committee on Empowerment of Women in its 12th Report on Plight of Indian Women deserted by NRI husband presented to the Lok Sabha on 13 August, 2007, had also expressed that all marriages irrespective of religion should be compulsorily registered.

CONTENTS

The new Law is indeed laudable and salutary. It defines "marriage" as a union solemnized between a male and a female belonging to any caste, religion or tribe and includes marriages solemnized under any custom, usage or law for the time being in force and also includes remarriages. The proposed new law makes it mandatory that every person shall get his marriage registered under the new Act or under any other Central or State law in force or under the Anand

Marriage Act, 1909. It further provides that the parties to the marriage whose marriage is registered under the new Act shall not be required to get their marriage registered under any other Marriage Law. Likewise, it is also stated that the provisions of the new law shall not apply to a person whose marriage has been registered under any existing law for registration of marriages and the validity of marriages registered previously shall not be affected. Furthermore, it is made clear that the provisions of the new law shall be in addition to, and not in derogation of any other marriage registration law in force and shall not affect any right recognised or acquired under any law, custom or usage by the parties. Specifically, the new law shall not apply to any matter or law relating to existing marriages including the Anand Marriage Act, 1909.

ENFORCEMENT MACHINERY

For bringing a stream lined, working and effective implementation method, the proposed marriage registration law amalgamates with the existing procedure and machinery created for Registration of Births and Deaths, thereby simplifying the process for providing a workable and effective mode for registration of marriages. The powers for registration, persons required to register marriages, duty of persons to inform marriages, provisions for refusal to register and delayed registration of marriages, corrections, cancellations or search in marriage registers, power of Registrars to obtain information on marriages and other related matters have been suitably added in the Registration of Births and Deaths Act, 1969, to empower the existing registration machinery to exercise these new powers for registration of marriages. The State Governments with the approval of the Central Government or the Central Government can make enabling rules or such provisions for implementation of the new provisions of the new marriage Act.

NEED OF THE HOUR

In enacting a composite secular and uniform marriage registration law applicable though out the country and implementing it through an existing workable mechanism, the legislators have done extremely well. It is now for countrymen to adapt to the proposed beneficial law and make it workable as for Births and Deaths. The applicability to all persons, regardless of religion professed is indeed commendable. At the same time saving of any existing State legislations providing for registration of marriages with liberty to avail of the new law is well meaning open minded proposition. Advantages of marriage registration, need to compulsorily register marriages and awareness of its benefits now needs to be made friendly to the common man. The duties of the administrators now require them to popularise the advantages which can be achieved to make the Marriage Registration Law a success. A friendly secular law will succeed with the acceptance of the people.

HIGHLIGHTS

The Registration of Births and Deaths (Amendment) Bill, 2012

- The Registration of Births and Deaths (Amendment) Bill, 2012 was introduced in Rajya Sabha on 7 May, 2012 and was passed by a voice vote on 13 August, 2013.
- The Registration of Births and Deaths Act, 1969 regulates the registration of births and deaths. The Bill amends the Act to include the registration of marriages within its purview and utilize the existing system for registration.
- The Bill requires that all marriages irrespective of religion shall be registered either under the Act or the Anand Marriage Act, 1909 or any other existing law, including any State or Central laws. Marriages already registered need not be registered again.
- The Bill defines marriage to include marriage solemnized between a male and female belonging to any caste, tribe or religion and includes re-marriages.
- Marriages registered under the Anand Marriage Act, any State laws or any other existing laws are not required to be registered under the new proposed law.
- The existing machinery of the Registrar General of India responsible for the registration of 'births and deaths', will also hold the portfolio for Registration of Marriages The Bill provides that the Registrar shall also be responsible for the registration of marriages.
- The Bill specifies the people who shall be eligible to submit information to the Registrar in order to register the marriage. It shall be the duty of the specified people to give the required information to the Registrar within the prescribed time period.
- The Act specifies that if the 'birth or death' is not registered within the specified time period, then the Registrar shall on the payment of a late fee, register the death or birth (a) within a period of 30 days (b) within one year only with the written permission of the prescribed authority; and (c) after one year only on the order of a first class Magistrate. The Bill states that the same provision applies to marriages as well.
- The Bill provides that if the Registrar seeks information from any person regarding any 'birth or marriage' then the person shall be bound to comply with such requirement.
- The Bill prescribes a penalty in case of (a) non-registration of 'marriage without a reasonable cause; (b) providing false information regarding the registration of marriage; and (c) refusal to furnish certain information, such as name and address.
- The Bill shall be in addition to and not in derogation of other existing laws. It shall not affect any rights recognised under any other law, custom or usage.

Domicile, Marriage and Divorce

THE PROBLEM

Hindu marriages solemnized on Indian soil being in the nature of a sacrament find an uphill road if sought to be dissolved on fault grounds before competent Courts under personal law of parties. Divorce by mutual consent requires both spouses to jointly petition the Court and maintain the unanimous decision to part for at least six months from the date of first hearing before the competent Court. Hence, when a traditional marriage of a Non Resident Indian breaks up overseas, the anxiety to dissolve it expeditiously is preferred to be done in the foreign matrimonial home of the spouses. The vexed question which then crops up frequently before Indian marital Courts is whether to accord recognition to such foreign divorce decrees or not as invariably such overseas dissolution is based on the ground of *irretrievable breakdown of marriage* which is not a ground for divorce under Hindu Marriage Act, 1955 (HMA).

RECENT DECISIONS

A recent reported verdict of the Delhi High Court in ***Pritam Ashok Sadaphule* v. *Hima Chugh,* 2014 (1) RCR (Civil) 697 (Del)** refused to give its imprimatur to a decree of divorce obtained by the husband from an English Court in UK. The marriage solemnized in New Delhi according to the Hindu rites was dissolved in UK on the ground of the marriage having been broken down irretrievably. The wife had represented to the English Court protesting that she was in India and was in acute financial difficulty to travel to London to contest the case. She requested the English Court not to grant divorce and had also petitioned the Delhi High Court for grant of a decree of permanent injunction against her husband from continuing with his divorce petition in UK. However, the English Court proceeded with the matter and dissolved the marriage.

The parties had met in England in 2004 and got married at New Delhi in 2005 to return to UK for work reasons. Developing matrimonial differences, the wife returned to India in 2010 to allege matrimonial cruelty. The husband petitioned for divorce in UK in 2010 and failing to injunct him in Delhi High Court through an anti suit injunction, in 2011 the wife also filed a petition for divorce in Delhi under the HMA, 1955 on the ground of cruelty. The husband appeared in the Delhi matrimonial Court alleging that since the English Court had already dissolved the marriage, the divorce petition in Delhi was not maintainable. The Delhi matrimonial Court rejected this plea of the husband which was challenged by him before the Delhi High Court. Relying on the

Supreme Court judgment in ***Y. Narashimha Rao's* case, (1991) 3 SCC 451,** the Delhi High Court rejected the challenge holding that the *ex parte* English divorce decree was not passed by a competent Court in accordance with Hindu Law and the wife had not submitted to the jurisdiction of the English Court. Hence, the divorce petition before the Delhi matrimonial Court by the wife was held to be maintainable.

In ***Rupak Rathi* v. *Anita Chaudhary,*** decided on April 9, 2014, in a path breaking euridte judgment rendered by Justice Rajiv Narian Raina of the Punjab and Haryana High Court and reported as 2014 (2) RCR (Civil) 697, principles were enunciated to decide on the validity of divorce decrees passed by foreign Courts on the ground of irretrievable breakdown of marriage. In this case, a Hindu couple had married in India according to Hindu rites and had set up a matrimonial home in United Kingdom. A Decree of divorce was granted by a U.K. Court on ground of irretrieable breakdown of marriage on a petition by the husband. Concluding, that the decree is not valid in India under The Hindu Marriage Act, 1955 as irretrivable breakdown of marriage is not a ground for divorce, it was held:—

"(i) No decree of divorce obtained from the English Court on a ground not available under the HMA, 1955 can be sustained on ground of irretrievable break down of marriage.

(ii) Where parties confer jurisdiction on the foreign Court, the said Court will assume jurisdiction available to a matrimonial Court in India but would remain confined to adjudicate the action in accordance with the matrimonial law of the parties i.e. HMA, 1955 and the grounds available therein.

(iii) The legal position is that when a Hindu couple tied by the nuptial knot according to Hindu rites travel abroad with intention to settle down and reside there to set up matrimonial home, they carry their personal laws on their back, off loading it in a foreign court for adjudication."

It was further held that a party producing a foreign Court matrimonial decree to contend that foreign court had already granted divorce was bound to follow the procedure laid down in the Civil Procedure Code (CPC) for seeking relief under Order VII, rule 11, CPC. The following guidelines were laid down to deal with such applications to safeguard interest particularly of Hindu Women married to Non Resident Indians. The guidelines were in the following terms:

"(i) If the spouse aggrieved by the foreign matrimonial decree has not submitted to the jurisdiction of the foreign court or consented to the passing of the foreign Court judgment, it ought not to be recognised being unenforceable under Section 13 CPC. This position of law ought to be applied to the facts of the individual case.

(ii) There may be occasions that a spouse relying upon the judgment of a foreign matrimonial court, upon receipt of a summon or notice from a court of competent jurisdiction under the HMA, 1955, may not choose to file a written statement in response to a petition seeking a matrimonial cause under HMA, 1955 in Punjab, Haryana or Chandigarh - Instead, the contesting spouse may prefer to move an application under Order VII, rule 11, CPC seeking to rely upon or invoke the

provisions of section 13, CPC - Thus, it may be contended before the court of competent jurisdiction under the HMA, 1955 that since the matrimonial action between the parties has already been decided and concluded by a Court in the foreign jurisdiction, the adjudication in the matter in issue between the same spouses based on the same matrimonial cause of action is barred by the principle of rs judicata and spouses are estopped in law from agitating the same again.

(iii) That wherever both or any spouse arrayed in a matrimonial cause in a matrimonial action under HMA, 1955 contest, dispute, question or oppose any above such application under Order VII, rule 11, CPC involving interpretation of the principles laid down under section 13, CPC thereby necessitating requirement of detailed pleadings and evidence of spouses, no summary decision may seem possible to decide the matter in the preliminary stage.

(iv) There may also be circumstances involving application of issues of domicile as also applicability of Sections 1 and 2 of the HMA, 1955 regarding extra territorial application of the provisions of HMA, 1955. Determination of these issues may also require parties to put their pleadings and testimony as well as the record of the Court of competent jurisdiction under the HMA, 1955.

(v) The application of the provisions of the CPC finding mention under section 21, HMA, 1955, the Court of Competent jurisdiction under the HMA, 1955 in Punjab, Haryana or Chandigarh may then be guided by the procedural law of pleadings contained in the Orders and Rules of the CPC and Punjab and Haryana High Court amendments, if any, for further proceedings in the matter. Accordingly, filing of a written statement, courter claim, rejoinder and/or other pleadings may be necessitated for having the factual matrix on record leading to the settlement of issues under Order XIV, CPC which can only be framed upon allegations made by parties to be read along with the contents of documents produced by spouses. Hence, this procedure may be necessary to be adopted to decide upon the warring claims of spouses relying on averments in support or against the judgment of the foreign matrimonial court between the parties.

(vi) Based on the above procedural requirements, the Court of competent jurisdiction under the HMA, 1955 may then examine the process, pleadings, grounds and other details in the passing of the judgment/decree of the matrimonial court of foreign jurisdiction to test it on the anvil of section 13, CPC and based on the principles laid down by the Apex Court in the third exception laid down in the judgment of the Apex Court in Y. Narasimha Rao *v.* Y. Venkata Lakshmi, *(1991) 3 SCC 451. Hence, in the event of a contest, dispute, opposition to the applicability of the foreign matrimonial judgment in the Indian jurisdiction, a summary disposal may not be possible. To do complete justice to both the spouses and to ensure that prejudice has not been caused to either of them as also that issues of maintenance, settlement of matrimonial property, child custody etc. arising in India have been completely settled between spouses based on provisions of HMA, 1955, the Court of competent jurisdiction under the HMA, 1955 may examine the matter on the lines suggested above.*

(vii) If the issue relating to the jurisdiction of Competent Court under the HMA, 1955 as also any bar to the matrimonial cause created by any existing law appears to

be established, the matrimonial court in Punjab, Haryana or Chandigarh may upon the facts and circumstances of the case take an appropriate decision under Order XIV, rule 2, CPC whether it needs to pronounce judgment on all issues or decide the issue of jurisdiction or maintainability as a preliminary issue. In such circumstances, the Competent Court under the HMA, 1955 may after forming an opinion take an appropriate decision on the facts of the case as to whether the issue of jurisdiction or maintainability is to be decided as a preliminary issue or pronounce judgment together on all the issues. Accordingly, based on the individual facts and circumstances, the Court ought to take a decision whether to decide the preliminary issue of jurisdiction or maintainability or postpone the settlement of other issues after such preliminary issues has been determined."

PREVIOUS PRECEDENTS

The Apex Court in its celebrated decision in ***Y. Narashimha Rao's* case** had laid down authoritative principles for recognition of foreign matrimonial judgments by settling that *"the jurisdiction assumed by the foreign Court as well as the grounds on which the relief is granted must be in accordance with the matrimonial law under which the parties are married."* Culling out exceptions when parties voluntarily and unconditionally submit to the jurisdiction of a foreign Court, where the contested decision is on a ground available under the law under which parties are married, the Supreme Court afforded protection to spouses to ensure that they were not saddled with *ex parte* decisions based on foreign law. The Supreme Court further in ***Neerja Saraph's* case, (1994) 6 SCC 461** went to the extent of advocating of the feasibility of an Indian legislation being made to safeguard interests of women so that no marriage between an NRI and an Indian woman solemnized in India may be annulled by a foreign Court.

The Delhi High Court in ***Harmeeta Singh's* case, 2003 (2) RCR (Civil) 197** has held that in the event of a decree of divorce being passed by a Court in America on an NRI spouse's petition, it would have to be confirmed by a Court in India in consonance with the principles of private international law embodied in section 13 of the Civil Procedure Code. Likewise, the Bombay High Court in ***Navin Chander Advani's* case, 2005 (2) HLR 582** held that the personal law of the parties will prevail. Similarly, the views of the Delhi High Court in ***Monia Khosla's* case, AIR 1986 Del 399** held that the Courts in India would not be ousted of their jurisdiction simply because one of the spouses was not resident in India.

DOMICILE CONFERS JURISDICTION

In another perspective, the Supreme Court in ***Sondur Gopal's* case, (2013) 7 SCC 426,** has whilst interpreting the extra territorial application of the HMA, 1955, authoritatively held that where both parties are Hindu by religion and have a permanent domicile in India, a matrimonial cause of action would be maintainable in India even if they reside outside India. It has been settled that the extra territorial application of the HMA, 1955 is linked to Hindus domiciled in India under the scheme of the HMA, 1955 and hence provisions of HMA, 1955 will apply to them.

IRRETRIEVABLE BREAKDOWN

The Apex Court in the case of ***Vishnu Dutt Sharma,* JT 2009 (7) SC 5,** and in ***Neelam Kumar,* AIR 2011 SC 193**, have held that since irretrievable breakdown of marriage is not a ground for divorce recognised by statutory law, no marriage can be dissolved on this ground under the HMA, 1955 and it is for Parliament to enact or amend the law on the subject. Therefore, any foreign court matrimonial decree dissolving a Hindu marriage on the breakdown principle does not find recognition in India. Consequently, whenever any such foreign divorce decree is thrust before a Indian matrimonial court in an attempt to avoid a matrimonial litigation of a divorce petition preferred by the local spouse on conventional fault grounds under HMA, 1955, the lack of maintainability has to be tested on judicial principles settled by the Apex Court. Invariably, attempts to avoid divorce trials in India on the basis of a foreign matrimonial decree do not find favour. Parties may be directed to file pleadings and establish facts by leading evidence upon issues being framed by the Indian Court. The crisis only perpetuates the misery of parties who can no longer live together.

A POSSIBLE RESOLUTION

With the influx of foreign matrimonial judgments being thrust before Indian Courts by a 30 million NRI population in 180 countries abroad, Parliament in its wisdom could well consider enacting a simplified irretrievable breakdown ground hedged with safeguards if one or both parties are resident abroad. Shifting the adjudicatory forum on Indian soil will aid and assist spouses to peacefully bury the hatchet on a equitable settlement fair to both parties on home turf without putting parties to expensive litigation abroad. This would also resolve the application of personal law issues being adjudicated by competent courts in India without a conflict of jurisdictions. Overseas spouses upon being offered a breakdown ground would prefer Indian matrimonial courts to settle issues so that parties are not in collision with law and domestic judgments so obtained would assume finality to conclusively settle aggravated matrimonial disputes without acrimony. If both spouses unanimously wish to terminate a matrimonial union, the breakdown principle in any case finds application even in divorces by mutual consent under the HMA, 1955. Therefore, landing credibility to irretrievable breakdown with legislative inputs will only define a recognised principle ingrained in the thought of dissolving a broken union. However, considering domestic conditions and to prevent spouses on Indian soil from being treated unfairly, issues relating to custody of children, maintenance and settlement of matrimonial property must be conclusively settled simultaneously. Friendly and speedy resolution of warring marital differences ought to be redressed by expeditiously setting up Family Courts under the Family Courts Act, 1984. A friendly law and a congenial atmosphere to resolve marital relationships gone sour is the epitome of any civilised set up. Peace at home brings happiness and stability. No sooner is this done, spouses will stop importing and imposing foreign matrimonial decrees against hapless partners pitted on Indian soil on uncomfortable terrain. A time has come to change for the better by incorporating what Courts offer abroad.

Hindu Marriages in Jammu and Kashmir

LAWS INVOLVED

The Hindu Marriage Act, 1955 (HMA) is an Act to amend and codify the law relating to Marriages among Hindus in India except in the State of Jammu and Kashmir (Jammu and Kashmir). However, it applies to Hindus domiciled in territories to which the HMA, 1955 extends. In view of the special status conferred upon Jammu and Kashmir by article 370 of the Constitution of India, the Jammu and Kashmir State Legislature has enacted the Jammu and Kashmir Hindu Marriage Act, 1980 (JKHMA) which extends to the whole of Jammu and Kashmir. The JKHMA is an Act to amend and codify laws relating to marriage among Hindus in Jammu and Kashmir. Like the HMA, 1955, the JKHMA prescribes solemnisation of Hindu Marriages by customary rites and ceremonies, leaving registration of Hindu marriages optional and which cannot be invalidated by omission of registration. Till date, there are no enforceable marriage registration rules in Jammu and Kashmir, though, The Jammu and Kashmir Hindu Marriage Registration Rules, 2012 have been circulated for eliciting comments/views/suggestions of public at large in pursuance to the decision of the Jammu and Kashmir Cabinet of Ministers of 28 June, 2012. However, till date, the said Rules have not been enforced in Jammu and Kashmir. The Special Marriage Act, 1954 (SMA), which is an Act to provide for special form of marriages and for divorces between any two persons in India, irrespective of religion or nationality, is not applicable in Jammu and Kashmir. However, SMA, 1954 is applicable to citizens of India from the Jammu and Kashmir who are domiciled in the territories to which the SMA, 1954 extends. Thus, if Indian citizens from the State of Jammu and Kashmir are domiciled in any other part of India, their marriage can be registered under SMA, 1954.

CONTENTS OF JKHMA

The JKHMA applies to any person who is a Buddhist, Jain or Sikh by religion and to any other person who is not a Muslim, Christian, Parsi or Jew by religion. The expression *"Hindu"* in the JKHMA shall be construed to include a person who though not a Hindu by religion, is, nevertheless a person to whom the JKHMA applies. A marriage between two Hindus can be solemnised between any two Hindus, *inter alia,* if the bridegroom has completed the age of 18 years and the bride the age of 15 years at the time of the marriage. If the bride has not completed the age of 18 years, consent of her guardian is necessary for marriage, which if not obtained can be a ground for annulment of the marriage. Other than age of majority, consent of Guardian and choice of place for filing matrimonial petitions, the JKHMA is similar to the HMA, 1955. However, The Jammu and Kashmir Hindu Marriage Laws (Amendment) Bill, 2012, for amending age of majority to 18 and 21 years for bride and groom besides omitting consent and concept of guardianship in marriage, are pending before the Jammu and Kashmir State Legislature for its consideration.

THE ANOMALY

The status of a Hindu marrying a Muslim is in quandary in the State of Jammu and Kashmir. Ceremonial marriages under personal laws cannot be possible between two persons of different religions and due to SMA, 1954 not being applicable in the State of Jammu and Kashmir, such a marriage cannot be registered. In the absence of their being no parallel religion free registration law like the SMA, 1954 or any other religion free registration rules in Jammu and Kashmir, no registration of an inter-religious marriage is possible in Jammu and Kashmir. Temporary shifting of residence outside the State of Jammu and Kashmir by such Indian citizens for seeking registration under the SMA, 1954 may be besotted with grounds of domicile, even though a 30 day residence period is statutorily sufficient to qualify for registration for notice of intended marriage before the Marriage Officer under the SMA, 1954. Couples waiting to unite in the matrimonial bond seek legislative solutions.

COMPULSORY MARRIAGE REGISTRATION LAWS IN JAMMU AND KASHMIR

The Apex Court in *Seema* v. *Ashwani Kumar,* AIR 2006 SC 1158, directed that "***marriages of all persons who are citizens of India belonging to various religions should be made compulsorily registrable in their respective States, where the marriage is solemnised***" In Jammu and Kashmir, the JKHMA empowers the Government to make rules to provide that Hindus shall have their particulars registered for facilitating proof of marriages. The draft Jammu and Kashmir Hindu Marriage Registration Rules, 2012 are pending approval of the Government in Jammu and Kashmir. As regards Muslims, section 3 of the Jammu and Kashmir Muslim Marriages Registration Act, 1981 provides that marriages contracted between Muslims shall be registered within 30 days of the Nikah ceremony but reportedly this Act has not been enforced. The Jammu and Kashmir Christian Marriage and Divorce Act, 1957, provides for registration of Christian marriages solemnised by the Minister of Christian Religion. However, till date there is no State enactment in Jammu and Kashmir providing for registration of marriages between two persons professing different religious faiths or beliefs.

THE PROBLEM COMPOUNDED

Marital discords between Hindu couples living outside Jammu and Kashmir and which have escalated from the tying of the vows of Hindu matrimony in Jammu and Kashmir face territorial objections of maintainability upon matrimonial petitions being instituted in Family Courts outside Jammu and

Kashmir. Harried spouses living in Jammu and Kashmir raise objections that marriages solemnised under JKHMA can only be dissolved in Jammu and Kashmir in proceedings under the JKHMA. A beleaguered opponent claims that as an Indian citizen living outside Jammu and Kashmir, the HMA, 1955 applies equally to Hindus domiciled outside the territories of Jammu and Kashmir irrespective of the solemnisation of the marriage in Jammu and Kashmir under JKHMA. The dilemma was resolved recently by the erudite pronouncement of the Bombay High Court in *Shashi Leekha* v. *Sheela Shashi,* 2012 (2) HLR 520 holding that there is no express provision in the HMA, 1955 to suggest that the presentation of such a petition would be barred. Conversely, if a Hindu who was a permanent resident of Jammu and Kashmir was to perform his marriage outside Jammu and Kashmir, he would still be governed by HMA, 1955. The Court also took notice of *"destination marriages"* evolved in contemporary times where parties may have married in Jammu and Kashmir, which would have an answer of an emphatic "no" if petitions for their dissolution were to be held to be maintainable only in Jammu and Kashmir. The Court held that there is no express bar or prohibition in the JKHMA for filing matrimonial petitions as per jurisdictional grounds available under the HMA, 1955 which permits a wife to file a petition in a court within whose jurisdiction she is residing on the date of the presentation of the petition. Moreover, due to disparity of jurisdictional grounds for filing a petition, a Hindu wife cannot be discriminated under the HMA, 1955, if the similar ground is not available under the JKHMA.

POSSIBLE SOLUTIONS

In Jammu and Kashmir, the enactment of a religion free marriage registration law on the lines of SMA, 1954 for all persons, under the aegis of the verdict of the Supreme Court in *Seema* v. *Ashwani Kumar,* could be the legislative solution for registration of all marriages which may be solemnised under such civil law or are sought to be registered as marriages celebrated in other forms. Registration of religious marriages under separate personal laws would alone not solve the problem and Indian Courts would continue to perform a yeoman function in resolving such human problems on a case to case basis. Religion free registration of marriages is the only breakthrough. Till then, the relaxation of the concept of domicile or residence outside the State of Jammu and Kashmir for permanent residents of Jammu and Kashmir, wanting to solemnize inter-religious marriages, is the only administrative answer for a practical and an amicable remedy to this impasse.

In so far the issue of malady of registration of marriages otherwise is concerned, the recently enacted Punjab Compulsory Registration of Marriages Act, 2012, would be the possible resolution if a ceremonial marriage has been performed in accordance with the personal law of either of the parties. This Punjab law provides for compulsory registration of marriages solemnized under any law governing the parties irrespective of their religion, caste, creed or nationality. Any marriage solemnised outside the State of Punjab can be registered at a place where parties have their temporary residence in the State of Punjab.

HIGHLIGHTS AT A GLANCE – FACT FILE

Hindu Marriage Act, 1955 (HMA) – An Act to amend and codify the law relating to marriage among Hindus. It extends to the whole of India except the State of Jammu and Kashmir. Applies to Hindus domiciled in territories outside. Provides ceremonial marriages in accordance with customary rites and ceremonies of either party. Registration of Hindu Marriages is optional leaving it to State Governments to make Rules.

- **Special Marriage Act, 1954 (SMA)** – An act to provide a special form of marriage between persons in certain cases, for the registration of such and certain other marriages and divorce. Extends to the whole of India except the State of Jammu and Kashmir. Applies to citizens of India domiciled in the territories to which the SMA, 1954 extends who are in the State of Jammu and Kashmir. Applicable to foreigners, Indian nationals and person of any religion. Provides solemnization of civil marriage and registration of marriages celebrated in other forms.
- **Jammu and Kashmir Hindu Marriage Act, 1980 (JKHMA)** – An Act to amend and codify the law relating to marriage among Hindus in the State of J&K. Does not apply to Muslims, Christians, Parsis and Jews. Provides ceremonial marriages by customary rites and ceremony between Hindus and registration is optional for which Government may make rules.
- **Jammu and Kashmir Hindu Marriage Registration Rules, 2012** – Provides for registration of Hindu Marriages solemnized in the State of J&K. Circulated for eliciting comments/views/suggestions of public at large in pursuance to a decision of the J&K Cabinet. However, have not yet been finalised or enforced.
- **Jammu and Kashmir Muslim Marriages Registration Act, 1981** – Provides for registration of marriages contracted between Muslims within thirty days of Nikah ceremony. Reportedly, this Act has not been enforced in J&K.
- **Jammu and Kashmir Christian Marriage and Divorce Act, 1957** – Provides for registration of Christian marriages solemnized by the Christian Minister of Religion.
- **However till date there is no Jammu and Kashmir State Legislation providing for solemnization or registration of marriages between two persons professing different religious faiths or beliefs like the SMA, 1954, applicable outside Jammu and Kashmir, there is no religion free marriage registration law in Jammu and Kashmir.**

Limping Marriages – Remedies and Solutions for Punjab

The Problem

Marriages on crutches need aid and attention. They limp and need intensive care treatment. Personal family law enactments prevalent today lack effective solutions. The problems are further compounded in NRI marriages in which parties import foreign matrimonial laws to unions solemnised domestically in India. An optional marriage registration law in India led the Supreme Court to pass orders on 14 February, 2006 and 25 October, 2007, making it mandatory that marriages of all persons who are citizens of India belonging to various religions should be compulsorily registerable in their respective States where the marriage is solemnised. Sadly, the State of Punjab, at one time had no compulsory registration of marriages prescribed under any enactment or rules made by Punjab. Moreover, compulsory registration of NRI marriages is urgently required to ensure that brides and grooms from the State of Punjab have proof and evidence of their marriage as also to prevent matrimonial frauds being practised commonly in this jurisdiction. Punjab has the discredit of about 30,000 abandoned "nowhere" brides with no succour or legal remedy. The Punjab State Commission for NRIs in a decision of 11 July recognizing this daily phenomenon of fraudulent marriages with overseas Indians leading to cruelty and harassment suggested that the menace need to be curbed with stern hands. The possible answers lie in a compulsory marriage registration law, setting up of Family Courts in the State of Punjab to deal with all aspects of disputes arising out of a matrimonial relationship and for meaningful amendments to give teeth to the Punjab State Commission for NRIs Act, 2011.

PUNJAB COMPULSORY REGISTRATION OF MARRIAGES ACT, 2012
COMPULSORY MARRIAGE REGISTRATION OF NRI MARRIAGES IN PUNJAB

The Hindu Marriage Act, 1955 (HMA) leaves it open for every State Government to enact compulsory provisions for Registration of Marriages. The Supreme Court in 2006 in *Seema* v. *Ashwani Kumar,* AIR 2006 SC 1158 issued a mandate to all States to make registration of marriage compulsory by enacting legislations. This directive led to the enactment of the Punjab Compulsory Registration of Marriages Act 2012, providing for compulsory registration of marriages solemnized under any law governing the parties irrespective of their religion, caste, creed or nationality. Any marriage solemnized in Punjab is now compulsorily registerable and even marriages solemnized outside the State of Punjab can be registered at a place where parties have their temporary residence in Punjab. However, if the marriage is already registered elsewhere, it shall not be registered again in the State of Punjab.

DEFINITION OF NRIs IN THE NEW LAW

The most prominent feature of the new marriage law is the definition of a *"non resident Indian"* to mean a person of Indian origin who is either permanently or temporarily settled outside India for employment, business, vocation or any other purpose indicating a uncertain or determined period of overseas stay. Likewise, a *"foreign national"* has been defined to mean a person who is not a citizen of India and shall include *Persons of Indian Origin* (PIO) and *Overseas Citizens of India (OCI)* who are defined under the Citizenship Act, 1955 and mean foreign nationals of Indian Origin who have earlier been Indian Citizens or qualify for Indian citizenship.

NRI MARRIAGES IN THE LOOP

The law in the making provides that every marriage between parties who are Indian nationals or NRIs or foreign nationals solemnized or performed in the State of Punjab, irrespective of religion, caste, creed or nationality shall also be registered in the State of Punjab. The most significant feature would be that for every NRI or foreign national, it would be mandatory to disclose in writing his/her passport number, country of its issue, period of its validity besides permanent residential/official address of overseas abode with social security number or any such permanent identification proof issued by his foreign country. All this information will be entered in the marriage certificate and the marriage register. Marriage would mean and include marriages solemnized or performed under Hindu Laws, Anand Marriage Act, Muslim personal law or under Indian Christian Marriage Act besides any other custom or personal law relating to marriages governing the parties.

REGISTRATION REGIME DEVISED

The new law with enabling Rules has notified Chief, District and Additional Registrars of Marriages or other Officers to be Registrar of Marriages for free and easy accessibility in cities, towns and tehsils. The new law notifies DC's, DRO's, Tehsildars and Naib Tehsildars for easy accessibility in cities, towns and tehsils. The Registrars so designated , shall upon scrutiny verify that the marriage between the parties has been performed in accordance with the personal law of parties to confirm their marital status and identities. A memorandum of marriage signed by the parties and their priest will be presented to the concerned Registrar within three months of marriage in the jurisdiction where the marriage was solemnised or where parties have temporary residence if they were married outside Punjab. Refusal to register shall be appealable and the Registrar may also *suo moto* or on notice call parties and register any marriage performed in his jurisdiction. Any erroneous or fraudulent entry in a marriage register may be corrected or cancelled after giving opportunity of hearing to persons concerned.

NON-REGISTRATION NOT TO INVALIDATE MARRIAGES

The new law states that no marriage shall be deemed to be invalid solely by the reason or the fact that it was not registered. This shortcoming is attributed to codified personal marriage laws of parties in India by which performance of essential ceremonies and not registration validates a marriage between parties. Hence, a State enactment cannot undo a law made by Parliament prescribing only ceremonies for recognition of a valid marriage. Consequently, resorting to compulsory registration may have to develop more as a accepted societal norm and practice for the law to gain recognition. Ailing The fact remains that Punjab has taken the lead to register NRI Marriages which will help in curbing matrimonial frauds to ameliorate the plight of ailing *"Nowhere Holiday Wives"*. Punjab would do equally well if it were to constitute Family Courts in every district in Punjab under the existing Family Courts Act, 1984, to provide speedy justice to abandoned spouses and deserted children as well. Prevention is better than cure but redressal of issues arising out of a broken or limping matrimonial relationship must be remedied too simultaneously.

Creation of Family Courts in Punjab

The Family Courts Act, 1984 which provides for the establishment of Family Courts with a view to promote conciliation in, and secure speedy settlement of disputes relating to marriage and family affairs is the appropriate forum where such matrimonial matters ought to be decided. The Act leaves it open to the respective State Governments to provide for Family Courts. The State of Punjab essentially needs Family Courts to provide fast-track, effective, meaningful and quick relief for abandoned spouses, deserted children and for resolving other disputes arising out of a matrimonial relationship. Under section 3, the Family Courts are required to be constituted by the State Government in consultation with the High Court. It is thus proposed that the Family Courts should be set up in every district in the State of Punjab so that all matrimonial disputes, particularly of NRIs, get effective, speedy and meaningful adjudication. As of now, the District Judge or his nominee under the Hindu Marriage Act, 1955 (HMA) entertains and adjudicates all matrimonial cases in their respective jurisdictions. Even though the HMA, 1955 contemplates day to day trial of matrimonial petitions and conclusion within six months, the statutory mandate remains an optical illusion being an impossibility. This deters NRIs from starting any matrimonial cause in Punjab. Hence, constitution of the Family Courts could prove to be a boon. Exclusively deciding matrimonial cases with conciliation, mediation and settlement procedures would put such matters in a better adjudicatory fast track mode for effective relief. Thus, every district in the State of Punjab particularly in the NRI segment would greatly benefit from it and abandoned spouses will have a expeditious relief giving Forum to plead their grievances, in person, if so desired.

Amendment of NRI Commission Act

The Government of Punjab enacted the Punjab State Commission for Non-resident Indians Act, 2011 (Punjab NRI Act) as an Act to provide for the constitution of a Commission for NRIs with a view to protecting and safeguarding the interests of NRIs in the State of Punjab and to recommend remedial measures for their welfare. The NRI Commission is fully functional, taking up matters with efficiency and performing excellently. However, the powers of the NRI Commission are stunted as it has been created prematurely without full powers. The NRI Commission can order or conduct an enquiry or investigation on a complaint with respect to NRIs but the Punjab NRI Act stops short. It leads nowhere. The NRI Commission cannot pronounce a decision or give any judgment because the Punjab NRI Act does not contain any provision by which it is empowered to do so. Hence, the exercise is in futility as the NRI Commission has no teeth. Therefore, it is recommended that the Punjab NRI Act should be amended with the following powers to be exercised after an enquiry or an investigation is conducted by the NRI Commission and which are:—

- Where the inquiry discloses, the commission or violation of rights of any law concerning parties of a serious nature, it may recommend to the Government or authority, the initiation of proceedings or prosecution of such action as the Commission may deem fit against concerned person or persons.
- Approach the Civil, Criminal or High Court concerned for such directions, orders or writs as the Court may deem necessary in the facts of the case.
- Recommend to the Government or authority for the grant of such interim relief to the victim or the members of his/her family as the Commission may deem necessary.

Unless and until the powers of enquiry and investigation of the NRI Commission is given the further statutory authority to take the matter to a logical end, the existence of the NRI Commission will remain an exercise in futility. Upon such empowerment, the NRI Commission will get statutory teeth to enforce their orders. Resultantly, beleaguered NRI spouses in distress can see their cases to a logical end only upon a legal remedy resulting from their complaint. NRI family disputes will no longer remain at sea.

Summing up

The State of Punjab which constitutes the maximum number of NRIs to the 30 million NRI population living in 180 countries abroad owes a moral duty to its brethren to give to them their due. It is a crying need that there should be redressal of family law problems in a proper legal framework. Rhetoric, empty promises, platitudes and non-remedial forums will not serve the purpose. The Government must act and perform. Punjabi NRIs have hope, faith and expectations. These additions and amendments for meaningful remedies of matrimonial problems must be met with without delay. At the same time, law must provide answers so that the NRI does not take recourse to foreign laws which defeats the very purpose and meaning of our domestic laws. The need of the day is to change for the better and to make amendments required for all.

FACT FILE

1. The Hindu Marriage Act, 1955 – An Act to amend and codify the law relating to marriage among Hindus. It provides that the trial of a petition under this Act shall be conducted from day to day until its conclusion unless the Court finds the adjournment of the trial beyond the following day for reasons to be recorded. Every petition under this Act shall be tried as expeditiously as possible and endeavour shall be made to conclude the trial within six months.

2. *The Family Courts Act, 1984* – *An Act to provide for the establishment of Family Courts with a view to promote conciliation in, and secure speedy settlement of disputes relating to marriage and family affairs and for matters connected therewith. It provides that the State Government after consultation with the High Court and by notification may establish Family Courts as it may deem necessary.*

3. ***Compulsory Registration of Marriages*** – *Registration of marriages be made compulsory – The Supreme Court in Transfer Petition (C) No.291 of 2005 –* Smt. Seema *v.* Aswini Kumar, *by judgment dated 14th February, 2006 has issued the directions that the central and State Governments shall take the following steps.*

- Marriages of all persons who are citizens of India belonging to various religions should be compulsorily be registered in their respective states.
- The procedure for registration should be notified by the respective states within 3 months.
- Thus it is now incumbent upon the states to provide for registration of marriages which needs to be implemented in case of NRI marriages taking place in India. Also marriage certificates for NRI marriages should be issued in duplicate copies and must carry social security number of the NRI spouse.

4. ***Judgment of Punjab State Commission for NRIs of 11 July, 2012*** –*"The phenomenon of the women being abandoned by the Bridegrooms, who happens to be an NRI is not new. Earlier also there have been such instances. Women trapped in such fraudulent marriages with overseas Indians are increasingly reported. The problem is not about the women being abandoned in India, but includes demand of dowry, cruelty and forms of harassment by her in-laws families. It is only when it is "Too Late" that the parents, who have possibly liquidated their assets to have their daughter enter into the so-called marriage, wake-up and approach the state authorities. This is a menace and needs to be curbed with stern hands."*

5. ***Possible Solutions—***

- √ Strict implementation of Punjab Compulsory Marriage Registration Law – Compulsory Registration of all marriages solemnised or performed in the State irrespective of religion, caste, creed or nationality. If either or both parties are NRIs or foreign nationals, passport details, foreign address, social security number or other foreign identification mandatory to be recorded in Register of Marriages.
- √ Creation of Family Courts in Punjab –The Family Courts Act, 1984 provides that the State Government may set up Family Courts in consultation with the High Courts. Punjab must accordingly set up Family Courts in every district for speedy settlement of disputes relating to marriage and family affairs where parties may have liberty to appear in person and seek redressal in a fast track mechanism.
- √ Amendment of Punjab State Commission for Non-Resident Indians Act, 2011 – A fully functional NRI Commission in Punjab, as of now, can

only order an enquiry or investigation. The Act does not empower the Commission with other powers. Thus, arming the Act with statutory powers of initiation of proceedings or prosecution, liberty to approach Civil, Criminal or High Court in individual cases and recommending Government to grant such interim relief as necessary, is required to make the NRI Commission an effective Forum with further powers.

NRI Marriage Law in a Limbo

On December 30, 2006, the Ministry of Overseas Indian Affairs had announced a scheme[available on *www.moia.nic.in*] to provide free legal and counseling services to NRI women as well as foreign citizens of Indian origin in distress as a welfare measure. To begin with this scheme was to be applicable in US, UK, Canada, Germany, Australia, Malaysia, New Zealand and the Gulf. It is now extended worldwide. Another proposal between the Overseas Affairs Minister and the Minister for Women and Child Development led the Indian Government to propose to stamp the marital status of Non Resident Indians on their passports. This was indeed a welcome development. But, it could not have been enough. Besides, the proposal of stamping passports was never implemented. Eight years have gone by and the same situation continues. Administrative remedies have failed to resolve these human problems.

The Ministry of Overseas Indian Affairs operates a Scheme to provide financial assistance to needy Indian women in distress due to desertion or divorce by their overseas spouses, for getting access to counseling and legal services. The counseling and allied services are provided through credible Indian Women's organizations, Indian Community Associations and NGOs empanelled with Indian Embassies abroad. It is stated that complaints regarding overseas marriages can be made to the National Commission for Women online at nricell-ncw@nic.in. Additionally, a complaint can also be made to the Ministry of Overseas Indian Affairs by email at dsds2.moia@nic.in. However, by the State wise data of the complaints received by the Ministry (Tabulated below as Annexure A), it does not seem that there is a very positive response or that such remedies are a success in practical relief oriented terms. These investigations which have no judicial sanctions, can at most result in recommendatory relief. The Ministry cannot cancel the visa of a person and revocation of the passport may itself be legally questionable.

Of a population of over 1.2 billion Indians, about thirty million are NRIs living worldwide. Times have changed but family law legislations enacted by the Indian Parliament in 1955 and 1956 have left family laws for NRIs where they were. The result, an influx of family law problems arising out of NRI marriages with no practical solutions in the legislative enactments as they exist today. To compound the problem, registration of marriages, which is optional under Hindu Family laws, though now made compulsory, has not been put into practice in most States in India including Punjab, as the rules for doing the same have not yet come into effect. The fallout: multiple marriages by the

NRI often without a previous divorce, invariably by duping the previous spouse and providing no maintenance to the abandoned wife and no support to the unfortunate child of such union if any. Foreign divorce decrees are not accepted by Indian Courts. Defending a matrimonial matter abroad sitting in India is an impossible task. Legal recourse in India is difficult, time consuming, expensive and complicated. Despite a Family Courts Act, 1984, most States have none despite 30 years having elapsed since this law was made. The end result : about thirty thousand abandoned women in Punjab alone fending for themselves in an uphill legal system which provides no solutions or answers. Then, there are issues relating to Inter parental child abduction. Court recourse is difficult, undefined and India not being a signatory to The Hague Convention on Child Abduction, there is practically no statutory law on the subject. Still further, inter country adoptions are governed by a maze of laws and procedures. Surrogacy also now sails in these unchartered waters How are all these NRI family law related issues to be resolved. Who will do it. How will it be done. Regardless, Courts resolve individual matters with beneficial interpretations.

In our country where we have a plural systems of family laws, multiple bigamous unions by NRIs are abound. Defending summary divorce proceedings of foreign courts initiated by an erring NRI with no legal assistance or maintenance makes the hapless deserted Indian spouse suffer in agony thereby compounding the problem. Caught in this cross fire are innocent children of such unfortunate marriages often bundled of against their wishes. Indian legislation provides no answers. There being no bilateral agreements or treaties with foreign countries, parallel court proceedings initiated on both sides in different countries leads to a conflict of jurisdictions and flouted court orders. Hague Conventions on marriage and divorce are not acceded to. The result undoubtedly is a total mess. The sufferers are fellow citizens in India and those on foreign soil.

In this stage and time, the Parliament seriously needs to enact a comprehensive legislation for NRI marriages and divorces applicable country wide which is a composite and wholesome answer to these social issues. Patchwork with isolated eyewash will not help. The need of the hour is a new law and not administrative remedies which are an exercise in futility. The purpose of making a new law is now very clear and needs no further elucidation. Simultaneously, State Governments must forthwith set up Family Courts and with the aid of trained mediators, attempt alternative dispute resolution methods which see finality with the seal of Family Courts upon expeditious and effective resolution.

ANNEXURE A

STATE-WISE NUMBER OF COMPLAINTS RECEIVED BY MINISTRY OF OVERSEAS INDIAN AFFAIRS DURING LAST THREE YEARS UPTO 18TH FEBRUARY, 2013

Sr. No.	Name of the State/Union Territory	Number of complaints during 2009-10	Number of complaints during 2010-11	Number of complaints during 2011-12	Number of complaints during 2012-13 (upto 18th February 2013)	Total
1	Andhra Pradesh	10	2	1	6	19
2	Assam	...	1	1	1	3
3.	Bihar	2	...	...	...	2
4.	Chandigarh	...	...	...	2	2
5	Chhatisgarh	...	...	...	1	1
6.	Delhi	6	7	3	10	26
7.	Gujarat	4	...	3	0	7
8.	Haryana	4	...	1	3	8
9.	Himachal Pradesh	1	...	...	...	1
10.	Jammu & Kashmir	5	...	...	...	5
11.	Karnataka	1	1	1	2	5
12.	Kerala	3	1	5	0	9
13.	Maharashtra	2	...	3	3	8
14.	Madhya Pradesh	2	NIL	2	0	4
15.	Punjab	6	1	6	13	26
16.	Puducherry (UT)	1	...	...	...	1
17.	Rajasthan	1	...	...	...	1
18.	Tamil Nadu	3	...	3	7	13
19.	Uttar Pradesh	3	...mm	1	3	7
20.	Uttarakhand	2	...	...	...	2
21.	West Bengal	...	2	1	2	5
	Total	56	15	31	53	155

Religious Conversion in NRI Marriages

THE DILEMMA OF REGISTERING A HINDU MARRIAGE

Foreign Embassies and Diplomatic Missions in India decline to process permanent settlement visa applications of local bridegrooms who wish to migrate to foreign jurisdictions after having married a foreign non-Hindu national under Hindu Marriage Act, 1955 (HMA) and have got registered such a Hindu marriage under the Special Marriage Act, 1954 (SMA) in India. The reason and logic in such refusal of a foreign High Commission is clear. Only two Hindus by religion can marry under the HMA, 1955 in accordance with the customary rites and ceremonies of either party thereto. Hence, a Hindu by religion cannot solemnize a ceremonial marriage with another non-Hindu in India who is not professing the Hindu faith or religion. Consequently, in the opinion of a foreign mission, registration of such a Hindu marriage under the SMA, 1954 as a marriage celebrated in other form is invalid. This stumbling block is irreparable since registration of such a marriage under the SMA, 1954 is deemed to be a marriage solemnized under the SMA, 1954 conferring the status of husband and wife between the parties which however is apparently not recognised or accepted by a foreign High Commission for considering a visa application of a Hindu Indian spouse. The marriage already solemnised under HMA, 1955 has been registered under the SMA, 1954 as a marriage celebrated in other form and cannot be re-registered again additionally as a marriage solemnized under the SMA, 1954 as a special marriage since the same marriage cannot be registered twice. The paradox poses a legal dilemma for the parties.

REGISTRATION UNDER THE SMA, 1954

The HMA, 1955 is an Act to amend and codify the law relating to marriage among Hindus by religion and in which only the ceremonial marriage is compulsory as registration under the HMA, 1955 is optional. The SMA, 1954 in contrast, is an Act to provide a special form of marriage in certain cases and for the registration of such and certain other marriages celebrated in other forms. Hence, civil registration of marriage is an essential requirement under the SMA, 1954. Thus, any two persons, irrespective of nationality or religion can perform and register their marriage as a marriage solemnized under SMA, 1954. However, SMA, 1954 also additionally provides only registration of marriages which have been celebrated in other forms. Therefore, marriages solemnized under the HMA, 1955 can be registered under the SMA, 1954 since HMA, 1955 itself does not provide for any compulsory registration. This, as a community practice is the course normally adopted by Hindus who marry non-Hindus as they register ceremonial Hindu marriages under the SMA, 1954 after the traditional Hindu marriage is solemnised by performing customary rites and ceremonies of either party thereto.

CONVERSION TO HINDU RELIGION

Traditionally and conventionally unless and until a marriage is solemnized in India in accordance with customary rites and ceremonies of either party thereto, it does not gain family or community acceptance. However, overseas travel or permanent migration to a foreign country entails compulsory registration and ceremony alone does not serve the purpose. Marrying under the SMA, 1954 by registration alone without ceremony also does not generally find acceptance in traditional Hindu culture. Therefore, for a non-Hindu spouse to convert to Hindu religion before solemnising a Hindu marriage is the only way to validate the Hindu marriage and to confer legal sanctity of its registration under the SMA, 1954. However, the dilemma is compounded if the non-Hindu spouse has not converted to Hindu religion before solemnising a ceremonial marriage under the HMA, 1955 and the folly is realised when the foreign High Commission declines to accept the marriage certificate issued under the SMA, 1954 which is accompanying the visa application for permanent immigration abroad. Retracing of steps for conversion of religion is difficult and fresh registration of the marriage again for the second time is impossible. Cancellation of the earlier registration is equally unworkable, cumbersome and may entail a lengthy process with negative results.

MODALITIES OF CONVERSION

The Constitution of India grants freedom of conscience and the right to profess, practice and propagate any religion of choice as a cherished ideal of secularism. The change from one religion to another is a consequence of an individual faith or belief and there is no precise definition of "religion". Conversion like marriage is a solemn act. The right to conversion connotes an individual right of a person to embrace a faith or a religion in preference to the one professed by him earlier and may occur at the time of marriage. Conversion affects rights of succession, marital status and may have other social consequences. Most non-Hindu persons voluntarily embrace Hindu religion before marrying a Hindu. However, law, as declared by the Supreme Court does not prescribe any particular formalities or rituals for conversion though some religious texts require ceremonies to be performed for conversion in some religions. The law on the point as declared by the Apex Court reads as follows:

➢ *In* Punjabrao *v.* Dr. D.P Meshram, *AIR 1965 SC 1179, a Constitution Bench of the Supreme Court, interpreting the expression "profess" held that if a public declaration is made by a person that he has ceased to belong to his old religion and has accepted another religion, he will be taken as professing the other religion. In the face of such an open declaration, the Supreme Court held that it would be ideal to enquire further as to whether the conversion to another religion was efficacious.*

- In Perumal Nadar *v.* Ponnuswami, *AIR 1971 SC 2352, the Supreme Court held that a person may be a Hindu by birth or by conversion and a mere theoretical allegiance or a bare declaration by a person does not convert him into a Hindu. But, a* bona fide *intention to be converted to the Hindu faith accompanied by his unequivocal intention may be sufficient evidence of conversion. However, no formal ceremony of purification or expiation is necessary to effectuate conversion.*
- In Kailash Sonkar *v.* Maya Devi, *AIR 1984 SC 600, while dealing with a case of reconversion, it was held that the main test should be a genuine intention to reconvert by a clear and a genuine intention to go back to the old fold and adopt the customs and practices of his erstwhile cast.*
- In M. Chandra *v.* M. Thagamuthu, *(2010) 9 SCC 712, the Apex Court held that it is a settled principle of law that to prove a conversion from one religion to another, two elements need to be satisfied. First, there has to be a conversion and second, acceptance into the community to which the person has converted. It is obvious that the need of conversion cannot be altogether done away with.*

A reading of the above clearly demonstrates that since no formal ceremony of conversion is prescribed under codified law, there seems to be a vacuum in statutory law for effectuating voluntary religious conversions. A non-Hindu may have willingly converted to the Hindu faith before solemnising a marriage as per customary Hindu rites and ceremonies, but no codified or statutory law will give him a conversion certificate. Thus, the need for enacting a process of law to afford an opportunity to produce documentary evidence of a declaration to substantiate the plea of conversion, is a necessity, more so in the realm of NRI marriages. This will end the stalemate of uncertainty of proof of conversion required in Hindu marriages for non-Hindu spouses who have registered it under SMA, 1954 and who have converted to the Hindu faith before solemnising a marriage under HMA, 1955. Like registration of marriages, even the question of recording and registering of voluntary conversions for marital purposes done before marriage could also be considered by the Parliamentarians.

VIEWS OF THE LAW COMMISSION OF INDIA

The Law Commission of India in Report No. 235, of December 2010, on *Conversion/Reconversion to Another Religion – Mode of Proof* has made serious salutary recommendations that proper guidelines on the subject of religious conversions will help avoiding conflicts. It is suggested by them that within a month of the date of conversion, the converted person can send a declaration to the Officer Incharge of the registration of marriages in the concerned area, who after public notice and entertaining objections can issue a declaration recording the conversion of religion. The Law Commission is inclined to think that a separate enactment or amendments to respective personal laws is not required in this regard and the process can be implemented administratively to give effect to its recommendations. The aim, objective and goal of the Law Commission clearly seems to be to obviate the necessity of enactment of any new law on the subject which in its view can be resolved by exercise of executive power by the Central Government by issuance of communications to State Governments and Union Territories, which in turn can be implemented by Registration offices administratively. The fact remains, whether by statute law or executive instructions, the problem needs resolution. NRI marriages of Non-Hindus cannot remain in limbo. The dilemma of proving conversion before marrying voluntarily must be simplified. The process of law must provide an answer for a consistent clear path to be followed which should be transparent, uniform and visible easily to all those who need it.

Secular Indian Marriages

A BENEFICIAL LAW

In the Budget session in 2012, Parliament proposal to amend the Registration of Births and Deaths Act, 1969, was passed by the Rajya Sabha to include compulsory registration of marriages without mentioning the religious denomination of parties. The proposal still to be passed by the Lok Sabha is based on the fact that infrastructure for registration of Births and Deaths is already available country wide and only addition of marriage registration to the existing law is required. The proposed Bill is stated to be beneficial to women by protecting them from unnecessary harassment in matrimonial and maintenance cases by providing handy proof of marriage. It is said to also provide evidence in matters of custody of children and protect rights of children born from wedlock besides providing legal protection to couples in cases of inter-religious matrimony. Above all, it is said to provide succour to brides or grooms who solemnize hasty marriages for fast track dreams of lives abroad by ensuring instant testimony of NRI marriages. This move is proposed to supplement efforts of State Governments to register NRI marriages especially of girls hailing from rural areas.

NO UNIFORM CIVIL LAW OF MARRIAGE

The Indian Parliament has enacted different family law legislations for different religious communities based on their personal laws. Article 44 of the Constitution requires the State to secure for the citizens of India, a uniform Civil Code. However, article 44 enshrined in Part IV of the Constitution dealing with Directive Principles of State Policy are non-justiciable and cannot be enforced. Accordingly, our nation is a unique blend and merger of codified personal laws of Hindus, Christians, Parsis and to some extent of Muslim laws. The Hindu Marriage Act, 1955 (HMA) is an Act to amend and codify the law relating to marriage among Hindus who include Buddhists, Jains or Sikhs by religion. In respect of persons who do not profess any particular religion or are foreigners, the Special Marriage Act, 1954 (SMA) governs all their matrimonial causes. Hence, any foreigner can marry another foreigner or an Indian under the SMA, 1954. The Foreign Marriage Act, 1969, makes provisions relating to marriages of citizens of India who are resident outside the territorial limits of India. There exists no uniform family related law in a single statutory book for all Indians which could be universally applicable to all religious communities who coexist in India. Polygamous relationships are not recognised except under Muslim Personal Law. Even though live in relationships may not be accepted in traditional Indian society, they have found legislative acceptance after the enactment of the Protection of Women from Domestic Violence Act, 2005.

POSITION OF LAW

The principal legislation *i.e.*, HMA, 1955 under which marriage is a sacrament lays down that a Hindu Marriage may be solemnised in accordance with the customary rites and ceremonies of either party. Registration of Hindu marriages is optional as State Governments may make rules providing for registration of marriages. However, this societal practice of optional registration is now not serving the test of time. This lack of will on the part of the Indian legislature to enact a compulsory law for registration of marriages had prompted the Supreme Court in *Seema* v. *Ashwani Kumar*, AIR 2006 SC 1158 to issue directions to all States in India in 2006 to promulgate rules for compulsory registration of marriages in a time bound period, irrespective of the religion of parties. This reform spearheaded by the National Commission for Women was on a progressive note to hinder child marriages, prevent marriages without consent of parties, check bigamy or Polygamy, enable women's rights of maintenance, inheritance and residence besides deterring desertion of spouses. However, despite eight years having gone by, this Court mandate has not been implemented by all States countrywide.

A UNIQUE ROLE MODEL

The family laws in force in Goa, Daman and Diu relating to marriage, divorce, children and succession are primarily contained in the Portuguese Civil Code of 1867. By the Goa, Daman and Diu (Administration) Act, 1962, Parliament has maintained the Portuguese laws in force in Goa, Daman and Diu before its liberation until amended or repealed by the legislature. Law of marriage as a civil contract is in force in the territories of Goa, Daman and Diu w.e.f. May 26, 1911. Goa today therefore has unity in diversity as marriage in the State of Goa is a civil contract solemnized between two persons of different sex with the purpose of legitimately constituting a family. The solemnisation of marriage is by a compulsory civil registration leaving it open to parties to undergo personal law ceremonies optionally. All Indian citizens and foreigners in Goa adhere to the Civil Family Law Code of Goa.

POSITION UNDER HMA, 1955 TODAY

HMA, 1955 mandates solemnisation of ceremonial marriage and performance of customary rites and ceremonies is compulsory whereas registration is optional. Questions relating to whether registration of marriage is substantial proof of Hindu marriage and whether a certificate of marriage being a public document allows a presumption of a valid marriage under the Indian Evidence Act, 1872, have often posed problems for parties. Elucidating the law, it may be commented that purpose of registration of Hindu marriages is to facilitate proof of a Hindu marriage and the parties to any such marriage may exercise the option of having particulars relating to their marriage entered in a Hindu Marriage Register. Clearly, entry in any such register is only optional and the validity of any Hindu Marriage shall in no way be affected by the omission to make such an entry. Therefore, a Hindu marriage solemnised by essential rites and ceremonies is to be proved independently by the performance of such customary practices and registration of a Hindu marriage is only for the purpose of facilitating the proof of such ceremonial unions.

PERFORMANCE OF CEREMONY ESSENTIAL

The registration pre-supposes performance of a valid ceremonial marriage. Thus, performance of *Saptpadi (that is taking of 7 steps by the bridegroom and the bride jointly before the sacred fire)* is a *sine qua non* for solemnising a Hindu marriage. Hence, the extract of the Hindu Marriage Register, which contains the statements of parties of such a marriage, is not substantial evidence to prove the marriage when one of the parties to the registration repudiates or denies the same. It may be a conclusive proof for all other purposes concerning third parties or all others. Noteworthy to say, any third party or a public authority cannot hold that a certificate of Hindu marriage is not substantial proof of the marriage itself . However, if one of the parties denies, repudiates or declines the entry in such a Hindu marriage certificate, then it is for the other party to prove the fact of solemnisation of marriage by establishing performance of customary rites and ceremonies which make it conclusive. In such a situation, merely because the Hindu marriage is registered or the particulars containing the marriage are entered in a Hindu marriage register, will not go to show that the marriage was solemnised in accordance with the conditions prescribed in HMA, 1955. Therefore, the registration of a Hindu marriage alone is not substantial proof of a Hindu Marriage, if one party repudiates, declines or denies the marriage. The effect of production of a marriage certificate is only to the extent that parties have made such statements before the Registrar of Marriages. The marriage certificate being a public document, favourable presumptions can be drawn under the Indian Evidence Act, 1872, subject to their being questioned by parties to the marriage themselves. However, for all others, the marriage certificate may be conclusive.

LAW IN A FLUX – THE DILEMMA REMAINS

The Haryana Compulsory Registration of Marriages Act, 2007 enacted to provide for compulsory registration of marriages solemnised in the State of Haryana irrespective of caste, religion and creed also authorise the Registrar of Marriages to decline registration of marriage if the marriage between the parties is not performed in accordance with the personal law applicable to parties. The Haryana Marriage law enacted pursuant to the 2006 Supreme Court directions pre-supposes performance of Hindu rites and ceremonies as an essential condition. Punjab has enacted the Punjab Compulsory Registration of Marriages Act, 2012. UT Chandigarh has not made any such compulsory Marriage Registration Act. If the registration of marriages is made compulsory under the Registration of Births and Deaths Act, 1969 without corresponding amendments to the HMA, 1955 or other personal laws, the dilemma will remain. Until and unless registration of marriages is also made mandatory and compulsory under the HMA, 1955 and other personal laws, the exercise will be incomplete. If parties to a Hindu marriage choose to resile, repudiate or contradict a proposed compulsory registration under the new proposed marriage registration law, the very solemnisation of marriage will have to be established under the

HMA, 1955 since registration alone will not serve the purpose. The escape route will still remain. Therefore, unless parallel amendments are also carried out in the HMA, 1955 or other personal laws, the new law may be an exercise in futility and the laudable purposes of the fast track registration process may be defeated. It is therefore, necessary and essential that HMA, 1955 and other personal laws are also brought in tandem with the proposed beneficial marriage registration law by also making registration compulsory under the HMA, 1955 and other personal laws. The Goan model which has survived the test of time for 450 years is a useful example for examination in this context. Our law makers would do well if they harmonise the proposed marriage registration law with other prevalent personal family law legislations applicable to make the registration laws a success. A wholesome overhaul is better than a piece meal exercise. The laudable purposes must not be lost in lofty announcements. The salient features of the Punjab Compulsory Registration of Marriages Act, 2012 provide a beacon to shed light in this arena to provide much needed guidance.

PUNJAB COMPULSORY REGISTRATION OF MARRIAGES ACT, 2012 – HIGHLIGHTS

It is an Act to provide for compulsory registration of marriages solemnized under any law governing the parties irrespective of their religion, caste, creed or nationality and for the matters connected or incidental thereto.

- *Every marriage between parties who are Indian nationals or NRIs or foreign nationals solemnized or performed shall be registered.*
- *Foreign nationals will mean any person who is not an Indian citizen and shall include PIOs and OCIs.*
- *To avoid any ambiguity , term NRI has been defined in the new Act to mean any person of Indian origin permanently or temporarily settled outside India.*
- *Whenever any party is an NRI, his passport and foreign address details, social security number as also relevant particulars about him shall be entered both in the marriage register as well as the marriage certificate.*
- *Any marriage solemnised outside Punjab shall also be registered in Punjab. However, if any marriage is already registered elsewhere, it shall not be registered again in Punjab.*
- *A complete mechanism and procedure for registration has been laid down and identified with nominated Registrars of Marriages.*
- *The marriage to be registered shall have to be solemnised in accordance with the personal law of the parties to the satisfaction of the Registrar of Marriages concerned.*
- *Non-registration will not invalidate the marriage as such because the new law is only for registration and cannot invalidate a marriage solemnised as per Central Laws.*
- *Memorandum of marriage duly signed by parties and the priest shall be presented within three months of marriage to Registrar of Marriages. Relaxation may be permitted by the Registrar wherever necessary.*
- *Registrar of Marriages may also* suo moto *(on his own) or on notice register any marriage taking place in his jurisdiction by calling parties.*

- *Any entry may be corrected or cancelled by Registrar of Marriages if obtained fraudulently or made in improperly within correct facts.*

PUNJAB COMPULSORY REGISTRATION OF MARRIAGES RULES, 2013 – HIGHLIGHTS

- *Rules for compulsory registration of marriages in the State of Punjab notified on June 27, 2013, provide for presentation of a Memorandum in a prescribed form before the Registrar of Marriages within three months of the date of marriage. If one of the parties to the marriage is an NRI, he shall furnish additional information as prescribed under the Rules.*
- *Memorandum for registration of marriage can be presented after expiry of period of three months, six months, or one year upon payment of late fee and after obtaining written permission of District Registrar or Chief Registrar of Marriages.*
- *Any person aggrieved by an Order of Registrar of Marriages may appeal within 30 days to the District Registrar of Marriages and thereafter to the Chief Registrar of Marriages within 60 days.*
- *Every Registrar of Marriages shall maintain a Marriage Register both in English and Punjabi language recording details of marriage solemnised which can be inspected by any person interested on payment of a fee.*
- *Registrar of Marriages may* suo moto *or on receipt of an application from any person correct or cancel any entry of a marriage made in erroneous form or made improperly or fraudulently after passing a speaking order upon affording reasonable opportunity to parties concerned of being heard before correction or cancellation.*

FACT FILE – REGISTRATION OF BIRTHS, DEATHS TO INCLUDE MARRIAGES

- The Union Cabinet has approved the introduction of a Bill in the Budget Session of Parliament to amend the Registration of Births and Deaths Act, 1969 to include registration of marriages as well, so that the existing administrative mechanisms will be able to carry out such registration of marriages in accordance with the specified procedures and be able to maintain necessary records and statistics for registration of marriages also.
- The Cabinet also approved introducing a Bill in Parliament to further amend the Anand Marriage Act, 1909 to provide for registration of marriages under this Act. As of now, marriages of all Hindus including Sikhs, Buddhists and Jains are solemnised in accordance with customary rites and ceremonies of either party under the Hindu Marriage Act, 1955, under which registration of such marriages is optional. Only performance of customary rites and ceremonies is mandatory under the Hindu Marriage Act, 1955.
- The proposed Bills are stated to be beneficial for women to prevent them from unnecessary harassment in matrimonial and maintenance cases. It will also provide evidentiary value in matters of custody of children, protect rights of children born from wedlock of couples whose marriage is registered as also provide proof of the age of parties to the marriage.

- The Supreme Court in its judgment of 14 February, 2006, in *Seema* v. *Ashwani Kumar*, AIR 2006 SC1158 had directed the State Governments and the Central Government that marriages of all persons who are citizens of India belonging to various religious denominations should be made compulsorily registerable in their respective States where such marriages are solemnized and *inter alia* directed that as and when the Central Government enacts a comprehensive statute, the same shall be placed before that Court for scrutiny.
- The Committee on Empowerment of Women (2006-2007) in its Twelfth Report (Fourteenth Lok Sabha) on "Plight of Indian Women deserted by Indian husbands" has viewed that all marriages, irrespective of religion should be compulsorily registered and desired that the Government to make registration of all marriages mandatory, making the procedure simpler, affordable and accessible.
- The 18th Law Commission of India in its 205th Report titled" Proposal to Amend the Prohibition of Child Marriage Act, 2006 and Other Allied Laws" in paragraph (iv) recommended that "registration of marriages within a stipulated period, of all the communities, *viz.* Hindu, Muslim, Christians, etc. should be made mandatory by the Government".
- The 18th Law Commission of India further in its 211th Report titled "Laws on Registration of Marriage and Divorce. A proposal for consolidation and Reform", recommending for a Parliamentary Legislation on Compulsory Registration of Marriages by enacting of a "Marriage and Divorce Registration Act" which may be made applicable to the whole of India and to all citizens irrespective of their religion and personal law and without any exceptions or exemptions".
- The Registration of Births and Deaths Act, 1969 is an Act to provide for the regulation of registration of births and deaths and for the matters connected therewith. Accordingly, provisions have already been provided in the said Act for a Registration establishment consisting of Registrar-General, Chief Registrar and Registration Division, District Registrars and Registrars.
- Further, procedures for registration of births and death and for maintenance of records and statistics are provided for in the said Act. Also, by virtue of the powers conferred under section 30 thereof, rules for compulsory registration of births and deaths have been framed by all the State Governments and Union territory Administrations. Therefore, if the said Act is suitably amended to include registration of marriages as well, then the existing administrative mechanisms will be able to carry out such registration of marriages in accordance with the specified procedures and be able to maintain necessary records and statistics for registration of marriages also.
- The registration of marriages of the parties under the proposed amendment of the Registration of Births and Deaths Act is stated to not affect any right recognized or acquired by any party to marriage under any law, custom or usage.

Settlement Sans Divorce-Post Nuptial Agreements

UNIQUE POSITION

In an inimitable decision rendered on 15 July, 2013, in *Pamela Sharda* v. *Rama Sharda* in Special Leave to Appeal (Civil) No. 11714/2012, the Supreme Court, accepting a tripartite settlement deed executed between the wife, husband and his mother through mediation, permitted parties to part ways upon a onetime payment of Rs. 45 lacs to the wife with the condition that both would not seek divorce on any ground. The couple married for 30 years agreed to withdraw all their pending litigations and the wife agreed not to cause any disturbance or invade the privacy of her husband and his 83 year old mother living in their household property. The sum of Rs. 45 lacs paid in full and final settlement to the wife was towards all her financial claims. Both parties living separately since 2009, agreed that they shall have nothing to do with each other's lives and will not undergo any divorce proceedings. The wife would also not claim restitution of conjugal rights or rights of residence in the household. However, in the event of remarriage of the husband, the agreement shall stand terminated and the wife would be entitled to revive her claim of maintenance or alimony for the present and future, since the sum of Rs. 45 lacs shall not be considered as an amount towards dissolution of marriage and payment of permanent alimony. The Apex Court accepting the *Settlement Deed* and the *Undertakings* of the parties, disposed off the matter and permitted parties to file the same before all Courts where litigations were pending with liberty to invoke the provisions of the Contempt of Courts Act, 1971 upon breach if any.

POSITION OF LAW

Under Hindu family laws where marriage is considered a sacrament and not a contract, pre-nuptial agreements do not find any recognition under existing matrimonial legislation or under other civil codified laws. Hence, pre-marital settlements between Hindus are alien to the present legal system. Regardless, if there be any pre-nuptial settlement, it would be tested like any other contract for its validity. Essentially, it should not be opposed to public policy, must not violate principles of natural justice, shall not be fraudulent, and must recognise rights of both the parties as also should be executed freely, voluntarily, without coercion and upon full disclosure of all relevant facts. As, traditionally, breakups are not discussed before marriages, there seems to be no reported decision testing the validity of a pre-nuptial termination agreement.

CHANGING SOCIAL MILLIEU

In a fast evolving society of urban set-ups and escalating cross border matrimonial unions, divorces settled through mutual consent petitions to avoid ugly, protracted and harmful litigations are being increasingly resorted to through the process of alternative dispute resolution and mediation centres now available in all Courts in India. Furthermore, invoking of punitive criminal proceedings against immediate family members and parents of spouses upon death of a matrimonial relationship often results in the entire family being implicated on trumped up charges as retribution to settle scores. Easy outlets to do so under the Indian Penal Code and the Domestic Violence Act often result in harassment to parties, even though they may have no role attributed to them. Likewise, adequate protection and financial support to an abandoned spouse needs to be secured in advance to avoid flights of fancy, leaving a hapless partner with nothing to survive on, if a marriage goes sour. Securing protection for children from inter-parental child removal is another dimension of breaking marriages when abduction of children is resorted to by parents to settle egos. Such facets of life of new generations makes the mind ponder to evolve solutions which as of now do not exist in the statute book but are now necessitated with the advent of time.

EXISTING LAW

As of now, mutual consent is the most resorted to method for divorce if parties are principally in agreement on the terms and conditions of termination of marriage which in itself reflects acceptable breakdown of marriage. However, the Parliament is looking at defining and bringing in irretrievable breakdown of marriage as a additional ground for divorce, through the process of legislation may be time consuming. Though, irretrievable breakdown of marriage is not recognised as a ground of divorce under existing matrimonial laws, the Apex Court, in exercise of its vast powers under article 142 of the Constitution of India may pass such decree or make such order as it is necessary for doing complete justice in any cause or matter pending before it. Hence, in a prolonged messy litigation, the Apex Court may bury the hatchet in the facts and circumstances of a case under its inherent jurisdiction. The Apex Court of India in two decisions *i.e., B.S. Joshi* v. *State of Haryana,* (2003) 4 SCC 675 and *G.V. Rao* v. *L.H.V. Prasad,* (2000) 3 SCC 693, has very eloquently emphasised the need to encourage court settlements in matrimonial disputes. The Court concluded "*...that the parties may ponder over their defaults and terminate their disputes amicably by mutual agreement instead of fighting it out in a court of law where it takes years and years to conclude and in that process the parties lose their "young" days in chasing their "cases" in different courts.*" Therefore, there is far greater emphasis in the Indian context to settle post-marriage matrimonial disputes in the event of divorce oriented litigation, rather than focusing on pre-nuptial agreements. Law, thus looks at the cure and not the remedy to prevent the problems.

NEW PERSPECTIVE

The Apex Court Judgment of July 15, 2013 opens a new window. It is in this breath that the need for pre-nuptial agreements needs a fresh thought with a new outlook. It comes at a time when surrogacy agreements are entered upon freely and have become acceptable in society. Thus, if the concept of a pre-marital settlement finds judicial acceptance and ultimate legislative sanction, matrimonial terms can be settled in advance optionally and alternatively to those who wish to do so. By no means would this be mandatory to offend those who do not wish to think of marital breakups before marriage by considering it as inauspicious or uneventful. Without disturbing sentiments, emotions or feelings of traditional mindsets, the thought process can possibly relax drawing up of pre-marriage agreements where double income independent spouses are comfortable in such mutual understandings. Protection of spouses and avoidance of inter-parental child removal are immediate benefits of it. Beneficiaries would include a large segment of the NRI population who either marry foreign spouses or relocate to overseas jurisdictions and need written understandings for mutual protection and easy implementation by courts in alien jurisdictions. Clash of parallel matrimonial disputes in Indian and foreign courts can easily be avoided by it.

CONCLUSIONS

Equally, the law does not forbid spouses to agree as to how they should live and conduct themselves as husband and wife, when they would consummate their marriage and how they would conduct themselves to each other. It is equally important that due respect should be given for adult autonomy, subject to proper safeguards and which could be tested by judicial discretion, when the need arises. The fact remains, that any matrimonial agreement made between husband and wife should not be illegal, immoral or opposed to public policy. The overhanging safeguard of the pre-marital settlement being adopted as a fair, free and just settlement will always be omnipotent. By no means or standard, it should be used as an instrument of oppression to take away rights of spouses which are guaranteed under existing laws meant to secure relief. The need for evolving a jurisprudence to develop a positive thought process for creating such friendly methods would require an educative process to familiarise the advantages of such a concept while also clearly identifying its negative traits. The chaff has to be separated from the grain to enjoy the dough which has to be kneaded and blended over a period of time to be consumed to become acceptable as a welcome change. The traditional and sacramental notion of marriage must be gently flavoured with a commercially sounding phrase of pre-nuptial agreements which is not to be viewed as an announcement of a break up of a marriage, even before it is solemnised. The path has to be tread carefully and slowly while administering the change. Changing times require that amicable settlements be arrived at by dispute resolution which can be aided and assisted if the parameters are penned down in advance.

Trial of NRI Matrimonial Criminal Offences

The vexed jurisdictional question for seeking relief in split NRI marriages for criminal wrongs has been set at rest by the Apex Court Judgment of 2 September in *Thota Venkateswarlu* v. *State of Andhra Pradesh,* (2011) 9 SCC 527, wherein it has been held that Indian Courts, with the prior consent of the Central Government, can try offences committed by an Indian citizen in a foreign country. The case related to a Hindu traditional marriage solemnized in Andhra Pradesh with allegations of torture meted out to the wife in Botswana. Accordingly, abandoned brides, jilted spouses, destitute children and offended families back home can now find solace with Indian Courts under criminal law.

Allegations of cruelty by the husband or his relatives, criminal breach of trust by misappropriation of a woman's personal property, dowry wrongs, criminal neglect to maintain spouse, children or parents, bigamous marriages and commission of adultery are commonly cited criminal offences in NRI marriages. Thirty million NRIs in 180 countries abroad makes their occurrence a high risk number. However, the process of criminal investigation and trial in India can be tardy and hedged with jurisdictional objections to thwart and delay award of punishment. In this bleak scenario, the Supreme Court judgment provides succor to unfortunate victims in dire straits on Indian Soil. Interpreting these provisions, the Apex Court has culled out a clear mandate of law providing an authoritative import to be followed by all Indian Courts as the law of the land.

In terms of section 4 of the Indian Penal Code (IPC), Indian criminal courts can try an accused Indian citizen even if the offence was committed outside India. Under section 188 of the Code of Criminal Procedure (Cr. P.C.), if a criminal offence is committed by an Indian citizen outside India, he may be dealt with in respect of such an offence as if it had been committed at any place within India at which the Indian citizen may be found. However, no such offence shall be inquired into or tried in India except with the previous sanction of the Central Government.

Considering a mixed bag of criminal wrongs of matrimonial cruelty, the Apex Court had crystallized the crux question whether in respect of a series of such offences, some of which were committed within India and some outside India, could such offences be tried together without the previous sanction of the Central Government as envisaged under section 188, Cr. P.C. Having done so, the salutary verdict of the Supreme Court, proceeds to conclusively decide the issue and an analysis of the settled law on the proposition can be interpreted to lay down the following conclusions:

- Stated offences under the Dowry Prohibition Act occurring within the territorial jurisdiction of the criminal courts in India can be tried without having to obtain the previous sanction of the Central Government.
- Alleged offences of matrimonial cruelty and criminal breach of trust committed by an Indian spouse outside India, where the couple resided, may be dealt with as if they had been committed in India. Previous sanction of the Central Government would be necessary in such cases.
- In respect of offences alleged to be committed outside India, previous sanction is required to be taken by the prosecuting agency before the trial can commence. However, this fetter is imposed only when the stage of trial is reached and no sanction is required till commencement of trial. It is only after the decision to try the offender in India was felt necessary, sanction would be required for trial to commence. Upto the stage of taking cognizance, no previous sanction is necessary.
- The Magistrate is free to proceed against the accused in respect of offences allegedly committed in India, complete their trial and pass judgment therein, without being inhibited by the other alleged offences for which sanction would be required.
- As the IPC extends to extra-territorial offences, Indian citizens would be amenable to Indian criminal law subject to limitations of sanction required under law.

The vivid, erudite and meaningful pronouncement will enable criminal courts in India to proceed with clarity in the dispensation of justice to wronged NRI marriages. The jurisdiction of the Indian courts in respect of NRI marital offences will no longer be lost by reason of the venue of the offence. Clearly, the object of prior sanction of the Central Government is only to prevent the accused from being tried over again in two different places for the same offence and not to escape the noose by jurisdictional immunity. Logically, the phrase "dealt with" for being proceeded with in India under criminal law does not impede or infringe the process of investigation into marital wrongs committed abroad. Axiomatically, the bar of sanction operates before the Magistrate in India after the investigating authority presents the charge sheet for the alleged offences. However, it can also be stated that for all overt criminal acts committed in India, in furtherance of a conspiracy and confabulation with NRIs abroad, sanction of Central Government of prosecution in India may not be necessary.

In, a different breath, in another previous decision, The Supreme Court, in *Fatima Bibi* v. *State of Gujarat,* AIR 2008 SC 2392 had earlier come to the rescue of a mother-in-law, a Mauritius national, who was accused by her Indian daughter-in-law in Gujarat of torture, intimidation and instigation, as offences under the IPC in respect of physical and mental cruelty faced at the hands of her husband while residing with him in Kuwait. The Apex Court allowing her appeal had quashed the criminal proceedings holding that since the offences were said to have been committed in Kuwait, the IPC or Cr. P.C. would have no application. Further, as a citizen of Mauritius, the mother-in-law was not liable for prosecution under the IPC in India for offences committed outside India. Substantial justice resulted thereupon.

Thus, marriages in vain abroad cannot be remedied or dissolved in India if they are not within the ambit of Indian law. The courts have drawn a well-defined dividing line. But then, such fractured and fragmented human relationships need to be resolved. If Indian law is beyond the scope and purview of application, the solutions and answers may lie elsewhere. Seeing to the phenomenal number of increasing Indian diaspora abroad, principles of private international family law seriously need to be debated to assemble mechanisms within legal frameworks of the respective countries who face these global family law problems. This needs urgent and immediate deliberation at international platforms for common unified humane solutions. The Apex Court judgments point to this much needed path of resolution.

MISCELLANEOUS

MISCELLANEOUS

- A Milestone Achieved – DNA Profiling Comes of Age
- Human Rights Law above Children in Norway
- New Punjab Laws – A Milestone Achieved
- The Triumph of the Human Spirit
- Victims Compensation Scheme
- Law, Films and the Sound of Music
- Law, Liability and Compensation
- Chinks in the Non-Resident Indian Armour

A Milestone Achieved – DNA Profiling Comes of Age

DNA Testing Enforceable

A valuable right of a party to prove paternity by DNA testing has been tried, tested and proved. A person can now be physically compelled to give a blood sample for DNA profiling in compliance with a Civil Court order in a paternity action. The erudite judgment of the Delhi High Court of 27 April, 2012 in *Rohit Shekhar* v. *Narayan Dutt Tiwari,* AIR 2012 Del 151, has held that once a matrimonial or civil court exercises its inherent power to order a person to submit to a medical examination or it directs holding of a scientific, technical or expert investigation, which is resisted or refused by a party, the Court is entitled to enforce such direction and not simply take the refusal on record to draw an adverse inference therefrom. The Court also settled the issue that such mandatory testing upon an unwilling person is not violative of the Right to Life or privacy of a person under article 21 of the Constitution though the power to direct a DNA test should be exercised after weighing all *"pros and cons"* and satisfying the *"test of 'eminent need'"*. However, this right has been restricted to the Civil Courts only by holding that the same reasoning cannot be applied in the context of criminal cases as the Supreme Court in *Selvi* v. *State of Karnataka,* (2010) 7 SCC 263 has held that Narco-analysis, Polygraph (Lie-detector) test and BEAP (Brain Electrical Activation Profile) conducted against the will of a person are impermissible under criminal law where an accused cannot be compelled to make self incriminating statements to be a witness against himself.

SOME PREVIOUS INSTANCES

√ On October 30, 2006, in *CBI* v. *Santosh Kumar Singh,* the Delhi High Court sentenced the accused to death for the rape and murder of a law student on January 23, 1996. The acquittal was turned into conviction by the High Court, amongst other grounds on the basis of the DNA Test conducted in the case by The Centre for Cellular and Molecular Biology, Hyderabad, which had clearly established the fact of rape even though the surgeon who had conducted the post mortem had ruled out rape. The Supreme Court has affirmed both the findings and the said sentence.

√ On December 6, 2005, in *Nirmaljit Kaur* v. *State of Punjab,* the Apex Court relying exclusively on report dated August 30, 2005, for "DNA Typing Evidence for Establishing Maternity" came to the conclusion that the child produced before the Court is not the real child of the petitioner and that the petitioner's real child is in the custody of the respondents elsewhere. The Supreme Court also held that "A perusal of the entire proceedings in this Court and the proceedings pending before the other Courts would only go to show the respondents' evil desire to grab the property and to make the life of the petitioner-a widow with a girl child miserable." The respondents' were also convicted for Contempt of Court.

√ On September 26, 2005, in *State of Uttar Pradesh through CBI* v. *Madhumani Tripathi*, the State of Uttar Pradesh through CBI aggrieved by the orders passed by the Allahabad High Court releasing the accused on bail, filed appeals before the Supreme Court in a case of murder where the DNA reports showed the accused as the father of a six month feotus found in the womb of the deceased. The Supreme Court while disposing off the appeals held that on the basis of material collected in evidence, the Supreme Court set aside the High Court orders and cancelled the bail bonds and directed the respondents to surrender forthwith.

√ In an international perspective in 2007, the Jamaican Police probing the murder of Pakistan's cricket team coach Bob Woolmer had sought the DNA samples from everyone in the hotel where the deceased was allegedly said to be strangulated. According to the police, as reported, DNA samples were sought from all the members of the West Indies, Ireland and Pakistani teams.

√ Maninder Pal Singh Kohli accused of murdering Hannah Foster in Hampshire in 2003 was apprehended in India and extradited to UK by British Police in 2007 after his wife consented to DNA testing from their two sons and Forensic Science Service was able to infer a DNA profile for the fugitive criminal from their DNA which matched the DNA of the semen of the accused found on the clothes of Hannah Foster.

In view of the above quoted instances, today, the most debatable question which generates thoughts amongst jurists, judges, scientists, lawyers and academicians, irrespective of any legal system, is as to how the present value based system of justice requires to be changed or modified or reoriented for the purposes of utilizing the advantages of modern scientific discoveries and technological advancements in the justice delivery system.

DNA FINGERPRINTING – INPUTS AND ADVANTAGES

This science is used as a new form of circumstantial evidence, which is placed on a higher pedestal than direct and ocular evidence because of its objectivity, scientific accuracy, infallibility and impartial character. Moreover, this new technology is also extensively applied in civil cases in order to determine paternity or maternity disputes, baby-swapping matters, succession disputes, maintenance proceedings and matrimonial disputes etc. For instance, in case of disputed paternity or maternity of a child, mere comparison of DNA obtained from the body fluid or body tissues of the child with his father and mother can offer reliable evidence of biological parentage within a short span of time. No other evidence or corroboration is required because timely medical examination and proper sampling of body fluids followed by quality forensic examination can offer irrefutable evidence, avoiding the need of protracted Court proceedings. Regardless of the fact that the science may be foolproof, but the fact remains that human action which controls the result of this scientific forensic examination may be questionable. There is also the lurking probability of manipulation and tampering of this scientific evidence. In instances of organized crime, rioting and public massacres, DNA samples can be fudged by deliberate action. This apart, the infallible results of the scientific process is otherwise apparently unassailable.

SOME CONFLICTING CASE LAW PROPOSITIONS

Depending on the individual facts and circumstances in different cases over lengths of time, varied views have emerged from the Apex Court vis-à-vis admissibility and credibility of DNA profiling as cogent evidence before Courts of law. Even though Medical Jurisprudence has immensely benefited the legal arena but the fact remains that DNA fingerprinting has no statutory recognition.

- In ***Goutam Kundu* v. *State of West Bengal,* (1993) 3 SCC 418**, the Supreme Court expressed the most reluctant attitude in the application of DNA evidence in resolving the paternity dispute arising out of a maintenance proceeding. In the said case, the father disputed paternity and demanded blood grouping test to determine parentage for the purpose of deciding whether a child is entitled to get maintenance under section 125 of the Code of Criminal Procedure from him. In this context, the Supreme Court held that where purpose of the application was nothing more than to avoid payment of maintenance, without making out any ground whatever to have recourse to the test, the application for blood test couldn't be accepted. It was also held that no person could be compelled to give sample of blood for analysis against his will & no adverse inference can be drawn against him/her for such refusal. The Apex Court held (at page 428 para 26):

  "That courts in India cannot order blood test as a matter of course; wherever applications are made for such prayers in order to have roving enquiry, the prayer for blood test cannot be entertained. There must be a strong *prima facie* case in that the husband must establish non-access in order to dispel the presumption arising under section 112 of the Evidence Act. The Court must carefully examine as to what would be the consequence of ordering the blood test; whether it will have the effect of branding a child as a bastard and the mother as an unchaste woman. No one can be compelled to give sample of blood for analysis."

- In a judgment of the Supreme Court in the year 2001, ***Kamti Devi* v. *Poshi Ram,* (2001) 5 SCC 311** the Court gave priority to social parentage over biological parentage and thereby rejected DNA evidence by observing that though the result of a genuine DNA test is said to be scientifically accurate it is not enough to escape from the conclusiveness of section 112 of the Evidence Act, 1872. Accordingly, it was held that under section 112 of the Evidence Act, non-access between the man and the woman is the only way to raise the presumption against legitimacy and the DNA result was not given any weight.

- However, in total contrast, in ***Sharda* v. *Dharmpal,* (2003) 4 SCC 493,** the Apex Court took a very positive view regarding the importance as well as the admissibility of medical evidence in matrimonial matters. The Supreme Court categorically summed up its conclusions as hereunder (at page 524, para 81):

  "*1. A matrimonial court has the power to order a person to undergo medical test.*

  2. Passing of such an order by the court would not be in violation of the right to personal liberty under article 21 of the Indian Constitution.

  3. However, the court should exercise such a power if the applicant has a strong prima facie case and there is sufficient material before the court. If despite the order of the court, the respondent refuses to submit himself to medical examination, the court will be entitled to draw an adverse inference against him."

  In the aforesaid case, the Supreme Court by distinguishing its earlier decision in *Goutam Kundu's* case further held that right to privacy under article 21 of the Constitution is not an absolute right and in a case of conflict between the fundamental rights of the two parties, the court has to strike balance between the competing rights.

- In a turn around, the Apex Court in ***Banarsi Dass* v. *Teeku Dutta,* (2005) 4 SCC 449,** following ***Goutam Kundu* v. *State of West Bengal,* (1993) 3 SCC 418,** while determining the question whether a direction can be given for conducting a DNA test in proceedings for the issuance of a succession certificate, declined the same and held that DNA test is not to be directed as a matter of routine. It was held by the Court that even though the result of a genuine DNA test is said to be scientifically accurate but it is not enough to escape the conclusiveness of section 112 of the Evidence Act. According to the Court if a husband and wife are living together during the time of conception but the DNA test revealed that the child was not born to the husband, the conclusiveness in law would remain unrebuttable. Therefore, in law, this presumption can only be displaced by a strong preponderance of evidence and not by a mere balance of probabilities.

- In ***Kamalanantha* v. *State of Tamil Nadu,* (2005) 5 SCC 194,** in a case of conviction for rape of 13 Ashram girls and murder of one of its inmates, the reliance on reports of DNA tests on dead foetus to establish paternity to prove rape was sought to be dislodged in appeal on different grounds. Rejecting the challenge, the Apex Court upheld the veracity of the DNA reports which were held to be good testimony for convicting the accused.

- In ***Nandlal Wasudeo Badwaik* v. *Lata Nandlal Badwaik* decided on January 6, 2014 and (2014) 1 SCALE 99,** reconciling the reports of a DNA test and the provisions of section 112 of the Evidence Act, the Apex Court held that section 112 of the Evidence Act does not create a legal fiction but provides for presumption. Relying on the report of the DNA test which scientifically indicated that paternity was not established, the Apex Court also utilized the factual aspect of denial of access to the alleged father from the mother of the child. Holding that, "Truth must triumph", the Court held that, "The husband's plea that he had no access to the wife when the child was begotten stands proved by the DNA test report and in the face of it, we cannot compel the Appellant to bear the fatherhood of a child, when the scientific reports prove to the contrary."

A perusal of some of the decisions in the last 20 years quoted above indicates that in the absence of any statutory recognition to DNA as credible evidence, its acceptance may vary at the discretion of the Court trying a civil or criminal case. Statutory inferences to the contrary dispel scientific results of DNA evidence. Hence, views vary on a case by case approach depending on the debated facts and circumstances which necessitate testing of credibility DNA evidence. The latest decision in 2014 by the Apex Court, however, shows strong reliance on a DNA test report for paternity purposes.

EXISTING STATUTES DEALING WITH MEDICAL EVIDENCE

- Several convictions have occurred in India where the scientific evidence (DNA) has been accepted under **section 45 of the Indian Evidence Act** dealing with opinions of experts. The Courts have opined that medical evidence is only an evidence of opinion and is hardly decisive not being substantive evidence.
- Likewise **section 293 of the Code of Criminal Procedure (Cr.P.C.)** deals with reports of certain Government scientific experts. Section 293(2) says that the Court may, if it thinks fit, summon and examine such expert as to the subject matter of his report. However, DNA finger printing and diagnostics is not specifically included amongst Government scientific experts mentioned in section 293(4) of Cr.P.C. which applies to specified government scientific experts.
- **Section 53 of the Criminal Procedure Code** provides some scope for the investigating officer to have the accused examined by a medical practitioner at the request of the police. This section too does not specifically say whether it would be applicable for DNA testing as well.
- To determine a child's parentage there is a statutory presumption under **section 112 of the Evidence Act** that any person born during the continuance of a valid marriage between his/her mother and any man, or within two hundred and eighty days after its dissolution, the mother remaining unmarried, shall be conclusive proof that he is the legitimate child of that man, unless it can be shown that the parties had no access to each other at any time when that child could have been begotten. Now, DNA testing may be attempted to rebut the said statutory presumption arising under the Act, or to establish evidence in the circumstances where no presumption arises. One may seek DNA parentage testing in order to obtain evidence that the person is not the father of the child. DNA

parentage testing may also attempt to provide evidence to show that a person has a biological connection with a deceased person and can be a proof in support of a succession claim. However, in the absence of any legislation regarding the status of DNA evidence, it is the discretion of the Court whether to accept or decline such evidence, which may be brought on the record of the Court.

CHANGE & REFORMS IN THE PRESENT SYSTEM: NEED OF THE HOUR

- The vigilant search for truth is the hallmark of our criminal justice system. Science and law, two distinct professions have increasingly become intermingled for ensuring a fair process and to see that justice is done. The legal system today has to deal with novel scientific evidence, which has posed new challenges for law. Many of these dilemmas arise from fundamental differences between legal and scientific processes. Scientific evidence has accurate fact-finding results without uncertainties, which accompany legal decision-making. However, if these scientific investigations do not find statutory recognition, their reports may or may not be accepted in the discretion of the Court. DNA profiling in criminal cases is one such paradox.
- The 185th Report of the Law Commission of India on the review of the Indian Evidence Act, 1872, dated March 13, 2003 has recommended that with reference to proof of paternity, section 112 of the Evidence Act be amended. Three other exceptions by way of blood group test, DNA investigations, and medical tests to prove impotency have been recommended to be introduced other than non access of parties to each other.

A reading of the above shows that if the above recommendation is accepted and incorporated in the Evidence Act, it may be the first Indian legislation to give statutory acceptance to DNA investigations conducted by consent of parties. Furthermore, it will dispel the existing requirement of proof where other than non-access of parties, even DNA investigations are not considered conclusive proof to rebut legitimacy. As of now if the DNA result does not match, the identity of the person is not established. But, surprisingly, the contrary is not true. May be the amended position will be a harmony in reality.

CONCLUSION: SO NEAR YET SO FAR

- In Western Countries, DNA test and profile is now widely employed. In our country too, systematic programme and scientific planning ought to be started for the use of DNA technology. Orientation programmes, seminars, workshops, publications and awareness campaigns ought to be carried out for popularizing and creating awareness of the benefits of DNA tests. All concerned functionaries in the civil and criminal justice delivery system in general and the police, Courts and correctional institutions in particular must be acquainted with this science. A fusion of knowledge of forensic sciences and new DNA technology will not only lead to quick detection of crimes but will also be useful in the prevention and control of crimes. Needless to add, civil disputes will also find quick resolution.

- A serious endeavour should be made to emphasize the need for recognition of an independent body which has been called the DNA Profiling Advisory Committee and implement quality control measures with reference to DNA profiling, to provide recommendation on the use of current and future DNA methods, to draft an appropriate legislation for all issues concerning DNA profiling, to safeguard the rights of individuals thereunder, and to create a National DNA Bank for aiding Criminal Justice System;
- Immediate steps should be taken to make suitable changes in the Code of Criminal Procedure 1973, Indian Penal Code, 1860, Indian Evidence Act, 1872, The Family Courts Act, 1984, and all other prevalent family law legislations in India to provide for statutory amendments to recognize results of DNA investigations and to provide for DNA tests and profiles as authentic modes of proof in matters of civil, criminal and matrimonial disputes.

In sum and substance, rather than leaving it to a case by case approach of the Courts, clear legislation is the need of the hour. How long will it take before DNA evidence can be universally accepted as reliable evidence, depends on the protagonists of change. It may also be said that the existing value based criminal justice system cannot be done away with and a balance has to be struck between the modern system and the existing pattern. It may be unsafe to convict or acquit a person exclusively on the basis of DNA evidence but, its scientific results cannot be ignored in achieving the truth for justice. It may be remembered that the DNA witness is unstoppable and given a chance it will speak the truth and only the truth. Despite vast benefits, in the field of law, medical jurisprudential techniques are not treated as primary or secondary evidence till date. The present Indian Evidence Act, continues to treat technical findings such as results of DNA tests as expert evidence. This stalemate will continue till a suitable legislation is enacted by the Parliament. It is sincerely hoped that the proposed Bill for recognizing DNA as evidence sees the light of the day at the earliest. Ends of justice demand that it should not be further delayed. To enable non-resident Indians to be benefited by DNA evidence in matters of determining paternity in surrogate arrangements and resolving consequential immigration issues, such amendments would be extremely beneficial. Likewise, in matters of ascertaining and establishing evidence in international crimes, DNA evidence would assist Indian law in clinching the culprits with certainty.

*****

SOME CONFLICTING CASE LAW PROPOSITIONS

Depending on the individual facts and circumstances in different cases over lengths of time, varied views have emerged from the Apex Court vis-à-vis admissibility and credibility of DNA profiling as cogent evidence before Courts of law. Even though Medical Jurisprudence has immensely benefited the legal arena but the fact remains that DNA fingerprinting has no statutory recognition.

- In ***Goutam Kundu* v. *State of West Bengal,* (1993) 3 SCC 418**, the Supreme Court held *"That courts in India cannot order blood test as a matter of course; wherever applications are made for such prayers in order to have roving enquiry, the prayer for blood test cannot be entertained. There must be a strong prima facie case in that the husband must establish non-access in order to dispel the presumption arising under section 112 of the Evidence Act. The Court must carefully examine as to what would be the consequence of ordering the blood test; whether it will have the effect of branding a child as a bastard and the mother as an unchaste woman. No one can be compelled to give sample of blood for analysis."*
- In ***Kamti Devi* v. *Poshi Ram,* (2001) 5 SCC 311**, the Supreme Court held that under section 112 of the Evidence Act, non-access between the man and the woman is the only way to raise the presumption against legitimacy and the DNA result was not given any weight.
- In ***Sharda* v. *Dharmpal,* (2003) 4 SCC 493, the Apex Court held that**

  "1. A matrimonial court has the power to order a person to undergo medical test.

  2. Passing of such an order by the court would not be in violation of the right to personal liberty under article 21 of the Indian Constitution.

  3. However, the court should exercise such a power if the applicant has a strong prima facie case and there is sufficient material before the court. If despite the order of the court, the respondent refuses to submit himself to medical examination, the court will be entitled to draw an adverse inference against him."
- In ***Banarsi Dass* v. *Teeku Dutta,* (2005) 4 SCC 449,** it was held by the Court that even though the result of a genuine DNA test is said to be scientifically accurate but it is not enough to escape the conclusiveness of section 112 of the Evidence Act. According to the Court if a husband and wife are living together during the time of conception but the DNA test revealed that the child was not born to the husband, the conclusiveness in law would remain unrebuttable.
- In ***Kamalanantha* v. *State of Tamil Nadu,* (2005) 5 SCC 194**, in a case of conviction for rape of 13 Ashram girls and murder of one of its inmates, the reliance on reports of DNA tests on dead foetus to establish paternity to prove rape was sought to be dislodged in appeal on different grounds. Rejecting the challenge, the Apex Court upheld the veracity of the DNA reports which were held to be good testimony for convicting the accused.
- In ***Nandlal Wasudeo Badwaik* v. *Lata Nandlal Badwaik* decided on January 6, 2014 and (2014) 1 SCALE 99,** reconciling the reports of a DNA test and the provisions of section 112 of the Evidence Act, the Apex Court held that section 112 of the Evidence Act does not create a legal fiction but

provides for presumption. Relying on the report of the DNA test which scientifically indicated that paternity was not established, the Apex Court also utilized the factual aspect of denial of access to the alleged father from the mother of the child. Holding that, "Truth must triumph", the Court held that, "The husband's plea that he had no access to the wife when the child was begotten stands proved by the DNA test report and in the face of it, we cannot compel the Appellant to bear the fatherhood of a child, when the scientific reports prove to the contrary."

A perusal of some of the decisions in the last 20 years quoted above indicates that in the absence of any statutory recognition to DNA as credible evidence, its acceptance may vary at the discretion of the Court trying a civil or criminal case. Hence, views vary on a case by case approach depending on the debated facts and circumstances which necessitate testing of credibility DNA evidence. The latest decision in 2014 by the Apex Court, however, shows strong reliance on a DNA test report for paternity purposes.

EXISTING STATUTES DEALING WITH MEDICAL EVIDENCE

- Several convictions have occurred in India where the scientific evidence (DNA) has been accepted under **section 45 of the Indian Evidence Act** dealing with opinions of experts. The Courts have opined that medical evidence is only an evidence of opinion and is hardly decisive not being substantive evidence.
- Likewise **section 293 of the Code of Criminal Procedure (Cr.P.C.)** deals with reports of certain Government scientific experts. Section 293(2) says that the Court may, if it thinks fit, summon and examine such expert as to the subject matter of his report. However, DNA finger printing and diagnostics is not specifically included amongst Government scientific experts mentioned in section 293(4) of CrPC which applies to specified government scientific experts.
- **Section 53 of the Criminal Procedure Code** provides some scope for the investigating officer to have the accused examined by a medical practitioner at the request of the police. This section too does not specifically say whether it would be applicable for DNA testing as well.
- To determine a child's parentage there is a statutory presumption under **section 112 of the Evidence Act** that any person born during the continuance of a valid marriage between his/her mother and any man, or within two hundred and eighty days after its dissolution, the mother remaining unmarried, shall be conclusive proof that he is the legitimate child of that man, unless it can be shown that the parties had no access to each other at any time when that child could have been begotten. Now, DNA testing may be attempted to rebut the said statutory presumption arising under the Act, or to establish evidence in the circumstances where no presumption arises. However, in the absence of any legislation regarding the status of DNA evidence, it is the discretion of the Court whether to accept or decline such evidence, which may be brought on the record of the Court.

Human Rights Law Above Children in Norway

As March 8, 2012 had drawn nearer, the clock ticked and the residence permits of Indian children Abhigyan and Aishwarya in foster care in Norway would have lapsed. Before they had been renewed against the consent of the Bhattacharayas in Norway, Indian Government ought to have acted as all ongoing diplomatic parleys had to be subject to the hearing before a Norwegian Court on March 23, 2013 which may still have decided to keep the Indian children in Norway and a *fait accompli* would have followed sealing the rights of the Indian parents. That should not have been allowed to happen. There is a law above Norway for children and that should have been invoked forthwith. We are missing the point of the legal avenue by venturing into diplomatic solutions.

Article 8 of the European Convention on Human Rights (hereafter, ECHR), which is the cornerstone of the right to family life, is as important in the European Union as right to life and personal liberty guaranteed as a fundamental right under article 21 of the Constitution of India. Article 8 of the ECHR can be applied to the benefit of the expatriate Indian parents in Norway, "whose family life has been severely disrupted," rather tormented on account of forced separation at the hands of Norway from their minor children. What has been unfairly done must be nullified by a superior legal process in an arena of human rights jurisprudence. Norway cannot be an end to itself.

The humanitarian and respected ECHR is an international treaty that has a charter of fundamental rights for the benefit of persons residing within the European region. Aggrieved persons whose treaty rights have also been violated in terms of article 8 of the ECHR can seek redressal of their rights against the member states by invoking the jurisdiction of the European Court of Human Rights, in Strasbourg, France. The Strasbourg system is so termed because of the geographical location of the Court and the institutions have adjudicated upon 40,000 individual cases and approximately 20 cases of member states *inter-se* between themselves.

Formal intervention for redressal under the provisions of the ECHR is called for in the Norway children case for suitable and fair redressal. Norway, is very much party to the ECHR. Hence, Sagarika and Anurup Bhattacharya, the aggrieved parents were very much entitled to institute proceedings before the ECHR not only for seeking to be reunited immediately with their two minor children but also for seeking costs and damages. This was on the basis of article 8 of the ECHR which provides as follows:

> "**Article 8. Right to respect for private and family life**
>
> 1. Everyone has the right to respect for his private and family life, his home and his correspondence.
>
> 2. There shall be no interference by a public authority with the exercise of this right except such as is in accordance with the law and is necessary in a democratic society in the interests of national security, public safety or the economic well-being of the country, for the prevention of disorder or crime, for the protection of health or morals, or for the protection of the rights and freedoms of others."

Clearly, there had been unnecessary and unwarranted interference by the Norwegian Child Protection Services, which had shown scant disregard for the private and family life of the Bhattacharyas. Hence, the infringement and disruption of their private and family life, vested with them with justifiable cause of action to invoke the jurisdiction of the ECHR. In the cases before the ECHR, presence of legal counsel is not mandatory, which in effect, would have facilitated the Bhattacharyas to directly invoke the jurisdiction of the ECHR without incurring enormous prohibitive legal costs.

Any complaint to the ECHR must qualify basic admissibility criteria, the complainant must be personally aggrieved from any such alleged violation. Prima facie, the Bhattacharyas certainly were the affected victims themselves. A duly completed form has to be returned to the Court with complete factual description, averments alleging convention rights, judicial domestic remedies exhausted and relief sought from the ECHR. Applicants must demonstrate that they have made efforts to avail a remedy for the alleged breach from the erring State, which of course had been unsuccessfully done so far by the Bhattacharyas. Adjudication through written arguments is generally the norm before the ECHR. Additionally, "Notes for the guidance of persons wishing to apply to the European Court of Human Rights" may be found at http://www.echr.coe.int/NoticesForApplicants/Noticeeng.htm.

Instead of mediating with the Norwegians and increasing the 10 month gap of the separation of the Bhattacharyas family in Norway, in retrospect it can be stated that it is time that India had taken up the matter in the ECHR or had assisted the family in doing so. The human rights of Indians which are sacrosanct in the Indian jurisdiction must be respected abroad equally. If India as a emerging global economic centre lends its intellectual property to European nations, reciprocity requires India to protect their honour and fundamental freedoms. What cannot be cured must not be endured. If the Norwegian judicial system had decided to keep the Indian children in foster care in Norway till they attain age of majority, article 8 of the ECHR would have been violated. Norway cannot violate a law by which it is bound. The internal adjudication in Norway by their local principles and domestic standards cannot override an international law which applies to nations. Norway cannot rule its own roost.

It seems shocking that India whose writ jurisdiction is a harbinger of human rights had permitted the Bhattacharayas in Norway to be compulsorily subjected to an internal closed door conventional Norwegian justice system obsessed with their ideologies of child care. Though, the argument of personal law application to Bhattacharayas in Norway had its own force independently, their right to private and family life could not have been flouted by Norway under article 8 of the ECHR. A public outcry, a media flare and human interest outrage had flooded all print and electronic news daily highlighting the injustice. The immunity of the Indian Government in being a subservient spectator did not serve the cause of 30 million non-resident Indians in 180 countries abroad.

New Punjab Laws – A Milestone Achieved

NEW LAWS DEFINED

The Punjab Compulsory Registration of Marriages Act, 2012 and the Punjab Travel Professionals Regulation Act, 2012, which have both been recently approved by the Punjab Legislative Assembly on 21 December, 2012 have become laws in State of Punjab. Both new laws seek a milestone to achieve. Punjab will be the first State of the country to enact a Human Smuggling Law to provide for the regulation of the profession of travel agents with a view to check and curb their illegal or fraudulent activities. Likewise, even though compulsory Registration of Marriages is now provided in most States, however, Punjab will be the first State to make marriages of Non-resident Indians and foreign nationals also compulsorily registrable in the State of Punjab. These initiatives are the product of a long exercise which will help resolving maladies plaguing the system intrinsically as a result of lack of legislations to curb new generation problems created by a migratory regime of 30 million NRIs living in 180 nations overseas.

PUNJAB COMPULSORY REGISTRATION OF MARRIAGES ACT, 2012

COMPULSORY MARRIAGE REGISTRATION OF NRI MARRIAGES IN PUNJAB

The Hindu Marriage Act, 1955 (HMA) leaves it open for every State Government to enact compulsory provisions for Registration of Marriages. The Supreme Court in 2006 in *Seema* v. *Ashwani Kumar,* AIR 2006 SC 1158 issued a mandate to all States to make registration of marriage compulsory by enacting legislations. This directive led to the enactment of The Punjab Compulsory Registration of Marriages Act, 2012, providing for compulsory registration of marriages solemnized under any law governing the parties irrespective of their religion, caste, creed or nationality. Any marriage solemnized in Punjab is now compulsorily registerable and even marriages solemnized outside the State of Punjab can be registered at a place where parties have their temporary residence in Punjab. However, if the marriage is already registered elsewhere, it shall not be registered again in the State of Punjab.

DEFINITION OF NRIs IN THE NEW LAW

The most prominent feature of the new marriage law is the definition of a *"non resident Indian"* to mean a person of Indian origin who is either permanently or temporarily settled outside India for employment, business, vocation or any other purpose indicating a uncertain or determined period of overseas stay. Likewise, a *"foreign national"* has been defined to mean a person who is not a citizen of India and shall include *Persons of Indian Origin* (PIO) and *Overseas Citizens of India (OCI)* who are defined under the Citizenship Act, 1955 and mean foreign nationals of Indian Origin who have earlier been Indian Citizens or qualify for Indian citizenship.

NRI MARRIAGES IN THE LOOP

The law in the making provides that every marriage between parties who are Indian nationals or NRIs or foreign nationals solemnized or performed in the State of Punjab, irrespective of religion, caste, creed or nationality shall also be registered in the State of Punjab. The most significant feature would be that for every NRI or foreign national, it would be mandatory to disclose in writing his/her passport number, country of its issue, period of its validity besides permanent residential/official address of overseas abode with social security number or any such permanent identification proof issued by his foreign country. All this information will be entered in the marriage certificate and the marriage register. Marriage would mean and include marriages solemnized or performed under Hindu Laws, Anand Marriage Act, Muslim personal law or under Indian Christian Marriage Act besides any other custom or personal law relating to marriages governing the parties.

REGISTRATION REGIME DEVISED

The new law will notify Chief, District and Additional Registrars of Marriages or other Officers to be Registrar of Marriages for free and easy accessibility in cities, towns and tehsils. The Registrars so designated , shall upon scrutiny verify that the marriage between the parties has been performed in accordance with the personal law of parties to confirm their marital status and identities. A memorandum of marriage signed by the parties and their priest will be presented to the concerned Registrar within three months of marriage in the jurisdiction where the marriage was solemnised or where parties have temporary residence if they were married outside Punjab. Refusal to register shall be appealable and the Registrar may also *suo moto* or on notice call parties and register any marriage performed in his jurisdiction. Any erroneous or fraudulent entry in a marriage register may be corrected or cancelled after giving opportunity of hearing to persons concerned.

NON- REGISTRATION NOT TO INVALIDATE MARRIAGES

The new law states that no marriage shall be deemed to be invalid solely by the reason or the fact that it was not registered. This shortcoming is attributed to codified personal marriage laws of parties in India by which performance of essential ceremonies and not registration validates a marriage between parties. Hence, a State enactment cannot undo a law made by Parliament prescribing only ceremonies for recognition of a valid marriage. Consequently, resorting to compulsory registration may have to develop more as a accepted societal norm and practice for the law to gain recognition ailing. The fact remains that Punjab has taken the lead to register NRI Marriages which will help in curbing matrimonial frauds to ameliorate the plight of ailing *"Nowhere Holiday Wives"*. Punjab would do equally well if it were to constitute Family Courts in every district in Punjab under the existing Family Courts Act, 1984, to provide speedy justice to abandoned spouses and deserted children as well. Prevention is better than cure but redressal of issues arising out of a broken or limping matrimonial relationship must be remedied too simultaneously.

PUNJAB TRAVEL PROFESSIONALS REGULATION ACT, 2012 – A LAW TO CURB ILLEGAL IMMIGRATION

THE PROBLEM

With the merchants of death running thriving rackets of human smuggling in Punjab at the cost of gullible youth trapped everyday with dollar dreams, the waiting worsens the plight of duped innocent citizens and this organized crime perpetuates horror and misery flourishing with daring impunity. Smuggled migrants are vulnerable to exploitation and their lives are often put at risk. They have suffocated in containers, perished in deserts, drowned at sea or herded as forced labour in slave camps. Smugglers of migrants conduct their activities brazenly without fear or favour with no regard for human life. Survivors tell harrowing tales of their ordeal, forced to sit in human waste, deprived of food and water, while others around them die and their bodies are dumped at sea or on road sides. The smuggling of migrants generates high net worth profits at the hands of criminals who fuel corruption and organized crime. The smuggling of migrants is a deadly business that must be combated as a matter of grave urgency and happily Punjab is the first State ready to combat it.

THE PROPOSED SOLUTION IN THE NEW LAW

The Punjab Travel Professionals Regulation Act, 2012 is described as a law to provide for the regulation of the profession of travel agents with a view to check and curb their illegal, fraudulent activities, and malpractices of the persons involved in organized human smuggling in the State of Punjab and for the matters connected therewith or incidental thereto. This new law has nine noteworthy features.

√ **It defines human smuggling and travel agent. It applies to travel agents, coaching institutes of IELTS, ticketing agents and general sales agents of airlines.**

√ **Provides for a licensing regime for travel agents. Debars persons from operating without a license under the Act. Requires licence number to printed in any advertisement or permission to be sought if unlicenced.**

√ **Gives power of search, seizure and arrest to Magistrates and Police Officials.**

√ **Prescribes power of investigation by DSP to be completed within two months and to be verified by S.P./SSP to be Nodal Officer for all investigations under the Act. Prior verification of complaint to be done by Deputy Commissioner from Additional Deputy Commissioner and Sub Divisional Magistrate concerned.**

- √ **In addition to imposing penalties, provides award of reasonable compensation to be paid to aggrieved person by travel agent.**
- √ **Identifies defined variable punishment for offences under the Act which may be extended upto 7 years.**
- √ **Authorises Courts to decide whether any illegally acquired property is liable to be confiscated.**
- √ **Provides for liability of Director, Manager, Secretary of Companies responsible for conduct of business when negligence can be attributed.**
- √ **Cheating shall have the same meaning as under the Indian Penal Code.**

"Travel Agent" is defined as a person in a profession that involves arranging, managing or conducting affairs related to sending people abroad. It includes consultancy for permanent emigration, obtaining education, work, travel for tourism, cultural entertainment or musical shows, medical treatment, spreading or preaching religion, participating in sport tournaments, issuing advertisements for travel, holding seminars and lectures to promote emigration, arranging matrimonial alliances for purposes of emigration, and arranging overseas travel for any purpose whatsoever. Dishonest misrepresentation with intention to have wrongful gain for inducing, deception, cheating or allurement for above activities is punishable under the Bill. If any travel agent wants to advertise or hold seminars, he will have to notify the competent authority in writing giving complete details of advertisement or seminars. It does not include recruitment agents carrying on the business of recruitment who are governed and registered under the provision of the Emigration Act, 1983

THE GRAVE END

Naive youth fell prey to agents and land up working as slave labour in ammunition dumps or fields in Iraq or end up condemned to live as illegal immigrants abroad in pitiable conditions with no hope of return if they manage to survive hazardous channels of death. Smuggling of migrants is a highly profitable business with a low risk of detection. For criminals, it is increasingly attractive to deal in human merchandise and this business of death is becoming more and more organized, in which professional international networks wantonly flourish transcending global borders and regions. India, as a nation, therefore, has a dire need to check this global menace. However, sadly, The Emigration Act, 1983, which is an Act to consolidate and amend the law relating to Emigration of citizens of India, neither defines human smuggling nor even looks at the problems connected with this deathly trade. Thus, the need for Parliament to legislate a Indian Human Smuggling law is a crying need. Piecemeal state legislations with limited ambit of application will restrict scope only to State territorial borders. A Central law is therefore, the composite solution. Initiatives of Parliament must set this ball rolling. Till then, any State legislation on the subject would be a welcome take off point and the Government of Punjab deserves kudos for this innovative pioneer excellent effort.

CENTRAL LAW IN EXISTENCE

The Emigration Act, 1983 provides for checks, controls, balances by enacting a licensing regime for "recruiting agents," for "emigration" purposes which find definition in the following words in the said Act.

- "Recruiting Agent" means a person engaged in India in the business of recruitment for an employer and representing such employer with respect to any matter in relation to such recruitment including dealings with persons so recruited or desiring to be so recruited.
- "Emigrate and Emigration" means the departure out of India of any person with a view to taking up any employment (whether or not under an agreement or other arrangements to take up such employment and whether with or without the assistance of a recruiting agent or a employer) in any country or place outside India.

The Emigration Act, 1983, creates a "Protector of Emigrants" for providing emigration clearance to ensure that conditions of employment of Indian citizens are not discriminatory, exploitative, unlawful, against public policy, violative of norms of human dignity & decency, besides, do not prescribe sub-standard working or living conditions. The ambit of the Act extends to Indian citizens only and exempts control of recruiting in India for service of foreign States. Clearly, the regulatory provisions of the Central Act, provides beneficial legislation to reign in Indian recruiting agents operating in India.

NEW PUNJAB LAW IN CONTRAST

In contrast, the Punjab Travel Professionals Regulation Act, 2012, enacted to provide a licensing regime for travel agents with penal provisions, has similar regulatory functions to check human smuggling. The words "travel agent" and "human smuggling" in the Punjab Act, find definition in the following words:

"Travel Agent" means a person doing the profession which involves arranging, managing or conducting affairs relating to sending persons abroad or which arise out of the affairs of persons sent to a foreign country, and shall include a range of activities covering diverse practices .

"Human Smuggling" shall mean and include illegally exporting, sending or transporting persons out of India by receiving money from them or their parents, relatives or any other persons interested in their welfare, by inducing, alluring or deceiving or cheating.

It is further stated in the Punjab Act, that "cheating" shall have the same meaning as assigned to it in sections 415 and 416 of the Indian Penal Code, 1860. Therefore, the Punjab *Travel Professionals Regulation* Act, looks at the menace of human smuggling by defining it as an offence and creates a process for its regulatory enforcement by compulsory registration and imposition of punishment upon violations through a legal process prescribed in the Punjab Act.

CONCLUSION

Hence, placing both the Acts *i.e.,* the Emigration Act, 1983 and the Punjab Travel Professionals Regulation Act, 2012, side by side clearly shows that they enshrine regulatory mechanisms for recruiting agents and travel agents separately. Viewed objectively, both carry complimentary purposes in their own spheres. To the author, they neither appear inconsistent or repugnant to each other. In fact, the two laws compliment each other as they provide similar objectives, aims and functions for recruiting and travel agents respectively. It does not appear that Punjab has enacted a law which will be in conflict or repugnant to the existing law already enacted by Parliament In fact, human smuggling is a silent issue in the Emigration Act. The authority of law vested in the State must be exercised to enforce this law. Punjab should proceed with its own initiative and lead the nation in its yeoman spirit.

PUNJAB TRAVEL PROFESSIONALS REGULATION ACT, 2012

➢ *The renamed Punjab Travel Professionals Regulation Act, 2012, passed by the Punjab Vidhan Sabha on 21 December, 2012 is an Act to provide for the regulation of the profession of travel agents with a view to check and curb their illegal, fraudulent activities, and malpractices of the persons involved in organized human smuggling in the State of Punjab and for the matters connected therewith or incidental thereto. This law has nine noteworthy features.*

√ **It defines human smuggling and travel agent. It applies to travel agents, coaching institutes of IELTS, ticketing agents and general sales agents of airlines.**

√ **Provides for a licensing regime for travel agents. Debars persons from operating without a license under the Act. Requires licence number to printed in any advertisement or permission to be sought if unlicenced.**

√ **Gives power of search, seizure and arrest to Magistrates and Police Officials.**

√ **Prescribes power of investigation by DSP to be completed within two months and to be verified by S.P./SSP to be Nodal Officer for all investigations under the Act. Prior verification of complaint to be done by Deputy Commissioner from Additional Deputy Commissioner and Sub-Divisional Magistrate concerned.**

√ **In addition to imposing penalties, provides award of reasonable compensation to be paid to aggrieved person by travel agent.**

√ **Identifies defined variable punishment for offences under the Act which may be extended upto 7 years.**

√ **Authorises Courts to decide whether any illegally acquired property is liable to be confiscated.**

√ **Provides for liability of Director, Manager, Secretary of Companies responsible for conduct of business when negligence can be attributed.**

√ **Cheating shall have the same meaning as under the Indian Penal Code.**

➢ *Travel agent is defined as a person in a profession that **involves arranging**, managing or conducting affairs related to sending **people abroad.***

- √ It includes consultancy for permanent emigration, obtaining education, work, travel for tourism, cultural entertainment or musical shows, medical treatment, spreading or preaching religion, participating in sport tournaments, issuing advertisements for travel, holding seminars and lectures to promote emigration, arranging matrimonial alliances for purposes of emigration, and arranging overseas travel for any purpose whatsoever except for business of recruitment governed by registration under provision of the Emigration Act, 1983
- √ Dishonest misrepresentation with intention to have wrongful gain for inducing, deception, cheating or allurement for above activities and cheating by personation is punishable under the Act as having same meaning as IPC. If any travel agent wants to advertise or hold seminars, he will have to notify competent authority in writing with complete details of advertisement of seminars.

➢ ***The words "travel agent" and "human smuggling" in the Punjab Act, find definition in the following words:***

- √ "Travel Agent" means a person doing the profession which involves arranging, managing or conducting affairs relating to sending persons abroad or which arise out of the affairs of persons sent to a foreign country, and shall include a range of activities covering diverse practices.
- √ "Human Smuggling" shall mean and include illegally exporting, sending or transporting persons out of India by receiving money from them or their parents, relatives or any other persons interested in their welfare, by inducing, alluring or deceiving or cheating.

HIGHLIGHTS OF THE EMIGRATION ACT, 1983

➢ **The Emigration Act, 1983 provides for checks, controls, balances by enacting a licensing regime for "recruiting agents," for "emigration" purposes which find definition in the following words in the said Act.**

- √ **"Recruiting Agent" means a person engaged in India in the business of recruitment for an employer and representing such employer with respect to any matter in relation to such recruitment including dealings with persons so recruited or desiring to be so recruited. Recruiting agents doing business of recruitment have to obtain compulsory registration under the Emigration Act, 1983.**
- √ **"Emigrate and Emigration" means the departure out of India of any person with a view to taking up any employment (whether or not under an agreement or other arrangements to take up such employment and whether with or without the assistance of a recruiting agent or a employer) in any country or place outside India.**

PUNJAB COMPULSORY REGISTRATION OF MARRIAGES ACT-HIGHLIGHTS

It is an Act to provide for compulsory registration of marriages solemnized under any law governing the parties irrespective of their religion, caste, creed or nationality and for the matters connected or incidental thereto.

- *Every marriage between parties who are Indian nationals or NRIs or foreign nationals solemnized or performed shall be registered.*
- *Foreign nationals will mean any person who is not an Indian citizen and shall include PIOs and OCIs.*
- *To avoid any ambiguity, term NRI has been defined in the new Act to mean any person of Indian origin permanently or temporarily settled outside India.*
- *Whenever any party is an NRI, his passport and foreign address details, social security number as also relevant particulars about him shall be entered both in the marriage register as well as the marriage certificate.*
- *Any marriage solemnised outside Punjab shall also be registered in Punjab. However, if any marriage is already registered elsewhere, it shall not be registered again in Punjab.*
- *A complete mechanism and procedure for registration has been laid down and identified with nominated Registrars of Marriages.*
- *The marriage to be registered shall have to be solemnised in accordance with the personal law of the parties to the satisfaction of the Registrar of Marriages concerned.*
- *Non-registration will not invalidate the marriage as such because the new law is only for registration and cannot invalidate a marriage solemnised as per Central Laws.*
- *Memorandum of marriage duly signed by parties and the priest shall be presented within three months of marriage to Registrar of Marriages. Relaxation may be permitted by the Registrar wherever necessary.*
- *Registrar of Marriages may also suo moto (on his own) or on notice register any marriage taking place in his jurisdiction by calling parties.*
- *Any entry may be corrected or cancelled by Registrar of Marriages if obtained fraudulently or made in improperly within correct facts.*

PUNJAB STATE COMMISSION FOR NRIs ACT, 2011

The enacted law labelled as "*The Punjab State Commission for NRIs Act, 2011*" is stated to be "*An Act to provide for the constitution of the Commission for NRIs in the State of Punjab with a view to protecting and safeguarding the interests of the NRIs in the State of Punjab, and to recommend remedial measures to State Government.*" It defines a "*Complaint*" by stating that it "*means all petitions/communications received in State Commission for NRIs from an NRI or any other person on his behalf, in person, by post, by telegram, by fax or by any other means whatsoever, alleging, disputes or violations or abetment thereof or negligence in the prevention of such dispute or violation, by a public servant or a private person or the material on the basis of which the Punjab State Commission for NRIs takes suomotu cognizance.*" The powers and the functions of the Punjab State Commission for NRIs are stipulated as follows:

"12. *Powers and Functions of the Commission*

(1) The Commission shall, while investigating any matter under this Act, have all the powers of a Civil court trying a suit and, in particular, in respect of the following matters namely:—

(a) summoning and enforcing the attendance of any person and examining him on oath;

(b) requiring the discovery and production of any documents;

(c) receiving evidence on affidavits;

(d) requisitioning any public record or copy thereof from any court or office;

(e) issuing commissions for the examination of witnesses and documents; and

(f) any other matter which may be prescribed.

(2) The Commission shall function by holding "sittings" and "meetings" at any place within the State of Punjab.

(3) The Members of the Commission including the Chairperson shall function in accordance with Rules framed by State Government.

14. *Power of the Commission to utilize the services of certain officers and investigating agencies for conducting investigating*

The Commission may conduct enquiry or investigation into the matters falling within its authority:

(a) either directly; or

(b) through an Investigating team constituted by the Commission; or

(c) through the Deputy Commissioner of the district concerned; or

(d) through the Government."

The Punjab State Commission for NRIs constituted by the Government of Punjab is the first NRI commission in the Country which is fully functional for the past one year and is receiving complaints in person, by post and by e-mail as well. The three Member Commission has its office premises in the Mini Secretariat on the ground floor in Sector 9 at Chandigarh and is working very successfully. It receives large number of complaints in its office which are taken up by the NRI Commission which holds daily sittings. Enquiries or investigations are conducted by NRI Commission through its directions to Government agencies and follow up reports are obtained to ensure compliance. This is a very effective means of redressal of complaints and the opportunity to parties to appear in person or through counsel has resulted in settlement of grievances of large number of NRIs and other persons. The NRI Commission has been able to resolve a large number of matrimonial, property, immigration and other related NRIs disputes in a short span of time with their regular sittings and meetings. They can be reached at nricommpb@gmail.com.

The Triumph of the Human Spirit

For nearly four hundred years colonial and apartheid rulers in South Africa banished those they regarded as political trouble makers or social outcasts of society to Robben Island, a 518 hectare rocky outcrop in Table Bay near Cape Town. From 17th to 20th Centuries, Robben Island served as a place of imprisonment, isolation and banishment. Today, from a maximum security prison, it is a world heritage site, a poignant reminder of the price paid for freedom by the present democratic South Africa.

On a visit by the authors to Cape Town for attending the 11th Annual Family Law Conference in 2009, the visit to Robben Island was strongly recommended. The experience was humbling, striking and captivating. It was a reminder of a grim reality practiced and perpetuated as a crime against humanity. At various times, the island's unwilling inhabitants included slaves, political and religious leaders who opposed Dutch colonialism in East Asia, indigenous leaders who resisted British expansion in South Africa, leprosy sufferers, mentally ill patients, prisoners of war and most recently, political opponents of the apartheid regime in South Africa and Namibia.

A visit to the cell in which Nelson Rolihlahla Mandela, Nobel Peace Prize Winner and South Africa's first democratic President was imprisoned for 28 years at Robben Island prison was a lifetime experience. To visualise that despite being chained, tormented, humiliated and subjected to inhuman conditions, he sustained his spirit of tolerance and humanity, is a feat no normal human can endure. His words reverberate in my ears when he says "I have fought against white domination, and I have fought against black domination. I have cherished the ideal of a democratic and free society in which all persons live together in harmony and with equal opportunities. It is an ideal which I hope to live for and to achieve. But if need be, it is an ideal for which I am prepared to die." Mr. Mandela in his poignant words is a man to emulate. Even if we can follow a minuscule part of it, we would be inching to being human. But, we seem to be miles away in ethics, morals, life and politics.

Bringing an end to apartheid was dependant on many things. Internal popular uprising, diplomatic international isolation of apartheid South Africa, underground organisation, armed resistance and the people's spirit all contributed to it. It is admirable to see that some of these freedom fighters and ex-political prisoners who spent 15 to 25 years in prison are now guides who accompany you on tours to Robben Island Prison. Their first hand encounters narrated to groups of tourists in guided tours sitting in their prisons cells, on their mattresses or bunker beds are touching and tearful. The prisoners crushed limestone, rocks and sea shells with bare hands in scorching sun with no protection. Forced to live in inhuman conditions, they endured and endeared with fellow prisoners bound as one. Unbelievable but these accounts are true.

Despite the brutality and harsh conditions, those imprisoned on the island succeeded in turning the prison into a symbol of freedom and personal liberation. Its most famous inmate Nelson Mandela emerged from prison in 1990 to lead South Africa to democracy with a message of reconciliation, tolerance, love and hope that moved the entire universe. There were no massacres, reprisals, retaliations or mass migrations. Today on Mandela's words, all people in South Africa co-habit in peace and unison. On 1 December, 1999, In recognition of Robben Island's historic role in overcoming injustice and the universal importance of its heritage, Robben Island was declared a World Heritage Site by UNESCO. Therefore, a visit to Robben Island is now a pilgrimage to humanity which evokes the triumph of the human spirit.

What is the message that this temple of human race and civilization leaves with you. What is it that touches your heart, body and soul? Why is it so grim and painful? The answers are difficult to find. But it undoubtedly permeates into you how mankind inflicts injuries upon itself. It also teaches you that love, patience and time heals these wounds. However, the most laudable feature is the forgiveness of the sufferers.

Victims Compensation Scheme

The Constitution of India solemnly resolves to constitute India into a Sovereign, Socialist, Secular, Democratic Republic and to secure justice, liberty, equality and fraternity to all its citizens. The non-justiciable Directive Principles of State Policy, contained in Part IV of the Constitution, enjoin that the State secure a social order for the promotion of welfare of people and provide, within limits of its economic capacity, assistance in cases of need and want. These goals, though laudable are still illusory.

THE PROBLEM IDENTIFIED

Lamenting on the plight of rape victims, in *Delhi Domestic Working Women's Forum* v. *Union of India*, (1995) 1 SCC 14, the Supreme Court in 1994 had noted a major shift in *"penelogical thinking, reflecting the growing importance attached to restitution and reparation over the more narrowly retributive aims of conventional punishment."* While propounding the thought requiring courts to consider the making of a compensation order, the Apex Court indicated broad parameters in assisting the victims of rape and felt that schemes will have to be evolved to wipe out the tears of such unfortunate victims and for implementation of which necessary steps be taken.

THE STATUTORY PROVISION

Section 357A of the Code of Criminal Procedure was inserted in 2008 making it mandatory that every State Government in coordination with the Central Government shall prepare a Scheme for providing funds for the purpose of compensation to the victim or his dependents who have suffered loss or injury as a result of a crime and who require rehabilitation. The salient features of this mandatory provision are:

- Whenever a recommendation is made by the Court for compensation, the District or State Legal Services Authority shall decide the quantum of compensation to be awarded under the Scheme of the concerned Government.
- If the Trial Court at the conclusion of the Trial is satisfied that compensation ordinarily awarded under existing law is not adequate for such rehabilitation, or, where cases end in acquittal or discharge and the victim has to be rehabilitated, it may make a recommendation for compensation.

- Where the offender is not traced or identified, but the victim is identified, and where no trial takes place, the victim or the dependents may make an application to the State or District Legal Services Authority for award of compensation.
- Upon receipt of a recommendation or an application, the District or State Legal Services Authority shall after due enquiry award adequate compensation by completing the enquiry within two months.
- The District or State Legal Services Authority, to alleviate the suffering of the victim, may order for immediate medical benefits or first aid facility to be made available free of cost on the certification of a Police Officer or a Magistrate or grant any other interim relief as deemed fit.

THE FACTUAL POSITION

The provision in law exists to ameliorate the plight of an unfortunate victim of rape. But, the actual relief is very far away. The Scheme of the Government, be it Punjab, Haryana or Chandigarh, if notified, is practically unknown and its actual benefits are not accessible to those victims who may actually need it. The laudable shift of thinking advocated by the Apex Court for making payment of compensation or providing rehabilitative aid thus still remains illusory. The slow pace of working of the criminal justice system for trying the offender further adds to the woes of the rape victim. The traumatised sufferer has neither the means nor the resources for the process to end and to wait for the Court to conclude that aid, assistance or compensation be finally awarded upon conclusion of the case and awarding of punishment to the offender.

COURTS TO THE RESCUE

In the situation as it exists, the Apex Court in 1993 in its erudite expression in *Nilabati Behera* v. *State of Orissa,* (1993) 2 SCC 746, has held that the Supreme Court and High Courts being the protectors of the Civil liberties of the citizens, have not only the power and jurisdiction but also an obligation to grant relief in exercise of its writ jurisdiction under articles 32 and 226 of the Constitution. The Apex Court clearly recognised the need for award of compensation in writ jurisdiction for contravention of Human rights and fundamental freedoms thereby providing much needed succour to unfortunate victims who cannot reach out to justice under conventional legal systems. Further, in 2012, in *Dr. Mehmood Nayyar Azam* v. *State of Chhattisgarh,* [2012] 8 SCR 651, the Apex Court in another salutary view observed that when the Court moulds the relief by granting "*compensation*" in writ proceedings for enforcement or protection of Fundamental rights, "*it does so under the public law by way of penalising the wrong doer and fixing the liability for the public wrong on the State which has failed in its public duty to protect the Fundamental rights of the citizens.*" The Apex Court further stated that "*the payment of compensation in such cases is not to be understood as it is generally understood in a civil action for damages under the private law but in the broader sense of providing relief by an order of making monetary amends under the public law for the wrong done due to breach of public duty by not protecting the fundamental rights of the citizen.*" Thus, our Constitutional Courts perform a yeoman service to underprivileged sections of society in culling out much needed relief whenever needed and for which the Courts act even *suo moto* to those in dire need.

THE END AND THE FUTURE

Rape is a heinous crime for which we need swift trial and stringent punishment. Simultaneously, compensation awarded to the victim may be programmed to be rehabilitative or tailored to suit the need of the victim and the child so born. In the furtherance of the progressive view and the thinking propounded by the Apex Court, such crutches of financial aid neither compound or condone the offence. The mandate of the Indian Constitution to secure social justice to have-nots must not be illusive and must be promoted. Law which provide so must be implemented with vigour.

Law, Films and the Sound of Music

"There's music in the sighing of a reed;
There's music in the gushing of a rill;
There's music in all things, if men had ears;
There's earth is but an echo of the spheres"

Lord Byron

THE HISTORY

William Shakespeare in *"Twelfth Night"*, Act II, Scene I, laments, "if music be the food of love.... play on" while the speaker is asking for music because he is frustrated in courtship. The *"Sound of Music,"* an American musical film made in 1965 containing several popular songs was filmed in exotic locations in Salzburg, Bavaria and California. It won five Academy Awards and the United States Library of Congress deemed it, "culturally, historically or aesthetically significant". Music theatricals at West End in London and epic musicals at Broadway theatre, New York have been hailed for historical shows of "Marry Poppins", "Les Miserables" and "King David". Traditional Indian music from "Gharanas" carrying rich cultural traditions and values of India have wafted from time immemorial carrying legacies through fables, legends and ballads. Music, the messenger, since the advent of mankind, has served the test of time for the human race. But, tested today, it is fraught with dangers from murky waters and storms emerging in modern society with new trends. Regardless, music is the only sensual gratification in which mankind in privacy may indulge in excess without injury to moral or religious feelings of others. Therefore, music regulated or unregulated is elevation to a happy state of mind.

THE PROBLEM TODAY

Today, music is in a dilemma. For some commercial adventurers through vulgar overtones, it has acquired a pitch crossing limits of decency and morality. Obscene and misogynist lyrics attacking the female gender using pseudonyms and vernacular phrases are hurled with a cocktail of westernized blends at misguided youth. Unmindful of social repercussions and moral norms, musical fortune hunters are making deep inroads into a rich cultural heritage of music unpolluted by time. The alarming pace with which this virus is infecting and plaguing society has no antidote.

CENTRAL LAWS IN EXISTENCE

Section 294 of *the Indian Penal Code, 1860,* punishes singing, reciting or uttering any obscene song in or near any public place with three month's imprisonment or fine or both. *The Copyright Act, 1957* does not permit any person to publish a sound recording unless it displays the owner of the copyright of such work, person who made the sound recording and the year of its publication. Entry 60 of The Union list of the Constitution of India empowers the Central Government to enact laws for sanctioning of cinematograph films for exhibition. Accordingly, *the Cinematograph Act, 1952,* provides for certification of cinematograph films and empowers the District Magistrate to revoke the certificate for a particular area in view of public health and safety. The Censor Board, in turn classifies a film for restricted or unrestricted public exhibition. Further, the Government of India, under the Union list, can enact laws for wireless, broadcasting and other like forms of communication. Besides, there are content restrictions for Cable television in the *Cable Network Act, 1995* and restraints for internet in section 67 of *the Information Technology Act, 2000* which prohibits publication of obscene material in electronic form. Internet content is also controlled by guidelines for internet service providers who are under an obligation to prevent any obscene, objectionable and unauthorized material over their networks.

PUNJAB LAWS IN EXISTENCE

Punjab Cinemas (Regulation) Act, 1952, governs the matter relating to licensing and regulation of cinemas in the territory of Punjab. *The Punjab Dramatic Performances Act, 1964,* provided for better control of dramatic performances in Punjab and empowers the District Magistrate to prohibit any objectionable dramatic performance in a public place. The *Music in Muslim Shrines Act, 1942* was enacted to control performances by girls in Muslim shrines and barred any woman or girl to either sing or dance in a Muslim shrine which is publishable with imprisonment of six months or fine or both. Other than this, music for society in general, is unregulated by any State enactment applicable in Punjab, primarily because it is within the domain of the Government of India to make a regulatory law applicable throughout the territory of India. Punjab laws alone may not apply outside its territory and lewd compositions will still haunt air waves if the lyricists or singers operate outside Punjab.

THE YAWNING GAP

Irrespective of the matter being a central subject, Entry 33 of the State list, under Schedule 7 of the Constitution of India, empowers the State Government to enact laws for theatres and dramatic performances, sports, entertainments and amusements. Since, sound recordings are not regulated by any central enactment like the Censor Board certification for films under the Cinematograph Act, 1952, the music industry goes unchecked as song content has no regulatory mechanism to check lewd lyrics. A song which is a combination of lyrics, compositions and voices of a performer recorded in a studio, the producer is its first owner under the Copyright Act, 1957. Regardless, pirated music sold at abnormally low costs rules the roost. However, offensive and vulgar lyrics do not find statutory road blocks other than section 294, IPC for punishing obscene acts and songs.

THE POSSIBLE REMEDY

The deep rooted societal impact of loud and bawdy music with double meaning overtones has become fashionable among misguided youth. It may precipitate and provoke actions amounting to criminal offences. Law ought not to permit this. Since, unethical singers are germinating and flourishing without abandon or fear, they ought to be checked in Punjab where this surrogate industry has developed irrespective of its territorial constraints. Under Entry 33 of the State List of the Constitution of India, the Government of Punjab is well within its powers to consider music as a part of *"entertainment"* and enact a new regulatory law to curb the communication of vulgar music to the public emanating from the State of Punjab. The *Music in Muslim Shrines Act, 1942* and *The Punjab Dramatic Performances Act, 1964* are examples of Punjab legislation which emulate this proposition to be put into this practice. New generation societal ills need fresh thought to check fresh maladies. Law has to catch up with offenders who take advantage of missing checks. An innovative perspective defining vulgar music compositions, checking lyricists, defining indecent songs and containing wholesome provisions in the new arena of music law is the need of the day. Punjab could well have a Music Sensor Board under a new Music Regulatory Law for sanctioning and certifying content of sound recordings on the same terms as films. If Punjab can make the start, other jurisdictions will follow. A positive start is needed. The job well begun will be half done. A new Law must check such indecent songs.

LAW ON FILMS AND MUSIC - HIGHLIGHTS

➢ **Indian Penal Code, 1860**

294. Obscene acts and songs.—*Whoever, to the annoyance of others—*

(a) Does any obscene act in any public place, or

(b) Sings, recites or utters any obscene song, ballad or words in or near any public place, shall be punished with imprisonment of either description for a term which may extend to three months, or with fine, or with both.

The said offence is cognizable, bailable, non-compoundable and triable by a Magistrate.

➢ **Copyright Act, 1957**

Section 52A.—Particulars to be included in sound recording and video films.—*(1) No person shall publish a sound recording in respect of any work unless the following particulars are displayed on the sound recording and on any container thereof, namely:*

(a) The name and address of the person who has made the sound recording;

(b) The name and address of the owner of copyright in such work; and

(c) The year of its first publication.

(2) No person shall publish a video film in respect of any work unless the following particulars are displayed in the video film, when exhibited, and on the video cassette or other container thereof, namely:—

(a) *If such work is a cinematograph film required to be certified for exhibition under the provisions of the Cinematograph Act, 1952, a copy of the certificate granted by the Board of Film Certification under section 5A of that Act in respect of such work.*

(b) *The name and address of the person who has made the video film and a declaration by him that he has obtained the necessary license or consent from the owner of copyright in such work for making such video film; and*

(c) *The name and address of the owner of copyright in such work.*

➤ **The Cinematograph Act, 1952**

Section 5A. Certification of films.—(1) *If, after examining a film or having it examined in the prescribed manner, the Board considers that*

(a) *The film is suitable for unrestricted public exhibition, or as the case may be, for unrestricted public exhibition with an endorsement of the nature mentioned in the proviso to clause (i) of sub-section (1) of section 4, it shall grant to the person applying for a certificate in respect of the film "U" certificate, or as the case may be, a "UA" certificate; or*

(b) *The film is not suitable for unrestricted public exhibition but is suitable for public exhibition restricted to adults or, as the case may be, is suitable for puhlic exhibition restricted to members of any profession or any class of persons, it shall grant to the person applying for a certificate in respect of the film an "A" certificate, or as the case may be, a "S" certificate; and cause the film to be so marked in the prescribed manner.*

Provided that the applicant for the certificate, any distributor or exhibitor or any other person to whom the rights in the film have passed shall not be liable for punishment under any law relating to obscenity in respect of any matter contained in the film for which certificate has been granted under clause (a) or (b).

(2) A certificate granted or an order refusing to grant a certificate in respect of any film shall be published in the Gazette of India.

(3) Subject to the other provisions contained in the Act, a certificate granted by the Board under this section shall be valid throughout India for a period of 10 years.

√ THE PUNJAB GOVERNMENT HAS ENACTED THE PUNJAB CINEMAS (REGULATION) ACT, 1952 AND THE RULES THEREOF TO GOVERN THE MATTERS RELATING TO LICENSING AND REGULATION OF CINEMAS IN THE TERRITORY OF PUNJAB.

√ **THE PUNJAB DRAMATIC PERFORMANCES ACT, 1964** – AN ACT TO PROVIDE FOR BETTER CONTROL OF DRAMATIC PERFORMANCES IN THE STATE OF PUNJAB. THE ACT EMPOWERS THE DISTRICT MAGISTRATE TO PROHIBIT ANY DRAMATIC PERFORMANCE IN A PUBLIC PLACE WHICH IS OBJECTIONABLE AS PER SECTION 2(1) OF THE SAID ACT.

√ THE PUNJAB GOVERNMENT HAS ENACTED A STATUTE TO CONTROL PERFORMANCES BY GIRLS IN MUSLIM SHRINES THROUGH THE **MUSIC IN MUSLIM SHRINES ACT, 1942**. THE ACT BARS ANY WOMAN OR A GIRL TO EITHER SING OR DANCE IN A MUSLIM SHRINE AND THE PERSON GUILTY SHALL BE PUNISHABLE WITH IMPRISONMENT OF 6 MONTHS OR RS. 500 FINE OR BOTH.

Law, Liability and Compensation

BACKGROUND POSITION IN CIVIL LAW

Torts as Civil wrongs for actionable claims are not codified under Indian Statute Law. However, the Apex Court since 1996, in the judgments rendered in *Indian Council for Enviro-Legal Action* v. *Union of India*, AIR 1996 SC 1446 and in *Vellore Citizens Welfare Forum* v. *Union of India*, AIR 1996 SC 2715, in the well founded wisdom of the Apex Court, has held that the *"Polluter Pays Principle"* and the *"Precautionary Principle"* are essential features of sustainable development. Applying them for activities which are hazardous or inherently dangerous more so in environmental matters, the Apex Court in its extraordinary writ jurisdiction has often come down with a heavy hand for urgent remedial compensatory measures in public interest. But, actionable claims in private interest for traditional, conventional and procedural proceedings for damages under ordinary Civil law can be tedious, cumbersome, expensive, protracted and riddled with technicalities of law. The individual common man has to tread this ordinary path.

VICTIM COMPENSATION SCHEME UNDER CRIMINAL LAW

In 2008, The Code of Criminal Procedure was amended by Parliament to incorporate section 357A to add the statutory mandate of the Victim Compensation Scheme under which every State Government was required to prepare a scheme for providing funds for compensation to a victim or his dependents who have suffered loss or injury as a result of a crime and who require rehabilitation. Even if the offender is not traced or identified, but the victim is identified, and no trial has taken place, compensation can be awarded upon due inquiry by the State or District Legal Services Authority. The purpose is laudable and salutary. The States of Punjab, Haryana and Union Territory, Chandigarh have notified Victim Assistance Compensation Schemes to offer succor but the actual monetary reliefs are either symbolic or beyond the reach of the ordinary mortal souls blissfully unaware of such schemes. Alas, retributive compensatory relief for the common man remains an illusory albatross.

EXTRA ORDINARY RELIEF IN WRIT JURISDICTION

The Apex Court under article 32 and the High Courts under article 226 of the Constitution can issue prerogative writs for enforcement of fundamental rights guaranteed under Part III of the Constitution. This right to constitutional remedies is a prerogative of the superior courts to enforce the rule of law and to ensure that the State as also other statutory authorities act in accordance with law. Not available in the case of disputed facts, these discretionary powers exercised by the superior courts are a hallmark of the judicial system. Tested over a span of 60 years, the nation is indeed proud of this exemplary justice system which has moulded out relief in innumerable cases involving violation of human rights and infringement of civil liberties. We have the unique distinction of this salutary concept of justice unknown in most jurisdictions. However, invoking it as an alternative to avoid conventional adjudication under statutory civil and criminal laws is often checked and deterred by the superior courts. Regardless, our Apex Court and the High Courts perform a yeoman service in securing justice by stretching out within the parameters of codified law when the conscience of the court is struck and per se violation of fundamental rights is perceived by the Court. This sense of justice attributed to the wisdom of the superior courts is unparalleled in any other justice system in different jurisdictions on the globe.

A NEW CONCEPT OF RELIEF

The Apex Court in *Nilabati Behera* v. *State of Orissa,* (1993) 2 SCC 746 and in *Dr. Mehmood Nayyar Azam* v. *State of Chhatisgarh,* JT 2012 (7) SC 178, enunciated that the Supreme Court and the High Courts being the protectors of civil liberties of citizens, have not only the power and jurisdiction but also an obligation to grant relief in exercise of their extra ordinary jurisdiction under articles 32 and 226 respectively of the Constitution. Award of compensation in writ jurisdiction for contravention of human rights and fundamental freedoms more so under article 21 dealing with life and personal liberty is thus innovated by the Supreme Court to repair damage and provide monetary aid, notwithstanding the rights of the citizen to enforce conventional civil or criminal proceedings for relief.

A PATH BREAKING JUDGMENT

By a landmark verdict of July 2 2013, in Raman v. *State of Haryana,* 2013 (3) 171 PLR 502, Justice Rajiv Narain Raina of the Punjab and Haryana High Court awarded a Rs. 60 lacs package for a four year old boy who suffered triple amputation of his limbs upon contact with live electric transmission wires passing over his home in District Panipat at Haryana. Relying upon the Apex Court's dictum of law for moulding relief in writ jurisdiction for payment of compensation for damages for making *"monetary amends"* under public law for wrong done for breach of public duty, the High Court upholding the principle of *"strict liability"* and consequential negligence in awarding compensation, awarded *"exemplary damages"* to this hapless little child upon whom fate had inflicted a cruel malady. The Court concluded that failure to provide statutory safeguards and protective devices against high voltage electricity of dangerous dimensions and not removing live overhead lines passing over roofs of houses, attract the principles of strict liability to *"invade the battle ground in fighting for the protection of life and liberty of our people under article 21 of the Constitution"*. The High Court in its well reasoned verdict issued salutary directions in quantification of monetary compensation, damages and other ancillary matters to secure the ends of justice. The High Court directed the Director General of Health Services, Haryana to take the assistance of all specialist medical institutions on humanitarian principles for making the minor child mobile through artificial robotic limbs including stem cell technology if possible. In order to secure the financial and monetary future of the minor, a sum of Rs. 30 lacs was directed to be locked in financial deposit till the child attained the age of 21 and was ordered to be put in a fixed deposit account towards loss of enjoyment of life, trauma suffered and to act as a guard against neglect or dependence on others, loss of employment, pain and mental shock besides irreconcilable damages suffered. Furthermore, another compensatory sum of Rs. 30 lacs was directed to be deposited in a separate interest bearing account to be invested to earn interest of Rs. 20,000 per month for requiring running income to meet the child's daily expenses and provide his day to day care. Separately, Rs. 2 lacs was awarded as compensation to the mother for trauma, mental shock, pain and agony besides costs of litigation. The Court further directed that permanent employment be offered to the minor boy on compassionate grounds upon attaining age of 21 years in which case Rs. 30 lacs compensation awarded would be put in his provident fund account. It was further ruled that *"as substantial monetary compensation on principles of strict and vicarious liability and on tortuous liability based on negligence had been awarded, it is ordered that no civil suit would lie claiming further compensation in any Court."* However, in Letters Patent Appeal (LPA) No. 1631 of 2013, titled *Uttar Haryana Bijli Vitran Nigam Limited* v. *Raman*, decided on October 30, 2013, both parties by a consent order agreed to a compensation of Rs. 30 lacs only being desposited in State Bank of Patiala, Panipat Branch within ten days to be converted into a fixed deposit receipt (FDR) in terms of the direction earlier issued by the learned Single Judge. It was further agreed between the parties that in so far the other direction for the deposit of another Rs. 30 lacs to earn interest of Rs. 20,000 per month is concerned, the same *"will stand substituted by a direction to pay a sum of Rs. 10,000 per month on or before 7th day of every month in advance, directly to the bank account already intimated and such payment will continue to be made till the minor attains the age of 21 years.* All other remaining directions issued by the Single Bench were retained. Thus, in effect the compensation were reduced from Rs. 60 lacs to Rs. 30 lacs. Regardless, of the *justification, if any, to substantiate the* reduction of the compensation, the innovation of the learned Single Judge to do substantial justice to a minor boy who suffered triple amputation of his limbs and who would remain hundred percent permanently disabled throughout his life, was commendable and laudable. Expanding the contours of the writ jurisdiction, the relief culled out was uniquely distinct to break the shackles and fetters of contributory negligence with the sound foundation of absolute liability. Further, without forcing the minor boy to go through a protracted, technical and procedural conventional litigation, the Court in its wisdom followed the path of the Apex Court to hold that the High Court being a protector of the civil liberties of citizens, have not only the power in jurisdiction but also an obligation to grant relief in exercise of jurisdiction under article 226 of the Constitution. The High Court found support in its verdict from the view of the Apex Court in Nilabati Behera and *Dr. Mehmood Nayyar Azam* (Supra) holding award of compensation in writ jurisdiction for contravention of human rights and fundamental freedoms to be recognized by the Supreme Court and the High

Courts. Hence, a sound principle of law has established a new compensatory principle in writ jurisdiction.

MEANS TO AN END

The High Court in its deep rooted wisdom and constitutional commitment to secure the ends of justice has innovatively culled out substantial relief by an unconventional mode under the judicial umbrella. Growing out of the shackles of the Victims Compensation Scheme and without relegating the hapless victim to a painful legal process which would have consumed substantial time, energy and finances, the High Court stretched its extraordinary jurisdiction to do extensive justice. It is an extremely well founded precedent in the hallmarks of justice which will open up vistas and avenues for those exceptional cases where remedial compensation would ensure survival. This precedent of law may be a good role model to emulate for rape victims, sufferers of acid attacks, victims of human trafficking, child abuse and kidnapping where protracted trials can be tedious and cumbersome. Settling new boundaries to advance the cause of justice with powers vested by the Constitution, the superior courts can ameliorate the cause of the downtrodden and under privileged sections of society to whom justice must be done. The cause of justice must be promoted to reach the common man.

Chinks in the Non-Resident Indian Armour

1900 delegates from 60 countries attended the 10th Pravasi Bhartiya Divas (PBD) from 7 to 9 January, 2012 at Jaipur with the usual fanfare of the ritual NRI jamboree. Even the successive PBDs in 2013 and 2014 were old wine in new bottles. Nothing new, nothing great. The themes of the session events looked at health, youth, investment in Research & Development, trade and industry besides parallel State sessions to attract Euros, Dollars, Pound Sterling and other currencies with foreign wings. Sadly, a session on NRI problems missed the bus. Lurking issues of 30 million overseas citizens on the horizon relating to voting rights, nationality issues, immigration problems, property paradoxes and new age dilemmas of family law conflicts found no platform for discussion at this NRI gathering in Jaipur. The disenchantment in discussing solutions or remedies ailing the foreign Indians drives the wedge deeper. Even window dressing of key issues without legislative changes would not bring respite to beleaguered overseas Indians disappointed with their homeland.

The 2010 PBD had a full day seminar on property related issues of Non-Resident Indians/Persons of Indian Origins which was a thumping success. Sadly, none was repeated thereafter in the realm of any other tenor or tone of ailing NRI issues. Regardless, the desire to fully tap the investment potential of NRIs and use their entrepreneurial skills to promote inclusive growth was exhorted at the 2012 PBD citing the example of Foreign Direct Investment in China from the overseas Chinese. Only the NRI investment was discussed without looking at what could be given back in return to the NRI. This chink in the NRI armour only soils the Indian cavalry.

The key issue which ought to have been discussed at the 2012 PBD striking the NRI chord today is the right to cast the ballot in the upcoming assembly elections in five States. The amendment to The Representation of People Act, 1950 to the phrase "ordinarily resident" allowing a person absenting himself from his place of ordinary residence owing to his employment, education or otherwise, outside India, whether temporarily or not, allowing an NRI to vote on account of his non resident status gives no solace. The reason, he has to be physically present for voting at an election at the constituency in India and has to register afresh as a voter to cast his franchise in the elections at his original address in the Indian passport. There is no provision or relaxation for casting his vote overseas at an Indian Embassy/High Commission where the NRI is temporarily resident, nor is there any provision for postal/electronic ballot. The law was not statutorily amended to make legislative changes in this regard and Punjab therefore finds only 47 new overseas electors who may or may not come to actually vote. The exercise is therefore in futility.

The principal issue remains. Both the Constitution of India and the Indian Citizenship Act, 1955, prohibit dual nationality. Thus, the right to vote is restricted to only Indian citizens resident abroad. Hence, only 11 million NRIs with Indian passports qualify for voting rights. The remaining 19 million NRIs may choose to become Overseas Citizens of India (OCI) but under section 7B of the Citizenship Act, 1955, an OCI shall not be entitled to registration as a voter under the Representation of People Act, 1950, not being a citizen of India. Disappointment galore, the PBD exercises announcing registration of NRI voters ends with a whimper even before it begins. To top it, it is not even discussed in the PBD. It is time that dual nationality was discussed as an option. Surely, India would gain more Indians and more investment if we thought so and did so.

The next fanfare announcement at the 2012 PBD for Indians living abroad was 3 fold:

- New pension and life insurance fund for overseas Indian workers with life insurance cover against natural death.
- E-migrate project providing end to end computerized solutions for all processes in the emigration system to link all key stakeholders on a common platform.
- Action plan to implement recommendations relating to repatriation, relief and rehabilitation of 5 million Indians affected by developments in West Asia.

Immigration law in India needs a statutory framework in Parliament. Piecemeal schemes, projects and plans without legislative sanctions will serve no purpose. Recent bone chilling occurrences of Indian workers in Dubai brought to the fore pitfalls of punitive foreign laws suffered by gullible youths besides Punjabi youth facing death in Iraq on account of illegal immigration and human smuggling not defined as an offence under any Indian law. The Emigration Act, 1983 needs a serious legislative overhaul for statutory remedies. Besides, India has an outdated Foreigners Act, 1946 and Foreigners Order, 1948 which does not serve the test of time. India has no work permit regime by which it can gain substantial revenue from business and work visas. Clearly, the PBD 2012 could have been an occasion to deliberate, discuss and ponder over problems of overseas Indians and inbound immigration for possible suggestions in making a stable, wholesome new immigration law to curb human trafficking and provide statutory provisions for protection of immigrant workers. Clearly, the PBD fell short of its role in not providing this exercise. We cannot gain if we do not consolidate what we have. If we do not even deliberate over it, we will be miles away from its potentials.

The third possible agenda before any PBD could have been a spotlight session on new age family law problems. Inter-country divorce decrees, abandoned spouses, removed children, surrogacy practices, pre-nuptial agreements, adoption hurdles, forced marriages and other private international law issues have mushroomed but find no solutions in the family laws made 55 years ago. NRIs export foreign court family law orders which defy legislative solutions in India leaving it to Courts to cull out relief judicially on equitable grounds. This imported NRI legal baggage of marital problems only disillusions the foreign Indian who wants to reconnect but finds no fulcrum. Parliament has no time to amend or make new family laws to keep pace with these requirements of a 30 million NRI community who find solace in foreign family laws. If the PBD also chooses to look the other way, we will only distance the foreign Indians.

If the PBD has to be a connecting thread to the roots of the migrated NRI, it has to become an occasion when his homeland can talk about him and not his assets. Till this is consciously done, the annual mega PBD event is an exercise in futility. It is therefore time that the Government plans the agenda of its next coming PBDs with the eye on the heart of the NRI and not on his pocket.

NRI ISSUES

NRI ISSUES

- Diplomats, Conflict of Jurisdictions and Anti Suit Injunctions
- Indian Citizenship for Stateless Persons
- Indian Passport Sans Citizenship
- Indians, Foreigners, Deportation and Dual Citizenship

Diplomats, Conflict of Jurisdictions and Anti Suit Injunctions

An interesting off shoot emerges in diplomat *Devyani Khobragade's* case *i.e.* – Civil Suit (OS) No. 1809 of 2013, titled *Devyani Khobragade* v. *Sangeeta Richard*. On September 20, 2013 the Delhi High Court had issued an *ex parte* anti-suit injunction restraining her former maid Sangeeta Richard and her husband Phillip Richard from "**initiating any action or proceeding or filing any suit or claims**" against Devyani in any Court/Tribunal/Forum in any country outside India arising out of or in connection with the employment of the maid. This class of litigation in the realm of conflicts of laws under private international law, by legal parlance, is labelled as an "**Anti-suit injunction**" and gives rise to an order issued by a Competent Court in India that prevents an offending party from commencing or continuing a proceeding in another jurisdiction or foreign forum. The Foreign Court cannot be and is not restrained in such process as Indian Courts cannot injunct a foreign court. However, if the opposing party contravenes such an order, a Contempt of Court may be issued by the domestic Indian Court against the offending party located in the foreign jurisdiction. Not very often invoked, anti-suit injunctions, are preferred in personal actions of matrimonial causes besides commercial matters and may be used to prevent forum shopping or checking oppressive and vexatious litigation in overseas jurisdictions to avoid conflicting judgments. Most often, its actual success is difficult. Regardless, it is a developing jurisprudence in a country with a 30 million diaspora in 180 countries over the globe contributing immensely to cross border litigations.

DIPLOMAT'S CASE

Undoubtedly, the matter related to employment issues between the parties and was an *ex parte* interim injunction. However, upon the matter being heard again on December 13, 2013 it is reported that the Delhi High Court was informed that the notice sent by the Court had not been served on Sangeeta in USA. Her husband who was served did not put in appearance and was proceeded *ex parte*. Accordingly, the Delhi High Court again ordered that the Court's summons be served upon Sangeeta afresh by an approved courier and through ordinary process. Meanwhile, Devyani Khobragade had already been arrested in USA on December 12, 2013 creating a diplomatic furore with cross allegations of human rights violations and domestic abuse charges. However, in 2014, a US court has itself dismissed visa fraud charges against Indian diplomat *Devyani Khobragade,* whose arrest and strip-search in New York sparked a bitter diplomatic row which was the very foundation of the relief sought in the anti-suit injunction. US judge Shira Scheindlin dismissed the case on March 12, 2014 on the grounds that Ms Khobragade was granted full diplomatic immunity when she was named a counselor to India's mission to the UN.

Earlier, when the Delhi High Court had been seized of the matter in September 2013 in the application for interim injunction, it was observed that Devyani posted as Deputy Consul General, Consulate General of India, New York, USA, had employed Sangeeta as a domestic help to take her to USA as India Based Domestic Assistant (IBDA,) which is a facility provided by the Government of India to diplomats serving abroad. A contract dated November 23, 2013 was executed at New Delhi between them whereby Sangeeta was to work only for Devyani in USA and was to return to India promptly upon leaving this employment. Sangeeta proceeded to USA with Devyani on an air ticket given by the Government of India. Reportedly, Sangeeta is stated to have left Devyani's household in USA on June 21, 2013 and had not returned.

PREVIOUS PENDING MATTER IN DELHI HIGH COURT

Whilst granting the anti-suit injunction in *Devyani's* case, the Delhi High Court placed reliance on a previous order of March 14, 2012 passed by it in another pending anti-suit injunction titled *Union of India* v. *Shanti Gurung,* CS (OS) 610/2012, whose facts were said to be somewhat akin to Devyani's case. In the previous pending matter, another employee i.e., *Shanti* was employed as a service staff member under the IBDA and was given a visa by the US Embassy to accompany a career Indian diplomat working on a official full time assignment in USA from 2006 to 2009. Reportedly, Shanti is said to have disappeared from the apartment of the diplomat in 2009 in USA and whereafter an official notification of which was made to the US authorities leading to official revocation of her passport by the Government of India.

The Delhi High Court order of March 14, 2012, in a anti-suit injunction, by the Diplomat and the Union of India, also records that Shanti filed a complaint in the United States District Court, Southern District, New York alleging mal-treatment, forced labour, trafficking, failure to pay wages etc., by the Indian diplomat and to which the Government of India responded in USA objecting to the jurisdiction of US Courts to try the said matter as also raising pleas of invalid service. Regardless, the US Court allowed the motion for default judgment on February 22, 2012 in favour of Shanti and against the diplomat awarding USD 1,458,335 in her favour. A period of 14 days from the service of this judgment was granted to file objections before the US Court.

CONTENTIOUS CLAIMS

It was averred before the Delhi High Court in the anti-suit injunction to restrain Shanti from pursuing further proceedings in the US Court, that the diplomat and the employee both being Indian citizens in employment of the Union of India, they would be governed by domestic laws of India. Furnishing proof of payments to Shanti in India at a bank in New Delhi, the Delhi High

Court observed that it cannot be prima facie conceived that she was trafficked or kidnapped from India. It was also urged that the Courts in United States had no jurisdiction to pass orders against an Indian diplomat posted officially for an assignment in the US on account of sovereign immunity for which reliance was placed on The *Hague Service Convention* and *The Vienna Convention on Consular Relations.* It was agitated before The Delhi High Court that if the US default judgment awarding damages was finally decreed, it would *"seriously interfere with judicial sovereignty of India besides the same being in violation of the Vienna Convention, the Hague Convention and the Foreign Service Immunity Act, 1976.*

OBSERVATIONS AND INJUNCTIONS OF THE COURT

The Delhi High Court in its anti-suit injunction order of March 14, 2012, without expressing any views on the truthfulness of the allegations levelled by Shanti leading to the passing of US default judgment, observed that it was incomprehensible as to why no complaint was made by Shanti till July 2010 specially when she had visited India with the diplomat on vacation in January 2007. The Court found force with the contentions that any order passed by the US Courts would tantamount to interfering in the right of Government of India to determine the terms and conditions of the employment of its diplomatic officers posted abroad including terms by and under which assistants are provided to such diplomats. Furthermore, for any alleged ill-treatment by any employee, the US Courts would have no jurisdiction and the remedy would lie with the Indian Courts as per the Standard agreement between the diplomatic agents and their domestic servants. Applying the tripartite test of prima facie case, balance of convenience and irreparable loss and injury, on March 14, 2012, the Delhi High Court granted an *ex parte* anti-suit injunction against Shanti and others from pursuing their complaint or relying upon the default US Judgment to get a final judgment or proceed to enforce the same. The Decree of the US Court was stated to be not executed. However, in 2014, a US court has itself dismissed visa fraud charges against Indian diplomat Devyani Khobragade, whose arrest and strip-search in New York sparked a bitter diplomatic row which was the very foundation of the relief sought in the anti-suit injunction. US judge Shira Scheindlin dismissed the case on March 12, 2014 on the grounds that Ms Khobragade was granted full diplomatic immunity when she was named a counselor to India's mission to the UN.

MATRIMONIAL DISPUTES

This class of litigation is now being also used in matrimonial matters as well. Hindu marriages said to be made in heaven and solemnized in India are now wantonly dissolved abroad. Sad but true. A prelude follows. Parties immigrate, fight abroad and litigate for the parallel adjudication of their matrimonial disputes in Courts simultaneously in India and abroad which activates a new *inter se* martial discord. This clash of jurisdictional battles also germinates a conflict amongst authority of Courts. Foreign Courts often impose penal sanctions oblivious of prior directions of existing Indian Courts of superior hierarchy. Rules of Private International Law offer little resolution. Spouses, children and extended families bear the brunt of multi-faceted parallel directives of Courts of different overseas territories.

The Supreme Court in *Neerja Saraph* v. *Jayant Saraph,* (1994) 6 SCC 461 proposed feasibility of enacting a legislation to ensure that no marriage between a NRI and an Indian which has taken place in India may be annulled by a foreign Court. Earlier in *Y. Narasimha Rao* v. *Y. Venkata Lakshmi,* (1991) 3 SCC 451, the Apex Court spelt out guidelines for recognition of foreign Court matrimonial judgments to decide when Hindu marriages solemnized in India were said to be dissolved by unenforceable foreign decrees.

The Bombay High Court in *Sondur Rajini* v. *Sondur Gopal,* 2005 (4) Mah LJ 688 affirmed by the Supreme Court in 2013 in *Rajini Sondur* v. *Gopal Sondur,* (2013) 7 SCC 426 ruled that a foreign domicile of parties will not take away the jurisdiction of Indian Courts to decide the annulment of their ceremonial Hindu marriage solemnized when they were domiciled in India. In *Navin Chander* v. *Leena,* AIR 2005 Bom 277, the matrimonial dispute of a ceremonial marriage of Hindus celebrated in USA, was held by the Bombay High Court to be amenable for adjudication by the Family Court, Pune. The Delhi High Court in *Veena Kalia* v. *Jatinder Kalia,* AIR 1996 Del 54, ruled that an *ex parte* decree of divorce of a foreign Court being a nullity, would not bar a subsequent petition for divorce in India even though maintenance had been accepted under the foreign judgment. In *Harmeeta Singh* v. *Rajat Taneja,* 102 (2003) DLT 822, the Delhi High Court temporarily restraining the foreign Court divorce proceedings held that even if the Hindu marriage is dissolved in USA, it would still have to be confirmed by an Indian Court. In *Moina* v. *Amardeep,* AIR 1986 Del 399, a foreign domicile was held by the Delhi High Court to be no deterrent to a divorce petition preferred in India to dissolve a Hindu marriage celebrated here. These authoritative and laudable verdicts clearly reflect that Indian Courts rightly have a prerogative to adjudicate matrimonial disputes falling in their domain. The majesty of the Indian Courts in implementing personal law must prevail after the Supreme Court decision in *Rajini Sondur* (Supra) holding that in the matter of a Hindu Couple settled in a foreign country, for deciding matrimonial issues, they would be governed by the provisions of Hindu Law *i.e.* the law of their permanent domicile irrespective of the foreign nationalities and overseas residences acquired by them.

ANTI-SUIT ACTIONS

In this backdrop, a new dimension of matrimonial litigation is coming in practice in the arena in the shape of anti-injunction Suits which is the remedy against filing of suits at different jurisdictions in respect of the same cause of action. A petition preferred in India for restraining an opposing spouse from pursuing or continuing with a complaint for matrimonial relief in a foreign Court would be such an anti-injunction Suit in matrimonial matters. Lack of jurisdiction, both regarding the corpus of the Hindu marriage and the physical presence of an Indian spouse in the territory abroad, are the grounds of such suits in India. However, even the reverse application now finds popular practice making anti-suit injunctions a two way street.

FOREIGN REACTIONS

An extreme view finds enunciation in a Judgment rendered on 20 September, 2010 in an anti-injunction Suit. The Federal Magistrates Court of Australia at

Canberra restrained the wife from taking any action, as also for causing, allowing or assisting any other person, to pursue a complaint in India against the husband under the Dowry Prohibition Act, 1961. Both parties were Australian citizens married according to Sikh rites in India. By Australian consent orders, settlement of maintenance, property and child custody were resolved. The Canberra Court found that on evidence presented, Ms. Singh had not established that a dowry was either requested or paid as alleged. Accordingly, the Court held "that the injunction acts *in personam* only in relation to Ms. Singh, and does not, either in terms or otherwise, purport to affect the administration of justice in India". The Judgment was said to be based on considerations of equity and justice. This was the foreign Court perspective.

NEED OF THE HOUR

In the above backdrop, the thought proposed for conscious deliberation which reverberates in the minds of those who live on home soil is the dire need for evolving an Indian jurisprudence in domestic litigation to deal with anti-injunction suits in India. If US authorities oblivious of the Indian legal system arrests and imprisons an Indian diplomat violating human rights, remedies under Indian law must develop to safeguard rights of Indians. Further, If an American Court imposes a fine of one lac US Dollars a day for not complying a US Court Child custody order contrary to an Indian Court order or a divorce petition on grounds of irretrievable breakdown of marriage is proceeded with in USA despite a pending Indian divorce litigation, such oppressive litigation must be restrained by the dictates of equity, good conscience and comity of Courts. Such unconscionable acts are estoppel by conduct. If foreign Courts can evolve principles, similar thinking must develop at home too.

CONCLUSION

Issues relating to applicability of Indian law in cases such as cited above and the authority of Indian Courts to adjudicate such disputes executed in India between employees and diplomats as also norms of judicial comity requires serious deliberation to avoid conflict of jurisdictions. Personal disputes originating on Indian soil must be determined in India. In the far reaching repercussions which tend to shake the foundations of strong traditional Hindu marriages, a foreign Court matrimonial order may at times invade the privacy of the home and leave the hapless Indian spouse to abject surrender without a remedy. Anti-Suit Injunctions are perhaps the only answer if there is an impending risk of conflicting judgments and if the proceedings in the court of foreign jurisdiction would perpetuate injustice or usurp the jurisdiction of a domestic Court. A blind eye cannot overlook vexatious or oppressive litigation. Thereafter, violation of an anti-suit injunction passed against an offending party should be seriously pursued in contempt jurisdiction. Surely, Indian Law must come to rescue. The yeoman verdicts of Indian Courts are a big crutch. However, the need for a preventive remedy is stronger than a powerful cure at the end. What can be prevented must be stopped. What should not be suffered should not be endured. Anti suit injunctions in such matters in fit cases must deter oppressive foreign Court orders without technicalities. The majesty of Indian law must prevail.

Indian Citizenship for Stateless Persons

LANDMARK DECISION

By a decision of August 7, 2013 the High Court of Karnataka in Writ Petition No. 15437 of 2013, *Tenzin Choephag Ling Rinpoche* v. *Union of India,* following an earlier precedent of the High Court of Delhi of December 22, 2010 in Writ Petition (Civil) 12179 of 2009, *Namgyal Dolkar* v. *Government of India* has held that a Tibetan refugee born in India to Tibetan parents between January 26, 1950 to July 1, 1987 would as a right entitle him to claim citizenship by birth under The Citizenship Act, 1955. The Courts rejected the contention of the Union of India that such Tibetan refugees born in India are said to have "renounced" their Indian citizenship acquired by birth, by holding that by virtue of their having a Tibetan identity certificate, it does not amount to renunciation of Indian citizenship. Following the mandate of the Supreme Court in *Satwant Singh* v. *APO, New Delhi,* AIR 1967 SC 1836 and *Maneka Gandhi* v. *Union of India,* AIR 1978 SC 597, that no Indian citizen could be denied a passport, except on specified grounds, it has been held by these Courts that Indian passports cannot be denied to such Tibetans born in India in the said period.

BACKGROUND

Reportedly, more than 1.5 lacs Tibetan refugees had taken shelter in India for an indefinite period following the footsteps of the 14th Dalai Lama in 1959. By a policy decision of the Ministry of Home Affairs, a Tibetan national who entered India after March 1959, could not be granted Indian citizenship by naturalisation under the Citizenship Act, 1955, which is a law to provide for the acquisition and determination of Indian citizenship. Such Tibetan nationals in India possess Tibetan *identity certificates* in lieu of passports, which are issued by Central Tibetan Administration running in exile in India. These certificates are required to be surrendered to the nearest Indian Passport issuing authority upon acquisition of Indian national passports upon gaining Indian citizenship by any of the modes prescribed in the Citizenship Act.

LAWS APPLICABLE

The Passports Act, 1967, is a law to provide for the issue of passports and travel documents. Travel documents can be issued under this law to *"stateless"* persons resident in India, including Tibetan refugees, as such documents issued under the authority of the Government of a foreign country are also recognised under this law. It was the contention of the Government of India that since Tibetan refugees were holding Tibetan identity certificates, they could not be treated as Indian citizens under the Citizenship Act, 1955 and could therefore not be granted Indian passports.

The Citizenship Act, 1955, was amended in 1986 to provide Indian citizenship to persons born in India after January 26, 1950 but before July 1, 1987, as a cut off date, and was thus meant to confer citizenship status acquired by birth as a matter of right, without requiring any such person to make an application for Indian citizenship. Hence, in view of the above verdicts, it has now been decided by the Courts that in the case of Tibetan refugees born in India during this period, irrespective of the fact that they held a Tibetan identity certificate, they could not be denied Indian Passports on the grounds of being Tibetan nationals. The Courts did not find favour with the argument that without there being an application by such Tibetan refugees under the Citizenship Act, the competent authority issuing an Indian Citizenship certificate, was entitled to decline the issue of an Indian passport since the nationality of such Tibetan refugees born in this period was indicated by them as Tibetan on their *"identity certificates"*. Hence, the Courts have now held that any Tibetan refugee born in India between January 26, 1950 and July 1, 1987 is to be automatically considered as a citizen by birth in India without a declaration or an application under the Citizenship Act.

A VIBRANT INTERPRETATION

The reasoning adopted by the Courts is laudable. The ostensible grounds for rejection of an Indian passport under the Passports Act on the ground that such persons are not citizens of India and that because they are not *"Indian nationals"* under the Citizenship Act, were duly analysed by the Courts. It was observed that the concept of *"nationality"* does not have legislative recognition in the Citizenship Act. The Ministry of External Affairs treats Tibetans as *"Stateless"* persons and thus recognises their Tibetan *"Identity Certificates"* answering the description of travel documents within the meaning of the Passports Act, whose absence would render Tibetans facing the prospect of being deported. Hence, the Courts have held that the holding of a Tibetan *"identity certificate"* or a declaration in an application form that the applicant was a Tibetan national, would not constitute valid grounds to refuse an Indian passport.

The Courts further held that the policy decision of the Ministry of Home Affairs not to grant Indian citizenship by naturalisation to Tibetans who entered India after March 1959, is not relevant to Tibetan refugees born in India between January 26, 1950 and July 1, 1987 as such persons are Indian citizens by birth under the Citizenship Act. Possessing any *"identity certificate"* answering the description of a Tibetan national and registration as such under the Registration of Foreigners Act, 1939, does not amount to waiver of the right to be recognised as an Indian citizen by birth and will not amount to renunciation of Indian citizenship under the Citizenship Act.

SUPPORTING REASONING

The Passports Act enjoins that a person is eligible to hold only one passport or travel document. An *"identity certificate"* answering the description of a travel document would clearly have to be relinquished upon the issue of an Indian passport. This, therefore, *per se* cannot constitute valid grounds to refuse issuance of an Indian passport. Hence, prior surrender of the *"identity certificate"* rendering a stateless person without a travel document, would not legitimately amount to a disqualification for an Indian Passport. However, subsequent surrender of the *"identity certificate"* upon issuance of an Indian passport is necessary for compliance of the Passports Act.

ANALYSIS AND CONCLUSION

The choice of the Tibetan youth refugees to amalgamate and merge in a land of their new birth by their independent conscious decisions deserves to be respected and honoured. Opening of windows to balance citizenship rights expressed in a democratic set up with progressive modern life standards for aspiring to achieve new professional avenues gained in a cosmopolitan environment reflects the true spirit of globalisation. Second and third generation Tibetan diaspora may now also no longer harbour feelings of living in exile in their new home land of birth. They find expression of their identity by adorning a new habitat offering opportunities of higher educational facilities, vocational training and an ultimate economic prosperity. The winds of change under the view propounded by the judicial umbrella only furthers, aids and assists such denizens in rehabilitating themselves in a land of their choice. The vibrant interpretations of their rights echo, resound and resonate constructively in times today. The rights of Tibetans born in India to vote as Indian Citizens is meaningful and well founded. Those who choose to join the stream of Indian citizens by being born in India have made a well meaning and conscious choice. Likewise, the decision of the Government of India to permit Tibetans to work or practice in India subject to professional qualifications and rules is a significant and beneficial drive.

FACT FILE

- THE CITIZENSHIP ACT, 1955 for acquisition and determination of Indian Citizenship provides four modes of acquiring citizenship in India. They are:
  - √ Citizenship by Birth (section 3)
  - √ Citizenship by Descent (section 4)
  - √ Citizenship by Registration (section 5)
  - √ Citizenship by Naturalisation (section 6)
- Sections 8, 9 and 10 provide for renunciation, termination and deprivation respectively of Indian citizenship.
- THE PASSPORTS ACT, 1967, provides for issuance of passports and travel documents to regular departure of Indian Citizens from India in the following provisions:

- √ Requirement of passport or travel document for departure from India (section 3)
- √ Making of applications for issue of passports etc., and consideration thereof by Passport authorities (section 5)
- √ Grounds on which Passport authorities shall refuse to issue passport or travel documents (section 6)
- √ Duration of passports and travel documents (section 7)
- √ Renewal of Passports (section 8)
- √ Prescription of conditions and forms in which passport or travel documents are issued (section 9)
- √ Power of passport authorities to vary, impound or revoke passports or travel documents on certain grounds (section 10)
- √ Offences and Penalties (section 12)

Indian Passport Sans Citizenship

A passport is a document which by its nature and purpose recognises a person as a citizen of the country granting it and is in the nature of a request to other countries for his free passage. It contains a recognition of the officially authorised agencies giving nationality to the citizen of the State issuing the passport upon necessary declarations being made to it by the holder. Therefore, a citizen is granted an Indian passport upon confirmation of Indian nationality. However, it can be impounded, revoked or cancelled under the Passports Act, 1967 upon certain prescribed conditions and following the requisite procedure under law. In *Satwant Singh Sawhney* v. *APO, New Delhi*, AIR 1967 SC 1836, the Apex Court has held that deprivation of a passport amounts to infringement of right to personal liberty under article 21 of the Constitution of India and in *Maneka Gandhi* v. *Union of India*, AIR 1978 SC 597, it was reiterated that an order impounding a passport must not contravene any fundamental right.

The Citizenship Act, 1955, which is an Act to provide for the acquisition and determination of Indian Citizenship, prescribes under section 9 that if any citizen of India voluntarily acquires the citizenship of another country, he shall cease to be a citizen of India. Section 9 of the Citizenship Act is a complete code as regards the termination of Indian Citizenship on the acquisition of the citizenship of a foreign country. In exercise of powers under the Citizenship Act, the Central Government has made the Citizenship Rules, 2009 to carry out the purposes of the Act. Under rule 40 of Citizenship Rules, 2009, the Central Government may determine the issues as to whether, when or how any citizen of India had acquired the citizenship of another country and in doing so shall have due regard to the rules of procedure specified in Schedule III prescribed under the Rules.

Schedule III of the Citizenship Rules stipulates salient considerations as hereunder:

1. *Where it appears to the Central Government that a citizen of India has voluntarily acquired the citizenship of any other country, it may require him to prove within such period as may be fixed by it in this behalf, that he has not voluntarily acquired the citizenship of that country; and the burden of proving that he has not so acquired such citizenship shall be on him.*
2. *For the purpose of determining any question relating to the acquisition by an Indian citizen of the citizenship of any other country, the Central Government*

may make such reference as it thinks fit in respect of that question or of any matter relating thereto, to its Embassy in that country or to the Government of that country and act on any report or information received in pursuance of such reference.

3. *The fact that a citizen of India has obtained on any date a passport from the Government of any other country shall be conclusive proof of his having voluntarily acquired the citizenship of that country before that date.*
4. *In determining whether a citizen of India has or has not voluntarily acquired the citizenship of any other country, the Central Government may take the following circumstances into consideration, namely:—*
   (a) whether the person has migrated to that country with the intention of making it his permanent home;
   (b) whether he has in fact taken up permanent residence in that country; and
   (c) any other circumstances relevant to the purpose

Clearly, the Central Government is vested with powers under section 9(2) of the Citizenship Act, 1955, read with rule 30 of the Citizenship Rules, 1956, as an exclusive jurisdiction to determine the question whether a person, who was a citizen of India, has lost that citizenship by having voluntarily acquiring the citizenship of a Foreign State. Further, under section 9(2) and rule 30 above, mere proof of the fact that the person has obtained a passport from a foreign country is not sufficient to sustain an order for deportation or prosecution, unless there has been a decision of the Central Government under section 9(2) of the said Act. Moreover, the enquiry by the Central Government under section 9(2) of the said Act is a *quasi*-judicial enquiry. This proposition of law is well settled by the following judgements of the Apex Court:

(i) *State of Andhra Pradesh* v. *Abdul Khader*, AIR 1961 SC 1467;
(ii) *Government of Andhra Pradesh* v. *Syed Md.*, AIR 1962 SC 1778;
(iii) *State of Uttar Pradesh* v. *Rehmatullah*, AIR 1971 SC 1382.

Let us apply the above principles to the case of X, a stated Indian citizen holding an Indian passport who travelled to England in 1962. X obtains British Citizenship and a British Passport in 1968 and travels to India in 1969 on the British Passport. In 1981, X obtains an Indian Passport which is renewed in 1994 in India. Further, in 1995 and 2004, X obtains fresh Indian Passports in India. Upon a question being raised in 2012 for determination of the nationality of X by the Central Government under section 9 of the Citizenship Act, it is stated by X that he never wanted to settle in UK permanently, he came back to India 1969 after surrendering his British Passport and renouncing British Citizenship which X had not acquired voluntarily in 1968 and that he had intimated all these facts to the Indian Authorities. X claims to have travelled to UK in 1995 and again thereafter on a British Visa since he had acquired an Indian Passport from 1981 onwards being an Indian Citizen living permanently in India.

The Central Government upon hearing X comes to the conclusion that it cannot be accepted that X got British Citizenship under duress in 1969 since he stayed in UK from 1962 to 1969. Thereafter, even though he acquired Indian Passports in 1981 and 2004, there is no record since 1981 onwards of X being granted Indian Citizenship. It is concluded that X automatically ceased to be a citizen of India upon acquisition of British Citizenship in 1968. X is now told that he is at liberty to acquire Indian Citizenship as per the due process of law.

In the opinion of the authors, the said determination by the Central Government falls foul of the principles laid down in Schedule III of the Citizenship Rules. It seems surprising that after 21 years of residence of X in India and without any confirmation from the British authorities of surrendering his British passport/ citizenship and without determining his permanent residence in India since 1981, an adverse conclusion has been drawn against X. It has not been determined whether X had at all migrated to UK to make it his permanent home, whether he has resided in UK permanently after 1969, and his travel to UK in 1995 and thereafter on a British Visa, stamped his Indian passport, has been totally over looked as relevant facts.

The error apparent on record seems to be to determine the nationality issue under section 9 of the Citizenship Act without invoking the procedure for revocation, cancellation or impounding of the Indian passport under the Passports Act, 1967. The moot question which seems to have escaped notice is that an Indian passport could not have been issued in 1981 and 2004 unless there was a determination of Indian nationality. If this was not the case, then, first, the Indian passport ought to have been revoked under section 10 of the Passports Act, 1967. Thereafter, the issue of determination of Citizenship could possibly have arisen. Perhaps, a more comprehensive and detailed procedural investigation ought to have been conducted before taking away the rights of X. A short circuit procedure neither satisfies the ends of justice nor is it equitable in law. Established rights can only be dislodged by the due process of law and cannot be taken away after 21 years summarily. Justice must not only be done but must seem to be done uninfluenced by other factors.

Indians, Foreigners, Deportation and Dual Citizenship

THE CONTROVERSY

As debates continue in India about using laws made during the British Raj, Great Britain itself is in the process of repealing 38 enactments which were legislated between 1849 and 1942 relating to construction and maintenance of Indian Railways network during British Rule. However, we are still not following suit. Even though the Parliament has enacted the Passports Act, 1967, the Citizenship Act, 1955 and in 2005, created *"Overseas Citizens of India"*, till date we still rely on the Passport (Entry into India) Act, 1920, the Registration of Foreigners Act, 1939, and the Foreigners Act, 1946, for various purposes. Most of such archaic legislations made during colonial rule are redundant, do not stand the test of principles of natural justice, confer unfettered, arbitrary and draconian powers, which seriously requires them to be taken off the statute book. But, we still carry on regardless.

A WHOLESOME LAW

The Passports Act, 1967, which is a comprehensive and wholesome law relating to issue of passports and travel documents, provides a statutory safeguard procedure for variation, impounding and revocation of passports with rights of appeal to aggrieved persons against offences and penalties levied under this Act. However, the simultaneous existence of the Passport (Entry into India) Act, 1920 and the Foreigners Act, 1946, conferring absolute and unlimited powers to remove or deport a person from India summarily without following the due process of law, are an anathema and an anti-thesis to the rule of law in a democratic nation with ample scope for judicial review. Powers of house arrest, detention, solitary confinement and summary removal from India under these 1920 and 1946 Acts clearly infringe the fundamental rights of life and personal liberty guaranteed by the Indian Constitution. The reasons, therefore, to retain these pre-independence laws seems to be misplaced and defy fundamental freedoms.

NEW CATEGORIES

1.2 billions Indians contributing 30 million non-resident Indians in almost 180 countries on the globe has led to compromises on dual nationality which is otherwise prohibited under article 9 of the Constitution of India and section 9 of the Citizenship Act, 1955. Categories of "Persons of Indian Origin" (PIO) and "Overseas Citizen of India" (OCI) were carved out to confer limited benefits on persons of Indian origin by amending the Citizenship Act, 1955 in 2005 and adding sections 7A to 7D for registration of Overseas Citizens of India besides conferment, renunciation and cancellation of Overseas Citizenship. Therefore, PIOs and OCIs now enjoy limited rights in India and can enjoy residence rights in India without any visa, registration, sanction or other permissions. Moreover, under article 5 of the Constitution, every person who has his domicile in India and was born in India or whose parents were born in India or who has been ordinarily resident in India for not less than 5 years preceding for commencement of the Constitution, shall be a citizen of India. Hence, inherent rights flow to presumption of Indian nationality by determination of law.

DETERMINATION OF NATIONALITY

Under the 1946 Act, disputes relating to questions of determination of nationality when a foreigner is recognised as a national of more than one country or it is uncertain as to what nationality is to be ascribed to a foreigner, such person may be treated as the national of the country with which he appears to be most closely connected. The 1920 and 1946 Acts permit removal or deportation of a person from India without providing any forum or procedure for determination of the question of the nationality of the foreigner or giving any statutory rights in this process. Tribunals to determine these questions are non existent. However, in the same breath today, now the Citizenship Act, 1955 and the Citizenship Rules, 2009 prescribe that if any question arises as to whether, when or how any person had acquired the citizenship of another country, the Central Government shall first determine such question. The Supreme Court interpreting these provisions has held that a person could not be ordered to be deported or removed from India unless the Central Government takes a conscious decision upon holding a quasi-judicial enquiry that a person has ceased to be an Indian citizen. A foreign passport simpliciter will not label a person as a foreigner and determination of his nationality is his fundamental right. It is time our Parliament reconciles this concept of freedom, personal liberty and natural justice inter-twined with determination of nationality.

DEBATABLE QUESTION

In the social milieu today, international Indians qualify to be PIOs or OCIs. If they wish to reconnect with their homeland, they ought not be bundled out as foreigners by invoking the colonial provisions of the 1920 and 1946 Acts which offend fundamental freedoms. The Citizenship Act, 1955 itself creates harmony. The retention of a foreign passport today cannot lead to deportation and summary removal from India. Why then, do we need to retain the 1920 and 1946 enactments which were enacted to regulate the entry of foreigners into India in circumstances prevailing in 1946. This is a serious issue which must engage the attention of Parliament.

NEED OF THE HOUR

Today, persons of Indian origin have matters relating to matrimonial differences between spouses of global origin or nationality issues arising out of foreign domiciles. The desirable approach in the proper perspective today therefore would be to create appropriate forums or authorities within the legal system who would address such resolvable issues by granting opportunity of hearing and redressal. Accordingly, deportation or removal of a person to a foreign jurisdiction would be an abject surrender to a foreign dominion. Having resolved to be a sovereign, socialist, secular, democratic Republic, we in India, are very capable and competent of adjudicating our nationality issues to provide redressal for Indigenous Indians. Our post independence laws provide the solutions which our vibrant judiciary interprets to protect fundamental freedoms guaranteed under the Constitution of India. Hence, pre-independence laws in conflict with rights today must go off the statute book. The process of reform must not be delayed. Our autonomous laws give us self dependence and we do not need to rely on archaic laws for better governance.

CITIZENSHIP AND FOREIGNERS LAWS AT A GLANCE

- *The Registration of Foreigners Act, 1939* – An Act to provide for the registration of foreigners in India.
- *The Registration of Foreigners Rules, 1992 issued in supersession of the Registration of Foreigners Rules, 1939* – Rules Made under the 1939 Act.
- *The Foreigners Act, 1946* – An Act to confer upon the Central Government certain powers in respect of foreigners.
- *The Foreigners Order, 1948* – An Order made under section 3 of the 1946 Act for power to grant permission to depart from India.
- *The Foreigners (Tribunals) Orders, 1964* – An Order made under section 3 of the 1946 Act to Constitute Tribunals to determine if a person is a Foreigner.
- *The Passport (Entry into India) Act, 1920* – An Act to take powers to require Passports of persons entering India.
- *The Passport (Entry into India) Rules, 1950* – Rules made under 1920 Act.
- *The Passports Act, 1967* – An Act to provide for the issue of Passports and travel documents to regulate departure from India.
- *The Citizenship Act, 1955* – An Act to provide for the acquisition and determination of Indian Citizenship.
- *The Citizenship Rules, 2009* – Rules made under Citizenship Act, 1955.

LAW SETTLED BY SUPREME COURT

Central Government is vested with powers under section 9(2) of the Citizenship Act, 1955, read with rule 30 of the Citizenship Rules, 1956, as an exclusive jurisdiction to determine the question whether a person, who was a citizen of India, has lost that citizenship by having voluntarily acquiring the citizenship of a Foreign State. Further, under section 9(2) and rule 30 above, mere proof of the fact that the person has obtained a passport from a foreign country is not sufficient to sustain an order for deportation or prosecution, unless there has been a decision of the Central Government under section 9(2) of the said Act. Moreover, the enquiry by the Central Government under section 9(2) of the said Act is a *quasi*-judicial enquiry. This proposition of law is well-settled by the following judgments of the Apex Court:

(i) *State of Andhra Pradesh* v. *Abdul Khader*, AIR 1961 SC 1467;

(ii) *Government of Andhra Pradesh* v. *Syed Md.*, AIR 1962 SC 1778;

(iii) *State of Uttar Pradesh* v. *Rehmatullah*, AIR 1971 SC 1382.

SURROGACY

SURROGACY

- Rewriting Surrogacy Laws
- Speed Breakers on the Road to Surrogacy
- Surrogacy Imported from India – Need for a Regulatory Law

Rewriting Surrogacy Laws

ISSUE AT STAKE

Recent meetings of Departments and Ministries of the Government of India on 6 and 7 March, 2014 to discuss and review divergent views on the draft Assisted Reproductive Technology (Regulation) Bill, 2013 (ART Bill, 2013), have resulted in a proposal to revise the draft ART Bill with significant changes. The most crucial proposal is to restrict surrogacy in India to "infertile Indian married couples" only and it would not be allowed to foreigners unless he/she is married to an Indian citizen. Non-resident Indians (NRIs), Persons of Indian Origin (PIOs) and Overseas Citizens of India (OCIs) shall, however, be eligible. The purpose of the object sought to be achieved is to prevent exploitation of Indian women who may be tempted to take the risk in the face of financial hardships.

EXISTING POLICY ON THE SUBJECT

The Indian Council of Medical Research (ICMR) working under the auspices of the Ministry of Health and Family Welfare finalised the National Guidelines for Accreditation, Supervision and Regulation of ART Clinics in India in 2005 after extensive public debate all over the country from all stake holders. Under these 2005 guidelines, there was no legal bar to the use of Artificial Reproductive Technology (ART) by a single or an unmarried woman and the child born would have legal rights on the woman or man concerned. Thereafter, the draft Assisted Reproductive Technology (Regulation) Bill, 2008 (ART Bill, 2008), the draft Assisted Reproductive Technology (Regulation) Bill, 2010 (ART Bill, 2010) and the draft ART Bill, 2013, stated to be revised based on the recommendations of the Ministry of Law and Justice, have consistently proposed that ART in India would be available to all persons including single persons and foreign couples. The Draft Bill, 2013, an exhaustive document containing 100 sections addressing various issues relating to ART is stated to be now "Top Secret" being a part of the Cabinet note as per the requirement and procedure of the handbook of the Cabinet Secretariat on Cabinet Notes. The exercise of drafting the 2008, 2010 and 2013 Bills was entrusted to a 12 Member Specialist drafting Committee besides constituting a National Advisory Committee on ART under the Chairmanship of the Director General, ICMR. The Draft Bills and Rules of 2008 and 2010 were extensively circulated for public opinion besides being sent to State Governments, institutions, statutory bodies, NGOs and other stake holders besides medical professionals. The 2013 Draft Bill was however not circulated or put in the public domain for discussion, comment or opinion.

REPORTED CASES

The only reported Judgment of the Supreme Court in surrogacy matters in *Baby Manji Yamada* v. *Union of India,* AIR 2009 SC 84 took due notice that in cases of "commercial surrogacy," an intended parent may be a single male when it had the occasion to consider the petition of a Japanese grandmother wanting issuance of a travel document for her Japanese divorced son's daughter. In another matter decided by the Gujarat High Court in *Jan Balaz,* AIR 2010 Guj 21 the matter in appeal is still pending in the Supreme Court and the decision of the High Court holding, that babies born in India to gestational surrogates are Indian citizens entitled to Indian passports, has been stayed by the Supreme Court. However, twin German children born to the German couple were permitted to leave India upon directions of the Apex Court to Central Adoption Resource Agency (CARA) to permit adoption of the children as a special case for them to leave India. The main issue of nationality and citizenship arising thereto, being of grave importance, is still undecided.

GUIDELINES RESTRICTING SURROGACY

The Ministry of Home Affairs by guidelines of 9 July, 2012 restricted surrogacy to foreign nationals *i.e.,* a man and a woman duly married for at least two years who would be required to take a medical visa for surrogacy in India. As of now, even though surrogacy as a subject is in the administrative concern and domain of the Ministry of Health and Family Welfare, regardless, it has been decided that till the enactment of a law on the ART Bill, 2013, the Guidelines issued by the Ministry of Home Affairs will prevail till then. Hence, foreign single parent surrogacy is as of now barred.

NEW PROPOSAL IN CONFLICT

The deliberations of 6 and 7 March, 2014 restricting surrogacy to infertile Indian married couples only and debarring all foreigners other than OCIs, PIOs and NRI married couples is a turnaround in the thought process. The suggestion barring foreigners from commissioning surrogacy in India is stated to be subject to their being no conflict with other Indian laws applicable to foreigners, such as those for adoption and other purposes. The most important contradiction and inconsistency seems to be the conflict arising with the Guidelines Governing the Adoption of Children, 2011 for inter-country adoptions which now have statutory sanction by virtue of them being having enacted under the Juvenile Justice (Care and Protection of Children) Act, 2000 which clearly provide that a Court may allow a child to be given in adoption to an individual irrespective of his or her marital status. Moreover, both the Guardian and Wards Act, 1890 and the Hindu Minority and Guardianship Act, 1956 permit a Court that where it is satisfied that it is for the welfare of a minor, a person may be appointed or declared as a Guardian. The bar on single parents to adopt is not statutory but can be a restraint in a particular case upon examination by a competent Court. Therefore, debarring single persons and foreign nationals from being parents will amount to re-writing laws in existence which have been enacted by Parliament.

RECENT DECISIONS

The Supreme Court in *Stephanie Joan Becker,* (2013) 12 SCC 786, permitted a single 53 year old lady to adopt a female orphan child aged 10 years by relaxing the rigor of the guidelines of CARA on the totality of the facts of the case that the proposed adoption would be beneficial to the child as the experts were of the view that the adoption process would end in successful blending of the child in the US. Likewise, in *Shabnam Hashmi* v. *Union of India,* (2014) 4 SCC 1, the Apex Court upholding the recognition of the right to adopt and to be adopted as a fundamental right has held that every person, including Muslims, irrespective of the religion they profess is entitled to adopt a child. The latest verdict of the Supreme Court in *National Legal Services Authority* v. *Union of India,* (2014) 5 SCALE 1 recognising transgender as the third gender have held *"that discrimination on the basis of sexual orientation or gender identity includes any discrimination, exclusion, restriction or preference, which has the effect of nullifying or transposing equality by the law or the equal protection of laws guaranteed under our Constitution."* Clearly, transgender persons having been granted a legal recognition as third gender would be entitled to rights of adoption, succession, inheritance and other privileges under law. The new enunciation is a path of rights.

CONCLUSION

The sum and substance therefore, is not to shut the door to surrogacy which is a accepted societal practice in India having grown slowly over the past almost two decades. Medical technology, advancement of science permitting free export of frozen embryos and other scientific methods have offered hopes to childless persons. The more pragmatic and practical approach would be to make a law hedged with safeguards, checks and balances. The appropriate and desirable method would be to create a mechanism to judge the suitability of proposed surrogate parents rather than to debar all single and foreign persons totally. This would also avoid any conflict with existing laws of adoption wherein foreign persons including single parents are allowed to adopt through a strict and rigorous mechanism provided by CARA and overseen by Indian Courts. Simply trying to shut out surrogacy for foreign nationals and single persons may not be the ideal way to stamp out the hopes of persons wishing to be a parent. Whether Indians or foreign nationals, law treats persons as individual parents when so required. A restrictive meaning to the word "person" cannot qualify or change the definition by restricting it to an Indian national. The celebrated view of the Apex court in widening the horizons to prevent discrimination on grounds of sex or gender identity is a new thought process based on international covenants of human rights. We cannot now permit our thinking to be retrograde simply because of the problems which come with surrogacy. Administrators cannot usurp law making functions to be a law unto themselves. This is the function of the Parliament. Mandarins cannot take over. The more apt approach would be to find solutions to handle and curb these problems. The mechanisms in law which can be created in India as is the case in the case of inter country adoptions is the best cited example. The approach is to restrict the entry and not shut the door altogether. Let us be wiser.

Speed Breakers on the Road to Surrogacy

BURGEONING SURROGACY INDUSTRY IS PROPELLED BY ABSENCE OF A COHESIVE LEGISLATION AND MUSHROOMING IVF & ART CLINICS WANTONLY ADVERTISING SERVICES FOR PROVIDING WOMBS ON RENT

The unregulated reproductive tourism industry procreating surrogacy is booming with India being the first country proposing to legalise commercial surrogacy. Whilst, the new *Assisted Reproductive Technology (ART) (Regulation) Bill and Rules, 2010,* are still in the womb, the non-statutory *Indian Council of Medical Research (ICMR) Guidelines, 2005,* rule the roost. The Indian entrepreneurial industry spirit has catapulted the business of providing *"wombs on rent"* to a whopping trade valued at Rupees Twenty Five thousand Crores. Despite legal, moral and social complexities that shroud surrogacy, economic necessity stimulates women to shake off their inhibition and fear of social ostracism to be lured by agents or corporate surrogacy consultants for international markets. Free availability of a large pool of women willing to be surrogates, a good medical infrastructure, fractional costs, less waiting time, close monitoring of surrogate mothers by over two lac In-Vitro Fertilization (IVF) Clinics and no check of any law restricting single, gay or unmarried couples becoming parents by surrogacy, has made this unethical trade in India skyrocket to spiralling heights.

NEW INDIAN MEDICAL VISA REGULATIONS WILL CAP SURROGACY

However, soon, the business of surrogacy will plummet and boomerang. As per latest and new Indian visa regulations, effective 15 November, 2012, onwards, all foreigners visiting India for commissioning surrogacy will be required to apply for *"Medical Visas"* and cannot avail of simple tourist visas for surrogacy purposes. The Ministry of Home Affairs by a letter of 9 July, 2012, has stipulated mandatory conditions for such medical visas, which if not fulfilled, will lead to visa rejection. These new medical visa Regulations stipulate that a letter from the Embassy of the foreign country in India or its Foreign Ministry should be enclosed with the visa application stating clearly that such country recognises surrogacy and that the child to be born to the commissioning couple through the Indian surrogate mother will be permitted entry into their country as a biological child of the couple commissioning surrogacy who will undertake to take care of their surrogate child. The treatment will be done only at registered ART Clinics in India recognised by ICMR and the foreign commissioning couple must produce a duly notarised agreement between them and the prospective surrogate Indian mother. After the surrogate baby is born, an exit permission by a commissioning couple before leaving India will be required from the Indian Foreigners Regional Registration Office (FRRO) to verify issuance of a certificate from the ART Clinic confirming discharge of liabilities of the Indian Surrogate mother and ensuring custody of child with the commissioning parents. Clearly, the safeguards, checks, balances besides moral and ethical dimensions, which till date remain unaddressed through any legislation, have been administratively put in place to temporarily regulate the surrogacy industry. The dam built with the strong bricks of the conditions of medical visas will prevent the gushing flow of unrestricted, pouring and muddled surrogate waters which had polluted India by becoming a bane for women's health, their basic dignity and human fundamental rights. However, imposing a ban by administrative instructions on single parent surrogacy, whilst statutory enactments allow single parent adoptions, is discriminatory and violative of fundamental rights guaranteed to all persons. Moreover, administrative instructions cannot usurp statutory functions to make laws.

MEDICAL VISA REGULATIONS WILL HARMONISE WITH EXISTING INDIAN AND FOREIGN LAW OF COUNTRIES OF COMMISSIONING PARENTS

Commercial surrogacy is illegal in UK, though permissible under British Law, on payment of reasonable expenses to the surrogate mother. In most US States, compensated surrogacy agreements are either illegal or unenforceable. In some Australian States, arranging commercial surrogacy is a criminal offence and surrogacy agreements giving custody to others are void. In New Zealand and Canada, commercial surrogacy is illegal, although altruistic surrogacy is allowed. In Italy, Germany and France, commercial or other surrogacy is unlawful, in Israel, commercial surrogacy is illegal and law only accepts the surrogate mother as the real mother. India, in total contrast, accepts commercial surrogacy and no law declares it illegal. The Supreme Court on 29 September, 2008, in *Baby Manji Yamada* v. *Union of India*, AIR 2009 SC 84, observed that *"Commercial Surrogacy"* reaching *"Industry proportions is sometimes referred to by the emotionally charged and potentially offensive terms: wombs for rent, outsourced pregnancies or baby farms."* However, the new Indian Medical Visa Regulations by disallowing Indian visas to foreigners whose countries prohibit surrogacy will ensure that we harmonise and fall in tandem internationally with those foreign nations whose overseas citizens wish to wrongfully patronise surrogacy in India Of our own, we have banned foreign single, unmarried or gay parents by restricting surrogacy to couples constituted by a foreign man and woman only who have been married for atleast two years. Recently, proposals indicate that surrogacy will be restricted to infertile married Indian couples only. This may not meet the test of law if such a proposition is tested on the judicial anvil in a challenge to fundamental rights guaranteed under the Constitution to all persons. Regardless, Operations of unethical, unregistered and unrecognised

ART shops cannot be availed of anymore. But, the fact remains that the proposed legislations of 2008, 2010 and 2013 on Artificial Reproductive Technologies to regulate surrogacy must find statutory approval as the ICMR Guidelines of 2005 cannot be a substitute for an enactment of law.

REACTIONS AND RESPONSES OF FOREIGN GOVERNMENTS

Most foreign embassies have indicated on their websites that Indian Government now requires medical visas for foreigners coming to India for surrogacy. Besides, stringent DNA tests are already in place to establish genetic connections for parentage and foreign nationality. Indian Consulates overseas and Visa Facilitation Services (VFS) have also notified that foreign nationals must ascertain beforehand whether their country permits surrogacy and that they cannot enter India for surrogacy purposes by tourist visas. The British High Commission, New Delhi, in advance preparation, by its letter of 30 October, 2012 to the India High Commission, London, states that the British Government recognises surrogacy and makes provisions for commissioning couples for children born overseas through surrogacy. The UK Human Fertilization and Embryology Act, 1990 is cited in support. It allows surrogacy if one parent is genetically related to the surrogate child and no money other than reasonable expenses are paid in respect of the surrogacy arrangement. Alternatively, the said letter also take support of the UK Human Fertilization and Embryology Act, 1990, for providing parental orders to commissioning parents. This letter is stated to be a request for entertaining applications for medical visas for purposes of surrogacy in India as per requirements of the new Indian Medical Visa Regulations.

CONCLUSION

Rather than Parliament catching up to make a law to regulate the unscrupulous surrogacy trade, the new Medical Visa Regulations have stepped in to do what the law ought to have done. Rather than permitting surrogate children to be born in India with the risk of being stateless persons and being denied entry into foreign countries where their commissioning parents reside, it is apt and necessary that such unethical practices leading to such disastrous situations must be pre-empted and prevented. The Indian Government in its administrative wisdom has stepped in at a time when the regulatory law is nowhere near the horizon. Recent instances of surrogate children from Germany, Japan and Israel born in India and leaving upon court intervention should well make legislators think of enacting a strict surrogacy monitoring law. The ART Bill, 2010, itself has legal lacuna, lacks creation of a specialist legal authority for determination and adjudication of legal rights of parties in addition to falling in conflict with existing family laws. The ART Bill, 2013 which is now stated to be a part of a Cabinet note to be put up before the Cabinet of Ministers of the Central Government, is now said to be a secret document beyond public domain. It was never put up for public discussion, debate or suggestions. Its contents remain unknown. A surrogacy law cannot be enacted in absentia of public thought. These pitfalls should not become a graveyard for a law which is yet to be born. Surrogacy needs to be checked and regulated by a proper statutory law. Till then, the much needed medical visa regulations will provide succour and relief. What cannot go on must not be allowed to be carried on if there is no law.

Surrogacy in India

New Indian visa regulations for commissioning parent(s) extracted from third party correspondence with the Indian Ministry for Home Affairs

Visa for foreign nationals intending to visit India for commissioning surrogacy

It may be noted that the foreigners visiting India for commissioning surrogacy are required to apply for Medical Visa with the following conditions:

i. The foreign man and woman are duly married and the marriage should have sustained for at least two years.

ii. A letter from the Embassy of the foreign country in India or the Foreign Ministry of the country should be enclosed with the visa application stating clearly that:

   a. the country recognizes surrogacy; and

   b. the child/children to be born to the commissioning couple through the Indian surrogate mother will be permitted entry into their country as a biological child/children of the couple commissioning the surrogacy.

iii. The couple will furnish an undertaking that they would take care of the child/children born through surrogacy.

iv. The treatment should be done only at one of the registered ART clinics recognized by the Indian Council of Medical Research (ICMR).

v. The couple should produce a duly notarized agreement between the applicant couple and the prospective Indian surrogate mother.

vi. Before the grant of visa, the couple needs to be informed that before leaving India for their return journey, an 'exit' permission from FRRO/FRO would be required. Before granting the 'exit' the FRRO/FRO will see whether the foreign couple is carrying a certificate from the ART clinic concerned regarding the fact that the child/children have been duly taken custody of by the foreigner and that the liabilities towards the Indian surrogate mother have been fully discharged as per the agreement.

vii. Further it may be noted, for drawing up and executing the agreement cited above at (5), the foreign couple can be permitted to visit India on a reconnaissance trip on Tourist Visa, but no samples may be given to any clinic during such preliminary visit.

viii. If the listed conditions are not fulfilled, the visa application shall be rejected."

A letter of support for you to submit along with your visa application confirming points ii a. & b.

GOVERNMENT OF INDIA, LAW COMMISSION OF INDIA NEED FOR LEGISLATION TO REGULATE ASSISTED REPRODUCTIVE TECHNOLOGY CLINICS AS WELL AS RIGHTS AND OBLIGATIONS OF PARTIES TO A SURROGACY – REPORT NO. 228 AUGUST, 2009

RECOMMENDATIONS

The draft Bill prepared by the ICMR is full of lacunae, nay, it is incomplete. However, it is a beacon to move forward in the direction of preparing legislation to regulate not only ART clinics but rights and obligations of all the parties to a surrogacy including rights of the surrogate child. Most important points in regard to the rights and obligations of the parties to a surrogacy and rights of the surrogate child the proposed legislation should include may be stated as under:

1. Surrogacy arrangement will continue to be governed by contract amongst parties, which will contain all the terms requiring consent of surrogate mother to bear child, agreement of her husband and other family members for the same, medical procedures of artificial insemination, reimbursement of all reasonable expenses for carrying child to full term, willingness to hand over the child born to the commissioning parent(s), etc. But such an arrangement should not be for commercial purposes.
2. A surrogacy arrangement should provide for financial support for surrogate child in the event of death of the commissioning couple or individual before delivery of the child, or divorce between the intended parents and subsequent willingness of none to take delivery of the child.
3. A surrogacy contract should necessarily take care of life insurance cover for surrogate mother.
4. One of the intended parents should be a donor as well, because the bond of love and affection with a child primarily emanates from biological relationship. Also, the chances of various kinds of child-abuse, which have been noticed in cases of adoptions, will be reduced. In case the intended parent is single, he or she should be a donor to be able to have a surrogate child. Otherwise, adoption is the way to have a child which is resorted to if biological (natural) parents and adoptive parents are different.
5. Legislation itself should recognize a surrogate child to be the legitimate child of the commissioning parent(s) without there being any need for adoption or even declaration of guardian.
6. The birth certificate of the surrogate child should contain the name(s) of the commissioning parent(s) only.
7. Right to privacy of donor as well as surrogate mother should be protected.
8. Sex-selective surrogacy should be prohibited.
9. Cases of abortions should be governed by the Medical Termination of Pregnancy Act, 1971 only.

Surrogacy – Imported from India – Need for a Regulatory Law

Glamour promotes surrogacy. British pop star Elton John and his Canadian film-maker partner David Furnish became parents of a baby boy born to a surrogate mother in California while our very own film Indian star Aamir Khan and Kiran Rao obtained a child through surrogacy aided by In-vitro Fertilization (IVF). Today, the reproductive tourism industry promoting surrogacy in India is estimated at Rs. 25,000 crores promoted by over 200,000 IVF clinics with websites offering wombs, sperms and eggs. Surrogacy packages which reportedly cost $100,000 in Europe or the US are easily available in India in the range of $10,000. Surprisingly, surrogate hiring of wombs exists in India even though The Transplantation of Human Organs Act, 1994, bans the sale of human organs, loaning of organs and any commercialization of the trade of human organs. Moreover, surrogates are nowhere as freely available as in India to single parents, gay or unmarried partners, despite the fact that same sex relationships are not permissible in India. The primordial urge to have a biological child of one's own flesh, blood and DNA, aided with technology and purchasing power of money coupled with the Indian entrepreneurial spirit has generated this flourishing Indian reproductive tourism industry.

AN ANOMALOUS LAW

In a developed country like the UK no contract or surrogacy agreement is legally binding. In most states in the US, compensated surrogacy arrangements are either illegal or unenforceable. In some states in Australia, arranging commercial surrogacy is a criminal offence and any surrogacy agreement giving custody to others is void. In Canada and New Zealand, commercial surrogacy has been illegal since 2004, although altruistic surrogacy is allowed. In France, Germany and Italy, surrogacy, commercial or not, is unlawful. In contrast, in Israel, virtually all surrogacy permitted for married couple only, is commercial and surrogates are paid an amount as per a written agreement to be approved by a special committee. What then prompts India to enact a proposed law to make surrogacy agreements legally enforceable is to protect the genetic parents, surrogate mother and the child.

Economic necessity fuels the surrogate trade. Ironically, medical data indicates that in India, there is a need every year of about 1,75,000 kidneys, 50,000 hearts and 50,000 livers for transplantation and each year about 1,40,000 people die waiting for a kidney. Life saving organs are not available but wombs on hire are. Even though commercial surrogacy is an anti-thesis of transplantation laws, but it is a medically accepted practice reflected in the 2005 Indian Council of Medical Research (ICMR) Guidelines and the Assisted Reproductive Technology Regulation Bill, (ART), 2010, prepared by the Health Ministry. Clearly, surrogacy flourishes legally because it is medically not illegal. No doubt, the Supreme Court in *Baby Manji Yamada's* case (2008) observed that "commercial surrogacy" reaching "industry proportions is sometimes referred to by the emotionally charged and potentially offensive terms wombs for rent, outsourced pregnancies or baby farms." India therefore, is set to be the only country to legalise commercial surrogacy through the proposed law which is already a glaring reality.

Recently, in December 2011, the High Court at London granted parental orders to a British couple under the British Human Fertilisation and Embryology Act, 2008, for their two children born to Indian surrogate mothers after both children were given British passports and allowed to leave India. Sir Nicholas Wall, speaking for the Court, held that "it is plainly in the interests of these two children that they should be brought up by Mr. & Mrs. A as their parents." The couple had paid £ 27,405 for a surrogacy package in India because of lack of surrogate mothers in UK as there was a three year waiting list in the UK. Earlier, even the Indian Supreme Court in September 2008 in *Baby Manji Yamada's* case had directed the Central Government to dispose off expeditiously the request of the grandmother permitting her to transport her surrogate granddaughter born in India through surrogacy. Resultantly, the surrogate baby whose parents had divorced was issued an "identity certificate" enabling her journey to Japan.

COURTS TO THE RESCUE

After a frustrating two-year legal battle in India on behalf of their surrogate sons – Nikolas and Leonard – German couple Jan Balaz and Susan Anna Lohald were allowed to return to Germany after the Supreme Court of India intervened and, in a court hearing on 26 May, 2010, the Indian Government agreed to provide them with exit permits. The twins were born in the State of Gujarat in January 2008 and registered as children born of a foreign couple through an Indian surrogate mother. Upon being declined birth certificates, Jan Balaz moved the Gujarat High Court, which ruled that since the surrogate mother is an Indian national, the children would also be treated as Indian nationals and would be entitled to Indian passports. The Judgment in *Jan Balaz* v. *Anand Municipality*, AIR 2010 Guj 21. It is under challenge in the Supreme Court of India by way of Special Leave to Appeal (Civil) No. 31639 of 2009, titled as *Union of India* v. *Jan Balaz* and is still pending final adjudication on the issue whether babies born in India to gestational surrogate mothers are citizens of India and whether they would be entitled to get Indian passports or not. However, the Government of India challenged this decision, stating that the toddlers, being surrogate children, could not be granted Indian citizenship, which rendered them stateless as they had neither German nor Indian citizenship. The German authorities had also refused visas to the twins on the ground that German law did not recognise surrogacy as a means to parent-hood. Ultimately, Jan Balaz and Susan Lohald went through an inter-country adoption process in India, upon which the Indian Government granted exit permits to the German surrogate twins to enable their journey back home to Germany. Clearly, Courts worldwide acting equitably lean to favourably interpret existing laws aiding parenthood for surrogate children. Surrogacy is also popularly resorted to by gay couples in India. Israeli gay couple Yonatan and Omer Gher became parents to a child born to them with the help of a Mumbai based surrogate mother in 2008. Subsequently, in 2010, Dan Goldberg and Arnon Angel from Israel, another gay couple to whom twin baby boys were born in Mumbai from an Indian surrogate mother, were stranded in India after the refusal of the Jerusalem Family Court to allow a paternity test to initiate the process for Israeli citizenship for the twins. The issue was debated in the Knesset (Israeli Parliament) where Prime Minister Benjamin Netanyahu had to intervene so that the infants could be brought to Israel following legal procedures. Ultimately, on appeal, the Jerusalem District Court accepted the claim that it was in the best interest to hold a DNA paternity test to establish that Dan Goldberg was the father of the boys, Itai and Liron. The DNA samples of Goldberg and the twins were brought to the Sheeba Medical Centre in Israel, which established Goldberg as the father of the infants. After being stranded in Mumbai for over three months, Goldberg and his twin baby boys returned to Israel in May 2010 after the children were granted Israeli passports. Thereafter, in 2011, a gay Spaniard couple Mauro and Juan became parents of female twins born to them through a surrogate mother in India. More such occurrences will follow in times to come.

A FLAWED LAW IN THE MAKING

The only face saving which can be pondered and deliberated is how to regulate surrogacy, prevent exploitation besides resolve issues of citizenship, nationality and parentage. In this context, the ART Bill, 2010 suffers from serious lacunas and shortcomings. Some questions left unanswered in the Bill are enumerated below:

- Remedies available to biological parents to obtain exclusive legal custody of surrogate children and waiver of rights of surrogate mother besides restricting rights of sperm or ovum donor.
- Mode of statutorily establishing genetic constitution of surrogate baby.
- Legal process of recording parentage of surrogate child.
- Process of determination of citizenship and nationality rights.
- Guardianship/adoption proceedings in respect of children born out of surrogacy agreements as Hindu laws do not allow non Hindu parents to adopt in India.
- Custodial rights of single/gay/unmarried/divorced parents.
- Legal validity of surrogacy agreements *vis-à-vis* existing Indian laws.
- Rights to prevent exploitation of surrogate mothers.

The ART Bill, 2010 is flawed. It has neither designated, nor authorized or created any Court or judicial forum to resolve issues which will require adjudication in problems arising out of surrogacy. The National and State

Advisory Boards created by the Bill will not serve the purpose to determine issues of parentage, nationality, issuance of passports, grant of visas and problems of disputed parentage. It is extremely necessary to create a statutory procedure for mandatorily adjudicating these issues before the surrogate child leaves India. Even rampant exploitation of surrogate mothers has to be curbed, checked and punished upon detection. The Bill does not address these issues.

It seems that the question whether India should be the surrogate motherhood capital of the world or not is now a far cry. Social and economic necessities besides medical professional sponsorships have ensured that surrogacy is here to stay. Therefore, an active legislative intervention to facilitate the correct uses of this new technology of ART may be a more plausible approach in grappling with commercial surrogacy. The proposed law has to also take care that the use of ART and IVF does not graduate to unethical practices of making designer babies by choosing traits or embryo selection now made possible by stem cell research and cloning. Medical personnel must be guided by a strict law to prevent any malpractices. Above all, trading of any form in human merchandise by other unethical agents in the so called business of babies must be curbed with a heavy hand. A regulatory law supported by a legislative machinery and effective rules to look at all the problems associated with surrogacy must be put in place. Besides, Embassies and High Commissions of Foreign Missions of different countries in India are also looking for a law which will help them make their own policies for adapting to surrogacy besides resolving issues of surrogate children born to their countrymen to enable them to achieve dreams of parenthood. Thus, a proactive, well drafted surrogacy law requires to be urgently put in place forthwith without any delay. This it seems is, now the call of the born surrogate child.

THE LATEST SURROGATE WEB – BABY EMPEROR'S CASE

- Seven weeks old surrogate child Emperor Kaioyus Van Buren Green was born to an unknown surrogate mother through in-vitro fertilization (IVF). His mother J. Pearl Linda came from the US with her husband Eric Dalton's sperm from a Cryo-Bank in New York. The ovum was donated in India and Emperor was born at a fertility centre in Hyderabad on December 7, 2011 using a surrogate mother.
- Hyderabad Regional Passport Officer (RPO), K. Srikar Reddy has declined issuance of a passport to Emperor till it is proved that Linda's husband is the child's biological father. Dalton, a Jamacian national had not come to India as he reportedly suffers from aerophobia (fear of flying by air). There is no Jamacian Embassy either in Delhi or in Hyderabad.
- J. Pearl Linda has three options to enable a travel document for Emperor.
  - Get Eric Dalton to Hyderabad for a DNA test to establish that he is the biological father of the Emperor and satisfy the RPO.
  - Approach the US Embassy to get Eric Dalton's DNA sampling report or blood sample to Hyderabad to ascertain his parentage.
  - Undergo the process of legal adoption/Guardianship proceedings.

- In the absence of the Assisted Reproductive Technology Regulation Bill (ART), 2010, still not a law, the 2005 Guidelines by the Indian Council of Medical Research are the only enabling provisions as per which one of the parents should establish the parentage of the surrogate child. Only a DNA test can prove this. Linda is not the biological mother. Hence, only Dalton's DNA test can do it.
- The RPO cannot issue a passport unless conclusive proof of parents is established. Under the Hindu Adoption and Maintenance Act, 1956 (HAMA), only Hindus by religion can adopt in India. Linda is not a Hindu and can only become a legal Guardian of Emperor under the Guardian and Wards Act, 1890 (GWA). However, without conclusive proof of who is the father, this petition may not be entertained or adjudicated by Courts in India.
- Will the precedents in the case of *Baby Manji Yamada* (Japanese case), *Jan Balaz* case (German matter) or Israeli and Spanish gay couple case help. It seems that invoking the prerogative writ jurisdiction of a High Court under the Constitution of India may perhaps be the only equitable solution possible.

ALL ABOARD FOR THE FERTILITY EXPRESS

- Transferring a fertilized egg cell through in vitro fertilization to a rented womb is the plain meaning of surrogacy. The sperm or the egg or both may be of biological parents. The availability of wombs may be commercial or altruistic. Under the Assisted Reproductive Technology Regulation Bill, 2010, "Surrogacy", means an arrangement in which a woman agrees to a pregnancy, achieved through assisted reproductive technology, in which neither of the gametes (sperm or oocyte) belong to her or her husband, with the intention to carry it to term and hand over the child to the person or persons for whom she is acting as a surrogate.
- In UK, no contract or surrogacy agreement in legally binding. In USA, compensated Surrogacy agreements are either illegal or unenforceable. In Australia, arranging commercial Surrogacy may be a criminal offence. In Canada and New Zeland, commercial Surrogacy has been illegal since 2004, although altruistic surrogacy is allowed. In France Surrogacy is unlawful. In contrast, in Israel, virtually all surrogacy permitted for married couple only, is commercial and surrogates are paid an amount as per a written agreement to be approved by a special committee.
- India is preparing to be the first country to legalise commercial Surrogacy. The Indian entrepreneurial spirit has generated the "reproductive tourism industry" estimated at Rs. 25,000 crores today. The Supreme Court in *Baby Manji Yamada's* case, JT 2008 (11) SC 150 stated that "Commercial surrogacy is sometimes referred to by the emotionally charged and potentially offensive terms "wombs for rent", outsourced pregnancies" or "baby farms"."
- Clinically called "Assisted Reproductive Technology" (ART). it has been in vogue since 1978 and today an estimated 200,000 clinics across the country offer artificial insemination, in-vitro fertilization (IVF) and Surrogacy.

- ART is widely canvassed for its scientific potential- may be by stem cell research or by cloning. If medically used, it can help detect diseases and find cures. If commercially misused, it can create trait selection features and designer babies or make cosmetic productions for unethical uses.
- The Transplantation of Human Organs Act, 1994, bans the sale of Human Organs, loaning of organs and any commercialization of the trade of Human Organs. In contradiction, commercial surrogacy, if practiced, will allow hiring of sperm, eggs and wombs.
- As yet, the Assisted Reproductive Technology Regulation Bill, 2010 has not become the law in India. Today, the 2005 Indian Council Medical Research Guidelines apply, but being non statutory, they are not enforceable or justiciable in a Court of law. Hence, a child born through surrogacy must be adopted by the biological parents. However, this is not possible for non Hindu foreign parents, who cannot adopt and be only Guardians in India.
- Arguments of morality, ethics and economic realities abound, India seems to be heading to be a surrogate motherhood capital. Only an active legislative intervention can facilitate the correct uses of medical technology aiding surrogacy. Safeguards, checks, balances and legislative protections must be put in place.

Suggestive Cross Border Perspectives and Safeguards for Proposed Surrogacy Law in India

Having elaborated upon the current legal position in India, with regard to surrogacy, we are now to advance the following suggestions for the proposed surrogacy law sought to be enacted in India at this moment in time, on the basis of draft 2013 Bill.

Certainly, larger awareness as to the draft 2013 Bill and more than that vigorous continued debate and discussion on surrogacy related private international law issues is urgently required. It is the dire need of the day. In the present situation, a proper meaningful public debate on the draft 2013 Bill has been negligible, rather conspicuously missing. This is of course a major reason for worry, as the legal inputs in this area of law have not been given the due attention which they deserve, especially with regard to the cross border perspectives. In light of the growing ramifications of the surrogacy industry, and with the large number of foreign commissioning parents wanting to use the services of surrogate mothers from India, hence, it becomes all the more important to look at certain key issues in the international perspectives. Accordingly, we are to advance the following suggestions that could well possibly be taken into consideration in the enactment of the proposed surrogacy legislation and the rules to be framed under the said legislation. The said suggestions are as follows:

CREATION OF EXCLUSIVE SPECIALIST FORUMS

There are already serious issues of determining parentage, nationality, issuance of passports, grant of visas and problems of disputed parentage. Corresponding amendments will have to be made in the Births and Deaths Act, 1969, as the same contains no provisions for children born out of surrogacy arrangements. There is no Forum defined, designated or created which will look into these problems or determine how they have to decided or dealt with.

PROPOSED LEGISLATION SHOULD PROVIDE FOR STATELESS CHILDREN

Clearly, the proposed legislation has to provide "for stateless children," in the absence of court intervention. A child cannot be left stateless. This is a very serious issue.

A POWERFUL DUE DILIGENCE MECHANISM SHOULD BE IN PLACE

There are no mechanisms at all in place to check credentials of commissioning parents. Clearly, there should be an accredited agency in a foreign country to check and verify backgrounds credentials of commissioning parents. Home study reports mandated under CARA guidelines in inter-country adoptions, could well possibly be applicable in cross border surrogacy arrangements.

MULTIPLE FORUM SHOPPING BY COMMISSIONING PARENTS SHOULD BE BARRED

The proposed legislation should prohibit simultaneous multiple forum shopping in different jurisdictions, expressly also prohibiting use of two surrogate mothers, whether in India or abroad leading to two surrogate children born at the same time.

CREATION OF REGULATORY ENVIRONMENT

The level of commercialisation seriously warrants a regulatory environment. The MCI should contemplate some sort of surrogacy regulators.

MEDIATION, ARBITRATION AND SURROGACY OMBUDSMAN

The proposed law should also provide for mediation and arbitration, in the event of disputes. If we can have a banking ombudsman, we could well have a surrogacy ombudsman.

SUFFICIENT ATTENTION TO INTERNATIONAL SURROGACY AGREEMENTS/ARRANGEMENTS

Surrogacy in India is legitimate because no Indian law prohibits surrogacy. To determine the legality of surrogacy arrangements, the provisions of the Indian Contract Act, 1872 would apply. Alternatively, the commissioning parents can also move an application under the Guardian and Wards Act, 1890, for seeking an order of appointment to be declared as the guardian of the surrogate child. In comparison, surrogacy contracts are unenforceable in the UK also in terms of reported decision Re *TT (Surrogacy)*, [2011] EWHC 33 (Fam). The point to be canvassed is that there should be a separate exhaustive chapter in the proposed legislation exclusively dedicated to international surrogacy arrangements, so as to attempt to create at least a basic minimum harmonisation process fraught without difficulties.

MANDATORY INSURANCE COVER FOR SURROGATE MOTHERS WITH U.S. DOLLAR BENCHMARKS BY OVERSEAS COMMISSIONING PARENTS, AS A PREREQUISITE TO THE ISSUANCE OF MEDICAL VISAS

The proposed law and the rules framed there under should provide that the potential overseas commissioning parents, should mandatorily take an approved insurance cover [with US dollar benchmarks] for the surrogate mother for the gestation period and till the time of the birth of the surrogate child, from approved/accredited Government and private insurance companies in India. Such insurance cover, should be mandatorily appended with the medical visa application lodged on behalf of intending commissioning parents, at the Indian Embassy/Mission overseas. Details of the Insurance cover should be recorded in the surrogacy agreement as well, including the bank account and aadhar card details of the surrogate mother, so as to attempt to ensure proper realisation in the event of any mishap, contingency, default or death of the surrogate mother.

ANONYMITY OF SURROGATE MOTHER NOT BEING MAINTAINED, WHICH LEADS TO OSTRACISATION AND INVISIBILIATION OF THE SURROGATE MOTHERS

In actual practice, on the basis of empirical data, it has been observed that the anonymity of surrogate mothers is not being maintained, hence leading to their social ostracisation. Consequently, stigma of being a surrogate mother leads to invisibiliation of the surrogate mothers. Hence, the point to be conveyed is that there should be sufficient safeguards and mechanisms in place, so as to adequately protect the anonymity of the surrogate mother in question.

LEGAL FEES TO BE PAID BY COMMISSIONING PARENTS

The proposed legislation should mandatorily provide that the legal fees, should be paid independently over and above all other bracketed costs by the commissioning parents.

COMPREHENSIVE CONSOLIDATED SURROGACY LEGISLATION, WITH EXTRA TERRITORIAL APPLICATION LIKE THE PROVISIONS OF THE HINDU MARRIAGE ACT, 1955

Given the fast changing socio economic conditions, technological advancements, an attempt should be made for one stop shop consolidated piece of surrogacy legislation, covering both domestic and international surrogacy arrangements, rather than creating an environment of cherry picking *i.e.*, selective reliance on scattered pieces of legislation.

LEGAL RIGHTS QUA USE OF GENETIC MATERIAL UPON TERMINATION OF MARRIAGE OF OVERSEAS COMMISSIONING PARENTS

The proposed legislation has to address the position of legal rights to use genetic material upon termination of marriage and in the event of the surrogate child not being claimed on account of divorce of foreign commissioning parents, stringent financial penalties with dollar benchmarks should be imposed on such separated parents.

ILLEGAL TRADING IN GAMETES/EMBRYOS SHOULD BE PUNISHABLE

Illegal trading in gametes/embryos should be punishable under the Indian Penal Code, 1860 or under a separately carved out offence of human smuggling.

The said legislation should also address the issue of baby breeding rings/ cartels, which are part of illegal cross border migration networks.

MOTHER RETRACTING HER CONSENT? CHANGE OF HEART

The proposed legislation and the rules have to seriously take into account certain unwarranted situations. One such major issue is as to what would happen if the surrogate mother, changes her mind during the gestation period? One of the serious issues in the case of a foreign commissioning couple is as to what law would be applicable in such a situation? Specific provisions with regard to choice of law and conflict of law will have to be incorporated in the proposed legislation. The mother could well argue, that parting with the child would be violative of article 21 of the Constitution of India.

AGGRIEVED SURROGATE MOTHER/IMMEDIATE FAMILY MEMBERS SHOULD BE EMPOWERED TO INVOKE THE JURISDICTION OF THE NATIONAL COMMISSION FOR WOMEN, NEW DELHI OR APPROPRIATE STATE LEVEL FORUMS

There should be a mandatory provision in the proposed legislation for an aggrieved surrogate mother and in the event of her inability, disability or restricted movement, in the alternative her immediate family members should be empowered to invoke the jurisdiction of the NCW, New Delhi, or appropriate State level forums during the gestation period and, "for a reasonable amount of time," after the birth has taken place. This is in the event of any mishap, contingency or disability of any sorts accruing to the surrogate mother, or in the event of the unfortunate death of the surrogate mother.

PROVISION FOR MANDATORY COORDINATION OF NCW, NEW DELHI OR APPROPRIATE STATE LEVEL FORUM WITH FOREIGN MISSIONS, IN CASE OF DEFAULT BY ERRING FOREIGN NATIONALS/COMMISSINING PARENTS

In such a situation, the NCW, New Delhi or the State level forum should be duty bound to enforce their findings, and the relief awarded by the NCW, New Delhi or the State level forum should be enforceable *qua* the commissioning parents, and in the case of foreign nationals, the concerned consular department of the foreign mission/embassy/consulate should be clothed/directed with the responsibility of enforcing attendance of such erring foreign nationals/ commissioning parents.

Also, in the event of any default, lapse, wilful error or cheating on part of the intending overseas parents during the currency of the surrogate agreement, and even after the birth of the child having taken place, the NCW, New Delhi or the appropriate State level forum, as a central nodal agency or the State level forum, as the case may be, should be statutorily vested for pursuing the cause/ case of the affected surrogate mother.

PLEA OF DATA PROTECTION LEGISLATION BY FOREIGN MISSIONS IN INDIA SHOULD NOT BE USED TO OBSTRUCT, THWART OR STALL THE ENQUIRY PROCESS

That on an institutional basis, the NCW, New Delhi or the appropriate State level forum should also be empowered and authorised to correspond, liaise and coordinate with the overseas commissioning parents, as also foreign missions both in India and abroad, both in normal circumstances or in the event of any default. And, such an enabling clause should be mandatorily recorded in the surrogacy agreement/contract, also explicitly providing consent of the foreign commission parents to the effect that the plea of foreign data protection legislation of the country of their habitual residence will not be allowed with a view to negate the fact finding process carried out by the NCW,

New Delhi or the State level forum, or to thwart/stall any such enquiry process so initiated.

COLLECTIVE RESPONSIBILITY OF GOVERNMENT STAKEHOLDERS

Also in so far relating to private international law issues, the rules framed under the proposed surrogacy legislation should provide for setting up a nodal agency comprising of representatives from various Indian Ministries *i.e.*, the Law Ministry, Legal and Treaties Division, Ministry of Women and Child Development and of course National Commission for Women, New Delhi for active meaningful dialogue and collaboration with the Hague Conference on Private International Law.

PROVISION FOR MUTUAL INTERNATIONAL COOPERATION

Internationally, there is already talk going on of having a Hague Convention on Surrogacy.

The Hague Conference on Private International Law has commissioned a study and released a report titled, "Parentage/Surrogacy Project" by the Permanent Bureau at the Hague in March 2014. Seventy Six Member States and the EU will decide in the next council meeting in March or April 2015, as to whether, and if so how this project should be continued.

The point to be conveyed is that the rules framed under the proposed legislation, should also provide for meaningful international dialogue with institutions like the Hague etc.

IMMIGRATION PERSPECTIVE: ARTICLE 8 OF THE ECHR, IS THE INVISIBLE ELEPHANT IN THE ROOM

Some of the foreign jurisdictions allowing surrogacy have now framed immigration rules for children born out of surrogacy arrangements.

Generally, all surrogacy applications are being lodged within the ambit of immigration rules, with lot of emphasis on comprehensive documentation, mandatory DNA testing.

Quite understandably checks, balances and concerns in processing surrogacy application voice concern of the member states, that flood gates should not be opened.

European member states are presumably worried at a potential interpretation of Article 8 of the European Convention of Human Rights, which talks of the right to family life, which has been given a very sweeping interpretation in the Stratsbourg jurisprudence. What if at a later point of time, the surrogate mother claims her right to be united with the surrogate child in a foreign land as a parent of such a surrogate child, who is firmly entrenched with the commissioning parents in the country of their domicile and habitual residence. This proposition has not been tested in the British Courts or any foreign court at this moment in time.

Different countries have conflicting legislation governing surrogacy and there are no international agreements covering surrogacy immigration applications.

CONCLUSION

We have to wait and watch, as to what shape the present draft 2013 bill will finally and eventually take place at the end of the day and as to what amount significant meaningful qualitative suggestions of legal nature and terminology are seriously and actually taken into consideration by the Government of India, from the so called feeble debate on the present bill.

SUBJECT INDEX

D

T

V

•••